Natural Resources and Economic Growth

The relationship between natural capital and economic growth is an open debate in the field of economic development. Is an abundance of natural resources a blessing or a curse for economic performance? The field of Economic History offers an excellent vantage to explore the relevance of institutions, technical progress and supply-demand drivers.

Natural Resources and Economic Growth contains theoretical and empirical articles by leading scholars who have studied this subject in different historical periods from the nineteenth century to the present day and in different parts of the world. The first three chapters present the theoretical issues and discusses the meaning of the "curse" and the relevance of the historical perspective. After that, the rest of the book captures the diversity of experiences, presenting thirteen independent case studies based on historical results from North and South America, Africa, Asia, Oceania and Europe.

This book emphasizes that an abundance of natural resources is not a fixed situation. It is a process that reacts to changes in the structure of commodity prices and factor endowments, and progress requires capital, labour, technical change and appropriate institutional arrangements. This abundance is not a given, but is part of the evolution of the economic system. History shows that institutional quality is the key factor to deal with abundant natural resources and, especially, with the rents derived from their use and exploitation.

This wide-ranging volume will be of great relevance to all those with an interest in economic history, development, economic growth, natural resources, world history and institutional economics.

Marc Badia-Miró is a lecturer at the Department of Economic History of the University of Barcelona, Spain.

Vicente Pinilla is Professor of Economic History, Faculty of Economics and Business Studies, University of Zaragoza, Spain.

Henry Willebald is Associate Professor, Instituto de Economía, Faculty of Economics and Business Administration, Universidad de la República, Uruguay.

Routledge explorations in economic history
Edited by Lars Magnusson
Uppsala University, Sweden

1 **Economic Ideas and Government Policy**
   Contributions to contemporary economic history
   Sir Alec Cairncross

2 **The Organization of Labour Markets**
   Modernity, culture and governance in Germany, Sweden, Britain and Japan
   Bo Stråth

3 **Currency Convertibility**
   The gold standard and beyond
   Edited by Jorge Braga de Macedo, Barry Eichengreen and Jaime Reis

4 **Britain's Place in the World**
   A historical enquiry into import controls 1945–1960
   Alan S. Milward and George Brennan

5 **France and the International Economy**
   From Vichy to the Treaty of Rome
   Frances M.B. Lynch

6 **Monetary Standards and Exchange Rates**
   M.C. Marcuzzo, L. Officer and A. Rosselli

7 **Production Efficiency in Domesday England, 1086**
   John McDonald

8 **Free Trade and its Reception 1815–1960**
   Freedom and trade: volume I
   Edited by Andrew Marrison

9 **Conceiving Companies**
   Joint-stock politics in Victorian England
   Timothy L. Alborn

10 **The British Industrial Decline Reconsidered**
   Edited by Jean-Pierre Dormois and Michael Dintenfass

11 **The Conservatives and Industrial Efficiency, 1951–1964**
   Thirteen wasted years?
   Nick Tiratsoo and Jim Tomlinson

12 **Pacific Centuries**
   Pacific and Pacific Rim economic history since the 16th century
   Edited by Dennis O. Flynn, Lionel Frost and A.J.H. Latham

13 **The Premodern Chinese Economy**
   Structural equilibrium and capitalist sterility
   Gang Deng

14 **The Role of Banks in Monitoring Firms**
The case of the Crédit Mobilier
Elisabeth Paulet

15 **Management of the National Debt in the United Kingdom, 1900–1932**
Jeremy Wormell

16 **An Economic History of Sweden**
Lars Magnusson

17 **Freedom and Growth**
The rise of states and markets in Europe, 1300–1750
S.R. Epstein

18 **The Mediterranean Response to Globalization before 1950**
Sevket Pamuk and Jeffrey G. Williamson

19 **Production and Consumption in English Households 1600–1750**
Mark Overton, Jane Whittle, Darron Dean and Andrew Hann

20 **Governance, the State, Regulation and Industrial Relations**
Ian Clark

21 **Early Modern Capitalism**
Economic and social change in Europe 1400–1800
Edited by Maarten Prak

22 **An Economic History of London, 1800–1914**
Michael Ball and David Sunderland

23 **The Origins of National Financial Systems**
Alexander Gerschenkron reconsidered
Edited by Douglas J. Forsyth and Daniel Verdier

24 **The Russian Revolutionary Economy, 1890–1940**
Ideas, debates and alternatives
Vincent Barnett

25 **Land Rights, Ethno Nationality and Sovereignty in History**
Edited by Stanley L. Engerman and Jacob Metzer

26 **An Economic History of Film**
Edited by John Sedgwick and Mike Pokorny

27 **The Foreign Exchange Market of London**
Development since 1900
John Atkin

28 **Rethinking Economic Change in India**
Labour and livelihood
Tirthankar Roy

29 **The Mechanics of Modernity in Europe and East Asia**
The institutional origins of social change and stagnation
Erik Ringmar

30 **International Economic Integration in Historical Perspective**
Dennis M.P. McCarthy

31 **Theories of International Trade**
Adam Klug
Edited by Warren Young and Michael Bordo

32 **Classical Trade Protectionism 1815–1914**
Edited by Jean Pierre Dormois and Pedro Lains

33 **Economy and Economics of Ancient Greece**
Takeshi Amemiya

34 **Social Capital, Trust and the Industrial Revolution 1780–1880**
David Sunderland

35 **Pricing Theory, Financing of International Organisations and Monetary History**
Lawrence H. Officer

36 **Political Competition and Economic Regulation**
Edited by Peter Bernholz and Roland Vaubel

37 **Industrial Development in Postwar Japan**
Hirohisa Kohama

38 **Reflections on the Cliometrics Revolution**
Conversations with economic historians
Edited by John S. Lyons, Louis P. Cain, and Samuel H. Williamson

39 **Agriculture and Economic Development in Europe since 1870**
Edited by Pedro Lains and Vicente Pinilla

40 **Quantitative Economic History**
The good of counting
Edited by Joshua Rosenbloom

41 **A History of Macroeconomic Policy in the United States**
John H. Wood

42 **An Economic History of the American Steel Industry**
Robert P. Rogers

43 **Ireland and the Industrial Revolution**
The impact of the Industrial Revolution on Irish industry and society, 1801–1922
Andy Bielenberg

44 **Intra-Asian Trade and Industrialization**
Essays in memory of Yasukichi Yasuba
Edited by A.J.H. Latham and Heita Kawakatsu

45 **Nation, State and the Industrial Revolution**
The visible hand
Lars Magnusson

46 **A Cultural History of Finance**
Irene Finel-Honigman

47 **Managing Crises and De-globalisation**
Nordic foreign trade and exchange 1919–1939
Edited by Sven-Olof Olsson

48 **The International Tin Cartel**
John Hillman

49 **The South Sea Bubble**
Helen J. Paul

50 **Ideas and Economic Crises in Britain from Attlee to Blair (1945–2005)**
Matthias Matthijs

51 Bengal Industries and the British Industrial Revolution (1757–1857)
Indrajit Ray

52 The Evolving Structure of the East Asian Economic System since 1700
Edited by A.J.H. Latham and Heita Kawakatsu

53 German Immigration and Servitude in America, 1709–1920
Farley Grubb

54 The Rise of Planning in Industrial America, 1865–1914
Richard Adelstein

55 An Economic History of Modern Sweden
Lennart Schön

56 The Standard of Living and Revolutions in Russia, 1700–1917
Boris Mironov

57 Europe's Green Revolution and Others Since
The rise and fall of peasant-friendly plant breeding
Jonathan Harwood

58 Economic Analysis of Institutional Change in Ancient Greece
Carl Hampus-Lyttkens

59 Labour-Intensive Industrialization in Global History
Edited by Gareth Austin and Kaoru Sugihara

60 The History of Bankruptcy
Economic, social and cultural implications in early modern Europe
Edited by Thomas Max Safley

61 The Political Economy of Disaster and Underdevelopment
Destitution, plunder and earthquake in Haiti
Mats Lundahl

62 Nationalism and Economic Development in Modern Eurasia
Carl Mosk

63 Agricultural Transformation in a Global History Perspective
Edited by Ellen Hillbom and Patrick Svensson

64 Colonial Exploitation and Economic Development
The Belgian Congo and the Netherlands Indies compared
Edited by Ewout Frankema and Frans Buelens

65 The State and Business in the Major Powers
An economic history 1815–1939
Robert Millward

66 Privatization and Transition in Russia in the Early 1990s
Carol Scott Leonard and David Pitt-Watson

67 Large Databases in Economic History
Research methods and case studies
Edited by Mark Casson and Nigar Hashimzade

68 **A History of Market Performance**
From ancient Babylonia to the modern world
Edited by R.J. van der Spek, Jan Luiten van Zanden and Bas van Leeuwen

69 **Central Banking in a Democracy**
The Federal Reserve and its alternatives
John H. Wood

70 **The History of Migration in Europe**
Perspectives from economics, politics and sociology
Edited by Francesca Fauri

71 **Famines in European Economic History**
The last great European famines reconsidered
Edited by Declan Curran, Lubomyr Luciuk and Andrew Newby

72 **Natural Resources and Economic Growth**
Learning from history
Edited by Marc Badia-Miró, Vicente Pinilla and Henry Willebald

Natural Resources and Economic Growth

Learning from history

Edited by Marc Badia-Miró,
Vicente Pinilla and Henry Willebald

LONDON AND NEW YORK

First published 2015
by Routledge
2 Park Square, Milton Park, Abingdon, Oxon OX14 4RN

and by Routledge
711 Third Avenue, New York, NY 10017

Routledge is an imprint of the Taylor & Francis Group, an informa business

© 2015 selection and editorial matter, Marc Badia-Miró, Vicente Pinilla and Henry Willebald; individual chapters, the contributors

The right of the editors to be identified as the authors of the editorial matter, and of the authors for their individual chapters, has been asserted in accordance with sections 77 and 78 of the Copyright, Designs and Patents Act 1988.

All rights reserved. No part of this book may be reprinted or reproduced or utilized in any form or by any electronic, mechanical, or other means, now known or hereafter invented, including photocopying and recording, or in any information storage or retrieval system, without permission in writing from the publishers.

Trademark notice: Product or corporate names may be trademarks or registered trademarks, and are used only for identification and explanation without intent to infringe.

British Library Cataloguing in Publication Data
A catalogue record for this book is available from the British Library

Library of Congress Cataloging in Publication Data
Natural resources and economic growth : learning from history / edited by Marc Badia-Miró, Vicente Pinilla and Henry Willebald.
   pages cm
    1. Natural resources–History. 2. Economic development–History.
   3. Economic history. I. Badia-Miró, Marc.
   HC85.N35353 2015
   333.7–dc23
                                          2014046165

ISBN: 978-1-138-78218-1 (hbk)
ISBN: 978-1-315-76935-6 (ebk)

Typeset in Times New Roman
by Wearset Ltd, Boldon, Tyne and Wear

Printed and bound in the United States of America by Publishers Graphics, LLC on sustainably sourced paper.

Contents

List of figures	xi
List of tables	xiii
Notes on contributors	xv
Preface	
THORVALDUR GYLFASON	xvii

1 **Introduction: natural resources and economic development – what can we learn from history?**   1
HENRY WILLEBALD, MARC BADIA-MIRÓ AND VICENTE PINILLA

2 **From resource curse to rent curse: a theoretical perspective**   26
RICHARD M. AUTY

3 **Scarcity, frontiers and the resource curse: a historical perspective**   54
EDWARD B. BARBIER

4 **Botswana: caught in a natural resource trap**   77
ELLEN HILLBOM

5 **Oil as sweet as honey: linking natural resources, government institutions and domestic capital investment in Nigeria 1960–2000**   100
HANAAN MARWAH

6 **The USA as a case study in resource-based development**   119
GAVIN WRIGHT

7 **Welfare states and development patterns in Latin America**   140
LUIS BÉRTOLA

Contents

8 Oil illusion and delusion: Mexico and Venezuela over the twentieth century — 160
MARÍA DEL MAR RUBIO-VARAS

9 Public finances and natural resources in Bolivia, 1883–2010: is there a fiscal curse? — 184
JOSÉ A. PERES-CAJÍAS

10 Long-run development in Chile and natural resource curse: linkages, policy and growth, 1850–1950 — 204
MARC BADIA-MIRÓ AND CRISTIÁN A. DUCOING

11 Mixed blessings: mining in Indonesia's economy, 1870–2010 — 226
PIERRE VAN DER ENG

12 Land abundance, frontier expansion and appropriability: settler economies during the first globalization — 248
HENRY WILLEBALD

13 The lucky country syndrome in Australia: resources, social democracy and regimes of development in historical political economy perspective — 271
CHRISTOPHER LLOYD

14 The institutional foundations of natural resource based knowledge economies — 294
SIMON VILLE AND OLAV WICKEN

15 Avoiding the resource curse? Democracy and natural resources in Norway since 1900 — 313
ANDREAS R. DUGSTAD SANDERS AND PÅL THONSTAD SANDVIK

16 Water scarcity and agricultural growth in Spain: from curse to blessing? — 339
IGNACIO CAZCARRO, ROSA DUARTE, MIGUEL MARTÍN-RETORTILLO, VICENTE PINILLA AND ANA SERRANO

Index — 362

Figures

3.1	The classic pattern of frontier expansion	58
3.2	Phases of frontier expansion in North and South America, 1500–1914	60
3.3	Phases of frontier expansion in Asia and the Pacific, 1500–1914	61
3.4	Phases of frontier expansion in Africa, 1500–1914	62
4.1	Gini for Botswana, 1921–2010	83
4.2	Agriculture, industry and services, value added, 1960–2013	84
4.3	Botswana's annual GDP growth, 1960–2013	85
5.1	Value of Nigerian exports 1900–1945, 1945–1964	103
5.2	Company planned capacity vs. actual cement production 1964–1970	113
6.1	Coal production, USA, UK, Germany 1850–1913	122
6.2	Oil production, USA and Middle East 1900–1912	130
7.1	Total wealth and types of per capita wealth in seven regions (2005)	143
7.2	Latin America and the "West" 1870–1930	143
7.3	Rents of natural resources as a share of per capita GDP, 1970–2010	153
7.4	Uruguay: land rents on agricultural and overall GDP, 1908–1966	154
7.5	Uruguay: real price of land (deflated by CPI) and estimation of income	155
8.1	Oil production and home consumption in Mexico and Venezuela 1901–2011	162
8.2	Oil exports as percentage of total exports by value, Venezuela and Mexico 1901–2011	163
8.3	Share of oil taxes in government fiscal revenue, Venezuela and Mexico 1901–1989	163
8.4	Share of the oil sector in total GDP conventionally measured, Venezuela and Mexico 1920–1992	164
8.5	Index of GDP per capita of six Latin American countries relative to Western Europe 1900–2000	175

xii *Figures*

8.6	GDP per capita ranking vs HDI ranking for 1913, 1939, 1950, 1973 and 1995 for thirty-six countries	176
8.7	Genuine savings of Mexico and Venezuela as percentage of GDP	178
9.1	Natural and non-natural resources revenues in Bolivia, 1883–2010	187
10.1	Copper and nitrates cycles, 1850–1950	206
10.2	Share of Chilean exports by sector, 1844–1950	206
10.3	Share of industrial production by type of product, 1914–1937	213
10.4	Share of imports by type of product, 1882–1950	215
10.5	Share of domestic production over total consumption by type of product, 1911–1935	216
11.1	Gross value added in mining, 1870–2010	227
11.2	Cumulative shares of key commodities in gross value added in mining, 1870–2010	229
11.3	Shares of mining commodities in exports and of mining gross value added in GDP, 1870–2010	230
11.4	Share of tax and non-tax income from mining in total central government revenue and in gross value added from mining, 1870–2010	239
11.5	Implicit price indices of GVA in mining, 1870–2010	242
13.1	Australia's export profile 2013	280
13.2	Australia's exports by sector 2004–07	285
13.3	Mining overtakes manufacturing; employment generation in mining backward linkage industries	286
13.4	Australian industry share of output	287
13.5	Australian exports	287
15.1	GDP per capita in Europe, 1900	315
15.2	Electricity production per capita	316
15.3	Norwegian aluminium exports, 1946–75	322
15.4	State revenue from the petroleum sector	331
15.5	Mill. Sm^3 oil equivalents per year	331
15.6	GDP per capita (PPP) in select countries, 2013	332
16.1	Long-term average annual rainfall, 1982–2002	342
16.2	Trajectory of irrigated area, 1935–2006	343
16.3	Percentage of crop production, ratios of rainfed to irrigated production	345
16.4	Regional distribution of agricultural crop production as percentage of the total, 1930	349
16.5	Regional distribution of agricultural crop production as percentage of the total, 2005	350
16.6	Average annual rainfall in Spain vs changes in the share of agricultural crop production	351
16.7	Change in the percentage of irrigated land on total agricultural area, 1916–2009	352

Tables

2.1	Per capita GDP growth 1960–2010, by resource endowment	27
2.2	Stylised rent stream properties and predicted political economy impacts, by rent source	33
2.3	Per capita income, structural change and domestic absorption, post-1973	35
2.4	Principal features of two stylised facts rent-driven development models	42
4.1	Colonial investments in Bechuanaland Protectorate 1930–1946	81
4.2	Colonial administrative expenditure in Bechuanaland Protectorate 1900–1966	81
5.1	Comparison of estimates of fixed capital formation 1948–1952	104
5.2	Gross fixed capital formation 1961/1962–1967/1968	112
6.1	US mineral production as percentage of world total, 1870–1913	121
6.2	Average metal content of copper ore	126
7.1	Wealth structure by region, 2005	144
7.2	Heterogeneity of structural productivity by groups of countries, Gini index	151
7.3	Heterogeneity of labor productivity in Latin America by major sectors, 1991–2006	152
7.4	Inequality-adjusted Human Development Index	156
9.1	Relative importance of natural resources revenues within total revenues, 1883–2010	186
9.2	Latin American central governments' spending in education and health as a share of GDP, 1900–2010	192
9.3	Primary school support ratios in Latin America, 1950–2010	194
9.4	Primary education support ratio over tertiary education support ratio in Latin America and other selected countries, 1965–2007	195
10.1	Copper production in thousands of tons	208
10.2	Nitrate production and labour productivity, 1880–1902	210

xiv *Tables*

10.3	Evolution of industry and the GDP in Chile, 1980–1938	213
10.4	Copper production by kind, selected years	218
11.1	Economic role and composition of mining in Indonesia, 1971–2010	228
11.2	Active exploration permits and mining concessions in Indonesia, 1890–1938	231
11.3	Outstanding contracts of work and mining permits, 2000	235
12.1	Gross agricultural product per worker, natural resources and institutions	258
12.2	Growth of gross agricultural product per worker, natural resources and institutions	259
12.3	Income distribution, natural resources and institutions	260
16.1	Decomposition of agricultural production	346
16.2	Crop production and percentage of group products in agricultural crop production	347
16.3	Percentage of rainfed production by group of products on total agricultural crop production	348

Contributors

Richard M. Auty, Professor, Lancaster Environment Centre, Lancaster University, UK.

Marc Badia-Miró, Lecturer, Economic History Department, University of Barcelona, Spain.

Edward B. Barbier, Professor, Department of Economics & Finance, University of Wyoming, USA.

Luís Bértola, Professor, Programa de Historia Económica y Social, Facultad de Ciencias Sociales, Universidad de la República, Uruguay.

Ignacio Cazcarro, Researcher, BC3-Basque Centre for Climate Change, Bilbao, Spain.

Rosa Duarte, Associate Professor, Department of Economic Analysis, University of Zaragoza, Spain.

Cristián A. Ducoing, Post-Doctoral Researcher, Economics and Business School EICO, University of Valparaíso, Chile.

Andreas R. Dugstad Sanders, Researcher, European University Institute, Italy.

Pierre van der Eng, Associate Professor, Indonesia Project, Crawford School for Public Policy, The Australian National University, Australia.

Thorvaldur Gylfason, Professor of Economics, Department of Economics, University of Iceland, Iceland.

Ellen Hillbom, Associate Professor, Lund University, Sweden.

Christopher Lloyd, Emeritus Professor, School of Business, University of New England, Australia and Guest Professor at Finnish Centre of Excellence for Historical Research, Tampere and Jyväskylä Universities, Finland.

Miguel Martín-Retortillo, Researcher, Department of Applied Economics and Economic History, University of Zaragoza, Spain.

Hanaan Marwah, PhD Oxford University, Independent Scholar, UK.

José A. Peres-Cajías, Assistant Professor, Escuela de la Producción y la Competitividad, Universidad Católica Boliviana San Pablo, Bolivia.

Vicente Pinilla, Professor, Department of Applied Economics and Economic History, University of Zaragoza, Spain.

María del Mar Rubio-Varas, Associate Professor, Economics Department, Universidad Pública of Navarra, Spain.

Pål Thonstad Sandvik, Professor, Norwegian University of Science and Technology, Norway.

Ana Serrano, Assistant Professor, Department of Economics, University of Girona, Spain.

Simon Ville, Professor, School of Humanities and Social Inquiry, University of Wollongong, Australia.

Olav Wicken, Centre for Technology, Innovation and Culture, University of Oslo, Norway.

Henry Willebald, Associate Professor, Institute of Economics, Universidad de la República, Uruguay.

Gavin Wright, William Robertson Coe Professor, Department of Economics, Stanford University, USA.

Preface

There was a time, not long ago, when abundant natural resources were commonly and unquestioningly viewed as an important pillar of economic progress and prosperity. Australia, Canada and the United States were undisputable cases in point. True, some other countries – e.g. Japan and Switzerland – had made rapid advances and reached high standards of living without the benefit of bountiful natural resource endowments, but they were the exceptions that proved the rule.

It was not until internationally comparable national accounts data became available for a large number of countries around the world that it became possible to reconsider on empirical grounds some firmly held views on economic growth and development, including, in particular, the view that economic growth resulted from technological progress and little else and also the view that abundant natural resources were always and everywhere an unmitigated blessing. The new data opened new vistas, new lines of inquiry.

Thus, it was only after 1990 when thirty years of national accounts data for most countries reporting to the World Bank – i.e. nearly the entire membership of the United Nations – had become available that it became feasible to revisit, with statistical methods, the received theory of economic growth that held long-run economic growth to be immune to political and societal institutions as well as the belief, inherited from old economic geography, that natural resources are always a blessing. (Not much attention was paid to the apparent inconsistency between those two views.)

Now, twenty-five years later, a good deal more is, or appears to be, known than before about economic growth and development, including some of the ways in which good policies and good institutions are good for growth. For example, inflation is much lower on average in Africa and Latin America today than twenty-five years ago partly because it is now commonly understood that high inflation tends to undermine economic efficiency and growth. Econometric research, supported by theoretical analysis as well as by historical case studies and vice versa, has similarly suggested that abundant natural resources, if not well managed, can prove to be a mixed blessing, or worse. Econometric cross-country studies have encouraged other approaches, including detailed comparative studies and case studies stressing historical developments and institutions.

There is, of course, nothing wrong with having abundant natural resource endowments, even if such endowments sometimes attract the wrong sort of people to politics. Rather, the issue at stake is the risk of mismanagement of the resource rents, especially in countries with weak institutions and without fully fledged democracy.

Norway (pop. 5.1 million) has since its oil discoveries around 1970 built up the world's largest sovereign wealth fund amounting currently to $170,000 for every man, woman and child in Norway. The fund is managed by Norway's independent central bank, kept by design at arm's length from politicians. One of the keys to Norway's success is its deep democratic tradition which made it unlikely if not impossible that socially corrosive rent seeking would arise around the oil sector. Norway's ten oil "commandments", adopted even before oil production began, established ethical guidelines for oil wealth management. Norway's example shows how good governance can be an effective remedy against rent seeking.

Comparative vocabularies of the languages of neighbouring nations can be suggestive. The terms "oil king" and "oil queen" are never heard in Norwegian public debate, in contrast to Russia where "oligarchs" loom large on the national scene. With "sea barons", "quota kings" and "quota queens" throwing their weight about in Iceland's political arena, Icelanders cannot help but notice the difference.

Insofar as democracy guided Norway's successful management of its oil wealth, the advance of democracy around the world in recent years bodes well for many other countries. In Africa, before 1990, there were five or fewer democracies compared with seventeen today. In 1961, of Latin America's ten countries, there were three democracies compared with eight today. In 1943, there were only five democracies in Europe compared with full house today.

There are some fundamental differences between natural resources and natural resource rents and other types of resources and rents. First, natural resource wealth is the sole component of national wealth giving rise to concerns about the need for diversification away from excessive dependence on it. Human resources and social capital do not generate comparable concerns. Second, resource rents differ from regulatory and other types of rent in that, by international law, including the International Covenant on Civil and Political Rights that supersedes national laws, natural resources and the rents derived from them belong to the people as a matter of inalienable human rights (Wenar 2008). Put simply, natural resources belong to the people. Democrats are less likely than dictators to try to grab natural resources, thus violating human rights to consolidate their political power.

This means that only fully fledged democracies – e.g. the United States – can lawfully bring the rights to the utilization of their natural resources exclusively into private hands. In some autocratic countries – e.g. Equatorial Guinea – the democratic legitimacy needed to justify the transfer of natural resource rents into private hands is missing. Citizens of countries where ordinary people are demonstrably deprived of their fair share in their countries' natural resources are not only badly treated from the point of view of social efficiency and fairness, but also – this is often overlooked – from the point of view of international human rights proclamations that prohibit discrimination in any shape or form. True, low taxes and generous transfers and subsidies tend to weaken popular demand for democracy in some resource-rich countries, even if such benefits amount to only a small fraction of each citizen's fair share of the nation's natural resource wealth, an imbalance that advancing democracy aided by international law can help rectify.

This volume brings together wide-ranging scholarly work on natural resources and their role in economic development around the world. The contributing authors expertly offer the reader a vast panorama that reaches far beyond statistical cross-country studies through a balanced blend of economic theory, history and institutions supported by incisive case studies from eleven countries on six continents – Botswana, Nigeria, the United States, Mexico, Venezuela, Bolivia, Chile, Indonesia, Australia, Norway and Spain.

Thorvaldur Gylfason

Reference

Wenar, Leif (2008), "Property Rights and the Resource Curse", *Philosophy and Public Affairs* 36, No. 1, Winter, 1–32.

1 Introduction

Natural resources and economic development – what can we learn from history?

Henry Willebald, Marc Badia-Miró and Vicente Pinilla

1 Introduction

Economic development is no longer regarded as dependent only on the accumulation of physical and human capital. Academics now argue that there is a third form of "capital" or "economic asset", which is important to the performance of the system of production, consumption, investment, saving and welfare. This distinct type of capital is the natural and environmental resource endowment available to an economy, and it is commonly referred to as "natural capital". Capital refers to any stock that yields a flow of valuable goods or services now and in the future. Standard growth models emphasize the role of capital produced by humans and three types can be identified: manufactured capital (factories, buildings, tools and other physical objects identified with means of production), human capital (the stock of education, skills, culture and knowledge stored in human beings themselves) and social capital (connections within and between social networks). However, there is increasing consensus that natural capital is a fundamental determinant of economic development.

Natural capital consists of the various ways that the environment encourages production and supports most aspects of human existence. Two kinds of natural capital may be differentiated. First, there is non-renewable natural capital like fossil fuels and mineral deposits, which do not recover on a time scale close to the rate at which people use them. For all practical purposes, fossil fuels are literally consumed by use. This type of natural capital generally yields no services until it is extracted. The second type is renewable natural capital, which is active and self-maintaining, and uses energy from the sun and the Earth's core. Ecosystems are renewable natural capital. A forest or marine ecosystem provides a flow or annual yield of timber or seafood, and this flow can be sustained in the long run if the ecosystem is not deteriorating. The generation of natural resources is just one function of natural capital, yielding a flow of ecosystem services when the system is left in place (Ayres *et al.* 1997).

Natural capital is important for sustainable economic development, but increasing economic dependence on natural resource exploitation appears to be an obstacle to growth and development in most low- and middle-income economies in the world (Barbier 2005). The recent literature reveals a negative relationship between economic growth per capita and some measures of natural capital, which has been described as the "curse" of the abundance of natural resources (Sachs and Warner 1995, 2001; Auty 2001a; Gylfason 2006, 2007). Why should an abundance of natural resources often be connected to poorer economic performance? Is an abundance of natural resources a "curse" for economic growth? Are we faced with a general pattern or do these phenomena depend on specific conditions (e.g. technology or institutions) in an economy, the characteristics of supply and demand, and the effect of different historical circumstances?

We divide this chapter into two sections following this introduction. In section 2, we review the literature on the analytical and empirical relations between natural resource endowments and economic growth from a long run perspective. First, we introduce some concepts and a general overview of the debate (section 2.1). Second, we present two theses that represent the "natural resources blessing hypothesis", which was a commonly accepted idea of economic growth in the mid-twentieth century (section 2.2). Next we present three perspectives from the so-called "natural resources curse hypothesis": the "productive structure approach" (section 2.3), the "crowding out approach" (section 2.4) and the "factor endowment and institutional change hypothesis" (section 2.5), considering the different channels of cause and effect that can be identified.[1] We then refer this analytical framework to the chapters of this volume and discuss the contributions made to the literature. Finally, in section 3 we present the "lessons from the history" for today's resource-rich developing economies and conclude.

2 Abundance of natural resources: which channels and what causality?

2.1 The debate: "curse" or "blessing"?

To discuss the impact of natural resources on economic development it is useful to distinguish between resource abundance (a stock measure of resource wealth), resource rents (the "windfall" flow of earnings derived from natural resources at some point in time) and resource dependence (the degree to which economies have access to alternative sources of income other than resource extraction). Obviously these concepts can be correlated, because economies with abundant natural capital may obtain high incomes from extraction, they may specialize in primary exports and they may become dependent on resource trading. However, some resource-rich countries are not dependent on resources and some relatively resource-poor economies are. As a consequence, there is much confusion about the exact meaning of the concept "resource abundance". This term may be used differently in different sciences and even in different areas of economics. For example, resource abundance usually means the amount of potentially exploitable natural resources in the natural sciences and in environmental economics, but in studies of growth economics, resource abundance means the amount of natural resources and reserves that have already been exploited (or are being exploited). The share of potential resources which eventually becomes economically exploitable depends on many factors such as economic and political conditions, and technological progress, and it is therefore an endogenous factor in the economic system.

In the literature of the 1990s, the "curse" was regarded as an almost unquestionable empirical fact. This idea was based on an index constructed in terms of primary exports as a share of GDP, but this is more a measure of dependence on natural resources than their abundance. In these terms, the analysis concentrated on the channels which connect the two processes (natural resource dependence and economic growth) based on the conventional factors affecting economic performance, such as the accumulation of productive factors and technological progress. However, the literature has advanced systematically in bringing institutional arrangements into the analysis, considering (i) that institutions have increasingly entered the mainstream of recent economic thought; (ii) that the ownership of natural resources, whether in terms of the assets themselves or of the rents derived from their exploitation, is a key issue; and (iii) that both interest groups and the state are key agents in the formation of the property system. The results have been mixed, but there is a general consensus in the literature that some kind of "conditionality" is involved. The idea is that the quality of institutions plays a central role in the curse or the blessing of natural resources, and even when there are abundant natural resources in an economy it can perform well if its institutions are "good" (this would involve some kind of curse-reversal). Finally, the latest contributions in the literature have reacted to this consensus. A number of authors distinguish between natural resource dependence and natural resource endowment or abundance, and take into account alternative indicators such as the stock of natural capital or total natural resource assets. Empirical studies in this analytical line challenge the traditional view in that they invert the relationship, according to which resource abundance positively affects growth and institutional quality, and identify "this apparent paradox [with] a red herring" (Brunnschweiler and Blute 2008). Does this assertion mean we are faced with a meaningless debate? On the contrary, the debate constitutes a real "research programme" and is especially useful to enhance our understanding of the economic performance of economies that are based on the successful exploitation of natural resources.

Our aim in this section is to review the literature on the relationships between abundant natural resources and economic performance. In recent years the debate has moved to less extreme positions, so that mixed results are now accepted and certain institutional aspects are actively considered. The discussion has also broadened the notion of economic performance to include concepts other than economic growth, like poverty, inequality and various welfare indicators. However, the debate has largely concentrated on analyses of the second half of the twentieth century, and new light can be shed on the discussion by applying these concepts in the long run and with an historical perspective.

2.2 Natural resource abundance as a blessing

In the last quarter of the nineteenth century and up to WWI many countries grew rapidly. This economic boom was closely associated with export-led industrial expansion in Western Europe and the United States, and the temperate regions of North and South America, South Africa and Australasia also benefited. Industrializing European countries needed cheap natural resources from the "New World" and the new settlement economies needed to import capital and labour to expand their capacity to provide resource-based exports. A key factor in this world development was the transport revolution at the end of the nineteenth century (O'Rourke and Williamson 1994; O'Rourke et al. 1996), which made it possible for these new regions to join the world economy.

According to Myint (1958), trade was the channel whereby idle resources – in particular natural resources – in new economies were brought into productive use and fuelled economic growth. According to the "staples theory", development in many countries has been built around the expansion of export sectors in general, and natural resource exports in particular. The "vent for surplus theory", a Smithian concept, suggests that trade was the means by which unexploited resources started generating wealth and economic growth (Innis 1930, 1940; Bertram 1963; Watkins 1963; Chambers and Gordon 1966; Smith 1976; Southey 1978; Altman 2003; Wellstead 2007). Both frameworks consider the presence of excess resources in the form of land and natural resources which are not fully exploited in a closed economy, and international trade allows these new natural resources to be exploited to increase exports and foster growth (Barbier 2005; and Chapter 5 (Marwah 2015) for the cashcrop export cycle).

In the "vent for surplus theory", Adam Smith analysed trade for a country which had been isolated but then entered international trade. Trade provided new effective demand for the output of surplus resources which would have remained idle had there been no external trade (so that exports can be increased without reducing output for the domestic market). Smith implied that internal demand was inelastic because there was zero growth in the demand for resources to enable society to benefit from the new market economy. According to Harold Innis, the economic history of countries with abundant natural resources has been dominated by the discrepancy between the centre and the margin of western civilization.

> The raw material supplied to the mother country stimulated manufacturers of the finished product and also of the products which were in demand in the colony. Large-scale production of raw materials was encouraged by improvement of techniques of production, of marketing, and of transport as well as by improvement in the manufacture of the finished product.
> (Innis 1956, p. 385)

In these terms, agriculture, industry, transportation, trade, finance, and even governmental activities tended to be subordinate to the production of the staple for a highly specialized manufacturing society. Therefore, the staple theory is a subset of the export-led growth hypothesis, and it is designed to explain the growth and economic development of resource-rich economies. Since the 1990s it has come in for heavy criticism (Altman 2003), but it remains an important contemporary framework for economic analysis and it can help answer some of the questions about the curse and blessings of an abundance of natural resources.

Meanwhile, the abundant literature on the development of the United States emphasizes the positive impact of resource endowments on welfare levels in the late nineteenth and early twentieth centuries (David and Wright 1997; Mitchener and McLean 2003; Wright and Czelusta 2004; Czelusta and Wright 2007). Wright (1990) connects the United States' leading role in manufacturing to technological progress and learning potential in the American mining sector. Similarly, David and Wright (1997), Wright (2001) and Wright and Czelusta (2004) claim that mining encouraged the creation of prestigious educational institutions and diffused knowledge to other sectors (Chapter 6, Wright 2015), an argument which has points in common with the idea of biased technological change induced by the abundance of natural resources (Boyce 2013). The literature has also examined other successful country cases in depth, such as Botswana (Chapter 4, Hillbom 2015) where state ownership and management of abundant natural resources has driven economic performance.

A number of authors have recently proposed models to represent how the opening-up of a previously closed economic region to staples-led trade can lead to economic development (Lundahl 1998). Some of them employ the concept of the "endogenous" or "moving" frontier (Hansen 1979; Di Tella 1982; Findlay and Lundahl 1994; Findlay 1995), and others extend the framework of the staple approach to include the nature of export staples, regional characteristics and institutional structure (Schedvin 1990). These models also offer an explanation as to why resource-based development may be initially successful but may not be sustainable in the long run. Various late nineteenth and early twentieth century economies specialized in primary exports while maintaining only a small manufacturing sector (an activity which does not usually expand in this type of economy), and the dynamic demand for primary products during the golden age (1870–1913) allowed them to continue to grow. However, they remained vulnerable to falls in international commodity prices relative to the prices of manufactured goods. Once a country specializes in resource-based exports it may find it difficult to move away from its primary specialization and take the path of modern manufacturing (Chapter 4 (Hillbom 2015), Chapter 8 (Rubio-Varas 2015), Chapter 10 (Badia-Miró and Ducoing 2015), Chapter 11 (van der Eng 2015)). Frontier-based development (Barbier 2007; Chapter 3 (Barbier 2015); Chapter 12 (Willebald 2015)) is symptomatic of a pattern of economy-wide resource exploitation that generates little additional economic rent, and the rents that are produced are not reinvested in more productive and dynamics sectors (Chapter 7, Bértola 2015). This form of economic life, which is typical of "new" economies, was able to offer high standards of living but only for as long as domestic resource supplies and world demand remained dynamic. Declines in demand or increases in supply would have severe consequences for the internal political economy of a country, leaving it weakly positioned to react to the challenge of finding a new basic product to trade. These economies face the risks of the "staple trap". In this sense, the small domestic market, and the factor proportion – an abundance of land relative to labour and capital – create a comparative advantage in resource intensive exports (staples).

> Economic development will be a process of diversification around an export base. The central concept of a staple theory, therefore, is the spread effects of the export sector, that is the impact of export activity on domestic economy and society.
>
> (Watkins 1963, pp. 53–54)

In this situation the creation of backward, forward and final demand "linkages" in the export of particular staples would be a key element in the success or failure of a country's long-run economic performance (as in the case of Indonesia, Chapter 11 (van der Eng 2015)), or the comparison between Mexico and Venezuela (Chapter 8, Rubio-Varas 2015) and between Argentina and Australia in the long run (Duncan and Fogarty 1984)). To sum up, these kinds of models involve notions where the export orientation of some economies presents lock-in effects whereby the main primary specialization blocks structural change and impedes economic growth.

Lastly, we need to consider the numerous theories which posit the positive outcomes from expanding fiscal capacity due to rising tax receipts in the context of a natural resources boom to provide an explanation of the natural resource blessing (Palma 2000; Hujo 2012) or, at least, a partial explanation of this process (Chapter 10, Badia-Miró and Ducoing 2015).

2.3 Productive structure approach: the curse and primary specialization

We may distinguish a couple of viewpoints in this approach. In the first place, the allocation of resources between productive sectors with different spillover effects on aggregate growth emphasizes the role of specialization in economic development. Economies in which production is based on natural resource abundance, where manufacturing and services account for only a small share of the productive structure, will grow more slowly. Manufacturing and services lead to a more complex division of labour and have more potential to incorporate knowledge into production and thus develop a sustainable growth trajectory. Second, the so-called Dutch disease is an important concept in the literature on the natural resource curse hypothesis. Economies with abundant natural resources are subject to periodic rises and falls in their performance because commodity prices on world markets are variable and from time to time new exploitable natural resources are discovered. This process generates volatility in export and fiscal earnings and a real appreciation in the value of the country's currency, hurting other export industries. These two viewpoints both refer to productive structure, but they emphasize different aspects when it comes to identifying the origin and the evolution of the curse. The first highlights the predominance of primary activities as a long-run process with cumulative changes, while the second offers an explanation for the kind of sudden change in which the movement of relative prices is the centre of the process.

2.3.1 Primary specialization and restrictions affecting structural change

In the Development Theory propounded in the 1950s, ideas about growth and structural change were closely related. The argument was that development involved the reallocation of productive factors from sectors with low productivity to activities with high productivity, which are characterized by increasing returns and complementarities (Rostow 1953; Lewis 1954, 1955; Myrdal 1957; Rosenstein-Rodan 1957; Hirschman 1958; Nurkse 1962). As the industrial sector was supposed to constitute the main activity where higher levels of productivity could be obtained, the process would involve changes in the economic structure of the economy, and manufacturing would gain a greater share of GDP and employment. Manufacturing generates productive spillovers, forward and backward linkages, and economic and technological externalities which maintain increasing returns in the long run. Hence, economic growth is hampered in countries with an economic structure based on a high share of primary activities, and the abundance of natural resources is a curse that impedes economic development. As Chapter 4 (Hillbom 2015) argues, specialization dependence poses significant challenges for the economy of Botswana, even though the country could be considered a successful case.

In the 1960s the theoretical and empirical centre of attention changed, and the focus shifted to modelling economic growth based on an aggregated production function (Solow 1956; Swan 1956). In this new approach, productive activities and structural change by definition played a secondary role, and the assumption of exogenous technical progress meant that less attention was paid to matters of sector performance. However, the subject came back into the limelight in mainstream theories of economic development in the 1980s with the New Theory of Economic Growth (NTEG) and the endogeneity of technical progress. These models have two or three sectors; there are increasing returns to intensive research and development (R+D); and there is greater productive diversification to obtain positive rates of growth in the long run. The new theories in the fields of international trade and the geographic location of productive activities (Krugman 1991; Grossman and Helpman 1994), the new theory of economic growth (Aghion and Howitt 1992) and the new theory of development (Ray 2000; Ros 2000) are clear of recent theoretical and empirical contributions to the subject (Cimoli *et al.* 2005). Given that primary activities do not by nature form endogenous cores of innovation and technical progress, economic dependence on natural resources results in low output growth. The historical evidence certainly confirms these theoretical insights where de-industrialization, induced by global forces, offers a potential offset to the gains from trade (Williamson 2011).

There are two alternative positions to the mainstream literature, which identify primary specialization with low economic dynamism. One of them is derived from the Marxist and structuralist tradition, and the other proposes a framework derived from the Schumpeterian analysis of the economic growth and innovation.

First, we consider the unequal development view, whose proponents include the Latin American Structuralist school and some pioneers of the Development Economics school (Prebish 1950; Singer 1950; Myrdal 1957; Seers 1962; Dixon and Thirwall 1975), as well as scholars identified with Marxism and Dependency theory (Baran 1957; Frank 1967; Furtado 1969; Emmanuel 1972; Wallerstein 1974; Amin 1975). This literature includes various models and many of the key elements feature in the North-South trade model (Krugman 1981). The idea is that if trade reinforces the economic supremacy of the leading region this is because "a small 'head start' for one region will accumulate over time, with exports of manufactures from the leading region crowding out the industrial sector of the lagging region" (Krugman 1981, p. 149). One of the main theories of the unequal development of the centre (industrial core) and the periphery, with its specialization in primary production, is the Prebisch-Singer Hypothesis. According to this idea, there is an inherent long-run trend for (non-oil) primary product prices to fall relative to manufacturing prices. This may not be a problem if it is the result of increased technical progress and the country concerned is able to export more and improve its position in world markets. However, worsening terms of trade will affect the economic growth of a developing country because the income elasticity of demand for manufactured goods is much greater than the income elasticity of commodities. This combination of relatively low income elasticity and worsening terms of trade means, then, that countries which rely on primary goods will grow more slowly than economies that are based on manufacturing industries.

Recent post-Keynesian and post-Kaldorian theories address this issue and formalize these limitations on the balance of payments and economic growth (McCombie and Thirwall 1994; McCombie and Roberts 2002) in terms of the differing income elasticities of demand for exports and imports, and the dynamics of the current account. A vast empirical literature has attempted to examine the main trends in the evolution of the terms of trade. Results point to an improvement for the exporters of commodities in the long nineteenth century. According to Williamson (2011), this strengthened export specialization in these products and hindered industrialization. In the short twentieth century, the economic crisis of the 1930s and the shocks of the 1970s caused a sharp deterioration in the terms of trade for commodity exporters (though not for oil exporters in the second crisis) (Ocampo and Parra-Lancourt 2010; Serrano and Pinilla 2011). Some authors have noted that the price volatility factor has probably been very damaging to the growth potential of countries which are highly dependent on exports of commodities (Williamson 2012).

In the 1960s, the concept of a gap in technological capacity emerged from the contributions of authors concerned with technological dynamics and their influence on international trade and economic growth (Posner 1961; Freeman 1963; Hirsch 1965; Vernon 1966). On this view, technological asymmetries are the key to explaining international movements of goods and services between countries, and national specialization patterns. Innovation is not diffused immediately, and technologically advanced countries enjoy an initial advantage and can expand their share in the world market. In this light, economic growth in the long run depends on a country's ability to narrow the technological gap. Modern models have improved the formalization of technological dynamics in the Neo-Schumpeterian tradition and have included the notion of heterogeneity between agents (Dosi 1988) and the analysis of aggregated economies (Dosi et al. 1990; Fagerberg 1994). Industrialization is a process of "accumulation of capabilities" which led from traditional, especially rural, economies to others driven by industrial activities (nowadays also advanced services) "able to systematically learn how to implement and eventually how to generate new ways of producing and new products under conditions of dynamic increasing returns" (Cimoli et al. 2005, p. 2). The Evolutionary School takes the "industrialist" ideas and emphasizes that technological change is the motor of structural change and the source of international specialization. In economies that successfully internalize new paradigms and technological trajectories, changes in sector composition appear and technical progress diffuses to the whole economy. This process needs the existence of connections between codified knowledge, tacit knowledge and various capacities to transform information into innovation and development (Nelson and Winter 1982). The notion of technical change and industrial dynamics as evolutionary process (Dosi and Nelson 2010) has led authors to consider the systemic relationships between enterprises, organizations and institutional structure. "National Systems of Innovation" have become a central concept of models (Freeman 1987; Nelson 1994; Cimoli and Dosi 1995), and there is a privileged level of analysis referring to the interactions and co-evolutionary dynamics between the sub-domains of scientific knowledge, development, improvement, and adoption of new techniques, political and legal structures, and cultural domain-shaping values, norms and customs (Dosi 2007, p. 2).

Like in the mainstream, heterodox views therefore focus on why economies that base their productive expansion on the exploitation of natural resources find it difficult to obtain high rates of growth. The "curse" is expressed as a permanent process of economic divergence.

2.3.2 The Dutch disease and volatility of natural resource prices

A resource price boom or windfall may lead initially to an expansion of the export sector. Nevertheless, the impact on the economy as a whole is uncertain. A real appreciation of the rest of the economy is observed (Corden 1984) when some of these windfall earnings are spent in the country (directly or indirectly through the state). In addition, increases in labour productivity in a booming export sector pull the work force and attract economic resources away from other economic sectors. This drives a de-industrialization process and reinforces real appreciation due to excess demand which the domestic market cannot satisfy (Gylfason 2001). As a result, the economy will in the long run become specialized in production and exports based on natural resources, and consequently economic growth will be slow and intermittent.

At the same time, primary-product exporters which exploit comparative advantage by specializing in one or two products expose themselves to higher price risk than those that have a wider range of export products (Blattman *et al.* 2007; Williamson 2011). Thus, the Dutch disease tends to reduce the level of total exports or bias their composition away from the kind of high-tech and high-value-added manufacturing and service sectors that may be particularly beneficial for economic growth (Chapter 10, Badia-Miró and Ducoing 2015). The fact that exchange rates are unstable causes uncertainty, and this may hurt exports, investment (Herbertsson *et al.* 1999; Sachs and Warner 1999a) and other trade activities including foreign investment (FDI), which suffers as investment opportunities other than natural resource exploitation dry up. Hence, natural capital tends to crowd out foreign capital (Auty 1997, 2001b; Gylfason 2007). Besides, industries based on natural resources can pay higher wages (Sachs and Warner 2001) and also higher interest rates than other export and import activities, which can become increasingly uncompetitive in world markets.

Turning to the effects of high volatility on commodity prices, countries with abundant natural resources undergo booms and busts at irregular intervals. Recent research into the endogeneity of resource dependence suggests that volatility may be the quintessence of the resource curse (van der Ploeg 2011). This evolution makes for irregular changes in export earnings and periodic real appreciation of the national currency, and it works to the detriment of other export industries and foreign capital inflows in a process that has come to be called the Dutch Disease (Corden 1984; Neary and Wijnbergen 1986; Krugman 1987; Torvik 2001; Drelichman 2005).

2.4 Crowding out: natural capital displaces other capital modalities

In the structure of recent models an abundance of natural resources or heavy dependence on them influences a variable "x" which hampers economic growth (Sachs and Warner 2001). So the task of theorists and empirical researchers has been to identify the mechanisms that connect these two processes. These channels can be seen in terms of crowding out: an abundance of natural capital tends to displace other kinds of capital and hinder the expansion of production (Gylfason 2004, 2007). We focus on rent-seeking activities, the influence of "bad" institutions, effects on the generation of human capital, and the expenditure and saving patterns associated with abundant natural resources.

2.4.1 Rent-seeking, weak institutions and appropriability

In many developing countries, large natural resource rents, especially in combination with badly defined property rights, imperfect markets (or the absence of markets) and permissive legal structures may lead producers to engage in uncontrolled rent-seeking. This diverts resources away from economic activities that are socially more fruitful and it may hamper economic growth (Gelb and Associates 1988; Tornell and Lane 1998, 1999; Ascher 1999; Baland and Francois 2000; Auty 2001b; Gylfason 2001; Torvik 2002).

Huge resource rents may lead to a concentration of economic and political power in the hands of elites which use their rents, once in control, to tilt income and wealth distribution in their favour and thus secure and perpetuate their hold on power. The consequences of this are persistent high inequality (Gylfason and Zoega 2003; Williamson 2011), weakened democracy and political instability, all of which slow growth (Karl 1997; Acemoglu et al. 2001; Collier and Hoeffler 2002, 2005; Dalgaard and Olsson 2008) where political clientelism constitutes the main expression of the natural resources "trap" (Collier 2007), Chapter 4 (Hillbom 2015) and Chapter 5 (Marwah 2015). Governments may be tempted to spoil markets by granting enterprises or individuals privileged access to common-property natural resources, or they may offer producers tariff protection or other favours at the public expense, creating competition for favoured treatment among rent seekers. Extensive rent-seeking may generate corruption in business and government (Krueger 1974; Gray and Kaufmann 1998; Leite and Weidmann 1999; Baland and Francois 2000; Torvik 2002), distort the allocation of resources, weaken fixed investment (by crowding out physical capital), lead to increased public spending (Ross 1999; Atkinson and Hamilton 2003), reduce economic efficiency and work against social equity. Moreover, abundant natural resources may induce a false sense of security among people and governments and cause the state to miss opportunities to impose good economic management and establish high institutional quality (Sachs and Warner 1999b; Auty 2001a, 2001b; Bulte et al. 2005; Sala-i-Martin and Subramanian 2013). In other words, abundant natural capital may crowd out social capital (i.e. the infrastructure and institutions of a society in the broad sense of culture, cohesion, law, legal system, rules, customs and so forth), dragging down economic growth (Gylfason 2004; Auty 2006). Corruption, inequality and the absence of political liberties can, then, be identified as the main channels through which rent-seeking corrodes social capital. Moreover, all three of these factors hinder economic growth and perpetuate poverty, and this effect is not independent of the political regime. In fact, the evidence indicates that the curse is more likely to occur in presidential regimes (and other non-democracies) than in parliamentary systems (Andersen and Aslaksen 2008).

According to Auty (2001b), different kinds of natural resource endowments may have different effects on economic performance. It is especially interesting to distinguish between "point resources" (e.g. mineral and energy resources, activities where the use of capital is intensive) and "diffuse resources" (e.g. cropland and livestock). The former generate greater opportunities for rent-seeking and corruption than the latter, and the negative consequences for economic growth are more serious. In this regard, Isham et al. (2005) argue that export concentration in point resources is strongly associated with weak public institutions, and these are in turn strongly linked to slower economic growth. In fact, as Woolcock *et al.* (2001) show, natural resources-rich economies and different types of resources put diverse pressures on community structures, institutional capacity and state-society relations. Economic growth is more likely to be undermined when natural resources and the rents derived from them (Chapter 2, Auty 2015) are more easily captured and controlled by a narrow elite. Bulte *et al.* (2005) propose similar empirical studies but evaluate the curse in terms of indicators of human welfare, showing that resource-intensive countries tend to have lower levels of human development. This implies that the resource curse phenomenon does not just affect economic growth but has wider impacts, and countries that rely on point resources tend to perform worse.

Boschini *et al.* (2007) demonstrate that the effect of natural resources on economic development is not determined by resource endowments alone but by the interaction between the type of resources available to a country and the quality of its institutions. This combination of factors is the "appropriability" of a resource, a concept which captures the probability that an abundance of natural resources will lead to rent-seeking, corruption or conflict, outcomes which in turn hobble economic development. In economies where resources are highly appropriable, the abundance of resources may have different effects on the dimensions of development (economic growth, inequality, structural change), and the curse may turn out to be a process that is conditioned by the influence of institutional arrangements (Chapter 12, Willebald 2015).

2.4.2 Human capital and skill intensity

Natural resource abundance may reduce private and public incentives to accumulate human capital because of high levels of non-wage income (e.g. dividends, social spending, low taxes) and because the predominant tendency in resource-rich economies is to underestimate the long-run value of education (Birdsall *et al.* 2000; Gylfason 2001; Wood and Mayer 2001; Bravo-Ortega and De Gregorio 2005). In others words, abundant natural capital may crowd out human capital. In terms of the productive structure approach, activities based on natural resources like agriculture, fishing and forestry are less high-skill labour-intensive and probably also less high-quality capital-intensive than other industries, and as a result they confer relatively few external benefits on other industries (Wood and Berge 1997), tending to impede learning by doing, innovation (Sachs and Warner 2001; Papyrakis and Gerlagh 2004), technological progress and economic growth in general.

2.4.3 Expenditure patterns: incentives for saving and investment

Natural resource abundance may prevent private and public incentives from promoting saving and investment (Papyrakis and Gerlagh 2006). As the owners of natural resources accumulate more, we expect the demand for capital to fall, leading to lower real interest rates and slower growth (Gylfason and Zoega 2006).

Manufacturing often enjoys increasing returns to scale and creates positive externalities. A decrease in the scale of manufacturing thus depresses the productivity and profitability of physical capital and accelerates the decline in investment (Gillis *et al.* 1996; Sachs and Warner 1999a). In other words, abundant natural capital may crowd out physical capital. Natural resource wealth reduces the need for savings and investment as the abundance of natural resources provides a continuous stream of future windfalls, and welfare seems less dependent on the transfer of man-made capital to future periods (Corden 1984; Gylfason and Zoega 2006). This process may be a contributing factor in retarded development of financial institutions, a state of affairs which discourages saving, investment and economic growth. Besides, it is not only the volume of investment that is important but also the quality of expenditures, and individuals or governments all too commonly invest windfall rents in unproductive projects.

In economies in which a large proportion of total wealth is held in the form of land, total savings can be used either to accumulate capital and attend to market demand or to invest in land (Kurz and Salvador 1995; Foley and Michl 1999). When land is still relatively abundant, the aim of investing in land is to reap the benefits that will come from future price rises. As land prices increase, capitalists invest a larger part of their wealth in it and this slows down capital accumulation. On the other hand, when land is not abundant and the frontier has already been occupied, increases in land rents depress profits and boost capitalist expenditure up to the point at which capital accumulation virtually stops. In both cases resources are diverted away from the alternative of capital accumulation. Since investment is the main source of growth and technical change, economies in which land rents and/or opportunities for land speculation are higher will grow less.

2.5 Factor endowment and the institutional change hypothesis

A last and very influential approach in recent economic historical research into the reasons why some resource-dependent economies have developed more successfully than others claims that the basic explanation of economic development is to be found in the interaction of critical exogenous factors such as geography, climate and institutional legacy. These factors may explain why certain recently settled regions in temperate areas, such as Australia, Canada, New Zealand and the United States, entered the twentieth century as "more developed" countries than the resource-dependent tropical plantation and peasant economies of Africa, Asia and Latin America (Barbier 2005).

Acemoglu *et al.* (2001) suggest that different European colonization strategies created different sets of institutions. "Neo-European" states were set up where colonial settlers tried to replicate European institutions, and the emphasis was on private property and controls against government power. But, at the other extreme, there were also "extractive" states in which these two aspects were not considered. Colonization strategy and settlement were influenced by geography, climate, disease and environmental factors. In less suitable places for settlement where malaria and yellow fever resulted in high mortality rates among settlers, it was more likely that extractive states would be formed. On the other hand, if European colonists could safely settle in an area they created better institutions. Long after European colonies became independent the colonial legacy of the institutional matrix persisted, and it has been a key factor in determining whether economic performance would be good or bad (path-dependence).

Engerman and Sokoloff (1997, 2002) argue that the key factor endowments were not just abundance of land and natural resources relative to labour in the New World, but also the soil, the climate and the size and density of native populations. Their view highlights the fundamental importance of the extreme differences so commonly found in New World societies, where inequalities in the distribution of wealth, human capital, and political influence due primarily to factor endowments (or initial conditions more generally) have persisted since the early days of the colonies. The causal relationship is between factor endowments, social and economic inequality and the generation of institutional arrangements that create the conditions for economic development. The proponents of this approach emphasize the role of factor endowments, arguing that the colonies that came to make up the United States and Canada were quite unusual in the New World, because their factor endowments predisposed them toward paths of development with relatively equal distributions of wealth, human capital and greater population homogeneity as compared with most regions of Latin America.

Other authors have studied the connection between specific environmental conditions (climate and tropical locations) and economic performance, presenting evidence that the former directly influenced the latter (Kamarck 1976; Bloom and Sachs 1998). However the predominant current view is that factor endowment explains economic growth but only through the indirect impact of institutional factors (Hall and Jones 1999; Easterly and Levine 2003), and that there are no convincing arguments for direct causality.

3 What can we learn from history?

Whereas the previous section of this introduction offered a brief review of the different analytical and empirical approaches dealing with the "curse" and "blessing" of natural resources as a conceptual context for our proposal, this section will highlight the "lessons from history" that can be drawn from a historical discussion and understanding of the past and present of resource-rich developing economies to obtain conditions for successful natural resources-based development (in the sense of Barbier 2011; Chapter 3 (Barbier 2015)).

The history of economic ideas concerning the relationship between natural resources and development has shifted from enormous confidence in natural wealth as a motor of economic growth, which continued until the mid-twentieth century, to an increasing conviction about the impossibility of creating sustainable conditions for resources-based development. This conviction took the form of difficulties associated with primary specialization (developmentalists, Latin

American structuralists, dependence theorists and neo-Schumpeterians) until the 1990s, when a new "orthodoxy" emerged in the debate. Since 2001, hundreds of academic studies have examined the "resource curse", meaning the claim that natural resource wealth tends to have perverse impacts on economic growth, equality and welfare conditions. The results have been mixed, but there is a general consensus in the literature that some type of "conditionality" is involved. The idea is that the quality of institutions plays a central role in the curse or the blessing of natural resources, and that an economy can perform well even when natural resources are present in abundance provided its institutions are "good". However, a number of scholars have recently questioned this view and cast doubt on the intensity of the effect and the causality of the relationship.

Stijns (2005) argues that natural resources can have both positive and negative effects on economic growth, and Domenech (2008) shows in a case study of Spain (1860–2000) that mineral resources had a positive effect on industrialization by 1920. Chapter 6 (Wright 2015) also stresses the important role played by natural resources in the economic development of the United States. Ding and Field (2004) use more appropriate indicators of natural resource abundance in the form of natural capital according to World Bank measures rather than the share of GDP represented by commodity primary exports to demonstrate that the impacts of natural resources on growth disappear under these conditions. Finally, Brunnschweiler (2008) and Brunnschweiler and Blute (2008) present evidence that overturns the causality hypothesis, proposing instead that resource abundance has positive effects on growth and institutional quality.

Can economic history contribute to this debate? Can long-run studies and historical episodes for different regions provide new insights to help us understand this apparent paradox?

> The analysis of resource rich countries draws on macroeconomics, public finance, public policy, international economics, resource economics, economic history and applied econometrics. It also benefits from collaboration with political scientists and historians.
>
> (van der Ploeg 2011, p. 407)

In other words, it is an interdisciplinary field where economic history has a central role to play. The conceptual core of our answer to those questions will be based on three key ideas drawn from our review and discussion of academic descriptions of the problem, analyses and results:

- Abundant natural resources are non-neutral for economic development.
- Abundance is an endogenous process.
- Institutional quality is the key factor to deal with abundant natural resources.

First, abundance of natural resources is closely associated with levels of economic development. At the beginning of the twenty-first century, only 5 per cent of total world wealth consisted of natural capital. However, divergence between regions was the dominant norm, and where the ratio was barely 2 per cent for high income OECD countries, it was 25 per cent for lower middle income and 30 per cent for low income countries. Evidently abundance of natural resources is non-neutral for development and the different cases we review are clear illustrations of this insight. As Edward Barbier states in his chapter, at some historical stage, all economies faced the scarcity of their natural resources and the ways in which they resolved the restriction could explain a lucky country trajectory (Chapter 13, Lloyd 2015), a litany of successive failures or the design of effective public policies to avoid the curse or strengthening the blessing (Chapter 5 (Marwah 2015), Chapter 9 (Peres Cajías 2015), Chapter 15 (Sanders and Sandvik 2015) and Chapter 16 (Cazcarro et al. 2015)).

As economic historians, we have the opportunity to address a promising research programme to assess the dimensions, evolution and impact of natural capital on economic development, which will in all likelihood end by obliging us to reconsider some of our historical interpretations from the Industrial Revolution to the present day. Regions such as Latin America and Africa, where natural resources were always a key factor for economic development, are especially attractive in this respect. Rents from natural resources in the sense defined by Richard Auty (Chapter 2, Auty 2015), the degree of appropriability of such rents (Chapter 12, Willebald 2015) and the resulting distribution among the different social classes comprise the central concepts for an interpretation of long-run development in peripheral economies. This approach will also provide a good framework to analyse the impact of backward and forward linkages in mining cycles on the economy as a whole. In this context, Chile made only slow progress with industrialization before the Great Depression, providing an example of a country which did not suffer "Dutch Disease" effects (Chapter 10, Badia-Miró and Ducoing 2015). For African cases, good institutions could foster economic growth (Chapter 4, Hillbom 2015 for Botswana) but bad government institutions and rent-seeking behaviours created barriers to growth in Nigeria during the oil cycle (Chapter 5, Marwah 2015).

Second, we emphasize that an abundance of natural resources is not a fixed situation. It is a process that reacts to changes in the structure of commodity prices and factor endowments, and progress requires capital, labour, technical change and appropriate institutional arrangements (see Chapter 11 (van der Eng 2015) for Indonesia and Chapter 8 (Rubio-Varas 2015) for Mexico and Venezuela). This abundance is not a given, therefore, but is part of the evolution of the economic system. This is an idea which is far from new but in fact goes back a long way. "Resources are highly dynamic concepts; they are not, they become, they evolve out of the triune interaction of nature, man, and culture" (Zimmerman 1933, p. 4, quoted in Ding and Field 2004, p. 2). Natural resources "should not be seen as merely a fortunate natural endowment, but rather as a form of collective learning, a return on large-scale investments in exploration, transportation, geological knowledge, and the technologies of mineral extraction refining, and utilization" (Czelusta and Wright 2007, p. 186).

The endogeneity of natural capital is as obvious in historical analysis (as Chapter 16 (Cazcarro et al. 2015) show for water and irrigation) as it is absent in the long-run interpretations in economics. History teaches us that "curses" and "blessings" are constructions – they are the result of the socioeconomic system – and the exploitation of natural resources means dealing with opportunities and challenges with profound consequences on the historical process in the societies concerned. Thus, successful experiences of economic development in countries like Australia and Canada highlight the fact that institutions promoting the interaction between enabling and receiving sectors are fundamental to science-based and innovation-driven growth in resource-based economies. It is crucial, therefore, to develop institutional structures to support knowledge capabilities in the growth of natural resource-based industries (Chapter 14, Ville and Wicken 2015).

Finally, history shows that institutional quality is the key factor to deal with abundant natural resources and, especially, with the rents derived from their use and exploitation.

> Most developing countries are resource-rich and natural resource abundance tends to foster predatory political states that use the rents to relax market discipline and buy political support, distorting their economies in the process so that competitive economic diversification falters and growth collapses.... Meanwhile, macro policy failure damages micro policies,... by distorting prices and incentives, depressing genuine saving rates and shortening time horizons to secure immediate survival.
>
> (Auty 2003, p. 15)

In other words, the ways in which natural resources interact with economic development are mediated by the performance of institutional arrangements in at least three dimensions (following Siddiqui and Ahmed 2013): (i) institutions' ability to limit rent-seeking opportunities that divert innovation and resources from productive avenues; (ii) political competition and participation relate to rules governing chief executive recruitment and selection, the fairness and impartiality of electoral processes, and constraints on executive power; and (iii) the characteristics of institutions that reduce transactional risk through proper enforcement of property rights.

In sum, history is very clear in showing that natural capital is non-neutral for economic performance but it is a systemic component of economic development where institutional quality is the key component to deal with and create "curses" and "blessings" of natural resources.

Note

1 This section follows van der Ploeg (2011); Willebald (2011).

References

Acemoglu, D., Johnson, S. and Robinson, J.A., 2001. The colonial origins of comparative development: an empirical investigation. *American Economic Review*, 91 (5), 1369–1401.

Aghion, P. and Howitt, P., 1992. A model of growth through creative destruction. *Econometrica*, 60 (2), 323–351.

Altman, M., 2003. Staple theory and export-led growth: constructing differential growth. *Australian Economic History Review*, 43 (3), 230–255.

Amin, S., 1975. *Accumulation on a World Scale: A Critique of the Theory of Underdevelopment*. New York: Monthly Review Press.

Andersen, J.J. and Aslaksen, S., 2008. Constitutions and the resource curse. *Journal of Development Economics*, 87 (2), 227–246.

Ascher, W., 1999. *Why Governments Waste Natural Resources: Policy Failures in Developing Countries*. Baltimore, MA: Johns Hopkins University Press.

Atkinson, G. and Hamilton, K., 2003. Savings, growth and the resource curse hypothesis. *World Development*, 31 (11), 1793–1807.

Auty, R.M., 1997. Natural resource endowment, the state and development strategy. *Journal of International Development*, 9 (4), 651–663.

Auty, R.M., 2001a. Introduction and overview. *In*: R.M. Auty, ed. *Resource Abundance and Economic Development*. Oxford: Oxford University Press, 3–18.

Auty, R.M., 2001b. The political economy of resource-driven growth. *European Economic Review*, 45 (4–6), 839–846.

Auty, R.M., 2003. *Natural Resources, Development Models and Sustainable Development*, Discussion Paper, No. 03–01, Environmental Economics Programme, June.

Auty, R.M., 2006. *Pattern of Rent-Extraction and Deployment in Developing Countries. Implications for Governance, Economic Policy and Performance*, UNU-WIDER Research Paper, No. 2006/16, February.

Auty, R.M., 2015. From resource curse to rent curse: a theoretical perspective. *In*: M. Badia-Miró, V. Pinilla and H. Willebald, eds. *Natural Resources and Economic Growth: Learning from History*. London: Routledge.

Ayres, R., Castaneda, B., Cleveland, C., Costanza, R., Daly, H., Folke, C., Hannon, B., Harris, J., Kaufmann, R., Lin, X., Norgaard, R., Ruth, M., Spreng, D., Stern, D. and Van den Bergh, J., 1997. *Natural Capital, Human Capital, and Sustainable Economic Growth*. MacArthur Foundation-Center for Energy and Environmental Studies at Boston University, Boston.

Badia-Miró, M. and Ducoing, C.A., 2015. Long-run development in Chile and natural resources curse: linkages, policy and growth, 1850–1950. *In*: M. Badia-Miró, V. Pinilla and H. Willebald, eds. *Natural Resources and Economic Growth: Learning from History*. London: Routledge.

Baland, J.M. and Francois, P., 2000. Rent-seeking and resource booms. *Journal of Development Economics*, 61 (2), 527–542.

Baran, P., 1957. *The Political Economy of Growth*. New York: Monthly Review Press.

Barbier, E.B., 2005. *Natural Resources and Economic Development*. Cambridge, MA: Cambridge University Press.

Barbier, E.B., 2007. Frontiers and sustainable economic development. *Environmental and Resource Economics*, 37 (1), 271–295.

Barbier, E.B., 2011. *Scarcity and Frontiers: How Economies Have Developed through Natural Resource Exploitation*. New York: Cambridge University Press.

Barbier, E.B., 2015. Scarcity, frontiers and the resource curse: a historical perspective. *In*: M. Badia-Miró, V. Pinilla and H. Willebald, eds. *Natural Resources and Economic Growth: Learning from History*. London: Routledge.

Bertola, L., 2015. Welfare states and development patterns in Latin America. *In*: M. Badia-Miró, V. Pinilla and H. Willebald, eds. *Natural Resources and Economic Growth: Learning from History*. London: Routledge.

Bertram, G.W., 1963. Economic growth and Canadian industry, 1870–1915: the staple model and the take-off hypothesis. *Canadian Journal of Economics and Political Science*, 29 (2), 162–184.

Birdsall, N., Pinckney, T. and Sabot, R., 2000. *Natural Resources, Human Capital, and Growth*. Carnegie Endowment for International Peace, Working Papers. Washington D.C.

Blattman, C., Hwang, J. and Williamson, J.G., 2007. Winners and losers in the commodity lottery: the impact of terms of trade growth and volatility in the periphery 1870–1939. *Journal of Development Economics*, 82 (1), 156–179.

Bloom, D.E. and Sachs, J.D., 1998. Geography, demography, and economic growth in Africa. *Brookings Papers on Economic Activity*, (2), 207–295.

Boschini, A.D., Pettersson, J. and Roine, J., 2007. Resource curse or not: a question of appropriability. *Scandinavian Journal of Economics*, 109 (3), 593–617.

Boyce, J., 2013. *Biased Technological Change and the Relative. Abundance of Natural Resources*. Department of Economics Working Papers, No. 2013–04, University of Calgary.

Bravo-Ortega, C. and De Gregorio, J., 2005. *The Relative Richness of the Poor? Natural Resources, Human Capital and Economic Growth*. The World Bank Policy Research, Working Papers Series, No. 3484, Washington D.C.

Brunnschweiler, C.N., 2008. Cursing the blessings? Natural resource abundance, institutions, and economic growth. *World Development*, 36 (3), 399–419.

Brunnschweiler, C.N. and Blute, E.H., 2008. The resource curse revisited and revised: a tale of paradoxes and red herrings. *Journal of Environmental Economics and Management*, 55 (3), 248–264.

Bulte, E.H., Damania, R. and Deacon, R.T., 2005. Resource intensity, institutions, and development. *World Development*, 33 (7), 1029–1044.

Cazcarro, I., Duarte, R., Martín-Retortillo, M., Pinilla, V. and Serrano, A., 2015. Water scarcity and agricultural growth in Spain: from curse to blessing? *In*: M. Badia-Miró, V. Pinilla and H. Willebald, eds. *Natural Resources and Economic Growth: Learning from History*. London: Routledge.

Chambers, E.J. and Gordon, D.F., 1966. Primary products and economic growth: an empirical measurement. *Journal of Political Economy*, 74 (4), 315–332.

Cimoli, M. and Dosi, G., 1995. Technological paradigms, patterns of learning and development: an introductory roadmap. *Journal of Evolutionary Economics*, 5 (3), 243–268.

Cimoli, M., Porcile, G., Primi, A. and Vergara, S., 2005. Cambio estructural, heterogeneidad productiva y tecnología en América Latina. *In*: M. Cimoli, ed. *Heterogeneidad estructural, asimetrías tecnológicas y crecimiento en América Latina*. Santiago de Chile, Chile: CEPAL-BID, 9–39.

Collier, P., 2007. *The Bottom Billion: Why the Poorest Countries Are Failing and What Can Be Done About It*. Oxford: Oxford University Press.

Collier, P. and Hoeffler, A., 2002. *Greed and Grievance in Civil War*. Centre for the Study of African Economies Working Paper, No. 1.

Collier, P. and Hoeffler, A., 2005. Resource rents, governance, and conflict. *Journal of Conflict Resolution*, 49 (4), 625–633.

Corden, W.M., 1984. Booming sector and Dutch disease economics: survey and consolidation. *Oxford Economic Papers*, 36 (3), 359–380.

Czelusta, J. and Wright, G., 2007. Resource-based growth past and present. *In*: D. Lederman and W.F. Maloney, eds. *Natural Resources: Neither Curse nor Destiny*. Washington D.C./Stanford, CA: World Bank/Stanford University Press, 183–211.

Dalgaard, C.-J. and Olsson, O., 2008. Windfall gains, political economy and economic development. *Journal of African Economies*, 17 (Supplement 1), i72–i109.

David, P.A. and Wright, G., 1997. Increasing returns and the genesis of American resource abundance. *Industrial and Corporate Change*, 6 (2), 203–245.

Ding, N. and Field, B., 2004. *Natural Resource Abundance and Economic Growth*. University of Massachusetts Amherst Resource Economics Working Paper, No. 2004–07.

Dixon, R. and Thirwall, A.P., 1975. A model of regional growth rate differences on Kaldorian lines. *Oxford Economic Papers*, 27, 201–214.

Domenech, J., 2008. Mineral resource abundance and regional growth in Spain, 1860–2000. *Journal of International Development*, 20 (8), 1122–1135.

Dosi, G., 1988. Sources, procedures, and microeconomic effects of innovation. *Journal of Economic Literature*, 26 (3), 1120–1171.

Dosi, G., 2007. *Technological Innovation, Institutions and Human Purposefulness in Socioeconomic Evolution: A Preface to Christopher Freeman "Systems of Innovation. Selected Essays in Evolutionary Economics."* LEM Working Paper Series, No. 2007/18. Laboratory of Economics and Management, Sant'Anna School of Advanced Studies, September.

Dosi, G. and Nelson, R.R., 2010. Technical change and industrial dynamics as evolutionary processes. *In*: B.H. Hall and N. Rosenberg, eds. *Handbook of the Economics of Innovation*. Amsterdam: North-Holland, 51–127.

Dosi, G., Pavitt, K. and Soete, L., 1990. *The Economics of Technical Change and International Trade*. London: Harvester Wheatsheaf Press/New York University Press.

Drelichman, M., 2005. The curse of Moctezuma: American silver and the Dutch disease. *Explorations in Economic History*, 42 (3), 349–380.

Duncan, T. and Fogarty, J., 1984. *Australia and Argentina: On Parallel Paths*. Melbourne, Australia: Melbourne University Press.

Easterly, W. and Levine, R., 2003. Tropics, germs, and crops: how endowments influence economic development. *Journal of Monetary Economics*, 50, 3–39.

Emmanuel, A., 1972. *Unequal Exchange: A Study in the Imperialism of Trade*. New York: Monthly Review Press.

Van der Eng, P., 2015. Mixed blessings: mining in Indonesia's economy, 1870–2010. *In*: M. Badia-Miró, V. Pinilla and H. Willebald, eds. *Natural Resources and Economic Growth: Learning from History*. London: Routledge.

Engerman, S.L. and Sokoloff, K.L., 1997. Factor endowments, institutions, and differential paths of growth among New World economies. *In*: S. Haber, ed. *How Latin America Fell Behind: Essays on the Economic Histories of Brazil and Mexico*. Stanford, CA: Stanford University Press, 260–304.

Engerman, S.L. and Sokoloff, K.L., 2002. Factor endowments, inequality, and paths of development among New World economies. *Journal of LACEA Economia, LACEA – LATIN AMERICAN AND CARIBBEAN ECONOMIC*, 3 (1).

Fagerberg, J., 1994. Technology and international differences in growth rates. *Journal of Economic Literature*, 32 (3), 1147–1175.

Findlay, R., 1995. *Factor Proportions, Trade, and Growth*. Cambridge, MA: MIT Press.

Findlay, R. and Lundahl, M., 1994. Natural resources, "vent-for-surplus", and the staples theory. *In*: G. Meier, ed. *From Classical Economics to Development Economics: Essays in Honor of Hla Myint*. New York: St. Martin's Press, 68–93.

Foley, D. and Michl, T., 1999. *Growth and Distribution*. Cambridge, MA: Harvard University Press.

Frank, A.G., 1967. *Capitalism and Underdevelopment in Latin America: Historical Studies of Chile and Brazil*. New York: Monthly Review Press.

Freeman, C., 1963. The plastic industry: a comparative study of research and innovation. *National Institute Economic Review*, 26.

Freeman, C., 1987. *Technology and Economic Performance: Lessons from Japan*. London: Pinter.

Furtado, C., 1969. *Teoría y política del desarrollo económico*. Siglo XXI Editorial.

Gelb, A.H. and Associates, 1988. *Oil Windfalls: Blessing or Curse?* New York: Cambridge University Press.

Gillis, M., Perkins, D., Roemer, M. and Snodgrass, D., 1996. *Economics of Development*. New York: Norton.

Gray, C.W. and Kaufmann, D., 1998. Corruption and development. *Finance and Development*, 35 (1), 7–10.

Grossman, G.M. and Helpman, E., 1994. Endogenous innovation in the theory of growth. *Journal of Economic Perspectives*, 8 (1), 23–44.

Gylfason, T., 2001. Nature, power and growth. *Scottish Journal of Political Economy*, 48 (5), 558–588.

Gylfason, T., 2004. *Natural Resources and Economic Growth: From Dependence to Diversification*. Discussion Papers, No. 4804.

Gylfason, T., 2006. Natural resources and economic growth: from dependence to diversification. *In*: H.G. Broadman, T. Paas and P. Welfens, eds. *Economic Liberalization and Integration Policy: Options for Eastern Europe and Russia*. Berlin; Heidelberg: Springer, 201–231.

Gylfason, T., 2007. *The International Economics of Natural Resources and Growth*. Minerals and Energy-Raw Materials Report, No. 22 (1 and 2).

Gylfason, T. and Zoega, G., 2003. Inequality and economic growth: do natural resources matter? *In*: T. Eicher and S. Turnovsky, eds. *Growth and Inequality: Theory and Policy Implications*. Cambridge, MA: MIT Press.

Gylfason, T. and Zoega, G., 2006. Natural resources and economic growth: the role of investment. *World Economy*, 29 (8), 1091–1115.

Hall, R.E. and Jones, C.I., 1999. Why do some countries produce so much more output per worker than others? *The Quarterly Journal of Economics*, 114 (1), 83–116.

Hansen, B., 1979. Colonial economic development with unlimited supply of land: a Ricardian case. *Economic Development and Cultural Change*, 27 (4), 611–627.

Herbertsson, T., Skuladottir, M. and Zoega, G., 1999. *Three Symptoms and a Cure: A Contribution to the Economics of the Dutch Disease*. CEPR Discussion Paper, No. 2364. London.

Hilibom, E., 2015. Botswana: caught in a natural trap. *In*: M. Badia-Miró, V. Pinilla and H. Willebald, eds. *Natural Resources and Economic Growth: Learning from History*. London: Routledge.

Hirsch, S., 1965. The US electronics industry in international trade. *National Institute Economic Review*, 34.

Hirschman, A.O., 1958. *The Strategy of Economic Development*. New Haven, CT: Yale University Press.

Hujo, K., ed., 2012. *Mineral Rents and the Financing of Social Policy: Opportunities and Challenges*. London: Palgrave.

Innis, H.A., 1930. *The Fur Trade in Canada: An Introduction to Canadian Economic History*. New Haven, CT: Yale University Press.

Innis, H.A., 1940. *The Cod Fisheries: The History of an International Economy*. New Haven, CT: Yale University Press.

Innis, H.A., 1956. *The Fur Trade in Canada: An Introduction to Canadian Economic History*. Second edn. Toronto, Canada: University of Toronto Press.

Isham, J., Woolcock, M., Pritchett, L. and Busby, G., 2005. The varieties of resource experience: natural resource export structures and the political economy of economic growth. *World Bank Economic Review*, 19 (2), 141–174.

Kamarck, A., 1976. *The Tropics and Economic Development*. Baltimore, MD: Johns Hopkins University Press.

Karl, T., 1997. *The Paradox of Plenty: Oil Booms and Petro-States*. Berkeley, CA: University of California Press.

Krueger, A.O., 1974. The political economy of the rent-seeking society. *The American Economic Review*, 64 (3), 291–303.

Krugman, P., 1981. Trade, accumulation, and uneven development. *Journal of Development Economics*, 8 (2), 149–161.

Krugman, P., 1987. The narrow moving band, the Dutch disease, and the competitive consequences of Mrs. Thatcher. *Journal of Development Economics*, 27, 41–55.

Krugman, P., 1991. Increasing returns and economic geography. *Journal of Political Economy*, 99 (3), 484–499.

Kurz, H.D. and Salvador, N., 1995. *Theory of Production: A Long Period Analysis*. Cambridge, MA: Cambridge University Press.

Leite, C. and Weidmann, J., 1999. *Does Mother Nature Corrupt? Natural Resources, Corruption, and Economic Growth*. IMF Working Paper, No. 99/85. Washington D.C.

Lewis, W.A., 1954. Economic development with unlimited supplies of labour. *Manchester School of Social and Economic Studies*, 22, 139–191.

Lewis, W.A., 1955. *The Theory of Economic Growth*. London: Allen and Unwin.

Lloyd, C., 2015. The lucky country syndrome in Australia: resources, social democracy, and regimes of development in historical political economy perspective. In: M. Badia-Miró, V. Pinilla and H. Willebald, eds. *Natural Resources and Economic Growth: Learning from History*. London: Routledge.

Lundahl, M., 1998. Staples trade and economic development. *In*: M. Lundahl, ed. *Themes of International Economics*. Boston, MA: Ashgate Publishing, 45–68.

Marwah, H., 2015. Oil as sweet as honey: linking natural resources, government institutions and domestic capital investment in Nigeria 1960–2000. *In*: M. Badia-Miró, V. Pinilla and H. Willebald, eds. *Natural Resources and Economic Growth: Learning from History*. London: Routledge.

McCombie, J.S.L. and Roberts, M., 2002. The role of the balance of payments in economic growth. *In*: M. Setterfield, ed. *The Economics of Demand-led Growth: Challenging the Supply-side Vision of the Long Run*. Cheltenham, UK; Northampton, MA: Edward Elgar, 87–114.

McCombie, J.S.L. and Thirwall, A.P., 1994. *Economic Growth and the Balance of Payments Constraint*. New York: St. Martin's Press.

Mitchener, K. and McLean, I., 2003. *The Productivity of U.S. States Since 1880*. NBER Working Paper Series, No. 9445.

Myint, H., 1958. The "classical theory" of international trade and the underdeveloped countries. *The Economic Journal*, 68 (270), 317–337.

Myrdal, G., 1957. *Economic Theory and Under-developed Regions*. London: Duckworth.

Neary, J.P. and Wijnbergen, S. van, 1986. *Natural Resources and the Macroeconomy*. Cambridge, MA: MIT Press.

Nelson, R. and Winter, S., 1982. *An Evolutionary Theory of Economic Growth*. Cambridge, MA: Harvard University Press.

Nelson, R.R., ed., 1994. *National Systems of Innovation*. Oxford: Oxford University Press.

Nurkse, R., 1962. Patterns of trade and development. *In*: G. Haberler and R. Stern, eds. *Equilibrium and Growth in the World Economy*. Cambridge, MA: Harvard University Press.

O'Rourke, K. and Williamson, J.G., 1994. Late nineteenth-century Anglo-American factor-price convergence: were Heckscher and Ohlin right? *The Journal of Economic History*, 54 (4), 892–916.

O'Rourke, K.H., Taylor, A.M. and Williamson, J.G., 1996. Factor price convergence in the late nineteenth century. *International Economic Review*, 37, 499–530.

Ocampo, J.A. and Parra-Lancourt, M., 2010. The terms of trade for commodities since the mid-19th century. *Revista de Historia Económica/Journal of Iberian and Latin American Economic History*, 28 (1), 11–43.

Palma, J.G., 2000. Trying to "tax and spend" oneself out of the "Dutch Disease": the Chilean economy from the War of the Pacific to the Great Depression. *In*: E. Cardenas, J.A. Ocampo and R. Thorp, eds. *An Economic History of Twentieth-century Latin America*. New York: Palgrave associated with St Antony's College, 217–264.

Papyrakis, E. and Gerlagh, R., 2004. *Natural Resources, Innovation, and Growth*. Nota di Lavoro, No. 129.2004. The Fondazione Eni Enrico Mattei (http://ssrn.com/abstract=609764), October.

Papyrakis, E. and Gerlagh, R., 2006. Resource windfalls, investment, and long-term income. *Resources Policy*, 31 (2), 117–128.

Peres Cajias, J.A., 2015. Public finances and natural resources in Bolivia, 1883–2010. Is there a fiscal curse? *In*: M. Badia-Miró, V. Pinilla and H. Willebald, eds. *Natural Resources and Economic Growth: Learning from History*. London: Routledge.

Van der Ploeg, F., 2011. Natural resources: curse or blessing? *Journal of Economic Literature*, 49 (2), 366–420.

Posner, M., 1961. International trade and technological change. *Oxford Economic Papers*, 13.

Prebish, R., 1950. The economic development of Latin America and its principal problems. *Economic Bulletin for Latin America*, 7 (1), 1–22.

Ray, D., 2000. What's new in development economics? *The American Economist*, 44, 3–16.

Ros, J., 2000. *Development Theory and the Economics of Growth*. Ann Arbor: The University of Michigan Press.

Rosenstein-Rodan, P., 1957. *Notes on the Theory of the Big Push*. WP Series C. Center for International Studies, Massachusetts Institute of Technology.

Ross, M., 1999. *Timber Booms and Institutional Breakdowns in Southeast Asia*. Cambridge, UK: Cambridge University Press.

Rostow, W.W., 1953. *The Process of Economic Growth*. Oxford: Clarendon Press.

Rubio-Varas, M. del M., 2015. Oil illusion and delusion: Mexico and Venezuela over the twentieth century. *In*: M. Badia-Miró, V. Pinilla and H. Willebald, eds. *Natural Resources and Economic Growth: Learning from History*. London: Routledge.

Sachs, J.D. and Warner, A.M., 1995. *Natural Resource Abundance and Economic Growth*. NBER Working Papers, No. 5398, National Bureau of Economic Research, Cambridge, MA.

Sachs, J.D. and Warner, A.M., 1999a. The big push, natural resource booms and growth. *Journal of Development Economics*, 59 (1), 43–76.

Sachs, J.D. and Warner, A.M., 1999b. Natural resource intensity and economic growth. *In*: J. Mayer, B. Chambers and A. Farooq, eds. *Development Policies in Natural Resource Economies*. Cheltenham, UK: Edward Elgar Publishing, 13–38.

Sachs, J.D. and Warner, A.M., 2001. The curse of natural resources. *European Economic Review*, 45 (4–6), 827–838.

Sala-i-Martin, X. and Subramanian, A., 2013. Addressing the natural resource curse: an illustration from Nigeria. *Journal of African Economies*, 22 (4), 570–615.

Sanders, A.R.D. and Sandvik, P.T., 2015. Avoiding the resource curse? Democracy and natural resources in Norway since 1900. *In*: M. Badia-Miró, V. Pinilla and H. Willebald, eds. *Natural Resources and Economic Growth: Learning from History*. London: Routledge.

Schedvin, C.B., 1990. Staples and regions of Pax Britannica. *The Economic History Review*, 43 (4), 533.

Seers, D., 1962. A model of comparative rates of growth in the world economy. *The Economic Journal*, 72 (285), 45–78.

Serrano, R. and Pinilla, V., 2011. The terms of trade for agricultural and food products, 1951–2000. *Revista de Historia Económica/Journal of Iberian and Latin American Economic History*, 29 (2), 213–244.

Siddiqui, D. and Ahmed, Q., 2013. The effect of institutions on economic growth: a global analysis based on GMM dynamic panel estimation. *Structural Change and Economic Dynamics*, 24, 18–33.

Singer, H.W., 1950. The distribution of gains between investing and borrowing countries. *American Economic Review*, 40 (2), 473–485.

Smith, S., 1976. An extension of the vent-for-surplus model in relation to long-run structural change in Nigeria. *Oxford Economic Papers*, 28 (3), 426–446.

Solow, R.M., 1956. A contribution to the theory of economic growth. *The Quarterly Journal of Economics*, 70 (1), 65–95.

Southey, C., 1978. The staples thesis, common property and homesteading. *Canadian Journal of Economics Studies*, 11 (3), 547–559.

Stijns, J.P.C., 2005. Natural resource abundance and economic growth revisited. *Resources Policy*, 30 (2), 107–130.

Swan, T., 1956. Economic growth and capital accumulation. *Economic Record*, 32, 334–361.

Di Tella, G., 1982. The economics of the frontier. *In*: C.P. Kindleberger and G. Di Tella, eds. *Economics in the Long View*. London: Macmillan Press Ltd, 210–227.

Tornell, A. and Lane, P., 1998. Are windfalls a curse? A non-representative agent model of the current account. *Journal of International Economics*, 44 (1), 83–112.

Tornell, A. and Lane, P., 1999. The voracity effect. *American Economic Review*, 89, 22–46.

Torvik, R., 2001. Learning by doing and the Dutch disease. *European Economic Review*, 45 (2), 285–306.

Torvik, R., 2002. Natural resources, rent seeking and welfare. *Journal of Development Economics*, 67 (2), 455–470.

Vernon, R., 1966. International investment and international trade in the product cycle. *The Quarterly Journal of Economics*, 80 (2), 190–207.

Ville, S. and Wicken, O., 2015. The institutional foundations of natural resource based knowledge economies. *In*: M. Badia-Miró, V. Pinilla and H. Willebald, eds. *Natural Resources and Economic Growth: Learning from History*. London: Routledge.

Wallerstein, I., 1974. *The Modern World-System*. New York: Academic Press.

Watkins, M.H., 1963. A staple theory of economic growth. *The Canadian Journal of Economics and Political Science*, 29 (2), 141–158.

Wellstead, A., 2007. The (post) staples economy and the (post) staples state in historical perspective. *Canadian Political Science Review*, 1 (1), 8–25.

Willebald, H., 2011. Natural resources, settler economies and economic development during the first globalization: land frontier expansion and institutional arrangement. PhD Thesis, Universidad Carlos III de Madrid, Departamento de Historia Económica e Instituciones, Archivo Abierto Institucional de la UC3M, Colecciones multidisciplinares, http://e-archivo.uc3m.es/handle/10016/12281.

Willebald, H., 2015. Land abundance, frontier expansion and appropriability: settler economies during the first globalization. *In*: M. Badia-Miró, V. Pinilla and H. Willebald, eds. *Natural Resources and Economic Growth: Learning from History*. London: Routledge.

Williamson, J.G., 2011. *Trade and Poverty: When the Third World Fell Behind*. Cambridge, MA: The MIT Press.

Williamson, J.G., 2012. Commodity prices over two centuries: trends, volatility and impact. *Annual Review of Resource Economics*, 4 (6), 6–22.

Wood, A. and Berge, K., 1997. Exporting manufactures: human resources, natural resources, and trade policy. *Journal of Development Studies*, 34, 35–59.

Wood, A. and Mayer, J., 2001. Africa's export structure in a comparative perspective. *Cambridge Journal of Economics*, 25, 369–394.

Woolcock, M., Prichett, L. and Isham, J., 2001. The social foundations of poor economic growth in resource-rich economies. *In*: R.M. Auty, ed. *Resource Abundance and Economic Development*. New York: Oxford University Press.

Wright, G., 1990. The origins of American industrial success, 1879–1940. *The American Economic Review*, 80 (4), 651–668.

Wright, G., 2001. Resource-based growth then and now. Prepared for the World Bank project *Patterns of Integration in the Global Economy*.

Wright, G., 2015. The USA as a case study in resource-based development. *In*: M. Badia-Miró, V. Pinilla and H. Willebald, eds. *Natural Resources and Economic Growth: Learning from History*. London: Routledge.

Wright, G. and Czelusta, J., 2004. Why economies slow: the myth of the resource curse. *Challenge*, 47 (2), 6–38.

2 From resource curse to rent curse

A theoretical perspective

Richard M. Auty

1 Introduction

A study of resource-driven development through 1960–97 reveals scant evidence of a resource curse in the 1960s when the average income per head of the population in resource-rich economies was 50 per cent above that of the resource-poor economies (Auty 2001, p. 5). This is what economists would expect because windfall rent from natural resources increases the propensity to invest, which if efficiently deployed will accelerate economic growth, while the extra foreign exchange from rent-rich exports boosts the capacity to import the capital goods required to build the infrastructure of a modern economy.

However, the economic perspective omits political pressures that skew the allocation of inputs away from the optimum economic pattern. This misallocation lies behind the protracted growth collapses that were triggered in many developing economies, particularly the resource-rich ones, during the heightened commodity price volatility of 1973–85. Khan (2000) notes that the *political* rationale for choosing policies that are economically sub-optimal is often compelling: governments in many newly independent countries find it necessary to deploy rents to secure political cohesion without which economic activity struggles. North *et al.* (2009) concur and argue that most developing country governments extract rent and deploy it to limit potential violence by co-opting into the elite those deemed capable of wielding violence.

The limited evidence of resource curse effects in the 1960s implies that the curse is not an inevitable outcome. But Table 2.1 suggests the resource curse effect intensified through the 1973–85 period of heightened commodity price volatility. Most resource-poor economies outperformed the resource-rich economies and continued to do so through 1985–97, raising their mean income per head well above that of the resource-rich economies. The growth-depressing effects of the resource curse then ameliorated through the commodity boom of the 2000s, which limited further widening of the income gap between resource-poor economies and resource-rich ones. However, the resource curse not only varies in intensity over time, it also varies across space. Resource curse symptoms appear to be stronger for small economies than large ones, and especially for mineral-driven economies, most notably oil exporters (Table 2.1). During 1973–85 the mineral economies had

Table 2.1 Per capita GDP growth 1960–2010, by resource endowment (%/yr)

Economic phases	Pre-shock global growth 1960–73	Acute commodity price shocks 1973–85	IFI-backed reforms 1985–97	Post-reform recovery 1997–2010
Resource poor[1,2]				
Large	2.4	3.7	4.7	3.4
Small	3.5	1.8	2.4	2.4
Resource rich				
Large	2.7	0.7	1.9	2.4
Small, non-mineral	1.6	0.7	0.9	1.9
Small, hard mineral	2.2	0.1	−0.4	2.1
Small, oil exporter	4.0	2.3	−0.7	1.8
All countries	2.7	1.6	1.5	2.2

Source: Derived from World Bank (2012). See Auty (2001, p. 4) for country composition of endowment groups.

Notes
1 Resource poor = 1970 cropland/head < 0.3 hectares.
2 Large = 1970 GDP > $7 billion (proxy for domestic market size).

the highest resource rent but the slowest GDP growth, with oil exporters having the highest rent and weakest growth of all.

This chapter presents a theory of rent cycling (Auty 2010) to explain these characteristics of the resource curse. The theory posits that low rent motivates the elite to increase their welfare by growing the economy, which promotes competitive diversification that propels rapid economic growth and political maturation. In contrast, high rent encourages the elite to pursue immediate self-enrichment by channelling rent through patronage networks at the expense of competitive markets. This locks the economy into a staple trap of over-reliance on rent to subsidise protected urban activity, which cumulatively weakens the economy and if unreformed causes growth to collapse. In addition, rent cycling theory conceptualises the resource curse as part of a broader rent curse because symptoms associated with the resource curse can be triggered by other forms of windfall revenue such as foreign aid (geopolitical rent), labour remittances (labour rent) and government manipulation of relative prices (regulatory rent).

The chapter is structured as follows. Section 2 reviews the resource curse literature, noting an explosion of statistical studies since the mid-1990s in response to the sharp increase in the global incidence of resource curse cases through 1973–85. It reveals the neglect by such studies of: changing fashion in development policy; sources of windfall revenue other than natural resources; and variations among natural resources that differentiate development outcomes. Section 3 then identifies systematic patterns as incomes rise of structural change and political change, the two basic components of rent cycling theory. It stresses the positive role played in the low-rent development trajectory by *competitive industrialisation*, which most high-rent economies failed to achieve. Section 4 builds two stylised facts models, namely low-rent competitive industrialisation and the high-rent staple trap, based upon the interaction between the scale of the rent and four development parameters: elite incentives, economic structure, social capital accumulation and political change. Section 5 summarises the findings.

2 The contested literature on the resource curse

Recent academic speculation about the existence of a resource curse was sparked by case study analysis of the deployment of the 1974–78 and 1979–81 oil windfalls, which revealed mostly disappointing outcomes (Gelb and Associates 1988; Karl 1997). Sachs and Warner (1999) triggered a surge of systematic statistical research from the mid-1990s, which after a promising start degenerated into contradictory claim and counter-claim that has failed to determine whether a resource curse exists or not. Rent cycling theory helps move beyond this impasse.

2.1 Inconclusive statistical analyses

The initial statistical studies focused on economic explanations of the curse, notably the so-called "Dutch Disease" effects stressed by Sachs and Warner. Basically, booming commodity revenue strengthens the real exchange rate, which causes the non-booming tradable sectors (agriculture and manufacturing) to contract so that when commodity prices eventually fall the economy may be less prosperous than it was before the boom occurred. This reflects the fact that adjustment to exchange rate shifts is asymmetric: tradable activity is rapidly destroyed in booms but revives much more slowly when a boom subsides (Gelb and Associates 1988). Sachs and Warner analysed data for 1970–89 and concluded that most governments of natural resource-rich countries closed their trade policy as their dependence on primary product exports increased in order to counter the employment-diminishing effects of Dutch Disease. Lal and Myint (1996) show, however, that protective trade policies repress markets, distort the economy and cause growth collapses.

Interestingly, the trade policy/resource export dependence curve traces an inverted U-shape because at very high levels of resource dependence trade policy re-opens. The "capital-surplus" oil-exporting Gulf monarchies account for this opening because their unusually high rent per head confers sufficient revenue to permit governments to subsidise employment in the bureaucracy and consequently to discount employment lost through Dutch Disease effects. Subsidies also embraced energy and food as well as public sector jobs. However, bureaucratic employment shields workers from pressures to boost productivity and acquire skills to engage in entrepreneurial activity. More usually, commodity exporters (including capital-deficient oil exporters like Algeria, Iraq and Iran), protected manufacturing and channelled some rent to diversify into state-led industry, much of which was inefficiently executed and unprofitable.

The economic explanations for the resource curse are deterministic, yet resource-rich economies as diverse as Botswana, Malaysia and Indonesia managed to avoid prolonged growth collapses and to sustain rapid per capita GDP growth. Such exceptions nurtured alternative explanations for the resource curse, notably weak institutions. Acemoglu *et al.* (2001, 2002) argue that the quality of institutions is more important than natural resources per se in determining whether resources are a blessing or a curse. In particular, they identify as detrimental to economic growth those extractive colonial institutions associated with (tropical) lands that were too unhealthy for significant European settlement. In contrast, yeoman farmers in the resource-rich temperate regions of the Americas and Oceania created more inclusive institutions that proved more beneficial for economic development. Yet Glaeser *et al.* (2004) relegate institutions to secondary status: they find that institutions improve as a consequence of rising incomes but do not cause that rise, which is explained by human capital and policy choice.

It does seem more likely that, consistent with North *et al.* (2009) institutions in *low-income* economies bend to accommodate political incentives rather than mould those incentives. For example Schlumberger (2008) identifies a patrimonial form of capitalism in oil exporting countries (with wider applicability), the primary feature of which is the deployment of informal institutions to repress formal ones rather than reinforce them. Consequently, although countries may score favourably on the quality of governance or business environment, formal rules are invariably bent for elite advantage. More specifically, patrimonial capitalism: (i) retains formal rules for application to elements disloyal to the regime (which weakens respect for the rule of law); (ii) emasculates competition policies and reforms that constrain patronage; (iii) guarantees property rights through patronage (which demands social investment by participants) rather than through law; (iv) raises transaction costs compared with a competitive market economy; (v) concentrates patronage on a favoured subset (which reinforces elite opposition to electoral governance); and (vi) prefers non-democratic governments so as to sustain a "shadow" political system that overrides the formal rules.

Acemoglu and Robinson (2008) subsequently recognise the ability of the elite to manipulate institutions. The World Bank (2009) provides further evidence: it reports that almost two-thirds of a sample of Middle East and North African civil servants view the private sector as rent-seeking and corrupt, dominated by a handful of well-connected firms that sustain quasi-monopolies by barring new entrants, bribing civil servants, lobbying for privilege and underreporting earnings. For their part, a majority of firms view regulation of the business environment as arbitrary and biased in favour of politicians and a relatively small number of their privileged business allies. Institutions in developing countries are malleable.

Two decades of statistical research have therefore failed to provide a definitive explanation for the resource curse and its very existence is contested (Lederman and Maloney 2007). This reflects the overly narrow perspective of statistical studies hitherto, which fails to account for the fact that: the global incidence of cases of the resource curse fluctuates over time; other forms of windfall revenue can reproduce symptoms of the resource curse; and the properties of natural resource rent streams differ systematically in their developmental consequences. These omissions are now examined.

2.2 The varied incidence of the resource curse over time

Global policy shifts help to explain temporal changes in the incidence of the resource curse. Statist policies gained favour through the immediate post-war decades. They extended state intervention, which misallocated inputs and thereby distorted the economy. More specifically, recourse to statist policies intensified after the termination of Lewis's (1978) First Golden Age of Economic Growth (1870–1913), during which many primary product exporters had prospered under expanding global trade. Two World Wars and the Great Depression disrupted global trading patterns and caused commodity-exporting countries to experience acute revenue volatility. Many Latin American countries underwent forced industrialisation by import substitution in the 1930s, a policy they retained after the Second World War although global trade re-expanded.

The policy appealed to newly independent economies of Africa and Asia as well as Latin America as a means of complementing political independence with economic independence. It was backed by economists like Prebisch and Singer who argued that the terms of trade were running against most developing countries over the long term so they needed to sell greater volumes of primary commodities to pay for constant volumes of industrial goods from the advanced economies. Since the industrial countries' first mover advantage impeded global industrial diffusion, developing country governments should override markets to promote manufacturing. They monitor imports to identify products for which domestic demand will support a local factory of minimum viable size. The government then grants a licence for local production behind protective import tariffs that are lowered once the infant industry matures.

In practice, however, infant industries had little incentive to mature because they could pass high costs on to the captive domestic market. Factory maturation rates typically measured several decades rather than the five to seven years regarded by Krueger and Tuncer (1982) as the maximum if the discounted costs of infant support are to be justified by the discounted benefits from the policy. The Achilles heel of industrial policies (whether import substitution, resource-based industrialisation or an industrial big push) is policy capture (Auty 1994). Most industrial policies degenerate into vehicles for rent extraction by politicians, bureaucrats, unions, managers and, if privately owned, shareholders at the expense of domestic taxes foregone as well as domestic consumers who pay higher prices than imports for shoddier goods.

The statist policies of the 1960s and 1970s effectively relied on rents extracted from the competitive resource-based sector, whether farming or mining, as well as from households, to subsidise a privileged urban elite. The transfers from competitive activity to inefficient activity weakened their economies through the 1960s so they were vulnerable to growth collapses when commodity price volatility increased through 1973–85. This process explains why per capita GDP growth rates show little evidence of a resource curse in the 1960s (Table 2.1), although case studies confirm that statist policies were already distorting high-rent economies (Krueger 1992). The commodity price shocks initially caused growth collapses in the least credit-worthy states from the mid-1970s, mainly sub-Saharan African (SSA) oil importers; then spread in the early 1980s to economies in Sub-Saharan Africa and Latin America that had been able to borrow recycled petro-dollars to postpone adjustment; before hitting the oil exporters in the mid-1980s after oil prices plummeted when global energy conservation nurtured by high energy prices curbed oil demand.

Many resource-rich governments initially resisted economic reform because it threatened the interests of rent-seekers. They thereby accumulated further debt and were eventually forced to turn to the International Financial institutions (IFIs) for assistance. The IFIs made trade liberalisation and market reform a condition of their loans, while aid donors pushed for political pluralism. The hardship of economic reform and structural adjustment impaired implementation of some reforms and sometimes caused programme failures, which delayed recovery and fed accusations that the IFI policies were unsound. In fact, both IFI policies and the associated surge in foreign aid were often captured by the elite and manipulated to yield rent, further postponing reform and economic recovery into the mid-1990s. Despite this many resource-rich developing country governments, but not all, eventually stabilised their economies so that GDP growth rates recovered through the 1990s and 2000s (Table 2.1).

The period 1960–2000 therefore proved to be a lengthy policy learning curve for the developing economies. This implies that research covering the period 1970–90 like that of Sachs and Warner captures the period of maximum global incidence of resource curse effects, whereas studies extending into 1990–2010 coincide with a diminution of resource curse cases. Consequently, statistical analyses that neglect the shift from statist economic policy to IFI-backed policy, risk drawing inaccurate conclusions. They do so by over-estimating the incidence of the resource curse if they stress early decades (Sachs and Warner 1999) or by querying its existence if they focus on later years (Brunnschweiler 2008). A further complexity arises from the fact that the foreign aid that accompanied structural adjustment often functioned like windfall rent. Moreover, some resource-poor economies in the Sahel also struggled with growth collapses (Auty and Pontara 2008).

2.3 *Different rent sources have different economic linkages*

Most statistical studies of the resource curse neglect windfall revenue streams other than natural resources although they can replicate resource curse symptoms. The other sources of windfall revenue include foreign aid (geopolitical rent), worker remittances (labour rent) and government manipulation of relative prices (regulatory rent), all of which can match natural resource rent in scale relative to GDP. In addition, natural resource rent itself can be divided into at least two categories according to its distribution across economic agents, with different development implications. The dispersed (diffuse) resource rent associated with peasant farming is potentially more beneficial for economic development than the concentrated (point) rent associated with modern mining.

Table 2.2 identifies the principal categories of rent in developing countries and compares them in terms of their key characteristics, which are: size relative to GDP; dispersal across economic agents; revenue volatility; and developmental impact. As subsequent sections explain, rent that is high, volatile and strongly concentrated (Isham *et al.* 2005) carries the greatest risk of maladroit deployment. It is strongly associated with mineral economies and especially the oil exporters. The remarkable capital intensity and large scale operation of mining ensure the rent is large relative to GDP, strongly concentrated on large mining companies and governments and also volatile. In contrast, rent that is dispersed across many economic agents on an individual small scale, such as rent from peasant cash crops, is likely to be saved and invested more carefully and flexibly, thereby reducing the boom and bust risk compared with rent that accrues to governments (Baldwin 1956; Bevan *et al.* 1987). It is also less vulnerable to theft by the elite.

The recognition of multiple sources of rent means that resource-poor countries like those of the Sahel can exhibit symptoms of the resource curse. For instance, during the first forty years of independence, Mauritania consistently generated rent of around two-fifths of GDP, at least half of which comprised foreign aid with the remainder split between natural resource rent from fisheries licences sold to the European Union and an iron ore mine on the Moroccan border. Yet the average rate of economic growth was minimal (Auty and Pontara 2008). Rajan and Subramanian (2011) find that domestic expenditure of aid within the public sector triggers Dutch Disease effects that stifle labour-intensive manufacturing. Boone (1996) shows how the effectiveness of foreign aid is often blunted. Data for 1970–90 suggest foreign aid did not increase the investment rate in recipient countries but went mostly into consumption and expanded government. Moreover, the increased consumption did not benefit the poor in any of the three types of political state that Boone analysed (autocratic, egalitarian and oligarchic laissez-faire). Foreign aid has frequently been abused by the elite both for personal enrichment and to maintain political power by biasing public expenditure to targeted goods, which deliver political support, rather than towards universal public goods that benefit supporter and foe alike. Yet, Table 2.2 suggests that overall the development outcomes from flows of aid are equivocal due to variations in the rigour of donor aid supervision: donors grew more discriminating over aid application in the 1990s (Collier 2006).

Regulatory rent is created by governments manipulating relative prices to favour one group over another (Tollison 1982). It is associated with trade policy closure and increased government intervention within the economy, which expand scope to extract regulatory rent (whereas economic reform shrinks it by expanding competitive markets). Regulatory rent tends to be concentrated and

Table 2.2 Stylised rent stream properties and predicted political economy impacts, by rent source[1]

	Concentrated natural resource rent	Diffuse natural resource rent	Regulatory rent	Remittances (labour rent)	Foreign aid (geopolitical rent)
Rent stream properties					
Scale (% GDP)	8–20+	5–15	5–20+	2–10	2–10+
Degree of rent concentration	High	Low	High	Low	High
Volatility (Standard Deviation)	High	Moderate	Moderate	Moderate	Low
Potential rent impacts: economic					
Investment efficiency	Falling	High	Low	High	Equivocal
GDP growth	Decelerating	Rapid	Decelerating	Moderate	Equivocal
Dutch disease effects	High	High	Moderate	Moderate	High
Market repression and corruption	High	Low	High	Low	Equivocal
Potential rent impacts: political					
Self-reliant social capital	Low	High	Low	Moderate	Equivocal
Proliferation of social groups	Constrained	High	Constrained	High	Equivocal

Note
1 Most economies generate more than one rent stream.

therefore easier to steal (Table 2.2). Moreover government price manipulation may extract not just the rent from economic activity but also part of the return to capital and labour. The revenue so extracted represses producer incentives and all too often is expended to subsidise activity that markets would not support, a situation that is unsustainable. Krueger (1992) reports how governments in sub-Saharan Africa in the 1970s and 1980s abused crop marketing boards to transfer rent from peasant farmers to urban elites. Such policies transformed beneficially diffuse crop rent into concentrated rent that was deployed inefficiently.

Finally, wage remittances are a diffuse form of rent that at low levels of income boosts domestic consumption, often of the poorest and also funds local investment where financial systems are underdeveloped (Giuliano and Ruiz-Arranz 2009). These positive impacts on economic growth attenuate as incomes rise however, because the adverse effects of remittances on work incentives strengthen and also financial intermediation improves. Moreover, as with other windfall revenues large remittance flows can trigger Dutch Disease effects that depress GDP growth (Rajan and Subramanian 2011).

Each rent source can comprise 10–20 per cent of GDP or more (Krueger 1992; Svensson 2000; World Bank 2006), potentially taking the *total* rent within the economy to one-fifth to one-third of GDP or more. It is therefore not surprising that rent has the capacity to distort the economy and profoundly affect development outcomes. Moreover, rent on this scale is sufficient to suggest that statistical studies of the resource curse that ignore the additional rent streams are at best impaired by background noise and at worst badly flawed in their conclusions. In this context, rent cycling theory can capture the temporal shifts in the timing of the resource curse, the presence of additional rent streams and the contrasting features of different types of rent. Section 3 next examines key components of such a theory through the literature on structural change and political maturation. Section 4 integrates them into two basic stylised facts models.

3 Components of a theory of rent cycling

Economic analysis extols parsimonious explanation, which however risks neglecting key variables. Political incentives are an important example. For instance, IFI prescriptions for the reform of collapsed economies in the 1980s omitted strategies for building political support for the reforms, an omission that impaired reform outcomes. Rent cycling theory incorporates political variables into economic analysis by analysing rent extraction, deployment and impacts. In this context, this section traces the relationship between rising per capita income and systematic changes in the two main components of rent cycling theory, structural change in the economy and political maturation.

3.1 Systematic patterns of structural change with rising income

Different patterns of industrialisation lie at the heart of the divergence in the performance of high-rent and low-rent economies: low-rent economies pursue competitive industrialisation whereas high-rent economies tend to subsidise manufacturing. Syrquin and Chenery (1989) identify the central role of manufacturing in economic development, using data from more than one hundred countries for 1950 to 1983 to summarise aggregate structural change as per capita income rises from below $300 to more than $4000, measured in 1980 dollars.[1] The initial dominance of low productivity agriculture gives way to manufacturing and then services become dominant (McKinsey 2012). More specifically, the share of agriculture in GDP declines from one-half at low-income levels to under one-fifth at mid-income levels, when manufacturing overtakes it (Table 2.3). Thereafter, rising incomes are associated with the contraction of agriculture, now highly productive, to 5 per cent of GDP or less while manufacturing falls towards 10 per cent of GDP. McKinsey (2012) confirm the decline of manufacturing in high-income economies, which peaks at 25–35 per cent of GDP and then falls (currently, to 16 per cent of GDP and 14 per cent of employment for the OECD).

These changes in the structure of production systematically vary the rate of growth in per capita income because historically agriculture, manufacturing and services differed in their contributions to productivity growth, with manufacturing being the most productive. The net effect is for the rate of economic growth to first accelerate and then slow down across the income range covered. Historically, GDP growth tripled to reach over 4 per cent per annum at mid income levels and then halved (Syrquin 1986, p. 233). Manufacturing is deemed

Table 2.3 Per capita income, structural change and domestic absorption, post-1973 (share of GDP)

	Income per capita (1980 US dollars[1])						
	<300	300	500	1000	2000	4000	>5000
Production							
Agriculture	0.48	0.39	0.32	0.23	0.15	0.10	0.07
Mining	0.01	0.05	0.07	0.08	0.08	0.06	0.01
Manufacturing	0.10	0.12	0.15	0.18	0.21	0.24	0.28
Construction	0.04	0.04	0.05	0.06	0.06	0.07	0.07
Utilities	0.06	0.07	0.07	0.08	0.09	0.09	0.10
Services	0.31	0.32	0.35	0.38	0.41	0.45	0.47
Final demand							
Private consumption	0.79	0.73	0.70	0.66	0.63	0.60	0.60
Government consumption	0.12	0.14	0.14	0.14	0.14	0.15	0.14
Investment	0.14	0.18	0.21	0.23	0.25	0.26	0.26
Exports	0.16	0.19	0.21	0.23	0.23	0.26	0.23
Imports	0.21	0.25	0.25	0.26	0.27	0.28	0.23

Source: Syrquin and Chenery (1989, p. 20).

Note

1 Since 1980 the US GDP deflator has risen by 2.52, so the income range rises to <$750 to >$12,600.

to confer faster economic growth due to strong externalities from learning by doing (Matsuyama 1992; Sachs and Warner 1997). Echevarria (1997) uses a dynamic general equilibrium model to confirm that manufacturing has displayed the fastest rate of productivity growth and services the slowest rate. She estimates the changing sectoral composition of GDP explains more than one-fifth of the observed variation in economic growth among countries. Wood and Berge (1997) concur: countries that export manufactured goods grow faster than countries that export primary products, which they attribute to manufacturing requiring more skills and so accelerating human capital formation. McKinsey (2012) note that although at high income levels manufacturing contributes negatively to employment growth (−24% 1996–2006), it still contributes more than its sector share of GDP to productivity growth (37%), total exports (70%) and private research and development (77%).

The changing role of manufacturing means that structural change first accelerates economic growth and then slows it down. Some caveats apply regarding the historically dominant contribution of manufacturing to economic growth, however, arising from the pro-industry bias in most development policies through the first three decades of the post-war era (Lipton 1977). This may cause the historical data of Syrquin and Chenery to overstate the role of manufacturing relative to agriculture and services compared with the outcome under more rational economic policies. More crucially for the rent-driven models introduced in Section 4, the data also fail to distinguish between competitive industrialisation and protected industry, with the former much more effective in sustaining productivity-driven growth and driving GDP growth rates faster than the Syrquin and Chenery averages.

Post-war development policies frequently discriminated against agriculture. Yet, as the largest sector in the early stages of development agriculture provides cheap food, cheap labour to the expanding cities, foreign exchange, tax revenues and inputs for manufacturing (Johnston and Mellor 1961). Agriculture also performs an important function neglected by many policy-makers focused on industrialisation. Farmers comprise by far the bulk of the population at low income levels, and form a potentially large market for locally manufactured farm inputs and household goods, provided policies boost farm efficiency and raise incomes. Mellor (1995) shows agriculture can drive rapid economic growth *in a well-managed economy*. East Asian experience reveals that agriculture in early development can grow at 4–6 per cent annually, which can propel total GDP at a rate of 7.5 per cent annually. Yet agriculture rarely met this potential in the post-war decades due to the widespread pro-industrial policy bias.

The contribution of services may now also be under-rated by the historical data of Syrquin and Chenery. Recent research suggests that the rate of productivity growth in services is accelerating while that of manufacturing slows (Ghani *et al.* 2012). India shows that services can match manufacturing for dynamism even at mid-income levels. India conforms to the Syrquin and Chenery pattern of structural change through 1950–90 when it prioritized industrialization: a 25 per cent fall in the share of agriculture in GDP by 1990 was offset by a

12 per cent rise in each of industry and services. But the share of manufacturing in Indian GDP then stabilised and services filled the gap as agriculture continued to shrink. By 2005, services generated 50 per cent of GDP (World Bank 2009), but employed only 26 per cent of the workforce, a ratio implying similar productivity to industry which then generated 32 per cent of GDP with 18 per cent of employment.[2] By the late-2000s, services provided 38 per cent of total exports in India compared with 15 per cent for Africa, 12 per cent for Brazil and 9 per cent for China (Borchert and Mattoo 2009, chap. 3).

A final caveat regarding the historical dominance of manufacturing in development concerns the contribution of the demographic cycle in accelerating economic growth at mid-income levels. Bloom and Williamson (1998) identify three distinct phases in the demographic transition as the ratio of dependants to workers adjusts the capacity of households to save and invest. First, as population growth accelerates with the diffusion of modern medicine at low income levels the number of dependants per active worker rises, which slows economic growth because it raises the share of income going on consumption at the expense of the share for saving and investment. But through the middle of the cycle urbanisation causes the birth rate to decline, which creates a generational surge of active workers that lowers the dependency/worker ratio to create a "demographic dividend" that boosts the capacity of households to save and invest, thereby raising the rate of economic growth. Lastly, the demographic cycle becomes growth-depressing again as workers in the surge cohort retire and boost the proportion of elderly dependants, which increases the burden on a workforce that has shrunk in relative size.

Importantly for the rent-driven development models, the demographic dividend differentially impacts high-rent and low-rent economies. This is because countries that embark upon the demographic transition early capture the benefits of the demographic dividend sooner, which raises their rate of saving and economic growth relative to countries that do not. Section 4 shows that low-rent countries industrialise at lower per capita incomes than high-rent countries so they urbanise earlier and therefore move sooner through the demographic cycle. The early demographic dividend means that all else being equal resource-poor economies are favoured to grow faster, provided they pursue their comparative advantage in competitive industrialisation. Industrialisation is therefore important to economic development, but perhaps not as much as post-war development planners believed (and many economists have come to accept), and the nature of industrialisation is critical: competitive industrialisation confers the strongest developmental benefits.

3.2 *Systematic patterns in political change with rising income*

The link between rising per capita income and political maturation in developing countries is less clear cut than the link of per capita income with structural change. In fact, some researchers dispute whether such a link exists at all (Przeworski *et al.* 2000). Once again, consideration of the resource endowment clarifies matters: the sharply increased frequency of growth collapses through the 1970s and 1980s impacted mainly resource-rich countries, rendering their governments more prone to destabilisation and political churning. In contrast, most resource-poor governments, which were far fewer in number, avoided growth collapses and their polities matured incrementally, driven by structural change, albeit with a lag in some Asian countries. The weak relationship of income and political maturation in the aggregate data for developing countries reflects the preponderance of resource-rich countries in the total.

Olson's (2000) work on the incentives for the elite to create wealth provides a starting point for teasing out the stylised facts of political maturation. His basic premise is that the incentive for a government to provide public goods (which reduce transaction costs and strengthen the incentives for efficient investment) increases as the political state encompasses the interests of a wider fraction of society. In developing his thesis, Olson identifies four basic categories of political state that tend to be sequenced in a shift towards political pluralism as the government caters to a wider set of political interests. Olson's sequence of political states comprises the roving bandit state (conceived as a pillaging warlord), the stationary bandit state (an autocrat), the oligarchic state and the democracy.

The roving bandit plunders a region with little regard for future revenue and moves on to the next region to repeat the strategy. This type of state offers little prospect for accumulating capital and sustaining rising welfare. In contrast, the stationary bandit adopts a longer time horizon because he needs to ensure a sustained revenue stream from the region of residence, which is the region being exploited. The stationary bandit therefore maximises his revenue by providing some public goods that facilitate exchange (such as law and order, income-related taxation and essential infrastructure) and leaving producers with sufficient revenue to retain an incentive to increase output, which he can tax.

The third step in the progression, an oligarchy, reflects the capture of the political state by a political group that administers rent in a more collegiate manner than either form of autocratic state. Importantly, the oligarchy will tax less than a stationary bandit does and will invest more in public goods because, unlike either of the bandit states, the elite in an oligarchy is a producer of goods as well as a consumer of revenue so it benefits directly from incentives to boost output as well as indirectly. The oligarchic state relies less than either autocratic state does upon siphoning off rents for its income so that the oligarchy encompasses a wider set of interests than they do. Finally, a democracy embraces still wider political interests than an oligarchy and as a result promotes conditions that are even more conducive to broad-based wealth creation.

Olson's typology can be usefully elaborated by observing how elite incentives respond to different levels of rent. North et al. (2009) argue that developing country governments need to create rent and restrict access to it so it can be deployed to neutralise opposition from those with the power to achieve violent political change. There is therefore, of necessity, a trade-off between political imperatives and economic goals, which economists sometimes forget. North's

Limited Access Order Society characterises most developing countries and skews economic and political opportunity towards a powerful elite. It contrasts with the Open Access Order Society of the OECD countries, which provides broad access to economic and political opportunity. In Olson's terms, the Open Access Society embraces the maximum encompassing interests.

The scale of the rent relative to GDP differentiates elite incentives and generates contrasting political trajectories. Low rent encourages wealth creation that fosters rapid structural change that drives an incremental shift towards political maturation. High rent encourages immediate enrichment through rent-seeking, which distorts the economy, risking a growth collapse and political instability. In the presence of high rent, immediate personal gain has a stronger appeal than the deferred reward from growing the economy, whose benefits may be garnered by later cohorts rather than the current elite. Rent is extracted by diverting rent through patronage channels at the expense of competitive markets. This undermines investment efficiency and distorts structural change. Common patronage channels include licences to monopolise domestic imports of (or to produce) a particular good and ministerial control of discretionary public expenditure, including subsidies and building contracts. In contrast, the pursuit of growth in low-rent economies requires the provision of infrastructure and the maintenance of incentives for efficient investment through the promotion of competitive markets. This drives rapid structural change that spawns social groups able and willing to contest policy capture by any one group and broaden the encompassing interests of the state.

More specifically, the pursuit of economic growth in low-rent economies drives rapid structural change into a widening range of manufacturing and service activity, much of it located in self-funding towns and cities. This boosts social capital accumulation and self-reliant social groups. Taking social capital first, most transactions in rural-based low-income economies occur over short (i.e. local) distances and are facilitated by bonding social capital that insures individuals against risk (Woolcock and Narayan 2000). However, bonding social capital can stifle innovative and entrepreneurial activity (Stiglitz 1995) because it carries group social obligations that require any gains accruing to an individual, whether from luck or diligence, to be shared among the group. This hampers wealth accumulation and depresses incentives to innovate. But urbanisation within a market economy permits individuals to substitute *linking* social capital for bonding social capital by extending social links through regional associations, which reduces risk but imposes fewer redistributive claims than bonding social capital. This more economically productive form of social capital accumulates faster in low-rent economies due to their early and rapid urbanisation. As development proceeds further, formal legal institutions displace linking social capital because large anonymous markets are more effective than (informal) networks based on contacts, since the "best" buyer or seller may not be part of a network (Serageldin and Grootaert 2000, p. 213). But anonymous markets require effective institutions, notably a reliable legal system and protection of property rights, which businessmen in low-rent economies demand.

Rapid structural change also multiplies self-reliant social groups, many with the skills and aptitude to challenge the monopoly of political power and prevent policy capture by any one group. The expansion of such groups steadily strengthens three sanctions against anti-social governance to drive an incremental democratisation: it challenges autocracies and dissolves oligarchies. First, the process of early urbanisation within competitive markets builds a self-reliant form of social capital and civic voice (Isham *et al.* 2005) because workers do not depend on government patronage.[3] Second, private firms protect their investment by lobbying for property rights and the rule of law (Li and Zhang 2000). The final sanction against anti-social governance derives from the fact that in the presence of low rent, governments must rely for their revenue on taxing income, profits and expenditure, which spurs demand from tax payers for public finances to be accountable (Ross 2001).

The rapid structural change generated by the low-rent model strengthens the importance of industrial interests relative to landowners so a low-rent oligarchy increasingly comprises industrialists rather than large landowners. Acemoglu and Robinson (2006) argue that industrialists are more likely to nurture a diffusing oligarchy than landowners because industrialists rely more heavily on workforce cooperation to sustain their wealth since factory assets are more concentrated and vulnerable to civil disturbance than landed estates. Nineteenth century Britain provides an example of how industrialisation created a diffusing oligarchy. Lizzeri and Persico (2004) argue that the concern of industrialists about the inadequate provision of urban public goods drove an incremental widening of the franchise in nineteenth century Britain. Through the early nineteenth century, rising urban mortality fuelled demands in Britain to redirect public funds from the pork barrel patronage of autocratic government towards improving public goods, notably urban sanitation. Lizzeri and Persico (2004) use the 1832 electoral reform as an example: public expenditure did not increase its share of GDP but rather shifted it towards local government and urban public goods provision. The redirection of public funds continued for a century and, consistent with Olson, was accompanied by the periodic widening of the franchise, which incrementally transformed a diffusing oligarchy into a democracy.

In contrast, high rent permits an autocracy or an oligarchy to use rent to sustain its monopoly of policy through a combination of co-opting the potentially powerful; subsidising urban interest groups (which tend to be a more coherent political force than dispersed peasant farmers are); and using military force if necessary. In addition, high rent tends to retard *competitive* structural change, partly by repressing markets in order to facilitate rent-seeking activity and partly through the over-rapid domestic absorption of rent and the consequent Dutch Disease effects arising from political contests for its capture. These two factors cumulatively weaken the economy, which not only retards structural change in high-rent economies and slows the proliferation of social groups but also dilutes all three sanctions against anti-social governance that help drive political maturation in low-rent economies. First, under high rent businesses benefit more from lobbying politicians for favours than from productive investment and are therefore less concerned about property rights and the rule of law because personal contacts are more effective guarantors of keeping their profits. Second, social capital is subservient rather than self-reliant, reflecting the dependence of the population in high-rent economies on government largesse such as subsidies and even employment, rather than the self-reliance learned in competitive markets. Third, the high-rent government's reliance on rent streams for revenue rather than direct and indirect taxation mutes public pressure for financial accountability. Consequently, autocratic and oligarchic power structures persist longer in high-rent economies, but their reliance on rent that may fluctuate renders them brittle.

In essence, rapid economic growth in the low-rent economy drives structural change, which spawns self-reliant social groups that contest power with other groups. Consequently, an elite social stratum that pursues economic growth also sows the seeds of its own eventual demise as the polity shifts towards a diffusing oligarchy and then a democracy that is consensual. In contrast, the hesitant structural change of the high-rent economy experiences slower proliferation of social groups, which risk co-option by rent. Moreover, social capital is dependent on government largesse rather than being self-reliant. Authoritarian governments may therefore persist, but they are brittle and vulnerable to a growth collapse. Political change in the high-rent economy may therefore be abrupt and possibly violent so that political maturation can regress as Przeworski *et al.* (2000) observe.

4 Two rent-driven development models

Rent cycling theory distils the systematic interaction between the scale of rent and structural change and political maturation to identify two stylised facts development models, the low-rent competitive industrialisation model and the high-rent staple trap (Table 2.4). In both models elite incentives shape the pattern of structural change that drives social capital accumulation and political change. The post-war success of the low-rent competitive industrialisation model furnishes an instructive counterfactual to help explain why so many resource-rich economies (but not all) struggled to achieve rapid economic and political maturation.

4.1 The low-rent competitive industrialisation development model

The competitive industrialisation model identifies the critical advantage of the low-rent economy as an early start on competitive industrialisation, which triggers virtuous economic, social and political outcomes. Early examples include Hong Kong, Mauritius, Singapore, South Korea and Taiwan while a more recent recruit, China, has lagged as a consequence of prioritising heavy industry in pursuit of extreme economic autarky (Auty 2013). The initial condition of resource paucity limits scope for the elite to expand primary product exports and

Table 2.4 Principal features of two stylised facts rent-driven development models

Low-rent competitive industrialisation model	High-rent staple trap model
Elite incentives	
Grow economy to increase wealth	Compete to siphon rent for personal gain
Promote public goods and efficient markets	Press for rapid domestic rent absorption
Align economy with comparative advantage	Lobby to sustain patrimonial capitalism
Economic trajectory	
Export labour-intensive manufactured goods	Over-rapid rent absorption fuels Dutch Disease
Early onset of labour market turning point	Expand inefficient protected urban industry
Rapid and competitive structural change	Rent subsidises employment and consumption
Early onset of demographic dividend	Rent-dependent growth and high inequality
Rapid, sustained and equitable PCGDP growth	Over-reliance on rent triggers growth collapse
Social capital	
Market encourages self-reliant social capital	Reliance on political links, not rule of law
Social capital switches from bonding to linking	Rent fosters dependent social capital
Increasing reliance on institutional safeguards	Flexible application of institutional safeguards
Political change	
Structural change proliferates social groups	Slow structural change constrains social change
Social groups oppose policy capture	Oligarchs slant policy to sustain rent siphoning
Firms lobby for strong institutional safeguards	Political connections outbid rule of law
Taxation feeds demands for accountability	Rent-reliance blunts accountability demands
Incremental democratisation	Authoritarian, but brittle, tendency: vulnerable

extract rent. Rather, to create wealth the elite must grow the economy and taxes, from which it derives the most benefit. Economic growth requires the efficient allocation of inputs so the economy pursues its comparative advantage, which in a low-income low-rent economy lies in labour-intensive manufactured exports. This competitive industrialisation requires governments to provide infrastructure and effective markets, which constrain scope for extracting regulatory rent. In Olson's terms, low rent aligns the interests of the elite with those of the majority in growing the economy to create wealth efficiently.

Early competitive industrialisation brings early urbanisation, which confers three economic benefits. First, it accelerates passage through the demographic cycle because an urban environment helps reduce family size by: offering a wider range of employment than the rural economy; facilitating rising family incomes; and placing a higher premium on space than rural living. Slowing population growth advances the onset of the demographic dividend as the dependent/worker ratio falls. A lower dependent/worker ratio absorbs less expenditure for consumption, leaving more for saving and investment. This higher investment is efficient in an export economy that is exposed to global competition so it generates high per capita GDP growth. This demographic dividend persists until the workers in the expanded cohort begin to retire when each worker must support a growing number of dependents so that a worsening dependent/worker ratio becomes growth depressing (Bloom and Williamson 1998).

Second, early urbanisation rapidly absorbs surplus rural labour, which advances the arrival of the Lewis (1954) labour market turning point. The experience of Taiwan and South Korea suggests that the labour market turning point arrives within a decade of launching the trade reform that ignites manufacturing-led export growth. The onset of labour shortages boosts wage costs economy-wide, which encourages government and employers to invest in improving worker skills so as to maintain competitiveness by raising productivity. In this way rising wages propel a sustained diversification into the production of more skill-intensive and capital-intensive goods, which drives rapid growth in per capita incomes. In addition, the elimination of surplus rural labour permits farm consolidation that allows for the more efficient use of rural land and labour, stimulating gains in agricultural productivity and rural incomes in low-rent economies, in contrast to many resource-rich economies.

Third, GDP growth in the low-rent economy is not only rapid but also relatively egalitarian because the elimination of surplus rural labour puts a floor under the wages of the poorest while the rapid diffusion of technological skills caps the skill premium (Londono 1996). The resulting egalitarian and high per capita GDP growth can transform a low-income economy into a high-income economy within two generations. The rate of per capita GDP growth may exceed 8 per cent per annum through mid-income levels, double the mean for the countries analysed by Chenery and Syrquin. This rate is sufficient to more than quadruple per capita income within twenty years.

Turning to social capital, structural change within a competitive economy builds a self-reliant form of social capital, as explained in Section 3.2. Structural change also engenders new professions and social groups that can and do contest policy capture by any single group. Moreover, the more egalitarian income distribution of low-rent economies helps cement social solidarity and limit political polarisation, in contrast to the income skew of most resource-rich economies. Income equality also eases pressure for redistribution so that changes in government tend not to result in sharp changes of economic policy that can be wealth-destroying.[4] The rapidly diversifying social structure also encourages democratisation by strengthening the three sanctions against anti-social governance as private firms lobby for property rights and the rule of law; competitive urbanisation strengthens self-reliant civic voice and social capital; and government reliance on taxes rather than rent spurs demand for transparent public finances. The net result is an incremental political maturation in low-rent economies with rising per capita income. In Olson's terminology, this can transform an autocracy into a diffusing oligarchy that gives way to a democracy that is consensual rather than polarised.

4.2 The high-rent staple trap development model

The high-rent economy risks falling into a staple trap of over-reliance for its economic growth on expanding rent from primary exports rather than on raising productivity (Table 2.4). The risk arises because high rent encourages the elite to seek immediate personal enrichment by pressing for rapid rent absorption that the elite can siphon off. This triggers Dutch Disease effects and state intervention to protect inefficient urban activity, so that the high-rent economy fails to experience early competitive industrialisation and forfeits the six developmental benefits it confers, namely:

i Alignment of elite and majority interests in prioritising GDP growth.
ii Early reliance on labour-intensive exports that trigger competitive diversification.
iii Early passage through the demographic cycle and capture of the demographic dividend.
iv Rapid absorption of surplus labour and skill diffusion that constrain income inequality.
v Accumulation of self-reliant social capital.
vi Strengthening political competition and sanctions against anti-social governance.

Instead, contests to capture rent deflect policy away from promoting economic growth and into proliferating ways to siphon off rent for personal gain. The end result is a staple trap that weakens the economy by transferring rent (and also some of the return to capital and labour) from a competitive primary sector to expand an uncompetitive protected urban sector. The transfers cumulatively misallocate inputs and intensify the rent dependence of a burgeoning protected urban sector that eventually outstrips the rent-generating capacity of the primary sector. A growth collapse may then be caused by over-taxing the primary sector, softening commodity prices or resource exhaustion. The essence of the staple trap is therefore the expansion of a rent-dependent and uncompetitive modern sector whose demand for rent outstrips supply. The staple trap development trajectory impedes competitive diversification of the economy, builds dependent social capital and weakens sanctions against anti-social governance.

More specifically, high rent fuels political pressure for the rapid disbursement of rent, which governments find difficult to resist so that rent deployment invariably exceeds the absorption capacity of the domestic economy and stokes inflation. This causes an appreciation of the real exchange rate that strengthens Dutch Disease effects whereby the non-boom tradables contract unless they are given protection, while limited international competition accommodates price rises in the service sector. The change in relative prices triggers a resource movement effect that shifts capital and labour out of the struggling tradables sector and into more profitable services.

Most governments respond to Dutch Disease effects by closing trade policy to protect domestic producers of tradables, especially manufacturing, whose urbanised presence strengthens its political influence compared with dispersed rural activity like farming. But import barriers reduce incentives to compete, since domestic producers can pass increased costs on to their captive domestic market. The policy therefore shifts the internal terms of trade against agriculture, mining and competitive manufacturing in favour of *protected* manufacturing, which is the very reverse of the required competitive diversification of the economy. Although agriculture generates the most employment at low incomes, in the high-rent economy it invariably functions as a reservoir of cheap labour, a supplier of cheap food and a potential source of rent rather than an engine of economic growth.

Dutch Disease effects and protection preclude labour-intensive export-led manufacturing so all three of its beneficial effects on development are foregone. First, the persistence of surplus labour mutes the impulse from rising real wages for rapid and sustained productivity-driven structural change. Second, the labour surplus depresses the wages of the rural poor while urban workers in protected activity tap rents to boost their wages, amplifying income inequality. Third, retarded urbanisation postpones the emergence of the demographic dividend and its associated boost to saving, while protection depresses investment efficiency, which slows economic growth. Gelb *et al.* (1991) document the counter-productive nature of urban subsidies in copper-rich Zambia. Fearing urban unemployment the government deploys mineral rent to subsidise urban jobs, which attract more rural workers from the neglected agricultural sector in a self-defeating cycle, especially since subsidised import substitution industry tends to be capital-intensive and provide little employment. The policy quickly degenerates into a vehicle for rent-seeking and government corruption, which in the case of Zambia starved investment in the state-owned mines and rendered them uncompetitive.

Household subsidies funded by rent foster a dependent form of social capital while retarded structural change impedes the emergence of self-reliant social groups that contest political power and drive an incremental shift towards political pluralism. Rather, all three sanctions against anti-social governance that strengthen under low-rent competitive industrialisation weaken in the high-rent staple trap model, as explained earlier. Public expenditure is skewed towards targeted public goods that can be allocated to maximise political support at the expense of universal public goods like health and education, which benefit supporters and foes alike.

Reliance on government largesse discourages both economic reform and political reform because reform shrinks scope for rent-seeking opportunities. This tends to ossify the political regime, sustaining income inequality and associated political tensions. A polarised society raises the stakes from policy change, which reinforces elite opposition to evolutionary political adjustment. But income inequality and vulnerability to price shocks render such political regimes brittle. The absence of timely economic reform risks a growth collapse, which tends to be protracted since the elite oppose reform because reform extends competitive markets that shrink their rent-seeking opportunities. Elite resistance makes it politically attractive for governments to squeeze more revenue from the primary sector by extracting returns to capital and labour as well as the rent. Even when debt service requirements force economic reforms, the elite may capture policy to turn it to advantage by, for example, promoting privatisation so they secure advantageous terms for buying privatised industry and then obstructing trade liberalisation that would threaten their newly secured monopolies.

Nevertheless, the staple trap model predicts that a growth collapse will be self-correcting. This is because a growth collapse further postpones the demographic transition, which prolongs high population growth that steadily shrinks the per capita rent endowment. Mauritius in the 1950s and 1960s provides an illustration as a mono-crop sugar producing island with high population growth that ran out of land. The elite responded to declining per capita income by forming a coalition government that introduced birth control policies and established an export processing zone, which in contrast to the country's failing industrial policy of import substitution, successfully diversified the economy into competitive manufactured exports (Auty 2010). Unusually at the time, the government taxed away very little of the windfall sugar rent in the mid-1970s and left a high share with the planters, which they invested successfully in economic diversification.

Recapping, high rent incentivises the elite to seek immediate personal enrichment by siphoning rent through patronage channels at the expense of competitive markets. Political pressure causes rent deployment to exceed domestic absorptive capacity, triggering Dutch Disease effects that preclude competitive industrialisation and expand a protected urban sector that requires more and more rent from the primary sector. The high-rent economy thereby loses the developmental benefits that competitive industrialisation confers, namely rapid structural change that sustains both productivity-driven economic growth and incremental political maturation. Instead it risks a protracted growth collapse and political ossification that is brittle.

4.3 Some variations around the development trajectories

Rent cycling theory is capable of further elaboration by recognising differences between natural resource linkages and also the impact of differing initial conditions. The linkages from different classes of natural resources systematically vary the development outcome: some primary exports are more prone to precipitate growth collapses than others (Table 2.2). The risks of an adverse outcome are higher: the higher the ratio of rent to GDP; the more concentrated the rent on a handful of economic agents; and the greater the volatility of the commodity price.

Mineral-driven economies are most at risk of a growth collapse, and the oil-exporting economies most of all, as Table 2.1 confirms. First, mineral rents tend to be high relative to GDP because mineral extraction tends to be heavily capital-intensive and undertaken upon a scale that is large relative to the economies of most developing countries. Moreover, revenue is concentrated on a handful of companies and because most of the domestic linkage is fiscal (taxation) it accrues directly to the government. Other forms of domestic linkage like further processing, production of domestic inputs and spending by management and labour are limited. Unfortunately, governments tend to be less likely to save and invest rents efficiently than dispersed economic agents are (Baldwin 1956; Bevan *et al*. 1987). Finally, mineral rent is especially volatile (Cashin and McDermott 2002; Cashin *et al.* 2000; van der Ploeg and Poelhekke 2009), which severely tests macroeconomic management. Primary commodity prices fluctuate the most if sunk investment is important as with perennial crops and especially capital-intensive mining. The acute volatility of mineral prices reflects long lead-times (four to ten years) between the decision to invest and the start-up of production, which render it difficult to match supply and demand. Global productive capacity either lags demand or runs ahead of it, which amplifies booms and busts (Auty 1987).

The corollary is that some natural resource rent is harder for rent-seekers to capture and therefore more conducive to the promotion of economic development. In particular, the rent generated by crop-driven economies: is usually a smaller fraction of GDP than mineral rent; exhibits less price and revenue volatility; and is dispersed across many economic agents who tend to save and invest rent more effectively than governments do. Baldwin (1956) develops a model of temperate yeoman farming, which has low capital requirements that permit ease of entry while also accommodating small increases in investment that steadily raise crop yields, productivity and incomes. Moreover, income tends to be evenly distributed across the entire population, which creates a society that supports taxation to improve the infrastructure, including local transport and education, because all can expect to benefit from it. Expanding incomes also create a growing domestic market for basic consumer goods and a widening range of increasingly sophisticated producer goods like farm machinery. Yeoman society provides a stream of entrepreneurs in the form of farmers' children who if they do not inherit the land have the capital to exploit new economic opportunities. Such an economy of small farmers has a high probability of evolving into a dynamic diversified mature economy, as occurred in the Mid West upon which Baldwin based his yeoman farm model. However, in the post-war years too many developing country governments abused their crop marketing boards to extract the rent, which transformed the sector's beneficial dispersed rent into concentrated rent that risked growth collapses.

In addition to variations in commodity linkages, rent cycling theory recognises that initial conditions mediate the risk of a growth collapse. Statist policies and high ethnicity furnish examples. First, statist policies amplify the adverse effects of high rent by boosting scope for governments to override markets and manipulate prices (Van de Walle 2001). Policies to increase state control of the economy through the 1960s and 1970s backfired by degenerating into a means of extracting rent that fed rent-seeking, distorted the economy and led to growth collapses. Second, ethnic tension reinforces incentives to use rent to win political support. Bridgeman (2008) identifies a strong statistical link between low growth in ethnically diverse economies and redistributive pressure that deflects resources from welfare enhancing activity. Montalvo and Reynal-Querol (2005, p. 294) find ethnicity is negatively associated with the rate of investment, the rate of economic growth and the quality of government.

5 Conclusions and policy implications

Rent cycling theory suggests that the resource curse is not a deterministic law but rather a consequence of mismanaged rent-seeking. Moreover, the symptoms of the resource case can be replicated by other forms of windfall revenue, notably foreign aid, worker remittances and government manipulation of relative prices as well as by natural resource rent. The resource curse is therefore a manifestation of a broader rent curse. These conclusions help explain why statistical research into the resource curse has produced contradictory findings and sown doubt about whether a resource curse exists or not. The statistical analyses have suffered from background noise at best, and at worst have inadequately addressed three key aspects: the varying incidence of resource curse symptoms over time; the existence of large non-resource rent streams; and systematic variations in outcomes for different natural resources.

Rent cycling theory provides a more nuanced approach than the statistical analysis has hitherto. It does so by tracing the impact of rents upon structural change and political change as per capita incomes rise. The theory is based on the assumption that low rent incentivises the elite to enrich itself by growing the economy. In contrast, high rent motivates the elite to compete for rent for immediate personal enrichment, which channels some rent through patronage networks at the expense of markets. These contrasting incentives generate two basic development trajectories, the low-rent competitive industrialisation model and the high-rent staple trap model. The models trace systematic patterns of structural change, social capital formation and political maturation.

Low-rent motivates the elite to grow the economy, which requires public goods and incentives for efficient investment. This aligns the low-rent economy with its comparative advantage in labour-intensive manufactured exports, which confers critical benefits that drive rapid productivity-driven economic growth and political maturation. The expansion of labour-intensive manufactured exports soon exhausts surplus rural labour, which triggers diversification of the economy into a widening range of competitive skill-intensive and capital-intensive manufacturing. Early industrialisation also brings early urbanisation that accelerates the demographic transition, which lowers the dependent/worker ratio so that the share of saving and investment in GDP rise and per capita GDP growth accelerates. In addition, competitive industrialisation is relatively egalitarian because the absorption of rural labour puts a floor under the wages of the poor while the diffusion of skills caps the skill premium. The resulting rapid structural change accumulates a self-reliant form of social capital and strengthens civic voice. It also multiplies the groups in society willing and able to contest policy capture by any one group. These trends strengthen three sanctions against anti-social governance (rule of law, self-help social capital and fiscal accountability to tax-payers) to drive an incremental political maturation.

The low-rent competitive industrialisation trajectory can build a high-income democracy within two generations and it provides a counterfactual to explain the resource curse in high-rent economies. High rent deflects the elite from prioritising economic growth and into competing for rent for immediate personal gain, so some rent flows into patronage channels at the expense of competitive markets. Governments succumb to political pressure to absorb the rent too quickly into the domestic economy, which triggers Dutch Disease effects that weaken the non-boom tradables sectors, notably the dominant agricultural sector, and elicit subsidies for urban activity, including protected manufacturing that has little incentive to compete. The labour-intensive competitive export phase of the low-rent model is therefore omitted. This prolongs reliance on the primary sector, retards competitive structural change, arrests passage through the demographic cycle and perpetuates surplus rural labour (and associated income inequality). The high-rent model promotes a rent-dependant form of social capital and delays the emergence of social groups prepared to challenge policy capture, which weakens all three sanctions against anti-social governance. The net effect is to create a staple trap whereby an inefficient urban sector expands by extracting higher subsidies from the primary sector, which eventually outstrip the primary sector's capacity to supply them. This leads to a growth collapse in the absence of economic reform, which the elite recipients of rent oppose so that economic recovery is protracted.

Rent cycling theory can explain the diverging performance of the developing countries since the 1960s (Table 2.1) that caused the per capita income of the resource-rich economies to be overtaken by the resource-poor economies. The roots of the divergence lie in statist policies that were forced on governments by the disruption of world trade during the 1930s and 1940s and then voluntarily embraced in the immediate post-war decades. These policies quickly degenerated into vehicles for rent extraction in resource-rich economies that triggered growth collapses during the heightened commodity price volatility of 1973–85. IFI loans to revive the collapsed economies came with the condition of economic reforms that precluded statist policies. The reforms eventually achieved an economic revival that the commodity super-cycle sustained through the 2000s.

The changing global intensity of resource curse effects over time shows that the resource curse is not deterministic and varies in response to both external events and country initial conditions. For example, resource-rich Chile and Malaysia avoided protracted growth collapses while the resource-poor economies of the Sahel serve to remind that low rent does not ensure economic growth. Ideology in Chile and concern for the lagging rural Malay majority in Malaysia prompted both governments to ensure that rent-seeking did not undermine economic growth. By contrast, statist-leaning governments in the Sahel augmented meagre rent from small farmers and mines with foreign aid and deployed it to appease ethnic rivalries at the expense of sustained economic development and lengthy growth collapses.

Rent cycling theory therefore demonstrates that policy matters. Governments in high-rent economies need to manage domestic rent absorption and limit scope for theft by the elite. Two measures to constrain rent capture are, first, to lower the rate of domestic rent absorption to match absorptive capacity (and shrink the appropriable rent); and second, to distribute rent across many economic agents (say, equally across households) so as to reduce the role of government in domestic rent deployment. The theory also shows that effective reform requires a political strategy to build a pro-growth political coalition because governments attempting top-down reform of rent-distorted economies risk overthrow by aggrieved rent-recipients. The experience of reforming economies as diverse as Malaysia, Mauritius and China favours dual track reform (Auty 2011). This policy grows a dynamic market sector in early-reform zones (Track 1), while pursuing gradual reform in the rent-distorted sector (Track 2) so as to postpone confrontation with the rent-seekers. Within two decades the dynamic market economy can dominate both the economy and the political debate and thereby co-opt erstwhile rent-seekers into the reformed economy.

Notes

1 The advanced economies' GDP deflator for 1980–2010 is 2.52, which applied to the Syrquin and Chenery data raises the income range to one of <$300 to >$4000 to one of <$750 to >$10,000 in 2010 dollars (IMF 2013).
2 In contrast, agriculture had 56 per cent of the workforce but only 18 per cent of GDP, which Mellor (1995) also attributes to long-standing pro-industry policies.
3 The World Bank (1997, p. 81) defines social capital as group knowledge and trust, backed by sanctions, that facilitate economic exchange by reducing uncertainty and risk. In economic terms social capital manifests itself in variations in transaction costs (Djankov *et al.* 2003), whereas in sociological terms the principal components of social capital are civic spirit and civic associations. Civic spirit is defined as the reluctance of individuals within society to take advantage of private misfortune or public administrative error. Civic associations are horizontal networks such as membership of societies for politics, professions, environment, arts, sport and trade unions that build trust.
4 However, East Asia provides evidence that populations experiencing sustained and rapid rises in personal incomes may forgo some political freedoms for longer than populations with slower growth rates of income.

References

Acemoglu, D. and Robinson, J.A., 2006. *Economic Origins of Dictatorship and Democracy*, New York: Cambridge University Press.
Acemoglu, D. and Robinson, J.A., 2008. Persistence of power, elites and institutions. *American Economic Review*, 98(1), pp. 267–293.

Acemoglu, D., Johnson, S. and Robinson, J.A., 2001. The colonial origins of comparative development: An empirical investigation. *American Economic Review*, 91(5), pp. 1369–1401.

Acemoglu, D., Robinson, J.A. and Johnson, S., 2002. Reversal of fortune: Geography and institution in the making of the modern world income distribution. *The Quarterly Journal of Economics*, 117(4), pp. 1231–1294.

Auty, R.M., 1987. Producer homogeneity, heightened uncertainty and minerals market rigidity. *Resources Policy*, 13, pp. 189–206.

Auty, R.M., 1994. Industrial policy reform in six large NICs: The resource curse thesis. *World Development*, 22, pp. 11–26.

Auty, R.M., 2001. *Resource Abundance and Economic Development*, Oxford: Clarendon Press.

Auty, R.M., 2010. Elites, rent cycling and development: Adjustment to land scarcity in Mauritius, Kenya and Côte d'Ivoire. *Development Policy Review*, 28(4), pp. 411–433.

Auty, R.M., 2011. Early reform zones: Catalysts for dynamic market economies in Africa. In T. Farole and G. Akinci, eds. *Special Economic Reform Zones: Progress, Emerging Challenges and Future Prospects*, Washington D.C.: World Bank, pp. 196–205.

Auty, R.M., 2013. Reforming China's development strategy and urban policy, Lancaster: Background paper prepared for the *World Bank China Urbanization Strategy Overview*.

Auty, R.M. and Pontara, N., 2008. A dual track strategy for managing Mauritania's projected oil rent. *Development Policy Review*, 26(1), pp. 59–77.

Baldwin, R.E., 1956. Patterns of development in newly settled regions. *Manchester School of Social and Economic Studies*, 24, pp. 161–179.

Bevan, D., Collier, P. and Gunning, J.W., 1987. Consequences of a commodity boom in a controlled economy: Accumulation and redistribution in Kenya. *World Bank Economic Review*, 1(1), pp. 489–513.

Bloom, D.E. and Williamson, J.G., 1998. Demographic transitions and economic miracles in emerging Asia. *The World Bank Economic Review*, 12, pp. 419–455.

Boone, P., 1996. Politics and the effectiveness of foreign aid. *European Economic Review*, 89(1), pp. 22–46.

Borchert, I. and Mattoo, S., 2009. *The Crisis-resilience of Services Trade*, Washington D.C.: World Bank.

Bridgeman, B., 2008. Why are ethnically divided countries poor? *Journal of Macroeconomics*, 30(1), pp. 1–18.

Brunnschweiler, C.N., 2008. Cursing the blessings? Natural resource abundance, institutions and economic growth. *World Development*, 36(3), pp. 399–449.

Cashin, P. and McDermott, C.J., 2002. The long-run behaviour of commodity prices: Small trends and big variability. *IMF Staff Papers*, 49(2), pp. 175–198.

Cashin, P., Liang, H. and McDermott, C.J., 2000. How persistent are shocks to world commodity prices? *IMF Staff Papers*, 47, pp. 177–217.

Collier, P., 2006. Is aid oil? An analysis of whether Africa can absorb more aid. *World Development*, 34, pp. 1482–1497.

Djankov, S., Glaeser, E., La Porta, R., Lopez-de-Silanes, F. and Shleifer, A., 2003. The new comparative economics. *Journal of Comparative Economics*, 31, pp. 595–619.

Echevarria, C., 1997. Changes in sectoral composition associated with economic growth. *International Economic Review*, 38, pp. 431–452.

Gelb, A.H. and Associates, 1988. *Oil Windfalls: Blessing or Curse?*, New York: Cambridge University Press.

Gelb, A.H., Knight, J. and Sabot, R., 1991. Public sector employment, rent seeking and economic growth. *The Economic Journal*, 101, pp. 1186–1199.

Ghani, E., Goswami, A.G. and Kharas, H., 2012. *Service with a Smile*, Washington D.C.: World Bank PREM.

Giuliano, P. and Ruiz-Arranz, M., 2009. Remittances, financial development, and growth. *Journal of Development Economics*, 90(1), pp. 144–152.

Glaeser, E.L., LaPorta, R., López-de-Silanes, F. and Shleifer, A., 2004. Do institutions cause growth? *Journal of Economic Growth*, 9(3), pp. 271–303.

IMF, 2013. *IMF World Economic Outlook Data*, Washington D.C.: International Monetary Fund.

Isham, J., Woolcock, M., Pritchett, L. and Busby, G., 2005. The varieties of resource experience: How natural resource export structures affect the political economy of economic growth. *World Bank Economic Review*, 19(1), pp. 141–164.

Johnston, B.F. and Mellor, J.W., 1961. The role of agriculture in economic development. *American Economic Review*, 51, pp. 566–593.

Karl, T.L., 1997. *The Paradox of Plenty: Oil Booms and Petro-States*, Berkeley, CA: University of California Press.

Khan, M., 2000. Rent-seeking as process. In M. Khan and K.S. Jomo, eds. *Rents, Rent-seeking and Economic Development: Theory and Evidence in Asia*, Cambridge, MA: Cambridge University Press, pp. 70–144.

Krueger, A.O., 1992. *The Political Economy of Agricultural Pricing Policy: A Synthesis*, Washington D.C.: World Bank.

Krueger, A.O. and Tuncer, B., 1982. An empirical test of the infant industry argument. *American Economic Review*, 72, pp. 1142–1152.

Lal, D. and Myint, H., 1996. *The Political Economy of Poverty, Equity and Growth*, Oxford: Clarendon Press.

Lederman, D. and Maloney, W.F., 2007. *Natural Resources: Neither Curse nor Destiny*, Stanford, CA: Stanford University Press.

Lewis, W.A., 1954. Economic development with unlimited supplies of labour. *Manchester School of Social and Economic Studies*, 22, pp. 139–191.

Lewis, W.A., 1978. *Growth and Fluctuations 1870–1913*, London: Allen and Unwin.

Li, S. and Zhang, W., 2000. The road to capitalism: Competition and institutional change in China. *Journal of Comparative Economics*, 28, pp. 269–292.

Lipton, M., 1977. *Why Poor People Stay Poor: Urban Bias in World Development*, London: Temple Smith.

Lizzeri, A. and Persico, N., 2004. Why did the elites extend the suffrage? Democracy and the scope of government with application to Britain's Age of Reform. *Quarterly Journal of Economics*, 119(2), pp. 707–765.

Londono, J.L., 1996. *Poverty, Inequality and Human Capital Development in Latin America*, Washington D.C.: World Bank.

Matsuyama, T., 1992. The market size, entrepreneurship and the big push. *Journal of Japanese and International Economics*, 6(4), pp. 347–364.

McKinsey, 2012. *Manufacturing the Future: The Next Era of Global Growth and Innovation*, New York: McKinsey Global Institute.

Mellor, J.W., 1995. *Agriculture on the Road to Industrialisation*, Baltimore, MD: Johns Hopkins University Press.

Montalvo, J.G. and Reynal-Querol, M., 2005. Ethnic diversity and economic development. *Journal of Development Economics*, 76, pp. 293–323.

North, D.C., Wallis, J.J. and Weingast, B.R., 2009. *Violence and Social Orders: A*

Conceptual Framework for Interpreting Recorded Human History, Cambridge and New York: Cambridge University Press.

Olson, M., 2000. *Power and Prosperity: Outgrowing Communist and Capitalist Dictatorships*, New York: Basic Books.

Van der Ploeg, F. and Poelhekke, S., 2009. Volatility and the natural resource curse. *Oxford Economic Papers*, 61(4), pp. 727–760.

Przeworski, A., Alvarez, M.E, Cheibub, J.A. and Limongi, F., 2000. *Democracy and Development: Political Institutions and Well-Being in the World 1950–1990*, Cambridge, MA: Cambridge University Press.

Rajan, R.G. and Subramanian, A., 2011. Aid, Dutch disease and manufacturing growth. *Journal of Development Economics*, 94(1), pp. 106–118.

Ross, M., 2001. Does oil hinder democracy? *World Politics*, 53(3), pp. 325–361.

Sachs, J.D. and Warner, A.M., 1997. *Natural Resource Abundance and Economic Growth*, HIID Working Paper, Cambridge, MA.

Sachs, J.D. and Warner, A.M., 1999. The big push, natural resource booms and growth. *Journal of Development Economics*, 59(1), pp. 43–76.

Schlumberger, O., 2008. Structural reform, economic order and development: patrimonial capitalism. *Review of International Political Economy*, 15(4), pp. 622–649.

Serageldin, I. and Grootaert, C., 2000. Defining social capital: An integrating view. In R. Picciotto and E. Wiesner, eds. *Evaluation and Development: The Institutional Dimension*. New Brunswick, NJ: Transaction Publishers, pp. 203–217.

Stiglitz, J.E., 1995. Social absorption capability and innovation. In B.H. Koo and D.H. Perkins, eds. *Social Capability and Long-Term Economic Growth*, Basingstoke: Macmillan, pp. 48–81.

Svensson, J., 2000. Where is the Wealth of Nations? *Journal of International Economics*, 51, pp. 437–461.

Syrquin, M., 1986. Productivity growth and factor reallocation. In H.B. Chenery, S. Robinson and M. Syrquin, eds. *Industrialization and Growth: A Comparative Study*, New York: Oxford University Press, pp. 229–262.

Syrquin, M. and Chenery, H.B., 1989. *Patterns of Development, 1950 to 1983*, Washington D.C.: World Bank.

Tollison, R.D., 1982. Rent seeking: A survey. *Kyklos*, 35(4), pp. 575–602.

Van de Walle, N., 2001. *African Economies and the Politics of Permanent Crisis, 1979–1999*, Cambridge, MA: Cambridge University Press.

Wood, A. and Berge, K., 1997. Exporting manufactures: Human resources, natural resources, and trade policy. *Journal of Development Studies*, 34, pp. 35–59.

Woolcock, M. and Narayan, D., 2000. Social capital: Implications for development theory, research and policy. *World Bank Research Observer*, 15(2), pp. 225–249.

World Bank, 1997. *Expanding the Measure of Wealth, Environmentally Sustainable Development*, Washington D.C.: World Bank.

World Bank, 2006. *Where is the Wealth of Nations?*, Washington D.C.: World Bank.

World Bank, 2009. *From Privilege to Competition: Unlocking Private-Led Growth in MENA*, Washington D.C.: World Bank.

World Bank, 2012. *World Development Indicators 2012*, Washington, D.C.: World Bank.

3 Scarcity, frontiers and the resource curse

A historical perspective[1]

Edward B. Barbier

Introduction

Today, we are becoming all too familiar with the term *resource curse*. It implies that countries that are overly dependent on natural resources for exploitation and export are destined to have slow growth and economic development. As summarized by Jurajada and Mitchell (2003, p. 130),

> the main upshot of this literature is two-fold: first, natural resources, if not well-managed in well-built markets, will impede growth through rent-seeking; and second, an abundance of natural resources leads to serious policy failures: for example, if the windfall from a natural-resource boom is poorly invested, it can have long-run detrimental effects.[2]

Support for this resource curse hypothesis is based on recent empirical evidence that countries with a high percentage of resource-based commodities to total exports or to gross domestic product (GDP) tend to have lower levels of real GDP per capita, lower growth rates, higher poverty levels and a higher proportion of their populations living in poverty.[3]

Yet, not long ago access to abundant natural resources, especially those valued on the world market, was considered to be a guarantee of economic success rather than an obstacle. For example, the period from 1870 to 1914 is often referred to as the "Golden Age" of Resource-Based Development.[4] The transport revolution and trade booms of the era were primarily responsible for unprecedented land conversion and natural resource exploitation across many resource-rich regions of the world. The result was a long period of global economic growth, in which many countries and regions benefited from this pattern of resource use and development. The United States was the prime example of such success; in only a few decades the US had exploited its vast natural wealth to transform its economy into an industrial powerhouse. But other resource-rich countries also boomed during this era, including Canada, Argentina and Australia as well as some tropical regions that benefited from export-led colonial agricultural development.

However, with the advent of World War I, followed by the Depression years and World War II, the Golden Age came to an end. Although the United States continued to rely on its abundant natural resources to spur industrial expansion, by the 1950s the US economy had also become dependent on foreign sources of raw materials, fossil fuels, minerals and ores to support this expansion. In the post-war world, possessing an abundant endowment of natural resources no longer guaranteed successful economic development. Over the past 50 years, increased trade and globalization has resulted in declining trade barriers and transport costs, fostered global integration of commodity markets, and severed the direct link between natural resource wealth and the development of domestic industrial capacity. As a result, if a developing country simply possesses valuable natural resources, exploiting such an endowment does not assure a straightforward path to economic development.

But why should many economies with abundant endowments of land, mineral and fossil fuel resources have such difficulty in sustaining development whereas in past historical eras access to resource abundance was not a "curse" on development efforts? The answer lies in understanding the changing role of natural resources in the process of economic development in past eras compared to the present. In particular, a key factor appears to be how new supplies, or *frontiers*, of natural resources are found, exploited and incorporated in various economies.

How economies have developed through natural resource exploitation, especially by exploiting new frontiers of land and natural resources, has received little attention in contemporary economics, compared to other disciplines. As noted by Findlay and Lundahl (1994, p. 70), the analysis of frontier-based development "has been used extensively by historians and geographers for a wide variety of times and places, but has been neglected by economists". Similarly, as argued by David and Wright (1997, p. 204):

> Resource development is a neglected topic in economic history. To be sure, no economist would be surprised to learn that resource abundance is a function of extraction and transportation cost as well as of physical availability, and the role of substitution in mitigating resource scarcity is widely appreciated.... But natural resources still are viewed as the last of the exogenous factors, governed by the principle of diminishing returns in an economic growth process whose other constituents have come to be treated both as endogenous and subject to increasing returns.

However, over 100 years ago, the recognition of the role of the frontier in economic development was widely appreciated, thanks to the *frontier thesis* put forward by the historian Frederick Jackson Turner. In his infamous 1893 address to the American Historical Association, *The Significance of the Frontier in American History*, Turner (1986, p. 1) argued that "the existence of an area of free land, its continuous recession, and the advance of American settlement westward, explain American development". Critical to this frontier expansion was the availability of "cheap" land and resources:

> Obviously, the immigrant was attracted by the cheap lands of the frontier, and even the native farmer felt their influence strongly. Year by year the

> farmers who lived on soil whose returns were diminished by unrotated crops were offered the virgin soils of the frontier at nominal prices. Their growing families demanded more lands, and these were dear. The competition of the unexhausted, cheap, and easily tilled prairie lands compelled the farmer either to go west and continue the exhaustion of the soil on a new frontier, or to adopt intensive culture.
>
> (Turner 1986, pp. 21–22)

Turner's frontier thesis was further extended by the historian Walter Prescott Webb to explain not just American but global economic development from 1500 to 1900. Webb (1964, p. 13) suggested that exploitation of the world's "Great Frontier", present-day North and temperate South America, Australia, New Zealand and South Africa, was instrumental to the "economic boom" experienced in the "Metropolis", or modern Europe:

> This boom began when Columbus returned from his first voyage, rose slowly, and continued at an ever-accelerating pace until the frontier which fed it was no more. Assuming that the frontier closed in 1890 or 1900, it may be said that the boom lasted about four hundred years.

Historians, geographers and social scientists have continued to modify the ideas developed by Turner and Webb to describe processes of frontier-based development in many areas of the world and for different eras (e.g., see (Agergaard et al. 2009; Barbier 2005a, 2005b; Barney 2009; Cleary 1993; Hennessy 1978; Richards 2003; Rodrigues et al. 2009; Savage and Thompson 1979; Wieczynski 1976; Wolfskill and Palmer 1983). Although there is considerable debate over whether the frontier thesis as envisioned by Turner and Webb is still relevant for all regions, a consensus has emerged in this literature over both the definition of a frontier and its significance for economic development. A frontier area is typically defined as "a geographic region adjacent to the unsettled portions of the continent in which a low man-land ratio and unusually abundant, unexploited, natural resources provide an exceptional opportunity for social and economic betterment to the small-propertied individual" (Billington 1966, p. 25). Or, as summarized by di Tella (1982, p. 212), throughout history "processes" of frontier-based development "were characterized by the initial existence of abundant land, mostly unoccupied, and by a substantial migration of capital and people".

The view of frontiers and development as expressed by di Tella is the focus of this chapter. Throughout much of history, a critical driving force behind global economic development has been the response of society to the scarcity of key natural resources. Increasing scarcity raises the cost of exploiting existing natural resources, and will induce incentives in all economies to innovate and conserve more of these resources. However, human society has also responded to natural resource scarcity not just through conserving scarce resources but also by obtaining and developing more of them. Throughout history, exploiting new sources, or "frontiers", of natural resources has often proved to be a pivotal human response to natural resource scarcity. That is, economics and economic history should learn from economic geography, and no longer ignore the relationship between natural resource scarcity, frontiers and development.

The concept of a natural resource frontier and its relationship to economic development must be carefully defined. The term *frontier*, as employed here, refers to an area or source of unusually abundant natural resources and land *relative* to labor and capital. Note that it is the relative scarcity, or abundance, of natural resources that matters to economic development, not their absolute physical availability. The process of *frontier expansion*, or *frontier-based development*, thus means exploiting or converting new sources of relative abundant resources for production purposes. As suggested years ago by Schumpeter (1961, p. 66), this process often contributes fundamentally to economic development, which he defined as "the carrying out of new combinations of the means of production", one of which is "the conquest of a new source of supply of raw materials ... irrespective of whether this source already exists or whether it has first to be created". As this chapter explores, such *resource-based development* has proved to be highly successful in the past for some economies and regions, but less successful for others.

In sum, the process of economic development has not just been about allocating scarce resources but also about obtaining and developing new frontiers of natural resources. This is particularly the case if the concept of a "frontier" extends "vertically downwards" to include mineral resources and extractive activities as well as "horizontally extensive as in the case of land and agriculture" (Findlay and Lundahl 1999, p. 26). When viewed in this way, frontier expansion has clearly been pivotal to economic development for most of global history.

To argue this case, this chapter first examines long-run patterns of frontier expansion that occurred over 1500 to 1914 in major regions of the world outside of Europe. These patterns have in turn informed many existing theories of successful frontier-based economic development, which are discussed and reviewed. Historical examples since the late nineteenth century is cited to illustrate these effects, drawing on evidence from a recent study of how natural resource exploitation has influenced economic development throughout different eras (Barbier 2011). Based on this review, a consensus on the necessary and sufficient conditions for successful frontier-based development is suggested, and the chapter concludes by discussing the lessons learned for resource-rich developing economies during the Contemporary Era.

The Great Frontier expansion

Most theories of successful frontier-based development draw on the historical legacy of the Great Frontier expansion from 1500 to 1914, as described by Webb (1964), for their inspiration. Over this 400-year period Western European economies benefited significantly from the exploitation of frontiers on a global scale. Many European countries gained a vast array of natural wealth, not only through new lands that provided an outlet for poor populations emigrating from Europe in search of better economic opportunities but also through new sources of fishing, plantation, mining and other resource frontiers. For example, as suggested by Jones (1987, pp. 80–82), during this era Europe had at its disposal four main global "frontiers" that provided "vast, varied, and cheap" supplies of "extra-European resources": ocean fisheries, including whale and seal fisheries; boreal forests around the Baltic, Scandinavia and Russia; tropical land for plantation and smallholder commercial crops, such as sugar, tobacco, cotton, rice and indigo; and temperate arable land for grains.

The general perception, too, has been that the exploitation of the Great Frontier from 1500 to 1900 eventually benefited the regions that contained the abundant endowments of natural resources and land. Such a beneficial frontier-based development process, as outlined in Figure 3.1, can be termed the *classic pattern of frontier expansion*.

As shown in Figure 3.1, the first phase involves initial exploration and discovery of the vast areas of land and natural resources, and small-scale extracting of natural resources, minerals and other raw materials. The second phase sees the development of large-scale extraction activities, usually for commercial export, and transportation networks. By the third phase, agricultural conversion of land and the establishment of permanent settlements are in full fruition. The final phase involves the development of industrial activities, large urban centers and modern commercial networks. Somewhere between the third and fourth phases, the abundance of land and natural resources relative to labor and capital has disappeared, and the former frontier region has effectively "closed".

Various phases of European exploitation of the abundant land and natural resource wealth of the New World from 1500 to 1914 appear to fit this classic

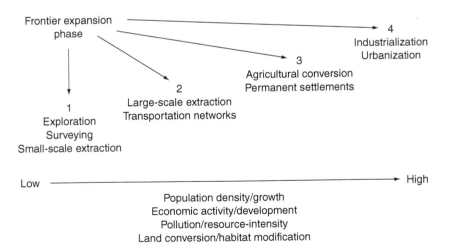

Figure 3.1 The classic pattern of frontier expansion.

pattern of frontier expansion (Barbier 2011). Meinig (1986, chap. 10) also distinguishes the development of "Atlantic America" into distinct phases, or "geographical interactions", that shaped simultaneously the geography and history of both Europe and the Americas. The first phase, from 1500 to 1640, included much of the initial exploration and conquest of the New World, as well as the establishment for the first important resource-extractive enclaves, the Spanish silver mines and "sugar economy" of Portuguese Brazil. The ending date of 1640 for this first phase of frontier expansion corresponds to the end of the first "global silver cycle", which according to Flynn and Giraldez (2002), occurred when profits to the Spanish from the silver trade just covered the costs of their New World mines. The second phase (1580 to 1860) corresponded to the spread of the slave-based plantation economy from Brazil to other tropical and subtropical regions of South America, the Caribbean and southern North America. This economy was an agricultural-based export enclave on an extensive scale, and became an important leg of the Atlantic "triangular trade" between Europe, Africa and the New World, by which slaves were sent from Africa to the Americas, raw materials from the New World to Europe, and manufactured products from Europe to the other two regions. Although colonization continued throughout the second phase, the mass immigration and frontier settlement boom occurred in the third phase, from 1830 to 1900. Immigration, settlement and expansion of the agricultural frontier took place mainly in the favorable temperate climatic and environmental zones of North and South America. Finally, the older "settlement" zones, especially in the northeastern US and Canada with favorable transportation and trade links, experienced the final frontier transformation of urbanization and industrialization, from 1870 to 1914. The Western frontier expansion and urban development phases interlinked in the late nineteenth century to foster successful resource-based development of the temperate regions of North America.

However, the classic pattern of frontier expansion is really only applicable to North America (Barbier 2011). Frontier-based development in Latin America did not fully complete the four phases outlined in Figure 3.1. For example, the "triangular trade" of the Atlantic economy contributed to economic development in the United States and Western Europe, whereas in contrast the economic benefits to Spain and Latin America of the silver "booms" were short-lived. In comparison to North America, the industrial "takeoff" of temperate South America failed to materialize, because during the Golden Age of Resource-Based Development (1870–1914), agricultural-based land expansion, settlement and exports did not mutually reinforce domestic manufacturing and urbanization in the region. Thus, a more realistic depiction of frontier expansion for North and South America is depicted in Figure 3.2. Whereas North America completed all four phases of successful frontier-based development, South America never really transformed beyond the first three phases. Thus, the region remained by and large an agricultural-based export enclave on an extensive scale from 1830 to 1914.

Frontier expansion in Asia and the Pacific also deviated from the classical pattern (see Figure 3.3). The first phase, from 1500 to 1750, was the era of the

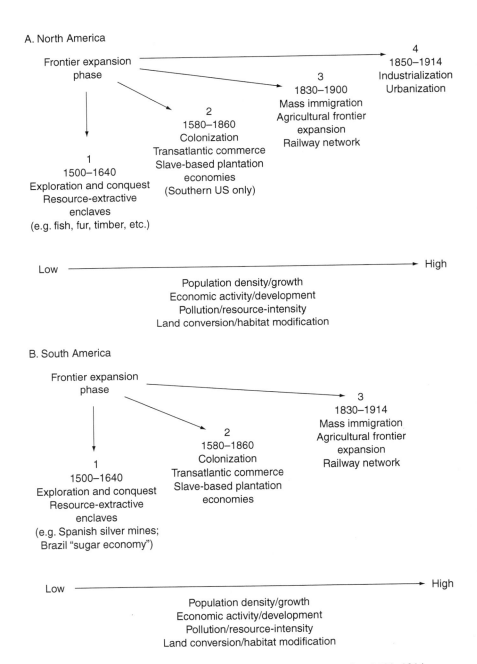

Figure 3.2 Phases of frontier expansion in North and South America, 1500–1914.

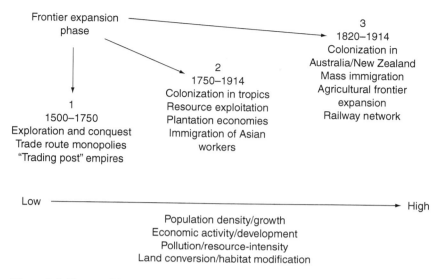

Figure 3.3 Phases of frontier expansion in Asia and the Pacific, 1500–1914.

trading post empires, when various European powers – notably Portugal, England and the Netherlands – used their naval and commercial shipping superiority to establish exclusive control over the spice and other Asian commodity trade routes. As the Europeans focused on accumulating wealth through monopolizing and extracting revenues from dominating these resource-products trade routes, very little direct frontier expansion by the European colonists occurred.[5] From 1750 to 1914, the European powers became territorial empires through colonizing much of Asia and the Pacific. During this second phase, considerable frontier land expansion and extension of agricultural cultivation took place. In the tropical regions, frontier-based development took the form of plantation economies specialized in a few key export crops. However, from 1820 to 1914, and only in temperate Australia and New Zealand, frontier land expansion was instigated through the third phase of farmer settlements, mainly by immigration from Britain and other European countries. But in Asia, the important "fourth phase" of industrialization did not occur as a result of this expansion. For example, Japan's rapid industrialization over the 1880 to 1914 period is attributed largely to its own efforts to emulate the West rather than as a direct result of European frontier and colonial expansion in Asia.[6]

Finally, the European pattern of exploiting the natural resource wealth of Africa from 1500 to 1914 shared many similarities to the pattern in Asia and the Pacific (see Figure 3.4). However, the first phase of creating a trading post empire lasted much longer in Africa, from 1500 until 1880. The trading post empire remained the dominant form of European involvement in Africa until the late nineteenth century for several reasons. First, as in other tropical regions of the Global Frontier, disease and inhospitable climate restricted any substantial

European settlement in much of Africa, and even the trading post enclaves in West Africa were sparsely populated by only a handful of Europeans.[7] Second, much of the interior of sub-Saharan African remained impenetrable; it had few navigable rivers, and remained largely unmapped until successful European expeditions in the mid-nineteenth century. Third, the Europeans did not need large settlements or territorial empires in Africa to exploit the slave, gold, ivory and other natural resource wealth of Africa because they could rely on procurement and trading routes established by powerful African states and empires.[8] In contrast, the establishment of settler colonies in southern Africa and the resulting agricultural frontier expansion occurred much earlier in Africa than in Asia, as the temperate climate and fertile soils in the southern cone of Africa encouraged permanent settlement by European immigrants. Thus, the British and Boer settlements of southern Africa, plus the more limited European settlement of Rhodesia at the turn of the twentieth century, represented the only true "agricultural frontier" phase of European expansion in Africa before 1914.[9] The true colonization of Africa through major territorial acquisition occurred fairly late, and this critical third phase meant that by 1914 most of Africa's commercial economies were based on resource commodity exports, such as plantation crops and minerals.

To summarize, by 1914 distinct regional patterns of frontier expansion had begun to emerge around the world. What is clear is that many parts of North and South America, Asia and the Pacific and Africa were unable to complete the full process of successful resource-based development, as exemplified by the classic pattern of frontier expansion (see Figure 3.1). Instead as noted by Schedvin

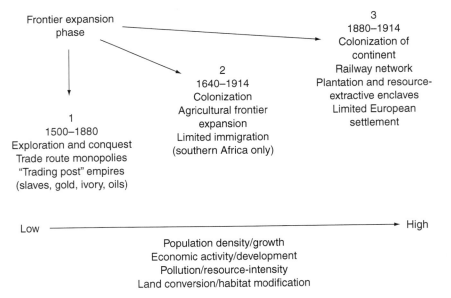

Figure 3.4 Phases of frontier expansion in Africa, 1500–1914.

(1990, p. 535), for most global frontiers, "the task of successful diversification from an original export base seems to have encountered more obstacles" than expected, especially when compared to the United States and other successful Great Frontier economies in temperate regions.

Theories of successful frontier-based development

The successful examples of frontier-based development from the nineteenth and early twentieth century have inspired some theories of how successful exploitation of natural resources can foster economy-wide development. These include the *staples thesis* and the *vent-for-surplus theory*. The staples thesis was originally put forward to explain Canadian economic development, and is usually credited to Innis (1940, 1956) and Mackintosh (1967). The modern vent-for-surplus theory is generally credited to Myint (1958).

The staples thesis maintains that the development of some countries and regions with abundant land and natural resources has been led by the expansion of key commodity exports, or "staples". The vent-for-surplus theory suggests that trade was the means by which idle resources, and in particular natural resources in underdeveloped countries and regions, were brought into productive use through the expansion of export opportunities. Both theories are relevant to the economic analysis of frontier-based development, because they focus on the existence of excess supplies of land and other natural resources that are not being fully exploited by a closed economy. International trade allows these surplus sources of land and natural resources that previously had no economic value to be exploited, for increased exports and growth.

Both the staples thesis and the vent-for-surplus theory were concerned mainly with the existence of surplus natural resources as the basis for the origin of trade and export-led growth during the Golden Age of Resource-Based Development (1870–1914). For example, the staples theory attempted to explain the substantial inflows of capital and labor into the "regions of recent settlement", i.e., Webb's "Great Frontier of Canada, the United States, Argentina and Australia, that occurred largely in the nineteenth and early twentieth centuries" (Findlay and Lundahl 1994, p. 70). According to Myint (1958), the classical vent-for-surplus theory of trade is a much more plausible explanation of the start of trade in an otherwise "isolated" country or region with a "sparse population in relation to its natural resources" such as "the underdeveloped countries of Southeast Asia, Latin America and Africa when they were opened up to international trade in the nineteenth century" (p. 316).

More recent theories characterize an "endogenous" or "moving" frontier as the basis for attracting inflows of labor and capital into a region or economy (Findlay 1995; Findlay and Lundahl 1994; Hansen 1979; di Tella 1982). Such economic development models assume that additional land or natural resources can be brought into production through investment of labor and/or capital, provided that the resulting rents earned are competitive with the returns from alternative assets. Thus frontier expansion becomes an endogenous process within the economic system, with the supply and price of land and other natural resources determined along with the supplies and prices of all other goods and factor inputs (e.g., capital and labor). As a consequence, changes in relative commodity and input prices, as well as exogenous factors such as technological change and transport innovations, can influence expansion of the land and natural resource frontiers. As with most economic theories of frontier-based development, these endogenous frontier models have been used mainly to explain the inflows of capital and labor into the "regions of recent settlement", i.e., Webb's "Great Frontier of Canada, the United States, Argentina and Australia, that occurred largely in the nineteenth and early twentieth centuries, and export-led colonial agricultural development in certain tropical countries during the Golden Age of Resource-Based Development" (Findlay and Lundahl 1994, p. 70). A variant of the endogenous frontier model has also been employed to explain the pattern of frontier-based economic development in low- and middle-income economies during the Contemporary Era from 1950 to the present (Barbier 2005a, 2005b).

However, if the process of frontier expansion has been pivotal to economic development for most of global history, then explanations of successful frontier-based development must look beyond models applicable just to the Golden Age or to the classic pattern of frontier expansion in North America.

One such theory that links frontier expansion with economic development in other historical eras and places is the *free land hypothesis* proposed by Domar (1970), which he viewed as "a hypothesis regarding the causes of agricultural serfdom or slavery". According to Domar (1970, pp. 19–20), abundant land and natural resources may attract labor, but "until land becomes rather scarce, and/or the amount of capital required to start a farm relatively large, it is unlikely that a large class of landowners" will be willing to invest in the frontier. Instead,

> most of the farms will still be more or less family-size, with an estate using hired labor (or tenants) here and there in areas of unusually good (in fertility and/or in location) land, or specializing in activities requiring higher-than-average capital intensity, or skillful management.

The economic reason for this outcome is straightforward: The abundance of land in the frontier assures that

> no diminishing returns in the application of labor to land appear; both the average and the marginal productivities of labor are constant and equal, and if competition among employers raises wages to that level (as would be expected), no rent from land can arise.

Thus, in the absence of opportunities to earn rent from frontier economic activities, owners of capital and large landowners have little incentive to invest in these activities.

In order to resolve this problem, and to foster large-scale investment and development of frontier lands, a deliberate intervention by the state is required.

Under certain conditions, the "ideal" intervention is to encourage methods of economic production suitable to exploiting abundant frontier resources without "free labor". That is why, as Domar maintains, in many frontier regions, such as the American South from the seventeenth to nineteenth century and the Russian Ukraine in the eighteenth century, institutions such as slavery and serfdom were often implemented in conjunction with frontier-based development. The scarcity of labor relative to land meant that the ruling elite could not afford to hire labor at the going market wage. In contrast, where land was not abundant, and subject to diminishing returns from employing more and more labor on the land, there was no need to employ slavery, serfdom or other methods of coercing labor to work. The scarcity of land relative to labor ensured that workers were paid a minimum, subsistence wage regardless of whether they were free or not.

There are periods and places in history that seem to fit Domar's hypothesis well (Barbier 2011). Some of the more successful examples of frontier-based development were accompanied by institutions such as serfdom and slavery that repressed "free labor" to ensure sizable surpluses. For instance, the Roman Empire (c.300 BC to AD 476) utilized slave labor in large-scale plantations and extractive industries to exploit fertile, unoccupied land as well as abundant mineral resources, timber forests and other natural resources that utilized slave labor. The feudal system was developed in tandem with the expansion of agricultural land in Great Britain and Western Europe in the centuries before the Black Death, from 800 to 1300. Russia instituted serfdom in the sixteenth century during its rapid "frontier expansion" across the Eurasian steppes. Finally, the rise of the Atlantic economy, from 1500 to 1860, and exploitation of New World land frontiers in the tropical and sub-tropical regions of South America, the Caribbean and southern North America was not possible without the adoption and spread of slavery-based plantation agriculture.

But Domar's free land hypothesis also contains a more general observation relevant to many other patterns of successful frontier-based development throughout history. The existence of an "abundant" frontier of land and natural resources does not in itself guarantee that it will be exploited for a windfall gain or profit. Instead, as pointed out by di Tella (1982, p. 212), realizing the potential economic gains from frontier expansion requires "a substantial migration of capital and people" to exploit the abundant land and resources, which can only occur if this exploitation results in a substantial "surplus", or "abnormal" economic rent. This observation is the basis of di Tella's *disequilibrium abnormal rents hypothesis*; i.e., since frontier expansion takes time, there must be "disequilibrium" periods in which abnormal rents (profits well in excess of costs) can be exploited to simulate further frontier investments.

Drawing on Latin American experience since the late nineteenth century, (di Tella 1982, pp. 216–217) agrees with Domar that one way such "abnormal rents" from frontier exploitation can be generated is "if the previous population can be enslaved, or through some other legal artifice made to work for a wage below its marginal productivity". But there are other ways of ensuring large profits or surpluses from frontier expansion, including "outright discovery of a new land, agricultural or mineral", "military pacification of the new lands", "technological innovation of the cost-reducing kind", and finally, "price booms" for land and minerals. Any of these factors can ensure that "the greater the rent at the frontier the more intense will be the efforts to expand it, and the quicker will be the pace of expansion". Moreover, such a process of frontier expansion through exploiting "abnormal rent" is applicable not just to agricultural land but also to minerals, oil and any abundant natural resource "frontier".

However, in order to earn substantial profits or surpluses, economic activities, institutions and technologies must also adapt to the varying environmental and resource conditions found in different frontier regions. The type of economies, institutions and technologies adopted in frontier regions can, in turn, determine whether the resulting frontier-based development is ultimately successfully in generating wider economic and social benefits. For example, the influence of differing environmental and resource conditions on the pattern of frontier-based development is relevant to an important puzzle in economic history: Why was slavery not adopted universally throughout the New World, such as in much of the temperate region of North America? These regions also had abundant land and other natural resources and scarce labor, so it seems perplexing that slavery was not used more widely as an economic solution to harnessing these frontier resources to create larger landholdings and commercial profits. In mid-eighteenth century Great Britain was the sole colonial power in North America, and given its dominance of the trans-Atlantic slave trade and the development of the slave-based "sugar" economy in the West Indies, Britain certainly had the means to introduce plantation economies and slavery in the North. Why then did Britain not intervene to do so?

One explanation of this paradox is the *factor endowment hypothesis* (Engerman and Sokoloff 1997; Sokoloff and Engerman 2000). The range of economic activities introduced and adopted successfully in frontier regions is determined not only by the *quantity*, or relative abundance, of land and resources but also by their *quality*, including the type of land and resources found and the general environmental conditions, geography and climate in frontier regions. These broader environmental conditions can also determine whether frontier expansion activities that generate substantial rents or surpluses lead to lasting, economy-wide benefits.

For example, the same environmental conditions that made tropical Latin American colonies – from Brazil to the West Indies – ideal for slave-based plantation systems and other resource-extractive activities also account for their poor long-term economic performance relative to the United States and Canada. Engerman and Sokoloff (1997, p. 275) consider that the relevant "factor endowments" influencing long-term development were not only the relative abundance of land and natural resources to labor in the New World but also "soils, climate, and the size or density of native populations". The extremely different factor endowments found from North to South America – i.e. the very different environments in which Europeans established their colonies in the New World – "may have predisposed those colonies towards paths of development associated with different degrees of inequality in wealth, human capital, and political power, as well as with different potentials for economic growth". That is, the key causal relationship is between differences in factor endowments (i.e., resource and environmental conditions), social and economic inequality and thus the development of key institutions that generate long-term economic development and growth.

Engerman and Sokoloff (1997, pp. 268 and 271–272) argue that, as a result, in the United States and Canada

> both the more-equal distributions of human capital and other resources, as well as the relative abundance of the politically and economically powerful racial group, would be expected to have encouraged the evolution of legal and political institutions that were more conducive to active participation in a competitive market economy by broad segments of the population.

This is "significant" because

> the patterns of early industrialization in the United States suggest that such widespread involvement in commercial activity was quite important in realizing the onset of economic growth. In contrast, the factor endowments of the other New World colonies led to highly unequal distributions of wealth, income, human capital, and political power early in their histories, along with institutions that protected the elites. Together, these conditions inhibited the spread of commercial activity among the general population, lessening, in our view, the prospects for growth.

Thus, the factor endowment hypothesis explains why some of the New World colonies, e.g., the United States and Canada, developed faster than others, e.g., Latin American and the Caribbean countries. But a major limitation of the hypothesis is that it still treats land, natural resources and general environmental conditions "as the last of the exogenous factors" in the economic development process. In contrast, successful resource-based development not only adapts and applies technologies and knowledge to exploit specific resource endowments but also creates backward and forward linkages between frontier economic activities and the rest of the economy (Barbier 2005b; David and Wright 1997; Gylfason 2001; Wright 1990; Wright and Czelusta 2004). The "fixed" land and resource endowments available to an economy must be transformed into endogenous components of the development process, thus generating constant or even increasing returns (David and Wright 1997).

Historical examples since the Golden Age

Various examples of successful resource-based development, from the Golden Age of Resource-Based Development to the present, highlight the three key factors in this process.

First, country-specific knowledge and technical applications in the resource extraction sector can effectively expand what appears to be a "fixed" resource endowment of a country. For example, Wright and Czelusta (2004) document this process for several successful mineral-based economies over the past 30 to 40 years:

> From the standpoint of development policy, a crucial aspect of the process is the role of country-specific knowledge. Although the deep scientific bases for progress are undoubtedly global, it is in the nature of geology that location-specific knowledge continues to be important ... the experience of the 1970s stands in marked contrast to the 1990s, when mineral production steadily expanded primarily as a result of purposeful exploration and ongoing advances in the technologies of search, extraction, refining, and utilization; in other words by a process of learning.

Second, there must be strong linkages between the resource sector and frontier-based activities and the rest of the economy. The origins of rapid industrial and economic expansion in the United States over 1879–1940 were strongly linked to the exploitation of abundant non-reproducible natural resources, particularly energy and mineral resources.

> Not only was the USA the world's leading mineral economy in the very historical period during which the country became the world leader in manufacturing (roughly from 1890 to 1910); but linkages and complementarities to the resource sector were vital in the broader story of American economic success.... Nearly all major US manufactured goods were closely linked to the resource economy in one way or another: petroleum products, primary copper, meat packing and poultry, steel works and rolling mills, coal mining, vegetable oils, grain mill products, sawmill products, and so on.
> (Wright and Czelusta 2007, pp. 184, 186)

Similarly, Findlay and Lundahl (1999, pp. 31–32) note the importance of such linkages in promoting successful "staples-based" development during the 1870–1914 era:

> not all resource-rich countries succeeded in spreading the growth impulses from their primary sectors ... in a number of instances the staples sector turned out to be an enclave with little contact with the rest of the economy.... The staples theory of growth stresses the development of linkages between the export sector and an incipient manufacturing sector.

Third, there must be substantial knowledge spillovers arising from the extraction and use of resources and land in the economy. For example, David and Wright (1997, pp. 240–241) suggest that the rise of the American minerals-based economy from 1879 to 1940 can also be attributed to the infrastructure of public scientific knowledge, mining education and the "ethos of exploration". This in turn created knowledge spillovers across firms and

> the components of successful modern-regimes of knowledge-based economic growth. In essential respects, the minerals economy was an integral part of the emerging knowledge-based economy of the twentieth century ... increasing returns were manifest at the national level, with important consequences for American industrialization and world economic leadership.

Wright and Czelusta (2004, p. 21) maintain that the development of the US petrochemical industry illustrates the economic importance of knowledge spillovers:

> Progress in petrochemicals is an example of new technology built on resource-based heritage. It may also be considered a return to scale at the industry level, because the search for by-products was an outgrowth of the vast American enterprise of petroleum refining.

There are many historical examples from eras other than the nineteenth and twentieth century that also fit the above necessary and sufficient conditions for successful frontier-based development.[10]

One such case was the Sung Dynasty in China from 960 to 1279 (Barbier 2011). Military conquest ensured that Sung China had amassed a huge "internal frontier" of agricultural land and other abundant natural resources, such as iron ore, coal, timber, fuelwood, salt, fish and metals. But Sung rulers did not just exploit these frontiers for windfall gains; they also invested the tax revenues earned from frontier expansion into developing canals, waterways and an effective inland transport system, as well as innovations in flood control and irrigated paddy rice production. These developments in turn fostered substantial floodplain and lowland arable land expansion throughout southern China, which sustained large increases in agricultural productivity as well as population growth. Tax revenues earned from the increased agricultural production funded further public works investments. Cheap and safe waterway transport facilitated long-distance marketing of agricultural products and induced further agricultural expansion into new frontier areas. New rice and sugar varieties were imported and cultivated in tropical southern China, suitable for both irrigated paddy and rainfed cultivation. These varieties allowed dryland rice farming to spread into hilly terrain, doubling cultivated area. By developing its abundant coal resources and blast furnace technology, a large iron industry grew in northern China, allowing the manufacture of weapons, farm implements and tools. Other technological innovations spurred new industries, such as the water-powered spinning wheel for textiles, mining technologies for salt production, new kilns, ceramic and glazing techniques for porcelain and advances in sericulture, spinning and weaving in the silk industry. By the end of the eleventh century, the iron industry in northern China was producing 125,000 tons annually. This iron output amounted to 3.5 to 4.3 pounds per person, a level of production that exceeded that of Western Europe until the Industrial Revolution seven centuries later.

So robust was Sung China's frontier-based development that economic progress survived the Mongol conquest and continued during the subsequent Yuan Dynasty (1260 to 1368). But, towards the end of the latter dynasty, the conditions for successful frontier-based development had ended, and by the onset of the Black Death (1330 to 1370) and its aftermath, China embarked on a long period of economic decline.

The Contemporary Era

However, in the Contemporary Era from 1950 to present, many economies with abundant endowments of land, mineral and fossil fuel resources have had difficulty in achieving successful resource-based development (Barbier 2005b, 2011). There are signs that four large emerging market economies, Brazil, China, India and Russia – the so-called BRIC economies – are beginning to reap economy-wide benefits from exploiting their vast sources of land and natural resources. But these economies are unusual compared to most developing countries because of the sheer scale of their populations, economies and resource endowments. Although since the 1990s the economic growth performance of the BRIC countries has been impressive, it is unclear whether this growth is the result of successful and sustainable management of their large natural resource endowments, or simply due to their having such large endowments to command for economic development.

Unfortunately, not many smaller resource-abundant economies have performed as well. For example, Gylfason (2001) has examined the long-run growth performance of 85 resource-rich developing economies since 1965. Only Botswana, Malaysia and Thailand managed to achieve a long-term investment rate exceeding 25 percent of GDP and long-run average annual growth rates exceeding 4 percent, which is a performance comparable to that of high-income economies. Malaysia and Thailand have also managed successfully to diversify their economies through re-investing the financial gains from primary production for export. Botswana has yet to diversify its economy significantly but has developed favorable institutions and policies for managing its natural wealth and primary production for extensive economy-wide benefits. Although many other developing countries still depend on finding new reserves or frontiers of land and other natural resources to exploit, very few appear to have benefited from such frontier-based development. It appears that the Contemporary Era is a historical anomaly that poses an intriguing paradox: Why should economic dependence on natural resource exploitation and frontier land expansion be associated with "unsustainable" resource-based development in many low- and middle-income countries today, especially as historically this has not always been the case?

One possible explanation of this paradox is the *frontier expansion hypothesis*, which is in effect a corollary to the above three factors for successful resource-based development outlined above (Barbier 2005a, 2005b, 2011). For frontier-based expansion to be ultimately successful, it must lead to efficient and sustainable management of natural resource exploitation capable of yielding substantial economic rents. Moreover, the earnings from such resource-based development must in turn be reinvested in productive economic investments, linkages and innovations that encourage industrialization and economic diversification. Thus the key hypothesis as to why the pattern of resource-based development and frontier expansion in many developing economies has failed to yield sufficient economy-wide benefits during the Contemporary Era is that one or both of these conditions have not been met. That is, in most of today's low- and middle-income economies, frontier expansion has been symptomatic of a pattern of economy-wide resource exploitation that: (a) generates little additional economic rents, and (b) what rents are generated have not been reinvested in more productive and dynamic sectors, such as resource-based industries and manufacturing, or in education, social overhead projects and other long-term investments.

Conclusion

Ever since Fredrick Jackson Turner formulated his frontier thesis in the late nineteenth century, most theories of frontier-based development derive their inspiration from a specific historical era or epoch. Nevertheless, there does appear to be a common set of themes across all these theories, from which it is possible to identify some necessary and sufficient conditions.

First, successful frontier-based development requires generating surpluses, or profits, from frontier expansion and resource exploitation activities. As noted above, this is di Tella's *disequilibrium abnormal rents hypothesis*. Since frontier expansion takes time, there must be "disequilibrium" periods in which abnormal rents can be exploited to stimulate further frontier investments, and as a result, "the greater is the rent at the frontier the more intense will be the efforts to expand it, and the quicker will be the pace of expansion" (di Tella 1982, p. 217).

Based on the various theories of frontier-based development, throughout history the necessary conditions for ensuring "abnormal rents" from investment in frontier land and natural resources depend on one or more of the following factors:

- Institutional developments, in the form of serfdom, slavery, draft labor and other means of "repressing" the returns to "free labor" (Domar 1970).
- Economic developments, such as "discoveries of land, agricultural or mineral, discoveries of technology, and restrictions on free competition", or additional windfall gains arising from "military pacification" of new lands and resources and "price booms" for land and primary commodities (di Tella 1982).[11]
- Adapting and developing specialized economic activities, institutions and technologies to accommodate heterogeneous frontier conditions and endowments (Engerman and Sokoloff 1997).

However, generating surpluses, or profits, from frontier expansion and resource exploitation may be a necessary condition for successful long-run economic development but it is not sufficient. The key to such success is that the overall economy does not become overly dependent on frontier expansion. Critical to avoiding such an outcome is ensuring that the frontier economy does not become an isolated enclave, first, by ensuring that sufficient profits generated by the resource- and land-based activities of the frontier are invested in other productive assets in the economy, second, by ensuring that such investments lead to the development of a more diversified economy, and finally, by facilitating the development of complementarities and linkages between the frontier and other sectors of the economy.

The dangers to long-term development of a frontier economy becoming an isolated enclave is also noted by (di Tella 1982, p. 221):

> One of the obvious factors which influence the impact of the frontier on the overall growth process is the relative economic importance of the expansion compared with the previous size of the economy. The smaller the economic significance of the frontier expansion and the larger the previous size of the economy, the greater will be the likelihood that growth will not suffer at the end of territorial expansion.

To illustrate this point, di Tella (1982, pp. 221–222) contrasts the development experience of the United States and Argentina during the Golden Age of Resource-Based Development, from 1870 to 1913. In the United States during this era, "the frontier expansion was huge in absolute terms, but its economic significance compared with the rest of the economy was not so great". In fact, "after the close of the frontier ... industry – the non-resource based activity" of the economy "will have attained considerable dimensions being able to become its leading sector." In contrast, for Argentina,

> at the end of expansion, the country's non-resource based sector was of only minor importance, so that, even despite that it grew at a significant rate, it was not in a position to replace the central role which the expansion of the frontier had had in the past.

As this chapter has shown, there are many historical examples that also fit the above necessary and sufficient conditions for successful frontier-based development. In contrast, in the Contemporary Era, most resource-rich developing economies are failing to implement these conditions for success. In fact, the tendency for lucrative frontier-based economic activities to become isolated enclaves is a major factor retarding the development of many resource-rich developing economies (Barbier 2005a, 2005b, 2011). A key issue is whether current economic development efforts for low- and middle-income economies, many of which rely on exploiting their abundant land and natural resources, can learn the lessons of past historical examples of successful frontier-based development.

Notes

1 I am grateful for comments provided by Henry Willebald.
2 Auty (1993) is often credited with naming this phenomenon a "resource curse". However, Auty (1994) gives credit to Mahon (1992) for also suggesting a "variant" of the resource curse theme as an explanation of why resource-rich Latin American countries have often failed to adopt sensible industrial policies.
3 For overviews of these findings and relevant empirical studies, see Barbier (2005a); Jurajada and Mitchell (2003) and van der Ploeg (2011).
4 See, for example, Barbier (2011); Crafts and Venables (2003); Findlay and Lundahl (1999); Findlay and O'Rourke (2007); Green and Urquhart (2010); O'Brien (1997, 2006); O'Rourke and Williamson (1999); Williamson (2009).
5 European monopolization and development of the Asian trade routes most likely encouraged frontier expansion indirectly, however. As Richards (2003, pp. 37–38) states, "Bengal's dynamic early modern economy rested solidly on frontier-driven growth.... Cheap abundant foodstuffs also encouraged rising industrial output in the province. Bengal's cotton and silk textiles found a ready and growing market in Asia and in Europe". There was also probably a backward-linkage between the trade-driven demand for textiles, the corresponding demand for industrial labor and cheap foodstuffs, and the need to bring additional land into production to cultivate more food crops.
6 Although the traditional view has been that Japan's drive to emulate Western industrialization received its impetus in the 1850s when Western powers forced Japan to "open up" to trade, scholars now suggest that the foundation for Japan's industrialization in the 1870s onwards lie in the achievements of Tokugawa Japan (1600–1868) during its long period of "closed economy" autarky between the mid-seventeenth century and the 1850s. These achievements include urbanization, road networks, the channeling and control of river water flow especially for irrigation, the development and expansion of rice cultivation, the encouragement of craft manufactures, and the promotion of education and population control. See, for example, Clark (2007); Jones (1988); Minami (1994); Mosk (2001); Richards (2003).
7 Meinig (1986, p. 22) draws an apt analogy between the impact of West African disease on Europeans and European diseases on Native Americans:

> It proved impossible to establish any substantial European enclave on the coast of West Africa because endemic diseases, especially yellow fever and malaria, proved as deadly to Europeans as European measles, smallpox, and pneumonia were to American Indians. The mortality of European residents and visitors was often eighty percent or higher. Hence they tended to stay on ships, work through African traders, and tarry as briefly as possible.

8 See Ehret (2002, chap. 9), who provides a detailed overview of the effects of the Atlantic slave trade on various African civilizations from 1640 to 1800. Obviously, the smaller and less powerful African states and tribes along the coast and in the interior that were victimized by the slave trade were more gravely affected than the more powerful states in West Africa who benefited either directly or indirectly from the trade.
9 Ehret (2002, pp. 438–445); Richards (2003, chap. 8); Weaver (2003).
10 See, for example, Barbier (2011) for detailed discussion of these historical examples.
11 Some of these economic developments leading to abnormal frontier rents, such as resource price booms and windfalls, are of course driven by demand factors in the wider world economy. For example, a major factor during the Golden Age of Resource-Based Development from 1870 to 1914 is that the world transport and trade boom of the late nineteenth century translated into a primary product export boom, mainly from periphery regions and colonies to industrialized Western Europe. As a

result, almost two-thirds of world exports consisted of primary products. Food accounted for 29 percent of world exports, agricultural raw materials for 21 percent and minerals 14 percent (Findlay and O'Rourke 2007, p. 411). In turn, the agricultural and raw material trade boom during the era fostered an unprecedented expansion of cropland and resource exploitation across many regions of the world, as documented in Barbier (2011; Findlay and O'Rourke (2007); Weaver (2003); Williamson (2009).

References

Agergaard, J., Fold, N. and Gough, K.V., 2009. Global-local Interactions: Socioeconomic and Spatial Dynamics in Vietnam's Coffee Frontier. *Geographical Journal*, 175(2), pp. 133–145.

Auty, R.M., 1993. *Sustaining Development in Mineral Economies: The Resource Curse Thesis*, London: Routledge.

Auty, R.M., 1994. Industrial Policy Reform in Six Large NICs: The Resource Curse Thesis. *World Development*, 22, pp. 11–26.

Barbier, E.B., 2005a. Frontier Expansion and Economic Development. *Contemporary Economic Policy*, 23(2), pp. 286–303.

Barbier, E.B., 2005b. *Natural Resources and Economic Development*, Cambridge, MA: Cambridge University Press.

Barbier, E.B., 2011. *Scarcity and Frontiers: How Economies Have Developed through Natural Resource Exploitation*, New York: Cambridge University Press.

Barney, K., 2009. Laos and the Making of a "Relational" Resource Frontier. *Geographical Journal*, 175(2), pp. 146–159.

Billington, R.A., 1966. *America's Frontier Heritage*, New York: Holt, Reinhart and Winston.

Clark, G., 2007. *A Farewell to Alms: A Brief Economic History of the World*, Princeton, NJ: Princeton University Press.

Cleary, D., 1993. After the Frontier: Problems with Political Economy in the Modern Brazilian Amazon. *Journal of Latin American Studies*, 25(2), p. 331.

Crafts, N. and Venables, A.J., 2003. Globalization in History: A Geographical Perspective. In M.D. Bordo, A.M. Taylor and J.G. Williamson, eds. *Globalization in Historical Perspective*, Chicago: University of Chicago Press, pp. 323–369.

David, P.A. and Wright, G., 1997. Increasing Returns and the Genesis of American Resource Abundance. *Industrial and Corporate Change*, 6(2), pp. 203–245.

Domar, E.D., 1970. The Causes of Slavery or Serfdom: A Hypothesis. *The Journal of Economic History*, 30(1), pp. 18–32.

Ehret, C., 2002. *The Civilizations of Africa: A History to 1800*, Charlottesville, VA: University Press of Virginia.

Engerman, S.L. and Sokoloff, K.L., 1997. Factor Endowments, Institutions, and Differential Paths of Growth among New World Economies. In S. Haber, ed. *How Latin America Fell Behind: Essays on the Economic Histories of Brazil and Mexico*. Stanford, CA: Stanford University Press, pp. 260–304.

Findlay, R., 1995. *Factor Proportions, Trade, and Growth*, Cambridge, MA: MIT Press.

Findlay, R. and Lundahl, M., 1994. Natural Resources, "Vent-for-Surplus", and the Staples Theory. In G. Meier, ed. *From Classical Economics to Development Economics: Essays in Honor of Hla Myint*, New York: St. Martin's Press, pp. 68–93.

Findlay, R. and Lundahl, M., 1999. Resource-Led Growth – a Long-Term Perspective:

The Relevance of the 1970–1914 Experience for Today's Developing Economies, Helsinki, Finland: WIDER.

Findlay, R. and O'Rourke, K.H., 2007. *Power and Plenty: Trade, War and the World Economy in the Second Millennium*, Princeton, NJ: Princeton University Press.

Flynn, D.O. and Giraldez, A., 2002. Cycles of Silver: Global Economic Unity through the Mid-Eighteenth Century. *Journal of World History*, 13(2), pp. 391–427.

Green, A. and Urquhart, M.C., 2010. Factor and Commodity Flows in the International Economy of 1870–1914: A Multi-Country View. *The Journal of Economic History*, 36(1), pp. 217–252.

Gylfason, T., 2001. Nature, Power and Growth. *Scottish Journal of Political Economy*, 48(5), pp. 558–588.

Hansen, B., 1979. Colonial Economic Development with Unlimited Supply of Land: A Ricardian Case. *Economic Development and Cultural Change*, 27(4), pp. 611–627.

Hennessy, A., 1978. *The Frontier in Latin American History*, Albuquerque, NM: University of New Mexico Press.

Innis, H., 1940. *The Cod Fisheries: The History of an International Economy*, New Haven, CT: Yale University Press.

Innis, H., 1956. *The Fur Trade in Canada: An Introduction to Canadian Economic History*, Second edn. Toronto, Canada: University of Toronto Press.

Jones, E.L., 1987. *The European Miracle: Environments, Economics and Geopolitics in the History of Europe and Asia*, Second edn. Cambridge, MA: Cambridge University Press.

Jones, E.L., 1988. *Growth Recurring: Economic Change in World History*, Oxford: Clarendon Press.

Jurajada, Š. and Mitchell, J., 2003. Markets and Growth. In G. McMahon and L. Squire, eds. *Explaining Growth: A Global Research Project*, New York: Palgrave Macmillan, pp. 117–158.

Mackintosh, W.A., 1967. *The Economic Background of Dominion-Provincial Relations*, Toronto, Canada: McClelland and Stewart.

Mahon, J.E., 1992. Was Latin America Too Rich to Prosper? Structural and Political Obstacles to Export-Led Industrial Growth. *Journal of Development Studies*, 28, pp. 241–263.

Meinig, D.W., 1986. *The Shaping of America: A Geographical Perspective on 500 Years of History*, New Haven, CT: Yale University Press.

Minami, R., 1994. *Economic Development of Japan: A Quantitative Study*, Second edn. London: Macmillan Press.

Mosk, C., 2001. *Japanese Industrial History: Technology, Urbanization, and Economic Growth*, Armonk, NY: M.E. Sharpe.

Myint, H., 1958. The "Classical Theory" of International Trade and the Underdeveloped Countries. *The Economic Journal*, 68(270), pp. 317–337.

O'Brien, P.K., 1997. Intercontinental Trade and the Development of the Third World since the Industrial Revolution. *Journal of World History*, 8(1), pp. 75–133.

O'Brien, P.K., 2006. Colonies in a Globalizing Economy, 1815–1948. In B.K. Gillis and W.R. Thompson, eds. *Globalization and Global History*, London: Routledge, pp. 248–291.

O'Rourke, K.H. and Williamson, J.G., 1999. *Globalization and History: The Evolution of a Nineteenth-century Atlantic Economy*, Cambridge, MA: The MIT Press.

Van der Ploeg, F., 2011. Natural Resources: Curse or Blessing? *Journal of Economic Literature*, 49(2), pp. 366–420.

Richards, J.F., 2003. *The Unending Frontier: An Environmental History of the Early Modern World*, Berkeley, CA: University of California Press.

Rodrigues, A.S.L., Ewen, R.M., Parry, L., Souza, J.C. and Verissimo, A., 2009. Boom-and-bust Development Patterns across the Amazon Deforestation Frontier. *Science*, 324(5933), pp. 1435–1437.

Savage, W.M. and Thompson, S.I., eds., 1979. *The Frontier*, Norman, OK: University of Oklahoma Press.

Schedvin, C.B., 1990. Staples and Regions of Pax Britannica. *The Economic History Review*, 43(4), p. 533.

Schumpeter, J.A., 1961. *A Theory of Economic Development: An Inquiry into Profits, Capital, Credit, Interest, and the Business Cycle.*, New York: Oxford University Press.

Sokoloff, K.L. and Engerman, S.L., 2000. History Lessons: Institutions, Factors Endowments, and Paths of Development in the New World. *The Journal of Economic Perspectives*, 14(3), pp. 217–232.

Di Tella, G., 1982. The Economics of the Frontier. In C.P. Kindleberger and G. Di Tella, eds. *Economics in the Long View*, London: MacMillan Press Ltd, pp. 210–227.

Turner, F.J., 1986. The Significance of the Frontier in American History. In F.J. Turner, ed. *The Frontier in American History*, Tucson, AZ: University of Arizona Press, pp. 1–38.

Weaver, J.C., 2003. *The Great Land Rush and the Making of the Modern World, 1650–1900*, Montreal and Kingston, Canada: McGill-Queen's University Press.

Webb, W.P., 1964. *The Great Frontier*, Lincoln, NE: University of Nebraska Press.

Wieczynski, J., 1976. *The Russian Frontier: The Impact of Borderlands upon the Course of Early Russian History*, Charlottesville, VA: University of Virginia Press.

Williamson, J.G., 2009. *Globalization and the Poor Periphery before 1950*, Cambridge, MA: The MIT Press.

Wolfskill, G. and Palmer, S., eds., 1983. *Essays on Frontiers in World History*, Austin, TX: University of Texas Press.

Wright, G., 1990. The Origins of American Industrial Success, 1879–1940. *The American Economic Review*, 80(4), pp. 651–668. Available at: www.jstor.org/stable/2006701.

Wright, G. and Czelusta, J., 2004. Why Economies Slow: The Myth of the Resource Curse. *Challenge*, 47(2), pp. 6–38.

Wright, G. and Czelusta, J., 2007. Resource Growth: Past and Present. In D. Lederman and W. F. Maloney, eds. *Natural Resources: Neither Curse nor Destiny*, Washington, DC: The World Bank and Stanford University Press, pp. 183–212.

4 Botswana

Caught in a natural resource trap[1]

Ellen Hillbom

Introduction

Botswana is by many considered to be one of few sustainable success stories in sub-Saharan Africa (Acemoglu and Robinson 2010; Acemoglu *et al.* 2003; Beaulier and Subrick 2006; Leith 2005; Lewin 2011; Mbabazi and Taylor 2005; Mkandawire 2001; Samatar 1999). Although the political system has not been uncontested, it is generally agreed that the political elite has shown an ability to both run a well-functioning multi-party state with democratically elected leaders and develop institutions with a high regulatory quality. The Botswana government has also stood out as a leading regional example in regard to investing significantly in education, health and infrastructure (Acemoglu *et al.* 2003; Leith 2005; Lewin 2011; Robinson and Parsons 2006; Transparency International 2014).

While the success story includes substantial political stability and significant social development, Botswana's most prominent feature has been its impressive economic growth record since independence in 1966. At that time it was one of the poorest countries in the world with a GNI per capita at US$70 (Lewin 2011, p. 81). Government revenue depended on low-value beef exports generated by a low-productivity cattle sector. Although a large section of the population held cattle wealth they were at the same time income poor and widespread malnutrition was reported (Hillbom 2008, 2010, 2014; Schapera and Comaroff 1991). However, in 1967 the discovery of diamond deposits was announced and once production started it was followed by four decades of the highest average long-term growth performance experienced anywhere in the world throughout history (Leith 2005, p. 4). Consequently, Botswana is currently classified as an upper middle-income country with an estimated GNI per capita of US$14,650 in 2012 (World Bank 2014). Although growth rates have levelled off to a GDP increase of roughly 4 per cent per capita per annum (World Bank 2014) there does not appear to be any immediate end to economic expansion.

The economic success story is, however, not without its challenges. Economic growth has consistently correlated with the long-term exploitation of diamond resources (Jerven 2010) with Botswana currently providing 20 per cent of all diamonds in the world (Bain and Company 2013). Meanwhile, there has been a failure to diversify the economy and getting any sector other than diamonds to really take off. Agriculture's share of GDP has plummeted from roughly 40 to 3 per cent during the independence era and manufacturing has stayed at roughly 5 per cent of GDP in the same time period. The only other sector, apart from mining, that has expanded is services which at present account for 50 per cent of GDP (World Bank 2014), however, this is primarily made up of low-productive services such as the public sector, hotels, restaurants, etc. With diamonds making up 89 per cent of export incomes (Botswana International Merchandise Trade Statistics (BIMTS) 2014, p. 9) and the diamond sector representing roughly one-third of both GDP and government revenues (CIA 2014) the economy is caught in a trap in the sense that it is unable to diversify away from its dependency on a single valuable natural resource.

This chapter will show that while Botswana has significantly profited from exporting its natural resources it has been unable to use this advantage as a window of opportunity to develop other sectors of the economy. Instead, it has become stuck in a state of natural resource dependency and export-led growth, lacking both the incentives and the ability to diversify the economy and develop alternative high-productive sectors. Moreover, we argue that explanations for current challenges to escape the natural resource trap can be found in structures rooted in the establishment of the colonial cattle economy. While there has been social development, the political system has matured and the low-productivity service sector has expanded, there has never been a structural transformation in economic terms between the cattle and diamond economies. In simplistic terms it can be argued that the only concrete difference between the colonial and the independence eras is that a low-value product has been replaced by a high-value one and therein lays the growth miracle. There are both geographical and institutional factors that have contributed to shaping the characteristics of Botswana's natural resource trap and they will both be discussed in the text.

For the presentation of Botswana's historical experience we apply a periodization based on changes in the overall economic structure (Hillbom 2014). Our first time period consists of the roughly 80 years between Tswana settlement, in the area presently known as Botswana, in the 1850s to the establishment of the colonial cattle economy in the 1930s. This is a period of subsistence farming paired with cattle rearing; a system of production that contains the initial conditions for the colonial cattle economy. It is followed by the colonial cattle economy 1930–1975 where efforts to develop a beef export industry created a mono-product export dependent economy, i.e. the pre-conditions for the natural resource trap. Subsequently, we have the switch to the diamond-led economy in the mid-1970s and the era of the growth miracle that has lasted until present. This is the time period where the natural resource trap is most clearly exposed as the economy has proven unable to diversify despite significantly improved financial opportunities to do so.

The disposition of the chapter is as follows. We start with three empirical sections divided according to the periodization presented above. These are followed by a reflection on how Botswana can be characterized and analysed based on the theoretical literature on natural resources dependency. We then discuss the challenges in diversifying Botswana's economy, the efforts that have been made and their outcomes. The last section is the conclusion.

The non-monetary cattle economy, 1850–1930

After a period of military conflict and migration in the mid-nineteenth century, in Southern Africa known as the Difaqane, eight Tswana groups settled in the area that is now Botswana. As they shared one language as well as a common history and customs they constituted the basis of reasonable homogenous population. The Tswana were sedentary agro-pastoralists, i.e. their agricultural system was based on a combination of crop farming and cattle rearing. The population was based in large and smaller villages, each surrounded by arable fields. Further away lay the communally held grazing range where their most valuable assets, the cattle, were kept. Household members moved according to season and labour tasks between the residential plot in the village, the arable fields and the cattle post (Mgadla 1998; Schapera 1994; Silitshena and McLeod 1998). Theory generally has it that African societies characterized by low population densities, land abundance and extensive farming systems also have had poor state capacity (Herbst 2000). However, due to their settlement patterns, with everyone belonging to and living part-time in organized villages under the control of traditional authority systems (Schapera 1994), these Tswana societies were relatively centralized with functioning political institutions. Several scholars have identified the heritage of good pre-colonial institutions and prudent governance as the key explanations for what separates Botswana of today from its less successful neighbours (see e.g. Acemoglu *et al.* 2003; Masire 2006).

The area where the Tswana settled had a subtropical desert climate characterized by great differences in day and night temperatures, very limited rainfall and overall low humidity. These climatic conditions defined the agricultural system of production. Being agro-pastoralists in a land-abundant dry area with limited opportunities for crop production meant that: first, an individual's ability to control or own cattle became the primary basis for both economic wealth and social status; and second, that the most valuable natural resource for a cattle holder to access and control was water.

In this natural resource dependent society accessing and governing agricultural resources was key for both survival and amassing political and economic power. Property rights systems were based on a mix between communal and private property as well as ownership, user rights and access. Starting with the land, this was communally held while individuals could turn to the chief to acquire private user rights to residency plots in the village, fields in the arable lands or cattle posts on the grazing range. Natural open waters such as pans and rivers were open access to all, but groups or individuals who dug wells to access ground water got private user rights to the site of the source and hence controlled the water coming from it. Finally, cattle were either held in common by the community and managed by the chief, or as private property belonging to wealthy members of society (Carlsson 2003; Hillbom 2014; Peters 1994; Schapera 1994). The cattle economy was then well established already in pre-colonial time, but both the community as a whole and single individuals lacked opportunities to turn cattle wealth into financial wealth or monetary incomes.

Colonial rule started with the establishment of the Bechuanaland Protectorate in 1885. The first half century was a time of establishment that saw only modest colonial strategies. Two changes did, however, occur during this time that would become intertwined in the future dependence on the cattle economy and beef exports. First, as wage opportunities were very limited in Bechuanaland many Tswana men looking for cash incomes went to work in the mines in neighbouring South Africa. As time went by labour migration diversified, involving women also, and offering new opportunities to work as farm hands, domestic servants, etc. Wage incomes were sent as remittances to families in Bechuanaland and to pay taxes, but more importantly for the continuous development of the cattle sector, they were used to invest in cattle upon the return home (Bolt and Hillbom 2013, 2015; Hillbom 2014; Schapera 1994). Second, in 1899, the colonial administration introduced taxes to raise its revenues and in 1920 a Native Fund Tax was added for the traditional authorities. Tax levels fluctuated throughout the colonial era, but it was usually between 20 shillings to £1, which meant that as a general rule they were kept low compared with other regions in the British Empire. However, they were significantly higher than those in neighbouring Southern African colonial territories (Bolt and Hillbom 2015; Frankema 2010). One explanation for the higher tax levels could be that although the Tswana were income poor, the majority held wealth in cattle, and this could be realized when taxes were due. We know that the large- and medium-scale cattle holders often sold cattle to pay taxes and that on average, the sale of one animal could pay seven times the annual tax (Bolt and Hillbom 2015; Schapera and Comaroff 1991). A dependency was established between the government's ability to collect tax revenues, on the one hand, and exploitation of natural resources within the agricultural sector, on the other hand. The connection cemented itself throughout the colonial era.

Development of the beef export industry, 1930–1975

From the 1930s onwards the British colonial ambition generally in Africa was significantly enhanced. It was a time when colonial administrations started forming policies for investments and made efforts to bring socio-economic development (Cooper 2002). Based on the existing systems of production and the climatic conditions in Bechuanaland it was decided by the colonial administration that ranching was the only potential comparative advantage of the territory. It was not, however, a unique resource and competition primarily from neighbouring South Africa was a challenge from the start (Parsons and Crowder 1988).

As Tables 4.1 and 4.2 show, there was an increase in British grants and loans and this was combined with a change in distribution of investments. While investments had previously been modest the parliamentary grant-in-aid in 1933

Table 4.1 Colonial investments in Bechuanaland Protectorate, 1930–1946 (£)

Year	Parliamentary grant-in-aid	Extraordinary revenue/Colonial Development Fund
1930–1931		11,594
1931–1932		12,826
1932–1933		4,631
1933–1934	177,000	1,902
1934–1935	98,000	2,689
1935–1936	50,000	15,870
1936–1937	60,000	25,873
1937–1938	25,000	69,508
1938–1939	35,000	57,026
1943–1944		15,879
1944–1945		43,770
1945–1946		105,571

Source: Makgala (2006, Table 1 and 2).

Table 4.2 Colonial administrative expenditure in Bechuanaland Protectorate, 1900–1966 (%)

	1900–1925	1926–1935	1936–1945	1946–1955	1956–1966
General administration	54.4	51.8	41.4	35.3	41.0
Police	37.1	20.0	11.5	10.8	6.6
Medical	1.7	7.5	9.4	9.9	5.9
Education	1.2	3.4	4.1	4.8	6.3
Veterinary & agriculture	3.4	10.9	12.8	12.6	10.0
Public works	2.2	5.8	9.5	12.9	4.9
Development expenditures	–	0.6	11.3	13.7	25.3
Total	100	100	100	100	100

Source: Colcough and McCarthy (1980, Table 1.1).

represented a staggering increase and financial support continued to flow into the Protectorate. Meanwhile, investments in veterinary services and agriculture together with development projects increased its share of colonial government expenditures from the mid-1930s onward and reached to above 35 per cent of the total in the 1960s. The lion's share of those investments was earmarked to benefit the expansion of the cattle sector and the beef export industry. This strategy meant the development of a mono-product economy based on beef exports and made the colonial administration dependent on beef for revenues to the point that at the time of independence it represented 85 per cent of total export earnings (Colcough and McCarthy 1980, p. 32; Harvey and Lewis Jr 1990, pp. 78–82).

The primary obstacle for the strategy to expand the cattle sector was access to water in the dryer areas of the grazing range. Tribal initiatives to drill modern boreholes had already started in the late 1920s and from the late 1930s colonial efforts also focused on borehole drilling schemes. Once constructed, both tribal and colonial boreholes were handed over as private or communal property to individuals and syndicates representing a limited number of relatively influential and wealthy members of Tswana society. This elite was considered to have the best opportunities to run and maintain boreholes and the result was an increasingly unequal division of water resources on the grazing range. After WWII drilling schemes continued and even increased in intensity in the 1950s and the 1960s. They were complemented with other efforts such as veterinary fences and the establishment of an abattoir in Lobatse in 1954 (Hillbom 2010).

A potentially unintended consequence of the establishment of the beef export sector was increasing inequalities among the Tswana. In the pre-colonial and early-colonial society commoners primarily held cattle to pay taxes and bride price, to gain in-kind incomes such as milk and to have access to draught power. Meanwhile, cattle wealth allowed the elite to gain social status, build patron-client relationships and secure political loyalty (Schapera 1994). In the 1940s, 90 per cent of all households held livestock (Hesselberg 1985, p. 182) and the distribution of animals was relatively equal with only the very top of the tribal elite, e.g. the chiefs, holding large herds. Investments in the cattle sector and opportunities to secure incomes from beef exports introduced monetary incentives that had not been present before. While the elite amassed resources, many medium-sized cattle holders saw their herds decrease and small-scale holders lost their cattle. Severe spells of drought and diseases in the 1930s and 1960s also affected the medium- and small-scale cattle holders negatively (Bolt and Hillbom 2013; Carlsson 2003; Peters 1994). In 1983 only roughly 60 per cent of households owned cattle and 30 per cent of the national herd was owned by 4 per cent of households (Arntzen and Silitshena 1989, p. 162).

A combination of opportunities to capitalize on cattle wealth, polarization of cattle ownership in the traditional sector and a significant increase in wages in the public sector, together led to rapidly increasing income inequalities (Bolt and Hillbom 2013). Figure 4.1 shows how the Gini coefficient was at a low 0.2 from the 1920s until the mid-1930s when it started to increase rapidly hitting 0.6 in the mid-1970s. In effect, this means that high levels of income inequality have their roots at the time when the colonial cattle economy was established, in the 1930s. Widespread poverty, high levels of inequality and amassment of wealth in the hands of the cattle elite and government officials, i.e. the two groups who relied the most on incomes from beef exports, also meant the absence of a basis for a demand-side-driven diversification of the economy. The same groups who profited from increasing natural resource dependency had the political influence and economic power to discourage the establishment of a dynamic private sector and the creation of an entrepreneurial class (Bolt and Hillbom 2015).

During the last decades of colonial rule development strategies were to a significant degree formulated in conjuncture with the Tswana cattle-holding elites, including future independence leaders, e.g. presidents Seretse Khama and Quett Masire. They came from the ranks of traditional leaders who had amassed cattle wealth, social status and political influence. While they did not represent a

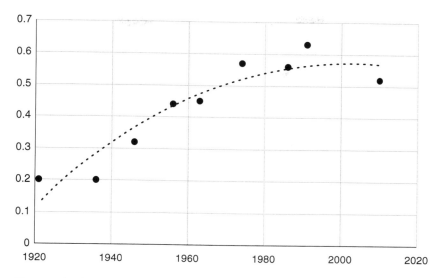

Figure 4.1 Gini for Botswana, 1921–2010 (sources: Colonial Blue Books and Annual Reports 1921–1965, World Bank 2014).

quest for equality they had generated principles for how to govern fairly and showing accountability, principles that might have been lost if they had been replaced by a new, unexperienced and unaccountable political elite. In some sense "benevolent chiefs" took over the new independence government and to a significant extent catered for the interests of their subjects as opposed to attempting to plunder the state. However, because the elite profited from the existing focus on the beef export sector it served their interests that development policies that had been generated within the colonial context stayed on and influenced development efforts during the first decades of independence (Masire 2006). Consequently, the independence government continued to invest in the beef export industry in the form of construction of water points, access to veterinary services, building veterinary fences and setting up the Botswana Meat Commission (a monopsonist buyer of cattle for export) (Acemoglu *et al.* 2003, p. 101; Lawry 1983, p. 14). Non-radical development efforts and socio-economic continuity between the colonial and early independence eras has often been quoted as a principal explanation to the subsequent success story in general and the stability of political institutions in particular (see e.g. Acemoglu and Robinson 2010; Acemoglu *et al.* 2003; Beaulier and Subrick 2006; Leith 2005; Samatar 1999). The downsides of continuity, however, also deserve to be discussed. First, while the consistency in the establishment of the elites has meant the survival of benevolent leadership it has also catered for an unequal amassment of wealth and influence favouring the old elite. Second, economic and political continuity has meant the absence of incentives and initiatives to instigate change and to break away from the existing natural resource dependency.

The diamond economy, 1975–present

After independence the newly founded government of Botswana vested all mineral rights under its authority. The South African company De Beers, one of the world leaders in mining and diamond specialists, immediately showed interest in prospecting. Possibly the government knew already before independence that valuable diamond deposits existed in Botswana. Notwithstanding, in 1967 such discoveries were announced and the government saw opportunities to negotiate a substantial share of profits from mining extraction. In 1969 it went into a 50/50 joint venture with De Beers and together they formed Debswana Diamond Company Ltd. in 1978, thus ensuring significant revenues for the country. Through this type of policy decision, the Botswana government has over the years managed to capture sizeable mineral rents, primarily from diamonds (Gaolathe 1997; Leith 2005).

After a few years of extraction diamonds took over as the primary driver of Botswana's economy. The mining sector, overwhelmingly dominated by diamonds, represented 8 per cent of GDP in 1974/1975, increasing to 53 per cent in 1988/1989, only to decline again to roughly 35 per cent in 2002, which is about the level it is still at (Leith 1997; Siwawa-Ndai 1997; World Bank 2014). Figure 4.2 shows how industry, which in effect in the case of Botswana is the equivalent to diamond mining, surpassed agriculture, measured as value added

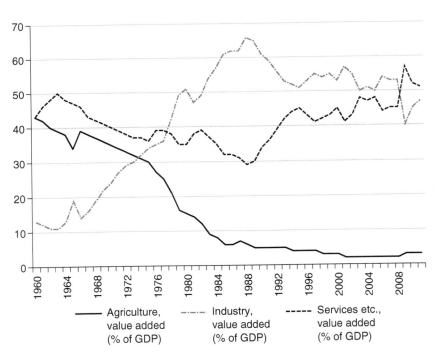

Figure 4.2 Agriculture, industry and services, value added (% of GDP), 1960–2013 (source: World Bank 2014).

percentage of GDP, in the mid-1970s and a few years later became the largest sector of the economy. We have therefore pinpointed the timing of the switch between the cattle economy and the diamond economy to the second half of the 1970s.

Diamonds are in many ways a perfect natural resource: they are valuable (as opposed to beef, for example); storable, which means that if you have the economic buffer you can hold back exports in times of low world market prices; cheap to transport, taking away the disadvantage that Botswana has as a landlocked country: and designated for the global market, nullifying any negative effects of overwhelming regional competition (in Botswana's case from South Africa). There is yet another important geographic aspect when discussing Botswana's diamond resources. Contrary to diamond resources in several West African countries such as Liberia and Sierra Leone, diamonds in Botswana are extracted through deep mining instead of being washed from river beds. This in turn means that diamonds cannot become open access for any interested party to extract using basic technology, something that invites conflict between agents. Instead access can be controlled by the state in its capacity as one of very few players who have the financial resources to set up the deep mining endeavours.

As Jerven (2010) has shown, the rate of diamond sector development correlates perfectly with Botswana growth figures and the only way to understand or explain Botswana's economic growth is to conclude that it is diamond-led. In terms of economic growth there is no question that the diamond economy has been a success. Figure 4.3 summarizes how during the overall period 1965–2005 the average real annual economic growth has been 9 per cent. This includes a staggering 25–26 per cent increase in GDP per annum in the years 1971–1972 as well as the period 1980–1989 which showed 13 per cent annual increase on average (Leith

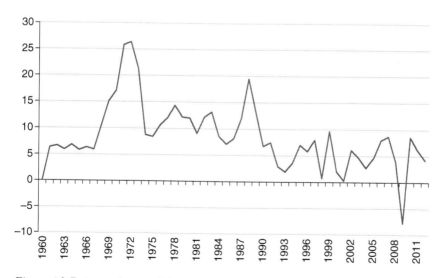

Figure 4.3 Botswana's annual GDP growth, 1960–2013 (source: World Bank 2014).

2005, p. 4; Samatar 1999; UNDP 2010; World Bank 2014). As mentioned in the introductory section of the chapter, this means that Botswana has had the highest long-term economic growth rate in the world and that is including the impressive performance of the Pacific Asian Tigers (Leith 2005, p. 4).

When discussing the transition from the cattle to the diamond economy we can see that the shift from one resource to another was a consequence of changing natural pre-conditions and that when state control over one low-value natural resource – beef – was replaced by that of a high-value resource – diamonds – significant economic growth occurred. While beef export lost its importance for national earnings, the cattle ownership continued to be of significance for income and wealth in the agricultural sector, as well as for rural and urban social status. Despite the fact that the cattle industry was the primary target for colonial investments and up until the present day has been the basis of the agricultural sector, productivity measured by off-take rates (percentage of animals slaughtered out of the national stock) has been modest in an international comparison. In 1967 off-take rates were at 9 per cent, after staying constant they declined to 7 per cent in 2007 where they remained, ergo there has been no productivity increase for 45 years in the country's most important agricultural sector. Meanwhile, in 2007 neighbouring South Africa had off-take rates at 22 per cent, Mongolia at 19 per cent and Argentina at 27 per cent respectively (Hillbom 2010). The government's interest in supporting the cattle sector in its current form can then be understood from a social and political perspective, but not from an economic point of view.

As Figure 4.2 shows, service is the other sector beside the diamond industry that has grown significantly since independence. This growth has been made possible by the expanding state and the general improvements in incomes, both of which in turn can be traced back to the diamond sector. The Botswana government has used a major part of diamond rents for investments in social development, primarily in infrastructure and human capital formation. Such investments have represented as much as 40 percent of GDP, thereby being among the highest in Africa and on a par with developed countries such as Norway (Acemoglu *et al.* 2003, p. 85; Leith 2005, p. 85). Such investments together with a swelling state apparatus have led to an enlarging public sector which makes up a significant section of the growing service sector. Another section that is expanding due to diamond incomes is hotels, restaurants, shops, repairs, etc. in the private sector which profits from the overall increase in individuals' incomes during the growth miracle (African Economic Outlook 2012). Both the public and the private sectors are made up of what Baumol (1967) calls "stagnant services". These are characterized by low productivity growth compared to the rest of the economy and consequent rising prices, but due to consistent increasing demand the output of these services grow proportional to the rest of the economy and so does the employment share. This development fits well with the Sachs and Warner (1999) argument that there is a general trend for natural resource rich countries to have larger service sectors and smaller manufacturing sectors.

In the midst of certain sectorial change the state has continued to receive significant revenues from natural resource exports. Currently diamonds represent almost nine-tenths of export revenues and roughly one-third of state revenues (World Bank 2014). State efforts have continued to be focused on developing exports of a few natural resources and the economy stays characterized as monoproduct with a high export dependency for securing government revenues. At the same time as the natural resource dependency has cemented itself, the political and economic elite has shown consistency. The cattle-holding elite and its associates have spread from controlling the traditional authorities to also dominating the independence government including being connected to the leading bureaucrats (Good 1994, p. 499). Their income basis has broadened from only being based on beef exports to also profiting from diamond revenues. For almost a century there has been a lack of committed strategies to encourage the private sector and flawed attempts to diversify the economy. Instead the government sector has dominated and in the last couple of decades it has become exposed to an increasing degree of elite capturing (Hillbom 2008, 2012; Makgala 2006). Notwithstanding, current leaders have been brought up in a tradition of accountability and prudent economic management and so far they have preserved a mostly well-functioning political institutional structure. As long as the current politico-economic elite is reaping the benefits from the existing institutional structure and controlling the state, there is really no reason to assume that they would act according to anything other than their own self-interest which means opting for a structural status quo (Kaufmann and Kraay 2002, p. 204).

Neither curse nor disease

It should be clear from the account above of Botswana's economic history from 1850 to present that the country's economy has consistently been dominated by the exploitation of natural resources and its growth has been export-led. It started off with subsistence agriculture combined with cattle keeping being the universal system of production. From this the beef export industry was developed in the 1930s, only to be replaced by diamond-led growth from the mid-1970s onwards. While this story of natural resource dependency and export-led growth is common, it also raises questions of whether to see natural resource abundance as a blessing or a curse. With the exception of a few city states virtually all countries have begun their economic development process with exploiting their agricultural resource base (Mikesell 1997). Taking advantage of one's natural resources for securing export revenues has also been a common strategy and the more valuable resources are, the bigger role have they played in economic processes. Then, however, there seems to be a divide in development trajectories. Certain countries managed to use the export-led growth based on valuable natural resources to instigate endogenous growth by investing revenues into human capital formation and modern technology. Subsequently, they diversified and even structurally transformed their economies away from natural resource dependency. Meanwhile, other countries appear to be stuck with vulnerable economies dominated by natural resources and many have even experienced paradoxical economic stagnation or even crisis in the midst of natural resource abundance. How are we to understand this difference in outcome and how should Botswana's experience be classified?

Until the 1970s economists in general had a favourable view of abundant natural resources (e.g. Habakkuk 1962; Nurkse 1953; Rostow 1960). Many developing countries that became independent in the decades after World War II possessed great wealth in primary products and this was understood as almost a guarantee for future growth. The actual outcome, however, was other than expected as the following decades saw the economic growth and development of the Newly Industrializing Economies in East Asia, stagnation in Latin America and economic and political failure in sub-Saharan Africa. The empirical evidence from resource abundant countries included: leaders that turned out to be corrupt selling off natural assets and pocketing the profits; individuals and international companies becoming wealthy while governments stayed poor; and financial policies unable to control increase in exchange rates and inflation. Meanwhile, in the numerous successful cases, low wages became a stronger comparative advantage than resource wealth (Auty 2010; van der Ploeg 2011). These empirical lessons, of course, came to influence the theoretical debate.

In theory abundant natural resources are still believed to be able to promote growth. As revenue raises wealth and purchasing power, this allows for increasing imports and investments in technology, infrastructure and human capital which can lead to improved growth rates. In a study covering the period 1970–1990 Sachs and Warner (1997) showed, however, that paradoxically there is instead generally a negative correlation between richness in natural resources and economic growth. The explanations given for the failure of many resource abundant countries varies and includes higher prevalence of indolence, rent seeking, conflict between stakeholders, corruption and predation compared to economies relying on other comparative advantages. The poor economic performance of natural resource rich countries has since repeatedly been shown empirically and discussed theoretically (Auty 2001; Gylafson et al. 1999; Leite and Weidmann 1999; van der Ploeg 2011; Sachs and Warner 1999). Empirical results have instigated a lively debate focusing on the negative aspects of resource abundance, a phenomenon often termed the natural resource curse. Despite decades of scholarly debate, it would, however, be faulty to state that we currently have a universally accepted theory or definition of what exactly constitutes the curse and how it develops. There are, however, some universal indications.

Part of defining the curse is to have an idea about how it relates to natural resource abundance, i.e. the stock of resource wealth, as well as natural resource dependence, i.e. the degree to which countries have alternative sources of incomes, specifically dependence on natural resource exports (Brunnschweiler 2008; Brunnschweiler and Blute 2008). Looking at Botswana it is clear that the cattle economy was based on accessing abundant land, but scarce water resources, and that it was an extensive agrarian system. It was also, of course, based on both a lack of agricultural alternatives due to the dry climate and an absence of valuable mineral finds. As the beef export sector was established any expansion of the cattle sector had to be paired with development of water sources to allow for the national herd to increase; notwithstanding, it stayed as an extensive system typical of abundant agricultural resources. Eventually the sector had expanded to the point that beef made up more than four-fifths of export revenues at the time of independence (Colcough and McCarthy 1980, p. 32), consequently making export dependence unquestionable. Moving on to the diamond economy, estimations state that Botswana is only surpassed by Brazil when it comes to having the biggest diamond deposits in the world. Again, abundance is uncontested. Also, export dependence is a clear-cut case from the 1980s onwards. Currently diamond revenues dominate export incomes even more than was ever the case with beef exports, they account for 45 per cent of total government revenue and roughly one-third of GDP (African Economic Outlook, 2012; Botswana International Merchandise Trade Statistics (BIMTS) 2014; World Bank 2014). Having concluded that Botswana has been natural resource abundant as well as export dependent during both the cattle and the diamond eras the question remains: Have these factors translated into a curse?

There are numerous examples around the world and throughout history of countries that have experienced both natural resource abundance and export dependency without a curse. For example, while Norway's discovery of abundant oil resources in the 1970s and the subsequent 40 years of oil extraction have been the basis for making the country world leading in terms of national wealth and standards of living, other productive sectors have also been developed and the economy has diversified (Gylfason *et al.* 2001). Meanwhile, other countries have instead experienced economic crisis and collapse in the midst of exploiting and exporting their abundant resources. In the middle of the oil crises in the 1970s when most oil producing countries secured significant export revenues, Nigeria managed to combine being a major oil exporter with having a severe economic crisis (van der Ploeg 2011). What sets the success stories and the failures apart appears to be the institutional quality and consequently this aspect must have a prominent place in any natural resource curse analysis. Taking it to its extreme, the claim can even be made that there could only be a curse when natural resource wealth is paired with poor institutional quality (Brunnschweiler 2008; Brunnschweiler and Blute 2008; van der Ploeg 2011). More specifically, Papyrakis and Gerlagh (2004) list corruption, low investments, protectionist measures, deteriorating terms of trade and poor educational standards as the probable main explanation as to why some countries do not benefit from their natural resource wealth. In the following paragraphs we will see how Botswana has fared in these terms.

Botswana's half-century of independent rule characterized by exceptional economic growth, significant social development and political stability would have not been possible without good institutional quality. It is clear that the state has been capable of developing a rule of law including secure property rights as well as a high regulatory quality while keeping levels of corruption modest. High institutional quality is, logically, often mentioned as the key explanation for Botswana's growth miracle. The claim is also often made that the origin of this good institutional quality is to be found in pre-colonial institutional structures and that colonial influence, potentially corrupting these structures, was limited. Specifically it is the tradition of public meetings, so-called kgotla meetings, where all male Tswana members in the community had the opportunity to be heard by the chief, as well as institutionalized negotiations between the traditional elite and their subjects that are commonly hailed as the basis for political stability, accountability and social development (Acemoglu et al. 2003; 2010; Masire 2006; Robinson and Parsons 2006). To fully appreciate what has safeguarded Botswana from becoming the victim of the natural resource curse we should, however, emphasize the broader explanations instead of focusing in on the phenomenon of the kgotla specifically. At the structural level it is the initial cultural homogeneity of the population together with the overall pre-colonial Tswana tradition of centralized governance and building state capacity that has been an important basis for developing lasting good political institutions.

That being said about the legacy of the pre-colonial era, we should be warned against excessively down-playing the influence that colonial efforts to develop the beef export industry have had on economic structures. These efforts to take advantage of existing natural resource abundance have led to natural resource export dependence and income inequality (Bolt and Hillbom 2013, 2015). Further, we need to remember that there is also well-founded critique against the institutional structure of the Botswana state in regard to elite capturing (Makgala 2006), high levels of inequality (Gulbrandsen 1996; Hillbom 2008), discrimination against minorities (Good 1993; Nthomang 2004), inability to battle the HIV/AIDS epidemic (Allen and Heald 2004; Heald 2006; Phaladze and Tlou 2006) and passivation of the poor (Lekoko and van der Merwe 2006). Still, it is beyond doubt that despite there being room for improvements, in both an African and a global comparison, Botswana's leaders have been relatively honest and elite capturing was rare until the 1990s. The presence of wise leaders is a reoccurring explanation for Botswana's success (Acemoglu et al. 2003; 2010; Masire 2006; Robinson and Parsons 2006) and it is doubtlessly true that the first generation of independence leaders were instrumental in setting up a standard for the political will to achieve development for the nation as a whole, although that standard may have been lowered in more recent years (Makgala 2006). Notwithstanding, it is positive to note that corruption continues to be kept at low levels even in an international comparison with the developed world (Transparency International 2014).

Moving on from the quality of the overarching political and economic institutional structure to the specific ability of the Botswana government to manage diamond incomes in a prudent fashion the picture becomes even clearer. The government has been keen to follow advice from the leading International Lending Institutions (IMF and World Bank) and has pursued a market oriented economic strategy with limited protectionist measurements. It has extracted diamonds wisely and its cooperation with De Beers has secured significant incomes for the country which have been used for ensuring positive terms of trade. The government has kept expenses consistent in boom years and even built up foreign exchange reserves thereby being able to compensate for bust years. This strategy combined with proper management of the exchange rate has meant that real exchange rate appreciations have been under control, which has been positive for the export sector. Through shrewd fiscal policy the government has avoided external debt problems and has maintained a stable growth rate over time (Hill 1991; Leith 2005; World Bank 2014). Consistent growth has enabled the government to make significant investments in key sectors such as infrastructure, education and health. Economic opportunities for this type of social development further separates Botswana from the economic crisis and persistent poor human capital and infrastructure that characterize countries infected by the natural resource curse.

A common trait in the theoretical thinking around the natural resource curse is that it is closely connected to a crowding out logic where abundant and valuable natural resources take away incentives and resources to develop other sectors of the economy. Income booms from natural resource exports create excess demand for non-traded goods which in turn drives up prices and wages. Profits in traded goods, i.e. manufacturing, are squeezed and consequently this sector does not take off (Sachs and Warner 2001). Perhaps the most famous theorizing on crowding out is the so-called Dutch Disease, so named after the implications experienced in the Netherlands after a sharp rise in natural gas exports in the 1970s. The term entails the idea that the economy is distorted by having a dominating and lucrative tradable natural resource sector that is supporting a growing non-tradable service sector while the tradable manufacturing sector is relatively economically weak. The greater the incomes from natural resource exports the higher the demands for the non-tradable sector and consequently the less capital and labour for the manufacturing sector (Corden and Neary 1982; Mikesell 1997; van der Ploeg 2011).

It is generally agreed that Botswana is not suffering from the Dutch Disease although all the typical pre-conditions are present. The country has a dominating and lucrative tradable natural resource sector that is supporting a growing non-tradable service sector while the tradable manufacturing sector is relatively economically weak at a few per cent of GDP (World Bank 2014). The greater the income from natural resource exports the higher the demands for the non-tradable sector and consequently the less capital and labour for the manufacturing sector (Corden and Neary 1982; Iimi 2006, p. 5). What sets Botswana apart from the typical Dutch Disease syndrome is the fact that manufacturing never took off, neither during colonial nor independence eras, and, consequently, there was nothing that could be ruined due to a re-allocation of capital and labour to other sectors. The crowding out theory is then only applicable in relation to limited incentives and opportunities for diversification and development of manufacturing from very low levels during the era of diamond-led growth. This is something that we consider to be an important aspect defining the natural resource trap, but it is inconsistent with the strict Dutch Disease definition.

While being the 18th largest resource exporter in the world (Iimi 2006, p. 6), it appears then that Botswana has managed to avoid both the natural resource curse and the Dutch Disease. The explanations can be found in a tradition of well-functioning political institutions that cater for a sound long-term plan for the extraction of natural resources and good policies for continued national growth (Hill 1991; Iimi 2006). This achievement makes it a member of a very exclusive group of developing countries (Sachs and Warner 1997). The country is, however, exposing both natural resource abundance and export dependency and as long as diamonds continue to dominate government revenues there is an indirect discrimination against a diversification of the economy, there are few incentives for diversified industrialization and productivity increase. Consequently, the process of structural change is hindered and this is the trap that the economy is locked into.

What characterizes the trap?

In theory, natural resource booms open up opportunities to instigate economic growth and development. Incomes from natural resource exports provide the financial basis for stimulating demand, e.g. by public spending and investments, and they can thereby help a low-income economy overcome the costs of industrialization (Sachs and Warner 1999). The growth of a stagnant service sector does not have the same type of linkages and cannot play an equivalent role. If we are content with only drawing a sketchy picture we can show that Botswana has experienced a quite substantial industrialization. Since independence, the industrial sector has grown by roughly 18 per cent per annum in the decade 1970–1980, 9 per cent in the years 1980–1993 (Siwawa-Ndai 1997) and 4 per cent in the years 2000–2012 (World Bank 2014). At present the sector constitutes roughly 35 per cent of GDP (World Bank 2014). However, industrial growth has primarily been driven by the expansion of the mining sector, i.e. diamond production, and in a small economy dominated by a high-value natural resource there are generally few linkages to other productive sectors or to the economy at large (Auty 2010; Hirschman 1958). Botswana and its diamond wealth is a perfect case fitting this argument. As diamonds have been exported unprocessed, mining has not contributed to any significant technological advances in the wider economy. Further, diamond production has engaged only 3 per cent of the labour force and, consequently, it has not provided any substantial employment opportunities (Gaolathe 1997; World Bank 2014).

For a more in-depth understanding of the development of Botswana's industrial sector as a strategy for diversification of the economy, it is not the primary production, but rather the manufacturing sector and the processing industry that are of relevance. They are expected to be the primary sources of technological progress as knowledge and skills generated here will spread to other sectors and affect them positively by contributing to increasing their productivity. The failure to promote them is commonly cited as the primary negative effect of resource abundance and dependency (Mikesell 1997). The fact that Botswana's manufacturing sector at no point has represented more than 5 per cent of GDP and that it has not increased its share since independence almost 50 years ago is worrying. In all fairness, it has to be remembered that part of the explanation of why development in the manufacturing sector has not resulted in an increasing share of GDP is that the rest of the economy has grown rapidly. However, while manufacturing has experienced substantial annual absolute growth, it will have to do better relative to other sectors if Botswana is to maintain its standard of living in the long run (Lewin 2011; Owusu and Ismail Samatar 1997). In comparison it can be noted that in South Africa, the oldest industrializing country on the sub-continent, manufacturing is 13 per cent of GDP and in Mauritius it is 17 per cent of GDP. Further, the fact that extraction of diamonds in the raw continues to constitute 90 per cent of the mining sector is also alarming (Mpabanga 1997; Republic of Botswana 2003; Siwawa-Ndai 1997; World Bank 2014).

The above exemplified types of deficiencies can, however, be countered by active state policies whereby the government transfers resources to stagnating sectors. From the start of the independence era, the importance of diversification was emphasized by the government and over the years a number of schemes to support entrepreneurial activities have been launched. The National Development Bank, NDB, was established in 1965 to provide loans to small-scale entrepreneurs in general and within the agricultural sector in particular. Botswana Development Corporation, BDC, was a venture capital company set up in 1970 to further complement the commercial banks. Both are owned 100 per cent by the Botswana government. The most high profile incentive program was the Financial Assistance Policy, FAP (running 1982–2001), which was projected to promote and expand employment-intensive and non-traditional businesses. There are differing opinions about the success of this government venture. According to Owusu and Ismail Samatar (1997) FAP has overall successfully managed to create manufacturing jobs, attracted industry to the rural areas and encouraged female entrepreneurs. However, the claim to success appears to be in relation to what would have happened without any efforts rather than in relation to achieving the set goals of creating job opportunities (8,000 instead of the intended 34,000) or diversifying the economy by expanding the manufacturing sector. Others claim that FAP as well as other government schemes aimed at encouraging private entrepreneurship have become subject to increasing abuse by both government employers and recipients, and subsequently they have failed to meet with initial expectations (Leith 2005).

When it has come to expanding beyond the traditional and well-established sectors, and away from natural resource dependency, Botswana has exposed itself as resembling other African countries, from which it is generally set apart (Hillbom 2008). Efforts have been made to identify explanations for Botswana's paradox of having successful macroeconomic management coexisting with government failure to implement policy instigating private sector development. Conteh (2008) claims that the last 30 odd years of policy programmes have been far too fragmented and, in some cases, even contradictory. There is, simply, a lack of an overarching ambition and a comprehensive, consistent strategy. The most recent endeavour in which the government puts its hope is De Beers' decision last year to move their cutting from London to Botswana's capital, Gaborone (Bain and Company 2013). While this appears to be an important step in the right direction, it is too early to say to what extent this processing industry will affect the rest of the economy.

Finally, what could be said about opportunities for demand-side-driven manufacturing constituting a basis for a diversification of the economy? To answer this question we have to consider poverty and inequality during the diamond economy. First, during the whole independence era there has been an increase in estimated GNI per capita from US$70 to US$14,650 and from 1986 to present poverty levels have declined from 59 to 19 per cent (World Bank 2014). Taken together this means that there has been an impressive increase in standards of living and the ability to consume. Second, if we recall Figure 4.1 summarizing changes in the Gini coefficient 1920–2010, it showed a peak in income inequality at 0.63 in 1993. After a slight increase in the first two decades of the diamond economy, income inequalities have since declined to presently being just above 0.5 (World Bank 2014). These changes are yet another indication that there should be improved opportunities for increased consumption of domestically manufactured goods. However, there are as of yet few signs that these opportunities have been realized and instead the market for basic consumption goods such as processed food, textiles and domestic utensils are, as before, dominated by imports from South Africa. Yet again, signs point to that the economic growth miracle is not transforming into an endogenous growth process and that the trap stays shut.

Concluding discussion

In this chapter we have argued that Botswana is a case of natural resource abundance and export dependency, but without a natural resource curse or the Dutch Disease. Instead, it is caught in a natural resource trap unable to use the window of opportunity provided by incomes from the spectacular diamond-led growth to diversify the economy and initiate a structural transformation. Our explanations for the creation of the trap goes back to the establishment of the beef export sector during the colonial era, they are of both a geographical and institutional nature and can be summarized as follows.

First, the climatic conditions of the subtropical desert area where Botswana is situated are undoubtedly essential for explaining how come cattle, and not crop farming, became the basis of the agricultural sector from the pre-colonial era onwards. Faced with the raison d'être of the existing agricultural system of production and not being able to produce any mineral finds of significance, the colonial administration's decision to focus its development efforts on establishing a low-value beef export sector is unsurprising. The only natural resource lacking for the further increase of the national cattle herd was water and scarcity was remedied with subsequent borehole drilling schemes. Although the carrying capacity of the grazing range as well as the sustainable extraction of water sources has been questioned during the last decades (Carlsson 2003; Colcough and McCarthy 1980; Hillbom 2010), climate cannot, however, be held responsible for the following poor profitability of the cattle sector. Explanations for low levels of productivity of the beef industry as well as the inability to diversify production into other types of meat (e.g. ostriches) and some processing industries must instead be found elsewhere.

Further, Botswana's position as being land-locked and situated next to the advanced South African economy has clearly affected its ability to export both agricultural and industrial products. From the colonial era onwards Botswana's dependency on its neighbour has e.g. manifested itself in labour migration and imports of consumption goods, something that has increased with improved standards of living. Diamonds have, in this regard, been a blessing as they have such a high value in relation to their volume and weight. Therefore the classic argument by Gallup *et al.* (1999) that one consequence of being land-locked is that transporting goods to the global market is generally too expensive and hinders economic growth has not applied. A further geographic condition, the need for deep-mining to reach diamond deposits, has also worked in favour of the government being able to control and exploit the country's diamond resources. Diamonds are, however, not the only type of minerals being mined and – which could be valuable for a land-locked country – there are also substantial reserves of gold, copper and nickel. The profitability of this production has, however, never taken off probably due to lack of incentives as it has never been able to compete with diamonds. In addition, the regional position of Botswana next to South Africa continues to constitute a significant challenge to any strategies for diversifying the economy away from its natural resource dependency.

Moving on to institutional explanations, we have argued that while good institutional quality has been the key explanation for avoidance of the curse, stagnant institutional structures may simultaneously be the key explanation for the trap. First, due to the initial homogeneity of the population and the traditional Tswana settlement pattern the pre-colonial period saw the building of centralized political institutions and state capacity, something that has formed the basis of the current institutional safeguard against becoming the victim of a curse. Second, the current politico-economic elite is to a large extent constant with the pre-colonial and colonial traditional elites, e.g. the current president Ian Khama is the son of the first president Seretse Khama who in turn, before independence, was the heir to the throne in the largest Tswana society. The consistency in benevolent leadership has been a positive force in the sense that there are established principles around accountability and responsibility between the leader and his subjects, principles that have ensured against the creation of a predatory state. The path-dependency in political institutions and leadership has, consequently, often been cited as preserving political stability (Acemoglu and Robinson 2010; Acemoglu *et al.* 2003; Robinson and Parsons 2006) and good governance. What must be remembered it that it is lacking incentives for the type of structural change that could take Botswana out of the trap. The Tswana elite during colonial days was made up of large cattle holders who benefited from the establishment of the beef export sector. Now their heirs are living well off diamond extraction. The elite has moved over from controlling the traditional authorities to controlling the state and as long as it benefits from the existing institutional structures it will opt for structural status quo. It is not until alternative interests also control the state that government policies can be expected to change and potentially seriously push for diversification and transformation of the economy.

Considering the political stability, successful social development and miraculous economic growth of Botswana since independence – how bad is the natural resource trap? It depends on how long the diamond deposits will continue to produce as they do today. No-one knows when Botswana will run out of diamonds. Some say in 20 years, others that there is no end in sight for the current export-led growth. What we do know is that as long as the country stays a case of pre-modern growth without structural transformation (Hillbom 2008) it is poorly prepared for that day whenever it comes.

Note

1 The author wishes to recognize the valuable comments from her colleagues Erik Green and Tobias Axelsson, at the Department of Economic History, Lund University.

References

Acemoglu, D. and Robinson, J.A., 2010. Why is Africa poor? *Economic History of Developing Regions*, 25(1), pp. 21–50.

Acemoglu, D., Johnson, S. and Robinson, J., 2003. An African success story: Botswana. In D. Rodrik, ed. *Search of Prosperity: Analytic Narratives on Economic Growth*, Princeton, NJ: Princeton University Press, pp. 80–119.

African Economic Outlook, 2012. Botswana, AfDB, OECD, UNDP, UNECA. Available at: www.afdb.org/fileadmin/uploads/afdb/Documents/Publications/Bostwana%20Full%20PDF%20Country%20Note.pdf.

Allen, T. and Heald, S., 2004. HIV/AIDS policy in Africa: what has worked in Uganda and what has failed in Botswana? *Journal of International Development*, 16(8), pp. 1141–1154.

Arntzen, J. and Silitshena, R., 1989. Access to land and farm income in Botswana. In K. Swindell, J.M. Baba and M.J. Mortimore, eds. *Inequality and Development: Case Studies from the Third World*. London: Macmillan Publishers Ltd., pp. 158–188.

Auty, R.M., 2010. Elites, rent cycling and development: adjustment to land scarcity in Mauritius, Kenya and Côte d'Ivoire. *Development Policy Review*, 28(4), pp. 411–433.

Auty, R.M., 2001. *Resource Abundance and Economic Development*, Oxford: Clarendon Press.

Bain and Company, 2013. *The Global Diamond Report 2013: Journey through the Value Chain*, Antwerp, Belgium: Antwerp Diamond Center.

Baumol, W.J., 1967. Macroeconomics of unbalanced growth: the anatomy of urban crisis. *The American Economic Review*, 57, pp. 415–426.

Beaulier, S.A. and Subrick, J.R., 2006. The political foundations of development: the case of Botswana. *Constitutional Political Economy*, 17(2), pp. 103–115.

Bolt, J. and Hillbom, E., 2013. *Social Structures and Income Distribution in Colonial sub-Saharan Africa: The Case of Bechuanaland Protectorate 1936–1964*, Lund, Sweden. Available at: www.aehnetwork.org/working-papers/.

Bolt, J. and Hillbom, E., 2015. The role of the formal sector in the Bechuanaland Protectorate economy, 1900–1965. *Economic History of Developing Regions* (in press).

Botswana International Merchandise Trade Statistics (BIMTS), 2014. *Monthly Digest Statistics Botswana, 2014/01*, Statistics Botswana.

Brunnschweiler, C.N., 2008. Cursing the blessings? Natural resource abundance, institutions and economic growth. *World Development*, 36(3), pp. 399–449.

Brunnschweiler, C.N. and Blute, E.H., 2008. The resource curse revisited and revised: a tale of paradoxes and red herrings. *Journal of Environmental Economics and Management*, 55, pp. 248–264.

Carlsson, E., 2003. *To Have and to Hold: Continuity and Change in Property Rights Institutions Governing Water Resources among the Meru of Tanzania and the BaKgtala in Botswana; 1925–2000*, Stockholm, Sweden: Almqvist and Wiksell International.

CIA, 2014. *World Fact Book*. Available at: www.cia.gov/library/publications/the-world-factbook/geos/bc.html.

Colcough, C. and McCarthy, S., 1980. *The Political Economy of Botswana: A Study of Growth and Distribution*, Oxford: Oxford University Press.

Conteh, C., 2008. Rethinking Botswana's economic diversification policy: dysfunctional state–market partnership. *Commonwealth and Comparative Politics*, 46(4), pp. 540–554.

Cooper, F., 2002. *Africa Since 1940: The Past and the Present*, Cambridge, MA: Cambridge University Press.

Corden, W.M. and Neary, J.P., 1982. Booming sector and de-industrialisation in a small open economy. *The Economic Journal*, 92, pp. 825–848.

Frankema, E., 2010. Raising revenue in the British empire, 1870–1940: how "extractive" were colonial taxes? *Journal of Global History*, 5(3), pp. 447–477.

Gallup, J.L., Sachs, J.D. and Mellinger, A.D., 1999. Geography and economic development. *International Regional Science Review*, 22(2), pp. 179–232.

Gaolathe, B., 1997. Development of Botswana's mineral sector. In J.S. Salkin *et al.*, eds. *Aspects of the Botswana Economy*. Gaborone: Lentswe La Lesedi, pp. 401–431.

Good, K., 1993. At the ends of the ladder: radical inequalities in Botswana. *The Journal of Modern African Studies*, 31(2), pp. 203–230.

Good, K., 1994. Corruption and mismanagement in Botswana: a best case example? *The Journal of Modern African Studies*, 32(3), pp. 499–521.

Gulbrandsen, O., 1996. *Poverty in the Midst of Plenty*, Bergen: Norse Publications.

Gylafson, T., Herbertsson, T.T. and Zoega, G., 1999. A mixed blessing: natural resources and economic growth. *Macroeconomic Dynamics*, 3, pp. 204–225.

Gylafson, T., Herbertsson, T.T. and Zoega, G., 2001. Nature, power and growth. *Scottish Journal of Political Economy*, 48(5), pp. 558–588.

Habakkuk, H., 1962. *American and British Technology in the Nineteenth Century*, Cambridge, MA: Cambridge University Press.

Harvey, C. and Lewis Jr, S.R., 1990. *Policy Choice and Development Performance in Botswana*, London: Macmillan in association with the OECD Development Centre.

Heald, S., 2006. Abstain or die: the development of HIV/AIDS policy in Botswana. *Journal of Biosocial Science*, 38(1), pp. 29–41.

Herbst, J., 2000. *States and Power in Africa: Comparative Lessons in Authority and Control*, Princeton, NJ: Princeton University Press.

Hesselberg, J., 1985. *The Third World in Transition: The Case of the Peasantry in Botswana*, Uppsala, Sweden: Scandinavian Institute of African Studies.

Hill, C.B., 1991. Managing commodity booms in Botswana. *World Development*, 19(9), pp. 1185–1196.

Hillbom, E., 2008. Diamonds or development? A structural assessment of Botswana's forty years of success. *The Journal of Modern African Studies*, 46(2), pp. 191–214.

Hillbom, E., 2010. Institutions, equity and distribution of resources in Kgatleng District, Botswana. *Development Southern Africa*, 27(3).

Hillbom, E., 2012. Botswana: a development-oriented gate-keeping state. *African Affairs*, 111(442), pp. 67–89.

Hillbom, E., 2014. Cattle, diamonds and institutions: main drivers of Botswana's economic development, 1850 to present. *Journal of International Development*, 26(2), pp. 155–176.

Hirschman, A.O., 1958. *The Strategy of Economic Development*, New Haven, CT: Yale University Press.

Iimi, A., 2006. *Did Botswana Escape from the Resource Curse?*, IMF Working Paper No. 138, Washington D.C.

Jerven, M., 2010. Accounting for the African growth miracle: the official evidence – Botswana 1965–1995. *Journal of Southern African Studies*, 36(1), pp. 73–94.

Kaufmann, D. and Kraay, A., 2002. Growth without governance. *Economica*, 3(1), pp. 169–229.

Lawry, S., 1983. *Land Tenure, Land Policy, and Small Livestock in Botswana*, Madison, WI: Land Tenure Center, University of Wisconsin.

Leite, C. and Weidmann, J., 1999. *Does Mother Nature Corrupt? Natural Resources, Corruption, and Economic Growth*, IMF Working Paper No. 99/85, Washington D.C.

Leith, J.C., 1997. Growth and structural transformation in Botswana. In J.S. Salkin *et al.*, eds. *Aspects of the Botswana Economy*. Gaborone: Lentswe La Lesedi, pp. 21–35.

Leith, J.C., 2005. *Why Botswana Prospered*, Montreal and Kingston, Canada: McGill-Queen's University Press.

Lekoko, R.N. and van der Merwe, M., 2006. Beyond the rhetoric of empowerment: speak the language, live the experience of the rural poor. *International Review of Education*, 52(3–4), pp. 323–332.

Lewin, M., 2011. *Botswana's Success: Good Governance, Good Policies, and Good Luck.*, Washington D.C.: World Bank.

Makgala, C.J., 2006. *Elite Conflict in Botswana: A History*, Pretoria, South Africa: Africa Institute of South Africa.

Masire, Q.K.J., 2006. *Very Brave or Very Foolish? Memoires of an African Democrat*, Gaborone: Macmillan Botswana Publishing Co (Pty) Ltd.

Mbabazi, P. and Taylor, I., eds., 2005. *The Potentiality of "Developmental States" in Africa: Botswana and Uganda*, Dakar: CODESRIA.

Mgadla, P.T., 1998. The kgosi in traditional Tswana setting. In W.A. Edge and M.H. Lekorwe, eds. *Botswana: Politics and Society*. Pretoria, South Africa: J.L. van Schaik Publishers, pp. 3–10.

Mikesell, R.F., 1997. Explaining the resource curse, with special reference to mineral-exporting countries. *Resources Policy*, 23(4), pp. 191–199.

Mkandawire, T., 2001. Thinking about developmental states in Africa. *Cambridge Journal of Economics*, 25(3), pp. 289–314.

Mpabanga, D., 1997. Constraints to industrial development. In J.S. Salkin *et al.*, eds. *Aspects of the Botswana Economy*. Gaborone: Lentswe La Lesedi.

Nthomang, K., 2004. Relentless colonialism: the case of the Remote Area Development Programme (RADP) and the Basarwa in Botswana. *The Journal of Modern African Studies*, 42(3), pp. 415–435.

Nurkse, R., 1953. *Problems of Capital Formation in Underdeveloped Countries*, Cambridge, MA: Cambridge University Press.

Owusu, F. and Ismail Samatar, A., 1997. Industrial strategy and the African state: the Botswana experience. *Canadian Journal of African Studies/La Revue canadienne des études africaines*, 31(2), pp. 268–299.

Papyrakis, E. and Gerlagh, R., 2004. The resource curse hypothesis and its transmission channels. *Journal of Comparative Economics*, 32(1), pp. 181–193.

Parsons, N. and Crowder, M. eds., 1988. *Monarch of All I Survey: Bechuanaland Diaries 1929–37*, Gaborone: The Botswana Society.

Peters, P., 1994. *Dividing the Commons: Politics, Policy, and Culture in Botswana*, Charlottesville, VA: University Press of Virginia.

Phaladze, N. and Tlou, S., 2006. Gender and HIV/AIDS in Botswana: a focus on inequalities and discrimination. *Gender and Development*, 14(1), pp. 23–35.

Van der Ploeg, F., 2011. Natural resources: curse or blessing? *Journal of Economic Literature*, 49(2), pp. 366–420.

Republic of Botswana, 2003. *National Development Plan 9 OR Agricultural Statistics Report 2001*, Ministry of Finance and Development Planning.

Robinson, J.A. and Parsons, Q.N., 2006. State formation and governance in Botswana. *Journal of African Economies*, 15(Supplement 1), pp. 100–140.

Rostow, W.W., 1960. *The Stages of Economic Growth: A Non-Communist Manifesto*, Cambridge, MA: Cambridge University Press.

Sachs, J.D. and Warner, A.M., 1997. *Natural Resource Abundance and Economic Growth*, HIID Working Paper, Cambridge, MA.

Sachs, J.D. and Warner, A.M., 1999. The big push, natural resource booms and growth. *Journal of Development Economics*, 59(1), pp. 43–76.

Sachs, J.D. and Warner, A.M., 2001. The curse of natural resources. *European Economic Review*, 45(4–6), pp. 827–838.

Samatar, A.I., 1999. *An African Miracle: State and Class Leadership and Colonial Legacy in Botswana Development*, Portsmouth, NH: Heinemann.

Schapera, I., 1994. *A Handbook in Tswana Law and Custom: Compiled for the Bechuanaland Protectorate Administration*, Münster-Hamburg: LIT Verlag.

Schapera, I. and Comaroff, J., 1991. *The Tswana*. Revised edition. London: Kegan Paul International.

Silitshena, R.M.K. and McLeod, G., 1998. *Botswana: A Physical, Social and Economic Geography*. Second edn. Gaborone: Longman Botswana Ltd.

Siwawa-Ndai, P., 1997. Industrialisation in Botswana: evolution, performance and prospects. In J.S. Salkin *et al.*, eds. *Aspects of the Botswana Economy*. Gaborone: Lentswe La Lesedi, pp. 335–367.

Transparency International, 2014. *Corruption Perception Index 2013*. Available at: http://cpi.transparency.org/cpi2013/results/.

UNDP, 2010. *Assessment of Development Results: Botswana – Evaluation of UNDP Contribution*. Available at: www.undp.org/evaluation/documents/ADR/ADR_Reports/Botswana/ADRBotswana.pdf.

World Bank, 2014. *World Bank Indicators*. Available at: http://data.worldbank.org/products/wdi.

5 Oil as sweet as honey

Linking natural resources, government institutions and domestic capital investment in Nigeria 1960–2000

Hanaan Marwah

Introduction: the oil curse in Nigeria

Nigeria was a classic example of a country with a "resource curse" in the four decades following its Independence from Britain in 1960. The Nigerian government received oil-derived revenues of more than $300 billion between 1960 and 2000, while real per capita income fell over the same period. Many of the symptoms of an "oil curse" are either consistent with the Nigerian case and in some cases were documented in detail by Nigeria scholars and then applied to resource-rich countries more generally. Scholars of the "curse", such as Collier, who has written more extensively than any other economist on long-run Nigerian economic growth trends (Bevan *et al.* 1999), have found that during the oil boom a typical curse pattern applied: there is some evidence of Dutch disease (Corden 1984, pp. 362–363; Ezeala-Harrison 1993, pp. 197–199; Sala-i-Martin and Subramanian 2008, p. 79), poorly managed oil price volatility (Bevan *et al.* 1992) and perhaps most prominently a negative shift in the quality of government institutions (Collier 2008, p. 47).

The economic effects of the "oil curse" in Nigeria can be seen most clearly and unambiguously in the changing pattern of domestic capital investment. Under healthy economic conditions, the revenues derived from oil – or any other commodity – need to be invested in domestically produced capital goods including physical infrastructure and buildings, which then form the basis for further, more diversified economic growth. Unlike equipment, which can be imported, buildings and other structures must be "produced" domestically, and the construction sector therefore has a pivotal role in supplying the non-tradable capital goods critical for economic growth (Bevan *et al.* 1990, p. 152). Any problems in transforming income into construction would also have affected returns on tradable capital goods, magnifying the impact of construction on economic growth. In Nigeria, however, the start of the oil boom in 1973 increased rent seeking by government officials, diverting most of the funds allocated for investment (Marwah 2014), and the quality of government institutions deteriorated, creating further barriers to investment and growth whose legacy has persisted, saddling the Nigerian economy with a long-term resource curse it has not yet overcome.

An examination of the connections between natural resources, domestic capital investment and government institutions illustrates the impact of oil revenues in the Nigerian context. The interactions between the three were shaped by specific historical circumstances, some specific to Nigeria, and others reflecting the prevailing international environment. This blend of historical circumstances, unconnected directly to the oil itself, created the conditions necessary for the "oil curse". These historical factors were so influential that in Nigeria at least, this chapter argues that oil greatly amplified some growth-hampering effects which would have happened anyway, as well as created a large opportunity cost by diverting resources from oil into other, less productive, forms of investment. The evolution of government institutions in particular bears mentioning. Although Nigeria as a case study fits well into the literature about the array of policy problems typical of natural resource booms (Gelb and associates 1988), the impact of rent-seeking elites in capturing oil resources from the state (Auty and Gelb 2001), while not unique to Nigeria, was extreme in the Nigerian case (Sala-i-Martin and Subramanian 2008, pp. 63, 76). This chapter's use of investment trends and resources offers a methodology with which to analyse the impact of this rent seeking, which by definition is illicit and ordinarily is therefore difficult to measure. It offers an outline of the timing and character of the rent seeking: it started significantly in the colonial period with the introduction of the "contracting system", before oil was discovered, and gradually increased using public sector "investment" contracts as a major mechanism to transfer rents to the private sector.

The structure of the chapter is as follows. First, it discusses the historical link between natural resources and investment in Nigeria and reviews the experience of previous resource booms. Second, it discusses the critical new elements of the oil "curse" and why they had such a negative impact on growth. Third, it concludes by discussing the nature of the three-part relationship between natural resources, government institutions and domestic capital investment. This chapter considers all major forms of non-agricultural fixed capital investment including buildings (houses and factories, social buildings including schools and hospitals) and construction (including infrastructure), as they had important roles in creating growth, but failed to develop in parallel with the expansion of the oil economy.

Nigerian experience with earlier natural resource booms

Natural resources were not always a "curse" in Nigeria. A long-run view of growth shows that earlier resource booms from exporting cash crops resulted in significant improvements in living standards due to increases in private sector domestic capital investment in buildings. The booms were driven by improvement in transportation links between Africa and Europe and within Nigeria. These improved the terms of trade for producers and incentivized a boom in the production of cash crops which were exchanged for imported consumer goods (Myint 1958, p. 327; Helleiner 1966, pp. 10–12; Austin 2008, p. 614).[1] As with oil later in the century, changes in world prices for the exported crops exacerbated fluctuations in incomes, but the positive impact of these booms on living standards is clearly demonstrated by the increased scale of imports of consumer and investment goods. On the other hand, although colonial government institutions were relatively strong and capable, they served imperial interests and not long-term Nigerian domestic interests, so there was little investment in social spending and no diversification of the economy from production into processing of primary products or other forms of manufacturing. While it was in imperial interests to boost the cash crop export market, which had a positive "trickle down" impact on farmers which generated investment, it was only in the 1950s – when the imperial ideology towards its colonies shifted and Nigerians gained more autonomy – that the funds from the boom were invested in social and industrial projects.

The first post-slave trade export boom began towards the end of the nineteenth century, and was catalysed by the introduction of a regular mail steamship service between Europe and West Africa from Europe in 1852 (Pedler 1974, p. 41) and up the Niger River from 1857 which increased access to and competition for the Nigerian market (Dike 1956, pp. 114, 213). This nineteenth century Niger Delta trade was initially dominated by mostly Liverpool-based companies exporting goods such as palm oil, ivory and timber and importing salt, textiles and other manufactured goods. At the same time, world demand was growing for palm oil, which had industrial uses and was a key ingredient in soap and the Niger Delta trade became hugely significant. The second export boom was catalysed by the building of a railway network between 1898 and 1916. This was paid for by the colonial territory itself on the strength of its export revenues, which again significantly widened the export market for Nigerian crops, which until then had been principally focused around the river system (Walker 1959, pp. 67–70; Williams 1976, pp. 18–19). The railway had an explosive impact on the terms of trade for exports coming from northern Nigeria, where groundnut production boomed (Pedler 1974, p. 168). Other changes such as improvement of the Lagos port facilities also helped to facilitate the rise in exports (Walker 1959, pp. 28–29; Olukoju 2004, pp. 15–17). Broadly, palm oil and kernels were exported from the east, cocoa and palm kernels from the west and groundnuts and cotton from the north. Volumes of exports rose almost continuously from 1900 until 1960 (Figure 5.1). Prices dropped in the 1920s and again in the 1930s during the worldwide depression, but overall there was a dramatic and almost continuous rise in import purchasing power during the twentieth century until Independence in 1960, with a particular increase during the commodity price boom after the Second World War (Helleiner 1966, p. 5; Kilby 1969, p. 8).

The colonial institutional framework for the early booms included the European trading firms, the colonial government, and later the government-run marketing boards. They were relatively effective in achieving their goals. From the early twentieth century expatriate trading firms made profits by buying export produce from Nigerian middlemen and farmers. Government-run marketing boards then took over control of exports in 1939 from the expatriate trading

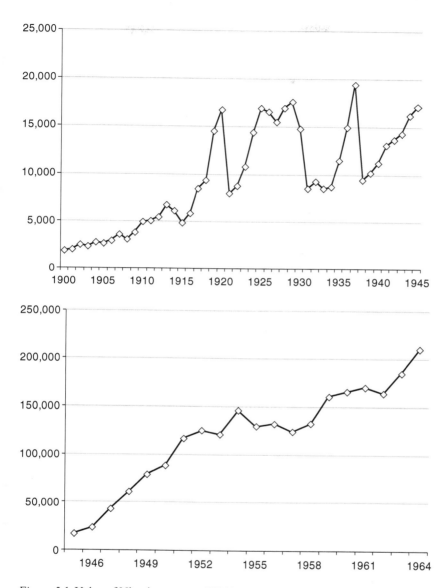

Figure 5.1 Value of Nigerian exports (£'000) 1900–1945, 1945–1964 (source: (Helleiner 1966, pp. 492–493, Table IV-A-1).

firms, in order to secure British access to raw materials during the Second World War. The boards were also supposed to smooth out export earnings for farmers by paying them a fixed price for their produce, insulating them from world market prices, though in practice they also became the primary instruments for taxing agricultural income, acting as a sales tax on exports. During the war, the buying prices of cocoa and other products were deliberately lowered by the colonial government in order to stockpile foreign exchange in London to reduce Nigerian demand for imports, to control inflation and thereby support the wartime metropolitan economy (Deutsch 1995, pp. 208–212). This caused a significant fall in producer incomes during the war; Deutsch shows in his study of the cocoa marketing boards that an index of incomes from cocoa measuring 100 in 1936/1937 was at 40 by 1947/1948 (Deutsch 1995, p. 221). After the war, prices received by farmers slowly rose and marketing boards, which in the 1950s changed into funding bodies for regional governments, received back the surpluses which had been stockpiled during the war. This led to another commodity boom, as farmers and governments benefited doubly from high commodity prices during the 1950s and gained access to previous surpluses. Some of the impact of this on investment trends can be seen in Table 5.1.

The colonial programme of investment was limited to its imperial goals. The export boom was encouraged to benefit British trading firms, and then colonial marketing boards, above all. The colonial government worked with the banks and trading firms to ensure that most African traders did not get access to bank lending which might have allowed them to compete with the firms (Williams 1976, pp. 18–19). The most significant action that the colonial government made in investment was in organizing the building of the railway; the agricultural market itself was owned and organized locally by Africans. Apart from this there was little "social" spending and no industrial investment. Indeed, a "modern" Nigerian manufacturing industry was discouraged by the British government, which did not want to crowd out manufactured imports already being made cheaply to scale elsewhere in the Empire (Dike 1956, p. 114). There was, in fact, almost no large-scale, mechanized industry in Nigeria until the 1950s as a result, and even in Lagos before 1951 there were fewer than 15 large industrial entities (Mabogunje 1968, p. 255). Foreigners who might have invested in Nigeria's vast internal market were barred from buying land in order to safeguard agricultural land for the export market (Liedholm 1970, pp. 55, 60). Therefore, even this commodity boom had elements of a resource curse, as colonial economic policies distorted the patterns of Nigerian investment. The best counterfactual for the type and volume of industry which might have developed had it been encouraged instead of suppressed by the colonial regime is the "explosion" of new industry that emerged when the government did start to encourage these projects

Table 5.1 Comparison of estimates of fixed capital formation 1948–1952 (£m)

Source	1948	1949	1950	1951	1952
Earlier (Unpublished) Official Series	13.6	20.8	17.8	22.8	
Prest and Stewart	36.6				
Hawkins	20.6	30.1			
International Bank and Official Series			36.6	42.0	55.7
Okigbo			30.8	42.0	54.0
Aboyade				41.8	55.3

Source: Aboyade (1966, p. 63).

in the 1950s, which ranged from manufacturing everything from textiles to metal products and are discussed later in the chapter. Of course, the 1950s had the particular benefits of a broader international postwar economic boom environment, but many products were made for the local market and are evidence of its attractions.

On the whole, however, in spite of limited public sector investment, higher agricultural incomes from the export booms led directly to increases in domestic capital investment, and higher land values. There was, for example, growing investment in mostly imported permanent building materials, such as the widespread shift towards the use of imported cement and iron (Inikori 2002, pp. 288, 456–458).[2] Thatched and flat mud roofs were already being replaced with corrugated iron roofing in towns by the end of the nineteenth century, but this accelerated hugely during this period, while imports of cement rose from 6,000 tons of cement in 1913 (Pugh and Ajayi 1990, p. 10), and 40,000 to 80,000 annually between 1925 and 1945 (Kilby 1969, p. 101), to 368,100 in 1954 (Federal Office of Statistics 1961). By the 1930s corrugated roofing and cement block walls were widespread, especially in cities, and economists in the 1960s remarked on the visible link between investment in buildings and Nigeria's export-led economic transformation. One noted that

> significant growth must have taken place in the decades following the First World War. For example, of the existing residential buildings in the towns, those constructed with corrugated iron sheets and aged between fifteen and forty years seem to dominate the sprawling landscape.
> (Aboyade 1966, pp. 13–14)

A farmer who left the Nigerian region of Ondo in 1910 noted on his return in 1926 that "many houses had iron roofs and people told him that the money to buy such roofs came from cocoa" (Berry 1970, p. 25). In agricultural southern Nigeria, in Ibadan the customary "rent" required for land use increased demand for cocoa growing land (Berry 1970, p. 21). This was part of a more general trend across West Africa where participation in the agricultural export market gave land "scarcity value" (Hopkins 2009, pp. 169–170). The introduction of new building materials also caused property values to increase, which had a trickle-down effect on farmers in towns across Nigeria, and encouraged others to invest similarly (Mabogunje 1968, pp. 209–210).

The colonial government only played a more active and productive role in investment in the 1950s for two reasons. The first was that colonial policy changed to encourage some industrial and social investment (Havinden and Meredith 1993). The second was that the colonial government increasingly gave some internal political autonomy to Nigerians, which accelerated in the mid-1950s. Some power was devolved to the three Nigerian regions, representing the north, east and west, with Lagos administered separately. When power was transferred to regional governments the agricultural marketing boards, previously organized by commodity, were reconstituted by region and the boards were the main funding sources for government investment spending. These "Nigerian" governments had a greater desire to invest. Schools, roads and electricity production started to be organized on a large scale in the 1950s, mostly funded from these taxes on agricultural exports. Free primary education was introduced in western Nigeria in 1955, which also helped drive the significant rural-urban migration in the 1950s and 1960s, particularly to booming industrial and administrative cities like Lagos, which helped drive even more domestic capital investment (Helleiner 1966, p. 39). More concentrated cities helped to develop economies of scale in infrastructure such as roads and electricity production. Spending on industry also increased during the 1950s. Investment largely came from the private sector but with strong government incentives, including tax holidays, tariff protection and the building of industrial estates. These government incentives were made even stronger after 1957 (Oyejide 1975, p. 22). From 1955 onwards a fall in export prices hurt the marketing boards and consequently restricted regional spending power to some degree (Aboyade 1966, pp. 145–146).

These pre-oil resources booms are therefore highly suggestive examples of some successful resource management. The governing institutions, the colonial government, trading houses and later marketing boards had an imperial rather than national concept of public service, but the two were also not wholly separate. To the extent that imperial and national economic priorities overlapped they therefore acted as effective institutions in implementing their projects. They also created an environment within which Nigerians developed the export market, and reinvested the proceeds, though they also suffered from a number of restrictions on their economic activity. The agricultural nature of the boom, which connected farmers closely to exports, assisted in helping ensure that the management of the boom was relatively transparent and that a wider group benefited, though clearly not as much as they could have had higher living standards been a primary government objective.

Why oil was different

Oil was discovered in commercial quantities in 1957/58, and by 1960 Nigeria was producing as much crude oil as it was consuming, though oil was only a small part of Nigerian government revenue for most of the 1960s. This changed when production expanded significantly before the civil war started in 1967 due in part to construction of pipeline infrastructure, making it the country's primary source of foreign exchange (Watts and Lubeck 1983, p. 106; Bevan et al. 1992, p. 7). There was a change again in October 1973 when the Arab oil embargo during the Yom Kippur war caused oil prices to rise exponentially, instantly transforming the country's fortunes. While broadly referred to here as the oil boom, Nigeria from 1973 to 1985 actually witnessed two extraordinary mini-booms, or oil price shocks, 1973–1974 and 1979–1980. The export component of GDP (in 1970 prices) was N1,855 million in 1970, and N3,295 million by 1973, where it stayed at approximately this level until the end of the decade

(Bevan et al. 1992, p. 9). The impact of more exports and higher prices was amplified by changes in the Nigerian government share of oil revenue during the oil boom, and over the 1970s the Nigerian government share of petroleum profit increased from 50 per cent to 85 per cent (Onoh 1983, p. 74). In addition, the Nigerian government borrowed against these revenues to further increase its funds available, which created significant problems when prices and production dropped in the 1980s, and Nigeria struggled to repay its debt. Unlike the earlier booms, the revenues from this boom flowed through the national oil company to various federal Nigerian government entities, to be transmitted onwards – in principle – to provincial and local authorities.

For mechanical reasons the increasing dependence on oil created new problems. Nigeria's balance of payments position was increasingly dictated by unpredictable oil prices and rapidly growing and difficult to control demand for imports, which affected spending power in all areas, including investment. This unstable position led to a volatile trade policy, which was tightened during the civil war (1967–1970), and was then actively managed in an attempt to maintain a balanced current account (Bevan et al. 1992, p. 14). This had important implications for the many sectors of the domestic economy which relied on imported materials and spare parts. In addition, other scholars have discussed the additional possible impact of Dutch disease which is not assessed in detail here. It is clear that during the 1970s and 1980s what had once been a buoyant agricultural export market and provided significant food crops for domestic consumption was at best stagnant and at worst had declined, while food imports grew exponentially (Watts 1983, p. 271).

Like the earlier booms, the oil boom caused an investment boom. There were two waves of spending during the 1970s, the first driven by an increase in government spending and the second funded by Nigerian industrialists and residential homebuilders in the late 1970s. Job lists from industrial contractors demonstrate that the same multinationals that invested in the early 1970s were reinvesting in the late 1970s, many of them extending factories built earlier. However, the ownership of many of those companies, because of the indigenization decrees of the 1970s, were by then increasingly Nigerian. Industrial investment towards the end of the 1970s and in the early 1980s was visible across urban areas including Kano and Kaduna (northern Nigeria), in Aba and Onitsha (eastern Nigeria) and in the western states and around greater Lagos (Forrest 1995, p. 41). Greater Nigerian involvement in industry in the late 1970s to early 1980s was facilitated by a combination of factors including the indigenization programme, banking reform, protectionist trade policy and easier credit (Biersteker 1987, pp. 245–253). In this respect, the Nigerian experience has often been seen as a typical, even stereotypical one, and broadly comparable with other oil-rich developing countries such as Algeria, Ecuador, Indonesia, Trinidad and Tobago and Venezuela, where Gelb says "a dominant common feature has been the speedy use of oil rents to fund domestic, and overwhelmingly public, capital formation". However, Nigeria stood out for its high private consumption relative to public consumption before the oil boom. Its initial public investment programme was focused on primary education and roads, before being expanded to industrial activity and higher education. In addition, the windfall of the first oil boom (1974–1978) was weighted more towards investment, whereas the second windfall (1979–1981) was spent more on consumption (Gelb 1986, pp. 56, 59, 62–64; Richards 1987, p. 94).

Unfortunately, though, this visible investment was a mere shadow of what it could have been. Only about a third of the construction investment recorded in national accounts between 1976 and 1985 actually took place. Public funds were diverted from their official channels into private hands, to the extent that most were never invested in the intended capital goods (Marwah 2014). This was largely linked to a clear deterioration in institutions during the oil boom, and construction not only suffered from this but was actually one of the key mechanisms through which this redistribution of funds from the public sector to the private took place. As Forrest observed, between 1974 and 1978 the "long oil boom" caused "a great expansion of trading and construction. All forms of public to private intermediary activity flourished (contracting, consultancy and commission agents) and 'arrangees' (in Nigerian parlance) had a field day" (Forrest 1995, p. 41). The impact of this lack of investment, and the deterioration of government institutions, was devastating for businesses and the population more widely, since the investment necessary to boost living standards and build the infrastructure needed for a growing, diversified private sector was simply not produced, while existing infrastructure deteriorated.

While it is possible that some of the second oil (and construction) boom of the period was rent-seeking elites spending their illicitly acquired wealth on capital goods, it is also clear that vast sums were spent on imports of consumer goods and even expatriated out of Nigeria. The more likely explanation for a first construction boom weighted towards investment and a second one weighted towards house and factories is that the enormous increase in public sector investment spending during the first oil boom building crowded out private sector investment. Evidence from the retail sector, using a combination of cement and roofing sheet sales data, suggests that affordability of materials was a key determinant of private sector building demand, and government crowding out was the primary influence on affordability (Marwah 2013). Private building, of both houses and factories, was only able to start later in the late 1970s. The public sector building boom started in 1974, weakened in the late 1970s and collapsed with oil revenues in 1983.

There are two obvious differences between the oil boom and the earlier resource booms. The first was that during the oil boom, income from oil flowed directly and almost entirely to Nigerian government entities instead of to farmers and traders as it did in the earlier booms. The Nigerian case fits neatly into the distinctions made by Auty between "point" and "diffuse" resources in his study of global booms, with the same predicted outcomes. Oil was a "point" resource with a more concentrated revenue and production pattern with the likelihood of poorer growth outcomes. Agricultural income was a "diffuse" resource, as land and production tended to be owned by smallholder farmers (although trading firms and government-controlled marketing boards had taken a portion of sales), with a greater likelihood of income benefiting a wider strata of society (Auty 1997). The second is that the scale of the oil boom was also stratospheric compared to the earlier booms. The impact of these differences was, moreover, particularly shaped by two additional, less obvious but equally important, differences. The first is that Nigeria was going through the painful transition to a completely new form of independent government which included national elections, a new federal structure and then a military government, as well as recovering from a deeply traumatizing civil war. The second is that neither the earlier booms nor the oil boom took place in a vacuum; the global environment was a critical factor. This section discusses these last two differences, the state of government institutions and the impact of the global environment, how they worked together and in particular their impact on investment trends.

In 1960 the Nigerian government was set up as a federal democracy, in which both the regions and the central government had allocations of power. However, in 1966, a military coup started an era of military domination of government which defined government and institutional leadership during the oil boom. It was punctuated by further coups, and a few years of occasional civilian rule (1979–1983). Regional politicians (political parties remained active), traditional rulers and the civil service were involved, but lost significant power relative to the increasingly centralized and relatively unaccountable military government (Bienen 1978). Even before the military takeover, however, the transition from a colonial government to national government had already caused significant shifts. As noted above, Nigerian institutions already had a greater degree of autonomy in the 1950s, but this was largely limited to regional and not national issues. In fact, the British colonial establishment deliberately created political structures which disadvantaged the nationalist leaders who had opposed them, to the benefit of regional populist politicians who lacked a national party strategy. Local politicians had largely only dealt with local social welfare. In the 1960s some contemporary writers attributed this fact to a colonial legacy of strong communal, and not national, political interests (O'Connell 1966, pp. 373–374).

One of the most significant, though gradual changes, arising from the military takeover was the centralization of power, and control of government revenue. The military regime which took control in 1975 had a programme of creation of new states that weakened regional centres of power in favour of the centre, a transition which had already begun with the growth of oil revenues, also apportioned from the centre. With its *1976 Guidelines for Local Government Reforms* the regime empowered local government to run basic services, but put local government under the ultimate authority of state governors (Vaughan 2000, pp. 139–140). This weakened traditional local authorities and existing mechanisms of political accountability. However, this centralization of power did not create a sense of public service or national economy. The sense of communal, and not national, welfare which characterized the newly independent civilian state did not go away, but went below the surface, as public officials turned their attention towards taking care of their personal and hometown networks to the disadvantage of the state, as is evidenced by the widespread diversion of public funds during the oil boom. When the oil boom began, Nigerian government structures therefore had something in common with the earlier colonial government. Like the colonial regime it had a central leadership which was not committed to the Nigerian national project, and no tested system of public accountability. In this case, though, it also lacked the discipline and order that had come with imperial rule, and which had allowed the colonial government institutions to implement their limited, though relatively successful projects. The new Nigerian government also had far greater access to resources.

The impact of this transition to a fragile and new government was a clear and gradual deterioration in government institutions, whose most obvious manifestation was that Nigerian public officials on a very wide scale used their access to government funds to divert those funds away from their officially intended use. In other words, rather than "trickling down" into the wider Nigerian economy these funds were misappropriated to benefit their own private, and intensely particular, networks. During the oil boom the scale of this diversion increased massively. Once diverted, the use of those funds could not be monitored by any formal or informal institution, creating often irresistible opportunities for state employees to appropriate funds for personal use. Richard Joseph has described this phenomenon as "prebendalism", in such effective terms that it has now become one of the most widely accepted lenses used to understand the nature of the state in Nigeria, though it has been updated by Peter Lewis and others who observed the increasing centralization and consolidation of state power during the oil bust from the late 1980s (Joseph1987; Lewis 1996, p. 80).

During the oil boom, public construction contracts in particular became a major avenue for prebendalism. Giving public construction contracts to private bodies started quite legally during the late colonial period. Before 1950 government buildings were generally built by the government-run Public Works Department to "strictly controlled standards" (Godwin and Hopwood 2000, p. 1). Over the decade of the 1950s, expenditure dramatically shifted from using outside contractors for only about 15 per cent of spending to 70 per cent by 1958 (Aboyade 1966, p. 124). Public projects had a well-established competitive tendering process, but a new policy emerged to make sure that "indigenously" run companies received the work, where possible, though even this tended to be smaller projects which required less experience and capital. The shift to contract work by newly formed companies was in some cases associated with a fall in "qualitative standards" and the rise in anecdotal "sizable contractor 'kick-back' payable to the treasury of the ruling political party and the politician responsible for the contract award" (Kilby 1969, p. 11). Between 1950 and 1963 construction costs rose 285 per cent against general inflation of 36 per cent. As Kilby argued:

> [t]he single largest component of this cost inflation can be traced to the shift from direct construction by the Ministry of Public Works of road and other public projects to contract tendering to Nigerian and, for the larger projects, expatriate construction firms.
>
> (Kilby 1969, p. 11)

Government "investment" in the agricultural sector during the same period is also widely thought to have served the same cash-transfer purpose as "investment" in construction, as did the creation of new states, which created new opportunities to reward allies with budgets, jobs and even more building contracts. Government loans served the same purpose, and Joseph notes that, "given the high level in Nigeria of the defaulting on 'development loans' from state agencies, such loan programmes can more appropriately be seen as instruments of private capital accumulation" (Joseph 1987, pp. 86–87). Many practices associated with these "ghost" contracts, including favouring certain areas for projects, over-budgeting for construction in development plans, and the avoidance of putting contracts out to bid, similarly "came to serve as effective instruments for privatizing public wealth" (Joseph 1987, p. 86). As the size of the cash payments available increased with increased government revenue from oil, their desirability increased and the rewards for political influence increased. Gaining political influence and therefore access to oil revenues became an occupation of its own and lowered the relative return of other more productive sectors, as occurred in other countries experiencing resource booms (Richards 1987, p. 97).

The problems of widespread division of government funds through investment projects were exacerbated by the contemporary international development ideology. This new thinking promoted large, centralized domestic capital investment projects which were particularly encouraged by the World Bank and International Monetary Fund. In Nigeria, this development ideology was mixed with the influence of the socialist and statist planning trends of the Soviet bloc and the postwar UK labour government (O'Connell 1966, pp. 375–376). There was no real commitment to socialism in a wider sense (O'Connell 1966, pp. 375–376) but the newly independent government enthusiastically embraced government ownership of industry. It was, however, a failure, although public investment in infrastructure before the oil boom had some success. Many of the same development planning trends adopted by Nigeria were also adopted by other countries also benefiting from resource booms at the same time, which among other effects led to high demand and shortages of certain key goods needed for investment including cement and international contracting capability, which drove up the price of investing. Although Nigeria published a series of planning documents starting in 1946 (Falola 1996, p. 47), the so-called First National Development Plan (1962–1968) doubled the budget of the preceding 1950s plan and expanded its scope. It was the planning vehicle for most government capital spending in the 1960s, which as it was written before the start of the oil boom, was designed to be funded significantly with foreign aid. Not all of this aid materialized, though not all the projects were ready to be started in any case (Dean 1972, p. 232). A series of additional "National Development Plans" followed.

The big, successful infrastructure projects in this first, pre-oil plan were over budget but mostly relatively well implemented; as Table 5.2 shows, as a consequence public sector capital investment strongly increased during the 1960s. They included the Kainji Dam project on the Niger River, which cost about £85 million, and was the size of planned expenditure for an entire region (Dean 1972,

Table 5.2 Gross fixed capital formation 1961/1962–1967/1968 (£m)

	1957 prices		Current prices	
	Public	Private	Public	Total private
1961/1962	55.5	84.7	60.3	92.2
1962/1963	55.0	82.2	64.5	95.3
1963/1964	54.8	98.2	63.4	113.6
1964/1965	58.2	108.8	68.0	127.0
1965/1966	71.8	128.8	83.8	150.3
1966/1967	77.8	130.0	90.9	151.7
1967/1968	71.3	165.5	81.3	136.1
National Plan Target			751.3	432.0
Realized Investment			453.9	664.5
Achievement of Target			60%	154%

Source: Dean (1972, pp. 208–209). Some of the data during the civil war from 1967 does not include the three eastern states.

Note
1967/1968 excludes the three eastern states.

p. 158). Construction started in 1964 and it started generating electricity in 1968. Its additional generation capacity of 320 Megawatts (MW) was supposed to allow the electricity needs of the whole country to be satisfied by 1969, and after its expansion, to satisfy demand until 1981 (Dean 1972, p. 159). Its planning and construction made it one of the most successful capital projects of the 1960s, and was to have "substantially" lowered electricity costs from the 3.5d per kwh charged in 1964/1965. A second major project in the national plan was the Second Mainland Bridge, constructed between 1965 and 1969 and an important transport link for Lagos (Dean 1972, pp. 170, 174). After the oil boom began, through a quirk of the contract system, larger projects were subject to more competition from international firms. This meant they were subject to more scrutiny, and so were less likely to become ghost contracts. As a result, some large investment projects did get built during the oil boom, and many transportation infrastructure projects were productive investments. On the whole however, most of the large government infrastructure programmes failed, in either not getting built or being built in a way that did not ultimately generate economic productivity, such as becoming failed businesses which did not cover their costs, or not were not maintained. Despite the early, pre-oil success of the Kainji dam, for example, the electricity sector was a failure during the oil boom. Over $3 billion was spent to build new electricity generation during the 1980s, but the existing generating plants were not maintained, leading to little net increase in generation and a near collapse of the state electricity company, creating a legacy of the necessity of private electricity provision that still remains today.

Government ownership of industry during the oil boom was even more problematic and unsuccessful. Government involvement in domestic cement production is a good example of this, all the more clearly so because the domestic cement industry *before* the oil boom was an example of both public and private sector industrial success. In 1966, the year before the Nigerian civil war began, domestic cement production rose to over one million tons per annum (TPA), with imports having dropped to less than 200,000 tons. In an example of mostly market-driven import substitution (though aided by government investment and tariff protection), a competitive domestic industry successfully supplanted imports during the 1960s, causing the real retail price of cement to decline (Kilby 1969, p. 13).

Although government entities made some dubious locational and design decisions about new cement plants during the 1960s before the oil boom, the problems facing domestic cement production worsened during the civil war, as Figure 5.2 shows, and accelerated after the war and during the oil boom, in spite of higher demand. Most plants, with the exception of West African Portland Cement (WAPCO, in which the government had some equity interest but not a controlling stake), were owned and controlled by one or more government entities. Nigeria started the oil boom in 1973 with five cement plants (WAPCO's Ewekoro, Nigercem, Sokoto, Ukpilla and Calabar) and by 1981 had added three entirely new ones (WAPCO's Shagamu, Benue and Ashaka). Diversion of public resources within the government cement companies caused them to gradually decline, functioning below theoretical capacity and suffering from unnecessary delays and shutdowns. A number of plants were built with an

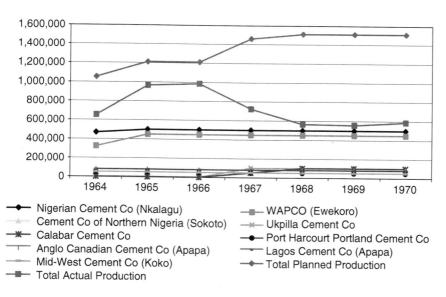

Figure 5.2 Company planned capacity vs. actual cement production 1964–1970 (tons) (sources: Total actual production: Federal Office of Statistics (1972, p. 38); Company planned production and individual company production: Ugoh (1966, p. 109)).

Note
Port Harcourt, Anglo Canadian, Lagos and Mid West companies were clinker grinding plants.

economically unviable design and/or location, making failure inevitable even with the most skilled management. Industry volume growth in the 1970s came mostly from WAPCO, which nearly doubled its capacity in 1978 to 1.45 million TPA. In contrast, the existing government-controlled plants of Nigercem, Ukpilla, Calabar and Sokoto, stopped producing or were operating much below installed capacity, and were not able to significantly contribute to production during the oil boom at all.[3]

The combined effect of these many government large-scale projects, as well as others not mentioned here in both infrastructure and industry, such as the steel production programme, had an additional negative impact of crowding out of the private sector that has been mentioned. The development theory embraced by Nigeria both relied on strong government institutions for implementation and ongoing maintenance and required careful supply and demand coordination in a range of goods and services, previously mentioned. Both of these things in the Nigerian context inevitably doomed them to fail, and significantly contributed to Nigeria missing out on the benefit of its oil boom.

Tripartite relationship: oil, government and capital investment

By the end of the 1980s, oil prices revenues declined and the Nigerian government was overburdened with debt it had taken on when times were good. In addition, because of institutional decline the Nigerian government leadership had largely lost control of the state. By the early 1990s, even when politicians wanted to invest in public goods and improve national infrastructure, they simply could not do so. For example, the Petroleum (Special) Trust Fund (PTF) was established in 1994 under the Abacha military regime as a direct response to the problem of shrinking provision of public goods. Officially, it was to channel funds directly from oil revenues to infrastructure works, principally roads, bypassing normal government procedures. Unofficially, this was an acknowledgement that if this money was channelled through federal ministries, the money would fall into the disparate patronage networks supported by individual ministries and not reach the intended targets. Similarly, the Nigerian government built the entirely new federal capital of Abuja during the late 1980s and early 1990s mostly "off budget" (Lewis 1996, p. 92), commissioning a German construction firm to build it, bypassing many government structures. Thus, resources from oil or other primary exports were a necessary but not sufficient condition for sustainable economic growth and higher living standards. Having strong, suitable government institutions was the key variable which would have allowed these resources to be used by the public sector for the capital investment necessary for growth, and managed this public investment so that it encouraged and did not crowd out private sector investment.

During the colonial era, Nigeria had colonial institutions, which emphasized process and control, and some resources from taxing exports, but made very little investment. The colonial government had little interest in boosting economic growth and living standards per se, and stifled industrial activity. However, the imperial project supported increased exports, since European trading firms and later colonial marketing boards took a share, and organized the building of the railway. Higher exports resulted in higher agricultural producer incomes. Investment was driven by the private sector investing, and was joined by the increasingly autonomous Nigerian government investing in social spending and industry, starting significantly from the 1950s. The pre-oil independent Nigerian government had the remnants of the colonial era institutions, some funding from agricultural exports and an ambitious investment plan. Although its institutions were not quite fit for purpose and had started to deteriorate, it showed some success in implementing necessary investment, and facilitating the private sector in doing the same. On the other hand, the oil-era Nigerian government was gifted with extraordinary resources, but deteriorated institutions. Although it had an even more ambitious investment plan, this left it almost incapable of implementing it, and equally even trying to without distorting private sector access to the market for construction and other goods and services needed for investment.

To what extent was the "oil curse" related to oil as a resource as compared to other natural resources? Oil flowed far more directly to the government, which made its use more vulnerable to government institutions, but this was not the only difference between the oil era and past resource booms. The process of decolonization and the shifting of Nigerian politics towards centralization and the military strongly impacted the need for those institutions. In addition, the international environment, and in particular trends in development planning, had a role in the design of state investment plans, which not only made this investment vulnerable to the weaknesses of this model in causing private sector crowding out, but also increased opportunity for funds to be diverted into private networks. In a sense, oil amplified and exacerbated what would have happened anyway.

In practical terms there was little that could have been done about the more fundamental problems faced by Nigeria such as the size and make-up of the country, its political character or its governance structure. The sheer volume of available oil revenue created an irresistible honey pot in the federal government which was and is too tempting to try to control intact, for the military and for civilian politicians. An early succession attempt in eastern Nigeria led to a bloody civil war which was relatively easily put down. Where Nigeria could have done better, though, was in managing its financial and investment policy. It sponsored a huge number of large projects through the 1970s and 1980s, paid for with both debt and oil. These projects could have been better selected and spread out, and timed so as to not drive up prices and crowd out the private sector, and to conserve government resources for future oil price fluctuations. This improved management would have been somewhat easier had investment projects not themselves been primary tools of patronage which helped maintain government control.

Notes

1 Most scholars use Myint's conceptual framework. See Helleiner (1966) for its application to Nigeria, though not all scholars agree on its extent; see Austin (2008).
2 In his examination of European goods exported to the West African coast prior to the nineteenth century, Inikori cites textiles and metal products (including nails) as significant but does not specifically cite the use of metal products as building materials.
3 "The Cement Crisis", Editorial, *Renaissance* [Nigerian newspaper], 12/9/73, 1. The article mentions the plants at Ukpilla, Sokoto and Calabar as not "effective".

References

Aboyade, O., 1966. *Foundations of an African Economy: A Study of Investment and Growth in Nigeria*. New York: Investments.

Auty, R.M., 1997. Natural Resource Endowment, the State and Development Strategy. *Journal of International Development*, 9 (4), 651–663.

Auty, R.M. and Gelb, A.H., 2001. Political Economy of Resource-abundant States. In Auty, R.M., ed. *Resource Abundance and Economic Development*. Oxford: Oxford University Press, 126–144.

Austin, G., 2008. Resources, Techniques and Strategies South of the Sahara: Revising the Factor Endowments Perspective on African Economic Development, 1500–2000. *Economic History Review*, 61 (3).

Berry, S.S., 1970. Cocoa and Economic Development in Western Nigeria. In Eicher, C.K., and Liedholm, C., eds. *Growth and Development of the Nigerian Economy*. East Lansing, MI: MSU Press.

Bevan, D., Collier, P. and Gunning, J.W., 1990. *Controlled Open Economies: A Neoclassical Approach to Structuralism*. Oxford: Clarendon.

Bevan, D., Collier, P. and Gunning, J.W., 1992. *Nigeria: Policy Responses to Shocks 1970–1990*. San Francisco: ICS Press.

Bevan, D., Collier, P. and Gunning, J.W, 1999. *The Political Economy of Poverty, Equity, and Growth: Nigeria and Indonesia*. New York: Oxford University Press.

Bienen, H. with Fitton, M., 1978. Soldiers, Politicians and Civil Servants. In Panter-Brick, K., ed. *Soldiers and Oil*. London: Frank Cass.

Biersteker, T.J., 1987. *Multinationals, the State, and Control of the Nigerian Economy*. Princeton, NJ: Princeton University Press.

Collier, P., 2008. Oil, Growth and Governance in Nigeria. In Collier, P., Soludo, C.C. and Pattillo, C., eds. *Economic Policy Options for a Prosperous Nigeria*. Basingstoke: Palgrave Macmillan.

Corden, W.M., 1984. Booming Sector and Dutch Disease Economics: Survey and Consolidation. *Oxford Economic Papers*, New Series, 36 (3).

Dean, E., 1972. *Plan Implementation in Nigeria: 1962–1966*. Ibadan: Oxford University Press.

Deutsch, J.G., 1995. *Educating the Middlemen: A Political and Economic History of Statutory Cocoa Marketing in Nigeria, 1938–1947*. Berlin: Verlag das Arabische Buch.

Dike, K.O., 1956. *Trade and Politics in the Niger Delta 1830–1885*. Oxford: Clarendon.

Ezeala-Harrison, F., 1993. Structural Re-Adjustment in Nigeria: Diagnosis of a Severe Dutch Disease Syndrome. *American Journal of Economics and Sociology*, 52 (2).

Falola, T., 1996. *Development Planning and Decolonization in Nigeria*. Gainesville, FL: University Press of Florida.

Federal Office of Statistics, 1961. *Annual Abstract of Statistics 1961.* Lagos: Federal Office of Statistics.

Federal Office of Statistics, 1972. *Annual Abstract of Statistics 1972.* Lagos: Federal Office of Statistics.

Forrest, T., 1995. *The Makers and Making of Nigerian Private Enterprise.* Ibadan: Spectrum.

Gelb, A.H., 1986. Adjustment to Windfall Gains: A Comparative Analysis of Oil-Exporting Countries. In Neary, J.P., and Van Wijnbergen, S., eds. *Natural Resources and the Macroeconomy.* Oxford: Basil Blackwell.

Gelb, A.H. and associates, 1988. *Oil Windfalls: Blessing or Curse?* New York: Cambridge University Press.

Godwin, J., and Hopwood, G., 2000. Construction Potential in Nigeria: 2000. *West Africa Committee Journal.*

Havinden, M., and Meredith, D., 1993. *Colonialism and Development: Britain and its Tropical Colonies, 1850–1960.* London: Routledge.

Helleiner, G.K., 1966. *Peasant Agriculture, Government, and Economic Growth in Nigeria.* Homewood, IL: Irwin.

Hopkins, A.G., 2009. The New Economic History of Africa. *Journal of African History*, 50 (2).

Inikori, J., 2002. *Africans and the Industrial Revolution in England.* Cambridge: Cambridge University Press.

Joseph, R.A., 1987. *Democracy and Prebendel Politics in Nigeria.* Cambridge: Cambridge University Press.

Kilby, P., 1969. *Industrialization in an Open Economy: Nigeria 1945–1966.* Cambridge: Cambridge University Press.

Lewis, P., 1996. From Prebendelism to Predation: The Political Economy of Decline in Nigeria. *Journal of Modern African Studies*, 34 (1).

Liedholm, C., 1970. The Influence of Colonial Policy on the Growth and Development of Nigeria's Industrial Sector. In Eicher, C.K. and Liedholm, C., eds. *Growth and Development of the Nigerian Economy.* East Lansing, MI: MSU Press.

Mabogunje, A.L., 1968. *Urbanization in Nigeria.* London: University of London Press.

Marwah, H., 2013. Investing in Ghosts: Building and Construction in Nigeria's Oil Boom and Bust c.1960–2000. Faculty of History, D.Phil thesis, University of Oxford.

Marwah, H., 2014. What Explains Slow Sub-Saharan African Growth? Revisiting Oil boom-era Investment and Productivity in Nigeria's National Accounts, 1975–85. *Economic History Review*, 67 (4).

Myint, H., 1958. The 'Classical Theory' of International Trade and the Underdeveloped Countries. *The Economic Journal*, 68.

O'Connell, J., 1966. The Political Class and Economic Growth. *Nigerian Journal of Economic and Social Studies*, 8, 129–140. Reprinted in Kilby, P., 1969. *Industrialization in an Open Economy: Nigeria 1945–1966.* Cambridge: Cambridge University Press [using its page numbers].

Olukoju, A., 2004. *The Liverpool of West Africa: The Dynamics and Impact of Maritime Trade in Lagos 1900–1950.* Trenton, NJ: Africa World Press.

Onoh, J.K., 1983. *The Nigerian Oil Economy.* New York: St Martin's Press.

Oyejide, T.A., 1975. *Tariff Policy and Industrialization in Nigeria.* Ibadan: Ibadan University Press.

Pedler, F., 1974. *The Lion and the Unicorn in Africa.* London: Heinemann.

Pugh, P., and Ajayi, J.F.A., 1990. *Cementing a Partnership: The Story of WAPCO 1960–90.* Cambridge: Cambridge Business Publishing.

Richards, A., 1987. Oil Booms and Agricultural Development: Nigeria in Comparative Perspective. In Watts, M., ed. *State, Oil and Agriculture in Nigeria*. Berkeley, CA: Institute of International Studies.

Sala-i-Martin, X., and Subramanian, A., 2008. Addressing the Natural Resource Curse: An Illustration from Nigeria. In Collier, P., Soludo, C.C. and Pattillo, C., eds. *Economic Policy Options for a Prosperous Nigeria*. Basingstoke: Palgrave Macmillan.

Ugoh, S.U., 1966. The Nigerian Cement Industry. *The Nigerian Journal of Economic and Social Studies*, 9 (1).

Vaughan, O., 2000. *Nigerian Chiefs: Traditional Power in Modern Politics, 1890s-1990s*. Rochester, NY: University of Rochester Press.

Walker, G., 1959. *Traffic and Transport in Nigeria: The Example of an Underdeveloped Tropical Territory*. London: HMSO.

Watts, M., 1983. *Silent Violence: Food, Famine and Peasantry in Northern Nigeria*. Berkeley, CA: University of California Press. [uses page numbers from the 2013, Athens, Georgia edition].

Watts, M., and Lubeck, P., 1983. The Popular Classes and the Oil Boom: A Political Economy of Rural and Urban Poverty. In Zartman, W.I., ed. *The Political Economy of Nigeria*. New York: Praeger.

Williams, G., 1976. Nigeria: A Political Economy. In Williams, G., ed. *Nigeria: Economy and Society*. London: RexCollings.

6 The USA as a case study in resource-based development

Gavin Wright

American development during the age of wood

North America's status as a "resource abundant" region was appreciated from the beginnings of European settlement. But little if any of the resource base was entirely a gift of nature to the economy. The temperate-zone areas of the continent were blessed with naturally fertile soils, but expansion of cropland throughout the eighteenth and nineteenth centuries required not only securing control from the native occupants but an arduous struggle to clear these lands of their forests. Thus, if any component of the country's natural resources had the character of an "endowment," it would be not minerals but forest products. Not only was timber plentiful, but the growth of supply was accelerated because it was a by-product of the ongoing process of clearing forests for farmland. Although trees are in principle renewable, from the viewpoint of the settlers the original forests seemed more like a one-time gift of nature.

As for minerals, North America was not thought to have any, or at least "none that are at present supposed to be worth the working," according to Smith (1776, p. 531). Writing in 1790, Benjamin Franklin declared: "Gold and silver are not the produce of North America, which has no mines" (quoted in Rickard 1932).[1] Northeastern cities relied on coal imports from the British Isles until the 1820s. At the same time, Great Britain was a major producer not only of coal but iron ore, copper, lead and tin, and "Britain was easily the most important mining nation in the world" until 1870 (Harvey and Press 1990, p. 65). Evidently mineral resources did not constitute a curse for the British economy in that era.

Thus it was that the first surge of industrialization in the US, though clearly following the technological lead of Great Britain, drew upon a distinctive material base. Sawmills proliferated across the countryside, making lumber the nation's second largest manufacturing industry by value added in 1860. The abundance of wood for buildings and machines was enhanced by technological progress in saws, such as the faster gang and muley saws of the 1840s, followed by the thick-bladed circular saws of the 1850s – albeit at the cost of high rates of kerf, or wastage (Rosenberg 1976). British engineers visiting in the 1850s were struck by the ubiquity of wood. The Committee on the Machinery of the USA (1855) stated: "In those districts of the United States of America that the

Committee have visited the working of wood by machinery in almost every branch of industry, is all but universal" (quoted in Hounshell 1984, p. 125). A notable example was the Blanchard lathe, invented in 1818 for the shaping of gunstocks, but adapted over time for reproducing other irregular shapes such as shoe lasts, hat blocks, spokes of wheels, and oars. Americans developed expertise in woodworking technology and a wood-based lifestyle unique in the world at that time. Even as timber prices rose over time in the east, as the frontier for forest "mining" marched steadily westward, Americans maintained their wood-using ways by transporting lumber across previously unheard-of distances, up to one thousand miles by the 1850s (Williams 1989).

Would the country's historical trajectory have been different, if the economy had not shifted from the "vegetable" to the "mineral" resource base across the nineteenth century? Perhaps less so than one might imagine. (Hounshell 1984, pp. 132–151) argues that there was no intrinsic incompatibility between wood and American mass-production techniques. Both the Singer sewing machine company and the Studebaker wagon and carriage maker deployed specialized machinery for long production runs of standardized wooden products, and Studebaker was sufficiently modern to move into wooden-bodied automobile manufacturing in the twentieth century. The largest single use of wood in the late nineteenth century was railroad construction, taking between 20 and 25 percent in most years.

But there is no need to carry the notion of an alternative wood-based American history to extremes. Despite its ostensible renewability, timber prices rose across the nineteenth century because of both growing scarcity and increasing distance to markets. As many interpreters of the British Industrial Revolution have argued, the replacement of wood by coal opened for human use a vast inventory of already-stored energy. Coal was a more efficient energy source per unit of weight and lent itself more readily to improvements in transportation.[2] The same shift in the US allowed Americans to adopt and extend British coal-using technologies, as the nation's mineral-exploration project progressed and opened up an ever-larger supply at constant or declining real cost. Nonetheless, although the early abundance of wood delayed the country's transition, the Age of Wood offers a vivid display of producers and technicians actively engaged in adapting European technologies to a very different American material environment. These traits were just as visible in the next phase of industrial development.

The rise of American minerals

George Otis Smith, director of the U.S. Geological Survey, wrote in 1919 that "the United States is more richly endowed with mineral wealth than any other country" (Smith 1919, p. 282). Smith had good reason for this assertion. In the World War I era, the country was the world's leading producer of virtually every one of the major industrial minerals of the time (Table 6.1). But was he right to refer to these resources as an "endowment?" David and Wright (1997) show that

Table 6.1 US mineral production as percentage of world total, 1870–1913

	1870	1890	1913	Rank in 1913
Bauxite		9.2	40	#2 to France
Coal	17	28	39	#1, surpassing Germany & UK
Copper	12	42	56	#1, surpassing Chile
Gold	47	27	19	#2 to South Africa
Iron ore	14	29	36	#1, surpassing Germany
Lead	5.7	22	37	#1, surpassing Spain
Petroleum	91	60	64	#1 from the start (1860)
Silver	25	41	31	#1, surpassing Mexico
Sulphur	–	–	52	#1, surpassing Italy
Zinc	2.8	17	37	#1, surpassing Germany

Sources: Adapted from Smith (1919, p. 288). Supplementary sources include *Basic Petroleum Data Book XIII* (American Petroleum Institute 1993); *European Historical Statistics* (Mitchell 1981), *International Historical Statistics: The Americas* (Mitchell 2003), *International Historical Statistics: Africa, Asia, & Oceania* (Mitchell 2003).

the US share of world mineral production in 1913 was far in excess of its share of world reserves, as estimated in the late twentieth century. For almost all economically important minerals, new deposits were discovered well into the twentieth century, and production continued to rise – not only through new discoveries but because advances in technologies of extraction, refining and transportation extended the nation's commercially viable resource base. Contrary to the intuition that the relative importance of natural resources should decline over time, the share of minerals in the labor force continued to rise until 1909, and its share in the GDP did not peak until the 1920s. The relative price of material inputs declined, and American manufacturing exports became more resource-intensive between 1880 and 1930, as the country moved into world leadership in both manufacturing and per capita income (Wright 1990). Over roughly the same period, Cain and Paterson (1986) find a significant materials-using bias in nine of twenty manufacturing industries, including many of the most prominent and successful cases.

Perhaps the best evidence that American mineral abundance was not a simple matter of endowment is that the size and importance of the sector emerged in historical time. Only during the 1820s did the search for gold in the eastern Appalachians attract substantial activity, at about the same time as a rush into lead mining in Missouri and the Galena district of the Upper Mississippi. In the same decade, regular shipments of anthracite coal into Philadelphia began, three decades after the initial discovery in the Lehigh Valley. Because anthracite was an unfamiliar form of coal, its exploitation required not just transportation infrastructure but development of appropriately adapted grates and furnaces, plus instructional booklets and advertisements with testimonials from satisfied customers. Chandler (1972) maintains that only with the opening of the anthracite fields were large-scale, steam-powered factories feasible in the US. The search for coal soon emerged as the largest and most profitable mineral project of the pre-Civil War era, with strong links to the emerging science of geology. Henry Darwin Rogers, professor of geology and mineralogy at the University of Pennsylvania, estimated in 1858 that Americans had discovered more coal than any other geologists in the world, "twenty times the area [of] all known coal-deposits of Europe" (quoted in Lucier 2008, p. 106). Figure 6.1 shows that US coal production grew rapidly thereafter, though world leadership was not achieved until the turn of the twentieth century.

The California Gold rush of the 1850s triggered a massive migration of labor and capital to the west, thereby launching a collective learning process of exploration and technological adaptation. Clay and Wright (2012) show that western settlements following the gold rush tracked a "mining frontier," driven by active exploratory efforts and advances in geological and metallurgical sciences. The spread of gold-seekers eastward led to the Comstock silver rush of 1859, which in turn generated searches for silver throughout the territories. It took several years after discovery of silver in Butte, Montana in 1875 for the managers to become aware that the silver mine was in fact one of the richest copper mines in the world! By 1882 investors in San Francisco financed a

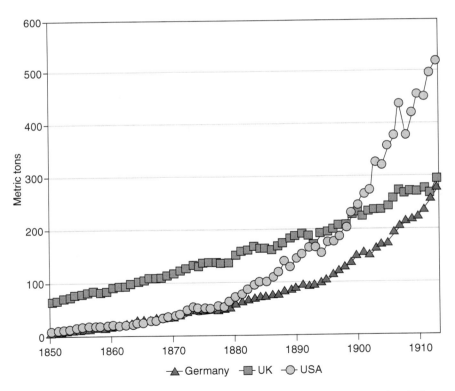

Figure 6.1 Coal production, USA, UK, Germany 1850–1913 (sources: *International Historical Statistics: Europe* (Mitchell 1992, pp. 4416–4421); *International Historical Statistics: The Americas and Australasia* (Mitchell 1983, pp. 399–400)).

project to mine and smelt copper on a mass production basis, and by 1887 Anaconda was the largest copper mine in the country, propelling the United States into world leadership in copper production. Between 1870 and 1910, the US assumed leadership or near-leadership in copper, iron ore, antimony, magnesite, mercury, nickel, silver and zinc, a correspondence in timing that can hardly have been coincidental (Schmitz 1979, pp. 9–17).

Unquestionably, geographic scale was a major factor, particularly the vast unexplored public domain that was opened for exploration after the Civil War. No isolated small country could have replicated the US minerals performance. But the record cannot be written off as a byproduct of western settlement, nor was it an automatic consequence of bigness per se. Some of the most rapid production growth occurred in older parts of the country: copper in Michigan, coal in Pennsylvania, oil in Pennsylvania and later Indiana. Even in the West, most discoveries were the result of purposeful exploration, often in areas remote from prior settlement. The large and growing US national market was indeed critical in providing incentives that underlay the process. From an economic perspective, however, the "extent of the market" was not mainly dictated by geographic area, but reflected the political unification of the country, the absence of trade barriers, the development of the internal transportation system, and effective standardization of the legal and regulatory regime pertaining to minerals. Other nations of comparable size did not begin to match US performance during this era, including Russia, China, Brazil, Australia, Canada, and for that matter, the entire British Empire – areas that we now know were as well-endowed geologically as the US, if not more so (David and Wright 1997, pp. 206–212). These comparisons suggest that a closer look at the institutional structures fostering American mineral development is in order.

American minerals and the knowledge economy

It is often asserted that the phenomenon known as the "knowledge economy" first appeared at the turn of the twentieth century, if not later. Abramovitz and David (2000) refer to the twentieth century as "the era of knowledge-based progress," while Goldin and Katz (1999, pp. 38, 43, 51) write that "something fundamental changed around the turn of the twentieth century," when "technological shocks" in scientific disciplines generated economically important findings that jolted the "knowledge industry." W.B Arthur, the theorist of Silicon Valley, has written (1990, p. 93) that

> parts of the economy that are resource-based (agriculture, bulk-goods production, mining) are still for the most part subject to diminishing returns ... [while] the parts of the economy that are knowledge-based, on the other hand, are largely subject to increasing returns,

listing computers, pharmaceuticals, missiles, aircraft, automobiles, software, telecommunications equipment and fiber optics as examples. An examination of the bases for American mineral expansion may lead us to question these popular historical demarcation lines: nineteenth vs. twentieth centuries, ideas vs. resources.

According to one conventional line of thought, an increase in output may be partitioned into a share attributable to the growth of inputs and another share attributable to the growth of output relative to inputs, the latter often identified with "technological progress." But applying such a distinction to the American minerals sector would be highly misleading. It is true that mining expansion was driven by the inputs of labor, capital and an expansion of geographic area. But the *successful* extension of the mining frontier also required advances in knowledge and technology, including the ability to recognize potentially valuable deposits, innovations in techniques of extraction, and metallurgical breakthroughs that revolutionized the separation of metals from ores, thereby vastly extending the country's commercially relevant mineral supply.[3] Over time these extensions increasingly drew upon higher-order forms of knowledge and individuals with advanced scientific training.

The growth of Comstock mining was facilitated by the Washoe pan amalgamation process for separating silver, developed in 1862 by Almarin Paul, who had come west from New Jersey in 1849. Paul began by transferring stamp-mill technology from California quartz mining and then extended it to incorporate heavy iron plates called "mullers" that would grind as well as mix the pulverized rock. The iron filings worn from the muller and pan proved to be an essential ingredient in the process, which reduced the working time from thirty days to four hours (Paul 1963, p. 66). But Paul was only the most successful of many gold rush veterans who were working along related lines. For example, when the Washoe process was found not to work well for ores with arsenic or antimony sulfides, a variant known as the Reese River process (in which the ore was roasted with salt to convert silver sulfides into silver chlorides) was developed and used in a number of new silver-mining districts. In the 1860s and 1870s, the Comstock became known as a world center for hard-rock mining techniques, the "mining school of the world" (Barger and Schurr 1944, p. 102).

Special geophysical challenges were posed by mining in Colorado, where the gold ores were found in chemical combination with sulfides, known as "sulpherets" or "refractory ores" that resisted amalgamation. Initially, the main adaptation was a local variation of the California stamp mill that gave a longer and finer crushing and a longer exposure to the action of mercury. These engineering methods were inherently limited in their ability to cope with what was in essence a metallurgical problem; hence they were commercially successful only with high-grade ores, which soon played out in the area. Numerous pseudoscientists, often self-titled professors, offered contraptions and processes to credulous mining companies, leading Rossiter Raymond, US commissioner of mining statistics, to declare that "desulphurization became the abracadabra of the new alchemists" (quoted in Fell 1979, p. 9).

Eventually Colorado investors turned to real scientists for a solution, recruiting Nathaniel P. Hill, a professor of chemistry at Brown University who supplemented his teaching with a vigorous consulting business. The answer was by no means straightforward, and after his initial trip to Colorado in 1864, Hill devoted several years to research, traveling to Britain and continental Europe to study techniques for smelting ore. In 1868 Hill built a smelter, modeled on a world-famous one that he had seen in Wales. Its costs were prohibitively high, however, and the real breakthrough came only in 1871 with the arrival of Richard Pearce, son of a Cornish miner who had studied at both the Royal School of Mines in London and in Freiberg. Pearce's new process provided the best method for separating gold from copper until electrolytic refining in the late nineteenth century. Remarkably, the method was never patented, but remained a company secret for the next thirty-three years. The success of Hill and Pearce provides a striking example of deployment of world-class scientific knowledge in the solution of a regional mining problem. Pearce's innovation quickly drew the attention of the scientific community, receiving extensive discussion in the *Transactions of the American Institute of Mining Engineers* during the 1870s.[4]

Successful development of Colorado smelting set the stage for the discovery of silver at Leadville in 1877, a bonanza in many ways endogenous to the emerging regional technology. Leadville in turn became one of the first priorities of the United States Geological Survey (USGS), newly established in 1879 as a consolidation of several existing agencies. The USGS monograph on Leadville, published in 1882, was known for years as the "miners' bible." It provided a comprehensive geological view of the structural conditions affecting the distribution of ores within a ten-mile radius. The survey's analytical maps led in turn to discoveries at Aspen and Rico, continuing the pattern of dynamic interaction among geological learning, processing technology and new discoveries (Rickard 1932, pp. 132–140). Within a few years, other mining districts were petitioning the USGS for similar surveys.

The rise of the US to world leadership in copper mining provides yet another illustration of the knowledge-based character of progress in minerals. Although the pure native coppers of the Great Lakes region were indeed a generous gift of nature, the discoveries in Montana emerged from the same exploratory process that spread gold and silver mining throughout the western states. The deeper source of national copper ascendancy, however, was a technological revolution. The major breakthroughs of the 1880s and 1890s were the adaptation of the Bessemer process to copper converting and the introduction of electrolysis to final refining on a commercial scale. Electrolysis allowed nearly complete recovery of the metal content of copper bullion, matching the naturally pure copper of Michigan. In the early twentieth century these advances were extended by use of the oil-flotation process in concentrating the ore, cutting milling costs sufficiently to allow commercial exploitation of low-grade porphyry copper ores (Schmitz 1986). In effect, advances in metallurgy created new American mineral resources by fostering rediscoveries of deposits long known but considered submarginal. Exploitation of this new resource potential in turn encouraged large-scale, nonselective mining methods, an approach first developed by Daniel Jackling, who graduated from the Missouri School of Mines in 1889 with a degree in metallurgy. The technological bases for American copper leadership were thus complex and interdependent: Jackling's method was effectively an intersectoral transfer of mass-production, high-throughput technology and organization from manufacturing to mining, made possible by prior revolutions in copper metallurgy.

Together these technological developments facilitated a steady reduction in the average metal content of American copper ore, as shown in Table 6.2. Considered in isolation, the falling share is ambiguous: it may simply indicate depletion and rising costs. But in the context of a long-term downward trend in the real price of copper, lower average metal content of ore is an index of technological progress. By contrast, in copper-rich Chile, where output was stagnant, shares averaged 10–13 percent between 1880 and 1910 (Przeworski 1980, pp. 26, 183, 197). Ultimately, however, American technology and organization were transportable internationally, and by the 1920s Chile's copper production was on its way back to world leadership. Command over technologies and organization, along with financial resources, gave American mining executives like the Guggenheim brothers great power and influence in countries like Chile that had not yet developed indigenous technical expertise and infrastructure (O'Brien 1989).

Well before the turn of the twentieth century, the payoff to higher-order knowledge in mining was recognized through indigenous institutions adapted to American conditions. Although advanced studies in geology and metallurgy were offered earlier at Harvard and Yale, the major advance on a national basis came in the wake of the California gold rush, with the 1864 opening of the first successful school of mines by Columbia College in New York City. Columbia dominated the national market for the next quarter century, sending its graduates to jobs and consulting trips throughout the western states and Mexico. An 1871

Table 6.2 Average metal content of copper ore (%)

Date	Location	Percentage copper
1800	UK average	9.27
1820–25	Cornwall	8.22
1850	UK average	7.84
1870	UK average	6.72
1880	Calumet and Hecla (Michigan)	4.81
1890	Calumet and Hecla (Michigan)	3.23
1900	Calumet and Hecla (Michigan)	2.61
1902	US average	2.73
1906	US average	2.51
1910	US average	1.88
1915	US average	1.66
1925	US average	1.54
1930	US average	1.43
1950	US average	0.89

Sources: Crowson (2012), p. 69; United States WPA (1940).

survey declared Columbia "one of the best schools in the world – more scientific than Freiberg, more practical than Paris" (Church 1871, p. 79). Training at Columbia was both theoretical and practical, interacting closely with the private sector. This market-oriented style contrasted with the European tradition of training mining engineers to serve as inspectors and in regulatory positions.

Despite Columbia's stature, and perhaps in emulation of its success, demands arose over time for mining schools in closer proximity to the mining districts. The Colorado School of Mines was the first to be set up as a separate institution, created by the territorial legislature in 1870 and open for instruction in 1873. Mining schools were subsequently established in California, Missouri, Michigan, South Dakota, Arizona, Nevada and New Mexico. At Berkeley, registration at the mining college grew tenfold between 1893 and 1903, supporting the school's claim to be "without doubt the largest mining college in the world" (Read 1941, p. 84). Although resistance to college-trained men continued to be voiced, the trend was clear. The *Mining and Scientific Press* wrote in 1915: "The fact remains that nearly every successful mining operation, old or new, is today in the hands of experienced technically trained men" (quoted in Spence 1970, p. 142). Graduates were increasingly prepared for managerial and executive as well as technical roles (Ochs 1992).

The age of petroleum

Oil is often identified as the prime candidate for "resource curse" effects of extractive activities. But in the US case, development of the petroleum industry exhibits many of the elements that were common to other minerals, as well as the evolving institutional relationships among government agencies, academic institutions and corporations. Edwin Drake's 1859 oil strike in Titusville, Pennsylvania, was in no way scientific, but it constituted one of several strategies being explored to find an inexpensive substitute for whale oil as an illuminant. The first such effort to achieve some success was a liquid distilled from coal, known as coal oil. The term "Kerosene" was coined in 1850 as the brand name for one type of lamp oil. Sold with a burner that became known as the "Kerosene lamp," the product enjoyed a boom between 1858 and 1860. One of the reasons petroleum was so quickly adopted was that it fit readily into an existing network of refineries, markets and distribution channels laid out for coal oil, not to mention the lamps themselves. Ultimately, kerosene became the generic term for all mineral-based lamp oils, including those made from petroleum (Lucier 2008, pp. 144–161, 233–237).

However rudimentary its origins, the increasing use of petroleum and the expanding range of by-products provided the "demand push" for the systematic deployment of scientific knowledge. As early as 1860–1861, J.P. Lesley included petroleum in his treatment of economic geology at the University of Pennsylvania. At Columbia, Francis L. Vinton's instruction in mining covered the drilling of artesian, brine and oil wells, while Charles F. Chandler, dean and professor of applied chemistry, devised the flash point test for kerosene and was the foremost chemical consultant for the petroleum industry at the time (Read 1941, p. 191). During the 1880s and 1890s, several pioneer geologists, notably Israel Charles White and E.B. Andrews, were employed as consultants by oil operators to help in the location of deposits in the Appalachian fields (Williamson et al. 1963, p. 441).

From Pennsylvania, the oil frontier moved westward and southward in a series of sporadic jumps, fears of exhaustion alternating with dramatic breakthroughs in new areas. The oil industry thus displayed the traits of American minerals generally, but in exaggerated fashion. One reason for this tendency to extremes is that oil is fugacious, and once a field was discovered, drillers were in fact pumping from a common pool. Extraction took place under the legal maxim known as the "rule of capture": the owner of the land on which drilling occurred was entitled to claim all of the oil extracted through that channel, regardless of its origins. This dictum has the virtue of simplicity (avoiding the disputes that would have arisen in an attempt to assign subterranean pools to various surface owners) and could be viewed as an extension of the "apex" rule in hard-rock mining, allowing those who undertook an investment to pursue the vein wherever it led. In the case of oil, however, the system generated major inefficiencies in the form of excessive drilling and extraction costs, and saddled the industry with extremes of instability in production and prices. Despite growing misgivings and conservationist concerns, the rule remained in place until the 1930s, when it was replaced by compulsory production controls (Williamson and Daum 1959, pp. 758–766; Libecap 1989).

An economist presented with a description of these institutional arrangements might well suspect that the history of American petroleum was a gigantic exercise in excessive resource-depletion, augmented by the urgency of a race to drain a common nonrenewable pool. Although aspects of such a scenario were at times on display, the record was also characterized by learning, technological improvements, and increasing deployment of advanced scientific knowledge and trained personnel. Employment of petroleum geologists dated from the 1860s, but advances were initially slow because of resistance from self-educated practitioners touting slogans such as "oil is where you find it" and "geology never filled a gas tank" (White 1970, p. 146). According to Williamson et al. (1963), much credit must go to the U.S. Geological Survey for its role in changing the attitudes of oil men towards geologists, by publishing reliable field data and popularizing the anticlinal theory of the structure of oil-bearing strata. The anticlinal theory was distinctively American in its origins and had been developed by scientists over many decades. But the theory had little practical payoff before the 1890s. A pivotal moment in industry history was the discovery in 1912 of the rich Cushing pool in Oklahoma, confirming the theory that anticlines were favorable places to find oil. In 1914 the Oklahoma Geological Survey published a structure-contour map of the Cushing field indicating that the line separating oil from water was parallel to the surface structure contours. For the next fifteen years most new crude discoveries were based on the surface mapping of anticlines (Williamson et al. 1963, pp. 45–46; Frehner 2011, pp. 98–201, 104–140).

The main advantage of oil over coal was transportability, both from the point of origin to the point of use and in moving vehicles themselves. Discoveries around Los Angeles and the San Joaquin Valley made California the nation's leading oil producer between 1900 and 1930, and the state became a symbol of the American high-mobility lifestyle of the twentieth century. Industrialization in California, which had been held back by an absence of coal, flourished under the new oil regime. Western railroad locomotives quickly switched to oil, saving more than 25 percent relative to expensive imported coal (White 1970, p. 142). The U.S. Navy also began to change fuels, quickly following Britain's historic 1911 decision to convert the battleships of the Royal Navy from coal to oil (Yergin 2011, pp. 264–265). But the primary driving force behind rising oil demand across the century was the automobile. On this frontier as well, California led the nation, dismantling its metropolitan rail systems in favor of highways and sprawling suburban developments. Although oil allowed great flexibility to firms and households, the country as a whole became quite committed to it through massive investments in an infrastructure of pipelines and roads and through its commercial and residential capital stock.

The contributions of oil-based technologies and products to American lifestyles and living standards went far beyond transportation. The rise of the US chemical industry to world leadership was closely associated with a shift in the basic feedstock for chemical plants from coal to petroleum. As technology developed, production of organic chemicals was carried on most effectively as a by-product of petroleum refining, hence closely associated with the location of petroleum supplies. Prior to the 1920s, there was little contact between petroleum companies and the chemical industry. In that decade, however, important connections emerged, through mergers, research establishments and industry-university associations. Working in close partnership with M.I.T., New Jersey Standard's research organization in Baton Rouge, Louisiana, produced such important process innovations as hydroforming, fluid flex coking and fluid catalytic cracking. Chemical engineer Peter Spitz writes:

> Regardless of the fact that Europe's chemical industry was for a long time more advanced than that in the United States, the future of organic chemicals was going to be related to petroleum, not coal, as soon as companies such as Union Carbide, Standard Oil (New Jersey), Shell and Dow turned their attention to the production of petrochemicals.
>
> (Spitz 1988, p. xiii)[5]

Petroleum-based pesticides, herbicides and fertilizers contributed directly and indirectly to unprecedented increases in American agricultural yields. The petrochemical industry has generated an astonishing number of new consumer goods: drugs, detergents, synthetic fibers, synthetic glycerin, synthetic rubber, and of course plastics. Pondering the ubiquity of oil-based products leads some social historians to assign cheap oil prime responsibility for the American ethos of mass consumption and disposability (Black 2012).

These consumption patterns were not disrupted when the US became a net oil importer in the 1950s and was then surpassed in production by the Middle East in the 1960s (Figure 6.2). But the national commitment to oil proved to be a burden after the price shocks of 1973 and 1979, brought on by production cutbacks coordinated by the Organization of Petroleum Exporting Countries (OPEC) and subsequently by the Iranian Revolution. Allowing for lags in adjustment, however, American firms and households displayed considerable flexibility and responsiveness to relative prices. Homes and industries moved away from oil in favor of natural gas or electricity (mainly generated by coal). Even the gas-guzzling American automobile increased its fuel efficiency, albeit prompted by federal legislation as well as by heightened consumer sensitivity to gas mileage. With the aid of hindsight, the crisis of the 1970s may be seen as a reflection of short-term vulnerability rather than impending long-term energy scarcity.

It is true that one of the background factors behind the crisis was the decline in US oil production after 1970. US reserves peaked in 1971 (when the Alaskan Prudhoe Bay discovery was recorded) and have generally declined since then.

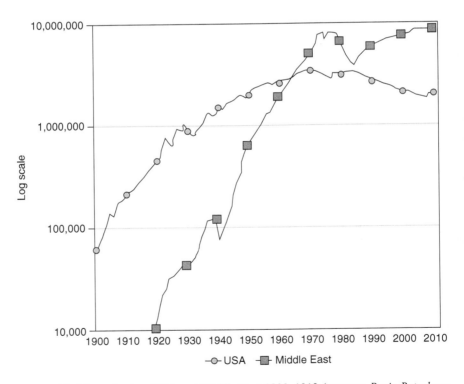

Figure 6.2 Oil production, USA and Middle East 1900–1912 (sources: *Basic Petroleum Data Book XIII* (American Petroleum Institute 1993); U.S. Energy Information Administration, *International Energy* (2013) – see www.eia.gov, accessed July 30, 2014).

This timing was predicted by geologist M. King Hubbert in a famous paper (Hubbert 1956), which subsequently attained a kind of cult status; "Hubbert's Peak" has become a popular name for forecasts of impending declines in global oil production. But in fact Hubbert's forecasts were quite far off, underestimating US oil output as of 2010 by a factor of four (Yergin 2011, p. 236). Hubbert's predictions for natural gas were equally inaccurate. Driven by new technological developments, US natural gas production has actually been rising since the mid-1980s, in contrast to the sustained decline from 1970 that Hubbert forecast (Gorelick 2010, p. 95).

Perhaps more important than production levels are the reasons for the decline in US oil production. As with other minerals, depletion is part of the explanation. The larger reasons, however, are discovery and development of oil deposits around the world, and reductions in the cost of transporting oil across long distances. The surge in US oil imports during the 1970s is better explained by the expansion of world supertanker capacity than by depletion of domestic supplies. As Edward Porter of the American Petroleum Institute wrote in 1995:

> The decline in U.S. supply after 1970 did not indicate that the U.S. was "running out" of oil, but rather that the cost associated with much of the remaining Lower 48 resources was no longer competitive with imports from lower cost sources worldwide. Consequently the decline in U.S. supply after 1970 represented not a signal of growing resource scarcity, but rather a signal of growing global resource abundance.
>
> (Gorelick 2010, p. 114)

In retrospect, the entire era of US leadership in oil production and technology was not based on geological endowment, but on precocious development of the nation's oil potential.

Recent developments in oil and gas technologies may call for revision of these statements about relative costs, but they strongly confirm the larger historical narrative. The most important innovations are horizontal drilling, 3-D seismic imaging and hydraulic fracturing. Improved control capability allows operators to drill to a desired depth and then veer at an angle or even sideways, thereby recovering a much higher yield of gas or oil from a given reservoir. Advances in microprocessing enable geophysicists to analyze vast amounts of data in three dimensions, leading to greatly improved seismic mapping of underground structures and improved success rates in exploration. Hydraulic fracturing refers to a technique by which a mixture of water with sand and chemicals is injected into a wellbore to create small fractures, along which oil and gas migrate into the well. Although the technique originated as a method for liberating "shale gas" (natural gas trapped within shale formations), after 2000 it began to be applied to the production of "shale oil" (also known as "tight oil") as well. These new techniques, which as in earlier episodes emerged from a combination of public and private research programs, opened up the prospect of commercial development of a vast oil formation known as the Bakken, which sprawls from the Williston Basin in the Dakotas across Montana into Canada. Numerous other shale formations offer oil and gas development prospects in various parts of North America (Yergin 2011, pp. 259–263, 325–332; Wang and Krupnik 2013).

These new technologies have fostered a boom in domestic natural gas output and forecasts that the US will regain its position as the world's leading oil-producing nation. Whether these scenarios are realized will depend on the outcome of the environmental debate over "fracking" and the ease with which these largely American innovations diffuse to other parts of the world. But taken together, these developments support the historical generalization that natural resources are not given by nature but by policy choices and human behavior.

The relevance of US mineral history for the resource curse debate

Many observers seem to feel that the American experience in resource-based development is too historically remote to have much bearing on contemporary policy discussions. Changes and contrasts in the economic and political context are indeed substantial, but it is more informative to try to identify these explicitly and take them into account than simply to assume irrelevance and dismiss the value of this history out of hand. This section discusses geographic size, transportation costs and environmental regulations.

It is certainly true that US leadership in mineral production, as depicted in Table 6.1 and Figures 6.1 and 6.2, is partly a function of the geographic area of the country. If we consider only countries rather than regional aggregates, the US would still be one of the top three producers of oil, coal, copper and gold even in the twenty-first century. But the country's historical record in minerals cannot be explained away as a simple consequence of size. David and Wright (1997) show that US mineral production in 1913 was far ahead of its share of world reserves, according to late twentieth-century estimates. This early development of mineral potential stood in contrast to that in other countries of comparable area, such as Canada, China, Brazil and Australia, or larger (Russia). The British government might have considered the entire British Empire as a base for exploration, but they did not, employing a total of just fifty-eight people in geological services overseas as late as 1947 (Warren 1973, p. 22).

It should also be recalled that the concept of "size" that is relevant here is *economic* scale, the space that is integrated into a unified national network for trade, migration and capital flows. Other things equal, sheer geographic size might well be a handicap for resource-based as well as other types of growth, because deposits may be too distant to be economically useful. But in the United States, the absence of internal barriers to trade and migration was enshrined in the Constitution, and prospectors could confidently explore remote parts of the country, confident that any major discoveries would soon be integrated into the national supply network. Improving access to minerals was an important motivation for extending the national rail system. Add to this the common language and relative commonality of mineral law on the federal public domain, and we arrive at the conclusion that much of US development reflected scale economies at the level of the nation. These scale economies were not given by geography, however, but instead were features of the national development process.

The dimension of scale most relevant for this chapter is that related to the knowledge economy. Surely the size of the US minerals sector provided backing for the work of the U.S. Geological Survey and professional societies such as the American Institute of Mining Engineers, with associated synergies and spillover effects. A smaller country could hardly have supported multiple degree-granting mining schools, which competed with each other for students and research support. These historical advantages must be acknowledged, but it should also be noted that in the modern era, smaller countries such as Australia, Chile and Norway have realized high returns to national investment in the knowledge foundations of resource-based development (Ville and Wicken 2013).

Another respect that differentiates the US historical experience from contemporary cases of resource-based development is that most American minerals were produced not for export but for domestic markets, and the sector grew in robust interaction with other parts of the economy, particularly cities and industry. Although little mineral exploration and development was actually sponsored by users, the extension of coal mining in the eastern states was linked to the construction of canals to supply urban markets. Canal builders were among the first aggressive promoters of the shift from firewood (which was rapidly rising in price) to anthracite coal as a home heating fuel (Adams 2014, pp. 55–70). Coal had even closer links to the nation's railroads, as the largest single item of revenue tonnage. Cheap coal provided the energy source for the iron and steel industries, which switched from charcoal to coke as fuel by the late 1850s, thereby tapping into one of the major technological trajectories of the Industrial Revolution (Allen 2009).

Complementarities among natural resources, urban growth and scale economies in production gave rise to the "American Manufacturing Belt," a contiguous area across much of the Northeast and Midwest, within which most of the nation's manufacturing was concentrated. This phenomenon is commonly cited by economic geographers as a case study in the historical persistence of industrial location (Meyer 1989; Krugman 1991). The region's centers of population and industry provided the major markets for the heavyweight producer and consumer goods produced within the region, giving the locational pattern an equilibrium character that persisted long after the center of national mineral production had shifted to the West (Klein and Crafts 2012). In its origins, however, the manufacturing belt clearly emerged from a system in which natural resources were crucial. The well-developed Great Lakes shipping system linked the iron range of northern Minnesota to the coal field of western Pennsylvania, adding the copper mines of northern Michigan as part of the bargain. The location of the automobile industry in Michigan (or at least somewhere within the region) was a logical outcome. For present purposes, the main point is that the growth of American minerals emerged not as a set of separate and distinct profit opportunities, but as an integral part of national industrial development. The process was one in which location was important, because natural resources were heavy and lost weight in processing, and transportation costs to final markets were large enough to matter.

The domestic-market orientation of most American minerals is related to the relatively small role played by foreign investment and management in the sector's development. To be sure, American mining drew upon and adapted technologies that originated abroad, and it certainly made ample use of skilled foreign-born mining labor. European investments in US mining were substantial after 1875, and foreign direct investment sometimes played a catalytic role. But in contrast to many developing countries, the American mineral industry was never dominated by foreign capital or management, and "backward integration" by outsiders to secure their own resource needs was almost unknown. For the relatively few direct investors that persisted in the US after 1900, the powerful draw of the domestic market was more likely to convert them into "American" firms than the other way around (Wilkins 1989, pp. 292–297).

In the modern global economy, the role of transportation costs in industrial location is sharply reduced. The shift from coal to oil was one of the early steps; the transformation of shipping through "containerization" was another milestone; recent revolutions in electronic communications have brought the economic "flattening" of world markets close to completion. The implication is that today's emerging resource-based economies cannot expect an easy or automatic linkage between primary production and industrial location, fostered by the "natural protection" of transportation costs. Minerals are more likely to be exported to remote users, sometimes aggravating the perception that such activities are not merely extractive but exploitative as well. But even in this setting, minerals can still generate positive linkages to other sectors in the host economy, often through services to mining and related activities.

Another important way in which times have changed is increased awareness of the environmental costs of extractive industries, accompanied by growing efforts to mitigate these costs through regulation and other policies. In nineteenth century America, environmental impacts of mining were barely recognized and rarely mentioned amidst the national and regional consensus that rapid development served the broader interest of the economy. National mining laws were silent on the environment, as were the curricula of leading mining schools (in Europe as well as in the US). When legal challenges were raised by those who suffered from externalities, the courts typically ruled in favor of the mining interest. A classic statement was by the Pennsylvania Supreme Court in 1886, in a case involving acid mine damages to private property:

> The trifling inconvenience to particular persons must sometimes give way to the necessities of a great community. Especially is this true where the leading industrial interest of the state is involved, the prosperity of which affects every household in the Commonwealth.
>
> (Smith 1987, p. 49)

Small wonder that litigation "was the handmaiden of mining," in the words of historian Malcolm Rohrbough (quoted in Bakken 2008, p. 73).

The results of this neglect were that streams in mining areas were filled with debris, mountains of tailings and slag were abandoned, forests were denuded of vegetation, fish life was destroyed by cyanide or mercury poisoning, and air was polluted by toxic discharge fumes from mills and smelters. Only when a substantial competing economic interest stood in opposition was there any possibility of slowing the mining juggernaut. One such case was the successful lawsuit by farmers in Maysville, California, against hydraulic mining, a particularly egregious technique in which the tops of hills were blasted off by powerful jets of water, in hopes of uncovering gold ore. Eschewing proposals for partial mitigation, a federal judge "perpetually enjoined and restrained" hydraulic miners from discharging or dumping into the Yuba River or its tributaries. Hydraulic mining subsequently went into decline and all but disappeared within the next few years (Smith 1987, pp. 68–73). This reversal was historic but exceptional for its time. Generally speaking, American mining regulation had little more than incremental impact prior to the federal legislative explosion of the 1960s – at which point the relative significance of the mineral sector for the national economy had markedly receded from its historic peak.

In light of these profound changes in the political and economic context, the reader may be inclined to conclude that this historical experience has little relevance for countries engaged in resource-based development in the twenty-first century. Despite a host of differences on specifics, however, some key principles still carry over. Perhaps most basic is the recognition that minerals should not be understood as mere "endowments" but as a resource base with potential for development. Realizing that potential requires investments of labor and capital, but above all, knowledge. To be sure, such investments can be made by profit-seeking multinational companies in their own interests. But even in the modern globalized economy, in which the mineral sector draws upon advanced frontiers of science-based technologies, useful forms of minerals knowledge still have strong geographically specific components. In general, countries that have exploited their resource potential successfully have been those that have invested in indigenous, country-specific knowledge and human capital pertaining to exploitation, extraction, processing, and sometimes usage of domestic resources. Because these learning processes have public-good properties, this sector deserves a legitimate place in the technology and engineering plans of developing countries with mineral potential.

The ascendancy of environmental awareness actually strengthens this case. No country today can or should expect to retrace the unregulated mineral-development path of the US. Mining companies from outside can be compelled to maintain environmental standards through taxes and other regulatory measures. But such companies will not have the same priorities as the host country, neither for environmental health nor the design of new technologies that ideally will enhance both environmental performance and industry productivity. There is substantial overlap in the technological expertise required for both of these missions, and indeed they should be viewed as a single unified undertaking. It is simply not the case that modern resource-based development is incompatible with environmental health, but the key is to internalize both goals in the process of technological development. Well-managed resource-based countries such as Australia, Canada, Chile and Norway have strong environmental movements and have taken the lead in developing environmentally friendly technologies.[6] There is no good reason why this list of success stories cannot be expanded.

Notes

1 In the eighteenth century, "mine" meant an outcropping or deposit of a mineral.
2 The major citations include Thomas (1980); Wrigley (1988, 2010); Allen (2009). Allen casts coal in the role of a "backstop" technology, whose potential was exploited through a sequence of improvements in steam engines and in iron-making. Wrigley adds that coal was "punctiform" rather than "areal," so that large volumes could move along a single route or a small number of routes.
3 A parallel process occurred in American agriculture, where the expansion of land in cultivation required ongoing innovations in cultivation practices, crop varieties and livestock, as farmers adapted to new soil and climate conditions. These processes are largely missed in analyses based on total factor productivity. See particularly Olmstead and Rhode (2008).
4 This paragraph draws on Fell (1979, pp. 11–46) and Paul (1960).
5 This paragraph draws on Nelson and Wright (1992, p. 1946).
6 For examples, see "Aussie Scientists Develop Cost-Effective Way to Treat Mining Wastewater," Mining.com (June 12, 2014); Global CCS Institute, "CCS [Carbon Capture and Storage] in Canada" (accessed July 16, 2014); Marion Tanguy, "Norway has set Europe an eco-example," *Guardian* (August 11, 2010); US AID and APEC, "Chile Environmental Industry 2011: Case Study." An example from recent US history is the extraction-electrowinnowing (SX-EW) process, which contributed to the revival of the copper industry in the 1990s, after it had been pronounced dead in the mid-1980s. The process separates the mineral from the ore more effectively and is especially useful for the leaching of mine dumps from past operations. Although the SX-EW process is now used globally, it is best suited for countries with stringent environmental regulations, which require recovery of sulfur emissions from smelting operations, this providing a low-cost source of sulfuric acid for the process (Tilton and Landsberg 1999, p. 131).

References

Abramovitz, M. and David, P.A., 2000. Growth in the Era of Knowledge-Based Progress. In S.L. Engerman and R.E. Gallman, eds. *The Cambridge Economic History of the United States*. New York: Cambridge University Press.

Adams, S., 2014. *Home Fires: How Americans Kept Warm in the Nineteenth Century*, Baltimore, MA: The Johns Hopkins University Press.

Allen, R.C., 2009. *The British Industrial Revolution in Global Perspective*, Cambridge, MA: Cambridge University Press.

American Petroleum Institute, 1993. *Basic Petroleum Data Book*, Vol. XIII, Washington, D.C.: API.

Arthur, W.B., 1990. Positive Feedbacks in the Economy. *Scientific American*, 262, pp. 92–99.

Bakken, G.M., 2008. *The Mining Law of 1872: Past, Politics and Prospects*, Albuquerque, NM: University of New Mexico Press.
Barger, H. and Schurr, S.H., 1944. *The Mining Industries, 1899–1939: A Study of Output, Employment and Productivity*, New York: National Bureau of Economic Research.
Black, B.C., 2012. Oil for Living: Petroleum and American Conspicuous Consumption. *Journal of American History*, 99, pp. 40–50.
Cain, L.P. and Paterson, D.G., 1986. Biased Technical Change, Scale and Factor Substitution in American Industry, 1850–1919. *Journal of Economic History*, 46, pp. 153–164.
Chandler, A.D., 1972. Anthracite Coal and the Beginnings of the Industrial Revolution in the United States. *Business History Review*, 46, pp. 141–181.
Church, J.A., 1871. Mining Schools in the United States. *North American Review*, 112, pp. 62–81.
Clay, K. and Wright, G., 2012. Gold Rush Legacy: American Minerals and the Knowledge Economy. In D.H. Cole and E. Ostrom, eds. *Property in Land and Other Resources*. Cambridge, MA: Lincoln Institute.
Crowson, P., 2012. Some Observations on Copper Yields and Ore Grades. *Resources Policy*, 37(1), pp. 59–72.
David, P.A. and Wright, G., 1997. Increasing Returns and the Genesis of American Resource Abundance. *Industrial and Corporate Change*, 6(2), pp. 203–245.
Fell, J.E., 1979. *Ores to Metals: The Rocky Mountain Smelting Industry*, Lincoln, NE: The University of Nebraska Press.
Frehner, B., 2011. *Finding Oil: The Nature of Petroleum Geology, 1859–1920*, Lincoln, NE: University of Nebraska Press.
Goldin, C.D. and Katz, L.F., 1999. *The Race between Education and Technology*, Cambridge, MA: Harvard University Press.
Gorelick, S.M., 2010. *Oil Panic and the Global Crisis*, Chichester, UK: Wiley-Blackwell.
Harvey, C. and Press, J., 1990. *International Competition and Industrial Change: Essays in the History of Mining and Metallurgy, 1800–1950*, London: Frank Cass.
Hounshell, D.A., 1984. *From the American System to Mass Production 1800–1932*, Baltimore, MA: The Johns Hopkins University Press.
Hubbert, M.K. 1956. "Nuclear Energy and the Fossil Fuels," presented at the *Spring Meeting of the Southern District Division of Production*, American Petroleum Institute.
Klein, A. and Crafts, N., 2012. Making Sense of the Manufacturing Belt: Determinants of U.S. Industrial Location, 1880–1920. *Journal of Economic Geography*, 12(5), pp. 775–807.
Krugman, P.R., 1991. History and Industry Location: The Case of the Manufacturing Belt. *The American Economic Review*, 81(2), pp. 80–83.
Libecap, G.D., 1989. *Contracting for Property Rights*, New York: Cambridge University Press.
Lucier, P., 2008. *Scientists and Swindlers: Consulting on Coal and Oil in America, 1820–1890*, Baltimore, MA: The Johns Hopkins University Press.
Meyer, D.R., 1989. Midwestern Industrialization and the American Manufacturing Belt in the Nineteenth Century. *The Journal of Economic History*, 49(4), pp. 921–937.
Mitchell, B.R., 1981. *European Historical Statistics, 1750–1975*, London: Macmillan.
Mitchell, B.R., 1992. *International Historical Statistics: Europe, 1750–1988*, Basingstoke, UK; New York: Macmillan; Stockton Press.
Mitchell, B.R., 1983. *International Historical Statistics: The Americas and Australasia, 1700–1975*, London: Macmillan.

Mitchell, B.R., 2003. *International Historical Statistics: The Americas, 1750–2000*, New York: Palgrave Macmillan.

Mitchell, B.R., 2003. *International Historical Statistics: Africa, Asia & Oceania, 1750–2000*, New York: Palgrave Macmillan.

Nelson, R.R. and Wright, G., 1992. The Rise and Fall of American Technological Leadership: The Postwar Era in Historical Perspective. *Journal of Economic Literature*, 30(4), pp. 1931–1964.

O'Brien, T.F., 1989. Rich Beyond the Dreams of Avarice: The Guggenheims in Chile. *Business History Review*, 63, pp. 122–159.

Ochs, K., 1992. The Rise of American Mining Engineers: A Case Study of the Colorado School of Mines. *Technology and Culture*, 33, pp. 278–301.

Olmstead, A.L. and Rhode, P.W., 2008. *Creating Abundance: Biological Innovation and American Agricultural Development*, Cambridge, MA: Cambridge University Press.

Paul, R., 1960. Colorado as a Pioneer of Science. *Mississippi Valley Historical Review*, 47, pp. 34–50.

Paul, R., 1963. *Mining Frontiers of the West, 1848–1880*, New York: Holt, Rinehart & Winston.

Przeworski, J.F., 1980. *The Decline of the Copper Industry in Chile and the Entrance of North American Capital, 1870–1916*, New York: Arno Press.

Read, T.T., 1941. *The Development of Mineral Industry Education in the United States*, New York: American Institute of Mining Engineers.

Rickard, T.A., 1932. *A History of American Mining*, New York: McGraw Hill.

Rosenberg, N., 1976. *Perspectives on Technology*, Cambridge, MA: Cambridge University Press.

Schmitz, C.J., 1979. *World Non-Ferrous Metal Production and Prices*, London: Cass.

Schmitz, C.J., 1986. The Rise of Big Business in the World Copper Industry 1870–1930. *The Economic History Review*, 39(3), p. 392.

Smith, A., [1776] 1976. *An Inquiry into the Nature and Causes of the Wealth of Nations*, Oxford: Clarendon Press.

Smith, D., 1987. *Mining America: The Industry and the Environment*, Lawrence, KS: University Press of Kansas.

Smith, G.O., 1919. *The Strategy of Minerals*, New York: D. Appleton and company.

Spence, C.C., 1970. *Mining Engineers and the American West, 1849–1933*, New Haven, CT: Yale University Press.

Spitz, P., 1988. *Petrochemicals: The Rise of an Industry*, New York: John Wiley & Sons.

Thomas, B., 1980. Towards an Energy Interpretation of the Industrial Revolution. *Atlantic Economic Journal*, 8, pp. 1–16.

Tilton, J.E. and Landsberg, H.H., 1999. Innovation, Productivity Growth, and the Survival of the U.S. Copper Industry. In R.D. Simpson, ed. *Productivity in Natural Resource Industries*. Washington D.C.: Resources for the Future.

United States Works Progress Administration, 1940. Technology, Employment and Output per Man in Copper Mining. *WPA National Research Project Report* No. E-12, Washington, D.C.

Ville, S. and Wicken, O., 2013. The Dynamics of Resource-based Economic Development: Evidence from Australia and Norway. *Industrial and Corporate Change*, 22(5), pp. 1341–1371.

Wang, Z. and Krupnik, A., 2013. A Retrospective Review of Shale Gas Development in the United States, *Discussion Paper DP 13-12, Resources for the Future*, Washington, D.C.

Warren, K., 1973. *Mineral Resources*, Newton Abbot, UK: David & Charles.

White, G.T., 1970. California's Other Mineral. *Pacific Historical Review*, 39, pp. 135–154.

Wilkins, M., 1989. *The History of Foreign Investment in the United States to 1914*, Cambridge, MA: Harvard University Press.

Williams, M., 1989. *Americans and their Forests.*, Cambridge, MA: Cambridge University Press.

Williamson, H.F. and Daum, A.R., 1959. *The American Petroleum Industry: The Age of Illumination, 1859–1899*, Evanston, IL: Northwestern University Press.

Williamson, H.F., Andreano, R., Daum, A.R. and Klose, G.C., 1963. *The American Petroleum Industry: The Age of Energy, 1899–1959*, Evanston, IL: Northwestern University Press.

Wright, G., 1990. The Origins of American Industrial Success, 1879–1940. *The American Economic Review*, 80(4), pp. 651–668.

Wrigley, E.A., 1988. *Continuity, Chance and Change: The Character of the Industrial Revolution in England*, Cambridge, MA: Cambridge University Press.

Wrigley, E.A., 2010. *Energy and the Industrial Revolution*, Cambridge, MA: Cambridge University Press.

Yergin, D., 2011. *The Quest: Energy, Security, and the Remaking of the Modern World*, New York: The Penguin Press.

7 Welfare states and development patterns in Latin America

Luis Bértola

Introduction

This chapter focuses on the study of the relationship between development patterns of Latin American economies, particularly those that have been based on the wide availability of natural resources, and welfare states. It attempts to shed light on the specific challenges that economic development faces in these economies, especially in the context of the emergence of social demands as societies become more democratic, and considering the very different production structures than those that were behind the development of industrialized countries.

The chapter first addresses the so-called modern economic development and its relation to natural resources, trying to shed light on how the availability of natural resources has often imposed restrictions on development, but also about how modern societies have lifted those restrictions. It then seeks to put the current debate on the environmental limits to growth into historical perspective.

Interdependence between regions is also discussed, focusing on the importance of international heterogeneity and its implications for development. The idea is to show how the existence of strong international asymmetries imposes specific demands to developing nations, which must not only address the causes for their delay, but do so in a highly competitive environment with more advanced nations.

Finally, the chapter addresses the demands of welfare arising through the development process and how welfare states and production structures intertwine, focusing on the challenges imposed on economies showing strongly heterogeneous, volatile production structures and large informal sectors. It is imperative to make a specific conceptualization effort for Latin American countries, and to creatively undertake the difficult task of facing at the same time development challenges, economic stability, welfare state development and the exploitation of natural resources without compromising environmental sustainability.

Economic growth and natural resources: a long-term perspective

The so-called modern economic growth has meant a huge leap in economic growth rates. Even in the nineteenth century it was very difficult to incorporate to the theoretical approaches and ideological visions the magnitude of the changes that were being processed. Many social and economic theories debated whether or not to consider the strong limitations to economic growth. Thus, despite its large methodological confrontations, the concept of scarcity and limits to growth were present in both David Ricardo and Robert Malthus.

However, since the agricultural revolution that occurred with the expansion of capitalist relations in the countryside and the successive industrial and transport revolutions, the supply of resources has constantly increased. While in the period that goes from 1500 to 2008, the world population multiplied by 15 and per capita income did in a similar way, the total economic output increased 205 times. In particular, when it comes to food production, it can be said that the agricultural sector has been able to respond to the claims submitted to it. Malnutrition, which is still suffered by millions of people, is not due to the absolute lack of food, but poor distribution. Moreover, it can be argued that we are in the presence of an overproduction of food (Federico 2005).

Undoubtedly, these achievements were not only the result of an expansion in resource extraction or the production of new renewable resources due to the increase in operating surface, but are largely explained by man's ability to learn, innovate and develop science and technology.

Despite the achievements, it is clear that this revolution and the voracity of growth during the last centuries have generated, and continue to generate, perverse effects. As the frontier expanded and subsoil was conquered, intensive growth has taken place, and nonrenewable resources have been exploited carelessly. We have also polluted the atmosphere, degraded the soil and expelled rural population to less well-endowed areas with little job opportunities. Furthermore, the environmental impacts generated have had different effects among countries and even in different sectors of society, with the poorest being the most affected.

This development pattern is not sustainable in the future, neither to maintain current development levels nor to enable disadvantaged regions to access the same level of wellbeing as the most favored. However, the legacy left by previous generations cannot be judged only in terms of these problems, but to be fair, we must recognize the great wealth of knowledge they left us, which can be used to solve development challenges in the future.

Unequal and interdependent growth: centers and peripheries

Almost all regions of the world have benefited from economic growth and contributed to it differently and have also suffered from excess and misdirection of development in different ways. Moreover, these different performances, far from being simply parallel paths, have formed a systemic whole, unequal and asymmetric.

Much has been debated about whether development in the center was possible due to the access of resources in the periphery and if the demand for resources from the center inhibited, promoted and shaped development in the periphery. It has even been suggested that development in the center took place at the expense of development in the periphery.

The answer is complex, but it could be argued that impact has been asymmetrical. Bairoch (1975) claimed that the imports of raw materials from the periphery did not fully determine the Industrial Revolution. Surely they contributed and expanded possibilities, but they were not the decisive determinants of the process. By contrast, the development of the center was decisive for the periphery and the dynamics of the central countries strongly determined the development in the periphery. This is where the concept of "dependency" arises in its many forms, some stronger and some more lax.

The strongest dependentist theories, like Gunder Frank's, have failed to stand the test of time and historical changes. It is not true that accumulation in the center has led to a permanent under-accumulation in the periphery. Most countries have experienced a certain kind of development that, even though not as strong as the center's, is somewhat promising. This is even truer in Latin American countries, China, India, and other countries that have experienced processes of fast economic growth and education and life expectancy improvements.

What is clear is that there is a universal tendency in the economic development process: a growing share of investment in physical capital in relation to the use of natural resources, and, in turn, an increasing role played by the accumulation of human capital and organizational, social and institutional knowledge. The World Bank has tried to group these components with the concepts of natural capital (i.e., the availability of natural resources), physical capital (i.e., the set of machinery, buildings and infrastructure) and intangible capital, which refers to different forms of knowledge and social innovations. Countries with the highest levels of per capita income are those who have advanced more rapidly in changing the capital structure, developing first an increase in physical capital in relation to the natural, and then increasing the intangible in relation to the other two, as shown in Figure 7.1. At the same time, Table 7.1 shows the capital structure by region, in which the precariousness of Latin American development becomes clear, being only higher than that of Africa.

One way to see these structures is through education, where Latin America shows a contradictory scenario. On the one hand, as a result of great efforts, there have been significant improvements in the average educational level, but those efforts appear as clearly insufficient when making international comparisons.[1]

Furthermore, Latin America has a feature that is central to the characterization of its development pattern: for each level of per capita income, educational level is lower than in other regions (see Figure 7.2). The main ideas that have

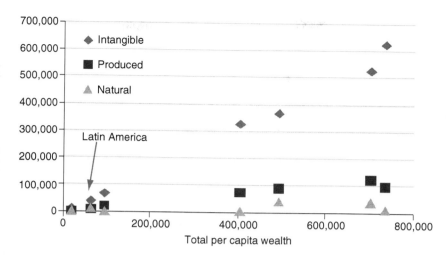

Figure 7.1 Total wealth and types of per capita wealth in seven regions (2005, 2005 dollars).

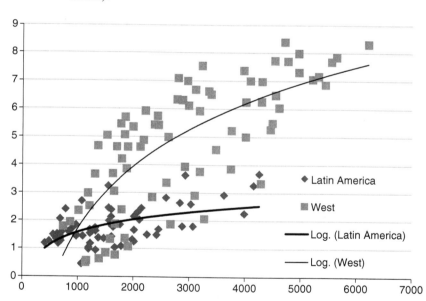

Figure 7.2 Latin America and the "West" 1870–1930: GDP per capita in 1990 PPP US$ (x) and average years of education in the population aged 15 and over (y) (source: Bértola and Ocampo 2012).

Table 7.1 Wealth structure by region, US dollars, 2005

	Total wealth	Total wealth	Intangible capital	Net external assets	Produced capital	Natural capital
1	23,324	100	54	−2	17	31
2	57,809	100	65	3	16	22
3	9651	100	74	−1	24	3
4	595,210	100	75	0	18	6
5	565,255	100	77	−1	18	6
6	613,205	100	75	0	18	6
7	734,195	100	85	−1	14	2

	Tangible wealth	Tangible wealth				
1	10,830	100		−4	37	66
2	20,278	100		−8	46	62
3	24,306	100		−4	91	13
4	147,137	100		1	75	24
5	127,826	100		−6	77	29
6	151,466	100		1	74	25
7	106,949	100		−6	94	13

1 Congo, D.R. Congo, Ivory Coast, Kenya, Nigeria, Senegal, South Africa, Zambia and Zimbabwe
2 Latin America and the Caribbean
3 China, India and South Korea
4 Spain, Greece, Italy and Portugal
5 Australia, Canada and New Zealand
6 Denmark, Findland, Norway and Sweden
7 USA

Source: World Bank (2012).

managed to explain this phenomenon have to do with social structures and power relations.

A complementary way to explain how is it possible for a population to produce more than would be expected from their human capital is by looking at the production function, which will be probably dominated by a high endowment of natural resources. The traditional Latin American path consisted in the export of commodities with relatively little added value but that is capable of generating income and it would be on the basis of a high per capita income in relation to the levels of human capital formation, which can be expressed through the level of education.

There is no simple causal link between natural resource availability and the level of education, but this relationship is mediated by the prevailing set of social relations in terms of economic and political power. For example, the countries of the southern South American border, while having a high availability of natural resources in relation to its population, were able to develop higher wage levels and social spending than other regions in which the endowment of natural resources per capita was not so high. When the provision of high natural resources was combined with a very high concentration of ownership and the existence of large populations with little education and little political power, educational delay may be even higher (Bértola and Ocampo 2012). Ultimately, the curse of natural resources is not inevitable in countries with abundant natural resources. What matters are the economic, social and political structures that are built in the process of its appropriation and exploitation.

Development and welfare states

Welfare states have emerged in a process of drastic structural change, first dominated by industrialization and then by the expansion of services. That process involved significant changes in the location of the population, the structure of families, the division of labor within family-groups, the consumption structure and in the distribution of time devoted to leisure, education and work. Throughout this process there was a shift in the risk structure, which meant that societies needed to reorganize their coverage.

It is important to note, however, that welfare states were built not only to respond to internal phenomena of different societies. They began to develop during the so-called first globalization, amid a restructuring of resources between different parts of the planet. Moreover, welfare states sought to assure the workers in a context of job insecurity and a changing economy. These trends occurred in migrant-sending countries like Germany and the Scandinavian countries, and migrant-receiving countries, like Australia, Canada and Latin American countries such as Uruguay. This leads us to emphasize once again the importance of the international dimension (Huberman 2012; Lloyd 2013).

However, it is not until after World War II that welfare states showed their full development in the more advanced countries. The work of Esping-Andersen has become a classic and is an inevitable reference for the study concerning this topic. His primary classification of three worlds of "welfare capitalism" (Esping-Andersen 1990) and its extension, review and discussion of more "varieties of welfare capitalism" (Esping-Andersen 1999), deserve to be discussed in detail.

The three worlds of welfare capitalism – the liberal, social democratic and corporate – differ in terms of the way they face similar structures of risks coverage with different conformations of the triad family, market and state. The liberal welfare capitalism assigned the state to a marginal role, where individuals or families, based on their income, deal with their needs, such as health care coverage and retirement, in the market. In the corporate welfare capitalism, which was developed in the postwar world in the Golden Age of capitalism, the risk coverage structure developed through a highly segmented labor market in different economic sectors, with specific forms of organization and differential access to risk coverage and quality. The third model, the socialdemocratic, is based on a comprehensive universal public coverage, which is accessed regardless of the position in the labor market, and the services quality levels are often much higher than the benefits of the marginal liberal capitalism system. This system represents a significant tax burden, which is functional to the broad participation of women in the labor market and an extensive provision of public services that are functional to this labor structure.

Understanding the genesis of these states is very important to understand their evolution. Contrary to expectations, the advance of globalization did not bring a tendency towards a unique pattern of social organization, but the varieties of capitalism have survived in different ways to face the crisis of the welfare state and its subsequent development.

According to Esping-Andersen, while the crisis of the welfare models until the 1980s was due to internal problems, the causes of the crisis from the 1980s and 1990s are exogenous, these being globalization and demographic changes. Globalization alters the development of autonomous monetary and fiscal policies and demands more flexible labor markets. Demographic changes create shifts in both the structure and stability of families, such as the aging population that transforms the risk structure (Esping-Andersen 1999).

Moreover, according to Esping-Andersen (1999), the welfare capitalisms are faced with the dilemma of choosing between societies with full employment, but with growing economic inequality between skilled and unskilled workers, and societies with high unemployment. What is interesting is the claim that this pressure is not so much due to globalization and the emergence of developing countries that produce industrial goods with much lower labor costs, but mainly due to the effects of the orientation of endogenous technological change of developed countries, which tends to reduce the demand for unskilled workers and rely on the creation of skilled employment, especially in the services sector.

These two claims seem to be rather contradictory. While it is clear that in Esping-Andersen there is a strong idea that welfare states are related to a specific production structure, with certain levels of productivity and technological contexts of important technological changes, in the analysis that the author makes about the crisis in the 1980s and 1990s, it seems that the link between welfare models and productive structure loses weight. In this sense, we must not forget that the origin of the welfare states, particularly in small open economies, stemmed from the need for stability in a population highly exposed to the ups and downs of the international economy. The configuration of welfare states is a national response to the collapse of the gold standard system and the crisis of the first globalization. Therefore, to consider globalization as an external shock to welfare models is misleading, as it finally detaches the welfare states of their production environment, losing this analytically critical relation.

Similarly, the claim that demographic changes are unrelated to the dynamics of the welfare state is debatable. The only way we can come to that conclusion is if we disassociate the welfare state from its socio-productive environment. The family structure is closely linked to the risk structure and labor market opportunities. It is also related to the services provided by societies to address these risks. Therefore, it seems implausible that the crisis of welfare states faced from the 1980s and 1990s is of an exogenous nature.

An alternative explanation can be found in regulationist approaches, even though they have not specifically focused on the study of the welfare state. Like Esping-Andersen, regulationists deny that there is a trend towards a unique pattern of social organization. However, this is not because the different worlds of welfare face external shocks maintaining its basic constitutive features, but because of the existence of inertia and *path dependence* in complex structural and institutional frameworks.

Regulationists provide a more comprehensive framework in which welfare states and regularities of reproduction of the different social sectors are articulated with a broader accumulation system, which includes both technical and social division of labor, the temporal dimension of capital accumulation, the regularities for the reproduction of the different components of demand and patterns of integration into the international economy.

Another approach that adheres to the idea of the persistence of various development patterns is the focus of the varieties of capitalism (VC) (Hall and Soskice 2001). Focused on the role of business in the competitive process, technological change and social construction, this approach argues that there are two types of capitalism: liberal market economies (LME) and coordinated market economies (CME), stylized from the study of the following dimensions:

- Industrial relations is the place for bargaining on wages and working conditions, which are intertwined and have an impact on productivity.
- Vocational training and education determine the competitiveness of enterprises.
- The forms of corporate governance are a complex web of relationships between shareholders, managers, family businesses, diversified business groups, vertically integrated business groups, etc.
- Relationships between firms are a central component of the relationship with customers and suppliers, determining levels of productivity, efficiency and competitiveness.

- Finally, the coordination of the employees is a central element in the cooperative strategies and the transmission of information.

The analysis stems from the concepts of institutions and organizations developed by North (1990), which recognizes the existence of tacit, informal institutions, with a strong cultural environment, which determine the behavior of agents. Based on the network of institutions and organizations, an array of institutional infrastructure that determines corporate strategy is built. This matrix is formed not only from market competition and hierarchy within companies, but also from a strong weight of components of cooperation and trust. At the same time, institutions are not the result of a choice by individual companies, but constitute a second order coordination problem of considerable magnitude: "the firms located within any political economy face a set of coordinating institutions whose character is not fully under their control "(Hall and Soskice 2001). Therefore, it produces a kind of institutional clustering, where different institutions are strengthened and conditioned. Thus, even within the CME there are differences, such as those that distinguish the complex Japanese groups that have a strong sectoral diversity and the German model of strong sectoral structure and vertical integration.

The VC approach, similarly to the regulationist, recognizes the limits of globalization as a creator of a unifying development model, and argues that nations are distinguished by their particular patterns of development based on the concept of institutional comparative advantage. While institutional matrices transform and evolve while countries globalize, internationalization processes hardly destroy their competitiveness institutional foundations. Therefore, according to this approach, there is a strong correspondence between the types of political economy developed, and the types of welfare states built. The welfare state, far from being an autonomous set of institutional arrangements, is closely linked to the general social and economic environment.

What could be concluded is that welfare states cannot be understood outside of a broader context of economic and social determinants. Moreover, their future does not seem to be determined as an unalterable fate of modern economic development. On the contrary, it is open, uncertain and it depends on economic determinants and the values and choices that different societies and the overall community develop over time. When discussing the future of the welfare state in Latin America, we cannot assume that their development is part of a universal and irreversible trend.

Welfare states and development in Latin America

As has already been extensively analyzed, the Latin American production structure is characterized by a limited industrial development, early deindustrialization in terms of the level of GDP per capita, a greater weight of primary exports, and an import structure dominated by highly technological goods. In the long term, trade balance deficit has become a trend and has imposed a restriction on growth, since as income grows, so does the tendency to consume goods with a higher technological content, which are mainly imported.

This trend in Latin America is not linear but has a strong cyclical component subject to various factors including financial volatility, cycles of technological creation and destruction, political cycles of the international economy, recurrent emergence of new expansive centers, depletion and discovery of natural resources, etc. Unevenly, and at certain times, some countries have appropriated mature technology and managed to close the gap in some strategic industries, but rarely did they manage to build productive development models that allowed them to reach the frontier of technological change. Thus, through successive waves of technological change, Latin America fell behind. The current growth cycle does not seem to be leading to a transformation in the productive structure that enables a different insertion of the region into the global economy.

Given this situation, and in the context of analyzing the development of welfare states, it becomes useful to identify the characteristics of the productive structure prevailing in Latin America in order to understand its variety of capitalism. However, we should keep in mind that the VC approach is designed for the study of developed countries, and therefore its application to Latin American demands considerable adaptation efforts. When we schematically analyze the five core components of the VC in the organizational-institutional complexities of Latin America, we might note the following:

- When it comes to the field of industrial relations the features are a high informality of the production system, a strong structural heterogeneity, large segments outside wage bargaining systems and salaries that, compared to developed countries, constitute a smaller part of the effective demand. Furthermore, patterns of wage bargaining are often unrelated to changes in endogenous productivity of the production process. The reason is that productivity gains tend to be often exogenous to businesses, because they are incorporated through foreign investment or included in capital goods.
- Education systems have shown to be strongly decoupled from production systems and exhibit comparatively low levels.
- As for the network of corporate governance, the Latin American case shows fragility due to the aforementioned structural heterogeneity. Large companies linked to exports have more sophisticated structures and are usually associated with foreign capital, like most large companies dedicated to provide modern services. The business sector is dominated by SMEs with very little capacity to generate innovation and productivity levels well below the average. Only in some countries has the state production survived the market reforms of the 1980–1990 years, and are powerful cores of accumulation and articulation with the productive sector.
- With the exception of some public enterprises and some endogenous nuclei, there is little interaction between the actors in the production structure. The most dynamic centers are subordinated to international value chains.

- In terms of the internal coordination of companies, large international companies transfer their practices of origin and large public companies hold specific dynamics that are relatively unknown and little studied.

All these aspects are in fact contained in two central features of the institutional and organizational formation of the Latin American economy: structural heterogeneity – see Table 7.2 which shows a Gini of inequality of GDP per worker among large sectors – and the characteristics of its capital – which, as already discussed, is featured by significant natural capital and poor development of intangible capital.

It could be argued that this high Latin American heterogeneity is mainly due to differences between countries in this group, but that is not the case. As displayed in Table 7.3, this heterogeneity is firmly rooted in the domestic structures of each of these countries.

The characteristics of the production sector in Latin America have been one of the great challenges in regulationist approaches. Based on the concepts of accumulation system and development models as a combination of structural and institutional elements that enable regularities that maintain stable accumulation process, regulationist approaches have had serious difficulties in achieving an acceptable explanatory framework of the development of Latin American economies.

These difficulties call us to make creative diagnoses and be careful with the application of analytic models that are designed and supported by very different historical realities, such as that of developed countries. In this sense, a way of approaching the dynamics of Latin American development is to identify five possible sources of economic growth and locate the social and economic forces that underlie the ways in which they articulate and how they influence each other and the growth pattern, as is done in Bertola (2012). These sources of growth are:

1. The Kaldorian growth induced by the expansion of the demand that fosters specialization and expansion of production scale, with corresponding impulses to increase productivity.
2. The Schumpeterian growth, as result of innovative efforts produced by the accumulation of scientific and technological knowledge and its application to the emergence of new products and new processes. This growth is strongly linked to research activities within companies, but also beyond them, in the scientific and technological system.
3. The growth produced by the international transfer of technology, which depends on the size of the technology gap. The greater the gap, the greater potential for growth. It also depends on the domestic social capabilities to seize the opportunities that the gap opens and the adaptation of exogenous technology. Nonetheless, catching-up as a development strategy has strong limitations, since it only allows for a process of conditional convergence, which can often be locked at a great distance from the level of development of the leaders if that process is not articulated with a Kaldorian and/or

Table 7.2 Heterogeneity of structural productivity by groups of countries, Gini index

Group	1991	1996	2001	2006	Average
1 LATAM (Argentina, Brazil, Chile, Colombia, Costa Rica, Ecuador, Mexico, Perú, Uruguay, Venezuela)	0.455	0.406	0.478	0.448	0.447
2 CORE EUROPE (Germany, France, UK, Belgium, the Netherlands, Switzerland)	0.168	0.191	0.158	0.180	0.174
3 ASIA (Korea, Japan)	0.318	0.314	0.332	0.281	0.311
4 SCAN (Denmark, Finland, Norway, Sweden)	0.198	0.220	0.234	0.259	0.228
5 LATPER (Spain, Italy, Portugal)	0.229	0.218	0.217	0.209	0.218
6 SETTLERS (Australia, Canada, New Zealand)	0.269	0.278	0.286	0.286	0.280
7 USA	0.211	0.211	0.221	0.233	0.219
8 All Europe	0.188	0.208	0.188	0.203	0.197

Group					
	Variation in percentage points				
1 LATAM (Argentina, Brazil, Chile, Colombia, Costa Rica, Ecuador, Mexico, Perú, Uruguay, Venezuela)	−4.8	7.1	−3.0		
2 CORE EUROPE (Germany, France, UK, Belgium, the Netherlands, Switzerland)	2.3	−3.3	2.2		
3 ASIA (Korea, Japan)	−0.4	1.8	−5.1		
4 SCAN (Denmark, Finland, Norway, Sweden)	2.2	1.4	2.5		
5 LATPER (Spain, Italy, Portugal)	−1.1	−0.1	−0.8		
6 SETTLERS (Australia, Canada, New Zealand)	0.9	0.8	0.0		
7 USA	0.0	1.0	1.2		
8 All Europe	2.0	−2.0	1.5		

Source: Bértola (2012).

152   L. Bértola

Table 7.3 Heterogeneity of labor productivity in Latin America by major sectors, 1991–2006

Country	1991	1996	2001	2006	Average
CRI	0.277	0.244	0.224	0.205	0.238
ARG	0.279	0.276	0.291	0.308	0.289
URY	0.311	0.310	0.335	0.302	0.314
BRA	0.353	0.290	0.338	0.355	0.334
PER	0.393	0.288	0.266	0.464	0.353
COL	0.371	0.334	0.352	0.378	0.359
ECU	0.394	0.374	0.322	0.417	0.377
CHL	0.405	0.372	0.396	0.452	0.406
MEX	0.467	0.478	0.402	0.404	0.438
VEN	0.408	0.478	0.399	0.475	0.440

Source: Bértola (2012).

Schumpeterian model, and if these two are not firmly rooted in the specific features of the country.

4   In the case of natural resource abundant economies, there is a constant rent-induced economic growth, a process that is based on the uptake of a price differential in the international market, which does not depend on an appreciation of a product by way of technological change, but by the monopoly of a natural resource in the context of extreme demand expansion without a correlate in the offer. This rentier growth tends to be subject to high volatility, because technological change enables the discovery of new reserves or increasing productivity in the case of reproducible goods. The ways in which these rents are generated and appropriated vary greatly depending on the characteristics of the sector, ownership structures, the international market, the network of marketing and transportation, etc. Such rentier growth overlaps with the Kaldorian dynamics.

5   Finally, Latin America has experienced episodes of economic growth induced by financial expansion. This type of growth is often short-lived and quickly leads to a particular form of the Dutch disease, perhaps the worst of all, since it is not based on the development of any productive sector.

The long-term divergent trend and volatility of the Latin American economy have been strongly linked to the predominance of the financial and rentier growth patterns. During its booms, growth models like *catching-up* were implemented, in which appeared Kaldorian and Schumpeterian activities, but without becoming the hegemonic and dominant growth patterns. The key question then is, what is the dynamics, in terms of political economy, that explains the volatile and lagged growth that prevents the strengthening of sectors that, in the long run, should lead the process of change.

Figure 7.3 shows the income of non-reproducible natural resources as a share of the GDP between 1970 and 2010 in some Latin American countries. As can

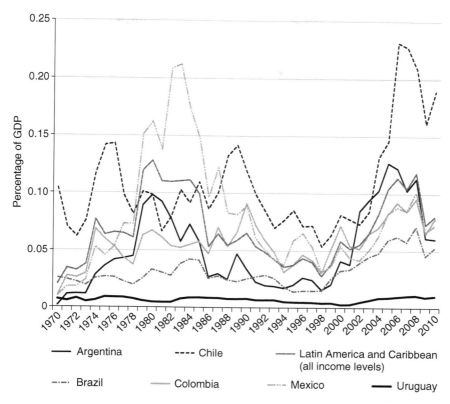

Figure 7.3 Rents of natural resources as a share of per capita GDP, 1970–2010.

be seen, the sharp fluctuations can hardly be seen as Schumpeterian movements but seem to be generated by demand shocks and even speculative components. On the other hand, a pro-cyclical component is observed in the share of these rents in the GDP. The importance of this type of income is much higher in the mining and oil countries than in countries with a large agricultural based economy, like Argentina and Brazil.

There is not too much information in the case of agro-based economies. Two examples of small and agro-based economies like the Uruguayan are shown only for the purpose of seeing the type of calculation that can be made.

Figure 7.4 shows trends in the period 1908–1966 in terms of agricultural income generation and its share in the GDP. Two observations can be made: (1) the share of income component of GDP (top line) shows very strong fluctuations that match with the movements of the terms of trade, especially its sharp decline towards the end of the 1950s and early 1960s; (2) the role of income in the agricultural GDP (bottom line) shows similar fluctuations but a more permanent downward trend which may be associated with changes in the growth model in favor of a strategy of technological catching-up, through industrialization and

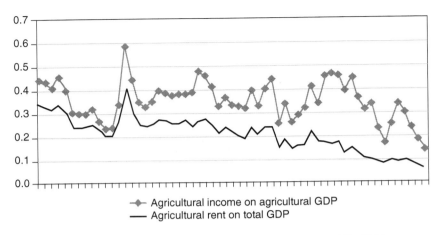

Figure 7.4 Uruguay: land rents on agricultural and overall GDP, 1908–1966.

agricultural development, at the expense of traditional cattle-breeding, which was the main source of rents.

Another perspective on this phenomenon can be visualized in Figure 7.5, where two indexes of land prices are presented: one is deflated by CPI (top line) and the other is further deflated by an index of productivity growth (bottom line). The bottom line, then, by eliminating the price increase due to technological change, reflects the rent of the soil. Interestingly, after a period of generalized inflation, that affected the value of land and severely impacted the agricultural sector, the last decade and a half was one of price stabilization, where paradoxically land prices rose significantly, largely surpassing the productivity gains in the sector. While there have been incentives to increase agricultural productivity in the last decades, due to the incorporation of innovations and structural change towards more investment- and knowledge-intensive industries, there has been a significant increase in the rent of the soil.

In short, even with marked and specific differences and logics, the generation of income from natural resources is a common process for both non-reproducible assets and for agricultural production. Both sectors experienced similar fluctuations in these revenues, fluctuations that are clearly pro-cyclical in relation to the movements of GDP.

The valuation of natural resources attracts investors seeking to appropriate these rents, which tends to concentrate land ownership. Moreover, the high volatility means that these processes are carried out in weak institutional contexts, so states are rarely able to impose conditions on those who exploit the lands. Therefore, in addition to processes of appropriation of assets and income, there is an unregulated use of these resources, which has perverse environmental and social consequences. The way that this expansion impacts the environment affects mostly the poorer sectors that live in eroded marginal areas with less access to

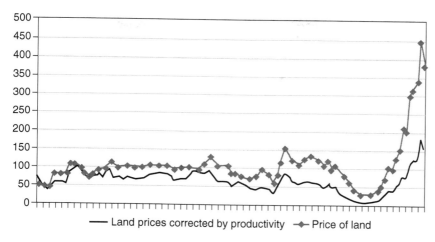

Figure 7.5 Uruguay: real price of land (deflated by CPI) and estimation of income (1913 = 100).

public goods and public services. The result is a marked increase in inequality of income and living conditions.

It is key to understand the political economy of (non) structural change, the patterns of development and its institutional arrangements. If the political and social system is organized around rent-seeking in the primary sector and around the defense of landowners' interests, it is easier to understand the limited support provided to development strategies of Keynesian or Schumpeterian type, and even catching-up. Moreover, environmental issues are always deferrable matters, compared to the need to meet immediate needs of the population.

Therefore, it is necessary to generate a mapping of economic and social structures comprising, first, a typology of resources from the point of view of their appropriability, reproduction, technological features, access, predominant forms of property, and their environmental and distributional impacts; and second, an economic, social and political weighting of the development of other sectors that includes, to give some examples, the importance of domestic and subsistence economies, the expansion of the industrial sector, the public sector, among others.

It is interesting to note, moreover, that the course of these patterns of growth in Latin America have been happening under a long-term trend, though not linear, of deepening of democratic life. The logic of reproduction of political systems in the context of democracy has been extensively addressed by the new political economy with a strong use of the concept of the median voter. What has not been done in the literature is study the link between these logics and the impact on the different strategies of economic growth in the context of societies with high levels of rent extraction of natural resources, high volatility thereof, and a strong structural heterogeneity. Or, in the words of the theories of VC, how the democratic expansion in Latin America is related to the various organizational and institutional environments of the private sector and the state.

In the midst of these processes, the Latin American welfare state has developed in different stages, starting in economies which are more open and exposed to international migration, consistent with the emergence of welfare states in developed countries and other new settlement economies (Lloyd 2011; Huberman 2012).

When addressing the discussion of the characteristics of the welfare state in Latin America, and based on the characterizations of Esping-Andersen, Filgueira (1997) correctly states that the Latin American tradition is framed predominantly in the tradition of conservative welfare state. Latin America has developed its welfare models based on a progressive expansion of benefits to various professional groups, starting with the state bureaucracy, especially the military, and progressively extending benefits to different professional groups, with marked differences in coverage and quality. The system is based on a formal sector in which the man is the main income earner, and the benefits to the rest of the population come through the family constitution.

Filgueira (1997) makes a stronger statement, which is in line with what has been developed in this work: strictly speaking, there is not a welfare state in Latin America, but *Social States*. The author seeks to characterize Latin American regimes not just in terms of their maturity level, à la Mesa-Lago, as if they were universal stages of a continuum, but seeking to identify structural features of the social functioning of Latin American states. Existing systems in the 1970s were then identified as stratified universalism (Argentina, Chile and Uruguay), dual systems (Brazil and Mexico) and exclusive systems (Bolivia, Ecuador and most of the Central American republics).

These forms of welfare states in Latin America are obviously related to the high level of inequality in the region. As shown in Table 7.4, Latin American countries are those with the highest levels of inequality in the global arena.

Table 7.4 Inequality-adjusted Human Development Index

	Southern Cone	Center	New Settlement	Spain-Italy	Scandinavia
1900			0.559	0.403	
1910			0.606	0.396	
1920		0.576	0.653	0.490	0.528
1930		0.641	0.711	0.548	0.562
1940		0.682	0.726	0.567	0.670
1950	0.344	0.755	0.689	0.587	0.767
1960	0.369	0.768	0.785	0.661	0.830
1970	0.361	0.789	0.803	0.727	0.867
1980	0.408	0.794	0.836	0.752	0.890
1990	0.428	0.768	0.798	0.794	0.887
2000	0.419		0.777	0.773	

Source: Bértola *et al.* (2010).

There are large sections of Latin Americans who are outside the welfare states because they belong to poorly formalized sectors, have precarious jobs, develop subsistence activities in marginal areas, participate in activities of high seasonality or in internal migration processes and inhabit areas where state presence is very marginal. They are outsiders not only in matters of social policy, but in the provision of public goods, including security itself.

As argued throughout this chapter, the characteristics of the welfare state cannot be separated from the broader characteristics of the production structure because they form a set of strongly interdependent interactions. The lack of welfare states and the existence of *Social States*, is the counterpart of the absence of developed economies, not only in the understanding that there is a quantitative relationship between the level of per capita income and social spending, but in the sense of how the welfare system is articulated with what the theory of the VC calls the comparative institutional matrix. The paths toward overcoming development constraints involve identifying actors, organizations and institutional arrangements that allow transforming the foundations of institutional comparative advantage.

As a conclusion

Latin America is going through an extremely favorable economic situation, which has been able to exhibit high rates of economic growth, poverty reduction and, in many cases, a significant reduction of inequality.

However, there are several unresolved issues on different levels. To summarize without establishing a hierarchical order of the obstacles to overcome – since they are strongly interrelated – listed below are the main challenges faced by Latin American countries:

1. Productive transformation. The key is to find a way to keep the export dynamics in the most competitive sectors, together with the urgent need to promote new export sectors, which will be impossible without a profound transformation of the entire production network, so as to markedly reduce structural heterogeneity. These objectives require a lot of resources from society in terms of the development of tools and capabilities to carry out industrial policies.
2. Social transformation. The eradication of indigence and the maximum reduction of poverty and alarming social inequalities require many resources. However, in the long run, they can stimulate economic and social dynamics by way of creating human capital. The universality of social benefits and the expansion of policies allowing extensive integration of women into the formal labor market are central objectives of development policies.
3. Environmental sustainability has become a cornerstone of any policy. It is not about compensating environmental damage but to stop it and reverse it, and in particular, to reduce the impacts of environmental degradation on the most vulnerable sectors. In this sense, environmental policies are inextricably linked to social policies.

4 The processes of economic and social development were not always hand in hand with political democracy. However, ultimately, the continued development coexists better with democratic regimes. The dilemma is how to build a credible, efficient system for creating more income and managing it in order to progress toward the goals of productive transformation, equity and environmental sustainability in the context of democracy. It is necessary to create the certainties and the political balance required, as well as facing excessive economic volatility. The volatile and cyclical nature of the economy has led to the development of pro-cyclical instruments and, even more dangerously, temporary social and political balances of weak sustainability. The political system must resist the temptation to build short-term scenarios of social welfare and social policies. In the long run, if there are not substantive achievements in the transformation of the productive structure and if social policies are not articulated with the capabilities of international competition, there will likely be episodes of short-lived wellbeing. These policies require a credible, reliable, moral state with a moral reputation and technical solvency.

5 The fifth critical area is the international, which requires exploration policies to expand into traditional markets and traditional items as well as new products and markets, where the processes of regional integration should play a strategic role. Regional integration processes should have a clear policy direction in order to build weight and regional political power for international negotiations. The reason is that this is the area where production and trade opportunities are conceived, international regulatory processes are discussed as well as trade and sovereignty, and access to knowledge and environmental management is gained.

The path for development and prosperity has not been easy to Latin America and no one can assure that the road will be easier in the future. Latin America has to rely on its own capabilities, from the development of its skills, social integration, harmony with its natural environment, the development of improved forms of political and social life and the strengthening of its international standing, in a framework of respect and tolerance.

Note

1 Latin America went from an average of 1.5 years of education in the early twentieth century to an average of 7.1 years in the late twentieth century. But Germany, France, United Kingdom and the United States showed an average increase of 12.5 years (Bértola *et al.* 2012).

References

Bairoch, P., 1975. *Revolución Industrial y Subdesarrollo*. México DF, México: Siglo XXI Editorial.

Bértola, L., 2012. *Informe de proyecto*. Santiago de Chile, Chile: CEPAL/ECLAC.

Bértola, L. and Ocampo, J.A., 2012. *The Economic Development of Latin America since Independence*. Oxford: Oxford University Press.

Bértola, L., Hernández, M., Rodríguez Weber, J. and Siniscalchi, S., 2010. *A Century of Human Development and Inequality: A Comparative Perspective*. Paper presented for the conference Historical Patterns of Development and Underdevelopment. CEPR and Universidad de la República. Montevideo, Uruguay.

Bértola, L., Hernández, M. and Siniscalchi, S., 2012. *Un índice histórico de desarrollo humano de América Latina y algunos países de otras regiones: metodología, fuentes y bases de datos*. Documentos de trabajo. Programa de Historia Económica y Social, Unidad Multidisciplinaria, Facultad de Ciencias Sociales, Universidad de la República, 28. Montevideo, Uruguay.

Esping-Andersen, G., 1990. *The Three Worlds of Welfare Capitalism*. Cambridge, MA: Polity Press.

Esping-Andersen, G., 1999. *The Social Foundations of Postindustrial Economies*. Oxford: Oxford University Press.

Federico, G., 2005. *Feeding the World: An Economic History of Agriculture, 1800–2000*. Princeton, NJ: Princeton University Press.

Filgueira, F., 1997. Tipos de welfare y reformas sociales en América Latina: Eficiencia, residualismo y ciudadanía estratificada. *In*: M.A. Melo, ed. *Reforma do Estado: A Mudança Institucional no Brasil*. Brazil: Editora Massangana.

Hall, P. and Soskice, D., 2001. *Varieties of Capitalism: The Industrial Foundations of Comparative Advantage*. Oxford: Oxford University Press.

Huberman, M., 2012. *Odd Couple: International Trade and Labor Standards in History*. New Haven, CT: Yale University Press.

Lloyd, C., 2011. The History and Future of Social Democratic Welfare Capitalism. *In*: P. Kettunen and K. Peterson, eds. *Beyond Welfare State Models*. Cheltenham, UK: Edward Elgar.

Lloyd, C., 2013. Welfare State and Capitalist Crisis. *In*: G Jónsson and K. Steffanson, eds. *Retrenchment or Renewal: Welfare States in Times of Economic Crisis*. Helsinki, Finland: Helsinki University.

North, D.C., 1990. *Institutions, Institutional Change and Economic Performance*. Cambridge, MA: Cambridge University Press.

World Bank, 2012. World Bank data [online]. Available from: http://data.worldbank.org/.

8 Oil illusion and delusion

Mexico and Venezuela over the twentieth century

María del Mar Rubio-Varas

Oil is fantastic and induces fantasies.
It created the illusion of a miracle;
it created, in practice, a culture of miracles.[1]

Introduction

Several studies have emphasised the problem that natural resource abundance allows countries to engage in excessive consumption that is not sustainable into the future (Davis 1995; Mikesell 1997; Rodríguez and Sachs 1999; Atkinson and Hamilton 2003; Neumayer 2004). The argument of this chapter is that even when Mexicans and Venezuelans of different epochs have not ignored the false prosperity of resource driven economies, they did continue to over consume due to the impression of opulence brought by oil. The resource curse in part arises because policymakers (and economists) do not take into account the different economic essence of wealth extracted from resource depletion. Such wealth from the depreciation of natural capital, if consumed rather than saved to replace the depreciated assets, leads to economic decline. In fact, the few countries that had overcome the resource curse have done so by appealing to savings (see Sanders and Sandvik 2015 for the Norwegian case).

This chapter demonstrates that Mexican and Venezuelan scholars have contemplated since very early on in the century the matter of the actual wealth of the country, the ephemeral prosperity delivered by oil depletion and the biases that oil cash introduced in the economic perception of the country. Yet they had no economic indicator that would substantiate their claims. The chapter also sets out the different approaches to oil exploitation in both countries in greater depth. While the Mexican government opted very early on for using oil to supply the domestic market with cheap energy, Venezuelan governments adopted the "sowing oil" slogan almost simultaneously, exporting oil and extracting rents (in the form of royalties and taxes). The implications of each strategy affected every aspect of oil exploitation: management, pace of exploration and exploitation, prices, costs of operation, etc.

Despite being aware of the illusory oil prosperity the contemporaries could not grasp the extent of the illusion. The second part of the chapter shows that the divergence between traditional GDP measures and alternative measures of prosperity, such as the Human Development Index or the genuine savings and income allow identifying the cases where resource curse may be arising. The final section points at the results of the environmental economist that show that in fact both Mexico and Venezuela endured negative savings (consumed beyond their means) over the twentieth century. Misleading economic indicators should be considered as a trigger of the resource curse that is hardly ever considered in the resource curse literature.

The historical setting: a century of oil in Mexico and Venezuela

It is somewhat surprising not to find many comparative historical studies of either the oil industries or the economic histories of Venezuela and Mexico. The comparative studies that are available appeared either in the first half of the century or in the post-oil boom crisis. It is true that most monographs about Venezuela start by emphasising the little attention that the country has attracted historically. According to Goodman, in scholarly terms,

> Venezuela had the least interesting combination of characteristics – exceptional and unexciting without being a likely model for others. It was too exceptional to be included in multi-country comparative studies of political or economic development, and it offered insufficient attraction as a single case to lure many students.
>
> (Goodman *et al.* 1995, p. 4)

In contrast, Mexico enjoys one of the largest historiographies of the continent.

Despite the deep contrasts between the two countries, particularly regarding their oil policies throughout the century, there are many links between the Venezuelan and Mexican histories. At the dawn of the twentieth century both Venezuela and Mexico based their economies on the primary sector, as did most of the rest of Latin America. Agriculture and mining (Venezuelan coffee and Mexican non-precious metals – copper, lead, zinc, silver, not yet oil) accounted for most of the productive effort and exports of both countries. There was relatively little artisan industry of the type to be found virtually everywhere in Latin America by the turn of the century. Two long dictatorships, Porfirio Díaz (1876–1911) in Mexico and Juan Vicente Gómez (1908–1935) in Venezuela, brought, in their time, the political stability that encouraged foreign investors to explore the countries' oil. The oil industry added to the "export-led" pattern of the early part of the century, just displacing some traditional products such as coffee and cacao in Venezuela and silver in Mexico.

In brief, one can divide the history of Mexican oil into three phases (see Figure 8.1). The first goes from the start of commercial crude oil production 1901–1938. Within this period, Mexico became the second largest producer of petroleum, after the United States, and the largest oil exporter. The second phase

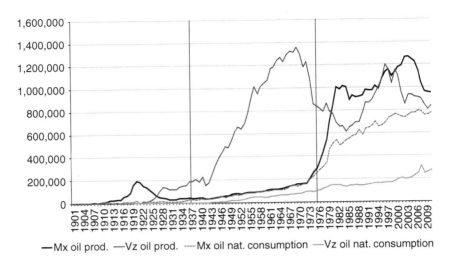

Figure 8.1 Oil production and home consumption in Mexico and Venezuela 1901–2011 (thousand barrels).

Note
Vertical lines mark the Mexican nationalisation of the oil industry in 1938 and the Venezuelan nationalisation in 1976. Data from Rubio (2002), Appendix A for the period before 1989, thereafter U.S. Energy Information Administration (EIA), retrieved from www.eia.gov/petroleum/data.cfm.

links the expropriation-nationalisation of the oil industry in 1938 with the mid-1970s. In this period, Mexico was producing mainly for its own internal consumption with negligible exports and became a net importer of petroleum by the late 1960s. Finally, the new era of Mexican energy development was launched by major oil discoveries in the south of the country in 1974, and the country's production and exports experienced an important thrust.

As for Venezuela, it is also argued that there were three different periods in its oil industry history. The first was the ultraliberal period, which gave the country the lead in the world's oil exports during in the inter-war period. A second period of emerging nationalism started during the post-war years, which led first to the creation of OPEC (1960) and finally to the nationalisation of the industry in 1976. The latter represents the starting point of the last period.

Oil exports became the main export product in Venezuela by the late 1920s, and by the 1930s already accounted for 80 per cent of total exports (see Figure 8.2). Indeed, from 1933 to 1985 the share was over 90 per cent, reaching levels close to 98 per cent in the years around 1950 and 1983. Even after nationalisation in 1976, the share stood at around 95 per cent. Only during the 1990s did the share of oil exports decrease below the 90 per cent mark, regaining it after 2005. In contrast, the Mexican oil exports share in total exports exhibits two peaks separated by a very long period of almost non-existent oil exports. Hydrocarbon exports accounted for half of total exports in 1921 and for more than 70 per cent in the early 1980s. In that sense, Mexico resembles more a classical

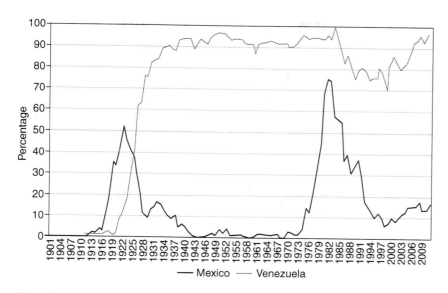

Figure 8.2 Oil exports as percentage of total exports by value, Venezuela and Mexico 1901–2011 (sources: Rubio (2002), Appendix B and UN COMTRADE data, retrieved from http://comtrade.un.org/db/).

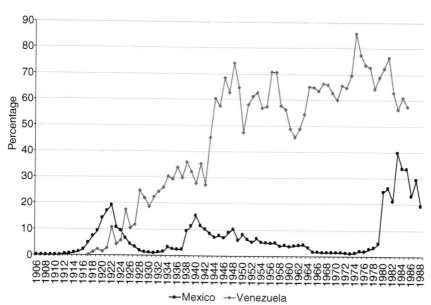

Figure 8.3 Share of oil taxes in government fiscal revenue, Venezuela and Mexico 1901–1989 (source: Rubio (2002), Appendix C).

Dutch Disease profile than Venezuela, which had a sustained dependence on oil revenues.

The claims about the different phases in Venezuela's oil history are better appreciated in the fiscal dependence figures of Figure 8.3. Since the implementation of the Hydrocarbons Law of 1943, Venezuelan governments obtained over half of their fiscal income from the oil industry, and as much as 85 per cent in 1974. The dependence of Mexican governments on oil taxes never exceeded 40 per cent (which constituted the maximum achieved in 1983). During the first oil boom in the early 1920s, oil taxes accounted for a mere 20 per cent of total government income. After nationalisation in 1938, the importance of oil taxes for government revenues continuously decreased and remained below 5 per cent.

Figure 8.4 shows the share of the oil sector GDP in total GDP conventionally measured in Venezuela and Mexico from the 1920s to the 1990s. As with the fiscal and trade indicators, it shows that historically the oil sector has been much more important for Venezuela than for Mexico as a consequence of their different strategies. The share of the oil sector in total GDP in Mexico remained well under 5 per cent throughout the century. According to these data, the oil sector in Venezuela represented between 15 and 25 per cent of the traditional GDP during the twentieth century. The implication of these figures is that the non-oil component of total GDP was calculated to be about 95 per cent in Mexico and between 75 and 85 per cent in Venezuela.

Governments have used the "non-oil-GDP" measure to demonstrate that the rest of the economy was gaining relative importance vis-à-vis the oil sector, which was as important as making public the increasing share of the nation in petroleum revenues. But in Venezuela the whole of the economy was impregnated from oil revenues that financed between 60 and 70 per cent of the public

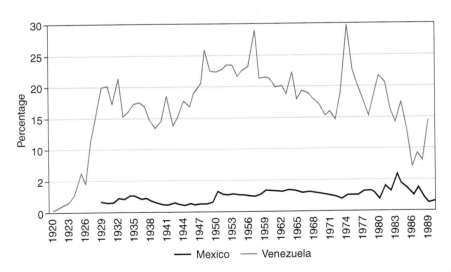

Figure 8.4 Share of the oil sector in total GDP conventionally measured, Venezuela and Mexico 1920–1992 (source: Rubio (2002), Appendix D).

sector. Thus the official non-oil GDP figures exaggerated the part of the economy independent from oil. Truth is, oil wealth impregnated much larger shares of the economic activity in both countries.

Mexico: the perception of the oil question during the century

The first oil boom: naive optimism

In the early days of the twentieth century Mexico was following the pattern of a typical export economy, which depended upon increasing exploitation of natural resources with cheap labour and foreign capital and technology to expand production for overseas markets. Due to the small amount of oil produced at this time (a maximum of 10,000 barrels), the government did not bother to give it any special tax treatment until 1912 (López Rosado 1963). This attitude slowly changed, partly due to the nationalism arising from the Revolution, and also to the increasing economic importance of oil for Mexico. Oil companies managed to isolate production from the effects of the Revolution, so that output in 1921 was fifty-three times greater than in 1910 (Maddison 1992, p. 145). At the beginning of the first oil boom, in 1917, the geologist Miguel Bustamante wrote a long report that can possibly be considered the first Mexican oil monograph (México 1917). The forecasts in 1917 were over-optimistic. The potential estimated production was 200 million barrels per annum. Mexico produced only thirty million barrels in 1916. The forecast multiplied the actual production times six. The forecasted production implied massive investment in infrastructure, and would allow the establishment of oil-related industries and other industries supported by national demand in the Republic. Furthermore, industries established abroad would come to Mexico due to the unlimited quantities of hydrocarbons available and the advantage of low wages. Oil could make it all possible, as the ultimate transforming force able to take the Mexican economy to a higher level.

The path towards economic success was through affordable energy for the country. Mexico wanted to take advantage of oil as a source of energy within the country from the very beginning. These ideals received their most famous – though not necessarily their most efficacious – assertion in the 1917 Constitution. Conservation and distribution issues were at the core of the article that would provide the constitutional basis for the oil expropriation. However, the immediate post-revolutionary governments maintained a hands-off policy with regard to American property, and the potential threat posed by the 1917 Constitution was not taken very seriously in the 1920s (Thorp 1989).

The nationalisation: facing reality (1938–1970)

The predicted production of 200 million barrels per annum would not be achieved until some sixty years later. What took place in the years immediately after Bustamante's article was the rise and fall of Mexican oil production (Rubio-Varas 2006). Production increased almost three fold in four years

(1917–1921). In the middle of the first historical oil shortage created by the final months of World War I and its aftermath, Mexico became the world's greatest exporter and second largest oil producer in 1921. By 1928 production was below what it had been ten years before and it did not recover the levels of the early 1920s until the 1970s.

The so-called limitless capacity of Mexican oil fields turned into fears of exhaustion in the 1920s and 1930s (Manterola 1937). From the companies' side, the government's increasing nationalist tendencies paralysed exploration and reduced production. The creation of national reserves – i.e. the retention of land for further exploration and potential exploitation by the state – exemplified the point made by the companies. As a consequence, capital started to flow away from Mexico, particularly to Venezuela. For the companies, Venezuela was a better recipient of capital since they found legislative facilities similar to those of Mexico before 1910 (Brown 1985).

Mexicans justified the decline of the oil industry in a different manner. The recent discoveries of oil in Venezuela attracted capital which otherwise would have been invested in further development of the Mexican industry, if Mexican oil fields had not been over-exploited beforehand. The general agreement among Mexican scholars was that oil exploitation could not be done in a sensible manner when there were several companies involved. According to this view, fields would be totally exhausted under private exploitation. The companies were accused of hiding profits (Silva Herzog 1938). The companies were said to be distorting information about their profit margins in order to evade taxes. They were not only exhausting Mexican oil, but also going away without paying any compensation.

According to one observer of the time, liberal countries were just generating a "misleading and ephemeral prosperity" by allowing rapid exploitation of their oil resources. It mirrored the environmental economist claims of the 1990s stating that "the expansion of economic activity as a consequence of accelerating the liquidation of subsoil assets is applauded as good economic performance and it is confused with the growth that comes from labour, capital formation, technological progress, and efficient organisation" (El Serafy 1989, p. 12). This is not to say that the agenda of the Mexican government and scholars matched green economists' concerns, but it is certainly true that the idea of the ephemeral prosperity brought about by resource exploitation was present as early as the 1930s.

What was on the agenda of the Mexican government was the nationalisation of the oil industry. In fact, it had long been contemplated. On 18 March 1938, the Mexican government expropriated by executive decree the property of seventeen foreign-owned oil companies without compensation. The companies judged the government incapable of running the industry in their absence. In truth it took PEMEX almost a decade to organise itself. From the foreigners' perspective the nationalisation was a failure in all respects. According to the companies, the mismanagement of the industry by the government made it inefficient and economically unsustainable, and failed to fulfil its aim of conserving the oil and improving living conditions in the country. The nationalisation process, or rather the whole debate over subsoil rights, seriously slowed the pace of economic growth (Haber 1989). The inefficiency of the national company has been established by the literature and even been recognised by PEMEX officials (PEMEX (Petróleos Mexicanos) n.d.; Philip 1982; Randall 1989).

By the late 1930s the Mexican government insisted on the path, initially suggested by Bustamante in 1917, of making productive use of their oil endowment within the country's boundaries. This doctrine shaped the principles ruling PEMEX's policy for the subsequent decades. These principles stated unequivocally that the Mexican government considered oil as a resource for national development in a very specific way: as a source of affordable energy for the country and of income for the oil workers (Báez 1939). The fact that those principles imposed a heavy burden on PEMEX, particularly on its finances, was considered just as a subsidy to the national economy (PEMEX (Petróleos Mexicanos) n.d.).

Partly as a consequence of conservation and self-sufficiency policies, and the weak financial situation of PEMEX, only 10 per cent of the potentially productive geological areas were explored between 1938 and 1970 (Sordo and López 1988). As a consequence, Mexico started importing oil products by 1956. By the 1960s PEMEX recognised that Mexico was on the edge of facing a real energy supply problem. Mexico's reserves to production ratio (R/P), in other words the life expectancy of Mexican oil fields, had been declining since 1960. Exploration needed to be urgently supported. The creation of the Instituto Mexicano del Petróleo in 1965 helped substantially to improve the gathering and systematic interpretation of the geophysical information available. The rebirth of the Mexican oil industry was on the way.

The second oil boom: bounded optimism and crisis (1970s–1980s)

The first results of the increasing exploration activity were visible by 1972. In 1974, Mexico produced enough oil to be able to export. Huge oil discoveries were announced two years later, together with the decision to export oil in meaningful amounts again. Oil continued being a core development resource for the Mexican government, but now not only as a supply of economical energy but also, for the first time since the nationalisation, as an earner of exports revenues. Several explanations are given for the change in policy of the 1970s.

> A change in administration in 1976 combined with serious economic problems. Other variations derive from unexpected frustration and unanticipated opportunities that emerged as the nation's export potential increased. Still another explanation is the novelty of the situation that saw the decision-makers confronted with new conditions that had not been carefully thought out.
>
> (Williams 1979, p. 42)

The change in oil policy had two phases. During the presidency of Echevarría (1970–1976), nationalistic sensitivities and domestic political discretion weighed heavily in favour of conservationist rhetoric, but evolving practice hinted at a less restrictive policy. After 1976, with the rise of López Portillo to the presidency, the official stance changed to emphasise increasing exports. Oil was expected to relieve the economy from both foreign and fiscal constraints. The public and private sectors went on an investment spree beginning in 1978, which was accelerated by an oil price rise and new oil discoveries in 1979 (Lustig 1992).

By the early 1980s, PEMEX played a strategic role in the country's economy and prospects. Oil exports accounted for 75 per cent of Mexico's total merchandise exports, making them the main source of foreign exchange. The oil industry contributed 26 per cent of fiscal revenues. In addition, almost a third of total public investment was directly carried out by the oil industry (Beteta 1987b). In the words of Ramón Beteta, head of PEMEX from 1982 to 1987, "oil wealth should bring Mexico beyond the reach of the ambitions of the powerful" (Beteta 1987a, p. 2). High expectations of future public revenues encouraged a rising fiscal deficit. For some time, this public-expenditure-led growth made it possible for the economy to grow at 8 and 9 per cent per annum. In 1981, with lower oil prices and higher interest rates, the deficit reached unprecedented levels. It was largely financed with more indebtedness in the erroneous belief that the decline in oil prices was temporary. The limit of external borrowing capacity was finally reached in 1982, following large devaluations of the peso, chaos in the financial markets and the beginning of the international debt crisis.

The oil boom did not produce the desired dramatic transformation of the economy and permanent improvement in living standards. On the contrary, crisis and increased poverty followed it. This forced a reconsideration of the role oil played in the Mexican economy. In a very brief period of time, oil passed from being once again the cure to all Mexican economic ills to being at the root of most problems. Yet we also know that, in comparative perspective, Mexico's history is not one of "petrodependency". This was only a relatively recent concern for Mexico. Not even in the 1920s did the Mexican government contemplate "petrodependency" as an issue. Nevertheless, it did not take too long for the old rhetoric of the 1930s, which had been abandoned in the late 1970s, to come back but with slight modifications. The finiteness of the oil endowment, the conservationist approach to its use and maintaining the level of autosufficiency had formed part of PEMEX's policy from the beginning of its existence. The main difference is that, from the 1970s, export and fiscal revenues from the oil sector re-emerged as contributions to the economic progress of Mexico. The ephemeral prosperity that this may entail was forgotten.

Over the twentieth century the Mexican strategy resulted in a slower pace of exploitation overall, which would be approved by "green" standards, and a better route to avoid resource curse. However, the reasoning leading to such a result was not inspired by environmental or macroeconomic principles, but on a nationalistic approach. Mexicans managed to avoid the resource curse for most of the century for the wrong reasons.

Venezuela: the illusion of oil wealth through history

The importance of oil for Venezuela is overwhelming. In the historical statements of politicians, experts and journalists, it is easy to identify the concerns about the "real gains" from oil, which emerged almost as soon as Venezuelans realised their dependence on oil. Nevertheless, since national accounting in Venezuela was not developed until the 1950s, there is no direct suggestion that the economic performance portrayed by national statistics may be misleading for Venezuela until the second half of the century.

The early years

The first reported application for an oil lease was in 1863 and the first two oil concessions were issued in 1866 (though asphalt concessions were granted as early as 1854). From 1878 to 1920, the government awarded 1,312 contracts for oil exploitation. Juan Vicente Gómez's dictatorial regime (1908–1935) relied on the new fiscal revenues generated by the oil concessions to confront the stagnant economy and the large foreign debt (Rubio-Varas 2002). The aim of one of the earliest Venezuelan ministers for industrial planning, Gumersindo Torres, was to obtain as much revenue from oil as Mexico did at the time. Yet, while the Mexican government was hinting at increasing the use of the resource domestically, the Venezuelan government dictated laws that facilitated the expansion of the oil industry by foreign companies. The law passed on 13 June 1922 gave the oil companies the incentives to redouble their exploration efforts (Salazar-Carrillo 1994). No major discoveries occurred in Venezuela until the blow out of well Los Barrosos No2 in December 1922, but important discoveries followed in the subsequent years. These led Venezuela's oil production to overtake that of Mexico by 1928, becoming the world's second oil producer after the United States and the major oil exporter, a position to be retained until the 1960s.

Nevertheless, there were criticisms of government policy on oil exploitation. For some, the concessions were nothing but the "surrender of national sovereignty to the imperialist capital". The overall perception was that "only the favourites of the dictator prospered. The petroleum enclave benefited foreigners and the dictator" (Allen 1977, p. 3). After Gómez's death in 1935, opponents of the petroleum industry were permitted to speak openly. The attacks were three-pronged: against Gómez's policy, against company behaviour and against the industry's dominant position in the national economy (Lieuwen 1954). They marked the onset of the shadows of nationalism that were to impregnate the late 1930s and were the prelude of the changes of the early 1940s.

In 1936, Arturo Uslar Pietri urged the Venezuelan government to "sow oil" (Uslar Pietri 1936). According to him, the cash received by the State from selling oil was not the result of any productive effort but a kind of "divine loan" with either terms or interest (Uslar Pietri 1989). Therefore, it should be employed precisely as a loan: prudently and sensibly, taking into account the returns and the possibilities of recovering the amount received. His concern was how to transform the transitory income from oil into permanent wealth for the nation, not whether Venezuela was obtaining a "fair share" (*participación justa*) of the petroleum profits (Pérez Alfonzo 1965; Rodríguez Gallad 1974).

Uslar Pietri's proposition set the basis of the national policy regarding the use of monetary resources obtained from oil in the promotion of development in its human, scientific and economic dimensions (Arcilla Farias 1989). Already in 1937, one finds echoes of "sowing oil" in speeches in Congress and in government publications (Ministerio de Hacienda. Venezuela. 1937; Venezuela. Cámara de Diputados 1937). Transforming the transitory income from oil into permanent wealth for the nation required treating oil income as "extraordinary resources" that should not form part of the ordinary national income flow but be set aside and reinvested (Arcilla Farias 1989). In this regard, Ulsar Pietri's concerns were identical to the environmental accounting literature of the 1990s.

Comprehending the reality of oil (1940s)

The nationalist voices that rose in Venezuela spurred on by the nationalisation of oil in Mexico were the prelude to the reforms that took place in Venezuela in the early 1940s. The balance of power shifted slowly from the companies towards the government side. The Hydrocarbon Law of 1943, which broadened the government's technical and administrative powers, made this obvious (Lieuwen 1954). The enforcement of the 1943 law had a special importance in the historic evolution of the petroleum industry, since it governed the industry with small modifications until nationalisation in 1976. It introduced the concept of income tax and raised royalties to $16^{2/3}$ per cent. This figure was calculated in order to assure the government of one-half of the net profits of the industry. Yet, in 1948, arguing that 1943 was a year of unusually low market price, thus royalties were insufficient to guarantee the government one-half of the profits, the Congress moved the 50–50 concept to the income tax. The 1943 law also introduced the principle of reversion. The idea of reversion had been introduced already in the law of 1920, but the companies rewrote it the following year. The 1943 law was clear and unequivocal: the companies could extract oil owned by the nation from the nation's property for a forty-year period after which everything, including all improvements and company property, belonged to the State (Allen 1977). Most of the reforms introduced in 1943 set the pattern for other oil countries' legislation in subsequent decades.

According to the Venezuelan government, "the system of taxing the oil industry did not come into existence spontaneously. It grew with the realisation that oil is a non-replaceable natural resource that belongs to the nation" (Venezuela. Ministry of Mines and Hydrocarbons 1962, p. 4). This recognition led the first Acción Democrática government (1945–1948) to attempt to reduce the amount of oil extracted in order to preserve future generations' income. It was all in vain, since its efforts did not offset the expanding market for Venezuelan oil in the post-war reconstruction of Western Europe. In addition, the government had an increasing need for funds to finance ambitious programmes of social reform and economic development (Lieuwen 1985). Accordingly, Venezuelan production almost doubled between 1945 and 1950.

The increasing production also increased the dependence of Venezuela's economy upon oil. The magnitudes involved at the end of the 1940s were greater than ever before. The share of oil exports in total exports rose from 90 per cent in 1935 to 97 per cent in 1948. The percentage of government income dependent on oil revenues had been about 30 per cent in 1935 but was over 60 per cent in 1948. Venezuelan governments progressively started to impose their authority over the oil industry during the 1940s. However, the strategy regarding oil exploitation still remained to be one of leasing the oil fields to the private sector in order to produce revenues for the State.

Measuring the gains (1950s–1960s)

The concerns about the "special" economic circumstances of the country and the possibly misleading indicators displayed by the incipient national statistics become apparent by the early 1950s. Within the country itself, the government admitted that "the circulation of such an extraordinary volume of wealth [that obtained from oil] injects a *special* bonanza to the country's economy" (Venezuela. Ministerio de Trabajo 1955, p. 141, emphasis added). Internationally, a 1955 survey on the post-war industrialisation of Latin America by the United Nations Economic Commission for Latin America (ECLAC) already emphasised the misleading nature of Venezuela's indicators (ECLAC 1956). Even if Venezuela's statistics looked similar to those of its neighbours, oil income affected Venezuela's indicators in such a way that they could not be taken at face value.

The cost associated with the depletion of the natural resources was not a totally neglected issue (Carrillo Batalla 1968). Venezuelans in fact assigned to the depleted resources the value of the fiscal intake by the State. The reasoning was as follows. The State owned the mineral resources by law. Therefore, when mineral products are sold, a national good is being traded and liquidated. Hereupon, the State should be compensated for the liquidation of the deposits. In this view, taxes upon oil extraction are not a fiscal obligation on nature, but the price received from the sale of a good that belongs to the national endowment. Taxes are the liquidation value of a pre-existing asset. Therefore, oil fiscal revenues should not form part of the national flow of resources available in any given year and should be reinvested in the promotion of economic development (Arcilla Farias 1989). These statements constitute the essence of the "sowing oil" rhetoric.

Scholars and policymakers have attempted to evaluate the success of "sowing oil" policies ever since its adoption as a generic slogan in the late 1930s. The general conclusion was much the same whenever the evaluation took place either in the 1950s, 1960s or the late 1980s: sowing oil had been a flawed project (Lieuwen 1954; Carrillo Batalla 1968; Balestrini 1989). It could be said that rather than "sow" it had been an oil spill. In general terms, the economic resources of the nation had only been marginally used (*The Economist* 1950).

In order to evaluate "sowing oil" policies, comparisons were drawn between the oil tax revenues collected by the government and public capital expenditure. The approach adopted was to consider that all of the fiscal receipts should have been invested in capital goods. As long as oil tax revenues exceeded public capital investment, they said, it was possible to talk of national impoverishment, given that the economy was failing to undertake investment equivalent to the fiscal resources received from the exploitation – i.e. depletion – of a non-renewable resource. From 1927 to 1963, the capital investment done by Venezuelan governments failed to match the fiscal tax receipts collected from oil exploitation. From 1917 to 1964 the amount under-invested annually, or rather the scale of the yearly impoverishment of Venezuela, ranked between 2 and 6 per cent of the actual GDP of the country for every year (Malave cited in Carrillo Batalla 1968, p. 79).

Nevertheless, public administrators and government employees defended the policy of not investing the whole of the oil tax revenue in capital goods. From their perspective, Venezuela did not have sufficient resources, other than oil, to support its current expenditures. The existing situation required the sale of oil and the expenditure of part of the fiscal receipts. They also pointed to the fact that bigger capital investment implied increasing current expenditures. "If we build more hospitals, we need to increase the number of doctors, nurses and resources needed for the maintenance of the service; if we build universities and schools, we need to pay the teachers..." (Carrillo Batalla 1968, p. 148). Some other authors pointed out later that the main problem of Venezuelan investment was indeed the fact that such investment was only profitable because part of the oil receipts were devoted to the consumption of goods produced by those investments (Baptista 1989, p. 135).

Despite limited achievements and persistent setbacks, it was generally believed that Venezuela had steadily progressed towards modernity since the end of the 1950s (Coronil 1997). At the same time, the evidence suggests that the first doubts regarding the adequacy of Venezuela's economic statistics and oil exploitation strategy surfaced in this period.

Illusion and delusion (1970s–1980s)

As a major oil producer and founder member of the OPEC, Venezuela's position in the mid-1970s seemed outstanding. Economically, the oil boom provided extraordinary resources. Just to give some idea of the dimensions of the impact of oil prices rises on the Venezuelan economy: the value of oil exports almost tripled between 1973 and 1974. Between 1973 and 1976, the fiscal income rose form 11,221 million bolivars to 28,991 million bolivars. Monetary liquidity increased from 21,300 million to 51,200 million bolivars. International reserves grew from $2,400 million to $9,300 million (Banco Central de Venezuela 1978). In addition, the Venezuelan data showed increasing income equality from the late 1950s until 1983 and a more equal income distribution than that found in the other large Latin American countries (Kuczynski 1977; Silva 1979; Urrutia 1991).

Nonetheless, there were simultaneously some critical voices already pointing to the illusory nature of the situation in titles such as *An Illusion of Harmony: Venezuela's case* (Naím and Piñango 1974). The rush of petroleum income temporarily postponed a critical assessment of Venezuelan development. It took almost a decade for these arguments to become mainstream opinions. The reason for such a delay was precisely the healthy appearance of most economic indicators and the confidence in continuing high oil prices. At this time of bonanza, the government planned to set aside half of current oil revenues for long-term and foreign investment through the Venezuelan Investment Fund in 1974 (Ewell 1984). Shortly after, the government of Carlos Andrés Pérez nationalised the oil industry in 1976. It was seen as the culmination of a slow process through which Venezuela progressively gained more control over the resource and the revenues it generated (Petras *et al.* 1977; Coronel 1983). Ambitious projects, waste and increased volume of luxury and capital imports gradually consumed a higher proportion of current revenues. Less was channelled into the Venezuelan Investment Fund, and more foreign loans were sought. High interest rates and inflation in the US and Europe contributed to inflation and a rising debt service in Venezuela. In 1977, the current account balance showed the first deficit since 1972 (Ewell 1984).

Nevertheless, it was not until well into the 1980s, when oil prices stabilised, that a serious analysis of the effects of the roller coaster of the 1970s took place (Coronil 1997). Moses Naím, Minister of Industry in the government of Carlos Andrés Pérez in the late 1980s, wrote that

> Venezuela's oil wealth no doubt encouraged the plunder by contributing to the widespread perception held by Venezuelans and foreign creditors alike that the country remained rich.... In sum, after decades of consuming more than they produced, to restore balance, Venezuelans' real incomes and consumption would have to decline.
>
> (Naím 1993, p. 28)

As Naím here, other authors (Mommer and Baptista 1983; Uslar Pietri 1985; Rodríguez and Sachs 1999) had also recognised that due to the nature of oil revenues an increasing gap opened between the real production capacity of that society and its earning and expenditure possibilities. Venezuela's exceptional financial wealth made it possible for the State to implement dazzling development plans that obscured structures typical of other Latin American nations (Coronil 1997). Karl (1997) recognised this when portraying the paradox of the plenty: oil producers were supposed to be rich but confronting very difficult realities. It was only after the 1980s' crisis that the effects of resource availability on the behaviour of economic agents began to be recognised and analysed.

Despite the problems that became evident by the early 1980s, the myth of Venezuela as a wealthy democratic nation steadily advancing toward modernity continued to hold into the 1990s. The myth endured currency devaluations, a prolonged decline in the standard of living, massive popular riots, and two abortive military coups in 1992. Nevertheless, the final recognition that Venezuela suffered from the political, economic and social problems common to most Latin American countries led to the "collapse of Venezuelan exceptionalism" in the mid-1990s (Coronil 1997). It was about then when Venezuela became the poster case of the "resource curse" literature. However, from a green economy perspective, the crisis that started in Venezuela in the 1980s and that has not yet seen an end, can be interpreted as the effect of having ignored the loss of natural resources in calculations of national income in the previous decades, which masked the true state of the economy.

Overall performance: which economic indicators?

The events of the 1980s questioned sustainability regarding the economic rather than the physical exhaustion of natural resources as sources of income for primary producers. It was at this time that environmental accounting came forward, claiming that traditional national accounting methods produce misleading indicators of economic performance for resource-based economies. For such economies, traditional accounting practices exaggerated income, encouraged unsustainable levels of consumption and obscured the necessity to implement greatly needed policy adjustments (El Serafy 1989; Repetto 1989; Hartwick 1990, 1995). Actually, it was not only the environmental literature that argued along these lines. Studies on rentier states put forward similar concerns about their national income accounts yet from a complete different perspective (Mahdavy 1970; Stauffer 1984).

Nevertheless, the economic histories of Mexico and Venezuela are still told in accordance with traditional accounting methods. In comparative terms, Mexico has had a fairly stable trajectory compared to most Latin American countries, remaining around 40 per cent of the European average income per capita. In contrast, Venezuela started the century with the second lowest GDP per capita of the six larger Latin American countries but by the 1940s it had surpassed them all, as shown in Figure 8.5. Furthermore, by the mid-1950s Venezuela had the seventh highest average income in the world, slightly greater than that in the United Kingdom and significantly higher than incomes in France and Germany.

Nevertheless, as Maddison (1995, p. 125) recalls, "it is useful to make plausibility checks, e.g. to see whether the apparent growth rates or levels of performance of a country in question make it an 'outlier'". After all, the hypothesis of environmental accounting is that that income is not being accurately calculated for economies based on natural resources. The problem is relevant to practically all countries where non-renewable resources are being run down without being restored by equivalent investment. Since both Mexico and Venezuela fit into such a description at some point in their histories, the first question is whether there is any indication that the GDP figures of these two countries may be a misleading indicator of their actual performance, and the resource curse was on its way.

Oil illusion and delusion in Mexico and Venezuela 175

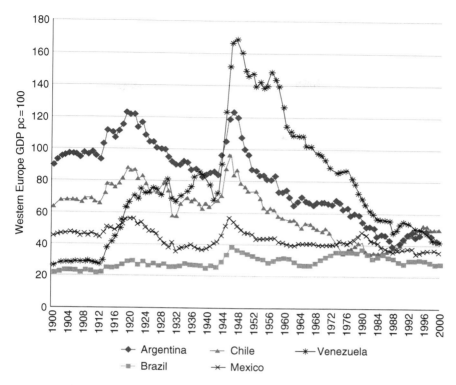

Figure 8.5 Index of GDP per capita of six Latin American countries relative to Western Europe 1900–2000 (source: based on the GDP per capita produced by Maddison (2010). Western Europe refers to the average GDPpc of the following twelve countries: Austria, Belgium, Denmark, Finland, France, Germany, Italy, Netherlands, Norway, Sweden, Switzerand and United Kingdom).

A preliminary way of enquiring along these lines is to consider indicators other than income-exclusive ones. Among those, the Human Development Index (HDI) is probably the most widely used (United Nations 1991). Figure 8.6 presents the ranking of a series of countries according to their GDP per capita versus their HDI index for 1913, 1939, 1950, 1973 and 1995. For each year, the diagonal represents the same GDP and HDI ranking among the countries represented. If a country is above the diagonal, it indicates that the country had a higher international ranking than its GDP ranking when a broader measure of development is taken (HDI). By contrast, when a country is below the diagonal, it signals that the country had a lower development (HDI) than its pure economic indicator suggests.

Mexico maintained a steady position in both rankings throughout the period considered. In contrast, Venezuela becomes an outlier when measuring its economic development in terms of HDI rather than in GDP per capita terms. In the extreme case of 1950, Venezuela had the world's fourth greatest GDP per capita

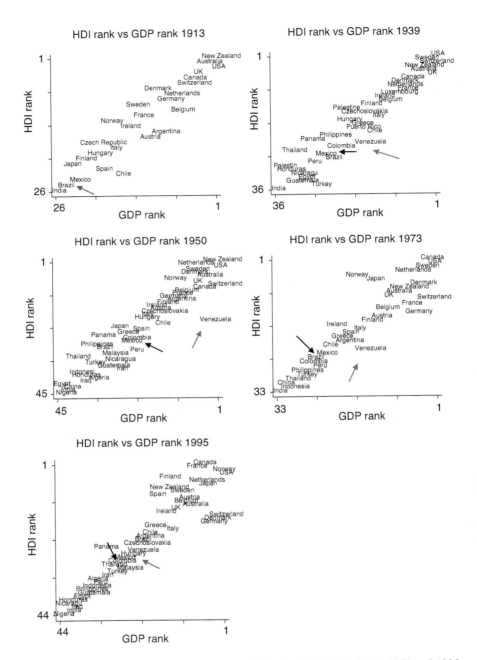

Figure 8.6 GDP per capita ranking vs HDI ranking for 1913, 1939, 1950, 1973 and 1995 for thirty-six countries (sources: Data for 1939 by Metzer (1998), the rest by Crafts (1997), GDP series by Maddison (2010)).

but its human development indicators push it down to the nineteenth position. Regarding their relative positions, the gap between Mexico and Venezuela is much smaller when development is measured by HDI rather than GDP. These results of the HDI index point in the direction suggested by the environmental accounting literature. The actual state of development of some economies is well below the position that their "income indicators" would suggest. Policymakers and society will be misled by untruthful economic indicators for decades before the true nature of the situation confirms. This would pave the way to economic, political and social disaster when the downward adjustment settled into place. In this sense, the resource curse would arise in part as consequence of this illusory wealth effect created by macroeconomic indicators unadjusted by environmental depletion and by ignoring the existing evidence: in fact Venezuela continuously lost ground for the second half of the twentieth century, in relative terms, with Western Europe, while Mexico kept a fairly stable distance with the West as shown in Figure 8.4. Such a continuous decline must have had an impact in society and institutions.

Living beyond their means

Existing studies analysing the resource curse hypothesis regress growth in gross domestic product (GDP) on some measure of resource intensity. This is problematic as GDP counts natural and other capital depreciation as income (Neumayer 2004). First Hartwick (1977) and then Solow (1986), building on the concepts of Hicks (1946), established that in order to achieve constant real consumption through time (the lower bound of sustainability) it is necessary to keep the underlying capital stock constant. It becomes a requirement that the value of the net change in the total capital stock (that is the *genuine savings*) must be equal or greater than zero. In principle, a country cannot therefore endure negative genuine savings for long periods of time without experiencing declining consumption, or the total collapse of its economy as time goes to infinity (Rubio-Varas 2004). The concept of *genuine savings* starts from the fact that the traditional measure of a nation's rate of accumulation of wealth is gross saving. This is calculated as a residual: GNP minus public and private consumption. Gross saving represents the total amount of produced output that is set aside for the future. Gross savings rates can say little about the ability to sustain future consumption, however, because productive assets depreciate through time: if this depreciation is greater than gross saving, then aggregate wealth is in decline. Net saving, total gross saving less the value of depreciation of produced assets, is one step closer to a sustainability indicator that guarantees future consumption, but focuses narrowly on produced assets. Environmental economists assimilate natural resources to man made capital, since a country's consumption may be mainly supported by draining natural resources, i.e. from the depreciation of natural capital. Traditionally computed net savings ignore the depreciation of natural capital. Once natural capital depreciation is also subtracted we arrive at the concept of genuine savings.

In addition to this, the national income literature has long noted the problem that traditional indicators "may not be a good indicator of national welfare in an open economy experiencing substantial change in its terms of trade" (Hamada and Iwata 1984, p. 752). This occurs because traditional measures of output and income fail to account for the impact of changing terms of trade on the consumption possibilities of the economy. This is particularly true for resource exporting economies. Therefore, the genuine savings shown for Mexico and Venezuela in Figure 8.7 are calculated both with and without the effect of the changes in the terms of trade.

Environmental economists have shown (Rodriguez and Sachs, 1999; Rubio-Varas 2004, 2007) that in fact both Mexico and Venezuela endured negative genuine savings (consumed beyond their means) over the twentieth century. The puzzling question is for how long a country can endure negative genuine savings before the eventual decline of well-being becomes apparent. Mexico managed to keep positive genuine savings for most of the twentieth century except for the years of the debt crisis in the 1980s, and in that decade declining consumption took place.

In contrast, in Venezuela negative rates of genuine savings occurred continuously for over forty years and yet, declining well-being was only apparent from the 1980s, and according to some authors, only from the 1990s onwards (see Goodman *et al.* 1995 and Coronil 1997). Traditional macroeconomic indicators explain that Venezuela had the best overall performance in Latin America throughout the twentieth century in terms of traditional GDP growth. Yet, going

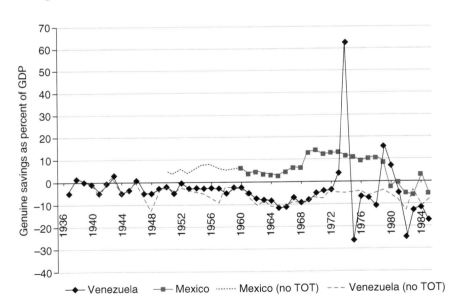

Figure 8.7 Genuine savings of Mexico and Venezuela as percentage of GDP (with and without the effects of the terms of trade) (sources: own elaboration from the data in the Supplementary Materials of Rubio (2004)).

back to the evidence of the previous section, the decline of Venezuela can be identified from as early as the 1950s in relative terms. Furthermore, the mismatch between the traditional macroeconomic indicators and the alternative indicators such as HDI, showed that Venezuela was suffering from resource curse much earlier than the GDP per capita figures would actually reflect.

Concluding remarks

Mexican and Venezuelan scholars and policymakers have contemplated since very early on in the twentieth century the matter of the actual wealth of the country, the ephemeral prosperity delivered by oil depletion and the biases that oil cash introduced in the economic perception of the country. But they were mostly unable to quantify their claims.

Historically the oil sector has been much more important for Venezuela than for Mexico. The different approaches to oil exploitation in both countries led to very different strategies, and in the long run, to different avenues into the resource curse. While the Mexican government opted very early on to use oil to supply the domestic market with cheap energy, Venezuelan governments adopted the "sowing oil" slogan almost simultaneously without truly implementing it. The Mexican strategy resulted in a slower pace of exploitation overall. However, the reasoning leading to such a result was not inspired by environmental or macroeconomic principles, but on a nationalistic approach. Mexicans managed to avoid the resource curse for most of the century but for the wrong reasons.

Despite being aware of the illusory oil prosperity the contemporaries could not grasp the extent of the illusion shown in the second part of the chapter: the divergence between traditional GDP measures and alternative measures of prosperity, such as the Human Development Index and the negative genuine savings. Faulty economic indicators should be considered as a trigger of the resource curse that is hardly ever considered in the resource curse literature. This should not be taken as an exoneration of policymakers: as the first part of the chapter shows, they knew, for the most part, that oil wealth was a mirage.

In general, the prediction of the resource curse literature is that countries with good institutions will not suffer a resource curse while those with bad institutions will. Yet in the case of Venezuela living beyond its means for over forty years paired with a long-term loss of relative position in the world economy. It can be argued that such conjunction gave rise to the wrong kind of institutions that we see today worsening the situation. Venezuela's relative position in the world economy has been in free fall since 1950 according to Figure 8.5 even if masked by growing GDP, apparently high rates of saving and investment, and deceptively stable or near stable prices. Back then Venezuela was treated as a political exception in Latin America, cited as a model of a successful transition to democracy or as having "consolidated" democracy (Coronil 1997). By any standard, Venezuela's institutions were of superior quality than Mexican ones for most part of the twentieth century. If anything, Venezuelan politics have gone down the drain while Mexican politics seems to have improved.

While most literature tends to view the resource curse as a matter of political will alone our research suggests that this approach fails to take the broader picture into account. Political will, like institutional capacity, and social reactions are the product of incentives. The usual economic indicators return mirages rather than realities in countries endowed with non-renewable resources creating the wrong incentives. This would pave the way to economic, political and social disaster that will worsen when the downward adjustment settles into place.

Note

1 Jose Ignacio Carbujas, a Venezuelan political commentator. As quoted in Coronil (1997, p. 1).

References

Allen, L., 1977. Venezuelan Economic Development. A Politico-Economic Analysis. *In*: E.I. Altman and I. Walter, eds. *Contemporary Studies in Economic and Financial Analysis*. Greenwich, CT: Jai Press.

Arcilla Farias, E., 1989. ¿En qué medida se ha cumplido el vaticinio de Uslar Pietri (Ahora, 1936) sobre el parasitismo rentista en la Venezuela petrolera?, ¿en qué medida se ha sembrado el petróleo?, ¿cuál es el significado del momento actual en esta evolución? *In*: F. Mieres, ed. *Hacia la Venezuela Post-petrolera [conference sponsored by la Academia Nacional de las Ciencias Económicas in 1985]*. Caracas, Venezuela: Academia Nacional de Ciencias Económicas, 123–130.

Atkinson, G. and Hamilton, K., 2003. Savings, Growth and the Resource Curse Hypothesis. *World Development*, 31 (11), 1793–1807.

Báez, J.D., 1939. Influencia de la guerra en el petróleo mexicano. *Revista de industria*, 5.

Balestrini, C., 1989. ¿Cuál ha sido el papel cumplido por la explotación petrolera en el proceso de modernización de la sociedad venezolana? *In*: F. Mieres, ed. *Hacia la Venezuela Post-petrolera [conference sponsored by la Academia Nacional de las Ciencias Económicas in 1985]*. Caracas, Venezuela: Academia Nacional de Ciencias Económicas, 195–202.

Banco Central de Venezuela, 1978. *La Economía venezolana en los últimos treinta y cinco años*. Caracas, Venezuela: Banco Central de Venezuela.

Baptista, A., 1989. ¿En qué medida se ha cumplido el vaticinio de Uslar Pietri (Ahora, 1936) sobre el parasitistmo rentista en la Venezuela petrolera?, ¿en qué medida se ha "sembrado el petróleo"? *In*: F. Mieres, ed. *Hacia La Venezuela Post-Petrolera [Conference Sponsored by La Academia Nacional De Las Ciencias Económicas in 1985]*. Caracas, Venezuela: Academia Nacional de Ciencias Económicas.

Beteta, M.R., 1987. Introduction. *In*: P.S. Falks, ed. Petroleum and Mexico's Future London: Westview Press.

Beteta, M.R., 1987. The Role of the Oil Industry in Mexico. *In*: P.S. Falks, ed. *Petroleum and Mexico's Future*. London: Westview Press, 124.

Brown, J.C., 1985. Why Foreign Oil Companies Shifted their Production from Mexico to Venezuela During the 1920s. *The American Historical Review*, 90 (2), 362–385.

Carrillo Batalla, T.E., 1968. *La evaluación de la inversión del ingreso fiscal petrolero en Venezuela [conference sponsored by Universidad Central de Venezuela. Foro Petrolero 1965]*. Caracas, Venezuela.

Coronel, G., 1983. *The Nationalization of the Venezuelan Oil Industry: From Technocratic Success to Political Failure*. Lexington, MA: Lexington Books.

Coronil, F., 1997. *The Magical State: Nature, Money, and Modernity in Venezuela*. Chicago and London: University of Chicago Press.

Crafts, N., 1997. The Human Development Index and Changes in Standards of Living: Some Historical Comparisons. *European Review of Economic History*, 1 (3), 299–322.

Davis, G.A., 1995. Learning to Love the Dutch Disease: Evidence from the Mineral Economies. *World Development*, 23 (10), 1765–1779.

ECLAC, 1956. *Economic Survey of Latin America, 1955*. Santiago de Chile, Chile: Economic Commission for Latin America and the Caribbean, United Nations.

Ewell, J., 1984. *Venezuela: A Century of Change*. Stanford, CA: Stanford University Press.

Goodman, L.W., Forman, J.M., Naím, M. and Tulchin, J.S., eds., 1995. *Lessons of the Venezuelan Experience*. Washington, D.C.: Woodrow Wilson Center Press.

Haber, S., 1989. *Industry and Underdevelopment: The Industrialisation of Mexico, 1890–1940*. Stanford, CA: Stanford University Press.

Hamada, K. and Iwata, K., 1984. National Income, Terms of Trade and Economic Welfare. *The Economic Journal*, 94, 752–771.

Hartwick, J.M., 1977. Intergenerational Equity and the Investing of Rents from Exhaustible Resources. *American Economic Review*, 67 (5), 972–974.

Hartwick, J.M., 1990. Natural Resources, National Accounting and Economic Depreciation. *Journal of Public Economics*, 43 (3), 291–304.

Hartwick, J.M., 1995. Constant Consumption Paths in Open Economies with Exhaustible Resources. *Review of International Economics*, 3 (3), 275–283.

Hicks, J., 1946. *Value and Capital: An Inquiry into Some Fundamental Principles of Economic Theory*. Oxford: Clarendon Press.

Karl, T., 1997. *The Paradox of Plenty: Oil Booms and Petro-States*. Berkeley, CA: University of California Press.

Kuczynski, P.P., 1977. The Economic Development of Venezuela: A Summary View as of 1975–1976. In: R.D. Bond, ed. *Contemporary Venezuela and its Role in International Affairs*. New York: New York University Press, 45–90.

Lieuwen, E., 1954. *Petroleum in Venezuela : A History*. Berkeley, CA: University of California Press.

Lieuwen, E., 1985. The Politics of Energy in Venezuela. In: J.D. Wirth, ed. *Latin American Oil Companies and the Politics of Energy*. Lincoln, NE: University of Nebraska Press.

López Rosado, D.G., 1963. *Curso de Historia Económica de México*. México D.F., México: Universidad Autonoma.

Lustig, N., 1992. *Mexico, the Remaking of an Economy*. Washington, D.C.: Brookings Institution.

Maddison, A., 1992. *Brazil and Mexico – The Political Economy of Poverty, Equity, and Growth*. Washington, D.C.: The World Bank.

Maddison, A. 1995. *Monitoring the World Economy, 1820–1992*. Paris: OECD.

Maddison, A., 2010. Historical Statistics. PIB and Population Data. Retrieved from www.ggdc.net/maddison/Historical_Statistics/horizontal-file_02-2010.xls.

Mahdavy, H., 1970. The Patterns and Problems of Economic Development in Rentier States: The Case of Iran. In: M.A. Cook, ed. *Studies in the Economic History of the Middle East*. Oxford: Oxford University Press, 428–467.

Manterola, M., 1937. La Situación de la Industria del Petróleo en México y su Reciente Nacionalización. *Revista de Economía*, I (1–6), 361–377.

Metzer, J., 1998. *The Divided Economy of Mandatory Palestine*. Cambridge: Cambridge University Press, 275.

México, 1917. *Secretaría de Industria y Comercio, El Petróleo En La República Mexicana*, ed. M. Bustamamte, Instituto Geológico De México, Boletín 35, México D.F.

Mikesell, R.F., 1997. Explaining the Resource Curse, with Special Reference to Mineral-exporting Countries. *Resources Policy*, 23 (4), 191–199.

Ministerio de Hacienda. Venezuela, 1937. *Memoria*. Caracas, Venezuela.

Mommer, B. and Baptista, A., 1983. *El Petróleo En Las Cuentas Nacionales: Una Proposición*. Working Paper IESA, No. 10.

Naím, M., 1993. *Paper Tigers and Minotaurs: The Politics of Venezuela's Economic Reforms*. Washington, D.C.: Carnegie Endowment for International Peace.

Naím, M. and Piñango, R., 1974. *El Caso Venezuela: una ilusión de armonía*. Caracas, Venezuela: Ediciones IESA.

Neumayer, E., 2004. Does the "Resource Curse" Hold for Growth in Genuine Income as Well? *World Development*, 32 (10), 1627–1640.

PEMEX (Petróleos Mexicanos), n.d. *Venta de Pemex 1950–1962*. México D.F., México: PEMEX.

Pérez Alfonzo, J.P., 1965. *La Dinámica del Petróleo en el Progreso de Venezuela [conference sponsored by Universidad Central de Venezuela. Foro Petrolero 1965]*. Caracas, Venezuela.

Petras, J.F., Morley, M., and Smith, S., 1977. *The Nationalisation of Venezuelan Oil*. New York: Praeger Special Studies in International Economics and Development.

Philip, G., 1982. *Oil and Politics in Latin America: Nationalist Movements and State Companies*. Cambridge: Cambridge University Press.

Randall, L., 1989. *The Political Economy of Mexican Oil*. New York: Praeger.

Repetto, R.C., 1989. *Wasting Assets: Natural Resources in the National Income Accounts*. Washington, D.C.: World Resources Institute.

Rodríguez, F. and Sachs, J.D., 1999. Why Do Resource-Abundant Economies Grow More Slowly? *Journal of Economic Growth*, 4 (3), 277–303.

Rodríguez Gallad, I., 1974. *El petróleo en la historiografía venezolana*. Caracas, Venezuela: Universidad Central de Venezuela, Facultad de Ciencias Económicas y Sociales, División de Publicaciones.

Rubio-Varas, M.d.M., 2002. Towards Environmental Historical National Accounts for Oil Producers: Methodological Considerations and Estimates for Venezuela and Mexico over the 20th Century. Ph.D. Thesis. London School of Economics.

Rubio-Varas, M.d.M., 2004. The Capital Gains from Trade Are Not Enough: Evidence from the Environmental Accounts of Venezuela and Mexico. *Journal of Environmental Economics and Management*, 48 (3), 1175–1191.

Rubio-Varas, M.d.M., 2006. The Role of Mexico in the First World Oil Shortage: 1918–1922, An International Perspective. *Revista de Historia Económica/Journal of Iberian and Latin American Economic History*, 24 (1), 69–95.

Rubio-Varas, M.d.M., 2007. Contabilidad nacional medioambiental para productores de petróleo. Estimaciones para México y Venezuela (1901–1985). *Investigaciones de Historia Económica*, 3 (8), 141–165.

Salazar-Carrillo, J., 1994. *Oil and Development in Venezuela During the Twentieth Century*. New York: Praeger.

Sanders, A.R.D. and Sandvik, P.T., 2015. Avoiding the Resource Curse? Democracy and Natural Resources in Norway since 1900. In M. Badia-Miró, V. Pinilla and H. Willebald, eds. *Natural Resources and Economic Growth: Learning from History*. London: Routledge.

El Serafy, S., 1989. The Proper Calculation of Income from Depletable Natural Resources. *In*: S. Ahmad and E. Lutz, eds. *Environmental Accounting for Sustainable Development: A UNEP–World Bank Symposium*. Washington, D.C.: The World Bank.

Silva, C.R., 1979. Bosquejo histórico del desenvolvimiento de la economía venezolana en el siglo XX. *In*: F.E. Mendoza, ed. *Venezuela Moderna: Medio siglo de historia 1926–1976*. Caracas, Venezuela: Fundación Mendoza, 765–861.

Silva Herzog, J., 1938. La expropiación de las compañías petroleras en México. *Revista de Economía*, II (7–12), 447–457.

Solow, R.M., 1986. On the Intergenerational Allocation of Natural Resources. *The Scandinavian Journal of Economics*, 88 (1), 141–149.

Sordo, A.M. and López, C.R., 1988. *Exploración, Reservas y Producción de Petróleo en México, 1970–1985*. Colegio de México, Programa de Energéticas.

Stauffer, T.R., 1984. *Accounting for "Wasting Assets": Income Measurement for Oil and Mineral-exporting Rentier States*. Vienna: OPEC Fund for International Development.

The Economist, 1950. Sowing Oil. 7 January.

Thorp, R., 1989. Latin America: Economy, 1914–1929. *In*: L. Bethell, ed. *Latin America Economy and Society 1870–1930*. Cambridge: Cambridge University Press, 57–82.

United Nations, 1991. *Human Development Report*. New York: United Nations Publications.

Urrutia, M., 1991. Twenty-Five Years of Economic Growth, 1960–1985. *In*: M. Urrutia, ed. *Long-Term Trends in Latin American Economic Development*. Washington, D.C.: Inter-American Development Bank, 23–80.

Uslar Pietri, A., 1936. *De una a otra Venezuela*. Caracas, Venezuela: Monte Avila Editores.

Uslar Pietri, A., 1985. Los males del petroleo. *El Nacional*.

Uslar Pietri, A., 1989. ¿En qué medida se ha cumplido el vaticinio de Uslar Pietri (Ahora, 1936) sobre el parasitismo rentista en la Venezuela petrolera? *In*: F. Mieres, ed. *Hacia la Venezuela Post-petrolera [conference sponsored by La Academia Nacional de las Ciencias Económicas in 1985]*. Caracas, Venezuela, Academia Nacional de Ciencias Económicas, 105–122.

Venezuela. Cámara de Diputados, 1937. Intervención del Senador Rojas Conteras. *Diario de Debates*.

Venezuela. Ministerio de Trabajo, 1955. *Realidades de la Seguridad Social*. Caracas, Venezuela.

Venezuela. Ministry of Mines and Hydrocarbons, 1962. The Petroleum Industry and Its Fiscal Obligations by A. Parra. *In*: *1st Venezuelan Petroleum Congress organised by the Venezuelan Society of Petroleum Engineers*. Caracas, Venezuela, 24–31.

Williams, E.J., 1979. *The Rebirth of the Mexican Petroleum Industry*. Lexington, MA: Lexington Books.

9 Public finances and natural resources in Bolivia, 1883–2010
Is there a fiscal curse?[1]

José A. Peres-Cajías

Introduction

The *rentier state hypothesis* (Ross 1999) is one of the most fashionable explanations of the natural resource curse. This idea suggests that natural resource exploitation has two straightforward but contradictory effects on the fiscal capacity of natural resources-rich countries: it increases public revenues in the short-term but it also reduces the state's incentives to increase its tax base – i.e., states become revenue satisficers rather than revenue maximizers. It is also alleged that these short-term increases in public revenues attract political pressure from different interest groups which distort states' expenditures on their own benefit. Therefore, according to this hypothesis, natural resource exploitation generates short-term increases in public revenues which tends both to hinder the long-term fiscal sustainability of natural resources-rich countries and to benefit particular individuals or groups rather than the entire population.

Empirical research has proved some of the mentioned ideas. Collier and Hoeffler (2005), for instance, found that an increase in natural resources revenues has a significant negative effect on long-term economic growth. In line with Moore's (2007) proposal, Collier (2006) explains this finding by arguing that a higher fiscal dependence on natural resources revenues reduces the government's accountability towards its citizens and, therefore, increases the space for discretionary public expenditure. Thus, this increase in public spending of poor quality would explain the smaller long-term economic potential of natural resource-rich countries.

Furthermore, by identifying a significant negative relationship between natural resources revenues and non-natural resources revenues, recent research stresses that natural resource rich-countries tend to reduce their domestic tax effort (Bornhorst *et al.* 2009; Thomas and Treviño 2013; Crivelli and Gupta 2014).[2] According to Ossowski and González (2012), this negative and significant relationship is also verifiable in Latin American countries: from 1994 to 2010, non-natural resources revenues in resource-rich countries were systematically lower than in non-resource-rich countries.[3] However, this negative relationship occurred in a context of a steady increase in non-natural resources revenues in both groups of countries. Thus, the lower fiscal effort in Latin American natural resource-rich countries does not necessarily mean that an increase in natural resources revenues *automatically displaced* non-natural resources revenues (Ossowski and González 2012, p. 11).

In this context, it must be considered that the *rentier state hypothesis* has been also challenged. For instance, Hujo (2012, p. 6) recalls that some results of the natural resource curse literature are sensitive to the empirical methodology used and the periods chosen.[4] So, by referring to different historical case-studies, she proposes that mineral-rich countries may effectively foster economic development by linking mineral revenues and both physical and human capital investment. In the same vein, different studies have identified the Chilean experience from 1880 to 1913 as a clear example in which the state used efficiently its natural resource revenues to foster economic growth (Cortes Conde 2006; Gallo 2008). Likewise, Braütigam (2008) has proposed that export taxes in Mauricio were beneficial both for state building and economic development throughout the twentieth century.

Taking into account these critical observations, this chapter aims at contributing to the debate by offering a new historical case-study. Specifically, it seeks to identify the plausibility of the *rentier state hypothesis* for the Bolivian case from 1883 to 2010. This analysis may be instructive because of the extreme and constant dependence of the Bolivian economy on natural resources exploitation. Indeed, from independence (1825) onwards, mining and hydrocarbon industries have not represented the biggest economic sector but certainly the most efficient of the Bolivian economy (Herranz and Peres-Cajías 2013).[5] Given this higher productivity (as well as the spatial concentration of the sector), it could be assumed that the Bolivian state was more tempted to collect money from these economic activities rather than to enforce taxes across the entire economy – i.e., to become a revenue satisficer rather than a revenue maximizer. However, the Bolivian experience also stands out as an interesting case because of the constant increase in the relative importance of social public spending within total expenditure from the late 1930s onwards (Peres Cajias 2014). Hence, despite a constant dependence on mining and hydrocarbon industries, it could be the case that the Bolivian government used its natural resources revenues for fostering human capital accumulation.[6]

These questions are explored through two different approaches. On the one hand, the chapter examines the plausibility of defining the Bolivian state as a revenue-satisficer by identifying *if* an increase in natural resources revenues *led to* a decrease in the domestic tax effort. On the other hand, the chapter looks at the evolution *and composition* of human capital spending in order to identify the impact of natural resources revenues on human capital accumulation.[7] Two main conclusions are obtained from these analyses: a) increases in natural resources revenues have not always been correlated with decreases in the Bolivian domestic tax effort; b) whereas natural and non-natural resources revenues have allowed increasing human capital spending, the expansion of these expenses did not necessarily benefit the vast majorities of the country. Both findings suggest that the *rentier state hypothesis* is not an inherent feature of the history of Bolivian public finances but a characteristic contingent to specific historical conjunctures and institutional designs; these are analyzed in the following sections.

Bolivian fiscal reliance: was there an offset between natural and non-natural resources revenues?

This section explores the plausibility of the *rentier state hypothesis* in the Bolivian case by analyzing the long-term interplay between natural and non-natural resources revenues. Following Haber and Menaldo (2011), the chapter considers as natural resources revenues those taxes and royalties paid by either privately owned or state-owned mining and hydrocarbon firms, as well as dividend payments or direct transfers paid to the government by state-owned firms; non-natural resources revenues are comprised of the rest of public revenues.[8] Likewise, following Bornhorst *et al.* (2009), Ossowski and González (2012) and Thomas and Treviño (2013), the fiscal pressure generated by both kind of revenues is measured as:

$$\text{Natural Resources Fiscal Pressure}_t = \frac{NRrev_t}{NRgdp_t}$$

$$\text{Domestic Tax Effort}_t = \frac{NNrev_t}{NNgdp_t}$$

where $\frac{NRrev_t}{NRgdp_t}$ and $\frac{NNrev_t}{NNgdp_t}$ denote the ratios of natural and non-natural resources revenues to the natural and non-natural GDP at time t.[9]

Table 9.1 allows identifying the Bolivian experience as a country-case where the relative importance of natural resources revenues within total revenues has considerably varied throughout time.[10] Indeed, during the last quarter of the nineteenth century, the ratio fell from a quarter of total revenues to less than

Table 9.1 Relative importance of natural resources revenues within total revenues (%), 1883–2010

	Mining revenues	Hydrocarbon revenues	Natural resources revenues
1883–1895	25.87		25.87
1896–1904	9.73		9.73
1905–1922	18.76		18.76
1923–1929	29.39		29.39
1930–1931	10.18		10.18
1932–1952	53.19		53.19
1953–1955	n.d.		n.d.
1956–1971	9.97		9.97
1972–1982	14.73	18.35	33.08
1983–1984	6.87	4.96	11.84
1985–1994	0.64	37.25	37.89
1995–2004	0.37	18.38	18.75
2005–2010	1.41	32.00	33.41

Sources: See text.

10 percent. Thereafter, the ratio increased thanks to the upsurge of tin exploitation. After the Great Depression crisis, the fiscal dependence of the Bolivian central government towards natural resources revenues achieved record levels; hence, 50 percent of total revenues, on average, were directly paid by the mining sector until 1952. This ratio has presumably lasted until the first half of 1956 because of the existence of some "shadow taxes" on mining activities (see below). The ratio fell thereafter but increased again during the early 1970s thanks to the increase in both mining and hydrocarbon fiscal revenues. From the late 1980s onwards, hydrocarbon activities consolidated as the most important revenue source and mining revenues played a marginal role. Anyway, the relative importance of natural resources revenues continued varying considerably.

Therefore, if we accept 20 percent as a fair threshold to define a country as fiscally dependent on natural resources revenues (Thomas and Treviño 2013, pp. 4–5), the new evidence stresses that the Bolivian fiscal dependence has not been constantly high. This is not an irrelevant finding since the experience of some Asian, African and Latin American oil producers suggests the opposite (Haber and Menaldo 2011). Likewise, the contrast between Table 9.1 and previous evidence stresses that the Bolivian fiscal reliance has not been necessarily among the higher in Latin America throughout the entire period under analysis. For instance, from the mid-1950s to the early 1970s, the Bolivian ratio was similar to the Chilean one and five times lower than the Venezuelan one (Haber and Menaldo 2011).

In the same vein, Figure 9.1 shows that a natural resources revenues increase has not been always followed by a decrease or even stagnation of non-natural resources revenues. Four main variables have been identified as the most

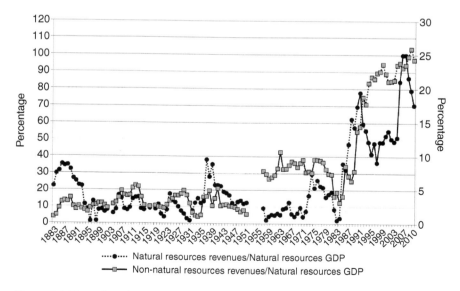

Figure 9.1 Natural and non-natural resources revenues in Bolivia, 1883–2010 (%) (sources: see text).

relevant for understanding this finding: the existence of structural restrictions which increased the costs and inefficiencies of any increase in the domestic tax effort; the composition of Bolivian mining and oil industries; the progression of international commodity prices; and, the effects of internal politics on the debate of private-ownership versus state-ownership of natural resources.

During the last quarter of the nineteenth century, silver export taxes accounted for more than 90 percent of natural resources revenues. Thus, the fall of natural resources revenues as a share of both total revenues and the mining/hydrocarbon GDP may be explained by the huge drop of silver international prices (early 1890s) and the subsequent reduction of silver export taxes.[11]

Whereas new export taxes were created in coincidence with the silver crisis,[12] natural resources revenues did not increase until 1905, once tin consolidated as the main mining product. As for the relative importance of these revenues on the mining and hydrocarbon GDP, Figure 9.1 shows the existence of two different periods of increase from 1904 to 1920 which were rapidly followed by a similar decrease. The upward trend of these cycles was driven by legislative changes, whereas the downward trend suggests the government's difficulty in maintaining this new higher fiscal pressure.[13]

A sharp increase in the fiscal pressure on natural resources took place thanks to the 1923 Fiscal Reform. Indeed, through this reform, the Bolivian government increased and created new export taxes, modified the mining transfer tax and finally imposed an effective profit tax on mining utilities.[14] As a consequence, natural resources revenues as a share of the mining and hydrocarbon GDP jumped from 5 percent in 1922 to 17 percent in 1924. Moreover, during these years, direct taxes accounted for the first time for more than 30 percent of the natural resources revenues. However, mining private-owners were subsequently able to impose their prerogatives in the political debate and tax pressure on the sector decreased during the late 1920s.[15]

As for the non-natural resources revenues ratio, its perfect synchronization with the evolution of natural resources revenues stands out from 1904 to 1920. This finding would be reflecting that export increases had also an indirect effect on taxation through certain non-natural resources revenues whose evolution was highly correlated with exports behavior – import duties are the most salient example. However, it also stresses that a natural resources revenues increase was not always accompanied by a decrease in the domestic tax effort. Indeed, notice that the non-natural resources revenues ratio also increased as a consequence of the 1923 Fiscal Reform and remained stable until 1929 – it jumped from 2.5 percent in 1922 to 5 percent in 1929. Thus, whereas the 1923 Fiscal Reform increased the relative importance of natural resources revenues, it also allowed the domestic tax effort to increase.

These facts suggest that the Bolivian government's dependence on certain revenues was not necessarily – or not only – explained by the lack of political will to increase the domestic tax effort but by different structural restrictions. Indeed, during this period of time, the Bolivian government followed a tax-system diversification which was based on an extremely fragile strategy of "extensive growth" (Peres Cajias 2012, p. 171). This strategy was characterized by the achievement of tax agreements with very specific economic agents on very specific economic activities. Because of this restricted nature, these agreements allowed diversifying the tax structure in terms of the number of taxes collected but not in terms of the amount of money collected.

As expected, the 1929 crash led to a dramatic decrease in both natural and non-natural resources revenues. The former, however, improved in 1932 because of the sanction of new mining taxes in the context of the Great Depression and the Chaco War (1932–1935).[16] Thereafter, territorial losses derived from this war fuelled the emergence and consolidation in power of new political groups which saw mining private-owners and "their antipatriotic behaviour" as the main cause of Bolivian economic underdevelopment (Contreras 1990). As a consequence, the Bolivian government amplified its intervention on the economy and tax pressure on mining increased considerably. Whereas the most radical administrations left office in 1939, the higher tax pressure on mining persisted, particularly until 1945. As for the non-natural resources revenues ratio, an initial upsurge from 1936 to 1939 was followed by a sharp decrease and a subsequent stabilization around the same levels which persisted since the last quarter of the nineteenth century –2.5 percent of the non-natural resources GDP. Both processes explain the Bolivian government's extreme dependence on natural resources revenues from 1932 to 1952. This, in turn, may be explained by three different factors: the necessity to deal with those short-term fiscal needs generated by political instability; the persistence of structural constraints (as well as the upsurge of new political restrictions) which restricted taxation beyond some easily identifiable economic activities; and the absence of any "fiscal solidarity" within Bolivian elites.[17]

The 1952 Revolution brought along a new economic model which has been labeled as "State's Capitalism" and lasted until 1985. Among other radical measures, the revolutionary leaders nationalized the three biggest mining companies – which accounted for three quarters of mining production – and created a new mining state-owned company (COMIBOL). Once again, short-term fiscal needs fuelled by political instability and the search of a new economic model, led both to maintain the high tax pressure on mining and to increase public expenditures.[18] Almost immediately, however, the new mining state-owned company ran into increasing losses, fiscal deficits widened and inflation yearly growth rates increased up to 100 percent.

As a consequence, an aggressive Stabilization Plan was implemented at the end of 1956 which removed the multiple exchange rate system, price controls and credits from the Central Bank to the government. Moreover, in order to guarantee the economic sustainability of the new state-owned company, the stabilization program designed a new export tax which replaced exchange rates earnings and ended an alleged over-taxation on the sector (CEPAL 1958, p. 82).[19] Meanwhile, a new tax reform was implemented which rationalized tax collection of indirect taxes. Thus, natural resources revenues decreased below 10 percent of the natural resources revenues GDP and non-natural resources revenues increased for the first time above 5 percent of their respective GDP.

No major changes took place during the 1960s.[20] By contrast, during the 1970s, natural resources revenues increased considerably. This process was driven by both legislative modifications and the change in the composition of the mining and hydrocarbon sector. Indeed, by claiming the lack of transparency of the Bolivian Gulf Oil Co. (the biggest Bolivian private hydrocarbon company at that time) and given popular repudiation towards the company, the Bolivian government decided to nationalize this company in 1969 and transfer its properties to the hydrocarbon state-owned company (Yacimientos Petrolíferos Fiscales Bolivianos, YPFB). Meanwhile, it enacted a new tax on hydrocarbon production which finally benefited the central treasury.[21] These changes allowed increasing natural resources revenues once gas exports to Argentina started in 1972.[22] Moreover, at the end of that year, the Bolivian government enacted an extra tax on both mining and hydrocarbon exports and, three years later, it also increased the tax rate of the original mining tax export.[23]

Meanwhile, the relative importance of non-natural resources revenues remained around those levels achieved immediately after the 1956 reform. This fact does not mean that the Bolivian government did not enact any tax measure concerning the non-natural resources sector, but that these efforts were not enough to generate any substantial increase in the domestic tax effort. These disparities in the political commitment towards taxation on natural and non-natural resources revenues, increased the Bolivian fiscal reliance on natural resources revenues and made it significant by international standards.

This higher fiscal reliance and the application of wrong fiscal and monetary policies explain the depth of the external debt crisis in Bolivia during the early 1980s.[24] As a consequence, the structural reforms implemented during the late 1980s stipulated a new fiscal regime on natural resources revenues. On the one hand, mining fiscal revenues were reduced in coincidence with the closing of COMIBOL (1986) and a new political economy which tended to attract foreign direct investment to the sector. On the other hand, the domestic price of gasoline was increased and a new transfer scheme from YPFB to the central government was implemented. This last measure explains the increase in natural resources revenues during the late 1980s and early 1990s.

Further changes were implemented at the end of 1994 when the Bolivian government enacted a new tax on the commercialization of oil and several fuels.[25] Two years later and as a consequence of the YPFB privatization, a new hydrocarbon law was sanctioned with the intention of attracting foreign direct investment to the sector; this legal modification explains the reduction in natural resources revenues during the late 1990s.[26] However, because of the widespread idea that private hydrocarbon companies were making extra profits and, given the results of a national referendum, a new hydrocarbon law was enacted in 2005. Furthermore, the nationalization of May 2006 stipulated that private-owned companies have to pay a participation share for the relaunched YPFB.[27] Thus, natural resources revenues increased again during the last years.[28]

Beyond these constant changes, non-natural resources revenues have steadily increased from the late 1980s onwards (see Figure 9.1). Furthermore, in contrast to the claims of Crivelli and Gupta (2014), the increase in natural resources revenues have not affected the collection of value-added taxes (VAT). Indeed, most of the increase in Bolivian non-natural resources revenues has been driven by the VAT created by the 1986 Fiscal Reform. Moreover, as has been already noticed by Ossowski and González (2012), there is evidence of significant and constant increases in the productivity and efficiency of VAT collection.[29] This suggests that the fiscal shortage inherited from the crisis and the trauma of the hyperinflation process led to the increase in both natural and non-natural resources revenues. Moreover, it shows that, despite the succession of governments of antagonist ideologies concerning natural resources exploitation, there has been a political consensus directed to constantly improve VAT collection.

Despite this positive trend, the relative importance of natural resources revenues achieved considerable levels during the late 1980s and late 2000s. In the same vein, the more recent increase in natural resources revenues has been mostly driven by the substantial rise in international prices, which increases the fiscal vulnerability of the country towards external shocks. Thus, whereas the progress of VAT collection represents a major improvement of Bolivian public finances, there is still space for further tax improvements that should be considered (Ossowski and González 2012). This is not an irrelevant issue, since as was previously suggested (Peres Cajias 2014), an extreme dependence on certain revenues may frustrate, through expenditure instability, the effective accomplishment of the state's intervention goals. The next section complements this view by arguing that it is *not only* necessary to smooth public expenditures but to carry out a good allocation of public expenses.

Escaping the curse through human capital spending?

Researchers focused on the evolution of developing countries' public finances have stressed that a dependence on certain revenues is not bad in itself; instead, it may allow collecting the money necessary to invest in physical or human capital accumulation (De Ferranti *et al.* 2004, pp. 132–140). By contrast, according to the natural resource curse literature, an extreme dependence on natural resources revenues may affect the economic long-term prospects of resource-rich countries through different channels (Ossowski and González 2012; Crivelli and Gupta 2014). This section does not explore all these channels but focuses on that stressed by the *rentier state hypothesis*: the existence of a positive correlation between the increases in natural resources revenues and the rent-seeking behavior of interest groups which tends to bias public expenditure to their own benefit.

This analysis is based in the evolution of education public spending since this is a growth-enhancing expenditure which achieved a significant importance in Bolivian public finances during the last decades (Peres Cajias 2014). Indeed, Table 9.2 shows that, until the first half of the twentieth century, both education and health spending in Bolivia were lower than 1 percent of GDP, well below their level in the rest of the countries.[30] From the 1960s to the 1980s, whereas the

Table 9.2 Latin American central governments' spending in education and health as a share of GDP (%, ten-year average), 1900–2010

	Bolivia		Chile		Peru		Uruguay	
	Education	Health	Education	Health	Education	Health	Education	Health
1900–1909	0.21	n.a.	0.86	n.a.	n.a.	n.a.	n.a.	n.a.
1910–1919	0.44	0.02	1.03	n.a.	n.a.	n.a.	1.09	0.56
1920–1929	0.40	0.02	1.36	n.a.	n.a.	n.a.	1.30	1.36
1930–1939	0.37	0.10	1.94	0.56	0.82	0.23	1.56	1.27
1940–1949	0.90	0.28	2.11	0.95	1.28	0.50	1.48	0.95
1950–1959	0.81	0.17	2.15	1.31	2.04	0.47	1.56	1.12
1960–1969	2.07	0.31	2.91	1.65	3.94	1.00	2.82	1.30
1970–1979	3.15	0.99	4.16	2.51	6.10	1.67	2.65	1.80
1980–1989	3.05	0.80	3.18	2.72	2.09	0.82	2.38	2.29
1990–1999	3.94	1.04	2.90	2.27	2.28	1.17	2.44	3.27
2000–2010	6.07	2.70	3.69	2.87	2.89	1.39	3.03	3.54

Sources: a) Bolivia: Peres-Cajías (2014); b) rest of countries from 1900 to 1989; Chile: Base de datos EH CLIO LAB, Iniciativa Científica Milenio Mideplan; Peru: (Portocarrero et al. 1992); Uruguay: (Azar et al. 2009); c) rest of countries from 1990 to 2010 from ECLAC database: www.eclac.cl.

Notes
n.a.: Not available.

relevance of health spending remained below 1 percent of GDP and well below the Chilean or Uruguayan ratios, Bolivian public spending in education increased substantially and became higher than the Uruguay one already in the 1970s. This process continued thereafter, and the Bolivian education ratio became higher than in the rest of the sample during the 1990s. Actually, at the eve of the twenty-first century, the Bolivian ratio was twice as high as the Peruvian and Uruguayan ones.

Thus, over the second half of the twentieth century, the ratio between Bolivian public spending in education and GDP has converged and then surpassed the equivalent figures in some of the most developmental countries of Latin America. This, obviously, must not be minimized. However, since the Bolivian GDP has been and is still among the lowest of Latin America, per capita public education spending in Bolivia remained below 70 percent of that of Chile and Uruguay throughout the second half of the twentieth century. More important, the growth of public education spending has not been in line with a general improvement in educational outputs. For instance, it was not until the 1990s that Bolivia achieved a full primary school enrollment, which shows a substantial delay both by regional and international standards.[31]

These facts can be better understood by trying to identify who benefited the most from the expansion of public education spending. These distributional analyses are commonly made through incidence analysis. However, the lack of micro data restricts the use of this methodology in the Bolivian case until the mid-1990s. As a consequence, the following analysis looks at the potential redistributive impact of public education spending through two indirect indicators.

To begin with, given that primary education tends to benefit a higher share of the population, the literature suggests that the higher the support to primary education, the higher the potential redistributive positive impact of education spending. A first indication of this potential bias is the tax support provided by the government to primary education in relation to the population's ability to pay. Lindert (2010, Table 9.2) has estimated this indicator for some Latin American countries from 1960 to 2002, showing that they have invested *less* in primary education than countries with similar incomes in other world regions.[32]

In order to assess if the Bolivian case fits into this description, I have estimated the tax support ratio for primary education as follows:[33]

$$\text{Tax support ratio for primary pupils} = \frac{\text{Subsidies}/\text{Attending student}}{\text{Income}/\text{Total populaton}}$$

Table 9.3 shows the evolution of this ratio in Bolivia and other Latin American countries from 1950 onwards. The table indicates that, during most of the period under study, the support to primary education by the Bolivian government was similar to the rest of the region. The 2010 figure appears as exceptionally high, which would suggest that the recent increase in natural resources revenues and the efforts carried out by the Morales administration (2006 onwards) to expand

194   J.A. Peres-Cajías

Table 9.3 Primary school support ratios in Latin America, 1950–2010 (%)

	1950	1965	1970	1975	1980	1986	1990	1996	2000	2006	2010
Bolivia	13.03	9.95	11.57	11.14	13.33	6.05[a]	7.00[b]	12.49	12.34	13.66	20.82
Chile	6.09	5.77	n.a.	5.59*	10.93	12.97[c]	10.66	n.a.	13.67	10.56	14.77
Peru		5.50*	10.90	11.17	10.97	6.76*	2.74	n.a.	3.21*	6.93	7.13	8.47
Uruguay	n.a.	11.32	12.40	n.a.	7.89	3.77	6.67	6.72	7.21	8.71	n.a.

Sources: Own elaboration based on: (a) *GDP per capita in national currency*: see Table 9.1. (b) *Public spending in primary school education*: UNESCO Statistical Yearbooks of 1963, 1973, 1994 and 1998. Data for 2000 onwards were taken directly from UNESCO Institute of Statistics webpage (www.uis.unesco.org/).

Notes
n.a.: Not available. (*) Values may be underestimated either because they only consider data from the Ministry of Education or because "other expenditures" or "non-distributed expenditures" represented a substantial share of total education expenditure. (a) In 1988; (b) in 1989; (c) in 1985.

educational services have effectively modified the amount of public money invested in primary education. Although this represents an important change, it is still too soon to fairly evaluate its long-term implications (see below).

Another criticism of the allocation of education expenditure in Latin America stresses the existence of a systematical favoritism towards tertiary over primary education – i.e., a favoritism towards a reduced share of the population. Authors like Frankema (2009) or Lindert (2010) have used the following indicator to test this claim:

$$\text{Primary tertiary double ratio} = \frac{\left(\text{Subsidy}/\text{student}\right) \text{ in primary education}}{\left(\text{Subsidy}/\text{student}\right) \text{ in tertiary education}}$$

I have reconstructed this ratio for Bolivia, some Latin American countries and some other countries which may constitute a good reference from 1965 to 2007 (Table 9.4).[34] Lindert (2010, pp. 390–395) suggests that the optimal level of this indicator would be at least 50 percent. Although very few countries reached that level in the mid-1960s, France or South Korea caught up rapidly with this figure during the 1970s. Among developing economies, while some African countries, such as Botswana or Zambia, still have very low ratios, some Asian countries, such as Thailand, have recently converged to that ideal level. The same applies in the Latin American case: whereas most countries were far away from the ideal value of 50 percent before the 1980s –Honduras being the only exception – many of them (including poor countries like Guatemala) reached it during the 2000s.

In the case of Bolivia, during the mid-1960s the priority of primary over tertiary education was similar to the Latin American average. Thereafter, the increase in the ratio in the early 1970s suggests that the initial expansion of natural resources revenues tended to benefit primary education more than tertiary education. However, this change would be temporary since the ratio decreased again

Table 9.4 Primary education support ratio over tertiary education support ratio in Latin America and other selected countries, 1965–2007

	1965	1970	1975	1980	2000	2007
France	10.82	19.12	19.79	34.39	59.42	50.72
United States	41.53*	63.66*	86.53*	62.15*	66.84	101.42
Korea, Republic of	16.93	27.04	24.77	54.23	220.05	188.20
Thailand	5.14	3.75	11.51	18.96	49.44	93.09
Botswana	n.a.	n.a.	1.38	n.a.	n.a.	4.92
Zambia	n.a.	n.a.	5.59	n.a.	4.36	n.a.
Argentina	22.30	11.02	13.54	19.74	72.06	93.90
Bolivia	9.62	27.10	22.58	14.49	26.22	29.75
Brazil	0.22[a]	n.a.	18.07*	13.96*	19.25	58.34
Chile	3.30	n.a.	8.55[a]	10.13	74.41	103.90
El Salvador	5.59	4.63	8.56	8.31	96.18	57.96
Guatemala	9.13	13.11	9.41	12.12[a]	n.a.	54.24
Honduras	6.19	n.a.	10.97	66.65	n.a.	n.a.
Paraguay	7.00	7.43	11.97	n.a.	23.09	41.36
Peru	11.94[a]	109.17[b]	148.58[b]	139.65[a]	32.95	66.32
Uruguay	13.85	n.a.	n.a.	29.20	47.46	47.00

Sources: Own elaboration based on UNESCO Statistical Yearbooks of 1973 and 1980. Data for 2000 and 2007 were taken directly from UNESCO Institute of Statistics webpage (www.uis.unesco.org/).

Notes

n.a.: Not available. (a) Probably underestimated because the share of "other expenditures" or "non-distributed expenditures" was higher than 20% of total education expenditure; (b) the original source indicates that expenditure in either first or third education was underestimated; (*) the original data adds in one single figure the expenditure made in both primary and secondary education. The 2000 figure in United States actually refers to 2001 and to 1999 in the case of Korea. The 2007 figure in Thailand refers to 2008 and to 2006 in the case of Uruguay.

between 1975 and 1980. More strikingly, the low levels of the ratio in the 2000s indicate a relative lack of support to primary education that is particularly noticeable even by Latin American standards. This would indicate that, despite its constant increase during the second half of the twentieth century, public education spending did not suffer any substantial change directed to particularly benefit the vast majorities of the country. Instead, it shows that a significant share of money has been constantly directed towards that reduced share of the population who was able to attend tertiary education.[35]

This finding can be explained – at least, partially – by the particular institutional relationship between the central government and public universities (Rodriguez 2000, pp. 91–161). Indeed, from independence to the early 1930s, this relationship was driven by a *Napoleonic* model by which the Bolivian central government controlled all aspects related to public tertiary education. However, after the university reform of 1928–1931, the model shifted to an *Autonomous* one which assured the autonomy of public universities in most aspects but not in financial issues. Since then, the Bolivian central government has neither an effective regulation nor a systematic control on universities and the only instrument of coordination between both entities has been the budget assigned by the central government. Moreover, this instrument has tended to be hardly flexible because of the unwillingness of university authorities to accept any budget reduction.[36] Thus, the significant relative importance of tertiary public education spending in Bolivia would be explained by this particular institutional design which restricts the central government's ability to reduce public subsidies in the sector.

Initially, natural resources revenues did not play any particular role in this relationship. Indeed, from 1928 to 1956, Bolivian public universities had a higher financial independence thanks to the existence of different taxes which were entirely devoted to them. After the 1956 Stabilization Plan, and in coincidence with the reduction in the relative importance of natural resources revenues, most of universities' revenues came from a specific share (2.5 percent) of Bolivian *total tax* collection. During the 1970s, this share was increased up to 2.8 percent of total tax collection (Rodriguez 2000, pp. 97–98). This suggests that public universities were able to take advantage of the increase in natural resources revenues.[37] This scheme persisted during the late 1980s when it was decided that 5 percent of total tax collection had to be devoted to public universities (Peres Cajias 2014).

This fiscal relationship, however, changed in 2005 due to the creation of the new direct tax on hydrocarbon production (Impuesto Directo a los Hidrocarburos, IDH). This tax was created in the context of a considerable political instability and, as a consequence, its legal distribution was not driven by technical criteria but by political agreements between the Bolivian central government and different groups of interests (Fundación Jubileo 2011a, p. 1). Within this broader debate, public universities achieved a share (8.6 percent of total IDH collection) which particularly benefited them. Indeed, the *effective* participation of public universities was around 8 percent of total IDH collection in 2011 and 2012 (the first years when detailed information is available) (Fundación Jubileo 2011a). This implies that the amount of money generated by the new tax and directed to public universities has been around 75 percent of that devoted to primary and secondary education. This is a significant share taking into account that total enrollment in public universities is equivalent to 18 percent of total enrollment in public primary and secondary education. More strikingly, the amount of money devoted to tertiary education is 20 percent higher than that invested in *total* public health spending. This suggests that public universities have obtained a disproportionate gain from the recent expansion in natural resources revenues.

Therefore, the strength of the favoritism towards tertiary education in Bolivia can be explained by two factors: the particular institutional relationship between the central government and public universities, and the political capacity of the latter to obtain a significant participation in the recent expansion of natural resources revenues. Both elements should be considered in order to improve the redistributive impact of public education spending.[38]

Conclusions

Mining and oil exploitation have been the most dynamic sectors of the Bolivian economy from independence onwards. This chapter analyzes if this dependence has affected the long-term evolution (1883–2010) of Bolivian public finances through the so-called *rentier state hypothesis* (Ross 1999). The chapter stresses that this hypothesis is not an inherent feature of the history of Bolivian public finances but a characteristic contingent to specific historical conjunctures and institutional designs.

First, the chapter shows that the relationship between tax pressure on natural resources revenues and the domestic tax effort has varied throughout time. The evolution of the former during the last quarter of the nineteenth century was led by the initial stabilization and subsequent downward trend of the international price of silver. During the first third of the twentieth century, the Bolivian government tried to increase tax pressure on mining. The results of these efforts, however, were not sustainable across time and each increase was rapidly followed by a new decrease.

This stresses that the state's ability to increase natural resources revenues must not be considered as an essential capacity of natural resources-rich countries but the result of political bargaining between different actors with different political strength. Indeed, those sharp increases in tax pressure on natural resources revenues which took place from the 1930s onwards (1930s, early 1970s, late 1980s and late 2000s) have been correlated with the Bolivian government's ability to impose its fiscal interests on the political debate.

As for the domestic tax effort, it stayed constant during the last quarter of the nineteenth century and increased sporadically during the first half of the twentieth century. Thereafter, sharp increases took place immediately after the big macroeconomic crises of the early 1950s and early 1980s. These increases were driven by the trauma generated by the crises and the upsurge of a new political consent towards the need to increase domestic taxation. Notice, however, that the subsequent evolution of the domestic tax effort diverged: it stagnated during the 1960s and 1970s, but it continuously increased during the 1990s and 2000s.

Second, whereas the chapter proves that both natural and non-natural resources revenues have allowed increasing human capital spending in Bolivia during the second half of the twentieth century, the lack of a systematic support to primary education and the high relative importance of tertiary education spending suggest that this expansion has not particularly benefited the vast majorities of the country. The origins of this favoritism towards tertiary education are not necessarily correlated with the abundance of natural resources and, by contrast, are explained by other institutional factors. However, the recent expansion in natural resources revenues (2005 onwards) and political pressure from public universities helps to understand why favoritism towards tertiary education has remained high in Bolivia until very recent years.

Summing up, if the Bolivian experience may offer policy lessons, it stands out that natural resource dependence does not automatically hinder the domestic tax effort in natural resources-rich countries. It also suggests that the usefulness of natural resources revenues as a developmental engine is related not only to the expansion of "good spending categories" but to its effective allocation. Both elements suggest that the *rentier state hypothesis* is not an inherent feature of natural resource-rich countries but an outcome contingent to certain economic and political restrictions.

Notes

1 This research has benefited from financial support from the University of Barcelona through the APIF (2008–2012) fellowship program; from the Catalonian Research and Universities Grant Agency through the BE-DGR 2011 fellowship program; from the Science and Innovation Ministry of Spain through the project ECO2012–39169-C03–03. The author specially thanks Alfonso Herranz-Loncán for his constant support and critical readings of previous drafts. The author also thanks Chris Absell, Marc Badia-Miró, Anna Carreras-Marín, Juan Flores, Alejandra Irigoin, Juan Antonio Morales, Mar Rubio-Varas and Henry Willebald for their valuable comments on previous drafts. The usual disclaimer applies.

2 Bornhorst *et al.* (2009) worked with a panel data of 30 hydrocarbon producing countries from 1992 to 2005; Thomas and Treviño (2013) worked with a panel data of 20 African countries fiscally dependent on natural resources from 2000 to 2011; Crivelli and Gupta (2014) worked with a panel data of 35 resource-rich countries from 1992 to 2009.

3 Natural resources-rich countries are: Bolivia, Chile, Colombia, Ecuador, Mexico, Peru, Trinidad and Tobago and Venezuela. The sample of comparison is comprised of Argentina, Brazil, Costa Rica, El Salvador, Honduras, Paraguay and Uruguay.

4 See Stinjs (2005); Brunnschweiler (2008); Haber and Menaldo (2011) for a discussion on this idea.

5 The composition of the mining and hydrocarbon sector has changed throughout time. From independence to the end of the nineteenth century silver exploitation represented more than three quarters of the sector and the remaining quarter was comprised of other minerals such as copper, tin or gold. During the first half of the twentieth century, tin exploitation became the main activity of the sector – 70 percent on average – and the relative importance of silver turned similar to the rest of minerals. From the mid-1950s to the mid-1980s the relative importance of tin decreased because of the upsurge of oil and natural gas exploitation. Thereafter, the hydrocarbon sector became the most important and, since the early 2000s, natural gas exploitation has represented around half of the sector.

6 Peres Cajias (2014) defines social public spending as the aggregation of education, health, welfare and other social public expenditures. Human capital spending is comprised of education and health spending.

7 Both analyses contribute to two branches of the natural resource curse literature which previous research defined as scarcely explored: the relationship between natural and non-natural resources revenues (Thomas and Treviño 2013, pp. 3–4) and the relationship between natural resources revenues and social policy (Hujo 2012, p. 7).

8 From 1883 to 1989, public revenues were obtained from Peres Cajias (2014) and refer to *total current* revenues of the Bolivian central government. The use of central government statistics is due to the lack of quantitative evidence on departmental (state) and local revenues. The representativeness of central government statistics of the overall evolution of Bolivian public revenues has been proved in Peres Cajias (2014). In contrast to Peres Cajias (2014), this chapter starts in 1883 because of the inability to disaggregate revenues in 1882. From 1990 to 2010, public revenues were obtained from UDAPE's website (www.udape.gob.bo); see Peres Cajias (2014) for a

discussion on the usefulness and shortcomings of this specific source. Revenues from 1990 to 2010 refer to *total revenues* of the Bolivian general government. The switch to general government statistics is explained by the availability of data and the need to account for the higher relevance of revenues both from municipalities (since 1995) and departamentos (since 2005).

9 From 1883 to 1950, GDP data was obtained from Herranz and Peres-Cajías (2013); from 1950 onwards, GDP data was obtained from the ECLAC website (www.eclac.cl). It was preferred to use the respective GDP rather than the aggregate GDP in order to discard any possible bias in the analysis. For instance, an increase on mining or hydrocarbon exploitation may increase the ratio on natural resources revenues to GDP as well as reduce the ratio on non-natural resources revenues just because of the GDP increase and not necessarily because of a lower domestic tax effort (Bornhorst *et al.* 2009, p. 443). Hence, the non-natural resources GDP may constitute a closer measure of the domestic tax base (Thomas and Treviño 2013, p. 11). Anyway, notice that natural and non-natural resources revenues are not perfectly independent. See Ossowski and González (2012, pp. 5–11) for a discussion on these issues.

10 Periods of Table 9.1 have been chosen taking into account different legislative changes which modified fiscal pressure on natural resources exploitation as well as some critical years for both mining and hydrocarbon industries.

11 Bolivian tax legislation tried to keep pace with the evolution of silver exploitation and its international price. In 1872, when silver production finally recovered its pre-independence levels, the Bolivian government enacted that silver exports must pay a tax of 50 cents per *marco* (*Ley del 8 de octubre de 1872*). Some years later, the silver export tax was increased up to 80 cents per *marco* (*Ley del 5 de agosto de 1881*). This tax was reduced to only 10 cents per *marco* in 1893 (*Ley del 16 de noviembre de 1893*) and modified once more in 1894, when it was decided that silver export taxes should be paid according to the exported quantities – the rate varied between 40 and 60 cents per *marco* exported (*Ley del 12 de noviembre de 1894*). This law was confirmed by another one enacted in 1897. However, due to the sector crisis, silver exports were declared free of taxes in 1902 (*Ley del 13 de diciembre de 1902*) and one year later a 5 percent *ad valorem* tax was imposed (*Ley del 22 de diciembre de 1903*). This quick reaction of tax legislation to the international economic context suggests that mining private-owners were able to impose their interests.

12 A tin export tax was created in 1889; it was 40 cents per *quintal* of bar exported and 20 cents per *quintal* of barrel exported (*Ley de 30 de octubre de 1889*); these rates were increased one year later up to 50 cents and 35 cents, respectively (*Ley de 26 de octubre de 1890*). New export taxes were also created for copper and bismuth.

13 Two different laws in 1906 and 1912 stressed that tin export taxes had to be paid according to its weight and the evolution of international prices (*Ley del 1 de enero de 1906*; *Ley del 18 de noviembre de 1912*). Whereas direct taxes on mining were imposed for the first time (a transfer tax in 1911, *Ley de 7 de febrero de 1911*; and a 3 percent tax on mining profits, *Ley del 1 de diciembre de 1911*), its effective contribution remained low. So, tin export taxes accounted, on average, for 80 percent of natural resources revenues from 1904 to 1920.

14 See Peres Cajias (2012, p. 173).

15 See Peres Cajias (2012, p. 174; 2014, p. 94) and the authors referenced in both works.

16 Oversupply characterized the tin market during the Great Depression. As a response, the International Tin Council (1931) was created. The aim of this cartel was to control tin supply through the assignation of production quotas for each country. The Bolivian quota was managed by the Bolivian government which meant that the government had to negotiate production shares with all mining producers. This increased the bargaining power of the Bolivian government towards private mining-owners. The Bolivian government was also able to increase mining taxation by alleging war efforts. See Peres Cajias (2014, p. 97 and footnote 32).

17 The increase in mining taxes was not contested by importers since they were satisfied with the tariff's decrease stipulated during this period of time (Gallo 1991, p. 142); nor by landowners who feared that any reduction in mining taxes had to be compensated by an increase in their long-term low tax pressure; nor by industrialists who were satisfied with the new tax scheme since it implied *cheap* foreign currency for them (Gutiérrez Guerra 1940, pp. 29–40).

18 This increase operated through a multiple exchange rate regime (Peres Cajias 2014, p. 98). This change cannot be seen in Figure 9.1 because of quantitative restrictions which prevented accounting for the effective amount of money generated by this "shadow tax"; see Gómez (1978, p. 140).

19 According to Gómez (1978, pp. 108, 125), the Bolivian central government had more than 104 mining taxes before the stabilization program. In 1957, these taxes were replaced by a single export tax which varied according to the international price of minerals and the ore content; further administrative modifications were implemented in 1965.

20 Despite the inexistence of detailed data, Gómez (1978, p. 126) suggests that most of mining revenues came from export taxes and a small proportion from direct taxes. Moreover, the relative stagnation of the natural resources revenues ratio should be explained by several tax exemptions on COMIBOL (Gómez 1978, pp. 141, 144), which accounted for 60 percent of mining production.

21 This tax was of 19 percent on both oil and gas production (*Decreto Supremo 8959 de 25 de octubre de 1969*). Before this measure, hydrocarbon taxes – which were not significant – benefited the departmental treasuries of the producing *departamentos* or autonomous national corporations. There were also taxes on gasoline consumption that have not been considered in the present estimation of natural resources revenues since they were paid by consumers.

22 Hydrocarbon industries represented no more than 1 percent of the Bolivian GDP before 1972. Thereafter, hydrocarbon industries achieved a relative importance between 4 and 7 percent of the Bolivian GDP. Likewise, whereas hydrocarbon exports accounted for no more than 10 percent of total exports from the early 1950s to the late 1960s, its relative importance increased up to one third from 1972 to 1980. See Klein and Peres Cajias (2015).

23 See *Decreto Supremo 10550 del 27 de octubre de 1972* and *Decreto Supremo 12879 de 24 de septiembre de 1975*. These constant tax changes can be understood by the fact that the considerable upsurge in mining and hydrocarbon international prices made it less costly to increase tax pressure on natural resources exploitation.

24 See Peres Cajias (2014, pp. 99–100) for more details concerning the causes of the crisis and the 1986 tax reform.

25 This is the *Impuesto Especial Directo a los Hidrocarburos*. This tax is not considered in the present estimation of natural resources revenues since is mostly paid by consumers.

26 This is the *Ley 1689 del 30 de abril de 1996*. This stipulated that those hydrocarbon camps which were operating before the sanction of the law had to pay royalties equivalent to 50 percent of hydrocarbon production; by contrast, new hydrocarbon camps had to paid a royalty of 18 percent of hydrocarbon production.

27 See Fundación Jubileo (2011b) for an explanation of hydrocarbon taxes and royalties from the early 1990s onwards.

28 Mining fiscal revenues maintained its marginal role during this period of time. This lack of significance can be explained by the relative importance of small Bolivian private-owners (called *cooperativistas*) and the political restrictions that they imposed on any government's essay to increase mining taxes.

29 The increase in the productivity of Bolivian VAT holds both for VAT on imports and VAT on internal consumption. Estimations are available upon author's request.

30 See Peres Cajias (2014) for a justification of the sample.

31 The only Latin American countries which evolved similarly to Bolivia were Guatemala and El Salvador. By contrast, countries like Zambia, Peru or Ecuador – mining producers – achieved full primary enrollment already in the 1970s (Frankema 2009, Table 9.4).
32 By suggesting that the rate of return of education investment has always been higher at the earlier levels of education throughout this period, Lindert (2010) stresses that lower investment in primary education has not been driven by demand-side factors but by a supply-side discrimination.
33 Lindert uses adult (instead of total) population in the denominator. However, the trends are the same if total population is used instead (Lindert 2010, p. 390).
34 No data is presented from the mid-1980s to the late 1990s because UNESCO statistical yearbooks do not offer detailed information for tertiary education spending in Bolivia.
35 Notice, however, that the limited evidence previously presented prevents saying that Bolivian public spending in education since the early 1950s *has only* benefited a reduced elite. Notice, moreover, that the composition of this elite has changed throughout time (Rodriguez 2000, pp. 31–90).
36 This can be explained by the fragile political power of university authorities. Indeed, after the 1952 Revolution and with the exception of the dictatorial periods of 1971–1978 and 1980–1981, both professors and students have the same political power concerning the major administrative and political issues of Bolivian public universities. This scheme is known as "University Co-government" (Co-gobierno Universitario). Beyond internal politics, university authorities have tended to deny any budget reduction by alleging constant increases in enrollment. This increase, in turn, has been driven by demographic changes as well as by institutional changes which have several times reduced those restrictions (qualitative and quantitative) established to attain public universities.
37 Furthermore, legislation changes determined that a share of departmental mining and hydrocarbon royalties had to be transferred to public universities of the producer *departamentos* (UDAPE 1985, pp. 273, 281). These revenues, however, were not significant and most of public universities' revenues came from total tax collection. The transfer of royalties from departmental treasuries to public universities was eliminated in 1980.
38 Two fiscal incidence analyses, which were carried using fiscal data from 2004 and 2009 (before and after the expansion of natural resources revenues) (Breceda *et al.* 2009 and Paz Arauco *et al.* 2013), have shown that the allocation of public education spending is fairly flat across quintiles or deciles. Looking at Paz Arauco *et al.* (2013)'s results and according to Lustig *et al.* (2013) this characteristic is explained by the high relative importance of tertiary education spending and its low progressivity.

References

Azar, P., Bertino, M., Bertoni, R., Fleitas, S., Garcia, U., Sanguinetti, C.,... Torrelli, M., 2009. ¿De quiénes, para quiénes y para qué?: las finanzas públicas en el Uruguay del siglo XX. Montevideo, Uruguay: Fin de Siglo.

Bornhorst, F., Gupta, S. and Thorton, J., 2009. Natural Resources Endowment and the Domestic Revenue Effort. *European Journal of Political Economy*, 25, 439–446.

Braütigam, D., 2008. Contingent Capacity: Export Taxation and State-building in Mauritius. *In*: D. Braütigam, O.-H. Fjeldstad and M. Moore, eds. *Taxation and State-Building in Developing Countries: Capacity and Consent*. Cambridge, MA: Cambridge University Press.

Breceda, K., Rigolini, J. and Saavedra, J., 2009. Latin America and the Social Contract: Patterns of Social Spending and Taxation. *Population and Development Review*, 35, 721–748.

Brunnschweiler, C.N., 2008. Cursing the Blessings? Natural Resource Abundance, Institutions, and Economic Growth. *World Development*, 36 (3), 399–419.

CEPAL, 1958. *Análisis y proyecciones del desarrollo económico. IV. El desarrollo económico de Bolivia.* México DF, México: Naciones Unidas, Departamento de Asuntos Económicos y Sociales.

Collier, P., 2006. Is Aid Oil? An Analysis of Whether Africa Can Absorb More Aid. *World Development*, 34, 1482–1497.

Collier, P. and Hoeffler, A., 2005. *Democracy and Natural Resource Rents.* Working Paper GPRG-WPS-016. Department of Economics, Oxford University.

Contreras, M.E., 1990. Debt, Taxes, and War: The Political Economy of Bolivia, c.1920–1935. *Journal of Latin American Studies*, 22, 265–287.

Cortes Conde, R., 2006. Fiscal and Monetary Regimes. *In*: V. Bulmer-Thomas, J.H. Coatsworth and R. Cortés-Conde, eds. *The Cambridge Economic History of Latin America.* Cambridge, MA: Cambridge University Press, 209–247.

Crivelli, E. and Gupta, S., 2014. *Resource Blessing, Revenue Curse? Domestic Revenue Effort in Resource-Rich Countries.* IMF Working Paper No. 14/5.

De Ferranti, D., Perry, G., Ferreira, F. and Walton, M., 2004. *Inequality in Latin America: Breaking with History?.* Washington D.C.: The World Bank.

Frankema, E., 2009. *Has Latin America Always Been Unequal?: A Comparative Study of Asset and Income Inequality in the Long Twentieth Century.* Leiden: Brill.

Fundación Jubileo, 2011a. *Renta hidrocarburífera más allá de las regalías y del IDH.*

Fundación Jubileo, 2011b. *A siete años del IDH. ¿En qué se gastan los recursos?.*

Gallo, C., 1991. *Taxes and State Power: Political Instability in Bolivia, 1900–1950.* Philadelphia: Temple University Press.

Gallo, C., 2008. Tax Bargaining and Nitrate Exports: Chile 1880–1930. *In*: D.A. Bräutigam, O.-H. Fjeldstad and M. Moore, eds. *Taxation and State-Building in Developing Countries.* Cambridge: Cambridge University Press, 160–182.

Gómez, W., 1978. *La minería en el desarrollo económico de Bolivia, 1900–1970.* La Paz, Bolivia: Editorial Los Amigos del Libro.

Gutiérrez Guerra, R., 1940. *Situación Económica y Financiera de Bolivia.* La Paz, Bolivia: Universo.

Haber, S. and Menaldo, V., 2011. Do Natural Resources Fuel Authoritarianism? A Reappraisal of the Resource Curse. *America Political Science Review*, 105 (1), 1–26.

Herranz, A. and Peres-Cajías, J.A., 2013. Tracing the Reversal of Fortune in the Americas: Bolivian GDP Per Capita Since the Mid-Nineteenth Century. *In*: *European Historical Economics Society Conference.* London.

Hujo, K., ed., 2012. *Mineral Rents and the Financing of Social Policy: Opportunities and Challenges.* London: Palgrave.

Klein, H.S. and Peres Cajías, J.A., 2015. Bolivian Oil and Natural Gas under State and Private Control, 1920–2010. *Bolivian Studies Journal*, 20, 141–164.

Lindert, P.H., 2010. The Unequal Lag in Latin American Schooling since 1900: Follow the Money. *Revista de Historia Económica – Journal of Iberian and Latin American Economic History*, 28, 375–405.

Lustig, N., Pessino, C. and Scott, J., 2013. *The Impact of Taxes and Social Spending on Inequality and Poverty in Argentina, Bolivia, Brazi, Mexico, Peru and Uruguay: An Overview.* Tulane Economics Working Paper Series, No. 1313.

Moore, M., 2007. How Does Taxation Affect on the Quality of Governance? *Trimestre Económico*, LXXIV (2), 281–325.

Ossowski, R. and González, A., 2012. *Manna from Heaven: The Impact of Nonrenewable Resource Revenues on Other Revenues of Resource Exporters in Latin American and the Caribbean.* IDB Working Paper, No. 337.

Paz Arauco, V., Gray Molina, G., Jiménez Pozo, W., and Yáñez, E., 2013. *Explaining Low Redistributive Impact in Bolivia.* Commitment to Equity, Working Paper, No. 6.

Peres Cajias, J.A., 2012. Public Revenues in Bolivia, 1900–1931. *In*: A. Carreras and C. Yañez, eds. *Latin-American Economic Backwardness Revisited.* London: Pickering and Chatto Publishers, 167–175.

Peres Cajias, J.A., 2014. Bolivian Public Finances, 1882–2010: The Challenge to Make Social Spending Sustainable. *Revista de Historia Económica – Journal of Iberian and Latin American Economic History*, 32 (1), 77–117.

Portocarrero, F., Beltrán, A. and Romero, M.E., 1992. *Compendio estadístico del Perú: 1900–1990.* Lima, Peru: Universidad del Pacífico, Lima (Peru); Consorcio de Investigación Económica.

Rodriguez, G., ed., 2000. *De la Revolución Universitaria a la Evaluación Universitaria. Cultura, discurso y política de educación superior en Bolivia.* La Paz, Bolivia: PIEB.

Ross, M., 1999. *Timber Booms and Institutional Breakdowns in Southeast Asia.* Cambridge: Cambridge University Press.

Stinjs, J.P., 2005. Natural Resource Abundance and Economic Growth Revisited. *Resources Policy*, 30 (2), 107–130.

Thomas, A. and Treviño, J., 2013. *Resource Dependence and Fiscal Effort in Sub-Saharan Africa.* . IMF Working Paper No. 13/188.

UDAPE, 1985. *Diagnóstico de Situación del Sistema Tributario en Bolivia.* La Paz, Bolivia: UDAPE.

10 Long-run development in Chile and natural resource curse

Linkages, policy and growth, 1850–1950[1]

Marc Badia-Miró and Cristián A. Ducoing

Introduction

The implications of natural resources in long-run growth remain as an open question (Barbier 2011, pp. 367–462; van der Ploeg 2011). On one hand, extended literature on the idea of natural resource curse points out that a country with plenty of commodities to export will fail to achieve development because economic agents have better incentives to specialize in natural resource activities or favour the emergence of rent-seeking attitudes adopted by elites.[2] Other work focused on global analysis also found a degree of correlation between high resource intensity and slow growth as Gregory (1976), Sachs (1999) and Sachs and Warner (2001). On the other hand, historical evidence shows that some countries escaped from natural resource curse and have achieved success in natural resource management.[3] Australia, New Zealand, Norway or the US are examples of strong forward and backward relationship between natural resources and the rest of the economy, which have allowed them to avoid the curse.[4]

In this discussion, we consider the analysis of Chile from a historical perspective, in hope it could shed some light about the curse of natural resources in those middle income countries which have benefited from natural resource boom cycles. In order to do so, first we describe the long persistence and importance of natural resources in the Chilean economy:

1 The nitrate cycle from the mid-nineteenth century up to the Great Depression (1880–1930) characterized by being labour intensive and highly concentrated.
2 A copper cycle from 1910 and onwards, geographically dispersed, with high levels of capital and technology requirements and a strong effort towards a higher degree of mineral manufacturing with the objective of adding value to exports.

Second, we want to analyse the differences among mining cycles and how they affected the characteristics and intensity of the forward and backward relationship in the Chilean economy.[5] Third, we review the literature surrounding the impact that public policies (or the lack of them) were implemented into the economy to manage the appearance of a NNRR boom. The appearance of tax surplus contributed to natural resource exploitation and thus their impact on infrastructure construction and on the economic boom in the long run.[6] Last of all, we want to analyse the economic performance of the Chilean economy during this period and discuss the hypothesis of the existence (or not) of a Dutch Disease problem during this period (Ville and Wicken 2013).

Corden and Neary (1982) and van Wijnbergen (1984) point out in their seminal work that countries with a natural resource boom experienced a strong process of de-industrialization due to the fact that an increase in the export sector attracted labour and investment and, at the same time, the service sector experienced a strong impulse due to the boom on the level of income. Parallel to that, higher wages on natural resources and sectors added to the appreciation on exchange rate reduced competiveness of the "traditional" export sector. In the end, the result is a less diversified economy, strongly dependent on evolution of natural resource prices (more volatile) and less potential growth. Interesting work on this issue has been published since then and interesting contributions were done on different countries.[7] From all of them, we highlight those studies with a more optimistic view, such as the one done by Davis (1995) on the positive performance of mineral-export and less developed countries compared with other less developed countries, and Mikesell (1997) who highlights that not all export booms imply Dutch Disease. Considering this framework, we shed some light on the hypothesis which links the backwardness of the country with the failure in natural resource management (Pinto 1996).

To accomplish these objectives, we are going to describe the export booms and check the possible existence of backward and forward relationships among natural resources and the rest of the economy, specifically the manufacturing sector and how this has affected economics in the long run.

Natural resources and economic development in Chile before 1950

Natural resource curse literature has identified a negative correlation between the share of the natural resource sector in the GDP and evolution of the economic performance in the long run (Barbier 2011, pp. 5–6). First, we have to confirm that the Chilean economy may be considered as a dependent economy.[8] In Figure 10.1 export figures show that before the War of the Pacific and the beginning of the nitrate cycle, mineral exports were the main item. More than 50 per cent of total exports were minerals from 1850 to 1875 reaching levels up to 70 per cent during the 1860s when the first copper cycle appeared. During this period, agricultural products (mainly wheat) and livestock were also important. The expansion of grain production in Australia and their exports to the west coast of the US were the main market for Chilean wheat exports.[9] After that, cereal exports decreased and Chilean production was oriented to the domestic market. The result was that the level of concentration on mineral products increased to more than 80 per cent of total exports until 1950 (see Figure 10.1 and Figure 10.2) and

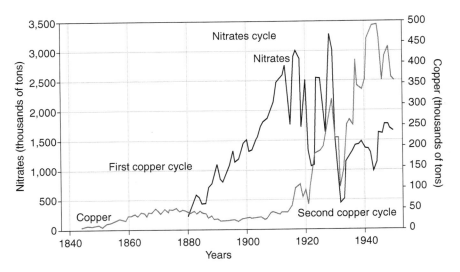

Figure 10.1 Copper and nitrates cycles. Production (thousands of tons). 1850–1950 (sources: Statistical Yearbook of Chile. Several years 1844–1950).

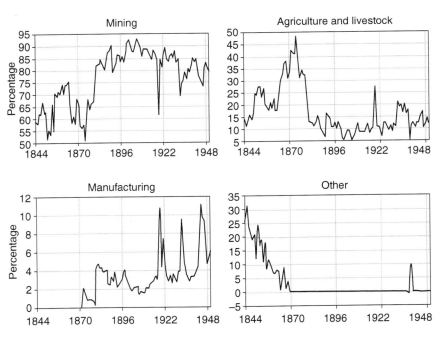

Figure 10.2 Share of Chilean exports by sector, 1844–1950 (source: Statistical Yearbook of Chile, several years).

resulting in an extremely high level of product concentration (Badia-Miró et al. 2012; Bulmer-Thomas 2003).

Product specialization was also accompanied by geographical specialization. During the 1870s Bolivia and Peru imported around 25 per cent of Chilean exports. The War of the Pacific changed this pattern deeply. Thereafter, up to the end of the nineteenth century, Germany, France, the UK and the US became Chile's most important partners and concentrated approximately 90 per cent of its exports. Exports to northern neighbours went down to less than 5 per cent. The expansion of the nitrate cycle in the following decades supported a light spatial diversification of exports with the incorporation of other destinations, such as Belgium, the US or Germany as main partners until the beginning of World War I (Badia-Miró et al. 2012).

Two minerals: one metallic – copper – and one non-metallic – nitrates – were the main players in Chilean mining cycles. Nitrate is related to the expansion of international demand as an agrarian fertilizer, in the nineteenth century (Miller and Greenhill 2006), and copper is due to the electricity revolution in the twentieth century. Although the nitrate cycle was shorter, it had an impressive effect on the economy due to the importance as a fiscal resource supplier for the Chilean state.

The appropriation of northern territories by the Chilean state crowded out investment and copper exports. The economic activity was centred in saltpetre production boosting mineral exports and, as we can see in Figure 10.2, forced a process of deeper specialization (more than 80 per cent of total exports were mining exports). As a result, there was an important decrease in total copper production and in the copper ore grade when we compare the 1870s and 1880s figures with the ones observed during the 1890s and the 1900s.[10]

Huge profits were obtained during the nitrate era. As Sunkel (2011) points out, the effects of nitrates on the Chilean economy (and its fiscal capacity) were enormous. Between 1890 and 1920, nitrate exports represented a minimum of 57 per cent of total exports and a maximum of 79 per cent. Considering fiscal revenues, by 1895, nitrate exports represented 56 per cent of State income and reached 60 per cent in 1915. Because of the War of the Pacific, Chile was able to obtain a stream of revenues that would have been difficult, if not impossible, to achieve otherwise.[11] The importance of fiscal impact forced a discussion among the elites around the possibility of keeping state monopoly over nitrates (Miller and Greenhill 2006). Nitrates also expanded those activities strongly linked with their exports. Examples of that are: (1) the expansion of the railways to transport nitrates to the coast; (2) supply goods and inputs to the offices; (3) the expansion of imports and the demand from other zones of the country, mainly Valle Central and the South (Cariola and Sunkel 1983); (4) the expansion of those industries connected to non-durable manufactured goods produced in the nitrate regions of Tarapacá and Antofagasta. Those firms were oriented to supply domestic demand expansion, which had relatively high wages, and all services were oriented to the transport of this product overseas such as banking, insurances and sea transport. As we can see in Figure 10.1, the effects of the nitrate boom were notably clear during the period 1880–1905, when copper production started a new cycle pushed by the effects of world electrification.

Copper extraction has been present in Chilean economic history since its origins (Méndez Beltrán 2004). The aborigines, the Spaniard conquerors and the new independent country entrepreneurs used it. The copper trade had a big push with the arrival of the industrial revolution due to copper's extensive use in several industries.[12] The first boom, in the mid-nineteenth century, finished at the end of depletion of the higher-grade ores (Ortega and Pinto 1990). Then, the nitrate cycle started after the War of the Pacific (1879–1884), a territorial dispute between Chile, Bolivia and Peru because of the Tarapacá and Antofagasta regions, both rich in nitrate minerals and copper (but this mineral was not the mineral in dispute). The territorial dispute ended with Chile occupying this zone as well as the region of Tacna.[13]

As we said, there were two main cycles of copper extraction and exports in Chile; the first one was a long cycle starting with the Spanish conquest of Latin America until 1880, and the second cycle started in 1906 with "*El Teniente*", an underground mine located in the O'Higgins region 80 km south of Santiago. The first cycle was linked to a traditional mineral exploitation, with high ores and labour-intensity rather than capital-intensity firms. This copper exploitation was concentrated on the northern part of the country, especially Huasco-Copiapó (Méndez Beltrán 2004). The main demand of copper was related to international commerce, with the uses of copper as ship sheathing, as stated by Harris (1966) and Staniforth (1985).

The second cycle was completely different both in production structure of the mining sector as well as the demand behind it. First, the labour-intensive production of the nineteenth century was replaced by capital-intensive firms, most of them from the US. Second, exports of raw materials during the nitrate cycle were replaced by a different sort of product with different levels of transformation and with differences in relative value per ton of mineral (see Figure 10.3 and Tables 10.1 and 10.4); the axis production (ore between 45 and 55 per cent) was progressively replaced by bars and raw mineral production. By 1938, close to 95 per cent of copper production was concentrated in bars (Statistical Yearbook of Chile: Mining Section, 1939).

This change in yield composition had a direct impact over linkages. There was an improvement in technology exploiting minerals, with more capital-intensive

Table 10.1 Copper production in thousands of tons (average)

Years	Yield
1870–1879	32,457,257
1880–1889	32,201,950
1890–1899	20,582,527
1900–1909	30.558.578
1910–1919	62,031,820
1920–1929	181,376,087

Source: Statistical Yearbook of Chile, several years and Sociedad Nacional Minera (1903).

technology applied. However, as we will see in the following sections, those improvements did not have an impact in other sectors of the economy.

The end of the War of the Pacific in 1884 was the starting point of the nitrate cycle, and the occupation of Tacna's provinces Tarapacá and Antofagasta in the Atacama Desert meant for Chile a virtual monopoly in world nitrates production. This monopoly gave government the possibility to tax nitrate exports and also the capacity to found a bigger state.[14] Even during the civil war in 1891, between parliamentary forces and the presidential power, the country's economy and nitrate production was not affected (see Table 10.2). However, the labour productivity of this industry declined at the end of the nineteenth century. In 1884 labour productivity reached 1.015 quintals per worker. Twenty years later, this value was transformed in half of the value reflecting one of the main problems of the nitrate sector. This, together with the fact that there was a lack of backward linkages to other sectors (only to the railway and transport sector), dismissed the possibility to expand the industry and diversify the Chilean economy. The nitrate industry requires less machinery for its extraction and transformation than copper; there were no foundries or smelters; nor steam motors.[15] Key inputs for nitrate industry were labour, TNT, water, coal, wood and transport to be exported. On the other hand, if we consider forward linkages, the situation is different. Home-market effects on nitrate zones (relatively higher wages and concentration of demand in Northern provinces) relied heavily on evolution of nitrates prices (Badia-Miró 2008; Badia-Miró and Yáñez (in press); Cariola and Sunkel 1983; Ortega 2005).

Why didn't nitrate activity generate a sustainable boom for the Chilean economy? Following the Dutch Disease framework, the result of an export boom is based on a simple premise: Natural resource activity generates an enormous surplus for the economy but at the same time, this profit does not materialize a structural change of the economy or incorporation of more value added in pre-existent sectors. At the same time, natural resource exports produce an exchange rate appreciation, hurting competitiveness of non-tradable sectors. Nitrate production was the main export in Chile during the period of 1880–1930 and its influence over the exchange rate was revisited by Palma (1979, 2000b) and Lüders and Wagner (2003). These authors confirm that there was never a clear relation between the exchange rate and Chilean dependency on saltpetre.

The failure in turning the Chilean economy into a sustainable economic boom during the predominance of nitrates must be analysed in a broader perspective. We have to consider its effect on the industry, in non-tradable sectors, the induced demand effect on domestic production (industrial and agrarian demand) and public investment derived by the boom of improvement of fiscal capacity due to nitrate taxation. When we observe government tax policy before and after the War of the Pacific, we could conclude that:

1   A severe decline in government revenues is observed during the 1870s.
2   As a consequence, Chile raised import rates and enacted an income tax and an inheritance tax (Sater 1986).

Table 10.2 Nitrate production and labour productivity 1880–1902

Year	Nitrate production	Workers	Labour productivity	Year	Nitrate production	Workers	Labour productivity
1880	2,239,740	2,848	786.4	1892	8,039,880	13,510	595.1
1881	3,557,180	4,906	725.1	1893	9,686,027	14,756	656.4
1882	4,922,460	7,124	691	1894	10,938,024	18,092	604.6
1883	5,897,200	7,077	833.3	1895	13,077,060	22,485	581.6
1884	5,589,000	5,505	1,015.30	1896	11,389,189	19,345	588.7
1885	4,359,880	4,574	953.2	1897	11,867,302	16,727	709.5
1886	4,510,300	4,534	994.8	1898	13,143,554	15,955	823.8
1887	7,127,000	7,201	989.7	1899	14,403,915	19,914	723.3
1888	7,637,720	9,180	832	1900	15,077,880	19,672	766.5
1889	9,513,720	11,422	832.9	1901	13,286,640	20,264	655.7
1890	10,751,580	13,060	823.2	1902	13,493,000	24,583	548.9
1891	8,619,940	11,657	739.5				

Source: Informe de la Minería de 1903 (Sociedad Nacional de Minería 1903).

However, between 1880 and 1900, the average import rate (import rate revenues divided by value of imports) fell by more than 25 per cent. Finally, income tax and inheritance tax, which never raised more than 200,000 pounds per year, were repealed in 1890.

Cariola and Sunkel (1983) observed that other internal taxes were eliminated during the 1880s. Sicotte *et al.* (2009) linked these changes in taxes to the nitrate boom and explained both impacts. Import rates and internal taxes imposed on one side and nitrate export tax on the other side maximize fiscal revenues. As Gallo (2008) described, the capacity of the state to maximize these revenues changed slightly at the beginning of the twentieth century and ended after World War I, where the monopolistic market power of Chilean production ended.

Industrial performance during the mining boom

Industrialization has been seen as a way of economic modernization opposite to natural resource dependence, in an export boom context. Since the 1980s, many authors suggested an early industrialization hypothesis in Latin America before the Great Depression, when the huge export boom benefited most South American countries (Suzigan 1988; Williamson 2011). This is a key point for effects on economic boom and implications on public policy.[16] In that sense, natural resource expansion could be responsible for industrial backwardness due to the effects of the so-called Dutch Disease effect and the impact on the competitiveness of the industrial sector.[17] Chilean bibliography provides opposite views of their existence during the nitrate boom. On one hand, Jeftanovic (1992) confirmed the existence of a slowdown in agriculture and industry during the beginning of the twentieth century due to draining of labour and investment in the saltpetre sector, from a model which considers three sectors (tradable, non-tradable and export). To confirm that, the author only considers the evolution of the real exchange rate and existing series of industrial GDP due to the lack of data.[18] Following this idea, Llona (1992) pointed out the existence of some degree of de-industrialization on copper refining during the Nitrate Era, as a way to confirm the existence of Dutch Disease. On the other hand, Palma (1979, 2000a, 2000b) claimed that the effect of the saltpetre trade was not negative on the economy and there was no evidence on dropping exchange rates during this period. However, the data used by Palma is considered aggregated, and do not split among tradable and non–tradable goods. He also pointed out the non-existence of Dutch Disease due to the active role played by the state in spending most of the surplus appropriated with their fiscal policy and the expenses of the productive process.[19] Other work on this topic was focused on analysis of the expansion of the copper sector during the twentieth century as Pereira *et al.* (2009) states. Later, Ugalde and Landerretche (2011) analyse the first decade of the twenty-first century and the impact of expansion of copper prices.

In the case of Chile, as far as we know, the nitrate cycle pushed the economy but it was not strong enough to reduce the gap between high- and middle-income countries. In that sense, one way to observe the capacity of the Chilean economy overcoming mining dependence is analysing what happened with industry. This is why, despite its economic expansion, we have a hypothesis that the country was losing competitiveness in the industry and, due to its forward and backward linkages, the potential boom was reduced during that period.[20] We also consider that this bad performance was reinforced during the copper cycle.

Generally speaking, figures for manufacturing were just 4 per cent during the beginning of the period and the peak (just over 10 per cent) was reached at the end of World War I and during the Great Depression. However, even during this period of "natural protection" due to the crash of foreign trade, the reaction of domestic manufacture was undersized in most South American countries (Albert 1988, p. 40; Carreras-Marín et al. 2013). To answer that question, we have to go deeper into the analysis of what happened with manufactured imports and their evolution during the whole period. We also have to check industrial performance on the long run following the new estimations provided by Ducoing and Badia-Miró (2013); they observed in detail the level of industrial diversification, its productivity and the capacity of domestic production to substitute imports.

As those authors pointed out and Bulmer-Thomas (2003) summarized, the performance of the industry at the end of the nineteenth century until the Great Depression is still not solved. If we summarize the main points under debate, Palma (1984) defended that the industrial performance is strong enough to become independent from the evolution of export demand and of imports of inputs and intermediate products. At the same time, the author showed that the share of machinery and intermediate goods increased during the 1920s.[21] Moreover, the percentage represented by local production of consumer goods over total consumption increased considerably. On the other side, Kirsch (1977) and Muñoz Gomá (1968) supported the view that industry and exports were strongly connected until the Great Depression. Muñoz Gomá (1968) justified the small structural change observed because of the strong dependence on consumer goods and consequently, because of the dependence on export performance. It was not until the 1930s when the industrial sector took the lead of the economy which was pushed by active state policies and culminated with the foundation of the CORFO in 1939 (Ortega et al. 1989). In that sense, Kirsch (1977) exposed that imports contraction caused an industrial bottleneck due to the dependence on combustibles and machinery, already during World War I.[22] Ortega and Pinto (1990), in a more pessimistic position, stated that the industry has problems adapting to more processed products and machinery equipment demanded by the mining sector.

New estimations on industrial production (Ducoing and Badia-Miró 2013), showed that the poor performance of the industry was not a driver of diversification for the Chilean economy. As we have stated, the peak is achieved around World War I and slightly exceeds 10 per cent (see Table 10.3). Although the growth of industrial output is greater than the growth of the GDP, we cannot confirm a transformation of the structure of the economy led by the industry as a driver of modernization.[23] The 11.8 share raised by the industry in 1938 is just 1 per cent more than in 1913, when Palma stated the best period for the industrial

Table 10.3 Evolution of industry and the GDP in Chile, 1980–1938 (%)

	1880–1913	1885–1913	1913–1929	1929–1938	1880–1930
Industrial GDP	3.8	4.1	1.7	2.8	2.8
GDP	3.2	3.3	2.2	0.7	2.1

	1880	1885	1913	1929	1938
Industry as a share of total GDP	8.4	8.7	10.5	9.8	11.8

Source: Ducoing and Badia-Miró (2013).

sector in Chile began. The higher rate of growth in the period 1929–1938 comparing industry and GDP is a bit misleading, because if we compare this rate with the previous periods, it is not higher than 1880–1913 and 1885–1913.

Figure 10.3 goes deeper into what happened in the industry during the whole period. Although the analysis in the figure only includes the period between the two World Wars, we observe a clear pattern of substitution of non-durables by semi-durable consumer goods. Other subsectors of the industry remained stagnated (durable consumer goods, intermediate goods and capital goods).[24] This figure depicts some degree of transformation of the Chilean industry towards a

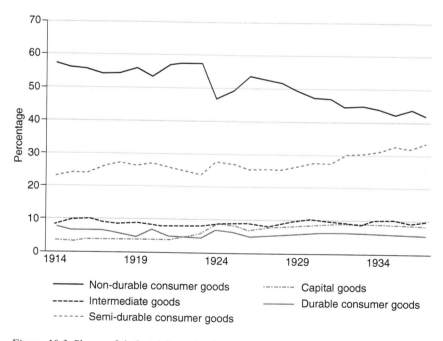

Figure 10.3 Share of industrial production by type of product, 1914–1937 (source: Muñoz Gomá (1968) corrected by the levels of Ducoing and Badia-Miró (2013)).

more diversified industrialization and notes this capacity of domestic production to react to the shortages of World War I reinforcing the production of consumer goods industry with low technology requirements (textiles, clothes, footwear and paper and printing). This figure coincides with Palma (1979)'s figures showing a duplication of weight of capital goods production over the whole industry. One question arises, considering that: was this expansion enough to state that Chilean industry started a process of transformation, towards a more diversified economy? From our point of view, it is opposite to what Palma defended; the growth is not high enough. Many reasons appeared to support this hypothesis: First, the importance of industry in the Chilean economy is very small, far from what we observe for European standards and even for South American countries. In that sense, the Ducoing and Badia-Miró (2013) figures contradict Palma (1979) who observed a strong expansion from World War I to the Great Depression. This supposed expansion is only a recovery from the shortages of the World War to the previous levels achieved in 1913, followed by an expansion during the beginning of the 1920s and stagnation during the second half of this decade.

If we consider what was happening with Chilean foreign trade, the reduction in consumer goods imports observed by Palma (1979, 1984) has to be shaded. The sector aggregation he proposed misled about some relevant aspects of what really happened during mining cycles. We have considered the dataset provided by Díaz and Wagner (2004) to analyse performance of imports during the nitrate cycle and the second copper cycle with further detail.[25] Our objective is to prove the existence of the structural change announced by Palma, among others, before the ISI period.

As we had expected, Figure 10.4 shows a decline in the share of consumer goods from 1880 to the beginning of World War I in parallel with a boom in the share of intermediate goods. From then on to the Great Depression we do not observe any variation of any type of product. This is something different from what Palma observed and goes in the opposite direction of the supposed early industrialization. From the Great Depression to 1950 a strong decline in consumer goods is compensated with an increase in intermediate goods. Although the copper cycle has started, the reason behind this change in import structure is related to the deep impact of the Great Depression, the crush of foreign trade, the beginning of industrialization led by the state and the protectionist turn of the economy.[26] If we observe in detail what was happening, what really drove the decrease of consumer goods was the evolution of food products, the most important item in the non-durable consumer goods category. Other consumer goods such as weaves, considered as semi-durable consumer goods, remained stagnated around 20 per cent of total imports. This showed that this decline in consumer goods is only concentrated in manufactured products with a small level of transformation. This result fits the hypothesis, developed in the next section, of an early industrialization in northern regions oriented to the production of food and beverages to supply the expansion of demand. At the same time, due to the fact that the expansion of the population and the impact of the home

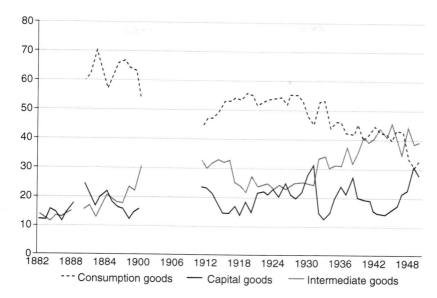

Figure 10.4 Share of imports by type of product, 1882–1950 (source: Díaz and Wagner (2004)).

market effect pushed the expansion of the industrialization, the end of the mining cycle ended the industrialization process.

Third and last, unlike what we have expected, the share of semi-durable goods increased during the 1920s to levels above what were seen before World War I. This trend compensated the reduction of the share of intermediate inputs and capital goods at the end of the war. In that sense, imports showed a good performance of those manufactured products, which incorporated some degree of transformation. Therefore, those domestic industries that could compete with this type of goods presumably had a bad performance and the whole industry was not able to advance to a higher level of modernization. To confirm that, we followed what Palma stated in his thesis. We calculated a sort of apparent consumption figure for each industrial sector to compute the share of consumption produced domestically. Unlike Palma (1979), we considered estimations for industrial GDP from Ducoing and Badia-Miró (2013) which clearly showed a different pattern during the 1910s and 1920s. We transformed the imports and exports from Díaz and Wagner (2004) into US$ in constant prices of 1995, following data provided by Díaz *et al.* (2007). For sectors figures, we only considered 1914–1935 from Muñoz Gomá (1968) because those are more reliable. Due to lack of export data we decided not to consider it, overestimating domestic production.[27]

Figure 10.5 shows stagnation in most of the sectors during the 1920s. This fact contradicts what Palma (1979) stated. In fact, his affirmation is based on lower levels of industrial production before World War I and the strong boom

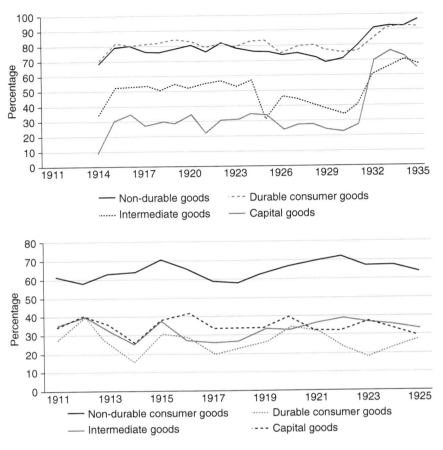

Figure 10.5 Share of domestic production over total consumption by type of product, 1911–1935 (top: Palma (1979) estimation, bottom: own estimation) (source: Palma (1979) and own elaboration based in Muñoz Gomá (1968); Ducoing and Badia-Miró (2013) and Díaz and Wagner (2004)).

after the end of the war. Our figures confirm that levels of domestic production of industrial consumption during the 1920s were so close to the ones observed before the war. Moreover, this pattern is very similar in all categories, even for intermediate goods and capital goods. It is not until the late 1930s that we observe a big change in share of domestic production due to the beginning of industrialization led by the state.

All the evidence provided in this section supports the idea that Chilean industry was not the leading sector during the nitrate cycle, and it was not able to transform the country into a modern economy country. In that sense, expansion of demand in some regions and weak linkages of mining activity to other sectors of the economy, specifically in industry, were not enough to push the economy to converge with the high-income countries. In that sense, the decline of the nitrate cycle and the emergence of the copper cycle could not change this pattern.

Mining linkages and economic performance

Although nitrate production was far more labour-intensive than capital-intensive, the boom in mining production in provinces of the northern part of the country attracted workers with relatively higher wages concentrated in few places,[28] both pushed the demand for consumption goods. As Badia-Miró (2008), Badia-Miró and Yáñez (in press) and Cariola and Sunkel (1983) also confirmed, the first response to the boom in purchasing power of the northern population was the import of low-quality manufactured goods, which also drove integration for national market. However, as an example of positive linkage of mining, industrial activities appeared, favoured by the distance of suppliers, both domestic and foreign and the advantage of production closer to the consumer. Apart from production of consumer goods for mine-labourers, there was also a need to handle and commercialize nitrate, which gave rise to secondary activities linked to mining and transport. Mechanization of mills and packaging systems, as well as spreading of railways as means of transport, led to a more upbeat pace of industrial activities in the mining zone.

During the period of economic boom based on nitrate exports, Chilean industrial activity was spatially quite disperse due to the legacy of the mid-1800s. Added to this, the effect of dynamism of nitrate provinces and a renewed strength with the zones of Concepción and Valdivia, in the south, helped to activate their industries. We can state that mineral exports pushed industry of some regions.

The end of the nitrate cycle changed this tendency. During this period, a change in economic policies, a change from relative liberalism to determined state intervention,[29] coincided with the mining cycle of copper, a spatially disperse activity, which was not capable of generating new geographic focal points of industrial activity, as nitrate mining had done before. Copper mining, being far more capital-intensive than labour-intensive, was founded on more advanced technological bases, but it neither generated a new population centre to attract industrial activities for consumption by the workforce, nor did it stimulate the appearance of industrial activities associated with mining activity, apart from metal foundries. Consequently, the geographic dynamic of industrialization was subject to the political economy of that time.

Natural resource cycles affected the Chilean economy, but without impulse or structural change in the economy. The export sector was concentrated in minerals, nitrates and copper, and the effect in the long run was limited. In Table 10.4, we can appreciate an important change in copper production, with predominance during the period of bars, a product with more value added than axis and minerals. However, during the same period (1910–1938) we cannot see a real improvement in manufactured share of GDP. The copper industry was an important sector for the economy but it lacked linkages, especially in the demand sector.

Table 10.4 Copper production by kind, selected years

	Bars			Axis			Minerals			Total	
	Tons	Ore (%)	Fine copper (tons)	Tons	Ore (%)	Fine copper (tons)	Tons	Ore (%)	Fine copper (tons)	Fine copper (tons)	% raw over total
1899	17,401	100.0	17,401	2,930	50.0	1,465	36,109	19.0	6,850	25,719	26.6
1913	20,150	98.9	19,937	18,510	47.2	8,737	72,537	18.7	13,586	42,000	32.3
1929	303,188	99.8	302,521				121,213	14.9	18,121	321,000	5.6
1938	338,294	99.8	337,516	24	56.5	13	100,371	13.9	13,932	352,000	4.0

Source: Statistical abstracts various years.

To confirm this assumption, we state that the boom of bar production, transforming 50 per cent more tons than axis and 80 per cent more than minerals, did not push the rest of the economy nor did it push machinery production (Ducoing 2012). At the same time, it had no impact on the demand due to the fact that it was an extremely concentrated activity (Badia-Miró and Yáñez in press).

Conclusion

Natural resources played an important role in the Chilean economy, mostly nitrates, and copper drove most of the booming mining cycles until the end of the nineteenth century. Nevertheless, its economy was unable to overcome its backwardness and remained as a middle-income country strongly dependent on commodities exports. This chapter shed some light on this discussion focusing on the analysis of industrial performance from the end of the nineteenth century up to 1950 and its linkages with mining cycles. In that sense, we confirm the existence of less dynamism in industrial performance, according with the Ducoing and Badia-Miró (2013) figures. We are not stating that there was no industrialization during this period; but that the performance of the mining sector was intensive enough to pull the industry and, as a result, the whole economy. This hypothesis is also confirmed by stagnation of domestic production in most industrial subsectors (both durable and non-durable goods) until the Great Depression.

Notes

1 Previous versions of this work were discussed in the WEHC 2012 (Stellenbosch) and AUDHE 2011 (Montevideo). We are very grateful for the comments of A. Carreras-Marín, H. Willebald, V. Pinilla, A. Tena and J. Díaz. M. Badia-Miró acknowledges the support of the Spanish research project ECO2012–39169-C03–03, the *"Xarxa de Referència en Economia i Polítiques Públiques"* financed by the Catalan government and the Consolidated Research Group in Economic History at the *Centre d'Estudis Antoni de Capmany* (2014SGR1345). C. Ducoing acknowledges the support of CONICYT Fund Project 82130021 *"Retorno de Doctores"*.
2 The term "natural resource curse" is used frequently to explain the poor growth performance of resource-rich countries during the second half of the twentieth century (Sachs and Warner 2001). Nevertheless, other work goes beyond the analysis of less developed countries analysing other countries such as Australia, following the discussion initiated by Gregory (1976) who defends the negative implications of natural resources on the non-tradable sector and continued by Snape (1977), who was more sceptical about problems in a macro-level dimension.
3 See David and Wright (1997) for the US, Greasley and Oxley (2010) for New Zealand, Mideksa (2013) for Norway and Ville and Wicken (2013) for Australia. For other countries see also Auty (1997) and Robinson *et al.* (2006).
4 Sachs and Warner (2001) point out the importance natural resources had on some economies during the nineteenth century. Nevertheless, natural resource intensity observed for Sweden, Australia and the US earlier never approached the level of natural resource intensity we see today in the Gulf States. In that sense, the argument presented in Habakkuk (1962) could be accepted for earlier periods when access to cheap power was essential. With the emergence of petroleum-based economy and global transport revolution, cheap energy could be easily accessed (Topik *et al.* 2006).

5 Labour-intensive mining cycles, such as nitrates, associated with relatively higher working-wages, pushed domestic demand (both external demand and consumer goods manufacturing). In that sense, in many course cases we observe an expansion of export demand due to the appreciation of exchange rate (one of the effects of the so-called "Dutch Disease"). What could nuance the curse is the capacity of domestic industry to satisfy it. During the copper cycle, some of the mining activities were able to add some degree of transformation. This could strengthen some linkages to the industry, such as the expansion of foundry and melting minerals, and to the service, such as expansion of the financial sector.
6 The positive view of Cariola and Sunkel (1983), Mamalakis (1976) or Palma (2000b) were shaded by the analysis of Frank (1967), Lüders and Wagner (2003) and, more recently, by Gallo (2008) whose work found a turning point of the effectiveness of natural resource taxation after World War I.
7 Alvarez and Fuentes (2006) and van der Ploeg (2011) have presented interesting surveys on this topic considering some of the most important approximations on this field and indicate most of the case studies in the world. For the oil boom cases, we could refer to Usui (1997).
8 Sachs and Warner (1999, p. 50) considered it a boom export economy when there was "a rise in the realized natural resource exports to GDP of at least 4% of GDP, from beginning to the peak of the boom, with a duration of at least three years".
9 Collier and Sater (2004) point out that wheat exports (and the product diversification of exports) ended around 1880, with the arrival of new competitors to the US (mainly Argentina and Australia). At this time, Chile lost its competitive advantage. Ortega (1981) also explains in detail the end of the first copper cycle.
10 See Sociedad Nacional Minera (1903). We also found a warning about the decrease of copper production, especially when it was compared with what happened in countries such as the US or Australia.
11 For a contra-factual study of effects of the War of the Pacific, see Sicotte *et al.* (2009).
12 Before the electrical revolution, copper was extensively used as coating for ships to protect them from worm ravages and encrustations of weed and barnacles (Harris 1966).
13 The War of the Pacific is still an issue of debate for the countries involved (Bolivia, Chile and Peru) and its legacy has created great problems for political and economic integration of the region. Chilean historical explanation about the war (Bolivia did not accomplish a legal agreement between the states and Chile defends its rights) is opposed to the Bolivian and Peruvian explanation (an aggressive attack by Chile in order to appropriate the saltpetre region). Opposite to these visions, Sater (2007) considered the war as a British movement to establish the saltpetre business in a more "friendly" environment for British companies (the Chilean government).
14 About nitrate taxation in Chile see Cariola and Sunkel (1983), Lüders and Wagner (2003), Palma (1979) and Sicotte *et al.* (2009).
15 Nitrate's mechanization was concentrated on main and bigger offices. Medium and small exploitations relied heavily on labour (Ortega and Pinto 1990).
16 See Hirschman (1958) for linkages between industry and economic growth.
17 A recent review of the theory for Latin America (Gregorio and Rodríguez 2011).
18 The author considers Industrial GDP from Ballesteros and Davis (1963) which is considered optimistic (Ducoing and Badia-Miró 2013).
19 Other authors as Díaz and Wagner (2004) and Lüders and Wagner (2003) reinforce this hypothesis.
20 Llona (1992) points out the de-industrialization in copper refining during the Nitrate Era as a way to confirm the existence of Dutch Disease in Chile.
21 Ducoing and Tafunell (2013) show that the machinery and equipment growth in the 1920s was the recovery from World War I, more than a sustainable improvement.

22 In spite of this bad performance, Kirsch (1977) considered the push of some sectors such as concrete production, due to the stimulus of the infrastructure expansion, sugar production or cotton weave.
23 In that sense, this view was consistent with what Carmagnani (1998) raised to explain the failure of the industry as a way to modernize the economy.
24 To build the figures we have considered the Ducoing and Badia-Miró (2013) estimations of industrial GDP and we have adopted the shares proposed by Muñoz Gomá (1968). For non-durable consumer goods, we considered food, beverages and tobacco. Textiles, clothes, footwear, paper products and printing were included as semi-durable consumer goods. For durable consumer goods, we considered wood and furniture. For intermediate goods, we considered leather and rubber products, chemical products and non-metallic minerals. Last of all, we considered metallic products as capital goods.
25 Díaz and Wagner (2004) provided data for imports for 15 aggregate sectors during the period of 1882–1900 and they also provided homogenized data for 83 sectors of imports during 1911–1966 as a percentage of total imports (see table 3.1–3.4).
26 For the period of 1882–1900, for consumption goods we considered food, wine and liqueurs, tobacco (non-durable consumer goods), weave, dress (semi-durable consumer goods), arts and science goods, arms and other (durable consumer goods). For capital goods, we considered machinery, transports and railways. For intermediate goods, we considered raw materials, mining products, drugs and other chemical products. For the period of 1911–1950, for non-durable consumer goods we considered food industries, beverages, liquors and manufactured tobaccos. For semi-durable consumer goods, we considered textile industries. For durable consumer goods, we considered transport products. For capital goods, we considered machines and tools and for intermediate goods, we considered chemical industries and the metallurgic industry.
27 As Carreras-Marín et al. (2013) stated, Chilean industrial exports were very small during the whole period, even during World War I. Palma (1979) figures showed that even for the highest exporting sector, the non-durable goods (food, beverages, tobacco, textiles and footwear) this value never reached the 5 per cent of total domestic production.
28 Pinto (1994, 1998). Wage figures of industrial workers were at their highest level during the Nitrate Era and fell later on.
29 During the 1940s and 1950s a maximum expansion of industry took place in a context of significantly intense GDP growth. The reorientation of the economy towards the domestic market and total immersion in state-directed industrialization in a context of policies encouraged substitution of a major part of importations, once more, it had a great impact on the local economy. During this period, a public organism embodied the state's active stance: "*Corporación de Fomento de la Producción*". This organism became one main economic agent, not only regarding industry, but it also played a decisive role in the development of energy sector, modernization of mining and promotion of agriculture.

References

Albert, B., 1988. *South America and the First World War: The Impact of the War on Brazil, Argentina, Peru and Chile*, Cambridge, MA: Cambridge University Press.
Alvarez, R. and Fuentes, R., 2006. El "Síndrome Holandés": teoría y revisión de la experiencia internacional. *Notas de Investigación Economía Chilena*, 9(3), pp. 97–108.
Auty, R.M., 1997. Natural resource endowment, the state and development strategy. *Journal of International Development*, 9(4), pp. 651–663.

Badia-Miró, M., 2008. *La localización de la actividad económica en Chile, 1890–1973. Su impacto de largo plazo*. Ph.D Thesis. Universitat de Barcelona.
Badia-Miró, M. and Yáñez, C., in press. Localization of industry in Chile, 1895–1967: mining cycles and state policy. *Australian Economic History Review*.
Badia-Miró, M., Carreras-Marín, A. and Rayes, A., 2012. La diversificación del comercio de exportación latinoamericano, 1870–1913. Ponencia presentada en CLADHE-IV, Argentina.
Ballesteros, M.A. and Davis, T.E., 1963. The growth of output and employment in basic sectors of the Chilean economy, 1908–1957. *Economic Development and Cultural Change*, 11(2), pp. 152–176.
Barbier, E.B., 2011. *Scarcity and Frontiers: How Economies Have Developed Through Natural Resource Exploitation*, New York: Cambridge University Press.
Bulmer-Thomas, V., 2003. *The Economic History of Latin America since Independence*, Cambridge, UK: Cambridge University Press.
Cariola, C. and Sunkel, O., 1983. *Un Siglo de historia económica de Chile 1830–1930: dos ensayos y una bibliografía*, Madrid: Cultura Hispánica.
Carmagnani, M., 1998. *Desarrollo industrial y subdesarrollo económico: El caso chileno (1860–1920)*, Santiago, Chile: Ediciones de la Dirección de Bibliotecas, Archivos y Museos.
Carreras-Marín, A., Badia-Miró, M. and Peres Cajías, J., 2013. Intraregional trade in South America, 1912–1950: the cases of Argentina, Bolivia, Brazil, Chile and Peru. *Economic History of Developing Regions*, 28(2), pp. 1–26.
Collier, S. and Sater, W.F., 2004. *A History of Chile, 1808–2002*, Cambridge, UK: Cambridge University Press.
Corden, W.M. and Neary, J.P., 1982. Booming sector and de-industrialisation in a small open economy. *The Economic Journal*, 92, pp. 825–848.
David, P.A. and Wright, G., 1997. Increasing returns and the genesis of American resource abundance. *Industrial and Corporate Change*, 6(2), pp. 203–245.
Davis, G.A., 1995. Learning to love the Dutch Disease: Evidence from the mineral economies. *World Development*, 23(10), pp. 1765–1779.
Díaz, J. and Wagner, G., 2004. Política Comercial: Instrumentos y Antecedentes. Chile en los Siglos XIX y XX. *Documentos de Trabajo – PUC*, 223.
Díaz, J., Lüders, R. and Wagner, G., 2007. Economía Chilena 1810–2000. Producto Total y Sectorial. Una Nueva Mirada. *Documentos de Trabajo – PUC*, 315.
Ducoing, C., 2012. *Inversión en maquinaria, productividad del capital y crecimiento económico en el largo plazo. Chile 1830–1938*. Ph.D Thesis. Universitat de Barcelona.
Ducoing, C. and Badia-Miró, M., 2013. El PIB industrial de Chile durante el ciclo del salitre, 1880–1938. *Revista uruguaya de Historia económica*, III(3), pp. 11–32.
Ducoing, C. and Tafunell, X., 2013. Formación bruta de capital en bienes de equipo en Chile, 1856–1930. Fuentes nacionales y extranjeras. *América Latina en la historia económica*, 20(1), pp. 5–34.
Frank, G., 1967. *Capitalism and Underdevelopment in Latin America: Historical Studies of Chile and Brazil*, New York: Monthly Review Press.
Gallo, C., 2008. Tax bargaining and nitrate exports: Chile 1880–1930. In D.A. Bräutigam, O.H. Fjeldstad and M. Moore, eds. *Taxation and State-Building in Developing Countries*. Cambridge, UK: Cambridge University Press, pp. 160–182.
Greasley, D. and Oxley, L., 2010. Knowledge, natural resource abundance and economic development: lessons from New Zealand 1861–1939. *Explorations in Economic History*, 47, pp. 443–459.

Gregorio Pineda, J. and Rodríguez, F., 2011. Curse or blessing? Natural resources and human development. In J.A. Ocampo and J. Ros, eds. *The Oxford Handbook of Latin American Economics*. Oxford: Oxford University Press, pp. 411–437.

Gregory, R.G., 1976. Some implications of the growth of the mineral sector. *Australian Journal of Agricultural Economics*, 20(2).

Habakkuk, H., 1962. *American and British Technology in the Nineteenth Century*, Cambridge, MA: Cambridge University Press.

Harris, J.R., 1966. Copper and shipping in the eighteenth century. *The Economic History Review*, 19(3), pp. 550–568.

Hirschman, A.O., 1958. *The Strategy of Economic Development*, New Haven, CT: Yale University Press.

Jeftanovic, P., 1992. El Sindrome Holandes: teoría, evidencia y aplicación al caso chileno, 1901–1940. *Estudios Públicos*, 45, pp. 299–331.

Kirsch, H.W., 1977. *Industrial Development in a Traditional Society: The Conflict of Entrepreneurship and Modernization in Chile*, Gainesville, FL: The University Press of Florida.

Llona, A., 1992. *Copper and Nitrate: A Case of Dutch Disease*, Buenos Aires, Argentina: Instituto Torcuato Di Tella, Centro de Investigaciones Económicas Buenos Aires.

Lüders, R. and Wagner, G., 2003. Export tariff, welfare and public finance: nitrates from 1880 to 1930. *Documentos de Trabajo – PUC*, 241.

Mamalakis, M.J., 1976. *The Growth and Structure of the Chilean Economy: From Independence to Allende*, New Haven, CT: Yale University Press.

Méndez Beltrán, L.M., 2004. *La exportación minera en Chile, 1800–1840: un estudio de historia económica y social en la transición de la Colonia a la República*, Santiago, Chile: Editorial Universitaria.

Mideksa, T.K., 2013. The economic impact of natural resources. *Journal of Environmental Economics and Management*, 65(2), pp. 277–289.

Mikesell, R.F., 1997. Explaining the resource curse, with special reference to mineral-exporting countries. *Resources Policy*, 23(4), pp. 191–199.

Miller, R. and Greenhill, R., 2006. The fertilizer commodity chains: guano and nitrate, 1840–1930. In S. Topik, C. Marichal and Z. Frank, eds. *From Silver to Cocaine: Latin American Commodity Chains and the Building of the World Economy, 1500–2000*. Durham, NC: Duke University Press.

Muñoz Gomá, Ó., 1968. *Crecimiento Industrial de Chile: 1914–1965*, Santiago, Chile: Instituto de Economía y Planificación.

Ortega, L., 1981. Acerca de los orígenes de la industrialización chilena (1860–1879). *Nueva Historia*, 1(2).

Ortega, L., 2005. *Chile en Ruta Al Capitalismo: Cambio, Euforia y Depresión 1850–1880*, Santiago, Chile: Lom.

Ortega, L. and Pinto, J., 1990. *Expansión minera y desarrollo industrial: un caso de crecimiento asociado (Chile 1850–1914)*, Santiago, Chile: U. de Santiago, Depto. de Historia.

Ortega, L., Norambuena, C., Pinto, J. and Bravo, G., 1989. *Corporación de Fomento de la Producción. 50 años de realizaciones, 1939–1989*, Departamento de Historia. Facultad de Humanidades. Universidad de Santiago de Chile.

Palma, J.G., 1979. *Growth and Structure of Chilean Manufacturing Industry from 1830 to 1935*. Ph.D Thesis. Oxford University.

Palma, J.G., 1984. Chile 1914–1935: De economía exportadora a sustitutiva de importaciones. *Colección de estudios del CIEPLAN*, 12(81), pp. 61–88.

Palma, J.G., 2000a. From an export-led to an import-substituting economy: Chile 1914–39. In E. Cardenas, J.A. Ocampo and R. Thorp, eds. *An Economic History of Twentieth-century Latin America*. London: Palgrave associated with St Antony's College.

Palma, J.G., 2000b. Trying to "tax and spend" oneself out of the "Dutch Disease": the Chilean economy from the War of the Pacific to the Great Depression. In E. Cardenas, J.A. Ocampo and R. Thorp, eds. *An Economic History of Twentieth-century Latin America*. London: Palgrave associated with St Antony's College, pp. 217–264.

Pereira, M., Pereira, M., Ulloa, A., O'Ryan, R. and de Miguel, C., 2009. Síndrome holandés, regalías mineras y políticas de gobierno para un país dependiente de recursos naturales: el cobre en Chile. *Series CEPAL*, 140.

Pinto, A., 1996. *Chile, un caso de desarrollo frustado*, Santiago, Chile: Lom.

Pinto, J., 1994. Historia y minería en Chile: Estudios y fuentes. *América Latina en la historia Económica*, 1, pp. 65–88.

Pinto, J., 1998. *Trabajos y rebeldías en la pampa salitrera: el ciclo del salitre y la reconfiguración de las identidades populares (1850–1900)*, Santiago, Chile: Editorial Universidad de Santiago.

Van der Ploeg, F., 2011. Natural resources: curse or blessing? *Journal of Economic Literature*, 49(2), pp. 366–420.

Robinson, J.A., Torvik, R. and Verdier, T., 2006. Political foundations of the resource curse. *Journal of Development Economics*, 79(2), pp. 447–468.

Sachs, J.D., 1999. Resource endowments and the real exchange rate: a comparison of Latin America and East Asia. In T. Ito and A.O. Krueger, eds. *Changes in Exchange Rates in Rapidly Developing Countries: Theory, Practice, and Policy Issues*. Cambridge, MA: National Bureau of Economic Research, pp. 133–154.

Sachs, J.D. and Warner, A.M. 1999. The big push, natural resource booms and growth. *Journal of Development Economics*, 59(1), pp. 43–76.

Sachs, J.D. and Warner, A.M., 2001. The curse of natural resources. *European Economic Review*, 45(4–6), pp. 827–838.

Sater, W.F., 1986. *Chile and the War of the Pacific*, Lincoln, NE: University of Nebraska Press.

Sater, W.F., 2007. *Andean Tragedy: Fighting the War of the Pacific, 1879–1884*, Lincoln, NE: University of Nebraska Press.

Sicotte, R., Vizcarra, C. and Wandschneider, K., 2009. The fiscal impact of the War of the Pacific. *Cliometrica*, 3(2), pp. 97–121.

Snape, R.H., 1977. Effects of mineral development on the economy. *Australian Economic History Review*, 21(3), pp. 147–156.

Sociedad Nacional Minera, 1903. *Estadistica Minera de Chile*. Santiago, Chile.

Staniforth, M., 1985. The introduction and use of copper sheathing – a history. *Bulletin of the Australian Institute for Maritime Archaeology*, 9(2), pp. 21–48.

Sunkel, O., 2011. *El presente como historia: dos siglos de cambio y frustración en Chile*, Santiago, Chile: Catalonia.

Suzigan, W., 1988. Estado e industrialização no Brasil. *Revista de Economia Política*, 8(4), pp. 5–16.

Topik, S., Marichal, C. and Frank, Z., eds. 2006. *From Silver to Cocaine: Latin American Commodity Chains and the Building of the World Economy, 1500–2000*. Durham, NC: Duke University Press.

Ugalde, M.G. and Landerretche, Ó., 2011. El "Efecto Holandés" en Chile: Heterogeneidad en competitividad y dinámica macroeconómica, Series: Documentos de Trabajo Facultad de Economía y Negocios. Universidad de Chile, 343. Santiago, Chile.

Usui, N., 1997. Dutch Disease and policy adjustments to the oil boom: a comparative study of Indonesia and Mexico. *Resources Policy*, 23(4), pp. 151–162.

Ville, S. and Wicken, O., 2013. The dynamics of resource-based economic development: evidence from Australia and Norway. *Industrial and Corporate Change*, 22(5), pp. 1341–1371.

Van Wijnbergen, S., 1984. The "Dutch Disease": a disease after all? *The Economic Journal*, 94(373), p. 41.

Williamson, J.G., 2011. Industrial catching up in the poor periphery 1870–1975. *NBER Working Paper Series*, 16809.

11 Mixed blessings

Mining in Indonesia's economy, 1870–2010

Pierre van der Eng

Introduction

Indonesia is currently one of the world's leading exporters of copper and nickel ore, refined tin and thermal coal, and a major producer of gold, natural gas, bauxite and oil. It was a major producer of tin for global markets by the mid-nineteenth century; much of the growth and diversification of its mining output took place since the 1890s. The development of the mining sector was part and parcel of the country's process of modern economic growth. Nevertheless, in recent economic histories of Indonesia, the development of the mining sector during the colonial era until the 1940s is eclipsed by the production of agricultural commodities, and the growth of oil production is used as a proxy for the sector as a whole (Booth 1998; Dick *et al.* 2002; Van Zanden and Marks 2013).

No studies offer a consistent discussion of the long-term economic development of Indonesia's mining industry and ready answers to questions relating to the role of the sector in Indonesia's economy, the effect of Indonesia's mineral resource abundance on the development of other economic sectors, and the combination of institutional, technological and market conditions sustaining the development of the sector. Most publications about mining tend to focus on the geological, technological and local aspects of mining, as well as the public administration of mining activities. Some offer snapshots of the political economy and economics of mining in Indonesia, but none offers a consistent analysis of long-term trends. Historical studies discuss individual mining companies (e.g. Lindblad 1985; Erman 2005), but it remains unclear whether these cases can be generalised. The oil sector has been the subject of several studies (e.g. Ooi 1982; Lindblad 1989), but these do not yield ready answers to the issues above.

This chapter starts with a quantification of long-term trends in the role of mining in Indonesia's economy to establish reference points for further discussion. It then offers a narrative of long-term trends in the expansion of Indonesia's mining sector, before discussing the institutional arrangements that governments in Indonesia created to maximise the share of society in the resource rents and quantifying the share of public revenue from mining in mining value added and the public revenues. Lastly, the chapter assesses issues

Mixed mining blessings. Indonesia (1870–2010) 227

relevant to the role of the mining sector in Indonesia's economic development, in terms of employment creation, forward linkages, and the impact of commodity price fluctuations on Indonesia's terms-of-trade and the international competitiveness of its other tradable goods.

Long-term trends in mining production and exports

Table 11.1 shows that the share of mining in GDP almost quadrupled from 7 per cent in 1971 to 26 per cent in 1980, before it decreased and stabilised at 11–12 per cent. The growth of oil and gas production during the 1970s, together with the rapid increase in international oil and gas prices are the main reasons for this development. Oil and gas production dominated the mining sector contributing 85 per cent to gross value added (GVA) in 1971, rising to 95 per cent in 1980, before declining when mining GVA diversified in favour of coal, copper ore and to a lesser extent gold, silver, iron and manganese ores. By 1980 85 per cent of oil and gas was exported, decreasing to 40 per cent by 2000 in favour of increasing domestic consumption of oil and gas. On average, Indonesia exported 40–45 per cent of total mining output. The remainder was processed in the manufacturing sector for domestic use or exports.

Figure 11.1 confirms the long-term domination of oil and gas in mining since the 1890s and the diversification of output since 2000. Figure 11.2 shows that

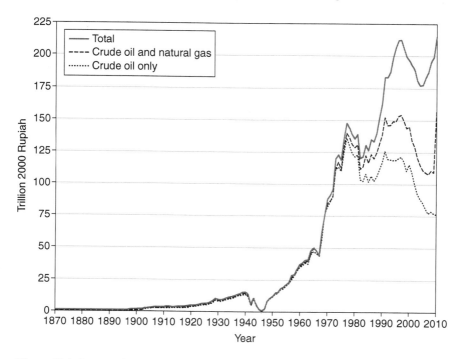

Figure 11.1 Gross value added in mining, 1870–2010 (trillion 2000 Rupiah) (sources: Van der Eng 2014: Appendix).

228 *P. van der Eng*

Table 11.1 Economic role and composition of mining in Indonesia, 1971–2010

	1971	1980	1990	2000	2010
A. Mining in the economy					
Mining GVA as % of total GDP	7.3	25.9	12.3	12.7	11.1
Mining exports as % of total exports	22.9	72.2	27.4	15.0	24.5
Mining as % of total employment	0.2	0.7	1.0	0.9	1.2
B. Sectors as % of total mining GVA					
Crude petroleum, natural gas	84.6	94.9	81.7	69.7	42.1
Coal	0.0	0.0	1.9	8.9	21.8
Copper ore	n.a.	0.4	2.7	5.6	11.4
Gold and silver ore	n.a.	0.0	0.6	4.7	5.6
Tin ore	4.4	1.7	0.7	1.0	1.4
Nickel ore	1.3	0.2	2.0	2.5	0.5
Bauxite	0.7	0.1	0.1	0.0	0.5
Other metallic ores*	0.2	0.0	0.1	0.1	0.6
Non-metallic mining and quarrying**	8.7	2.6	10.2	7.5	16.0
Total mining sector	100.0	100.0	100.0	100.0	100.0
C. Exports as % of gross output					
Crude petroleum, natural gas	62.2	84.4	50.9	38.8	39.0
Coal	0.0	37.6	47.4	56.9	70.0
Copper ore	n.a.	104.0[#]	96.7	94.2	62.2
Gold and silver ore	n.a.	0.0	0.1	0.0	0.0
Tin ore	53.1	14.1	1.1	0.0	0.3
Nickel ore	94.0	56.9	80.3	59.9	84.0
Bauxite	100.0	89.5	67.5	76.4	90.9
Other metallic ores*	59.4	21.9	19.2	2.3	40.2
(Sub-total metallic ores)	(64.1)	(36.1)	(67.6)	(49.8)	(42.0)
Non-metallic mining and quarrying**	0.0	0.6	2.6	4.6	2.7
Total mining sector	56.5	80.7	46.6	39.6	41.6

Source: Calculated from IDE (1977) and BPS (1975–2010); the 2010 share in employment is from Indonesia's National Labour Force Survey (Sakernas).

Notes
Calculated from data in current market prices; excludes GVA in related manufacturing (e.g. oil refining, LNG production, basic metals manufacturing, etc.); data from the 2010 I-O Table are provisional.
* Mainly iron and manganese ores.
** Includes copper, gold and silver ore in 1971.
\# Number exceeding 100 implies exports of stockpile.

the production of tin ore and concentrate dominated GVA in mining in the late nineteenth century. Tin production remained significant until the 1960s, when it slumped. It recovered in the late 1970s and after, but by then most output of tin ore and concentrate was processed in Indonesia and counted as GVA in basic metal manufacturing, which is not included in Table 11.1 and Figures 11.1 and 11.2. Figure 11.2 confirms that Indonesian mining production diversified significantly during the last 20 years, and that particularly the shares of coal and copper ore in GVA increased.

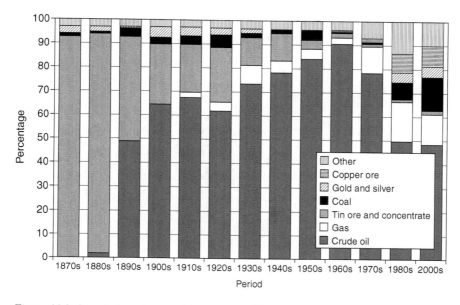

Figure 11.2 Cumulative shares of key commodities in gross value added in mining, 1870–2010 (ten-year averages, current prices) (sources: Van der Eng 2014: Appendix).

To assess the role of the mining sector in the Indonesian economy, Figure 11.3 contains two estimates of the share of mining GVA in GDP since 1880. One is based on GVA in mining in 2000 prices. However, the 2000 price of particularly oil and gas overestimates the contribution of GVA in mining in this series before at least the 1970s, which explains the discrepancy between the shares of mining in GDP in 2000 prices and in current prices from the input-output tables. A compromise series values oil and gas at "pre-1973" shadow prices. Both series are indicators of the degree to which mining GVA contributed to GDP and they are broadly comparable to the current price estimates. They confirm that mining output already increased faster than GDP during the 1950s and 1960s, when the sector's share increased from 5–10 per cent in the early 1950s to 15–30 per cent by the late 1970s. For 1900–40, both estimates in Figure 11.3 suggest a gradual increase in the share of mining GVA in GDP by a factor of four to 5–10 per cent by 1940.

Figure 11.3 also confirms that the trend in the share of mining commodities in Indonesia's exports was driven by crude oil and refined oil products, joined in the late-1970s by liquefied natural gas (LNG). Until 1900, the share of mining products was less than 10 per cent, rising to an average of 25 per cent by the 1930s and increasing further to a substantial 62 per cent during the oil boom of the 1970s, and 65 per cent in the 1980s, before decreasing to 32 per cent in the 1990s and 2000s. Since shares exceeded 25 per cent in the 1930s, Indonesia's export earnings have been highly dependent on mining commodities.

230　*P. van der Eng*

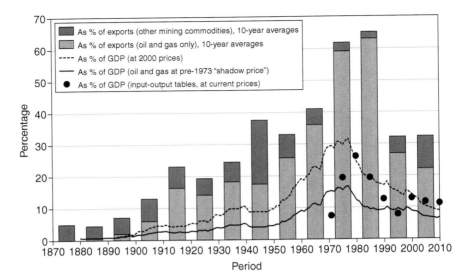

Figure 11.3 Shares of mining commodities in exports and of mining gross value added in GDP, 1870–2010 (percentages) (sources: Shares in exports calculated from Indonesia's foreign trade statistics 1870–2010; Shares in GDP in current prices from IDE (1977) and BPS (1975–2010), in 2000 prices see Figure 11.1, GDP 1880–2010 from van der Eng (2010), replacing the previous estimates of total GVA in mining with those in Figure 11.1).

Notes
No data for foreign trade 1942–45 and GDP 1942–48. The share of oil and gas GVA in GDP in 2000 prices is also estimated with just 40 per cent of GVA in oil and gas as a pre-1973 "shadow price" of the contribution of oil and gas to total GVA.

The long-term expansion of mining production and exports

Indonesians have mined metal ores (gold, silver and tin) and other minerals (such as diamonds and other precious stones) in different parts of the country for many centuries. These were small operations, employing basic technologies, and producing small quantities. Mining activity increased in the course of the nineteenth century.[1] Until 1850, the Dutch colonial government banned private mining operations in order to maximise its share in the resource rents. Effectively, it usurped the seigneurial rights of local rulers, as areas gradually came under colonial rule. The government expected to establish mining ventures, but it opened just one coal mine in Southeast Kalimantan in 1846. It realised that the involvement of private enterprise was required to mobilise the required finance and manage operations.

The next section explains that the principles that mining served fiscal purposes and required private sector involvement were contained in Indonesia's mining legislation after 1850. In 1872, the government institutionalised its involvement in the sector by establishing a Mining Service. It hired geologists and mining engineers to study mineral deposits across the country and identify their productive potential. The Service also managed state-owned mining ventures and sales of their produce, and it administered mining concessions of private firms. Publications by geologists, as well as discoveries of local public servants, adventurers and would-be entrepreneurs in various regions of Indonesia led to a growing interest in mining opportunities.

The Mining Service granted increasing numbers of exploration licences and exploitation concessions. Only around 25 per cent of applications for exploration licences were successful, but Table 11.2 indicates that there was a spate of speculative interest in exploration permits during 1897–1909. Most related to oil, following the high profitability of the first few oil companies in Indonesia. Most exploration licences did not lead to concessions, and most concessions never reached production stage. Explorations revealed that deposits were less promising than expected, or entrepreneurs failed to raise investment capital for ore production facilities and/or infrastructure needed for basic processing and transport to ports. Roughly 55–70 per cent of concessions lapsed because they failed to reach production stage.

Apart from tin, mining production included coal (particularly after 1870), gold and silver (in greater quantities since 1880), crude oil (1889), copper iodine (1897), wolframite (1897), manganese ore (1904), lead ore (1904), natural gas (1915), asphalt (1928), sulphur (1928), phosphate rock (1929), bauxite (1935), monazite (1936), copper ore (1937), nickel ore (1938), platinum ore (1938), and a range of quarrying products such as sandstone, marble, limestone, volcanic trass, kaolin clay, sand, and also quicklime for cement production.

As exploitation of mineral deposits increased, some companies evolved into sizeable ventures operating multiple concessions. By the late-1930s, these

Table 11.2 Active exploration permits and mining concessions in Indonesia, 1890–1938

	Exploration permits	Mining sites				
		Concessions	Article 5a	CoWs	Public-private JVs	Total
1890	109	19	–	–	–	19
1895	268	31	–	–	–	31
1900	2,758	89	–	–	–	89
1905	2,122	153	–	–	–	153
1910	741	177	–	–	–	177
1915	66	146	–	–	–	146
1920	191	220	–	–	–	220
1925	619	259	–	12	2	273
1930	1,267	271	20	10	4	305
1935	1,754	273	57	10	4	344
1938	1,412	274	64	5	4	347

Source: Calculated from *Jaarboek van het Mijnwezen* (1872–1939).

Notes
Article 5a, see main text; CoW = contract of work, JV = joint venture.

included the Bangka and Belitung tin mining ventures. The first was operated by the Mining Service, the second became majority government-owned in 1924, and operated by minority shareholder *NV Billiton*. Also operated by the Mining Service were the Ombilin (West Sumatra), Bukit Asem (Palembang) and Pulau Laut (Southeast Kalimantan) coal mines – producing coal for the Navy, interisland steam shipping and the state-owned railways. The main private firm was a subsidiary of the oil company *NV Koninklijke Maatschappij tot Exploitatie van Petroleumbronnen in Nederlandsch-Indië*, which in 1907 had merged with UK company *Shell* in 1907. It produced over 75 per cent of all oil. At the other end of the scale were many small, unregistered operations run by local groups of Indonesian miners and/or immigrant Chinese. The most significant ones yielded diamonds, gold and silver in Kalimantan and Sulawesi. Others produced coal in Kalimantan.

Indonesia's independence after 1945 brought continuity and change in mining operations.[2] The government continued the institutional arrangements for the mining sector until 1960 and there was continuity in the administration and monitoring of mining operations, even though the Mining Service in 1959 became a government department. This continuity and the Korea War commodity boom underpinned the quick recovery of tin ore, oil, manganese and bauxite production to pre-war levels in the early 1950s. Oil production doubled by 1960, but production of other commodities remained below pre-war levels.

Foreign-owned firms experienced difficulties regaining control over their mining concessions. Regional insecurity or the occupation of mining assets by local interests prevented them from resuming activities. Companies baulked at raising new investment capital to recover production facilities damaged during the Japanese occupation and the war of independence. Ventures that had not resumed production were *de facto* nationalised in 1956–57, and put under the management of the local military, before being converted into state-owned enterprises (SOEs). The public-private joint ventures were converted into SOEs as well, such as the Belitung tin and the Jambi oil joint-ventures, as were all mining ventures operated by the Mining Service. Compounding this trend were the nationalisations of the ventures of all Dutch-owned companies in Indonesia during 1957–58.

These SOEs often operated in close association with the local military that had the capacity and manpower to organise these ventures, as well as an interest in the off-budget revenues they raised for military expenditure (Purwanto 2009). Deficiencies in capital and expertise were overcome through "Contract of Work" (CoW) arrangements between SOEs and foreign companies, which generally included production sharing arrangements (Gibson 1966). This became the predominant mode to engage foreign firms.

Following amalgamations of mining SOEs in 1968, four controlled around 90 per cent of mining activity: *PN Pertamina* (oil and gas), *PN Aneka Tambang* (bauxite, gold, nickel, diamonds and iron ore), *PN Tambang Timah* (tin) and *PN Tambang Batu Bara* (coal). Each engaged foreign companies under CoWs in the exploration and exploitation of new and existing mineral deposits in Indonesia on the basis of the 1960 and 1967 mining laws (see the next section). Foreign firms made available technological expertise and investment capital for the purchase of equipment. They recouped their investments with revenues from exported produce, before sharing the remainder with SOEs (Darmono 2009, pp. 182–190). SOEs exported or processed their share and used proceeds for various investments, including facilities to produce concentrates, crude metals, oil derivatives or LNG.

By 1970, there were 217 non-oil mining sites in Indonesia (Departemen Pertambangan 1971), which compares to a total of 350 pre-war sites. Few new sites were added during intermediate years, so that the balance comprised sites producing oil and gas.[3] Of these 217, the largest 23 were operated by SOEs, which together employed 46 per cent of all workers in non-oil and gas mining, 96 were operated by smaller private companies and 98 by very small informal local enterprises, particularly in gold, diamonds and quicklime mining.

Despite economic stagnation in Indonesia during the 1950s and 1960s, production and export of mining commodities continued to increase, as Figure 11.1 and 11.3 showed. Much comprised oil production, but output of some other commodities increased as well; particularly bauxite (since 1963), nickel and iron ore/sands (since 1965), iodine, copper and silver (since 1973), gold (since 1980) and also coal (since 1986). This development involved increasing numbers of foreign companies under CoWs. For example, copper ore production increased since 1973, after US firm *Freeport Sulphur Co* invested on the basis of CoWs in the exploration and exploitation of copper and gold deposits in West Papua.

Foreign direct investment (FDI) for non-oil ventures was small relative to FDI that international oil companies poured into Indonesia under CoWs for exploration and exploitation of oil and gas deposits. From 1968, *Pertamina* handled all government interests in oil and gas and became by far the largest of the mining SOEs. Until its monopoly was dismantled in 2001, *Pertamina* was a "state within a state" (Booth 1998, p. 319). It exported crude oil, but it also refined and shipped oil, distributed oil-based products such as petrol and kerosene, and engaged in non-oil pursuits ranging from property development to manufacturing. *Pertamina*'s surpluses benefited the government budget and facilitated an increase in discretionary government spending. The company also facilitated off-budget spending benefiting the military.

In 1970, *Pertamina* administered 42 CoWs, rising to 55 in 1975, 78 in 1985 and 92 in 1995 with foreign oil and gas companies (Moenir 1985, pp. 315–323; Darmono 2009, p. 224). The contracts were for surveying, exploration, production, both on and offshore, or the construction of *Pertamina*'s processing facilities. They specified how physical production of oil and gas was shared and what bonuses foreign contractors were entitled to. Upon completion of the contract, all equipment and fixed production facilities of the foreign company would generally fall to *Pertamina*. The same applied to non-oil and gas operations involving CoWs between foreign and the SOEs that held the mining permits.

FDI inflows and Pertamina's reinvested earnings carried the accelerated expansion of oil production from 175 million barrels per year (mby) in 1965 to a peak of 615 mby in 1978. Production stabilised at around 550 mby until 1998, broadly in line with the quota allocated to Indonesia by the Organisation of Petroleum Exporting Countries (OPEC), of which Indonesia became a member in 1962. Indonesia struggled to meet its OPEC quota after 2002 and later left the organisation. The slump in oil production to 345 mby in 2010 was largely due to flagging FDI. Uncertainties caused by legal changes since 1999 (see the next section), caused foreign companies to limit investment in exploration of oil deposits in Indonesia. Oil production decreased as existing sites became depleted.

Tin and coal were exceptions to the growth of mining output since the 1950s. Tin and coal ventures were inefficiently run by SOEs *PN Tambang Timah* and *PN Tambang Batu Bara*. Their managers tended to be political appointees without mining experience. They were also treated as cash cows in the 1960s; their contributions to state coffers in the form of taxes, levies and royalties were over 45 per cent of revenues (Hunter 1968, pp. 75, 81–82). Including contributions to off-budget expenditure, that share may have been 80 per cent (Gillis and Jenkins 1978, p. 135). Consequently, funds for salary payments and investments in new technology to improve efficiency were limited until the 1970s (Nikle 1970, p. 70).

Rising tin prices during the 1970s helped *PN Tambang Timah*. Indonesia's tin production soon followed tin prices due to FDI inflows under CoWs involving a fleet of new large dredges for off-shore tin mining. New investment also rehabilitated *PN Tambang Timah*'s Bangka refining facilities, eliminating Indonesia's tin ore exports in favour of tin (Lloyd 1975, pp. 336–337).

Coal production remained below pre-war levels due to management inefficiency, deterioration of equipment and a lack of capital and foreign exchange to restore it, because coal was not exported. Domestic demand for coal decreased when the state railways phased out steam locomotives after 1967. But in the 1980s, the government reconsidered its energy policy, acknowledging the need for coal for electric power and cement plants. Subsequent rehabilitation of the Ombilin, Bukit Asem and Pulau Laut mines increased coal production, but most of the increase was due to FDI in new coal mines, particularly the large *PT KalTim Prima Coal* venture in East Kalimantan since 1982.

Increases in mining permits held by SOEs and local private companies and in CoWs with foreign companies underpinned the expansion and diversification of mining production since the 1970s. By 1975 the total number of permits was 321 (Lloyd 1975, p. 330), rising to 597 by 2000, as Table 11.3 shows. The 2009 Mining Law phased out the CoW system in favour of a licensing system. By 2012, the total number of issued licences was 10,673, of which 50 per cent was for production and the rest for surveying and exploration (MEMR 2013, pp. 65–71). More than 99 per cent had been issued by provincial and district governments and included very small operations that had hitherto been informal and/or illegal. Given high commodity prices in recent years, the number is reminiscent of the speculative boom in exploration permits issued prior to World War I, as Table 11.2 showed.

Table 11.3 Outstanding contracts of work and mining permits, 2000

	CoWs	Coal CoWs Foreign	Coal CoWs Domestic	Mining permits
Issued during 1967–2000	235	16	103	597
Concluded before 2000	132	0	0	0
Expired before 2000	17	0	0	0
Remaining in 2000, for:				
Surveying	20	0	0	21
Exploration	39	0	7	293
Feasibility study	6	0	18	0
Construction	6	0	15	0
Production	15	16	64	283
Total	86	16	103	597

Source: DESDM (2001).

Institutional arrangements to distribute resource rents

Mining activities generated resource rents, particularly at times when international commodity prices were high. To secure a fair share of those rents for the benefit of Indonesia's society, governments created legal institutions that sought to maximise this share. Such arrangements necessarily had to leave sufficient guarantees that foreign companies would be able to recoup their investments and pay for foreign expertise, as well as generate a reasonable return on FDI during the life of a venture. This section assesses the essence of these institutional arrangements.

Government regulations of 1850 and 1873 determined the general conditions under which private mining firms operated in Indonesia. They separated subsoil and surface rights for specified minerals and made exploration and exploitation of their deposits dependent on permits. Concessions for the exploitation of deposits stipulated the conditions that applied to operations, such as a due date for production to start, and the annual royalty to be paid to the government after starting production. These principles and an accumulation of clarifications were included in the 1899 Mining Law. Exploration licences were granted for three years and exploitation concessions for a maximum of 75 years and a maximum of 2,000 hectares. Holders of exploration licences and concessions paid annual fees and royalties depending on the value of production.

This legislation offered the certainty that private companies required to invest in exploration and exploitation of mineral deposits, as Table 11.2 showed. But with high prices and rich deposits, the terms proved generous to some enterprises. For example, first investors in oil production made windfall profits when oil prices were high and demand for petrol for motor vehicles expanded quickly. To prevent such cases, the government introduced changes to the legislation to increase its share in the resource rents. For example, it reserved concessions with rich deposits for state exploitation upon expiry of existing concessions. It denied new concessions in areas where deposits seemed rich and exploitation by the government was deemed preferable, and introduces an amendment that required companies to pay additional royalties and profit tax. Such arrangements indicate that political opinion shifted in favour of greater state control over exploitation of mineral deposits.

A change confirming this policy stance was the "Contract of Work" (CoW), effective in 1924. It was based on the notion that the government should maintain control over mining ventures, but that the expertise of private enterprise was necessary to manage such state-controlled operations. Explorations or concessions by private firms took place under a contract specifying conditions in order to maximise returns to the government. Consequently, mining operations increasingly took place by state-owned ventures, state-controlled joint-venture companies or by private firms under CoWs. Thus, the conditions of contracts and concessions became subject to fierce negotiations between government and private companies. The outcomes depended on the commercial merits of a case, and the degree of mutual dependence.

Variations in the conditions under which private firms operated in Indonesia makes it is difficult to state what on balance the share of government and firms was in the resource rents. For example, American oil company *Standard Oil* estimated that its subsidiary in colonial Indonesia shared around 50 per cent of its revenues with the government before World War II, comprising 4 per cent of the gross value of crude oil production, a 20 per cent tax on net revenues under Article 5a, and a general corporate income tax of 20 per cent (Higgins 1957, p. 41).

After independence, mining operations resumed operations on the basis of the pre-war legislation. However, the government imposed a moratorium on new explorations and concessions until a new mining law. Indonesia's parliament passed Law 37/1960 on Mining and Law 44/1960 on the Mining of Oil and Gas. The first ended the system of mining permits and concessions and decreed that mining could only be carried out by Indonesian companies and in the case of "strategic" minerals only by government agencies such as SOEs, albeit that foreign companies could be engaged under CoWs (Redfern 2010, p. 161). Law 44/1960 contained similar rules, tailored to the oil sector. Nevertheless, most firms waited with new commitments until after the enactment of Law 1/1967 on Foreign Investment and the concomitant Law 11/1967 on the Basic Provisions for Mining.

Law 1/1967 granted foreign firms exemptions from duties on imported machinery, equipment, tools, etc. It also permitted repatriation of profits and accelerated depreciation of a company's fixed assets in Indonesia. Law 11/1967 reiterated that domestic legal entities (private companies, SOEs, cooperatives) and individuals could engage in mining on the basis of permits issued by the Ministry of Mining, but reserved the mining of "strategic" minerals to government agencies, such as SOEs. Permits were required for prospecting, exploration and exploitation (up to 30 years for oil companies), as well as processing, transportation and the sale of mining commodities. Foreign firms could only operate in the mining sector on the basis of a CoW issued by an SOE or a government agency that held the relevant mining permit. The CoW included a production sharing agreement by which the SOE or agency received a minimum of 60 per cent of production. A CoW required the contractor to finance the project, although such costs could be recovered from the value of production.

Together, these 1967 laws provided reasonable security for foreign mining firms, as well as competitive and predictable royalty rates. FDI in Indonesian mining increased quickly. The basis for new CoWs was revised several times, for example in relation to income tax and tax concessions, royalties and duties on imported capital goods. This created several "generations" of contracts with increasingly restrictive conditions for foreign firms (Emerson *et al.* 1984, pp. 114–118; Darmono 2009, p. 189; O'Callaghan 2010, p. 220).

Law 11/1967 did not prescribe how production was shared. In oil production, after foreign firms had recovered their cash operating costs, capital depreciation and interest payments in the form of a percentage of annual production, the remainder was generally split 60–40 per cent or 65–35 per cent in favour of *Pertamina*. After income tax, the *Pertamina*/government-foreign enterprise distribution was around 85–15 per cent for oil and 70–30 per cent for natural gas (Emerson *et al.* 1984, pp. 114–115; Bahl and Tumennasan 2004, p. 211). As international oil prices increased in the 1970s, the details of new CoWs were adjusted to include production sharing arrangements more favourable to *Pertamina*.

Pertamina was a source of inefficiency and blatant rent seeking related to its selective awarding of contracts to local firms for e.g. the trade and transport of the company's oil supplies and the distribution of derivatives. This was only mitigated after the abdication of President Soeharto in 1998 and the first unfettered elections in 1999. Soon after, new laws changed conditions for the activity of domestic and foreign mining companies in Indonesia. For example, Law 22/2001 on Oil and Gas required *Pertamina* to give up its control over CoWs and production sharing arrangements for oil (but not gas and LNG production), in favour of a tender system supervised by a new regulatory agency. *Pertamina* became an SOE operating production sharing contracts on a commercial basis, competing with other domestic firms.

In addition, Law 22/1999 on Regional Autonomy ended Indonesia's highly centralised administrative system and delegated responsibilities to regional authorities of 27 provinces and 341 districts and municipalities. Subsequently, Law 25/1999 on Fiscal Decentralisation and Law 33/2004 on Fiscal Balance specify that regional governments could retain 80 per cent of the net tax revenues from mining, forestry and fisheries operations in their territories, as well as 30 per cent from natural gas and 15 per cent from oil (Agustina *et al.* 2012, pp. 5–6). Other clauses require mining companies to engage in environmental protection and community development in areas in the vicinity of their mining ventures. Law 34/2000 on Regional Taxes and Levies enables regional governments to impose additional local taxes on mining companies, while Government

Regulation 75/2001 allows district governments to issue mining permits for all minerals.[4]

Consequently, large mining companies had to associate more with local communities and local governments, which imposed numerous *ad hoc* taxes and regulations affecting mining operations (Bahl and Tumennasan 2004, pp. 206–207; O'Callaghan 2010, p. 222). Firms found that regional governments had limited administrative capacity. Inconsistencies between central and local legislations compounded the uncertainties they faced (Rusli and Duek 2010). Local support for rapidly expanding small-scale mining operations, often illegal and encroaching on the large mining ventures, enhanced the new issues that foreign firms faced (Spiegel 2012). Some foreign firms divested their interests in Indonesia; others put new projects on hold, awaiting the enactment of the 2009 Mineral and Coal Mining Law.

Hence, at a time when international mining commodity prices increased, FDI inflows in mining in Indonesia fluctuated significantly. They decreased from US$3.0 billion in 1998 to US$500 million in 2004, peaked at US$3.6 billion in 2006 and fell again to US$1.9 billion in 2010 or just 14 per cent of total FDI inflows (Darmono 2009, p. 356; BI, various years). Foreign companies became increasingly reluctant to enter new CoWs, particularly for greenfield exploration of deposits. Non-oil exploration indeed attracted a very low annual average of US$24 million per year in the 2000s (PWC, various years).

Given these institutional changes, what shares of the resource rents did governments in Indonesia capture on behalf of society? Figure 11.4 shows that the share of mining-related income in government revenue was just 2–5 per cent up to the late-1890s; mostly related to tin mining in Bangka and Belitung. During 1899–1927 public revenue from mining increased, but the share remained 5–15 per cent. Global oversupply caused commodity prices to plummet during 1928–32, before revenues recovered to on average 10 per cent. During 1948–68 the share was broadly similar, before the oil boom caused a rapid increase in public revenue from oil so that during the 1970s and 1980s, 45–50 per cent of the budget was mining-related, decreasing to an average of 30 per cent.

Figure 11.4 also shows government revenue from mining as a percentage of GVA in mining. This is an imperfect indicator of the distribution of the resource rents, as GVA accounts only for current inputs, not the cost of capital and labour that mining companies and contractors had to incur in order to generate the rents. During 1870–89, the average share was 52 per cent; the same as during 1970–2010. The share decreased to 23 per cent in the 1910s as oil production increased. This is partly explained by oil ventures requiring capital investment in exploration, exploitation and particularly processing facilities, as almost all oil was long refined domestically for export and domestic consumption.[5] This investment necessitated payments of interest and dividends before the resource rents were allocated to government and private companies.

The increase in the 1920s has two explanations. A spike in the tin price to 1927 in relation to the cartelisation of global tin production (Hillman 2010, pp. 55–59) boosted government revenue from tin ventures. In addition, new

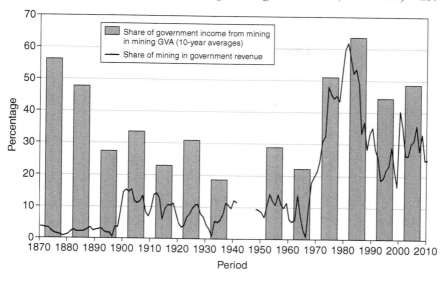

Figure 11.4 Share of tax and non-tax income from mining in total central government revenue and in gross value added from mining, 1870–2010 (percentages) (sources: Mining GVA in current prices, see the Appendix; government income 1870–1940 calculated from *Encyclopedia* (Vol. 1: 750–758; Vol. 7: 154–163), Mulder (1938), and budget papers included in *Bijlagen bij de Handelingen van de Staten Generaal* (1870–1940) and *Bijlagen bij de Handelingen van de Volksraad* (1918–42); 1948–2010 from *Nota Keuangan Negara* (1948–59), *Statistik Keuangan* (1960–89), BI (1990–2010)).

Notes
No data for 1942–47. 1870–1940 comprises net government income from tin, coal, gold and silver mining, revenues from mining concessions, dividends from NIAM and GMB joint ventures, oil industry crisis levy in the 1930s, mining export duties and mining company tax (both estimated from totals in proportion to the share of mining in exports), and excludes income from the government salt monopoly; 1948–2010 comprises 1948–66 mining company tax, 1948–2010 mining-related export duties (both estimated from totals in proportion to the share of mining in exports), 1952–59 net transfers from all SOEs, 1960–72 net transfers from SOEs *Permina* and *Pertamina*, 1967–89 oil company tax, 1990–2010 non-tax revenue from mining, 1994–2010 net profit transfers by SOEs (mining SOEs were predominant), 1999–2010 income tax from oil and gas firms.

arrangements, particularly CoWs and public-private joint-ventures, and changes in the distribution of resource rents, increased the government share. The 1929 crisis and its aftermath intervened. In line with commodity prices, net revenues of mining companies decreased, and the government's share in mining GVA fell, before recovering to around 25 per cent in the late-1930s. During the 1950s and 1960s, the average share was 29 and 22 per cent respectively, suggesting that nationalisations of foreign companies and making CoWs mandatory did not make much difference. But this takes no account of off-budget spending that mining SOEs facilitated. The share increased to an average of 52 per cent during 1970–2010, due to higher commodity prices and new generations of CoWs.

Mining and the wider economy

Apart from contributions to GDP, export earnings and government revenue, what significance did mining activity have for the wider economy? To start, employment in the mining sector grew significantly, but remained marginal. It increased from 44,000 (or 0.4% of total employment) in 1930, to 87,000 (0.4%) in 1961, 712,500 (1.0%) in 1990 and 1,255,000 (1.2%) in 2010.[6] Densely populated Java has long had a labour surplus, but most mining ventures were located in distant regions. During the colonial era, migrant labour was attracted to mining sites; initially from China and later also from Java. But large-scale mining operations were generally more capital-intensive than labour-intensive for technological reasons, which restricted labour absorption in mining. Recruitment of skilled migrant workers was relatively costly due to the need for investment in amenities comparable to urban areas. This sustained the creation of relatively well-endowed enclave economies that were not well-embedded in the regional economy. Large companies had their own transport infrastructure, steam- or diesel-driven electric power stations, as well as in-house facilities to produce charcoal for smelting of ores and timber for underground support. Mining services were supplied in-house, or purchased from distant, urban-based engineering companies, thus limiting the local backward linkages.

There also were limitations to the forward linkages of mining activities. Panel C in Table 11.1 indicated that the share of output not exported and processed domestically, changed from 43 per cent in 1971 to just 19 per cent in 1980, before increasing to 58 per cent in 2010. Most of value adding was in oil and gas. When domestic consumption of oil started to exceed exports, more crude oil was refined for domestic consumption. For metallic ores, Table 11.1 shows an increase from 36 per cent of output processed domestically in 1971 to 64 per cent in 1980, largely due to the phasing out of tin ore exports in the 1970s. The decrease to 32 per cent in 1990 was related to the rapid increase in the production of copper ore and bauxite, before investment in processing facilities for particularly nickel and copper brought the share to 58 per cent in 2010. Most domestic processing involved the production of basic metals, rather than refined metals, basic metal products and the use of minerals as inputs in other production processes, such as in the chemical industry.

Over time, various initiatives sought to maximise the forward linkages of mining production in Indonesia. The high unit cost of handling, transporting and shipping long weighed heavily on unprocessed commodities with low unit values. Depending on such costs, the available technologies and associated processing costs, and the conditions imposed by governments on concessions and CoWs, firms became more interested in processing minerals in Indonesia during the first half of the twentieth century. Particularly the large tin mines and oil companies, as well as smaller ventures producing gold and silver invested in processing facilities. Nevertheless, by 1940 many opportunities for domestic processing remained, albeit that not all were economical (Van Bemmelen 1940).

Of the metallic ores, only gold and silver ore have always been processed for the domestic market. Tin ore was partially processed since the mid-nineteenth century until in the 1970s *PN Tambang Timah* expanded its processing capacity, as mentioned above. In the case of nickel, the capacity of the two smelters operated since 1978 by *PT Inco* and *PT Aneka Tambang* sufficed to process just 25 per cent of nickel ore. Likewise for copper, the capacity of the smelter of *PT Smelting Gresik* opened in 1996 covers around 30 per cent of copper ore. Plans to process all of Indonesia's bauxite production into aluminium existed since the late-1930s. However, the capacity of the 1982 smelter of state-owned *PT Indonesia Asahan Aluminium* is still insufficient for that purpose.

From the outset, most crude oil was refined in Indonesia; about 60 per cent of production during 1900–11, increasing to 90 per cent during 1912–40. It was initially processed into kerosene for the domestic market, but production diversified to include other derivatives, such as petrol, aviation gasoline, kerosene, diesel, lubricants, paraffin and asphalt for domestic use and export (Lindblad 1989, pp. 66–70). By the late-1930s, there were five large and three smaller oil refineries with a capacity of 60 mby. Oil refining capacity increased to around 90 mby in 1963 (Redfern 2010, pp. 165–166). But the subsequent expansion of crude oil production and the increase of domestic consumption of oil derivatives necessarily implied increasing exports of crude oil. By the late 1950s 65 per cent of crude production was processed, falling to 25–30 per cent in the 1970s and 1980s. *Pertamina* increased its processing capacity to 150 mby in 1971 and about 300 mby in 2010, comprising nine refineries. Some ageing refineries cannot operate at full capacity, but the share of crude oil processed domestically rose, as oil exports decreased in favour of domestic consumption.

Indonesian ventures long also processed phosphate into fertiliser, and the chemical industry utilised mining products (e.g. sulphur, copper-iodine and other salts) as did the ceramic and construction industries (e.g. kaolin, quartz sand, marble, feldspar, sandstone, trass). Most of this produce was destined for domestic markets. However, their indirect contributions to value adding in manufacturing and constriction remained relatively small.

A major issue was the impact of significant changes in international commodity prices on Indonesia's real exchange rate and on the competiveness of other trade-exposed economic sectors, particularly manufacturing. This effect was compounded or mitigated by the fact that Indonesia was also a major exporter of a wide range of agricultural commodities, particularly sugar, rubber, copra and tapioca before World War II, and rubber and palm oil after the war until oil and gas dominated exports since the 1960s, as Figure 11.3 indicated.

Figure 11.5 shows changes in the average prices of mining commodities. The price of oil fell significantly until just before World War I, before peaking in the late-1910s, and then plummeting again. A response of oil companies in Indonesia was to invest in processing facilities and reduce the relative cost of transporting oil. Hence, the unit price of oil increased in the late-1920s, because it is a weighted average of crude and processed oil products. The prices of other mining commodities, particularly tin ore, increased until a peak in 1927. As noted, this

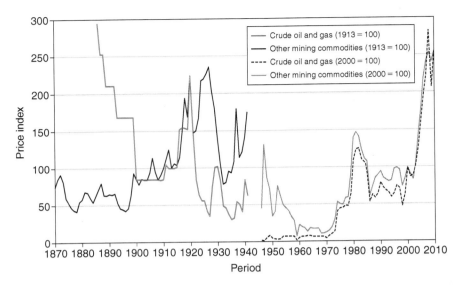

Figure 11.5 Implicit price indices of GVA in mining, 1870–2010 (1913 and 2000=100) (sources: Van der Eng 2014: Appendix).

Note
For 1946–1974 "deflated" with the official US$ export exchange rate, and for 1975–2010 with the market US$ exchange rate.

drove changes in the institutional arrangements that allowed the government to capture a larger share of the resource rents. The price movements of oil and tin ore may have cancelled each other out. After 1929 all commodity prices dropped, but oil prices decreased faster. One reason was that Indonesia joined the international tin cartel in 1931 (Hillman 2010, pp. 115–118). Restrictions of tin production halted the fall of the tin price.

For 1946–2010, Indonesia's domestic prices in Figure 11.5 are expressed in US dollars, because Indonesia experienced episodes of high inflation that are difficult to capture in the chart. Indonesia also had a multiple exchange rate system during 1949–74 for the purpose of restricting imports and implicitly taxing exports. High inflation eroded the value of the Rupiah, because official exchanges rates were not adjusted accordingly. The official exchange rate that applied to exports clearly reduced the price incentive for export producers. However, firms found ways around this. Small ventures may have benefited from smuggling to Malaysia and Singapore, while large companies simply repatriated only part of their foreign exchange earnings. SOEs also worked around the multiple exchange rates, as production sharing agreements helped to prevent disagreements about the applicable exchange rate. SOEs also engaged in barter arrangements with Japan, exchanging e.g. bauxite for metal imports. As soon as such foreign exchange restrictions were eased in the 1970s, the US dollar equivalents of the prices of both oil and non-oil mining commodities rose significantly, as Figure 11.5 indicates. They decreased during the early 1980s, stabilised by the 1990s, and increased very significantly during the commodity boom of the 2000s related to China's rapid economic development.

To the extent that export earnings depended on mining commodities, the price changes in Figure 11.5 impacted on Indonesia's terms of trade. During 1878–1936, Indonesia had a gold exchange standard and its nominal exchange rate was stable relative to the gold-based Dutch guilder (Van der Eng 1999). This was partly offset by the inability of the exchange rate to depreciate and accommodate adverse price changes of Indonesian exports. Higher commodity prices therefore tended to increase the general domestic price level relative to countries that did not export such commodities, and *vice versa*. At times, the higher domestic cost of living raised labour costs to make imports cheaper than domestic produce, reducing the competitiveness of trade-exposed non-commodity sectors, particularly manufactured goods. Consequently, Indonesia's real exchange rate fluctuated to the degree that domestic prices differed from international prices. Instability in the real exchange rate made it difficult for entrepreneurs to plan non-commodity production ventures. This was one reason why Indonesia did not see a significant development of a competitive textile industry until the 1930s, when it embraced import-replacing industrialisation (Van der Eng 2012).

The stance in trade policy continued after independence, when Indonesia experienced increasing foreign exchange shortages to cover its current account deficits. The oil boom of the 1970s relieved these difficulties. And with 45–50 per cent of the public revenue related to mining in the 1970s and 1980s, the rapid increase of oil revenues facilitated unprecedented increases in public expenditure on infrastructure and development (Hill 2000, pp. 46–60). It also facilitated the pursuit of import-replacing development of rice agriculture and industrialisation to create new employment and income opportunities and thus avoid the worst of the "Dutch disease" effects of the oil boom. This worked reasonably well until the early-1980s, when the prices of Indonesia's mining commodities decreased, as Figure 11.5 shows. In response, the government embraced policies to support export-oriented industrialisation and encourage a diversification of exports and government revenues away from dependence on oil and gas, as Figure 11.3 indicates (Hill 2000, pp. 49–52, 80–84, 164–167).

Conclusion

By quantifying mining production in Indonesia, this chapter has shown that the mining sector contributed a relatively small part to the economy until the 1970s, despite the development of some large mining ventures. Quantification showed that, despite the diversity of production, mining was long dominated by tin and oil until diversification of output into particularly gas, coal, copper and nickel ore since the 1970s. Apart from the development on some large mining ventures controlled by Indonesia's SOEs, the process engaged growing numbers of foreign enterprises as contractors as well as small privately owned domestic companies.

From the outset in the early nineteenth century, the government in Indonesia sought to maximise its share in the resource rents that mining ventures generated. But it realised that the investment capital and technology that private companies could muster were indispensable to mining development. The general principles for private sector involvement in mining were established with legislation passed in 1852, 1872 and 1899, although private sector involvement did not start to increase significantly until the 1890s. In that process, the government regularly changed the conditions under which private firms operated when market conditions shifted the balance in favour of private firms. Where commercial opportunities were limited, as in coal, the government operated ventures itself. Other ventures were operated by private companies as contractors.

During the 1950s and 1960s, conditions in Indonesia were unsettled and few foreign companies were willing to invest, except three foreign oil companies. The 1960 Mining Law created more certainty, facilitating the operations of foreign companies under two arrangements. The CoW continued past practice, and proved an acceptable compromise to government and foreign companies in the context of Indonesia's 1945 Constitution. The production sharing arrangement was a pragmatic response to Indonesia's foreign exchange shortages and controls, as well as the role of SOEs in Indonesia's mining sector. Nevertheless, it took until after 1967 before the mining operations expanded; first in the oil sector and later in other mining operations. Both institutions maximised the government share in resource rents, particularly in the wake of the 1973 oil boom.

The oil boom and the subsequent diversification of mining production facilitated a drastic expansion of public spending to spur economic development. Import-replacing agricultural and industrial development shielded the Indonesian economy from the worst "Dutch disease" consequences in the 1970s and early 1980s. When this effect subsided, the revenues from mining exports supported a more broad-based development strategy.

The expansion of mineral production exceeded the growth of processing capacity, particularly in oil. Large foreign companies were reluctant to invest in processing facilities in Indonesia, as they had their own processing facilities overseas. Based on the involvement of foreign firms as contractors, Indonesian SOEs took up processing mining commodities for growing domestic markets as well as exports. With the exception of tin and LNG, the capacity to process minerals before exports remained insufficient in the face of sustained growth in output. Reluctance among foreign firms to invest in such facilities and in new ventures increased when administrative decentralisation took hold in Indonesia after 1999.

Notes

1 Unless indicated otherwise, the descriptive discussion until 1941 draws on Encyclopaedie (1918–41) (Van Bemmelen 1941; Ter Braake 1944) and *Jaarboek van het Mijnwezen* (1872–1939).
2 Unless indicated otherwise, the descriptive discussion draws on Sigit *et al.* 1969; Moenir 1985; Darmono 2009) and USGS (1963–2012).

3 The remaining number is 231. Ooi (1982, p. 135) notes that Indonesia had 237 oil fields in 1976, which includes new fields identified during 1960–76 that may have compensated depleted and abandoned fields.
4 In addition, Law 44/1999 on Forestry banned open pit mining operations from forested areas. It also made other mining operations in forested areas subject to permission from the Minister of Forestry, leading to an effective ban on explorations in such areas by foreign companies.
5 Indeed, annual investment in mining increased from an estimated low f2 million (5% of total) in 1900 to f76 million (25%) in 1929, before slumping to f5 million in 1933 (14%) and recovering to f30 million (26%) in 1940 (estimates, based on Creutzberg 1977, pp. 54–59).
6 Calculated from the 1930, 1961, 1990 population censuses and 2010 national labour force survey.

References

Agustina, C.D., Ahmad, E., Siagian, D. and Nugroho, H., 2012. *Political Economy of Natural Resource Revenue Sharing in Indonesia*. LSE Asia Research Centre Working Paper. No. 55.

Bahl, R. and Tumennasan, B., 2004. How Should Revenues from Natural Resources Be Shared in Indonesia? In: J. Alm, J. Martinez-Vazquez and S.M. Indrawati, eds. *Reforming Intergovernmental Fiscal Relations and the Rebuilding of Indonesia: The "Big Bang" Program and its Economic Consequences*. Cheltenham, UK: Elgar, 199–233.

Booth, A., 1998. *The Indonesian Economy in the Nineteenth and Twentieth Centuries: A History of Missed Opportunities*. Basingstoke: St. Martin's Press.

Creutzberg, P., 1977. *Changing Economy in Indonesia: Expenditure on Fixed Assets*. The Hague, Netherlands: Martinus Nijheff.

Darmono, D., 2009. *Mineral dan energi kekayaan bangsa: sejarah pertambangan dan energi Indonesia*. Jakarta: Departemen Energi dan Sumber Daya Mineral.

Departemen Pertambangan, 1971. *Data Sensus Pertambangan 1968–1970*. Jakarta: Departmen Pertambangan.

DESDM, 2001. *Laporan Tahunan 2000*. Jakarta: Departemen Energi dan Sumber Daya Mineral.

Dick, H., Houben, V.J.H., Lindblad, J.T. and Thee, K.W., 2002. *The Emergence of a National Economy: An Economic History of Indonesia, 1800–2000*. Honolulu: University of Hawaii Press.

Emerson, C., Garnaut, R. and Clunies, A., 1984. Mining Taxation in Indonesia. *Bulletin of Indonesian Economic Studies*, 20 (2), 107–121.

Erman, E., 2005. *Membaranya batubara: konflik kelas dan etnik Ombilin-Sawahlunto, Sumatera Barat, 1892–1996*. Jakarta: Desantara.

Gibson, J., 1966. Production-Sharing. *Bulletin of Indonesian Economic Studies*, 2 (3, 4), 52–75, 75–100.

Gillis, M. and Jenkins, G.P., 1978. *Performance Evaluation of Public Sector Enterprises: The Case of Mining in Bolivia and Indonesia*. Development Discussion Paper. Kingston, Ontario, Canada, No. 1978–1. Kingston (Ontario): Queen's University.

Higgins, B., 1957. *Stanvac in Indonesia*. Washington D.C.: National Planning Association.

Hill, H., 2000. *The Indonesian Economy*. Melbourne, Australia: Cambridge University Press.

Hillman, J., 2010. *The International Tin Cartel*. London: Routledge.

Hunter, A., 1968. Minerals in Indonesia. *Bulletin of Indonesian Economic Studies*, 4 (11), 73–89.

IDE, 1977. *Input-Output Table Indonesia, 1971.* Tokyo: Institute of Developing Economies.

Lindblad, J.T., 1985. Strak Beleid and Batig Slot: De Oost-Borneo Maatschappij, 1888–1940. *Economisch- en Sociaal-Historisch Jaarboek*, 48, 182–211.

Lindblad, J.T., 1989. The Petroleum Industry in Indonesia before the Second World War. *Bulletin of Indonesian Economic Studies*, 25 (2), 57–77.

Lloyd, B., 1975. Indonesia's Mineral Resources. *Resources Policy*, 1 (6), 326–342.

MEMR, 2013. *Indonesia Mineral and Coal Statistics 2012.* Jakarta: Ministry of Energy and Mineral Resources.

Moenir, A.S., 1985. *40 Tahun Peranan Pertambangan dan Energi Indonesia 1945–1985.* Jakarta: Departemen Pertambangan dan Energi.

Mulder, W., 1938. *Het Tweede Tiental Begrootingen met den Volksraad: 1929–1928.* Batavia: Landsdrukkerij.

Nikle, T., 1970. Oil and Mining Developments. *Bulletin of Indonesian Economic Studies*, 6 (1), 61–72.

O'Callaghan, T., 2010. Patience is a Virtue: Problems of Regulatory Governance in the Indonesian Mining Sector. *Resources Policy*, 35 (3), 218–225.

Ooi, J.-B., 1982. *The Petroleum Resources of Indonesia.* Kuala Lumpur: Oxford University Press.

Purwanto, B., 2009. Economic Decolonization and the Rise of Indonesian Military Business. *In:* J.T. Lindblad and P. Post, eds. *Indonesian Economic Decolonization in Regional and International Perspective.* Leiden: KITLV Press, 39–58.

Redfern, W.A., 2010. Sukarno's Guided Democracy and the Takeovers of Foreign Companies in Indonesia in the 1960s. University of Michigan. PhD Thesis, University of Michigan.

Rusli, R. and Duek, A., 2010. *The Natural Resources Industry in Decentralised Indonesia: How Has Decentralisation Impacted the Mining, Oil and Gas Industries?.* CREA Discussion Paper 2010–25. Luxembourg: Centre for Research in Economic Analysis, University of Luxembourg.

Sigit, S., Purbo-Hadiwidjojo, M.M., Sulasmoro, B. and Wirjosudjono, S., 1969. *Minerals and Mining in Indonesia.* Jakarta: Ministry of Mines.

Spiegel, S.J., 2012. Governance Institutions, Resource Rights Regimes, and the Informal Mining Sector: Regulatory Complexities in Indonesia. *World Development*, 40 (1), 189–205.

Ter Braake, A.L., 1944. *Mining in the Netherlands East Indies.* New York: Arno Press.

Van Bemmelen, R.W., 1940. Delfstoffen van Nederlandsch-Indie als Grondstoffen der Inheemsche Industrie. *Natuurwetenschappelijk Tijdschrift voor Nederlandsch-Indië*, 101 (1), 11–19.

Van Bemmelen, R.W., 1941. De Beteekenis van den Nederlandsch-Indischen Mijnbouw. *Koloniale Studiën*, 25, 186–200.

Van der Eng, P., 1999. The Silver Standard and Asia's Integration into the World Economy, 1850–1914. *Review of Asian and Pacific Studies*, 18, 59–85.

Van der Eng, P., 2010. The Sources of Long-Term Economic Growth in Indonesia, 1880–2008. *Explorations in Economic History*, 47 (2), 294–309.

Van der Eng, P., 2012. Why Didn't Colonial Indonesia Have a Competitive Cotton Textile Industry? *Modern Asian Studies*, 47 (3), 1019–1054.

Van der Eng, P., 2014. Mining and Indonesia's Economy: Institutions and Value Adding,

1870–2010. *PRIMCED Discussion Paper No. 57.* Tokyo: Institute of Economic Research, Hitotsubashi University.

Van Zanden, J.L. and Marks, D., 2013. *An Economic History of Indonesia: 1800–2010.* London: Routledge.

Serials

BI, *Statistik Ekonomi dan Keuangan Indonesia.* Jakarta: Bank Indonesia (1990–2010).
BPS, *Tabel Input-Output Indonesia.* Jakarta: Biro/Badan Pusat Statistik (1975, 1980, 1985, 1990, 1995, 2000, 2005, 2010).
Bijlagen bij de Handelingen van de Staten Generaal (1870–1940).
Bijlagen bij de Handelingen van de Volksraad (1918–42).
Encyclopaedie (1917–1941) *Encyclopaedie van Nederlandsch-Indië* [Encyclopaedia of The Netherlands Indies]. The Hague: Nijhoff/Brill (11 volumes).
Jaarboek van het Mijnwezen in Nederlandsch-Indië (1872–1939).
Nota Keuangan Negara (1948–59).
PWC, *Review of Trends in the Indonesian Mining Industry.* Jakarta: Pricewaterhouse-Coopers (2003–12).
Statistik Keuangan (1960–89).
USGS, *United States Geological Survey Minerals Yearbook* (1963–2012).

12 Land abundance, frontier expansion and appropriability

Settler economies during the first globalization[1]

Henry Willebald

1 Introduction

A new literature has emerged, inspired by the work of Sachs and Warner (1995), that focuses on the so-called "resource *curse* hypothesis", a puzzling paradox that suggests resource-rich countries tend to grow more slowly than resource-poor ones. However, over a long period there was a consensus among economists that abundant natural resource endowments made for economic strength. Natural resources (coal, iron) played a central role in the emergence of the "modern economic growth" that started in the eighteenth century. In addition, in the nineteenth century wide areas of new land were incorporated into the expansion of world capitalism and participated in international trade, which showed that other resources besides minerals were a *blessing*. The Second Industrial Revolution had far-reaching consequences in extensive regions in South America, Australasia and Africa where technological changes like railways, refrigeration and reduced freight costs combined with a temperate climate and fertile soils suitable for the production of commodities such as wheat, wool and beef.

Rather than being a general pattern, the curse seems subject to the influence of supply and demand conditions, technological progress and institutional structure with strong historical specificities. As abundant-natural resource regions, the settler economies are an interesting "natural experiment" in this sense. I select six economies, namely Argentina, Australia, Canada, Chile, New Zealand and Uruguay (Willebald 2007), and evaluate their performance during the First Globalization (1870–1913). This was a period of strong economic expansion (Denoon 1983; Lloyd and Metzer 2013) based on dynamic participation in international trade (Schedvin 1990) and characterized by increasing income inequality (Williamson 2000; Greasley *et al.* 2007).[2]

The consequences of the First Globalization followed a common pattern in the settler economies, but when we examine these countries in greater depth it emerges that they reacted in strikingly different ways, and this probably determined their varying performance in subsequent decades. Although these economies based their production on primary activities, they achieved levels of development close to the industrial "core" at around the time of the First World War (WWI). However, in the former British possessions (Australia, New

Zealand, Canada) income per capita was higher, inequality was worsening less, and economic specialization was relatively less concentrated on primary activities (Willebald 2007) than in the South American Southern Cone (Argentina, Chile and Uruguay) (Williamson 2002; Willebald 2013a). The former British colonies were more blessed and less damned by their abundant natural resources than the other ex-colonies.

One of the main analytical branches of the curse hypothesis concerns the role of institutions in economic relations. I use the appropriability hypothesis to consider the idea that different types of natural resources interact with different levels of institutional quality and produce dissimilar results. I evaluate the curse in terms of productive expansion and income distribution in agriculture, which was the sector that made the most intensive use of the main natural resource of settler economies, namely land.

The settler economies had similar natural resources, but incorporating the idea of land "quality" introduces interesting insights in the analysis. A classification of land into different types by agricultural aptitude enables us to consider a gradient of appropriability possibilities ranging from high quality land (with greater possibilities to generate rental differentials) to low quality land. In terms of production, an abundance of natural resources was a blessing for the settler economies, but they suffered the curse of increasing inequality. These two processes functioned with varying degrees of intensity within the club, and this is explained by differences in use by type of land. Economies that moved their frontiers onto high agricultural aptitude land welcomed the blessing of agricultural expansion but suffered the curse of agrarian rents being concentrated in the privileged classes. However, resources did not perform alone but interacted with various different institutional arrangements. To gauge institutional quality we consider the enforcement of contracts and ownership rights – with contract-intensive money as a proxy on the "macroeconomic level" – and the configuration of the land ownership system (agents' behaviour on the "micro level").

I employ two approaches. First, I estimate the relationships between growth, income distribution, natural resources and institutions. For this analysis I use panel data estimation and include the interaction between the two last-mentioned variables in the six economies, considering annual data from 1870 to 1913. Second, I adopt a complementary approach based on a historical description of the distribution of land rights – from the beginning of the nineteenth century to WWI – and the institutional arrangements governing land ownership in the River Plate and Australasia. My discussion focuses on the role of national (or state) authorities and the definition and enforcement of land rights, and I attempt to identify two "models" – the "British" and the "Hispanic" – that made for different distributive patterns.

First, in Section 2 I review the concept of the curse of natural resources and present the appropriability hypothesis. In Section 3 I present my empirical strategy, analytical model and explanatory variables. In Section 4 I present the statistical results. In Section 5 I note the main shortcomings of this analysis, propose a second approach and consider the notion of appropriability to guide the depiction of the historical formation of land ownership systems. In Section 6 I draw my conclusions and make some final remarks.

2 Institutional quality and the appropriability hypothesis

Since the end of the twentieth century economic growth is no longer considered to be dependent only on the accumulation of physical and human capital. Academics now recognize that a third form of "capital", namely natural and environmental resource endowments or "natural capital", plays a key role in economic performance. However, although natural capital is important for sustainable economic development, the literature that covers the period from the 1960s to the end of the twentieth century shows a negative relationship between economic growth and some measures of natural capital, and this is considered the "curse" of natural resources (Sachs and Warner 1995, 2001; Gylfason 2007).

2.1 Institutional explanation and the appropriability hypothesis

Large natural resource rents, especially in combination with wrongly defined ownership rights, imperfect markets and permissive legal structures, may divert resources away from economic activities that are more fruitful in social terms and nurture economic growth (van der Ploeg 2011; Willebald 2011). The literature brought institutional arrangements into the centre of the analysis. The results have been mixed, but there is a general consensus that some kind of "conditionality" is involved. Quality of institutions plays a central role in the curse or blessing of natural resources, and even when there are abundant natural resources countries can perform well if institutions are "good".

Different kinds of natural resources may have differing effects on economic performance, and a distinction is made in the literature between "point resources" such as mineral and energy resources that make intensive use of capital, and "diffuse resources" such as cropland and livestock which require low capital concentration (Auty 2001). "Point resources" generate greater opportunities for rent-seeking and corruption, and the consequences are more adverse (Woolcock *et al.* 2001; Bulte *et al.* 2005; Isham *et al.* 2005). This focus on the intrinsic characteristics of natural resources gave rise to an examination of the quality of institutions in terms of their capacity to enhance or reduce the appropriability possibilities of incomes generated from natural capital.

Boschini *et al.* (2007) show that the effect of natural resources on economic development is not determined by resource endowments alone, but rather by the interaction between the type of resources and the quality of institutions. "Appropriability" concerns the factors that govern the innovator's ability to get returns generated by an innovation. In economies where resources – and the corresponding rents – are highly appropriable, it might be expected that abundance could hinder economic development.

The appropriability hypothesis is conceived in terms of technical and institutional dimensions. The technical dimension is the "intrinsic" character of natural resources, and the institutional dimension is the capacity of institutions that may interact with natural resources to counteract the curse. The basic idea here is that natural resource abundance is negative for economic performance only when institutions are of poor quality. The technical dimension is the idea that the impact of low institutional quality and abundant natural resources is more pronounced the more technically appropriable natural resources are.

Boschini et al. (2007) test these hypotheses with the following specification:

$$g_i = X'_i \alpha_0 + \alpha_1 NR_i + \alpha_2 Inst_i + \alpha_3 (NR_i \times Inst_i) + \varepsilon_i \qquad (1)$$

Where g is the average growth of GDP (country i), X' is a vector of control variables, NR is a measure of natural resources and $Inst$ represents institutional quality. $NR \times Inst$ is the interaction between natural resources and institutional quality. Authors use four different measures of natural resources to capture a gradual increase in physical and economic appropriability (the technical dimension) from the broadest to the narrowest measure (referred to as α_1). They employ the average of different indexes for institutional quality (Knack and Keefer 1995) (referred to as α_2) and show that whether natural resources are good or bad for a country's development depends crucially on the interaction between institutional setting and the types of resources (α_3). In contrast to the traditional curse hypothesis, they propose that the impact of natural resources is non-monotonic in institutional quality. Countries rich in minerals are cursed only if they have low quality institutions, while the curse is reversed if institutions are sufficiently good (when the negative impact of NR is countered by the positive effect of $Inst$ and the joint effect of $NR \times Inst$).[3] With different analytical options it is possible to arrive at compatible conclusions through other channels. This is the case of a recent article – García-Jimeno and Robinson (2011) – that shows a renewed interest in land frontier expansion.

As land frontier expansion is associated with the incorporation of land into production (natural resource) and is accompanied by the constitution of a new system of ownership rights (institutional arrangements), the connection with my area of research is obvious. These authors analyse the classical Frontier (or Turner) Thesis for the Americas from the middle of the nineteenth century to 2007. They suggest that if political institutions were deficient at the time of frontier settlement, the existence of such a frontier might lead to worse outcomes because it is a resource which non-democratic political elites can use to cement themselves in power. Bad institutions and abundant natural resources might lead to worse economic performance, and land frontier can be a proxy for abundance.

García-Jimeno and Robinson (2011) propose a model similar to the following:

$$g_i = \beta_0 + \beta_1 F_{i,t} + \beta_2 C_{i,t} + \beta_3 (F_{i,t} \times C_{i,t}) + \varepsilon_i \qquad (2)$$

Where g_i is the dependent variable of interest considering GDP per capita in 2007, the average democracy score (1950–2007 and 1990–2007), and the Gini coefficient. $F_{i,t}$ is the proportion of the country which was frontier land in period t and $C_{i,t}$ is the constraints on the executive from *Polity IV* ($t=1850$). If this analytical relation is reinterpreted considering that the occupied territory represents a measure of the natural resources available for production, the model is comparable with that used in Boschini et al. (2007).

2.2 Natural resources and land frontier expansion

Natural resources are special economic goods because they are not produced and they will yield economic profits – rents – if properly managed. Once exhaustible resources have been discovered they can only be depleted, and to consume rents is, quite literally, to consume capital. Live resources are different because they are a potentially sustainable source of rents. In these terms, natural resources may be conceptualized as "stocks of materials that exist in the natural environment that are both scarce and economically useful in production or consumption, either in their raw state or after a minimal amount of processing" (WTO 2010, p. 46).

A critical driving force behind global economic development throughout much of history has been society's response to a scarcity of natural resources (Barbier 2015). Increasing scarcity raises the cost of exploiting existing natural resources and encourages conservation and innovation to obtain "new" natural resources. Since the agricultural transition (over 12,000 years ago), exploiting new sources or "frontiers" has often proved to be a pivotal human response to natural resource scarcity (Barbier 2011). A "frontier" is an area or source of unusually abundant natural resources and land relative to labour and capital. It is this relative scarcity (or abundance) of natural resources that matters in economic development, not their absolute physical availability. The process of frontier expansion, or frontier-based development, means exploiting new sources of relatively abundant resources for production purposes.

3 Empirical strategy

Settler economies are characterized by an abundance of land and excellent conditions for the competitive production of agricultural commodities.[4] During the First Globalization, the settler economies expanded strongly and income distribution worsened. I look for evidence that the incorporation of abundant land had a significant impact on both these trends in agriculture and that the intensity of the effects was related to land aptitude. We test two hypotheses: (i) different degrees of appropriability determine the magnitude of the impact of abundant resources on economic performance; (ii) "good" institutions, especially in interaction with natural resources, lead to a reversal of the curse (or reinforce the blessing). I consider different types of land depending on agricultural aptitude, and construct a gradient of appropriability possibilities that ranges from high agricultural aptitude land to low aptitude. In terms of these hypotheses, I should expect "worse" long-run results when economies incorporate high quality land more intensively than low quality land.

3.1 Empirical model

Three dimensions are considered to make the notion of "economic performance" operational: level and growth of income (product) per worker and income distribution (the rentals/wages ratio derived from functional income distribution). It is necessary to have a theoretical approach to conceptualize the equations to be estimated.

In a previous study (Willebald 2011), I present an analytical model (in the tradition of specific factors models) that describes three main stylized facts of settler economies, namely primary export-led growth, worsening income distribution and deindustrialization (or primarization). I propose modifications to the theoretical formulation of Findlay and Lundahl (2001) and Findlay (1995) and introduce the effect of different land qualities. I consider an agricultural sector (A) with two sub-sectors (A_H) and (A_L) that work on high aptitude (N_H) and low aptitude land (N_L) respectively, and labour endowments L_H and L_L respectively, where technology is represented by a homogeneous of degree one production function. In intensive terms, product per worker is a function of the corresponding land-labour ratios (η),

$$\frac{A_H}{L_H} = a(\eta_H) \tag{3}$$

$$\frac{A_L}{L_L} = a(\eta_L) \tag{4}$$

Product per agricultural worker (A/L) can be represented as a weighted average of the product per worker for high and low land quality depending on the corresponding land-labour ratios.

In addition, land is a finite resource and the possibility of incorporating each type of land depends on availability. I use an indicator of the amounts of land incorporated into agriculture to represent these restrictions (the shares of already incorporated land by type). These conditions represent an idea of initial endowments and indicate the scale of production.

Lastly, I consider institutional quality so as to evaluate the direct and indirect influence of institutions on income per worker. I compare the parameters of estimations with institutions acting alone and with institutions acting together with natural resources.

Then I estimate five specifications to test the curse of natural resources. I use panel data for the period 1869–1913 (annual data).

$$agdppw_{it} = \gamma_0 + \gamma_1 nh_{i,t} + \gamma_2 nl_{i,t} + \gamma_3 hw_{i,t} + \gamma_4 lw_{i,t} + \gamma_5 Inst_{i,t} + \varepsilon_{it} \tag{5}$$

$$agdppw_{it} = \gamma_0 + \gamma_1 nh_{i,t} + \gamma_2 nl_{i,t} + \gamma_3 hw_{i,t} + \gamma_4 lw_{i,t} + \gamma_5 (Interaction_{i,t}) + \varepsilon_{it} \tag{6}$$

Where $agdppw_{it}$ is the (log) agricultural output per worker in 1913 constant dollars for country i in period t, with $t = 1869, 1870, \ldots 1913$. I consider four explanatory variables related to land quality: land-labour ratios corresponding to high (*nh*) and low (*nl*) quality and the proportion of land incorporated into production corresponding to high (*hw*) and low (*lw*) aptitude (weighted by the total endowments). Finally, I include an indicator of institutional quality (*Inst*) to capture the direct effect of institutions on agricultural income level – equation (5) – and evaluate its indirect effect through natural resources in equation (6) with,

$$Interaction = nh_{i,t}*Inst_{i,t}; nl_{i,t}*Inst_{i,t}; hw_{i,t}*Inst_{i,t}; lw_{i,t}*Inst_{i,t}$$

When considering land expansion – which is measured as land-labour ratios because abundance is a relative concept – the appropriability hypothesis of the curse of natural resources in terms of the technical dimension will not be rejected under the following results:

$\gamma_1 < 0$, $\gamma_2 < 0$ and $\gamma_1 < \gamma_2$: the effect of the land-labour ratio is negative and the impact is greater in the case of more appropriable natural resources.

$\gamma_1 < 0$, $\gamma_2 > 0$: the effect of the land-labour ratio is negative for high quality land and positive for low quality land.

In line with the literature, I expect that better institutions will have a positive effect on income level ($\gamma_5 > 0$) and I test the institutional dimension of the curse by comparing these parameters. When the parameters in equation (6) exceed that in equation (5) and those corresponding to the best lands result higher, I prove that the greater influence of institutions on income level occurs indirectly through the natural resources and institutional dimension works for income level.

Finally, as regards absolute land expansion, I evaluate the effects of scale factors in the evolution of agricultural income. I expect positive coefficients in both cases but with a greater influence for high quality land ($\gamma_3 > 0$, $\gamma_4 > 0$ and $\gamma_3 > \gamma_4$).

Annual change in agricultural income per worker (*ga*) can be expressed as the weighted sum of the corresponding rates of variations (*g*) in the components related to land (*nh*, *nl*, *hw* and *lw*), and also the interactions of levels to consider the effect (direct and indirect) of institutions on growth (equations 7 and 8).

$$ga_{it} = \gamma_0 + \gamma_1 gnh_{i,t} + \gamma_2 gnl_{i,t} + \gamma_3 ghw_{i,t} + \gamma_4 glw_{i,t} + \gamma_5 Inst_{i,t} + \varepsilon_{it} \quad (7)$$

$$ga_{it} = \gamma_0 + \gamma_1 gnh_{i,t} + \gamma_2 gnl_{i,t} + \gamma_3 ghw_{i,t} + \gamma_4 glw_{i,t} + \gamma_5 (Interaction_{i,t}) + \varepsilon_{it} \quad (8)$$

Initially, the hypotheses are the same as those tested in the case of income level, but caution is needed. Land is a finite resource and therefore it cannot increase indefinitely (components *ghw* and *glw* would tend to zero in the long run).

Lastly, I compare total land rents (R) and total wages (W) in agriculture to represent the evolution of income distribution (RW).[5] Land rents depend on the quantity of land incorporated into production (N) and land rental rates (q). In addition, assuming perfect labour market and an agricultural sector where the wage rate (w) is given by the manufacture (urban) sector, differences between types of lands are related to the quantity of labourers. I consider indicators of income distribution by type of land:

$$\frac{R_H}{W_H} = \frac{q_H N_H}{w L_H} = \frac{q_H}{w} \eta_H \tag{9}$$

$$\frac{R_L}{W_L} = \frac{q_L N_L}{w L_L} = \frac{q_L}{w} \eta_L \tag{10}$$

The rents-wages ratio in agriculture is a weighted average of the rents-wages ratios for high and low quality land, which depend on land-labour ratios. As land is a finite resource, the possibility of incorporating each type of land depends on respective availability. Finally, the direct and indirect impact of institutions on income distribution is considered. I propose the following model (variables in original values):

$$RW_{it} = \gamma_0 + \gamma_1 nh_{i,t} + \gamma_2 nl_{i,t} + \gamma_3 hw_{i,t} + \gamma_4 lw_{i,t} + \gamma_5 Inst_{i,t} + \varepsilon_{it} \tag{11}$$

$$RW_{it} = \gamma_0 + \gamma_1 nh_{i,t} + \gamma_2 nl_{i,t} + \gamma_3 hw_{i,t} + \gamma_4 lw_{i,t} + \gamma_5 (Interaction_{i,t}) + \varepsilon_{it} \tag{12}$$

In accordance with the appropriability hypothesis, in terms of the technical dimension, I expect positive effects on inequality (worsening income distribution) and $\gamma_1 > \gamma_2$ associated with the higher degree of appropriability of the most productive land. The coefficient γ_5 should show a negative effect on RW that would indicate an improvement in equality stemming from "good" institutions. Evidence in favour of the institutional dimension of appropriability would require finding more intensive effects of institutions when we estimate equations (12) for the best lands.

Finally, I expect positive effects of scale factors ($\gamma_3 > 0$; $\gamma_4 > 0$). The greater the proportion of land in production the less land is available for new landowners – less "free land" is available in Turner's sense – and economies face higher rents related to other factor returns. I expect that this process will be more intensive in the case of high quality land ($\gamma_3 > \gamma_4$) because this is the most attractive land for production.

3.2 Explanatory variables

Natural resources

In a previous work (Willebald 2011) I propose several measures of land frontier expansion according to land aptitude. My starting point was the García-Jimeno and Robinson (2011) *F* index, but my indicators measure the proportion of occupied land that is grassland allocated to raising livestock instead of all non-occupied land as a proportion of a country's total surface area. In Willebald and Juambeltz (2013) we construct indicators for ten-year periods from 1860 to 1920 to reflect the dynamism of the process. I use these indicators as proxies in the econometric exercises.

I propose to represent the gradient of different appropriability conditions with indicators corresponding to different land aptitudes. I classify land as high or low aptitude[6] and analyse the evolution of each frontier according to the type of the endowment. I consider the total land of high (N_h) and low (N_l) aptitude by 1,000 km² incorporated into production. I also examine the relation between these areas and the population settled in them to represent the land-labour ratio – n_h and n_l. I classify land with less than two people per square mile as frontier land ("open frontier") and land incorporated into production as the "closed frontier". Better land – the most productive land – opens the possibility of generating and appropriating rents when they are applied to production and then they are more prone to generate appropriability problems.[7]

In addition, I consider the shares of land incorporated into production by type of land (N_h and N_l) as a proportion of the total endowments of each type (N_H and N_L) and thus obtain ratios of land used in production (*h* and *l*). These ratios are weighted by each country's structure of endowments (*hw* and *lw*).

Institutional quality

Government has four crucial roles to play in contract enforcement and the protection of ownership rights (Clague *et al.* 1999): (i) it provides third-party enforcement when no self-enforcing mechanism exists; (ii) it may be the entity that communicates the terms to the parties of the contract; (iii) it may enforce the arrangements that private agents employ to constitute themselves as a formal group; and (iv) the government ensures peace. These are precisely the characteristics that apply in the creation and distribution of landowner rights and the enforcement of the property system. To capture the potential gains of activities intensive in contract enforcement and property rights I consider the concept of "contract-intensive money" (CIM). This indicator is the ratio of non-currency money to the total money supply, or $CIM = (M_2 - Curr)/M_2$, where M_2 is a broad definition of the money supply and *Curr* is currency held by people (Román and Willebald 2015). The application of these ideas to settler economies is not new (Prados De La Escosura and Sanz-Villarroya 2009; Fleitas *et al.* 2012) and the evidence is convincing.

4 Results

My sample is small, only six economies, and with annual data for 1869–1913 the estimators may have consistency problems. My aim, therefore, is to find sound evidence and complement it with the historical trajectories of the club members.

I estimate different panel data models that are fixed (FE) and random effects (RE), and ordinary least square (OLS), and perform specific tests to choose the most suitable model. The discussion is based on FE models.

Initially, I consider agricultural product per worker, which are referred to as models (1)–(5) in Table 12.1. I include a time-trend to control for the trend in the dependent variable.[8]

The land-labour ratios (η_j) present statistically significant coefficients in all specifications, with a positive sign for high aptitude land and a negative sign for low aptitude land ($\gamma_1 > 0$ and $\gamma_2 < 0$). Abundance is a curse only in the case of low quality land, while high aptitude land is a blessing. In this sense, I reject the technical dimension of the appropriability hypothesis because the land that is potentially subject to higher degrees of appropriability is the best to achieve higher levels of income per worker. This last condition also includes the high aptitude land in absolute terms (*hw*) while low quality land is positive but significant only in one case (model 2).

The influence of institutional quality is positive and statistically significant (at 10 per cent) when it is in interaction with land-labour ratios (*nhcim* and *nlcim*). The impact of institutions is similar regardless of the type of land (3.9 and 4.5)[9] and so we do not find evidence in favour of the institutional dimension. The direct effect of institutional quality is not significant (*cim*) in this case or when it interacts with the availability of land (*hwcim*, *lwcim*). Institutional quality acts through the land-labour ratio (abundance) and not through the available land.

The effects on economic growth per worker are given in Table 12.2. The coefficients of land-labour ratios (*gnh* and *gnl*) are not statistically significant – with the exception only of *gnh* in model 2 – so we reject the technical dimension of the appropriability hypothesis because the abundance of land by type does not explain growth. In contrast to this outcome the growth rate on high aptitude land (*ghw*) turns out to be positive and significant to explain agricultural expansion. The determinant factor of agricultural growth in the settler economies is the increasing use of high quality land (changes in the scale of use of the main factor) regardless of its relation with labour.

As before, the direct effect of institutional quality (*cim*) is not statistically significant while the interaction with natural resources turns out to be significant – models (2) and (4) – when we consider high aptitude land. This effect is negative for the relative indicator (*nhcim*) and positive for the index in absolute terms (*hwcim*). Institutional quality contributes positively to agricultural growth when it acts through the expansion of high aptitude land. However, its influence is negative when it acts through the land-labour ratio, which shows there are decreasing returns in the agricultural production. Institutions only have

Table 12.1 Gross agricultural product per worker, natural resources and institutions. Panel data analysis (fixed effects model). Dependent variable: Gross agricultural product per worker [lngdpapw]

	(1)	(2)	(3)	(4)	(5)
Variables					
nh	8.194***	6.037***	7.967***	8.222***	8.742**
	[1.361]	[1.349]	[1.456]	[1.508]	[2.345]
nl	−9.406***	−10.47***	−12.95***	−9.498**	−9.956**
	[1.608]	[1.903]	[2.870]	[2.388]	[2.917]
hw	3.905***	4.183***	4.058***	4.323**	3.947**
	[0.696]	[0.731]	[0.648]	[1.470]	[1.189]
lw	7.152	7.187*	6.242	8.082	7.394
	[3.971]	[3.446]	[3.545]	[4.288]	[4.204]
year	0.00119	0.000447	0.00104	0.00262	0.00184
	[0.00437]	[0.00423]	[0.00361]	[0.00527]	[0.00613]
cim	0.382				
	[0.267]				
nhcim		3.903*			
		[1.771]			
nlcim			4.528*		
			[1.967]		
hwcim				−0.842	
				[2.313]	
lwcim					0.682
					[1.686]
constant	3.673	5.362	4.361	1.173	2.650
	[7.971]	[7.830]	[6.773]	[9.786]	[11.34]
Rsq					
Within	0.85	0.85	0.86	0.84	0.84
Between	0.33	0.30	0.29	0.41	0.36
Overall	0.11	0.10	0.09	0.15	0.13
F-stat	242.82	252.05	259.38	221.86	223.52
(Prob)	0.00	0.00	0.00	0.00	0.00
F all u_i=0	161.33	179.12	180.09	151.77	158.92
(Prob)	0.00	0.00	0.00	0.00	0.00
Hausman	655.33	996.90	885.84	714.48	1308.15
(Prob)	0.00	0.00	0.00	0.00	0.00
Observations	270	270	270	270	270
Number of countries	6	6	6	6	6

Notes
Robust standard errors in brackets.
p-values indicated with asterisk where *** $p<0.01$; ** $p<0.05$; * $p<0.1$

an influence in the case of high aptitude land, and this constitutes evidence of the institutional dimension of appropriability. That is to say, there are differential effects by type of land.

Finally, exercises about income distribution show that abundant resources have significant and positive coefficients that do not reject the curse hypothesis (Table 12.3).

Table 12.2 Growth of gross agricultural product per worker, natural resources and institutions. Panel data analysis (fixed effects model). Dependent variable: Growth rate of agricultural product per worker [g]

	(1)	(2)	(3)	(4)	(5)
Variables					
gnh	−1.912	−1.711*	−1.928	−1.805	−1.937
	[1.094]	[0.794]	[1.056]	[0.932]	[1.027]
gnl	2.077	1.770	2.132	1.868	2.108
	[1.423]	[1.041]	[1.408]	[1.241]	[1.355]
ghw	1.982**	1.831**	2.005**	1.879**	1.999**
	[0.757]	[0.547]	[0.745]	[0.651]	[0.717]
glw	−1.829	−1.509	−1.873	−1.600	−1.838
	[1.265]	[1.007]	[1.252]	[1.181]	[1.204]
cim	−0.000688				
	[0.0156]				
nhcim		−0.308*			
		[0.152]			
nlcim			0.0568		
			[0.146]		
hwcim				0.0892**	
				[0.0311]	
lwcim					0.0412
					[0.0919]
constant	0.00698	0.0245	0.00311	−0.00234	0.00392
	[0.0152]	[0.0159]	[0.0151]	[0.0126]	[0.0121]
Rsq					
Within	0.93	0.93	0.93	0.93	0.93
Between	0.96	0.74	0.96	0.90	0.92
Overall	0.91	0.88	0.91	0.90	0.91
F-stat	668.96	695.95	669.91	685.44	670.97
(Prob)	0.00	0.00	0.00	0.00	0.00
F all u_i=0	7.00	8.26	7.04	8.30	7.22
(Prob)	0.00	0.00	0.00	0.00	0.00
Hausman	36.94	44.63	22.68	26.82	26.62
(Prob)	0.00	0.00	0.00	0.00	0.00
Observations	264	264	264	264	264
Number of countries	6	6	6	6	6

Notes
Robust standard errors in brackets.
p-values indicated with asterisk where *** $p<0.01$; ** $p<0.05$; * $p<0.1$.

The land-labour ratio for high aptitude land (n_h) turns out to be positive and significant in three models –(1), (2) and (3)– and the corresponding ratio for low quality land (nl) in only one – model (1) – and with a negative sign. We find evidence in favour of the appropriability hypothesis because expanding the frontier onto better land, and considering the labour used in production, reduces equality more intensively. The former trend repeats for the absolute indicators where both coefficients – of high (hw) and low (lw) aptitude land – are positive and significant, but the latter turns out to be greater. As I expected, more land in

Table 12.3 Income distribution, natural resources and institutions. Panel data analysis (fixed effects model). Dependent variable: Land rents/Wages [rw]

	(1)	(2)	(3)	(4)	(5)
Variables					
nh	13.42*	18.22**	13.85*	13.58	9.391
	[5.398]	[5.125]	[6.398]	[8.228]	[5.009]
nl	−5.674*	−3.644	0.900	−3.652	−2.955
	[2.270]	[3.147]	[6.443]	[4.507]	[2.644]
hw	5.573***	5.197***	5.292***	6.847**	4.779***
	[0.466]	[0.640]	[0.629]	[2.534]	[0.585]
lw	22.37*	22.22*	23.18*	21.38*	23.88**
	[9.046]	[10.05]	[10.29]	[9.962]	[7.385]
cim	−1.061*				
	[0.416]				
nhcim		−8.444*			
		[3.384]			
nlcim			−7.490		
			[6.356]		
hwcim				−2.091	
				[3.456]	
lwcim					−5.554***
					[1.182]
constant	−0.550	−1.336	−1.521	−1.405	−0.929
	[1.297]	[1.300]	[1.383]	[1.499]	[1.068]
Rsq					
Within	0.5196	0.5156	0.5022	0.4819	0.5365
Between	0.5346	0.5707	0.5318	0.4995	0.5846
Overall	0.4305	0.4589	0.4262	0.4038	0.4761
F-stat	54.72	53.85	51.04	47.06	58.57
(Prob)	0.00	0.00	0.00	0.00	0.00
F all u_i=0	40.12	33.73	40.29	34.11	22.58
(Prob)	0.00	0.00	0.00	0.00	0.00
Hausman	862.24	299.65	468.3	287.96	127.75
(Prob)	0.00	0.00	0.00	0.00	0.00
Observations	264	264	264	264	264
Number of countries	6	6	6	6	6

Notes
Robust standard errors in brackets.
p-values indicated with asterisk where *** $p<0.01$; ** $p<0.05$; * $p<0.1$.

production is "bad" for income distribution because absolute availability diminishes. However, and contrary to what I expected, the impact of low aptitude land is more intense.[10] One possible explanation of this paradox has to do with the timing of the expansion. This was not a lineal process and sometimes we may find "islands" of movement in the territory. For instance, when we consider productive specialization and the key role of ports, the progressive radial expansion from Buenos Aires that Argentina underwent to take possession of the high aptitude land of the Pampas meant low aptitude land was incorporated. This was similar to what occurred in Australia, where the land became more arid the farther from the coast the producer moved, or in Canada, where the highly productive prairies were 2,000 km from the east coast. In other words, the way to incorporate the best land was first to people land of lower quality and, together with the timing of the process, this affected income distribution (Willebald 2011, 2013b).

As I expected, institutional quality directly improves income distribution – negative coefficient – and institutions also have an influence when we evaluate the indirect effect of *CIM* interacting with the land-labour ratio of high aptitude land – *nhcim* in model (2) – with a higher coefficient (−1.1 vs −8.4). On the other hand, the interaction coefficient for low quality land (*nlcim*) is not significant. This means that the type of land onto which land frontier expansion occurs has an effect, and this is evidence that supports the institutional dimension of the appropriability hypothesis. Finally, the coefficient of the interaction with the absolute land expansion onto low aptitude land – *lwcim* in model (5) – turns out to be negative and significant, and counteracts the trend to worsening income distribution.

I shall now consider five highlights of the analysis:

i I reject the hypothesis that an abundance of natural resources in settler economies is a curse for income per worker and growth rates in the agricultural sector, but I do not reject the curse hypothesis as regards income distribution.
ii The technical dimension of the appropriability hypothesis does not operate for agricultural production but it has significant effect in terms of income distribution. In other words, better land (which can generate greater rents to appropriate) is more favourable for agricultural production but increases inequality more intensively.
iii Institutional quality by itself does not make for higher incomes per worker or higher growth rates in agriculture, but it has positive effects on income levels when it interacts with both high and low quality land abundance. In other words, institutional quality is important in agricultural income regardless of the type of land in question.
iv Institutional quality has different effects on agricultural growth depending on the type of land. It operates negatively for high aptitude land-labour ratios and positively for the absolute expansion of land.
v Good institutional quality by itself improves agricultural income distribution, and the interaction with high aptitude land abundance intensifies the positive effects. Therefore the institutional dimension of appropriability operates in distributive terms.

These exercises are far from conclusive, basically because the database is small, but they give rise to some interesting insights. The most important shortcomings have to do with the treatment of institutions insofar as (i) the complexity of institutional arrangements is reduced to "one number"; (ii) I consider institutions as an exogenous component, but there is extensive literature that emphasizes the endogeneity of institutions; and (iii) statistical exercises based on a "macroeconomic" level do not deal with the agents' behaviours.

The way to remedy these deficiencies at least partially is to adopt a complementary approach. I identify the specific institutional arrangements that formally or informally regulate the appropriability conditions of land, and consequently of rents. Following previous studies (Álvarez *et al.* 2010; Willebald 2013b), I describe the process of the distribution of land ownership rights and the characteristics of the land tenure systems from a historical and comparative perspective considering four economies: Argentina, Australia, New Zealand and Uruguay.

5 Appropriability and the formation of the land ownership system

Land tenure has to do with the collection of rights and obligations under which land is held, used, transferred and inherited. The specification (definition and interpretation) and enforcement of land ownership rights constitute two fundamental dimensions in the appropriability of natural resources because they affect the timing of settlement and the use of land.

Land ownership systems can be categorized in line with three essential points: (i) whether or not there are formal land deeds, which involve the registration of land ownership rights with a government authority, (ii) the extent of landowner and landholder rights to voluntarily contract for use of the land, and (iii) the spectrum of private-communal ownership rights. Arrangements governing land ownership rights vary depending on who specifies and enforces them, and the possible actors range from the first person that claimed ownership of the land to the State that is interested in the "agrarian question".

Usually it is the State that defines (legislative function), interprets (judicial function) and enforces (police function) land ownership rights. These functions entail costs, and in consequence the State may leave some rights as open access (*de jure* or de facto). In the economies of recent European settlement, the colonizer state had an additional function. There was a doctrine that underlined the traditional view of settlement where "new" areas were "*terra nullis*". European rulers adopted the position that territories without political organization or systems of authority could legitimately be annexed. For decades there was debate about tenure systems, prices and land taxes, and the authorities established a variety of instruments, which yielded differing results.

In my contrast, I identify two models. One of them – closer to the "British model" – is characterized by an active State with developmental features that promote a pattern of greater equality. The other – the "Hispanic model" – is dominated by a State pressured by financial difficulties, recurring administrative disorder and a high degree of intervention by the agrarian oligarchy in political power, all of which promoted income concentration.

5.1 Australasia vs the River Plate

Australasian historiography has emphasized that land distribution in Australia and New Zealand was highly idiosyncratic and was a factor that contributed to the emergence of an agrarian society with high standards of living and democratic values. The distribution of land constituted a political and economic resource that the State used widely to promote better uses of land and more intense settlement. The British colonial regime established a strong State that regulated the settlement of the European colonists and attempted to promote equitable land distribution. This process was governed by a legal framework that transferred ownership rights from the Crown to colonists, which ensured the effective ownership of land and moderated land concentration. In both Australia and New Zealand the State had enough political and institutional power to guarantee secure ownership rights, and this enabled the productive factor markets to function in a suitable way. The fact that these markets worked properly made for higher wage shares in the agriculture sector ("salarization" as is proposed in Willebald 2013a), and this evidently contrasts with the way markets in the River Plate region developed.

In Australia and New Zealand land was considered an important economic resource and this was expressed in public policies. It was a source of fiscal income and involved the transference of land ownership rights and different tenure regimes such as leasing, grants, sale by auction, etc. Leasing systems made it possible for small producers without enough capital to access land. In addition, state limitations on the size of estates moderated the trend towards land ownership concentration (Álvarez 2007).

In Argentina and Uruguay land distribution started before the wars of independence and therefore developed under the Spanish legal regime.[11] Land was not very valuable because the main economic resource was wild cattle. Large estates (*latifundia*) came into being because populations were very small and the Spanish armed forces were politically weak and mainly concerned with combating resistant native populations and the expansion of the Portuguese Empire. According to land laws, colonists were supposed to physically occupy the land and to produce on it, but in practice these conditions were not fulfilled.

Most land frontier expansion and the distribution of land ownership rights occurred after Argentina and Uruguay became independent. This process involved the transfer of public land from the State to settlers through a variety of different legal regimes that moved incoherently between direct sales and leasing. Direct sales were inspired in liberal principles and were aimed at transferring land to the private sector, and leasing was an effort to retain public land as a support for fiscal income and public debt. However, it turned out that neither Argentina nor Uruguay benefited from the transfer of land. Both countries lacked the political power to make an ordered distribution of land. Until the last quarter of the nineteenth century both States were weak in political, institutional and military terms, and the land distribution process favoured local elites. During the First Globalization land became much more valuable because of its connection with rising international commodity prices, and large estates consolidated their position. These elites supported the oligarchic regimes that dominated the political scene up to WWI.

5.2 Similarities and differences

Land frontier expansion and the configuration of a new land ownership regime were dominated by four principles (Willebald 2013b):

i   The creation of a private land tenure system whereby, depending on the period and with differing intensity, land ownership was transferred to the colonizers.
ii A new population should be brought onto the land so as to create a society based on immigrants.
iii Authorities were increasingly convinced that land constituted the nation's wealth and that land settlement was the source of prosperity.
iv Equality in land distribution was valuable in the construction of an independent and democratic nation.

Under these principles, the authorities in the different countries faced similar problems:

i   Strictly speaking, land was not "empty" because the expansion of the frontier meant displacing native populations. The prevailing rationale was that land had to be brought into civilization and put to use, and the best results would be obtained by bringing in settlers to establish a sedentary society of farmers (Williams 1975, p. 63).
ii There was a certain amount of theory involved,[12] but basically the way land was administered and how ownership rights for public land came into being was a matter of trial and error. It was very difficult to define land boundaries because of ignorance and information asymmetries, and there were problems too with determining the size of estates and their productive aptitude.
iii Land policies were dominated by conflicts among interest groups. Occupiers used their wealth and influence to evade attempts to reallocate land, and many evasion methods were used including "dummying", "peacocking" and forcing auctions. Land oligarchies usually participated actively in the various levels of government and fostered legislation that furthered their own interests.

There are two main models, and there are four main differences between them:

i   The colonial heritage (in the sense of Acemoglu *et al.* 2001 and Engerman and Sokoloff 2002) in the River Plate contrasts with the delayed institutional development of Australasia. Here, the absence of "path-dependence" allowed a really "new" system to be created, close to the British tradition and with the North American system as a model.

ii Oligarchic elites in the River Plate exerted broad control over land, and with the development of constitutional government they consolidated their political power. This contrasts with the pastoral economy of Australasia that was motivated by democratic values and shaped by rules imposed by a bureaucracy that was relatively disinterested and involved the active political participation of small farmers (Denoon 1983).

iii In Australasia the various States participated in the "agrarian question", and a well-organized public administration made it possible to implement and enforce autonomous action. In contrast, chronic fiscal deficits in the River Plate and continuous political struggles prevented the implementation of long-run policies. The governments in Australasia set up administrative and institutional arrangements that were closer to the notion of a developmental State (Lloyd 2013, 2015).

iv Australia and New Zealand shared the same fragment culture, and reforms reflected the same fundamental egalitarian, communally focused, working-class radical values that immigrants brought with them. The colonial social hierarchy lacked the appearance of permanence, and change of status was a relatively common experience. These factors shaped a socio-political context in which the land question as one of the main issues in public policy, and politicians, theorists and common citizens identified these concerns quite early (Rosecrance 1964; Paulson 1988; Lloyd 2013).

There were profound differences between the two systems, notably that the governments in the River Plate had little capacity to enforce regulations, and that elites whose power was based on land ownership influenced state policy, a feature derived from a strong colonial heritage. The authorities in Australasia created a more favourable environment for colonization and land settlement because they had the power to enforce regulations, they were guided by notions of development from the colonial government, and they enjoyed a context that was more stable economically and politically. The conditions of appropriability were clearly different and more intense in the River Plate, and this had an effect on income distribution (Willebald 2013a) rather than income generation (growth) – as the econometric model confirms – and was accompanied by idiosyncrasies that reinforced the consequences of natural resource endowments.

According to the appropriability hypothesis, the environmental factors – represented by the landholding system – that control the innovator's ability – the holder's capability – to get returns generated by an innovation – the incorporation of "new" land – characterized two different "models". Under similar economic growth conditions, one of these models resulted in an income inequality pattern with high concentration and rentier societies (the Hispanic model), whereas the other model led to a more egalitarian pattern with a greater share for wages and broader markets that functioned more efficiently and encouraged greater equality (the British model).

6 Conclusions and final remarks

In this chapter I analyse the effect of natural resource endowments on agricultural production and functional income distribution, and to guide the discussion I consider the hypothesis that natural resources can be a curse. Settler economies are characterized by abundant natural resources, but natural capital is not homogeneous as regards its composition (different soils, temperature, roughness) or intensity of use, and this makes for differences in terms of development. I focus on the abundance of natural resources in a country and the quality of its institutions in terms of the appropriability of a resource.

I reject the notion that an abundance of land was a curse for agricultural production during the First Globalization but I do not reject this notion as regards income distribution. The technical dimension of the appropriability hypothesis does not work for production but it operates in terms of inequality. This means that better land (that can potentially generate greater rents) had a positive influence on the level of income per worker but worsens income distribution.

As Australia, Canada and New Zealand expanded their land frontiers onto relatively worse land (Willebald and Juambeltz 2013) income distribution worsened, but not as much as in the Southern Cone of South America (Williamson 2002; Willebald 2013a). However, as natural resources do not act alone, some intra-club differences could be associated with other factors.

Better quality institutions made for higher agricultural production per worker and reduced inequality. The indirect influence of institutions by type of land led to similar consequences and encouraged production. That is to say, the institutional dimension of appropriability does not work in terms of the level of production but it does work for more egalitarian income distribution.

The authorities in Australasia inherited a more stable economic and political context and created an environment more conducive to land settlement. The conditions of appropriability were clearly different from those in the River Plate region, with the negative consequences for equality noted above. It seems that institutional land ownership arrangements foster high product levels in the agriculture sector, but do not promote more egalitarian societies.

Differences in land aptitude produce different incentives and possibilities for agents to appropriate rents from varying types of land. The appropriability problem is more intense when higher aptitude land is occupied because there are more possibilities to extract greater rents. However this situation is affected by the action of institutions and the path dependence of the settlement. A combination of better institutions and the expansion of the frontier onto (relatively) worse land made natural resources a blessing in Australasia and in Canada in that production was enhanced and the negative effects on income distribution were not so severe.

Notes

1 This chapter comes from my PhD Thesis in economic history at the Universidad Carlos III, Madrid, Spain (UC3M). I would like to thank the Instituto Laureano Figuerola, UC3M, for supporting my research as a PhD candidate, and also the members of

the projects "Nuevas Interpretaciones sobre la Integración Económica de las Periferias Europeas y Latino Americanas entre 1850–1950" (UC3M) and "Historical Patterns of Development and Underdevelopment: Origins and Persistence of the Great Divergence (HI-POD)". I am grateful to my supervisor Leandro Prados de la Escosura for his comments and suggestions, and to the members of my thesis committee Colin Lewis, Branko Milanovic, Pablo Astorga, Alfonso Herranz and Isabel Sanz-Villaroya. I am also grateful for the comments made by some participants at several seminars and conferences where I presented initial versions, especially Paola Azar, Luis Bértola, Christopher Lloyd, Inés Moraes, Esteban Nicolini, Alan Olmstead and Vicente Pinilla. Carolina Román helped in the econometric exercises and I thank her for her careful reading.
2 See recent comparative studies in Lloyd et al. (2013).
3 Mehlum et al. (2006) and Robinson et al. (2006) also present concepts of a non-monotonic relationship.
4 Even in the case of Chile, evolution previous to the incorporation of mineral wealth – in the 1880s – had several features common to economies that produce food and raw materials. Denoon (1983) argues that Chile and South Africa constitute *"limit cases"* of settler economies.
5 Instead of comparing wages and land rental rates as proposed in the more extended literature (Williamson 2000, 2002), I contrast the evolutions of total wages and rents (Willebald 2013a). Rising trends mean worsening income distribution.
6 I classify land according to biome types of potential vegetation (Klein Goldewijk and Van Drecht 2006).
7 I use "aptitude" instead of "quality" because the latter concept would include considerations about distance to "centres of gravity" in the territory (Willebald and Juambeltz 2013).
8 Boyce and Emery (2011) do a similar control.
9 We contrast the confidence intervals, which at 95 per cent are, respectively, [−0.65 8.46] and [−0.52 9.58], and the difference between the coefficients is not statistically significant.
10 The confidence intervals at 95 per cent for the coefficient hw [3.55 6.84] do not include the number 22.2 of lw (i.e. model 2).
11 The wars of independence took place in the second and third decades of the nineteenth century.
12 Edward Wakefield and Henry George are among the authors that discuss the land question in the nineteenth century.

References

Acemoglu, D., Johnson, S. and Robinson, J.A., 2001. The colonial origins of comparative development: An empirical investigation. *American Economic Review*, 91 (5), 1369–1401.
Álvarez, J., 2007. Distribución del ingreso e instituciones: Nueva Zelanda y Uruguay (1870–1940). In: J. Álvarez, L. Bértola and G. Porcile, eds. *Primos Ricos y Empobrecidos. Crecimiento, distribución del ingreso e instituciones en Australia-Nueva Zelanda vs Argentina–Uruguay*. Montevideo, Uruguay: Fin de Siglo, 273–303.
Álvarez, J., Bilancini, E., D'Alessandro, S., Porcile, G. and Alvarez, J., 2010. Agricultural institutions, industrialization and growth: The case of New Zealand and Uruguay in 1870–1940. *Explorations in Economic History*, 48 (2), 151–168.
Auty, R.M., 2001. The political economy of resource-driven growth. *European Economic Review*, 45 (4–6), 839–846.
Barbier, E.B., 2011. *Scarcity and Frontiers: How Economies Have Developed through Natural Resource Exploitation*. New York: Cambridge University Press.

Barbier, E.B., 2015. Scarcity, frontiers and the resource curse: A historical perspective. *In*: M. Badia-Miró, V. Pinilla and H. Willebald, eds. *Natural Resources and Economic Growth: Learning from History*. London: Routledge.

Boschini, A.D., Pettersson, J. and Roine, J., 2007. Resource curse or not: A question of appropriability. *Scandinavian Journal of Economics*, 109 (3), 593–617.

Boyce, J. and Emery, J.C.H., 2011. Is a negative correlation between resource abundance and growth sufficient evidence that there is a "resource curse"? *Resources Policy*, 36, 1–13.

Bulte, E.H., Damania, R. and Deacon, R.T., 2005. Resource intensity, institutions, and development. *World Development*, 33 (7), 1029–1044.

Clague, C., Keefer, P., Knack, S. and Olson, M., 1999. Contract-intensive money: Contract enforcement, property rights, and economic performance. *Journal of Economic Growth*, 4, 185–211.

Denoon, D., 1983. *Settler Capitalism: The Dynamics of Dependent Development in the Southern Hemisphere*. Oxford: Clarendon.

Engerman, S.L. and Sokoloff, K.L., 2002. *Factor Endowments, Inequality, and Paths of Development among New World Economies*. NBER Working Paper Series No. 9252.

Findlay, R., 1995. *Factor Proportions, Trade, and Growth*. Cambridge, MA and London: MIT Press.

Findlay, R. and Lundahl, M., 2001. Natural resources and economic development: The 1870–1914 experience. *In*: R.M. Auty, ed. *Resource Abundance and Economic Development*. Oxford: Oxford University Press, 95–112.

Fleitas, S., Rius, A., Román Ramos, C. and Willebald, H., 2012. *Economic Development and Institutional Quality in Uruguay: Contract Enforcement, Investment and Growth since 1870*. DT 01/13, Instituto de Economía, Universidad de la República, Uruguay.

García-Jimeno, C. and Robinson, J.A., 2011. The myth of the frontier. *In*: D. Costa and N. Lamoreaux, eds. *Understanding Long-Run Economic Growth: Geography, Institutions, and the Knowledge Economy*. Chicago: University of Chicago Press, 49–88.

Greasley, D., Inwood, K. and Singleton, J., 2007. Factor prices and income distribution in less industrialised economies 1870–1939. *Australian Economic History Review*, 47 (1), 1–5.

Gylfason, T., 2007. *The International Economics of Natural Resources and Growth*. Minerals and Energy-Raw Materials Report. No. 22 (1 & 2).

Isham, J., Woolcock, M., Pritchett, L. and Busby, G., 2005. The varieties of resource experience: Natural resource export structures and the political economy of economic growth. *World Bank Economic Review*, 19 (2), 141–174.

Klein Goldewijk, K. and Van Drecht, G., 2006. HYDE 3: Current and historical population and land cover. *In*: A.F. Bouwman, T. Kram and K. Klein Goldewijk, eds. *Integrated Modelling of Global Environmental Change: An Overview of IMAGE 2.4*. Bilthoven: Netherlands Environmental Assessment Agency, 93–111.

Knack, S. and Keefer, P., 1995. Institutions, and economic performance: Cross country test using alternative institutional measures. *Economics and Politics*, 7 (November), 207–227.

Lloyd, C. 2013. Institutional patterns of the settler societies: Hybrid, parallel, and convergent. *In*: C. Lloyd, J. Metzer and R. Sutch, eds. *Settler Economies in World History*. Leiden: Brill, pp. 545–578.

Lloyd, C., 2015. The lucky country syndrome in Australia: Resources, social democracy, and regimes of development in historical political economy perspective. *In*: M. Badia-Miró, V. Pinilla and H. Willebald, eds. *Natural Resources and Economic Growth: Learning from History*. London: Routledge.

Lloyd, C. and Metzer, J., 2013. Settler colonization and societies in world history: Patterns and concepts. *In*: C. Lloyd, J. Metzer and R. Sutch, eds. *Settler Economies in World History*. Leiden: Brill.

Lloyd, C., Metzer, J. and Sutch, R., eds., 2013. *Settler Economies in World History*. Leiden: Brill.

Mehlum, H., Moene, K. and Torvik, R., 2006. Institutions and the resource curse. *The Economic Journal*, 116, 1–20.

Paulson, R.E., 1988. Review: The Antipodeans connection: New Zealand liberalism and American progressivism. *Review in American History*, 16 (2), 272–277.

Van der Ploeg, F., 2011. Natural resources: Curse or blessing? *Journal of Economic Literature*, 49 (2), 366–420.

Prados De La Escosura, L. and Sanz-Villarroya, I., 2009. Contract enforcement, capital accumulation, and Argentina's long-run decline. *Cliometrica*, 3, 1–26.

Robinson, J.A., Torvik, R. and Verdier, T., 2006. Political foundations of the resource curse. *Journal of Development Economics*, 79 (2), 447–468.

Román, C. and Willebald, H., 2015. Contract enforcement in Uruguay during the First Globalization: Indicators and comparisons. *Revista Uruguaya de Historia económica*.

Rosecrance, R., 1964. The radical culture of Australia. *In*: L. Hartz, ed. *The Foundations of New Societies*. New York: Harcourt, Brace & World, Inc.

Sachs, J.D. and Warner, A.M., 1995. Natural resource abundance and economic growth. *National Bureau of Economic Research Working Paper Series* (5398).

Sachs, J.D. and Warner, A.M., 2001. Natural resources and economic development: The curse of natural resources. *European Economic Review*, 45 (4–6), 827–838.

Schedvin, C.B., 1990. Staples and regions of Pax Britannica. *The Economic History Review*, 43 (4), 533.

Willebald, H., 2007. Desigualdad y especialización en el crecimiento de las economías templadas de nuevo asentamiento, 1870–1940. *Revista de Historia Económica – Journal of Iberian and Latin American Economic History*, (2), 291–345.

Willebald, H., 2011. Natural resources, settler economies and economic development during the first globalization: Land frontier expansion and institutional arrangement. PhD Thesis, Universidad Carlos III de Madrid, Departamento de Historia Económica e Instituciones.

Willebald, H., 2013a. *Distributive Patterns in Settler Economies: Agrarian Income Inequality during the First Globalization (1870–1913)*. DT 05/13, Instituto de Economía, Universidad de la República, Uruguay.

Willebald, H., 2013b. Are institutions the whole story? Frontier expansion, land quality and ownership rights in the River Plate, 1850–1920. *In*: E. Hillbom and P. Svensson, eds. *Agricultural Transformation in a Global History Perspective*. London: Routledge Explorations in Economic History, 51–85.

Willebald, H. and Juambeltz, J., 2013. Land frontier expansion in settler economies (1830–1950): Was it a Ricardian process? *In*: U. of G. Paul Bairoch Institute of Economic History, ed. *Séminaire avancé de recherche, automne 2013*. Geneva, Switzerland: Paul Bairoch Institute of Economic History, University of Geneva.

Williams, M., 1975. More and smaller is better: Australian rural settlement 1788–1914. *In*: J.M. Powell and M. Williams, eds. *Australian Space: Australian Time*. Melbourne, Australia: Oxford University Press, 61–103.

Williamson, J.G., 2000. *Land, Labour and Globalization in the Pre-industrial Third World*. NBER Working Paper Series 7784, National Bureau of Economic Research, Cambridge, MA, July.

Williamson, J.G., 2002. Land, labour and globalization in the Third World, 1870–1940. *The Journal of Economic History*, 62 (1), 55–85.

Woolcock, M., Prichett, L. and Isham, J., 2001. The social foundations of poor economic growth in resource-rich economies. *In*: R.M. Auty, ed. *Resource Abundance and Economic Development*. New York: Oxford University Press.

WTO, 2010. *World Trade Report 2010: Trade in Natural Resources*.

13 The lucky country syndrome in Australia

Resources, social democracy and regimes of development in historical political economy perspective

Christopher Lloyd

Are there lucky and unlucky countries? The importance of historical contingency

The historical experience of economic and social development of the resource-dependent economies (especially the settler economies) has been "unbalanced" (in Hirschman (1958) terminology), to a greater or lesser extent, being heavily skewed towards commodity exports. But that has not necessarily meant they could not achieve developed, more balanced, modern, egalitarian societies. Part of the explanation for the differing experiences is the differing good or bad luck of factor endowments but that cannot get us very far. A simple materialist explanation is more or less meaningless without a socio-institutional-historical argument to frame it.[1] Another way to put it is that luck or good fortune has to be constructed through institutional and political processes rather than simply anticipated (Mehlum *et al.* 2006; Robinson *et al.* 2006). "Luck" is too limited a concept, of course, because national "good fortune" is a complex mixture of endowments, investments, institutions and, moreover, contingent historical events and processes. And, as is well known, natural resources are not necessary for economic development as many European and Asian countries have shown.

A rich material factor endowment, or, more precisely, a dominance in the economy and in exports of commodities such as agricultural, mineral or energy products, can lead to very uneven development and severe policy distortions and/or dysfunctional states, as the literature on resource curse tries to show. On the other hand, there have been marked successes of resource-based development. Furthermore, that a country's development process is always uneven and unbalanced has been recognized by economic historians ever since Adam Smith's observations of the unevenness of Scottish development in the mid-to-late eighteenth century, and was a central proposition in Hirschman (1958)'s theory of development. Regional, industrial, sectoral and class imbalances exist everywhere but in the early stages and during the process of development these differences are much more marked than in economically mature and modernized societies. Of course, such imbalances are incompatible ultimately with modernization in the long run for they can lead to political violence and dislocation.[2]

The problem has long been understood, in some theoretical traditions at least, as one of how to achieve national growth and development in an unbalanced way, at least to begin with, and then spread the development more widely. The variety of success and failure of "unbalanced countries" (most of which are former colonies or quasi-colonies) in achieving development and modernization over the past century, despite great variations in their factor endowments, should lead to scepticism about the value of resource-curse theorizing to explain the variations.[3] And good fortune in the senses of unpredicted, contingent, events and outcomes, such as mineral and energy discoveries, lack of natural disasters and enlightened leadership, could have something to do with it but perhaps not decisively so.

It might be considered that Australia, as a key example, has had a good "accident of history" to have a small-to-medium-sized population inhabiting a whole continent with all its supposed natural resources. A similar argument can be made about some other successful cases of large land areas with sparse populations and natural resource abundance, such as Canada and Western United States. But there are other cases of similar land-resource/population ratios (e.g. Argentina, Chile, Mongolia, Kazakhstan) that have not been so successful, at least so far, and other cases of large land areas and large natural resources but unsuccessful or only partially successful development, at least hitherto, such as Nigeria, Brazil and Russia.

The value, then, of the ironic Australian concept of "the lucky country"[4] is that it not only focuses attention on the developmental significance of commodity wealth in the particular Australian historical context but also its relevance to other similar societies that have experienced commodity dependence. Australia is not the only lucky country, in either the neutral or ironic senses of the term. On the other hand, there may well have been comparatively unlucky countries when viewed through a world-wide and historical perspective on commodity dependence. Commodity dependence, according to the Prebisch-Singer hypothesis, is supposed to lead to long-term relative decline because of the long-term adverse terms-of-trade problem (Toye and Toye 2003). But studying the short- and long-run economic, social and political effects of commodity dependence in any national context of the past two centuries or so is not simply a matter of examining the supposed negative effects of terms of trade or sudden natural resource booms à la "Dutch disease" or "resource curses". The literature on booming sectors, Dutch disease and resource curse/blessing is often too overgeneralized, too ahistorical and focused too much on cursed cases rather than blessed cases to capture the full complexity of these phenomena and their effects.[5] And the terms of trade issue is related to the type of commodity and the time scale being examined (Ocampo and Parra-Lancourt 2010). A commodity price cycle rather than a secular long-run decline is perhaps the more fundamental phenomenon of the world economy in the long run (Erten and Ocampo 2012). Furthermore, being commodity dependent is not the same as experiencing a new booming sector, and which does not have to be a primary commodity sector, as the Japanese, South Korean and Chinese cases of booming industrial exports of the past 50 years shows. Booming sectors can, sooner or later, collapse or they can stabilize at a new structural normality.[6] And their effects are very much contextualized by institutional and political frameworks.

A historical political economy perspective, and one, moreover, that also takes into account social, cultural and ideological developments, à la Polanyi, Hirschman and Moore, focuses attention on wider issues than just economic factors in abstraction from the rest of the historical-societal context and focuses on actual historical conditions and experiences of particular societies. And such a more inclusive (less abstract) approach should also go beyond the New Institutionalist perspective for it too misses essential social and cultural elements in this complex history.[7]

Commodity dependence is actually fundamental to the entire history of economic and social development for, after all, just about every country and society has at some stage been "commodity dependent" in a general sense of reliance on commodity production as the foundation of the economy and also the export profile.[8] The history of the earliest economically developing countries and regions – Britain and the Low Countries and later the Rhine, Baltic and New England regions – was one of commodity dependence at the earliest stages of growth, whether it was wool, fish, marine animal oil, forestry, coal, minerals, grain, or meat and other animal products. Indeed, as the transformative process of economic growth and development has spread around the world from the eighteenth century it has often begun from a foundation in commodity exports. Over time, the central issue always became, of course, of how to achieve diversification, greater efficiency and sectoral change in order to achieve ongoing development, prosperity and modernization. And, furthermore, *developmental* success or failure has always been more than the achievement or absence of high average incomes per capita (Sen 1999; Stiglitz *et al.* 2009; HDI 2014). There have been many cases of high average incomes per capita from resource wealth that have not led to development and modernization.[9] The resource curse can, of course, take many forms, including persistent widespread poverty in the face of seeming plenty (i.e. great inequality), high average incomes but with lack of human social and political development, especially in post-colonial contexts.[10]

The centrality of a developmental state: the importance of linkages and political embeddedness

Even a casual observation of the political, institutional, social and cultural consequences of long-term primary export dependence, including booms and busts, in some developed countries, such as Australia, Canada, New Zealand, Finland, Sweden, Denmark, Norway and Iceland, reveals that it has indeed been possible to ride the commodities roller-coaster to beneficial effect with industrial-modernization outcomes,[11] despite the prevalence in many places at certain times of resource squatting, rent-seeking and cartelization. Importantly, the countries listed above comprise two distinctive groups – Anglo settler societies and Nordic societies – both of which shared in the nineteenth and early twentieth centuries the important characteristics of resource abundance, social egalitarianism, relative labour scarcity and emergent-to-actual democratic constitutions. Moreover, they all developed, out of this background, versions of a developmental state that was able, as an institutional structure, to engineer the transition from commodity dependence to developed modernization. Why and how such a state emerged in these countries and why it couldn't in other cases is a basic question (Auty 2001). And why such a state then successfully developed in other advanced societies, not always peacefully, such as most of Western Europe, Japan and now other countries in East Asia, is part of the larger problematic.[12]

The Anglo settler and Nordic regions seem to have little in common with other groups of commodity-dependent countries in the twenty-first century, such as the African oil-exporting LDCs (e.g. Angola, Nigeria), the Middle Eastern oil and gas exporters (e.g. Saudi Arabia, Kuwait, Qatar, UAE) and Russia and Central Eurasian (e.g. Azerbaijan, Kazahkstan) oil and gas exporters. Thus when the long-run, world-wide, history of commodity dependence and the successes and failures of transformations to prosperous modernization is viewed as a whole (which is actually the economic history of the world during the past several centuries), it's very obvious that over-generalized theory and inappropriate comparisons have been roadblocks to a better understanding of the experiences of particular groups of countries and individual countries. Many commodity exporters did make the transformation to modernity and high human development. Some LDC commodity-dependent countries are continuing to make that transformation (more or less successfully), such as Malaysia, Chile, Mauritius and Botswana. Thus the historical picture is one of both contrast and similarity such that certain generalizations can be made but only within a context that takes complexity, uniqueness and comparison seriously. Reliance on a rational/institutionalist, public choice and governance approach is not very helpful (see Robinson (2009) for an example), because it often avoids the very question it should be trying to answer, through a historical analysis, of why there is good governance or its lack in particular places.

Thus, key to understanding the current economic situation in Australia and elsewhere is to see the significance of the forces that determined the evolution of its political and social institutions in the long run, particularly the emergence of a "developmental state" ideology and organization from the early twentieth century. This grew out of the combination of the cultural and institutional inheritance and historical experience of the Australian settler process. The contingent intersection of British imperial influence and institutional framework (including Liberalism), the natural resource endowment, the indigenous presence and response, and the peculiar Australian settler colonization process, resulted by the early twentieth century in a home-grown and pioneering form of Social Democratic Welfare Capitalism (SDWC) that had an agenda of economic diversification and modernization and which has more or less survived until the twenty-first century. This form of capitalism has morphed through several regimes since the late nineteenth century but has retained certain key elements.

Whether this political economy can survive the recent resource boom and its aftermath and the Euro-American economic crisis is the subject of much current debate, addressed at the end of this chapter.

The resource/commodities curse argument can be summarized by the following propositions:

> The flow of export income from a rich commodity sector has the potential to cause fundamental distortions in economy, society and government and a failure of development because:
>
> i Distortion of economic sectoral investment and employment – over-concentration in the resource export sector at the expense of other sectors, especially agriculture and import-replacing manufacturing. A very unbalanced economy results if the state is unable to redirect investment to other sectors.
> ii The distortion is caused partly by exchange rate appreciation caused by the high income-earning export sector.
> iii The flow of export income causes rent-seeking, corruption and criminality in the government sector, reducing state capacity to provide infrastructure and developmental assistance to other sectors. A rentier state can result that is captured by self-enriching elites who have no interest in national development.
> iv The over-dependence on a single or small number of commodity exports makes the country vulnerable to price shocks because commodity prices are highly volatile.
> v Ultimately, a resource export economy is vulnerable to the long-term terms of trade problem.

Five closely interconnected forces seem to be crucial in determining whether a commodity-dependent exporting country is characterized by resource curse or is able to avoid the problem to achieve a balanced developmental outcome. The history and situation of each state today is a consequence of this matrix of forces and a good understanding can only be had by examining all of them together. The relative influence of each differs in every case.

i The political and governance framework (including ideologies and cultures) that were inherited and have evolved from the distant past.
ii The material foundations of particular commodities, which affect the types and strength of linkages they have with the rest of the economy and society.
iii The strength of the linkages of particular commodities to the wider national and world economy.
iv The global context of economic regimes, policies and geopolitics, and their ideological justifications.
v Contingent historical events and processes within each polity, colony, nation and state.

Democratization, liberalization and the transparent rule of law are essential contexts for an institutional structure for avoiding resource curse for they are the only political framework that is more or less certain to prevent overwhelming corruption in the long run. The power of corruption in today's interlinked world is far greater than in earlier times.[13] "Benign" dictatorships have never succeeded in eliminating corruption and have always declined into a cycle of rent-seeking, inequality, violent repression and lack of dynamism or were forced to give way to democratic forces that enabled transparency and rule of law. In the early modern era of the nineteenth century it is noteworthy that those commodity-dependent countries that succeeded in transformative economic and social modernization did so within a framework of liberalizing constitutions and emergent de facto democracy. Civic engagement became possible and this in turn began to act as a break on corruption and rent-seeking by elites. Such a political context then enabled class pressure towards the establishment of a democratic developmental state and one, moreover, that engendered consensus about the possible nexus between growth, development, equality and social welfare. Emergence of such a consensus – a historic compromise around a "win-win" strategy rather than an ongoing class struggle – was highly successful in producing versions of a distinct form of SDWC (Lloyd 2011) in Australasia and the Nordic region.

A developmental state is essentially one in which democratic pressure from below and/or elite-driven policies from above are directed towards national economic development rather than just the elite rent-seeking, corruption and class exploitation that was the norm for most of civilizational history. The old hegemonic and exploitational elitist regimes were broken in various places and in various ways, often through violent revolutions in the eighteenth and nineteenth centuries. The emergence of states focused on development could only occur once "development" became a possibility in the nineteenth century with industrialization. Of course corruption and elitist enrichment can sometimes go hand-in-hand for a time with a developmental state and in fact may be the main motivation of developmental elites, especially in states that are not democratic or transparent. That has clearly been the case in many instances, notably Nazi Germany in the 1930s, the Soviet Union in the interwar decades, Peron's Argentina, Pinochet's Chile and Park's South Korea. But these were highly unstable situations and did not endure. CP-ruled China today, a developmental state, is also increasingly unstable. On the other hand, some developmental states (such as Australia and New Zealand) have pursued a democratic agenda of redistribution and equality. This began in the late nineteenth century and politicians of the era were very aware of their developmental and socio-political function in constructing "state experiments", as Reeves pointed out as early as 1902 (Reeves 1902). It could be hypothesized that autocratic developmental states have a tendency to evolve in the direction of democracy because of the democratic empowerment that can flow from the success of the developmental process. This seems to have been the case in, for example, South Korea and Taiwan in recent decades. But this is a highly controversial topic – the development/democratization nexus – and there is no space for a discussion here.

However, a developmental state cannot by itself guarantee the transformation of a commodity-dependent country or region. Some essential degree of market functionality and a dynamic interrelationship between markets and states should exist (as Polanyi (1944) argued) and economic linkages have to be possible and then institutionally fostered. Not all commodities are alike in their linkages to their wider economic contexts. The Innis/Hirschman[14] theory shows that the macroeconomic effects of particular staples or commodities are quite different, depending, *ceterus paribus* institutionally, on their material, technological and employment nature. Energy exports are quite different in terms of their backward, forward and final demand linkages from agriculture, base metals, forestry and fishing, all of which tend to promote greater in-country processing than energy production. And the backward and forward linkages from economically leading commodity sectors – commodity extraction, production and exports – are always significantly different from those from other leading sectors of manufacturing and services. Final demand linkages effects are also crucial – these depend on distribution of income, general wage levels and consumption patterns, which in turn are strongly affected by the institutionalization of the labour market.

Thus commodity dependence has certain basic effects on the structure of a domestic economy and society. Nevertheless, the strengths of these linkages and their potential for promoting development do depend, in turn, on institutional frameworks. For example, wheat export industries in Australia, Canada and Mid-West USA in the nineteenth century all had strong backward linkages to industrial development and stronger final demand linkages to consumption patterns because of wage structures, compared especially with other major wheat exporters such as Argentina and Poland. These differing linkages were the product of socio-institutional contexts in these regions and global geopolitical contexts affecting these regions. Land ownership patterns (independent family farmers versus tenants or serfs on large estates) were crucial as were regulated imperial trading connections, financial institutions and merchant networks. The stimulation of farm machinery manufacturing in Australia, Canada and Midwest USA in the late nineteenth and early twentieth centuries was instrumental in laying the foundations for industrial development in these places (Page and Walker 1997; Meyer 2010) thanks in part to protection of manufacturing. This development was also supported by the final demand linkage in the sense of the provision of an ever-cheaper food supply to urban industrial areas due to the technological revolutions in agriculture.

Another example is of the forestry products sector in Sweden and Finland in the nineteenth and early twentieth centuries, in which strong backward linkages to machinery manufacturing developed. The Nokia company is one striking instance of this backward linkage effect of a forestry company leading to the emergence over time of a major industrial conglomerate that then concentrated on high tech manufacturing by the late twentieth century.

Because of their seeming promise of riches but checkered history, "unbalanced" commodity-exporting countries have been perhaps the most affected by one or other of the two main ideological frameworks of development[15] that have influenced policy for most of the past century or more: (a) *laissez faire/free trade*, leading to specialization on grounds of comparative advantage, enabling high commodity productivity and dynamic efficiency, but with *unavoidable backwardness* in non-exporting sectors; or (b) *diversification through import replacement*, with wide-based self-sufficiency, state promotion of industrial development and growth of an urban middle class, through protection of industries, but with *unavoidable inefficiency* and probable gradual national comparative decline. How to steer a line between these ideologies has been a chief task for policy makers.[16]

Protectionist import-replacement and some form of active market interventionism was the preferred policy of almost all countries from the middle of the nineteenth century until the 1950s or even as late as the 1980s in some cases, but protectionism gave way in the 1970s and 1980s to neo-liberal inspired free-marketization and globalization, leading supposedly to specialization through comparative advantage and elimination of rent-seeking from state elites, a policy that was hoped would not only achieve higher growth but permit the benefits of greater (but specialized) trade to spread somehow through the wider society. Nevertheless, despite the ideological shift, much protectionism remained, even in the advanced heartlands of the world economy. For commodity-dependent exporters the effect of the neo-liberal strategy depended in turn on the strength of local institutions and the capacity to compete in the global trading system, a system, moreover, in which there were still many distortions and forms of protectionism, especially through agricultural subsidies in advanced countries and currency manipulation. State protectionist policy has long used such measures.

Indeed, one of the foundational components of policy ever since "economic growth policy" (rather than just mercantilism) was first seen to be a task of governments from the early nineteenth century, was currency regulation. Manipulations of metallic standards did enable governments to debase currencies until the more or less universal adoption of the gold standard in the late nineteenth century. This era of stable and fixed currency values and then the adoption of the Bretton Woods system of fixed exchange rates from the late 1940s, following the unregulated monetary turmoil of the interwar period, enabled governments to pursue protectionist policies within a developmental state agenda. Once the Bretton Woods system dissolved and was replaced with a supposedly free trade system of purely fiat currencies, widespread from the 1980s, the "self-adjustment" mechanism was supposed to prevent protectionist policies and enable commodity exporters, in particular, to avoid inflationary pressures flowing from booming sectors or to make orderly, automatic, adjustments when booms collapsed. Of course not all countries have joined the free currency system[17] and, moreover, it has become quite clear that the international forex market follows its own cyclical and stochastic logic without a close correlation with the fortunes of individual economies. The naïve exchange rate theory of market-driven convergence, according to international balance of payments and growth of particular economies, has been shown to be delusional by the experience of real world financialization and speculation in recent decades. All floated currencies are now open to speculation and several major currencies are now completely commoditized in the sense of being objects of trade and speculation more or less completely outside of the real economies that issue them.[18] Some countries have experimented with fixed exchange rates even during the post-Bretton Woods era, sometimes with spectacular failings (e.g. Argentina's dollarization) and at other times with much success for a period, such as China's pegged RMB and Hong Kong's pegged dollar.

Currency regulation and state manipulation as a form of strategic intervention is what Hirschman argued for in 1958, as has Krugman (1991, 1994) more recently. Central to both their theories is a concept of economic linkages. These linkages take the form of flows of capital investment, goods, labour and profits between industries and sectors within an economy conceived as a complex web or structure of exchanges. This structure is held together by sets of social relations that are expressed as a combinations of formal contracts, informal social relations, social norms, networks of social power and relatedness, and ideational expressions of all these formal and informal exchanges.

The Innis/Hirschman/Krugman theme of linkages can be conceptually related to the Polanyian idea of embeddedness in the sense that economic relations, decisions and behaviour are enveloped through linkages of a social relational kind such that the economic aspects take place within a larger social structure. The economy, in other words, is a *social* structure. This social structure is in part economic in its manifestation and socio-political in its framing of the context for economic exchange. Linkages of demand, supply and investment between sectors take place within institutional structures that are enabled and developed by social and political networks and governance institutions. Institutions are rarely invented *de novo* but almost always evolve out of prior structures and contexts. The settler societies, those neo-Europes or fragments of the Old World, born in the early modern period, are somewhat exceptional in the sense that they were newborn societies but even they carried the definite marks of their parentage. This was certainly the case with Australia, born within the British Empire and its evolving institutional structure of the late eighteenth and early nineteenth centuries, which had a profound effect on the subsequent history of the country.

Foundations of Australia: a settler capitalist society with special characteristics

Colonial Australia was founded as an urban service colony for the British Empire, in the sense of a state-directed and controlled establishment of a prison. The role of the state was fundamental from the beginning (Lloyd 2002, 2003). But a private entrepreneurial sector soon developed in a land of vast natural resources, beginning with seal and whale oil. Commodity dependence and export booms and busts have been a persistent feature of Australia's history ever since the late eighteenth century. The category of "commodities" includes agricultural, marine, mineral and energy products and flows and collectively these have always been the dominant component of exports, rarely falling below 50 per cent of the value of all exported goods and services and in 2011 constituting more than 67 per cent (as indicated in Figure 13.1 – DFAT 2014).

Furthermore, it can be argued that the ongoing primary export dependence has been key to Australia remaining in some respects as a settler society ever since European colonization in 1788 until the present. The settler legacy continues to dominate the economy and society and its politics and this has been the product, it is argued here, of the continuing commodity dependence. The reliance on large-scale immigration of skilled labour, the low household savings ratio (but now high compulsory private pension savings), high propensity to consume, high capital import needs, high commodity export ratio, and the unresolved indigenous impoverishment and marginalization problem, are all continuing features.

Squatting is a further feature that is still significant. Settler society processes in most of the world from the eighteenth century or earlier always had as a central dynamic the violent seizure and appropriation (or theft) of land and other resources, the monopolization of natural resources by the settler elite, a subsequent contestation for resource domination between these ruling elites and local and imperial states, a dependence henceforth on the export of commodities,

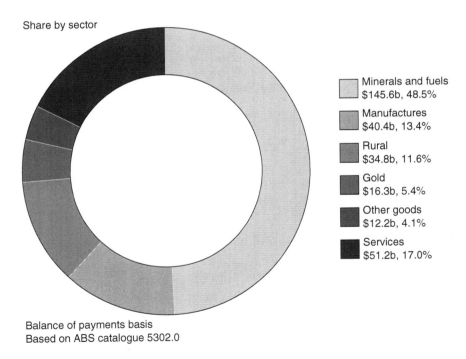

Figure 13.1 Australia's export profile 2013.

Note
Balance of payments basis.

and a consequent stunting of economic transformation towards modernization. Thus frontier squatting is fundamental to understanding these societies, not least Australia. Surprisingly perhaps, what is in effect squatting continues to be a crucial element in Australia's mineral and energy export sector today in the form of the virulent opposition to state regulation and taxation by the large oligopolistic mineral and energy corporations. Reaping the benefits of monopoly rents have been the *raison d'etre* of squatter settler capitalists for centuries.

However, the other side of the "Lucky Country" argument springs from the contingency of history for in spite of the power of the resource endowment and the other features of settlerism, including the atavistic squattocracy and the commodity export dependence, Australia did achieve economic and social modernization and was, indeed, for a time, a pioneer of the Social Democratization of capitalism as a regulatory regime and developmental strategy. How could that have come about, especially when Australia is compared with some other settler regions?

The political economy of Australia 1788–1914: emergence of an effective developmental state

Following the brief but spectacular marine oil era of the early nineteenth century there was the "pastoral age" of a rapidly expanding wool production economy, exploiting the natural grassland resource. The foundational *raison d'être* and the subsequent resource expansion with imported capital contributed to the engendering of a largely urbanized, port-city, society. That society was fed by immigration from British lower-middle-class society with values of social mobility and a growing sense of egalitarianism. The fact that all of Australia (occupied by several British colonizing foundations) remained as elements of the British Empire was significant for it meant that British Colonial Office policies drove the evolution of governance structures towards liberalization. Philosophic Radical/Wakefieldian ideas gained ascendancy in the Colonial Office by the early 1830s (Semmel 1961) and Chartist ideas were important among the immigrants arriving in the colonies. Wakefieldian systematic colonization was the central policy framework from the early 1830s in NSW, South Australia and later New Zealand. This policy met opposition among squatters and other atavistic elements in the colonies but by 1841 transportation of convict-labour to NSW ceased under the influence of liberal urban forces in Sydney and the atavistic frontier forces were eclipsed by the urban reformers. By the early 1840s the wool boom had collapsed. The depression of the early 1840s was a major turning point for not only were the political fortunes of the frontier defeated by the urban reformers but the wool producers lost economic power to the London-based merchants and banks (McMichael 1984).

The 1840s marked the consolidation of an effective local state in each of the colonies, one that was able henceforth to build a different kind of socio-political structure, moving away from the influence of landed interests and towards a society of family farmers, urban industries and promotion of middle-class suburban life by transferring frontier rents via high wages. The huge gold rushes from

1851 consolidated this emergent pattern and reinforced the push for liberal constitutions and electoral democracy. Once the gold began to decline in the 1860s political pressure grew for economic policies to promote employment and generate government revenue. The shift from laissez faire to protectionism was spreading around the world (except in Britain) and the Australian colonial dominions were no exception on the whole. New South Wales was an exception, remaining one of the few free trading regions in the world by the late nineteenth century. That case reflected the greater power of pastoral interests in the local parliament and also the greater abundance of good land for sale to small farmers as the chief source (rather than import duties) of government revenue.

The era from 1851 to 1891 witnessed the emergence in Australia of an effective, liberal constitutional state with *de jure* and de facto democracy, thanks to universal malehood suffrage, secret ballots and free and fair elections. This was crucial for what followed because the long, post-gold rush, mid-Victorian era of prosperity crashed in 1890–91 into a severe depression. The early 1890s crisis was fundamental for not only consolidating the local state structure but for the emergence of a new regime of capitalist regulation. The foundations for this regime were laid in the response to the depression and class-conflict of the early 1890s, thanks to the strength of liberalism and labourism that had developed in the preceding decades.[19]

Commodity dependence and regimes of development since 1914

The first decade of the twentieth century witnessed the development in Australia of a "state experiment", as Reeves put it in 1902, and which we should now call the development of a rudimentary form of Social Democratic Welfare Capitalism (SDWC), the central interlinked institutions of which were the Court of Arbitration and the industrial protection policy. The Harvester Judgment of that Court in 1907 established the principle of "wage justice" as being that "fair and reasonable wages" for workers in a "civilized society" were to be measured by family needs rather than capacity to pay or market conditions. Employers in the already large public sector adopted the principle and firms in the emerging import-replacing manufacturing sector (the sector was about 12 per cent of GDP in 1910) that wanted tariff protection had to pass on the implied higher profitability, resulting from the shelter, in the form of higher wages. This radical proposition, which became implemented throughout the labour market over subsequent decades, represented the conscious attempt to transfer via the industrial protection and wage-setting systems the wealth that had accumulated from the previous century of commodity export abundance into well-paid urban industrial and service employment. The highest average incomes per capita in the world of 1900 were to be made into the egalitarian reality via state action. In addition, the emergent welfare system was tied to the employment system in what Castles rightly called the "wage earners welfare state" (Castles 2002).

Together the two central institutions produced a system we can call labourist-protectionism (Lloyd 2002, 2003) which became an all-encompassing, hegemonic, regime of economic and social development throughout the period until the crisis of the 1970s. This regime, a form of SDWC, was explicitly designed by a loose coalition of Liberals and Labor as a developmental state response to the fundamental problems of diversification in a resource-dependent economy and the maintenance of the high standard of urbanized, middle-class, living that had already developed in the second half of the nineteenth century on the basis of resource-abundant exports, labour scarcity and capital inflows. The regime suffered a crisis during the Great Depression but a combination of protectionism, imperial preference and temporary wage suppression and, then, crucially, the full employment of the Second World War, enabled the regime to not only survive but be further developed by the Labor Party government of 1941–49. The conservative governments of 1949–72 did not abandon the regime, for it produced political and social stability and had a powerful political path dependency. Successive resource export booms in the 1950s and 1960s enabled the redistribution system, via higher wages and full employment, to continue to maintain the "suburban dream".

The other central institution invented in the early twentieth century was, of course, federation. But the federal system struggled in the early years to come to terms with fiscal federalism for the founders had not envisaged the central government being stronger than the states. The weakness of the centre threatened to destroy the federation because of states' rights and states' discontent. Unequal development and finance were the key problems. But solutions were found because the federal constitution was able to be subverted due to its complexity and sometimes contradictory provisions, despite the almost impossibility of revising it. The federal state was stabilized through key institutional developments in the late 1920s to 1940s era that consolidated the central fiscal authority and enabled horizontal fiscal equalization among the states while allowing vertical fiscal inequality.[20] The states have gradually become mere expenditure agents of the Commonwealth Treasury. The achievement of horizontal fiscal equality through the Commonwealth Grants Commission (CGC) was a crucial aspect of the stable development state structure that was designed to spread the wealth from the booming export sectors. Later in the twentieth century the poorer states erstwhile themselves experienced resource abundance and some of their wealth has been redistributed via the CGC process.

The current crisis of the Eurozone shows what can happen when there is the absence of a central developmental state. Europe introduced a common currency without the institutional framework of a centralized federal state that could regulate the economic behaviour and introduce stable growth policies in the regions (states or nations) within the union. The ten-year failure of institution and policy development leading up to the crisis of 2010–14, during which the EU papered over the lack of central authority to go with the common currency (with the important exception of the ECB) has now exposed the significance of developmental state power to go with a common currency. Other federations, including the US, Canada and Australia, had to learn this important lesson in their early history when implementing a new central system of currency with an emerging centralized monetary, fiscal and development management system. In Australia's case there were stumbling steps along the way but by the late 1920s the centralized framework of a stronger federal state began to emerge and by the early 1940s the whole structure of essential central control was in place with monetary and fiscal policy then more or less taken out of the hands of the states, which were and sometimes continue to be fiscally irresponsible, being much more prey to rent-seeking and pork barrelling than the federal government.

In two fundamental respects the labourist-protectionist system must be considered a success – industrialization and socio-political stability. Australia achieved full industrialization in the sense of sectoral shares of the domestic economy by the 1960s when the manufacturing sector reached about 28–30 per cent of GDP and the growth rate of the sector outstripped the rest of the economy in the postwar years (Attard 2010). Protection succeeded in the sense of industrial promotion of a full range of manufacturing, including a substantial motor vehicle industry.

By the 1970s the labourist-protectionism system was in crisis due to slow growth, stagflation and some Dutch disease effects from the new boom of the minerals and energy export sector.[21] Ad hoc arrangements to maintain the system failed and the hoped-for "rescue" of a new resource boom in the early 1980s also failed (the "lucky country" syndrome again) with the plunge into a severe recession in the early 1980s. The election of the Hawke/Keating government in 1983 saw the beginnings of the abandonment of the labourist-protectionist system to be replaced over the next decade by elements of a neo-liberal regime.

Commodity dependence, political economy and quality of life in the twenty-first century: from unbalanced development to a balanced outcome

Australia shared in the long boom of the 1992–2008 era with a rising standard of living, achieving near (official) full employment and continual growth, with no recession throughout the global crisis since 2008. By 2005 almost all public debt had been eliminated and Australia became a creditor nation. Commodity exports dominated the export profile on the eve of the financial crisis (Figure 13.2) and since then the commodity dependence has actually increased, thanks to the Chinese demand for raw materials (see Figure 13.1).

Australia has recently experienced an increased commodity dependence in terms of exports but not in terms of economic structure. The minerals and energy sector accounts for about 10 per cent of output but only 2 per cent of employment. Thus the question arises of whether Australia experienced a form of resource curse during the recent boom? Very substantial currency appreciation from 2010 impacted negatively on traditional exporting sectors (some parts of agriculture, most notably the wine industry) and more so on import-competing manufacturing. On the other hand, these are now so comparatively shrunken in sector shares of the total economy that the impact is much less than in earlier

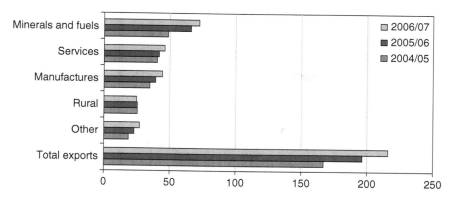

Figure 13.2 Australia's exports by sector 2004–07 (A$bn) (source: DFAT (2008)).
Note
Balance of payments basis.

resource booms. The highly efficient agricultural sector employs almost nobody and, as with all mature economies, the services sector now employs 80 per cent of the workforce and, with important exceptions, is not a highly trade-exposed sector (see Figure 13.4). Some parts of the services sector, notably higher education, one of the most dynamic and largest export sectors in recent decades, and tourism, have suffered from some loss of international competitiveness through the exchange rate effect but have proven resilient thanks to Chinese demand. Figure 13.5 shows the shift in composition of exports in recent years. With the decline in value of the A$ in 2015 export competitiveness has revived.

A fundamental point to make in conclusion, indeed made several times in this chapter, with regard to the whole international trading context of the mining "boom" in Australia in the twenty-first century, is the power of the linkage effect. Some attempts have been made to measure this effect and estimate its future potential in terms of employment generation in backward linkage industries (Figure 13.3). This shows that the linkage effect has great potential to grow just as mining is overtaking manufacturing as a share of GDP, the first time this has been the case for more than a century. The backward linkage effect is largely into highly skilled services and it is that area that has the most potential, along with the high-wage mining employment itself, to generate significant final demand linkages (Taylor 2011).

These structural considerations go some of the way towards explaining the "puzzle" of Australia's relatively slow growth in 2011 in the midst of a supposed resources boom. In their excellent discussion of this phenomenon, Gregory and Sheehan (2011) argue that the rise in the exchange from 2010 has had the effect of redistributing incomes towards households via lower import prices but that, on the other hand, the deleterious effect of traditional exporting and import-replacing sectors of agriculture, higher education, tourism and manufacturing, has been significant but probably not producing a full-blown case of Dutch

286 C. Lloyd

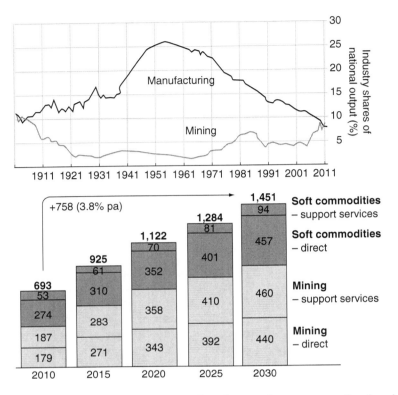

Figure 13.3 Mining overtakes manufacturing; employment generation in mining backward linkage industries (source: Kehoe et al. (2012), based on Taylor (2011)).

disease. The long-run shift in the Australian economy, as with all mature post-industrial economies, towards tertiary and particularly quaternary sectors has meant that there is less of a dislocational employment shock, à la Dutch disease, than in earlier eras. The finance sector now provides more than 10 per cent of GDP, thanks in part to the growth of the superannuation funds industry. It seems, then, that Australia is riding its luck again but ensuring the final demand linkage and productivity increases play their full role is partly a matter of public policy, especially regarding taxation and investment in infrastructure. But that's another story (Lloyd 2012).

Australia in 2015 presents a mixed picture of a mature economy with an advanced, "balanced" institutional structure very comparable with alike OECD countries, but again with an "unbalanced" export profile compared with other OECD countries. The trajectory of development over the past 120 years has been one of similarity to other countries that achieved development from a similar starting point in "unbalanced" commodity dependence (Anglo settler societies and Nordic societies) but a contrast with those (Hispanic settler

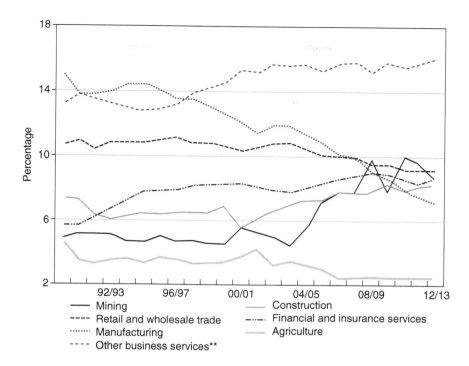

Figure 13.4 Australian industry share of output (source: RBA (2014, p. 13)).

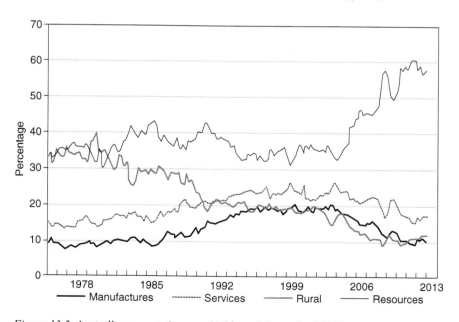

Figure 13.5 Australian exports (source: (Atkin and Connolly (2013)).

societies, especially) who did not make such a transformation for most of the twentieth century (especially the 1930s–1980s period). The inability to move towards a successful developmental state model after the early twentieth century seems to have been crucial there but in the twenty-first century that now seems to be happening. It can be argued (Lloyd 2013) that indeed the Anglo and Hispanic settler societies are actually on the same long-term path of institutional development. That one group is well ahead of the other does not mean that convergence is not happening. Good government, strong de facto civic participation, de facto democracy, equality, welfare and economic development seem to form an embedded structure of mutually reinforcing elements that are difficult to create but can emerge out of contingent historical experiences and institutional good fortune. Once they have developed and matured they are almost impossible to destroy.

Notes

1 This chapter is in the spirit of the critical realist socio-political-economy tradition of historical research into past and present of Karl Polanyi, Albert Hirschman and Barrington Moore, a tradition that was eclipsed some decades ago by rational choice, ahistorical, political economy, but which still has much to offer. Polanyi's rejection of economic abstractionism and his conceptualization of the formal/substantive distinction seems to be essential to the study of long-run socio-economic history. Attempts to understand the present crisis of the world economy could do worse than adopt the interdisciplinary outlook of Polanyi and of Hirschman, neither of whom could ever have been pigeon-holed into a single box such as economic development theorist or political theorist or economic historian. Hirschman's attempts to understand the complexities of macro-social processes over time showed an exemplary scepticism about simplistic models and spurious quantification of over-aggregate variables, and a constant concern to study the local specifics of cases within a theoretical framework that rejected the abstraction of the economy from culture, society and politics. Similarly, Moore was a theorist and historian of routes to development and modernity who was concerned with the intersection of social and political systems in producing alternative historical trajectories (Moore 1966). An approach in the tradition of these thinkers focuses on the role of social classes, the state and policy in the process of socio-economic change and development. In particular, the concept of the "developmental state" is now an essential component of theorizing the comparative history of commodity-dependent countries as much as of other types of countries, such as those in the Nordic region and in East Asia. Moreover, the uni-linear thinking of much development literature has been blinkered about the several alternative paths that have succeeded in producing modern, rich, societies and the possibilities that many developing countries still have open to them. Much of the "resource curse" literature exhibits uni-linear, ahistorical, thinking. The varied histories of types of capitalist development is still an under-researched project. The argument that material conditions, including labour and capital supply, have been very important, within an institutional framework, in the comparative history of the settler capitalist societies, has been made in Lloyd (2013).
2 "Modernization" is a key concept when it refers to institutional, political and cultural development that is centred on democracy, pluralism, tolerance and social stability. Modernity also contains the idea of individualism, which in turn is closely interrelated with the aforementioned characteristics of modernization.
3 The rapid development of China is repeating the pattern with very large imbalances

now between development and standard of living in urban and rural areas and coastal and hinterland regions. But the rapidity and scale of transformation and the possibility of massive migration, the largest in history, is perhaps the largest case of "the great transformation" ever experienced, greater even than the North Atlantic in the late nineteenth to early twentieth centuries. Whether and how the economic transformation will result in socio-political modernization is becoming one of the great questions of our time. That some other East Asian cases (Japan, South Korea, Taiwan, Singapore) have become or are becoming modern, not always peacefully or to a full extent, is significant.

4 The term "The Lucky Country" was coined by Horne (1964) to describe, in an ironic and critical manner, the syndrome whereby Australia remained rich due to successive waves of resource discoveries, which had the effect of always postponing the motivation and will to reform institutions, policies and attitudes, and which was, therefore, in his eyes, industrially, socially and politically backward in the early 1960s. In other words, the "luck" of constant resource windfalls was not luck at all but a stultifying influence that hindered progress. Nevertheless, he understood that Australia was a wealthy country; but one squandering its wealth, in his eyes. Forty years later (Horne 2004) he saw that significant change had occurred in the direction he hoped for. From today's perspective we can see that Horne's analysis was superficial and lacking in theoretical and scientific analysis but nevertheless was perceptive about what we would now call "resource curse". A similar argument has recently been made by Cleary (2011), trying to update Horne's classic, with a similar journalistic and unrigorous tenor, explicitly emphasizing what he takes to be resource curse and proposing policies to overcome it.

5 The seminal Sachs and Warner writings (1995, 2001) could be understood as hindering the debate because of their lack of a long-term perspective going back to the nineteenth century and their focus on the poorest countries. Moreover, an approach that uses only aggregated, short-term data and regression analyses of supposedly purely quantifiable variables is bound to miss what could be some fundamentally important factors, such as local power structures, formal and informal institutions, ethnic conflicts, cultures, corruption, criminality, and so on. Orthodox economics does not provide, in my view, the best approach to historical questions of socio-economic-institutional experience and change in the long run. Furthermore, the Dutch disease phenomenon, which, actually, turned out to be not a lasting illness but one which the Netherlands and later the UK overcame quite quickly, is very specifically the result of a booming new commodity export sector (such as oil and gas) within an already industrially mature (non-commodity-dependent) advanced economy. Such specificity means the phenomenon is not actually found in traditionally commodity-exporting economies that have always been commodity dependent.

6 Stabilization seems to be the case with Australia in 2014. That is, the boom investment phase in iron ore, coal, gold, CSG and LNG moderated and there seemed to be a new stability at a much higher level of mineral and energy exports, higher terms of trade and a higher exchange rate (Stevens 2010; Connolly and Orsmond 2011; Kearns and Lowe 2011). However, the collapse in raw materials prices in late 2014 has impacted greatly on Australia and similar countries. From then a new phase has begun of lower exchange rates and structural adjustment.

7 New Institutionalism, deriving from the work of Douglass North, is too imbued with the Rational Choice and Public Choice nostrums to capture the real complexities of the Polanyian substantive structures of power, decision-making and collective behaviour.

8 Edward Barbier's extensive work has developed this argument (Barbier 2011).

9 One of the most notorious and saddest cases is that of Nauru, which for a time had one of the highest average incomes per capita from its phosphate exports but is now a completely failed society and state. More pertinent are several oil-rich exporters with very high average incomes but low socio-political development (HDI 2014).

10 The conclusion by Easterly and Levine (2003, p. 37) of their econometric study of endowments, tropics and germs, among many other factors, is a telling one:

> These kinds of cross-country results are only a beginning to telling the story of colonial experiences, political conflict and consensus, institution-building, and economic development for each unique case. Still, we are struck by the way that endowments and policies have no independent effect once we control for institutions, contrary to a number of stories, and that institutional quality seems to be a sufficient statistic for accounting for economic development.

Of course what they could have added is that, in turn, institutional quality is itself the result of the long-run historical experience of each unique case, especially during the European colonial era that affected the whole world and had such a long-lasting and often quite damaging effect on most of the LDCs today. Furthermore, institutions are certainly not unchanging, including in the poorest LDCs, and that process is itself a consequence of the unique experience of each country, albeit within an increasingly globalized context.

11 The UN HDI has consistently ranked Australia, Norway, Canada and Finland at or near the top. The OECD's How's Life Index (OECD 2011) has Australia in first place, closely followed by Canada, if all 11 variables are rated equally. Various other international rankings (some more objective than others) of countries and cities always have Australia at or near the top in terms of quality of life.

12 Most likely the spread of a SDWC regime to all advanced capitalist economies during the second half of the twentieth century was a product of a combination of institutional transmission and more fundamental socio-political processes originating in mature democratic societies (Lloyd 2011).

13 Abjorensen (2011) quotes disturbing data from African Union and UN sources to the effect that 25 per cent of GDP is wasted in Africa each year through corruption; and illicit outflows from the global south amount to 1.3 trillion dollars or more each year. Most of these illicit flows are to the benefit of developed countries through their banking, property and consumption systems. Banking privacy in developed countries is partly to blame.

14 Innis (1930) and Hirschman (1958) developed the linkages argument in different ways. Innis' staple theory showed how export commodities linked with the wider economy and Hirschman took this further in a political economy perspective.

15 These are rightly called ideologies rather than theories for they are ex-cathedra-type statements of a quasi-philosophical kind that express a priori faith rather than inductively derived general concepts of causal connections.

16 A rich commodity export industry, such as wool, wheat, gold, oil, coal, iron ore or gas, has always been a magnet for ambitious politicians and other elites who wish to engineer national and/or personal outcomes.

17 Even Switzerland, a supposed bastion of the free market ideology, until January 2015 semi-pegged its currency to the Euro from September 2011.

18 The Australian dollar is one of the most notorious examples, 97 per cent of trades in which are for speculative/investment purposes. Currency trading requires volatility to be profitable, but volatility is detrimental to international trading in goods and services because of the added uncertainty and consequent risky necessity to hedge against price fluctuations, due to currency fluctuations, by many internationally trading corporations, such as airlines.

19 The 1890s development in Australia contrasted markedly with the US, both of which had witnessed a significant development of labour organization and mobilization in the prior decades. American labour suffered a historic defeat in the late nineteenth and early twentieth centuries from which it never fully recovered. The much greater scale and power of corporations in the US is part of the explanation.

20 The Loans Council and Financial Agreement of 1927 centralized and regulated public

borrowing, the 1933 Commonwealth Grants Commission guaranteed horizontal fiscal equalization, the Commonwealth Bank took on growing central banking powers from the late 1920s, the federal government became fiscally dominant with the uniform income tax of 1942, and in 1945 the Commonwealth Bank became a fully fledged central bank.

21 The 1965–75 decade witnessed a massive increase in minerals and energy exports from under 10 per cent to over 50 per cent of exports.

References

Abjorensen, N., 2011. The Corruption Pipeline. *Inside Story*. 10 November, Melbourne.

Atkin, T. and Connolly, E., 2013. *Australian Exports: Global Demand and the High Exchange Rate*. RBA (Reserve Bank of Australia). Available at: www.rba.gov.au/publications/bulletin/2013/jun/1.html.

Attard, B., 2010. The Economic History of Australia from 1788: An Introduction. *EH Net Encyclopedia*.

Auty, R.M., 2001. *Resource Abundance and Economic Development*. Oxford: Clarendon Press.

Barbier, E.B., 2011. *Scarcity and Frontiers: How Economies Have Developed through Natural Resource Exploitation*. New York: Cambridge University Press.

Castles, F.G., 2002. Australia's Institutions and Australia's Welfare. *In*: G. Brennan and F.G. Castles, eds. *Australia Reshaped: 200 Years of Institutional Transformation*. Cambridge, MA: Cambridge University Press.

Cleary, P., 2011. *Too Much Luck: The Mining Boom and Australia's Future*. Melbourne, Australia: Black Inc.

Connolly, E. and Orsmond, D., 2011. The Mining Industry: From Bust to Boom. *In*: *Reserve Bank of Australia Conference on Australia in the 2000s*. Sydney, Australia.

DFAT, 2008. *Australia in Brief*. Canberra, Australia: Department of Foreign Affairs and Trade (Australian Government). Available at: www.dfat.gov.au/aib/trade_investment.html.

DFAT, 2014. *Trade at a Glance*. Canberra, Australia: Department of Foreign Affairs and Trade (Australian Government).

Easterly, W. and Levine, R., 2003. Tropics, Germs, and Crops: How Endowments Influence Economic Development. *Journal of Monetary Economics*, 50 (1), 3–39.

Erten, B. and Ocampo, J.A., 2012. Super-Cycles of Commodity Prices Since the Mid-nineteenth Century. *DESA Working Paper* (110).

Gregory, B. and Sheehan, P., 2011. The Resources Boom and Macroeconomic Policy in Australia. *In*: *Australian Economic Report*. Melbourne, Australia: Centre for Strategic Economic Studies, Victoria University.

HDI, 2014. *Human Development Report 2012*. New York: UNDP.

Hirschman, A.O., 1958. *The Strategy of Economic Development*. New Haven, CT: Yale University Press.

Horne, D., 1964. *The Lucky Country*. Melbourne, Australia: Penguin Books.

Horne, D., 2004. Still Lucky but Getting Smarter. *The Age*. 28 August, Melbourne.

Innis, H.A., 1930. *The Fur Trade in Canada: An Introduction to Canadian Economic History*. New Haven, CT: Yale University Press.

Kearns, J. and Lowe, P., 2011. Australia's Prosperous 2000s: Housing and the Mining Boom. *In*: *Reserve Bank of Australia Conference on Australia in the 2000s*. Sydney, Australia.

Kehoe, J., Forrestal, L. and Wiggins, J., 2012. New Industries Defy Hollow Cries of Decay. *Australian Financial Review*, 3–4, pp. 44–45.

Krugman, P., 1991. Increasing Returns and Economic Geography. *Journal of Political Economy*, 99 (3), 484–499.

Krugman, P., 1994. The Rise and Fall of Development Economics. *In*: *Rethinking the Development Experience: Essays Provoked by the Work of Albert O. Hirschman*. Washington, D.C.: The Brookings Institution.

Lloyd, C., 2002. Regime Change in Australian Capitalism: Towards an Historical Political Economy of Regulation. *Australian Economic History Review*, 42 (3), 238–266.

Lloyd, C., 2003. Economic Policy and Australian State-Building: From Labourist-Protectionism to Globalisation. *In*: A. Teichova and H. Matis, eds. *Nation, State, and the Economy in History*. Cambridge, MA: Cambridge University Press.

Lloyd, C., 2011. The History and Future of Social Democratic Welfare Capitalism. *In*: P. Kettunen and K. Peterson, eds. *Beyond Welfare State Models*. Cheltenham, UK: Edward Elgar.

Lloyd, C., 2012. Resource Rents, Taxation, and Political Economy in Australia: States, Public Policy, and the New Squatters in Historical Perspective. *Australian Policy Online*, 28 May.

Lloyd, C., 2013. Institutional Patterns of the Settler Societies: Hybrid, Parallel, Convergent. *In*: C. Lloyd, J. Metzer and R. Sutch, eds. *Settler Economies in World History*. Leiden: Brill.

McMichael, P., 1984. *Settlers and the Agrarian Question: Capitalism in Colonial Australia*. Cambridge: Cambridge University Press.

Mehlum, H., Moene, K. and Torvik, R., 2006. Institutions and the Resource Curse. *The Economic Journal*, 116, 1–20.

Meyer, D.R., 2010. The Roots of American Industrialization, 1790–1860. *Encyclopedia of Economic History*, EH Net, Economic History Association.

Moore, B., 1966. *Social Origins of Dictatorship and Democracy*. Boston: Beacon Press.

Ocampo, J.A. and Parra-Lancourt, M., 2010. The Terms of Trade for Commodities since the Mid-19th Century. *Revista de Historia Económica/Journal of Iberian and Latin American Economic History*, 28 (1), 11.

OECD, 2011. *How's Life: Measuring Well-Being*. París: OECD Publishing.

Page, B. and Walker, R., 1997. From Settlement to Fordism: The Agro-Industrial Revolution in the American Midwest. *Economic Geography*, 67 (4), 281–315.

Polanyi, K., 1944. *The Great Transformation: The Political and Economic Origins of Our Time*. Boston: Beacon Press.

RBA, 2014. *Pack 2014 Chart*. Sydney, Australia: Reserve Bank of Australia. Available at: www.rba.gov.au/chart-pack/regions-industry.html.

Reeves, W.P., 1902. *State Experiments in Australia & New Zealand, Volume Two*. London: G. Richards.

Robinson, J.A., 2009. Botswana as a Role Model for Country Success. *WIDER Research Paper*, UNU-WIDER, Helsinki (2009/40).

Robinson, J.A., Torvik, R. and Verdier, T., 2006. Political Foundations of the Resource Curse. *Journal of Development Economics*, 79 (2), 447–468.

Sachs, J.D. and Warner, A.M., 1995. Natural Resource Abundance and Economic Growth. *National Bureau of Economic Research Working Paper Series* (5398).

Sachs, J.D. and Warner, A.M., 2001. The Curse of Natural Resources. *European Economic Review*, 45 (4–6), 827–838.

Semmel, B., 1961. The Philosophic Radicals and Colonialism. *The Journal of Economic History*, 21 (4), 513–525.

Sen, A., 1999. *Development as Freedom*. Oxford: Oxford University Press.

Stevens, G., 2010. *The Challenge of Prosperity*. RBA (Reserve Bank of Australia). Available at: www.rba.gov.au/publications/bulletin/2010/dec/pdf/bu-1210-9.pdf.

Stiglitz, J.E., Sen, A. and Fitoussi, J.P., 2009. *Report by the Commission on the Measurement of Economic Performance and Social Progress*. Paris.

Taylor, A., 2011. Port Jackson Partners: "Earth, Fire, Wind and Water": Economic Opportunities and the Australian Commodities Cycle. *ANZ Insight*, 1.

Toye, J.F.J. and Toye, R., 2003. The Origins and Interpretation of the Prebisch-Singer Thesis. *History of Political Economy*, 35 (3), 437–467.

14 The institutional foundations of natural resource based knowledge economies

Simon Ville and Olav Wicken

There was a turning point in the discussion of the "resource curse" around the turn of the millennium, strongly influenced by historical work on American economic development. Gavin Wright (in collaboration with various researchers) produced a series of papers which documented how natural resource based industries (NRBI) could be analysed and perceived as modern knowledge based production. In his early work, Wright (1990) created a link between the resource expansion and America's international economic success. His analysis of the factor content of trade in manufacturing exports showed that it was characterised by intensity in non-reproducible natural resources, and that the resource intensity had increased during the period c.1880–1930. With the arrival of Sachs and Warner's thesis of a resource curse, Wright used his historical knowledge of American history to challenge the arguments underlying the resource curse theory. In collaboration with Paul David (David and Wright 1997), they argued that a country's resource abundance was not given by the natural environment. Instead, the natural resource base may increase by investing in knowledge and technology to search for minerals, extract them, and process or market them. The stocks of natural resources are not fixed, but rather they are the dynamic output of investments in various types of knowledge, including science, education, technologies and organisations. This is the basis for the argument that the NRBI typified modern knowledge based economies, particularly in the form of positive feedback to investments in knowledge, spillover benefits between mining categories, complementarities between public- and private-sector discoveries, and increasing returns to scale. (David and Wright 1997, pp. 204–205). This is the basis of natural resource based knowledge economy (NRBKE).

The positive role of natural resources for long-term industrial and economic development, as observed in the USA, has also been the case for other economies. Wright and Czelusta (2004) particularly point to Norway (an oil economy) and Australia as the "most successful story" of any natural resource based economies. Ville and Wicken (2013) argue that the basis for the long-term success of Australia and Norway was the establishment of a diverse and wide knowledge base relevant for future dynamics of natural resource based industries. In many ways the description of the development in Australia and Norway resembles that of the USA (but far more limited). The analysis of the mining sector in the USA describes a mature industrial economy with strong and well-developed producer organisations and firms; technology providers; science and education system; policy institutions and infrastructure which supported innovation and technological development within the NRBI. Similar developments are observed in the Australian and Norwegian cases. However, none of the studies discuss the institutional foundations for the establishment of knowledge organisations relating to natural resource based industries. This gap in the research agenda of NRBI is the topic of this chapter.

The historical origins of natural resource based knowledge economy: useful knowledge

Our approach takes as its point of departure studies interested in the "Historical Origins of the Knowledge Economy" (the subtitle of Joel Mokyr's book *The Gifts of Athena*, 2002). We draw on the concept of *useful knowledge*, which was first used by Simon Kuznets, and presented as the main source of modern economic growth and development (Kuznets 1965, pp. 85–87). In historical work by Mokyr useful knowledge is defined as technology; or tools used by humans to manipulate nature. His project is to understand how the stock of useful best-practice knowledge increased, and how new types of knowledge entered the economy during "The Industrial Enlightenment" (Mokyr 2002, chap. 1). Useful knowledge is described by Mokyr as two sub-categories of knowledge: propositional[1] (beliefs about natural phenomena and regularities) and prescriptive knowledge (defined as techniques). In principle, the idea is that the stock of propositional knowledge was what changed the direction of history. It made possible new technologies, but even more important became a knowledge base for long-term improvement of existing technologies and industries. Propositional knowledge is about nature and can be used to manipulate the natural environment into new natural resources, much in line with the development of the US economy described above. Mokyr argues that this was at the centre of the Industrial Revolutions when the "organic economy" using plants and animals, supplemented with water and wind as energy sources, shifted the material and energy resources towards an economy based on minerals and fossil fuels; and where iron and steel gradually replaced wood, and coal replaced animal and human energy (Mokyr 2009, p. 6). A central part of the Industrial Revolution was the creation of new natural resources used in the economy (minerals, fossil fuels) and the transformation of old NRBI (agriculture).

We approach the emergence of a NRBKE in Australia and Norway through a three-step analysis. We start with the Industrial Enlightenment phase of development (from the late eighteenth century), studying movements which promoted the idea of useful knowledge in both countries. This is based on the argument that, in order for industrialists to use propositional knowledge, it was necessary that they believed in its usefulness.[2] We emphasise the existence of these enlightenment movements in Australia and Norway and analyse the extent to which they promoted knowledge relevant for NRBI. Both nations were in a formative period, and the movements promoting knowledge and industrial development became part of nation building.

The second step in our analysis is how elites and social groups created organisations and institutions which improved (and reduced costs related to) *access of knowledge*. Most of the early developments took place in a few core economies in Western Europe, primarily in the UK. Even with a belief in the usefulness of the emerging new knowledge and technologies, it was not obvious how industrial actors in countries like Australia and Norway would get access at costs which were acceptable. This could be done through various mechanisms; both through transfer of texts on new knowledge, through physical transfer of objects (like machines); but primarily through human mobility and visits to the locations where the new technologies and knowledge flourished. In the analysis we focus particularly on knowledge transfer linked to NRBI.

The final step of analysis is linked to the gradual improvement of *local knowledge capabilities* in Australia and Norway; and to what extent this was linked to knowledge relevant for local NRBI. We discuss how the early build-up of scientific organisations was directed towards supporting development of NRBI; then analyse the relationship and interaction between researchers in these organisations and the relevant industries.

Australia

Australia experienced very rapid economic development in the nineteenth century. From near subsistent standards of living in the years after settlement as a British convict colony in 1788, she had emerged as part of the developed western world by the time of Federation in 1901. By the 1860s Australian per capita incomes were probably the highest in the world (Madsen 2015, p. 36). What made this fast development relatively unusual was that it was based heavily upon the export of primary products rather than the manufacturing "take-off" more typical of most high wealth nations including Britain, the United States and Germany. Beginning with fisheries in the early nineteenth century, then wool, gold, coal, iron ore and many other commodities, streams of new and modified natural resources of economic value have continued to be produced (Ville and Wicken 2013, p. 1352). While services became the largest sector of the Australian economy, frequently in support of primary industries, resource exports have continued to drive many aspects of Australian economic development into the twenty-first century. Far from being the one-shot resources boom of some modern petrol economies or the passive precursor of modern industrial economies, resource based industries have regularly re-invented themselves as a self-sustaining and technologically sophisticated leading sector of the Australian economy.

It was apparent within a few decades of colonial settlement that Australia's comparative advantage lay in the abundant potential of her vast natural resources. However, the ability to exploit that potential and sustain its importance in a cost-effective manner over a long period of time has been a complex, and far from inevitable, story. In this section we explain how for Australia, as for Norway, the development of technological knowledge was critical to progress by linking science with output in a resource based economy. Their national narratives challenge the frequent assumption that such a relationship, among science, technology and economics, was largely the preserve of manufacturing industry.

The foundations of propositional knowledge

Critically, it was the growing realisation that settlers faced an all-consuming and harsh natural environment, lacking the more obvious bucolic charms of the old country but promising rich rewards for hard endeavour, which helped to foster a prevailing belief in the pursuit of useful knowledge. The soil was generally of poor quality, the dominant bush land was not suitable without investment for agricultural and pastoral systems, and rainfall was highly unpredictable – in poet Dorothea McKellar's words, "droughts and flooding rains"! The battle with a harsh and untamed environment, that offered promise but also threats, bred a challenge and response mechanism, similar to the concept of "creative adaptation" described by White for Australian society as a whole (White 1992, pp. 157–158).

The much older Aboriginal society had recognised the importance of harnessing the richness of the land and managing resources in a diverse and sustainable manner. Our modern historiography has increasingly acknowledged that a thriving, not declining, Aboriginal society and economy existed on the eve of European settlement (Butlin 1993). As an extension of that perspective, it has become clear that the interaction between settlers and indigenous groups was complex and multi-faceted. It included shared knowledge and settlers learning from Aboriginal people how best to harvest the valuable but difficult resources of the Australian continent. This particularly included the practice of "firestick farming" – the intentional burning of native vegetation to promote new dense plant growth – and knowledge of native plants and foods vital for living in the bush. Hunter (2015, p. 77) notes that the technological legacy from Aboriginal society "included knowledge of raw materials, the construction and use of equipment, seasonality and distribution of resources, and methods for tracking game and otherwise finding food". Aboriginal people were also involved in the first known resource export from Australia – the trepang trade – in the eighteenth century.

British settlers – convicts, emancipists and free migrants – arrived from the most economically advanced nation of the late eighteenth and early nineteenth centuries, the so-called workshop of the world. Far from the traditional myth of being recidivist criminals, they brought with them a breadth of industrious, innovative and entrepreneurial skills, learned against the backdrop of enlightenment thinking that focused on scientific solutions to real world problems (Meredith and Oxley 2015; Mokyr 2009). This equipped them well to turn their attention to a very different economic and business environment – a commercial as well as geographic antipodes (Ville 1998). The set of factor inputs to production – scarce labour and capital but abundant land – was the converse of Britain. Existing knowledge had to be applied in new contexts and often with new resources. Thus, early settlers searched for new sources of limestone from which lime could be extracted for use in building mortar. Leather making had to find new sources of tannin in wattle bark and then work out how to extract it. In addition to this search and adaptation process, settlers then turned their minds to establishing possible uses for many resources which were new to them, or at least in a level of abundance not previously encountered. A long process of experimentation established the valuable uses for eucalyptus oil (Magee 2015, pp. 126–127).

The drive to seek wealth through "natural capital" was enhanced by the realisation that resource exports provided the ideal complementary trade for the manufacturing exports of the north. This meant that rather than rely upon resources merely to support the needs of a small local population, comparative advantage encouraged specialisation in resource production as a "vent for surplus". Australian exports had already begun to occupy a major position in the London wool auctions by the 1840s. Given the relatively small labour needs of sheep stations and the "reproducible" capital of sheep, wool production and export expanded rapidly. By the end of the nineteenth century, Australia had become the global leader in wool exports and the market had begun to relocate from Europe. Since then the application of propositional knowledge diversified to the extracting, modifying and export of a wide range of commodities.

The application of propositional knowledge

The Australian colonies in the nineteenth century lacked a well thought out development strategy to guide these attitudes and aspirations. The British Empire did not provide economic leadership to its colonies in anything but a self-serving manner. However, the desire of the British, within a few decades of settlement at Botany Bay, to mitigate the financial burden of the Australian colonies motivated the development of a private sector and a search for the sources of sustainable development. For the colonies themselves, with very limited financial or education/research resources or rights of governance and facing great uncertainty, their initial thoughts were mostly focused on survival. Until the later nineteenth century, any development strategies were more piecemeal than the national independence movement in Norway after 1814.

Ironically, this void of governance and resources created the opportunity for the "democratisation of invention" (Magee 1998; Sokoloff and Khan 1990). In Australia, as in Norway, it was individuals as part of local communities who frequently took the lead in harnessing the natural resources informed by practical knowledge. They came from many walks of life and rarely possessed specialist skills or scientific knowledge derived from formal education and training. Even among the more prolific individual inventors for the resource based industries, practical skills and knowledge predominated (Magee 2015, pp. 136–137).

Embedded in local communities enriched with deep veins of social capital, their knowledge base drew on occupational experience, trial and error, which they exchanged with others in a shared battle with a demanding but promising natural environment. However, the church, while a regular and largely cohesive part of rural life, did not feature in the same way as it had in Norway. Local community organisations that fostered useful knowledge were predominantly secular and viewed the taming and harvesting of the natural environment as a practical real world problem.

Agricultural and pastoral societies were being established in rural communities by the 1820s and soon showed their value as receptacles of information dissemination. These were communities with a strong sense of bonding social capital developed through interaction in many forms. In addition to the many agricultural and pastoral societies, social and sporting clubs, charity groups, religious gatherings and farmers' clubs were all to be found in most pastoral districts of south-eastern Australia by mid-century. Social capital also accrued to high levels of kinship in extended families that settled together in rural towns. Finally, a tradition of informal social gatherings at festivals and fairs created a sense of community and place on which trust and cooperation could be based (Keen 1999; Raby 1996, pp. 114–137).

The opportunities presented by the mid-nineteenth-century economic expansion along with the simultaneous movement towards self-governing colonies provided the foundations for greater government facilitation and direction of research through agricultural research bodies and a growing range of museums, libraries, botanic gardens and observatories focusing on aspects of the natural environment (Inkster and Todd 1988; McLean 1982). After Federation, Australia, as a single nation gaining increasing de facto independence from Britain, began to design national institutions to facilitate economic and social modernisation. Foremost among these for the resources sector was the formation of CSIRO (Commonwealth Scientific and Industrial Research Organisation) in 1949 and its predecessor CSIR (Commonwealth Scientific and Industrial Research, 1926) to foster scientific research (Schedvin 1987). Through its network of laboratories and field stations, it engaged with the challenges and opportunities facing the primary industries, particularly where national solutions were necessary such as countering pests and building value in export industries.

Access to international knowledge networks may have appeared less propitious for Australia than Norway, the latter being nestled within north-western Europe. The opportunities for technological exchange had always existed with Britain but the very different natural environment and sectoral focus limited its value. However, the growth of Australian overseas trade in the second half of the nineteenth century, supported by major advances in international transport and communications, provided much improved access to global sources of technology relevant to Australia's burgeoning primary industries. Accompanying this was the expansion of international business as a receptacle for knowledge, particularly the free-standing companies that arrived from Britain as part of the supply chain for commodity exports.

Consistent with the tradition established in Scandinavia by Carl von Linné, Australians began to map their natural environment – botanical, zoological and geological data provided a valuable knowledge base and an increasing awareness of useful knowledge. Australian public organisations – museums, libraries, botanic gardens and the like – joined with private sector enterprises and individual collectors in a large-scale global trade of mapping, cataloguing and amassing natural history specimens (Coote 2014). Sometimes accompanying the much larger wool trade, birds, animals types, shells and many other items were traded. Australian museums – including the Australian Museum, the Macleay Museum, the South Australian Museum and the Museum of Victoria – built up substantial collections for educational and curatorial purposes. There were also many private collectors, those seeking natural specimens as household ornaments, and a booming millinery trade in bird feathers. The scale of the business of natural history was immense. Up to 1906, 48 different individuals and organisations had supplied specimens to the bird collection of the British Museum, whilst the National Museum of Natural History (the "Smithsonian") in Washington DC acquired from Australia over 500 items for its bird collection.

The mining industry

We turn our attention to how these questions – what motivated a useful knowledge approach and how science, technology and production interacted to facilitate cost-effective production in resource industries – played out in a key Australian resource, mining. Coal was mined within a decade of British settlement near Newcastle and, today, coal and iron ore are Australia's largest export earners. The principal mineral booms before Federation were copper in South Australia in the 1840s, gold in Victoria in the 1850s, gold in Queensland in the 1860s, silver and lead in New South Wales in the 1880s, copper in Tasmania in the 1880s and gold in Western Australia in the 1890s.

The earliest exploitation of coal was unsurprisingly driven by local needs – cooking, heating and the manufacture of simple metal implements. The knowledge source could be traced back to Britain where coal mining had been the major primary industry. Copper's properties of malleability, anti-corrosion, thermal conductivity, both in pure form and as an alloy, meant it was valued for a wide range of uses from cooking pots to sheathing the hulls of wooden vessels. Again, the British tradition of copper mining and manufacture would have encouraged the search for value in Australia. Gold was somewhat different. Its practical uses were limited but its great monetary value was well known. This value was largely realised through export rather than deployment into local and subsistent needs. Like wool, the market was apparently endless. Blainey (1970) has argued that the search for gold was often motivated by a downturn in other trades. The interaction with the pastoral frontier was clear – gold booms diverted labour and capital from wool production. Moreover, the relative price of gold motivated technical change as companies sought more efficient methods of extracting difficult veins.

The mid-nineteenth-century market for mining technology had become highly internationalised. Australian prospectors drew widely upon practice and research initiated in Europe or North America. The 1840s Californian gold rushes heightened interest in searching for gold elsewhere. The discovery of gold in Victoria in 1851 motivated a rush across the Pacific by prospectors from many countries, which doubled Australia's population. They brought with them the knowledge required for the simple panning techniques in the search by individuals for alluvial gold. Within a few years, these easily accessible sources had been largely exhausted and more complex and capital intensive techniques were required for quartz and deeper underground mining. Very quickly the means of acquiring and applying that knowledge shifted from the informal and personal to mediation through corporations and knowledge institutions. Mining equipment and servicing firms grew up in and around Melbourne, utilising their proximity to address the new technological needs of the miners. By 1864 three large foundries had established close to the goldfields boom town of Ballarat (the Victoria Railway Foundry, the Phoenix Foundry Company and the Soho Foundry), which produced pumping, puddling, winding and stamping gear together with stationary engines (Linge 1979, pp. 189–190).

The technology of quartz-crushing was largely European in origin but was adapted for Australian purposes (Menghetti 2005). This appears to be an important feature of knowledge application in Australian mining – the willingness to experiment with and modify off-the-shelf technology acquired from the international market. Indeed, corporate failure sometimes resulted where technology was imported without careful consideration of its appropriateness to Australian conditions and the process for adaptation and modification.

Colonial Australians, while drawing upon international innovations, increasingly provided their own solutions to the challenges of extracting minerals from the ground and converting them into an economically beneficial form. Historians have described examples of these improved local knowledge capabilities including the Hancock jig to treat low-grade copper ores, Ullrich's magnetic separator to recover lead and zinc from sulphide ore concentrates, and the flotation process for separating minerals from their ores, which were all domestically generated and additionally exported for use in other mining nations (Magee 2015; Menghetti 2005; Mouat 1996).

The pressure for continued success in gold prospecting and supported by investors on the London Stock Exchange, motivated institutional advances particularly the introduction of the no-liability mining company in Victoria from 1871. The latter, an apparently unique innovation in Australia, encouraged experimentation in new untried methods by removing investors from any further liability on a partly paid-up share in the case of the firm going bankrupt. A rush to incorporation produced 1000 mining companies in Bendigo by the end of 1871 (Blainey 1963, pp. 75–76). However, most miners remained small with limited resources and expertise until the Broken Hill (New South Wales) boom of 1887–8, which attracted significant inter-colonial investment providing the resources and connections to enable firms to undertake significant sustained investment in experimentation. BHP (Broken Hill Proprietaries) built up in-house technological capabilities by hiring engineers and metallurgists to follow through on the imaginative strategies of its leaders, particularly Essington Lewis and G.G. Delprat. They paid high salaries to American mining engineers such as William Patton which enabled the firm to dominate the building and operation of concentrating mills and smelting plants (Ville 1998). Menghetti (2005, p. 216) has argued that Australian conditions were propitious for innovations by locally domiciled foreign mining scientists and engineers suggesting innovators faced less bureaucratic and technocratic obstacles than in the USA. This is supported by the econometric interrogation of Victorian patent data by Magee who concludes that "in the mining industry foreign technology ... worked to complement and stimulate local inventive activity" (Magee 2000, p. 119).

Alongside the growth of corporate intermediation came the expanding role of quasi-public bodies focused on education and research. By the later nineteenth century, scientific advances and a greater commitment of formal science to the exploitation of natural resources were providing benefits. New scientific knowledge and technical equipment enabled a more effective geological mapping of the environment. Systematic searching for minerals was crucial for the continued growth of Australia as a major producer and exporter of minerals. Geological surveys were formed in each colony (Victoria 1852, Queensland 1868, South Australia 1882). Engineering tertiary courses commenced at the University of Melbourne in 1860, a professor of engineering was appointed in 1882 (W.C. Kernot) and a bachelor's degree commenced there a year later. Schools of Mines located in major mining centres were founded at Ballarat (1871) and Bendigo (1873). However, even allowing for the influx of foreign trained engineers their total numbers were small and their training focused primarily upon the civil engineering projects being built across Australia in the late nineteenth century – roads, bridges, harbours and public buildings. However, when the 1890s gold boom in Western Australia contrasted to the gloom elsewhere in the economy, mining engineering emerged as an important new specialisation and the Australasian Institute of Mining and Metallurgy was established in 1893. The number of newly qualified engineering graduates only expanded to significant numbers after World War I (Edelstein 1989, pp. 276–297).

Norway

Norway's economic development during the nineteenth century was more problematic than that of Australia. Maddison's calculations indicate that Norway's productivity level (GDP per capita) in 1890 was among the lowest in Europe. Norway did not experience an abundance of natural resources, but rather resource scarcity. High population growth until 1870 critically challenged the old industries' – agriculture, fisheries, forestry and mining – role as a foundation for social welfare and economic development. Large parts of the rural population left home and many migrated to America, with more than 800,000 people leaving Norway before World War I. As a percentage of the population only

Ireland experienced a higher emigration of the European countries. The situation during the "Long Depression" resembled a resource curse – specialisation in natural resources combined with low economic growth and social problems.

Norway remained an NRBE during the twentieth century by the end of which she had one of the world's highest GDP per capita. This was the result of a qualitative change in natural resource based industries (Wicken 2009). The old NRBIs became transformed into new types of knowledge based production where propositional knowledge became central. It was characterised by the emergence of knowledge organisations which enabled innovation and increased efficiency in old industries, but also supported the development of new NRBI (Ville and Wicken 2013). The transformation took place in a relatively short period of time (c. 1890–1920) but was possible because of the long term build-up of belief in useful knowledge, and systematic development of organisations and institutions that promoted this type of knowledge.

The belief in useful knowledge

We start from the attempts to create a belief in the role of useful knowledge for economic development from the late eighteenth century. The focus is on an elite movement which promoted systematic collection of data and observations of local natural environment, codifying the data, and diffusing it to potential users. This movement became of political importance during the formative years of the Norwegian state, and as part of the independence movement to break away from the union of Denmark during the Napoleonic Wars. When Norway got its constitution in 1814 and entered a political union with Sweden (until 1905) the elites promoting the role of propositional knowledge became part of the national state establishment (Bjerke 2008).

The point of departure for the movement was the perception that there was a large potential for exploiting the natural environment to increase production in old industries and to establish new production. The Norwegian economy contained small scale production units owned by individuals and families, with most of the population living in rural areas. Farming was the main occupation, often combined with income from other sources (fishing, forestry, shipping), or other local services. There was a tradition of localism and collective industrial activities, reflecting social capital (Thue 1994). The old production system was not static; in all natural resource industries small improvements occurred. People experimented with using the environment to improve the welfare of the household or for commercial transactions. However, there were limitations in the ability to manipulate the environment for economic purposes, and the economy often entered into setbacks and crisis due to changes in the natural environment.

The emerging movement to promote useful knowledge argued that a close relationship existed among useful knowledge, economic growth and social welfare. They regarded technology as applied science and technology was seen as central to industrial development (Bjerke 2008, p. 20). The study of nature – propositional knowledge – became a driving force for technological and industrial development, and a basis for an industrial strategy where useful knowledge was central. The movement systematically collected data on the natural environment to detect how nature can form a basis for industrial production. In addition to mapping the environment, the elite movement searched for "best practice" production methods and technologies – prescriptive knowledge. It was influenced by the "natural history" tradition of Carl von Linné, who became the leading representative in Scandinavia. This attempted to map and organise botanical, zoological and geological data – as well as data on economic and cultural practices – of specific regions.

These beliefs were not limited to a small elite. Interesting new inventions and improvements of production methods and technologies came from among farmers and peasants. Individuals with special technological skills – often called "mechanicus" – constructed new tools/equipment and machines which were used locally. Mechanical and commercial skills were widely distributed among non-educated farmers. This was recognised in competitions organised by the elite movement. They invited local farmers and non-educated people to present their own ideas for new methods and (Amdam 1985). An alternative movement promoting useful knowledge among wider social groups of the society emerged and was headed by a farmer, Hans Nielsen Hauge. Hauge wanted to show that farmers and other non-elite groups could use modern knowledge and technology to increase production and improve welfare – independent of the involvement of the elite. He used his own experiences from travelling abroad (Denmark, Sweden) to suggest changes in production technology; and to initiate new industrial activities in various parts of Norway. He suggested that coastal farmers should move from grain production to livestock (sheep); that inland farmers should move to potatoes and vegetables; proposed improvements to fertilising and irrigation systems; as well as introducing mechanisation. To illustrate the potential for improvements, he turned his farm into a model for modern farming including a grain mill and a saw mill (Breistein 1955, pp. 154, 160–163). Hauge also initiated new industrial production. An early attempt (1800) was to start a paper mill on a farm of one of his followers using a new business model based on community ownership. The national elite opposed the idea of a communal industrialisation from below, but some of his followers managed to get permission to start a paper mill. In spite of opposition from the elites, the project succeeded, and the Hauge movement soon started more paper mills, printing works, brickworks, copper mine, grain mills and saw mills (Breistein 1955, pp. 120–149).

Ideas of using new knowledge and technology to improve production and welfare were widely diffused, and not only to the elite. Useful knowledge was seen as an important aspect of the economy, social welfare and politics. This belief was a basis for the establishment of instruments to collect and diffuse useful knowledge in Norway.

Organisations and institutions for useful knowledge

One of the instruments established to collect data on local practice and the environment was competitions. The Academy of Sciences received funding from the king (state) to award prizes to the best theoretical/scientific papers written by the educated elite and best ideas and technology presented by farmers and non-educated persons. Competitions were organised by local civil servants who reported best ideas to the Academy for decision on prize winners. More prizes were given to new technologies and products than planned, at the expense of scientific papers. Agricultural societies also organised local competitions to collect data on local technologies, practices and methods of production (Amdam 1985).

A national topographical society organised the collection of data on the natural environment, where journeys were undertaken to systematically map existing species and minerals. They resulted in detailed reports which were frequently printed, often including suggestions for potential new industries or for improvements in existing practices. As there was insufficient funding for many journeys, most data collection was by civil servants and priests in various parts of the country. In Trondheim, Bishop Johan Ernst Gunnerus invited all priests in his diocese to write scientific texts about their local regions. Gunnerus also initiatied the first Academy of Science in Norway (1760). This role of the church was in line with the policy of the Danish state. It was proposed that priests could – in addition to theological studies – follow teaching in natural science and economics (Collett 2011, pp. 27–28). Some priests were linked to international scientific networks. A local priest, Jacob Nicolai Wilse, published scientific texts in Germany and became accepted as a corresponding member of the Science Society in Göttingen. Later a local priest in Western Norway, Michael Sars, published scientific texts in German and Scandinavian journals and became the first professor in zoology at the University of Oslo as already an internationally recognised scientist (Collett 2011, pp. 52, 471).

Access to the collected data, technologies and methods were controlled by the associations and societies. Most members of these organisations were civil servants and commercial traders, but the information was to a large extent directed to be used by uneducated peasants, farmers, fishermen, forestry owners and mining industrialists. While some scientific papers and descriptions of technologies appeared in newspapers or as separate publications, the main instrument for diffusion was direct contact between representatives of the elite and potential users. The local priest became a main agent of diffusion of knowledge. Priests would often receive printed material on prize winners' ideas, methods and technologies, and would inform his congregation at the Sunday sermon. Many priests promoted specific new ideas, exemplified by the introduction of potato during the last part of the eighteenth century; often nick-named "potato priests". Others illustrated the potential of using new technologies, methods and crops through local church farms. In a society where 90 per cent of the population were land owners and defined as farmers/peasants, farming was the core industry if people's welfare should be improved.

As a small society with limited resources and knowledge bases, the long-term development of the economy was dependent on transfer of knowledge and technology from abroad. Norway, in contrast to Australia, was located close to the leading economies of the nineteenth century enabling local industries to directly access new knowledge. This is well documented in mining and illustrated by the development of the silver mines in Kongsberg. The mining system was transformed over a very long period of time through incremental innovations where each part of the production system was improved (Berg 1994, p. 485). The small step strategy was based on a continuous flow of knowledge and specific technologies from other European countries. New ideas, knowledge and technology made it possible to extend the mines horizontally and vertically with the introduction of iron to strengthen old mechanical equipment and improved water power systems. The combination of improved material quality and energy supply – in addition to the use of powder – created the basis for long-term incremental innovations (Berg 1994, pp. 462, 484–485). The training and education of managers and skilled personnel in the mines gradually improved. From 1733 future managers and key personnel began visiting mines in central Europe, and the stays abroad could last for years. This was part of a socialisation process for Norwegian mining managers and skilled experts who became an integrated part of a European professional community where exchange of knowledge was a central part of practice. However, shorter travels often involved search and transfer for specific technologies. Berg concludes that "knowledge played a key role" for the long-term profitability and survival of the mines (Berg 1994, pp. 327, 465, 485).

From the nineteenth century Norwegian governments established strategies to access information on industrial-technological development in Europe (Bruland and Smith 2010). The main instrument was still travel and journeys to other countries. Funding of journeys with the intention to learn from abroad was initiated by the Danish–Norwegian government from the 1760s, and the Norwegian government continued to fund travels after independence in 1814. During the second half of the nineteenth century more than 1000 travel grants were handed out by governments, and almost 200 grants to technicians (Bruland and Smith 2010, p. 72). In addition managers, traders and skilled workers travelled around Northern Europe as part of ordinary work and training. For sons of rich traders travel was part of their training, and they often continued to visit colleagues in other countries. Export industries (timber, fish) demanded close contacts with trading companies in the main export markets and close relationships between export companies and importers in other countries emerged. Gradually, an increasing number of people received formal technical and commercial education abroad, mainly in Germany, Sweden, England and Switzerland. Norwegian managers often recruited foreigners with specific knowledge or experience to work for the company. While access to technological and commercial knowledge publications developed rapidly, for Norway journeys linked to education, work experience, trade, general or specific search for information remained central to technology and knowledge transfer.

Organisations for propositional knowledge: science-industry relations

The government also supported establishment of new organisations for promoting propositional knowledge. The first initiative was linked to the mining community. In 1757 a Mining Seminar was established inspired by the many Mining Academies in Europe. With the Academy of War (established 1750), the Mining Seminar became Norway's leading institution for technical education. The education combined theoretical (mathematics) and practical studies (mechanics, technical drawing). However, it remained limited and only 20 candidates received a diploma from the Seminar before it moved to the University of Oslo in 1814 (Myrvang 2014, p. 46). An objective of the elite movement promoting useful knowledge was to establish a university in Norway, and in 1811 Oslo University was founded. Until the second half of the century natural sciences played a minor role in the university, and there was little systematic research. The first build-up of a research group was in zoology, and closely linked to the old natural resource based industries, agriculture, forestry and fisheries (Collett 2011, p. 466). It was only after the 1860s that the university became a research oriented scientific organisation. The teaching of the Mining Academy was moved to the University, and during the second half of the nineteenth century research in various sub-disciplines of geology reached international standards. Similar developments occurred within marine biology, where Norwegian scientists became world leaders (Kyllingstad and Rørvik 2011; Schwach 2000).

In addition to this, new organisations providing relevant knowledge for natural resource industries emerged: Norwegian Geological Survey (1859), Agricultural University College (1859/1897), Ocean Research Institute (1904, precursor from 1860), Bergen Museum (geosciences from 1880s) and the Norwegian Institute of Technology (1910). The expansion of local scientific institutions did not make industries less dependent on the transfer of technology and ideas from abroad. However, they created local competence relevant for the specific challenges in local farming, fishing, mining, forestry and other natural resource industries in Norway and formed links between local industry and foreign expertise.

The scientific communities worked closely with industry to solve problems, improve productivity and production. The relationship between professors in geology and mining companies or marine biology researchers and the fishing industry involved active participation and interaction; combining theoretical studies with empirical and practical projects in close collaboration with industry. During the late nineteenth century the importance of science for economic and social development was widely accepted in society and in politics. This ideology gave direction and expectation to how scientists should contribute to national development and welfare. In mining, many companies now employed managers and skilled expertise with formal education, normally engineers. This eased communication and interaction between companies ("engineer-managers") and scientists ("professor-consultant") (Børresen 2011, p. 210; Schwach 2011, p. 391).

The active role of the scientific profession in industrial processes is illustrated by the attempts to revitalise the mining industry c.1880–1920. Many of the old mines struggled to remain competitive and profitable, and approached scientists for advice to raise efficiency and productivity. The contacts between companies and professors were often established through meetings in the field. Geology professors and researchers travelled to various parts of Norway during the summer season to undertake geological surveys, and also visited mines to collect samples for laboratory studies. Industry also approached scientists as result of publications in the media on modern mining methods. The result was a type of consultancy role of the scientist/professor; often formalised in paid reports to companies suggesting practical solutions to existing problems. Professors Johan H.L. Vogt and Waldemar C. Brøgger at the University of Oslo became leading professor-consultants in the mining industry using data from the mapping of the mineral content of ore. They developed plans for the transformation of the largest Swedish nickel mine in Klefva; and Vogt was a leading force in revitalising Norway's largest nickel mine in Evje by introducing modern Bessemer production technology. When Norway's oldest, largest and most technologically advanced mine in Røros entered into financial problems in the 1890s, Brøgger chaired a commission whose task was to assess the future of copper mining in the region. The commission suggested a radical reorganisation with new management of geological-technical experts, that is, experts educated by Brøgger and Vogt at the University of Oslo. The new management implemented many of the modernisation ideas of the commission, and the mines remained profitable for most years until the end of World War I (Børresen 2011, pp. 212–217).

The professor-consultants also played a direct role in promoting entrepreneurship in the mining industry. Vogt's active role in the revitalisation of the Evje nickel mine illustrates his ambition to support industrialisation. Similarly, Brøgger and Vogt attempted to establish a company for mining valuable minerals (marble) and cutting/polishing stone into consumer products. Inspired by observations made in Italian marble mines, the professors were commissioned by an industrialist to develop plans for the new industry. The attempt illustrates the active role of scientists in the development of natural resource industries (Børresen 2011, pp. 212–217).

A successful entrepreneurial role was played by professors and researchers in marine biology, exemplified by the establishment of the shrimp industry. The development process was linked to instruments used in mapping of marine resources. Danish marine biologists had constructed special equipment for catching plankton and small specimens in deep water living just above the bottom of the ocean, and this was used by the Norwegian scientists mapping shrimps. The mapping of shrimps in the Oslo Fiord was successful. The scientific study turned into experimental commercial fishery and systematic development of a shrimp trawl, in close collaboration with local fishermen. The main driving force of the process was Professor Johan Hjort at the University of Oslo, and he also supported the diffusion of the industry to wider parts of Norway and also internationally (Schwach 2011, pp. 390–401).

Conclusion: the institutional basis of NRBKE

In this chapter we have built on studies of the emergence of a natural resource based knowledge economy (David and Wright 1997; Ville and Wicken 2013) with strong knowledge organisations and capital goods industries (enabling sector) that established institutions to promote future industrial development. The intention of the chapter is to look at how this type of economy emerged in Australia and Norway during the nineteenth century. Our approach is to follow processes that supported the build-up of knowledge capabilities. Based on the concept of useful knowledge, we observed three types of processes: those that promoted the belief in useful knowledge as the basis for improving welfare and creating a "good society"; those that promoted organisations and institutions to gain access to useful knowledge (technology transfer); and those which promoted new scientific and technological (propositional) knowledge, and its interaction with industrial actors (university-industry relations). In both cases a section on the mining industry provides some depth and focus to the broader story.

Both countries experienced similar type of processes until the early twentieth century, but the specifics of each process varied due to differences in local contexts. In the late eighteenth century Norway was an established Western society; British immigration to Australia had just started. Norway was located close to the leading economies of the period; Australia was distant to the emerging industrial economy of Northern Europe. Australia experienced a natural environment with resource abundance which became the basis for world leading productivity of the economy; Norway from the late nineteenth century struggled to create an economic basis for a growing population due to resource scarcity. The emerging knowledge economy is reflected in the differences. The belief in useful knowledge was promoted differently, but still in an efficient way which gradually came to permeate the whole society. Technology transfer was important for both countries, but Australia was more dependent on technologies adapted to the local environment. Australia's relatively limited population could prosper by expanding and improving efficiency in established NRBI. Norway's economic future was dependent on a more radical transformation of old industries (forestry into pulp and paper) and the creation of new natural resources (transforming waterfalls into hydropower). The output was the establishment of knowledge organisations and institutions adapted to support local NRBI to increase production, improve production efficiency and create new natural resource industries. We therefore argue that the processes we studied should be seen as the institutional foundation for long-term growth and development in natural resource based economies.

Notes

1 Propositional knowledge is regarded as wider than what is normally defined as science, and includes both (1) observation, classification, measurement and cataloging of natural phenomena; and (2) natural laws that govern the phenomena observed and described.

2 The role of belief in useful knowledge: "[T]he beginning of modern economic growth depended a great deal on what people knew and believed, and how those beliefs affected economic behavior" (Mokyr 2009, p. 1).

References

Amdam, R.P., 1985. *Den organiserte jordbrukspatriotismen 1769–1790 – en jorbruksreformistisk reformrørsle?* Masters Thesis. University of Oslo.

Berg, B.I., 1994. *Gruveteknikk ved Kongsberg Sølvverk 1623–1914*, Kongsberg: Norsk Bergverkmuseum.

Bjerke, E., 2008. *Uavhengighet gjennom vitenskap. Naturhistorien som økonomisk og politisk redskap I opplysningstidens Danmark og Norge*, Masters Thesis. University of Oslo.

Blainey, G., 1963. *The Rush that Never Ended: A History of Australian Mining*, Melbourne: Melbourne University Press.

Blainey, G., 1970. A theory of mineral discovery: Australia in the nineteenth century. *The Economic History Review*, 23(2), pp. 298–313.

Børresen, A.K., 2011. *Bergtatt. Johan H.L. Vogt. Professor, rådgiver, familiemann*, Trondheim: Tapir Akademisk Forlag.

Breistein, D., 1955. *Hans Nielsen Hauge. "Kjøbmand i Bergen". Kristen tro og økonomisk aktivitet*, Bergen: John Griegs Forlag.

Bruland, K. and Smith, K., 2010. Knowledge flows and catching-up industrialization in the Nordic countries. In H. Odagiri et al., eds. *Intellectual Property Rights, Development, and Catch-Up*, Oxford: Oxford University Press.

Butlin, N.G., 1993. *Economics and the Dreamtime: A Hypothetical History*, Cambridge: Cambridge University Press.

Collett, J.P., 2011. Universitetet I Oslo 1811–1870: Universitet I nasjonen. In J.P. Collett et al., eds. *Universitetet i Oslo 1811–2011*, Oslo: Unipub.

Coote, A., 2014. "Pray write me a list of Species ... that will pay me best": The business and culture of natural history collecting in mid-nineteenth century New South Wales. *History Australia*, 11(2).

David, P.A. and Wright, G., 1997. Increasing returns and the genesis of American resource abundance. *Industrial and Corporate Change*, 6(2), pp. 203–245.

Edelstein, M., 1989. Professional engineers and the Australian economy, 1866–1980. In D. Pope and L. Alston, eds. *Australia's Greatest Asset*, Annandale: The Federation Press.

Hunter, B., 2015. The Aboriginal legacy. In S. Ville and G. Withers, eds. *Cambridge Economic History of Australia*, Cambridge, MA: Cambridge University Press.

Inkster, I. and Todd, J., 1988. Support for the scientific enterprise, 1850–1900. In R.W. Home, ed. *Australian Science in the Making*, Melbourne: Melbourne University Press.

Keen, S., 1999. Associations in Australian history: Their contribution to social capital. *Journal of Interdisciplinary History*, 29(4), pp. 639–659.

Kuznets, S., 1965. *Economic Growth and Structure: Selected Essays*, New York: Heinemann.

Kyllingstad, J.R. and Rørvik, T.I., 2011. Vitenskapenes universitet 1870–1911. In J.P. Collett, ed. *Universitetet i Oslo 1811–2011*, Oslo: Unipub.

Linge, G.J.R., 1979. *Industrial Awakening: A Geography of Australian Manufacturing 1788 to 1890*, Canberra: Australian National University Press.

Madsen, J., 2015. Australian economic growth and its drivers since European settlement. In S. Ville and G. Withers, eds. *Cambridge Economic History of Australia*. Cambridge, MA: Cambridge University Press.

Magee, G.B., 1998. The face of invention: Skills, experience, and the commitment to patenting in nineteenth-century Victoria. *Australian Economic History Review*, 38(3), pp. 232–257.

Magee, G.B., 2000. *Knowledge Generation: Technological Change and Economic Growth in Colonial Australia*, Melbourne: Australian Scholarly Publishing.

Magee, G.B., 2015. Technological change. In S. Ville and G. Withers, eds. *Cambridge Economic History of Australia*, Cambridge, MA: Cambridge University Press.

McLean, I.W., 1982. The demand for agricultural research in Australia, 1870–1914. *Australian Economic Papers*, 21(39), pp. 294–308.

Menghetti, D., 2005. Invention and innovation in the Australian non-ferrous mining industry: Whose technology? *Australian Economic History Review*, 45(2), pp. 204–219.

Meredith, D. and Oxley, D., 2015. The convict economy. In S. Ville and G. Withers, eds. *Cambridge Economic History of Australia*, Cambridge, MA: Cambridge University Press.

Mokyr, J., 2002. *The Gifts of Athena: Historical Origins of the Knowledge Economy*, Princeton: Princeton University Press.

Mokyr, J., 2009. *The Enlightened Economy: An Economic History of Britain, 1700–1850*, New Haven, CT: Yale University Press.

Mouat, J., 1996. The development of the flotation process: Technological change and the genesis of modern mining, 1898–1911. *Australian Economic History Review*, 36(1), pp. 3–36.

Myrvang, C., 2014. *Troskap og flid. Kongsberg Våpenfabrikks historie 1814–1945*, Oslo: Pax Forlag.

Raby, G., 1996. *Making Rural Australia: An Economic History of Technical and Institutional Creativity, 1788–1860*, Oxford: Oxford University Press.

Schedvin, C.B., 1987. *Shaping Science and Industry: A History of Australia's Council for Scientific and Industrial Research 1926–49*, Sydney: Allen & Unwin.

Schwach, V., 2000. *Havet, fisken og vitenskapen. Fra fiskeriundersøkelser til havforskningsinstitutt 1860–2000*, Bergen: Havforskningsinstituttet.

Schwach, V., 2011. *Til havs med vitenskapen. Fiskerrettet havforskning 1860–1970*, Ph.D. Thesis dissertation, Faculty of Humanities, University of Oslo.

Sokoloff, K.L. and Khan, B.Z., 1990. The democratization of invention during early industrialization: Evidence from the United States, 1790–1846. *The Journal of Economic History*, 50(2), pp. 363–378.

Thue, L., 1994. *Statens Kraft 1890–1947. Kraftutbygging og samfunnsutbygging*, Oslo: J.W. Cappelen.

Ville, S., 1998. Business development in colonial Australia. *Australian Economic History Review*, 38(1), pp. 16–41.

Ville, S. and Wicken, O., 2013. The dynamics of resource-based economic development: Evidence from Australia and Norway. *Industrial and Corporate Change*, 22(5), pp. 1341–1371.

White, C.M., 1992. *Mastering Risk: Environment, Markets and Politics in Australian Economic History*, Oxford: Oxford University Press.

Wicken, O., 2009. The layers of national innovation systems: The historical evolution of a national innovation system in Norway. In J. Fagerberg, D.C. Mowery and

B. Verspagen, eds. *Innovation, Path Dependency and Policy: The Norwegian Case*, Oxford: Oxford University Press.

Wright, G., 1990. The origins of American industrial success, 1879–1940. *The American Economic Review*, 80(4), pp. 651–668.

Wright, G. and Czelusta, J., 2004. Why economies slow: The myth of the resource curse. *Challenge*, 47(2), pp. 6–38.

15 Avoiding the resource curse?
Democracy and natural resources in Norway since 1900

Andreas R. Dugstad Sanders and Pål Thonstad Sandvik

Introduction

When scholars discuss the "resource curse", oil-rich Norway is often portrayed as one of the few outliers that somehow escaped the curse. After Philips Petroleum discovered oil on the Norwegian continental shelf in 1969, the country's economy has surged past its Nordic neighbours. Yet Norway seems to have largely avoided or at least limited the "Dutch Disease". The profitable oil and gas sector has not crowded out all other export industries. Moreover, Norway has not experienced a marked increase in corruption or had its political system replaced by an autocratic regime or a self-serving oligarchy, a fate that has befallen so many other petro states.

In order to learn from this apparent success story, scholars have sought to identify a set of key factors that have turned Norway from being "resource cursed" to "resource blessed". A recurring factor has been the country's sound macroeconomic policies after the oil boom, and particularly the decision to hoard much of the petro earnings into a sovereign wealth fund, which at the time of writing stands at a mind-boggling US$175,000 per capita.[1] Some, like Maloney (2007), have highlighted the importance of human capital. This meant that the country was better able to reap the full benefits of the resource boom than many other resource rich countries, while also providing the foundation for a more diversified economy. Perhaps the most popular explanation, fronted by a wide range of scholars, put this success down to the pre-existence of democracy and "high quality institutions" when oil was discovered in 1969.[2]

Norway offers an excellent case study for how a democratic resource rich nation has dealt with resource abundance. Not only has Norway has been a stable democracy for well over a century, but its economy relied on natural resources long before North Sea oil. While we agree with the notion that good institutions and a well-functioning democracy have contributed greatly to Norwegian success, it is in our view a somewhat blunt and deterministic simplification, that obfuscates the importance of Norwegian resource policies. High quality institutions do not automatically generate good resource policies. Nor do they explain the content and the outcomes of those policies. They can vary considerably between different countries, even between countries with sound institutions.

When oil was discovered, Norwegian politicians had more than 50 years of experience with comprehensive regulation of natural resources. Norwegian politicians had by that time already faced many of the challenges which are common to all countries with large natural resource sectors, including how to control foreign investment, how to secure and distribute (parts of) the resource rent, how to respond to income volatility, how to increase economic spill-over effects and economic diversity, etc.

This chapter examines the development of the Norwegian regulatory regime for natural resources. What have been the key political aims and how have they changed over time, e.g. in times of high economic volatility? Last, but not least, what results have been achieved?

We begin our account at the resource booms during the turn of the twentieth century, when the nation state became the central regulator of access and ownership of natural resources. From this point onwards, we trace a continuity in Norwegian natural resource policy, marked by a willingness to rely on natural resources for economic growth, despite the sometimes volatile nature of the sector. This willingness to rely on natural resources has been combined with strong, but pragmatic and adaptable, resource nationalism. The rents from the country's natural resources have played an important part in funding the Norwegian welfare state, which has reinforced popular support for an active role for the state in the natural resource sector.

The rise of state regulation

To properly understand the Norwegian debates on resource regulation at the beginning of the twentieth century we need to take into account the broader backdrop of the country's political and economic development. By 1900, Norway had developed strong democratic traditions. The country's liberal constitution from 1814 had granted around 40 per cent of adult men the right to vote; in 1898 the franchise was extended to all men, and in 1913 also to all women. The population was well educated. As a small country depending on access to world markets Norway supported free trade. However, as the following pages will show, commitment to laissez faire was clearly weakening. Norwegian politicians and the electorate had a strong belief in the benevolent potential of state regulation. The state bureaucracy was generally perceived as honest and competent and it enjoyed a high degree of popular legitimacy.

An oft repeated misrepresentation is that Norway was one of the poorest countries in Europe at the beginning of the twentieth century. Indeed, Norwegian GDP per capita was significantly less than the more prosperous parts of Europe, such as Great Britain and the Netherlands. But according to Angus Maddison Norway was more prosperous than Italy, Spain and Eastern Europe (Maddison 2010) (Figure 15.1). However, the country was probably more egalitarian than most, if not all, other European countries. The mid-income social groups were relatively larger, and the under and upper classes smaller than other places.

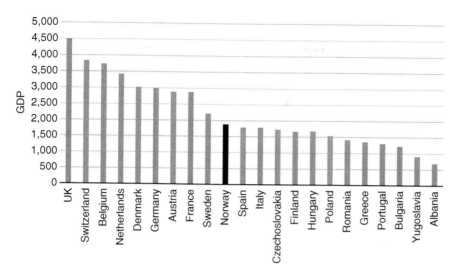

Figure 15.1 GDP per capita in Europe, 1900 (source: Maddison 2010).

Fish and forestry products accounted for more than half of Norwegian exports around 1900, while the non-resource based shipping industry accounted for much of the remaining. The country also had a rather diverse industrial sector. While the industry expanded at a brisk pace in the late nineteenth century, it was not as large or sophisticated as in neighbouring Sweden.

The fisheries were dominated by independent fishermen, who owned their own boats and equipment. This rather egalitarian structure was to some degree supported and protected by state policies, i.e. by granting subsidized loans to fishermen. Resource rents (which were rather modest) were thus widely spread. Forestry was less egalitarian. While much of the forests was owned by farmers, substantial tracts of forests were also owned by big forestry companies (Sogner and Christensen 2001; Sandvik 2007). Timberjacks tended to be relatively poor. In forestry, conflicts over resource rent emerged in the late 1890s, between farmers and forestry companies, in the following decades also between timberjacks and the owners of the forests.

At the turn of the century, the country experienced a boom in a set of new resources. The numerous waterfalls flowing down from the high mountain plateaus became a potential source for cheap and abundant hydroelectricity, which served as a vital input to the burgeoning electro-chemical industries (Figure 15.2).[3] New technology and increased demand also revived the Norwegian mining industry. Norwegian pyrites, which had long been an ore for the country's copper industry, became a source for sulphur for the European chemical industries (Hodne 1981, pp. 356–357). However, both the mining and the hydroelectric industry were very capital intensive. Thus, mining and electro-chemical industries were mostly financed and owned by non-Norwegian investors (Stonehill 1965, pp. 33–41).

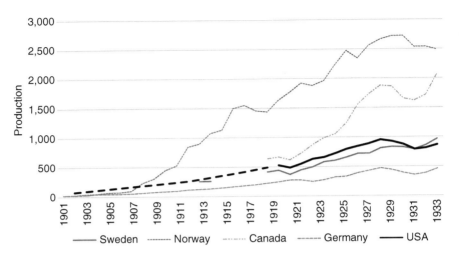

Figure 15.2 Electricity production per capita (kwh) (source: Etemad and Luciani 1991; Maddison 2010).

Note
The dotted line signifies an estimated kw per capita, based on the data for 1902, 1912 and 1917, as the source does not provide continuous annual data for electricity production in the US before 1920.

The rapid growth in the new industries and the influx of foreign investment caused some apprehension in Norway. The increasing level of foreign ownership proved especially controversial. Anecdotes of how foreign capitalists had undermined countries' sovereignty in Spain and Transvaal abounded. Even for the less fatalistic, it seemed that much of the country's natural wealth would benefit rich foreigners. As many of these new industries were located in remote places with little previous settlement, the foreigners could not only reap high profits, but perhaps also act as local lords over resource enclaves. As to hydroelectric resources, there was also the fear that a foreign owned company could monopolize power resources, and then earn excessive profits by selling electricity to Norwegian households and small-scale industry. On the other hand, it was widely acknowledged that the new resource industries brought new opportunities and jobs to the rapidly growing population, which might entice many of those who left for the New World to instead consider a future in the mother country (Annaniassen 1983, pp. 184–189; Dugstad 2011, pp. 12–24).

These concerns would in 1906 result in a set of concession laws, which introduced radical new legislation on natural resource ownership. By the end of 1906, all acquisitions of riparian rights, mineral claims or forested lands by foreigners or joint stock companies were subject to a government concession. But the government rarely blocked any foreign appropriation of riparian rights or mineral claims. Instead it soon became government policy to set terms to concessions. While this option was not initially specified in the law, it served as a useful compromise between the desire for economic growth through further foreign direct investment and the desire for some sort of government control (Annaniassen 1983, pp. 23–24).

The concession terms were designed to serve several purposes.[4] One of them was to restrict the power of the large resource companies, both towards their workers and the communities where they operated. This included regulations that secured housing and essential welfare requirements for the workers and their families. Power companies also had to provide a certain amount of cheap power (usually about 10 per cent of their production) to the local municipality. This was to ensure that power companies did not exploit their local monopoly, and to provide cheap power for households and small-scale businesses. The concession law also set time limits for when a company had to commence and complete a hydropower development. This limited the ability of a company to acquire resources as a speculative investment or to lay a dead hand on resources to prevent them from ending up in the hands of competitors.

The concession terms were also designed to increase rent capture from the resource industries. In order to increase the spill-over effects from the resource industries, the new concessions laws demanded that the companies used Norwegian-made machines and materials, provided that they didn't cost more than 10 per cent more than similar foreign products. The companies had to use Norwegian workers and managers. Later, the Norwegian government also introduced special concession taxes.

The most controversial concession clause was undoubtedly the so-called *right of reversion.*[5] This clause stated that that hydropower plants and mines would pass to the state after a set number of years (usually between 60 and 80) without remuneration. Inspired by similar laws in Switzerland,[6] the right of reversion would ensure that foreign ownership over the country's richest resources would not be permanent. It was thought that this would have little or no negative effect on the levels of investments, as investors did not operate with time frames of more than half a century. Thus, Norwegians would prevent permanent foreign ownership and eventually reap the benefits of cheap public-owned hydropower in perpetuity. However, detractors claimed that having a time limit on mining concessions would encourage mining companies to exhaust mines before they reverted to the state. More importantly, they saw it as a gross breach of established property rights and even the Norwegian constitution.

Foreign-owned companies were the main target of the concession laws, but the laws also applied to Norwegian-owned companies. The Norwegian government initially sought to differentiate between foreign- and domestic-owned companies. But when the first permanent concession law was passed in 1909, the Norwegian government opted for a principle of equal treatment (Haaland 1995, pp. 63–76). Only Norwegian municipalities and the state were exempt from the laws. It was difficult for the Norwegian government to control who owned the shares of a company at any given time, or if foreign investors used Norwegian straw-men (Mjeldheim 2006, p. 91; Dugstad 2011, p. 17). The equal treatment of domestic and foreign investors also reflected that natural resources were perceived as a common good, and the benefits should be shared and regulated in the interests of the society at large no matter the nationality of the owners.

The dual desire to restrict foreign ownership and prevent any private monopolization was also reflected in the concession laws for forests passed between 1906 and 1909. In contrast to the energy intensive industries and mining, the Norwegian forestry industry was less dependent on foreign capital. Consequently, unlike more liberal laws on hydropower and mining, the forest law prohibited any further purchases of forests by companies that could not prove that all its shares were owned by Norwegian citizens. However, this did not prevent foreign-owned companies from keeping the forests they had obtained before the law was passed. The law also contained clauses aimed to prevent single owners from becoming too dominant in one region, and to prohibit the sale of forests owned by local farmers to non-residents. In a parallel development, in 1908 trawlers were not allowed to fish in Norwegian coastal waters in order to protect Norwegian fishermen (and fish stocks) from foreign-owned trawlers (Christensen and Hallenstvedt 2005, pp. 103–115). In short, it became government policy to support the existing small-scale producers' access to natural resources that could be extracted by less capital-intensive means. For the resources which required more capital, the government would allow new big – mostly foreign-owned – companies to operate, if they would submit to the government's terms.

Consequences of the concession laws

The country's political economy was utterly transformed during the resource boom of the early twentieth century. With the concession laws state interventionism in the economy increased at an unprecedented rate, which came with a whole new set of challenges.

As the concession laws were enabling laws, which allowed the government to differentiate from case to case, they could in theory have become breeding grounds for nepotism, preferential treatment and corruption. Indeed, the Norwegian concession laws did come to benefit those who knew how to work the political system, and provided many well-paid opportunities for the small segment of Norwegian business lawyers (Dugstad 2011, p. 49). However, there is no evidence of graft in the source material. Concession negotiations between government and companies were channelled through bodies consisting of civil servants and a selection of politicians of all major parties in parliament. The largest hydropower concessions even needed parliamentary approval, in full view of the country's press. In other words, Norwegian concession policy was subject to considerable democratic oversight, a fact that minimized the opportunities for corruption.

The democratic openness was not a perfect shield against rent seeking. Factions could exploit the public concession debates in parliament in order to increase the public rent capture beyond what had been agreed between the investing company and the government. The clearest case of this was a concession to the British-owned fertilizer company *AS Aura* in 1913, where the powerful farmer faction of the Liberal Party managed to include a clause that compelled the company to sell cheap fertilisers (10 per cent below export prices) to Norwegian farmers.[7]

The somewhat arbitrary nature of the concession process was softened by a continuous desire by governments and civil service to provide a predictable concession policy. The laws of 1909 and 1917 gave a list of terms a concessionaire would be subject to, and what other terms the government could demand. Concession taxes were also given a minimum and a maximum rate. In addition, the concession law was not applied retroactively. This meant that all mines, hydropower plants and forests developments that had taken place before the laws were introduced in 1906 were not subject to the concession laws. There were also no forced renegotiations of existing concessions.[8] In some respect, this gave an "unfair" advantage to the first movers. But it was considered necessary for the credibility of the system that the investors could trust that the concession terms they accepted were final.

It is also important to bear in mind that the resources of the early twentieth century boom in Norway were not of the kind most typically associated with the resource curse. Nor were they on a scale that would easily lead to Dutch Disease effects. The Norwegian mining industry was mostly based on pyrites or low grade iron ore. These ores usually required substantial downstream processing to make them into sulphur, copper or iron concentrates. In other words, they were not the easily exploitable high windfall resources most commonly associated with the resource curse. The type of the resources ensured in part that much of the resource rent would spread windfalls to the rest of the economy.

The preferences for Norwegian-made machinery and material naturally spurred growth in the electro-technical industries. These industries were not developed from scratch, but output as well as technological sophistication increased at dizzying speed from around 1910 (Christensen and Rinde 2009, p. 55). Thus, the concession laws modestly increased technological spill-over, and helped diversify the Norwegian economy.[9] As Norway was already a rather developed country with a well-educated population and broad, if not very advanced, industrial sector, it was well situated to make use of such measures.

It is more difficult to assess how the concession laws affected economic growth. From when the first concession laws were passed in 1906 until the outbreak of the First World War, most investors seem to have accepted the government's terms, and investment in the resource intensive industries remained high (Lange 1977; Annaniassen 1983). However, the interwar era came to usher in a very different situation for the Norwegian resource industries. They were hit hard by the post-war depression, and would continue to struggle for much of the interwar period. Foreign investments fell dramatically. Many contemporaries came to blame the concession laws for having scared off foreigners and stifled investments with stringent rules and unreasonable taxes (Keilhau 1938, pp. 139–158).

While one should not take accusations of the opponents of the concession laws at face value, resource policy remained a challenge for Norwegian politicians throughout the interwar era. In particular, it was difficult for the regulators to know exactly what demands they could and should make to strike a desired balance between rent capture and investments. In hindsight, it is clear that Norwegian politicians and the public at large came to overestimate the value of Norwegian resources, and hydropower in particular. The First World War only augmented this trend. Aided by enormous profits from wartime shipping as well as a boom in energy intensive industries, the war saw the creation of the first large private Norwegian-owned metallurgical companies. In addition, Norwegian investors bought some of the country's largest foreign-owned industrial companies. This intensified calls to differentiate between Norwegian-owned companies and foreign-owned companies. When the concession law was reworked in 1917, the new law stated that foreign-owned companies would only be allowed to obtain hydropower in "singular circumstances".

At the same time, public investment in natural resources accelerated. Between 1917 and 1920, the Norwegian government bought a half-finished hydropower plant, a number of waterfalls, the country's largest unworked pyrite claim, as well as large forest tracts. The government not only wanted to secure Norwegian ownership over the resources, but it also believed that the investments would be profitable (Thue 2006, p. 322). Norwegian municipalities also spent enormous sums on power generation projects, expecting great demand for power in the immediate future (Thue 2003).

The euphoria surrounding Norwegian natural resources collapsed with the onset of the post-war depression in 1920. In Norwegian historiography the 1920s is known as the "lost decade", due to a series of economic problems (Hodne and Grytten 2002, p. 116). Besides a general downturn in all the resource-heavy industries, the Norwegian competitive advantage of cheap hydropower was substantially reduced. Before the war, much of the hydropower acquired by foreign investors had been obtained for the production of nitrates.[10] However, the war had proved the viability of BASF's new ammonia process (Haber-Bosch), which required significantly less energy than alternative processes (Haber 1971, p. 203; Leigh 2004). This made cheap electricity less of an all-decisive factor, and most of the nitrate works planned in Norway before the war were never completed. The reduced competitiveness for the energy intensive industries in Norway was further exacerbated by the fact that the war had proved that nitrate production, as well as aluminium, the other big energy intensive growth industry in Norway, were industries of great strategic importance. After the war, several of the former belligerents took action to secure domestic production of nitrates and aluminium, often effectively shutting out Norwegian production (Andersen 2005, p. 270; Storli 2010, pp. 148–149).

The combined effects of the post-war depression, competition from the new ammonia process and increased protectionism hit the resource industries hard, especially the Norwegian-owned companies. Many were practically bankrupt and had to be refinanced. The government's investments in hydropower, mines and forests also turned into expensive failures. The downturn was a stark reminder of how vulnerable the country's natural resource based exports were to changes in the international economy. With hindsight, it is clear that the allure of high rents led to a disproportionate allocation of capital to natural resources from both the private and public sector. Many of the municipalities that had invested heavily in hydropower found it difficult to repay their debts (Hodne and Grytten 2002, p. 98). The problems also came to aggravate the post-war banking crises, as a number of banks suffered enormous losses on their loans to the resource industries (Knutsen 2007, p. 170; Sogner 2012, pp. 194–195).

With this in mind, it is possible to argue that in the years of resource euphoria, the country experienced minor variants of one of the symptoms of "Dutch Disease", where a profitable but volatile natural resource sector crowded out investments in other sectors. However, the problems were magnified by a deflationary monetary policy in the 1920s. The Great War was enormously disruptive to the whole international economy, in ways it would have been difficult to predict at the time. In other words, the Norwegian "lost decade" was due to a lot more than just an overreliance on natural resources.

In order to improve the situation, foreign investments were again welcomed by the government, if somewhat reluctantly (Stonehill 1965, pp. 45–55; Dugstad 2011, pp. 78–80). The ambitious nationalist resource policies of the boom days were largely abandoned, and taxes and other concession terms were lowered to ensure that reinvestments took place. The Norwegian governments of the interwar era found economic growth more important than national ownership. However, the governments' concession practice was only relaxed up to a point. There was no big reform of the concession laws, and no government dared to tamper with the *right of reversion*, which remained a fundamental principle.

It was less easy for the Norwegian governments to find appropriate concession terms for greenfield investments. These investments often had to be approved by parliament, which tended to be more nationalistic and somewhat less pragmatic towards foreign ownership than the government. A long and uncertain concession negotiation progress was part of the reason why several planned investments were scrapped in the 1920s (Sandvik and Andresen 2000, pp. 70–73; Storli 2010, pp. 185–189; Dugstad 2011, pp. 108–109).

From this evidence, it is possible to conclude that the rent seeking of the Norwegian resource policies backfired. The effect of the right of reversion and concession taxes was not as large and beneficial as originally envisioned. However, when explaining the problems in the Norwegian resource industries in the interwar era, domestic policy only played a minor role. Market conditions and technological development were more important. Within the boundaries of the concession laws, resource policy was for the most part carried out in a pragmatic fashion. But even through this pragmatic approach, the commitment to the principle of the public and democratic prerogative over natural resources prevailed. Despite the lobbying from Norwegian business leaders to wrest the authority of the laws from government and parliament over to the courts, the law remained unchanged.

The post-1945 model; state-led resource development

After the Second World War, the state came to play a much more direct role in the Norwegian economy. Norway was occupied by Germany from 1940 to 1945. While Norway suffered less destruction than most other European countries, the war still had profound effects on the Norwegian political system, government-business relations and not least the political economy of the resource based industries. The electorate was radicalized, and the Labour Party won all elections and ruled Norway from 1945 to 1965, only with a short interruption in 1963. The Labour governments believed that state planning and state led industrialization would speed up growth, help finance social reforms and thus create a fairer, more egalitarian and prosperous society. It is important to note that there were no nationalizations of domestic industries as in Great Britain or France. The Norwegian Labour Party accepted private ownership of enterprises, but it ensured that all vital parts of the economy were strongly regulated.

Natural resources, especially hydropower, played a key role in the Norwegian post-war modernization drive. The advantages of cheap and abundant hydropower were to be exploited, both to electrify the whole country, but also to expand the energy intensive electrometallurgical industries. The country's production of electricity was almost quintupled from 1946 to 1970 (Historisk statistikk 1978: Table 48) (Figure 15.3). In 1970, the metallurgical industries consumed 45 per cent of all electricity, while households consumed 30 per cent. The production of aluminium rose from 45,000 metric tons in 1950 to 520,000 tons in 1970. As global demand for aluminium rapidly expanded this was a rewarding strategy. In 1971 Norway accounted for 18 per cent of the world's primary aluminium exports (Sandvik 2008, pp. 241–247). In 1972, non-ferrous metals constituted 15.7 per cent of Norwegian exports (Historisk statistikk 1978:

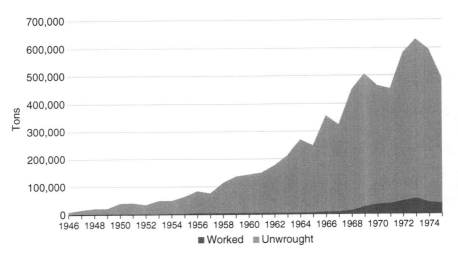

Figure 15.3 Norwegian aluminium exports, 1946–75 (tons) (source: Historisk statistikk 1978).

Table 158). In addition Norwegian output of ferro-alloys and other metallurgical products increased at a rapid rate.

The growth in electricity production was achieved without scrapping the concession laws and relinquishing the principle that the public should control the use of natural resources. Instead, the state and municipal utilities became the main producers of hydroelectric power, where the state took primary responsibility for supplying the energy intensive industries. While the private sector constructed a few new hydropower plants, they lost much of their previous significance (Skjold 2006, pp. 27–30, 41–43). Instead of seeking rent from the production of electricity, the state would now rather provide cheap power leases to entice the electrometallurgical industry to expand, and instead reap benefits from company and income taxes. Foreign-owned aluminium companies were also invited to invest in smelting plants in Norway, in joint ventures with domestic enterprises. To this day, Norwegian hydroelectricity production is almost exclusively public owned.

The post-war Labour party government did not just provide the input factors to the private sector, but it also established two large state-owned electrometallurgic companies. In 1946 the parliament unanimously decided to build a large – hydropower based – integrated steel mill in Mo i Rana in Northern Norway. This steel mill was Norway's only large example of "import substitution industrialization" and it soon became an economic failure. The export oriented state aluminium company, *ÅSV*, fared much better. At its inception in 1947 there were calls to develop a model enterprise, with sort of utopian company towns which were to embody socialist visions of a harmonious and classless society. This, however, came to nothing. With government blessing ÅSV developed into a quite hard-headed and profit oriented enterprise. Calls for creating a truly independent and vertically integrated national aluminium producer were also discarded. Instead, ÅSV focused on only one part of the value chain in which it had a competitive advantage (the electricity intensive smelting) and entered into close cooperation with the industrial behemoths Alcoa and Alcan in order to procure raw materials and market outlets. At a later date, in 1966, Alcan was allowed to acquire half the shares in ÅSV (Myrvang 1997, p. 84; Rinde 1997, pp. 132–151). For the government, the overriding aim was to generate industrial growth, other issues were of secondary importance.

Foreign-owned aluminium companies were also invited to invest in Norway, in joint ventures with domestic enterprises. As the state-owned ÅSV, the joint ventures gained access to hydropower on very advantageous terms, mainly from the state electricity company. The joint ventures were not offered the opportunity to acquire and develop hydropower resources (Skjold 2006, pp. 149–189). While the government actively sought foreign investments in industrial plants, foreign ownership of hydropower remained politically unacceptable.

The state also played an active role in the mining industry. It granted cheap credits and different types of assistance to the mining companies. In addition, the state also came to own and operate a number of mines. The state sequestrated the German-owned mining companies in 1945 (along with all other enemy property) and in the following year it acquired the British-owned Rana Gruber in order to furnish the newly established state-owned steel mill with iron ore. In addition to this, the government began exploiting its large pyrite claims, which it had acquired during the First World War. The state also invested heavily in the Spitsbergen coalfields (Anonymus 1957, pp. 109–292). The state mining enterprises seem to have been relatively efficient. However, it is worth noting that compared to hydropower, mining only had secondary importance in post-war Norway.

The fisheries followed a different trajectory from power generation and the mining industry. In the 1950s, fish still accounted for 12–15 per cent of Norwegian exports. In the post-war era the state supported a wide range of measures to increase output and productivity, restrictions on trawlers were somewhat softened, but it was still state policy to protect independent fishermen against capital intensive fishing companies (Christensen and Hallenstvedt 2005, pp. 104–115). Norway followed a much more restrictive policy on trawlers than Iceland, a Nordic country that also had bountiful fisheries (Jónsson 2009, p. 166). As we noted earlier in the case of forestry regulations, social considerations thus played a role in Norwegian resource policy.

While the resources endowments were important to the Norwegian post-war modernization effort the government also actively promoted growth outside the resource-heavy sectors. In particular, the government did its very best to foster the country's metal working and shipbuilding industries. This diversification policy was rather successful. In the 1950s and 1960s Norway's exports of industrial products rose more rapidly than exports of raw materials; the country was in other words becoming somewhat less dependent on its natural resources. In 1972 the largest resource-heavy sectors, non-ferrous metals and fish constituted 15.7 per cent and 8.2 per cent of exports respectively (Historisk statistikk 1978: Table 158). The resulting economic growth was also quite impressive, on average 4.2 per cent in 1950–1973, almost as high as the Western European average of 4.6 per cent.

Unlike in many other natural resource dependent economies, the Norwegian state did not opt for import substitution industrialization. It did not squander resource rents on fostering inefficient home market oriented industrial companies. Instead, the state did its very best to promote exports. Thus, the economy remained more outward oriented during the protectionist post-war era than in resource rich countries in Latin America and Australia (Maloney 2007, pp. 158–161).

From hydropower regulation to offshore oil and gas

In the early 1960s Norwegian authorities became aware that there might be oil and gas fields in the North Sea. While Norway did not make the same mistake as Denmark, which allocated its whole continental shelf to a single private company, it did not initially encourage Norwegian companies to invest in oil exploration. It was evident that any extraction would be capital intensive, risky and technically challenging. No domestic companies had at this point in time sufficient capital or the necessary technical capabilities. For Norwegian authorities, the overriding aim was to entice international oil companies to explore the country's continental shelf. Domestic industrial- development and ownership issues were of second priority. The initial state oil policy was in this respect quite different from its hydropower policy. All exploration licences were allotted to international oil companies. The terms were generous and tax rates were lower than in the British part of the North Sea (Ryggvik 2000, pp. 71–80; 2009, pp. 9–21).

However, one of the largest Norwegian industrial companies, Norsk Hydro, a producer of synthetic fertilizers and metallurgical products, became a junior partner in an exploration consortium consisting of French oil companies. With a stroke of luck Norsk Hydro thus became a minor shareholder in the huge Ekofisk field in 1969, the first oil discovery on the Norwegian shelf. In the following years Norsk Hydro made colossal investments (for a firm of its size) and became the first Norwegian company directly involved in the offshore oil activity (Johannessen et al. 2005, pp. 257–278, 319–332).

Ekofisk was soon followed by other discoveries. When oil prices were quadrupled in 1973 the potential resource rent from the North Sea increased spectacularly. The Norwegian negotiating position vis-à-vis the international oil companies was thus significantly improved. Simultaneously, patriotic passions ran high in Norway following the rejection of EEC membership in a plebiscite in 1972. As a result of all this, Norwegian oil policy was strongly altered in the early 1970s; it came to be more similar to the country's hallowed hydropower policies (Hanisch and Nerheim 1992, pp. 127–186).

Just as in the earlier concession laws, there was a broad political consensus that the resource rents should be secured to benefit the country at large. First of all, the state wanted stronger national control over the oil industry, both through state ownership and participation by domestic firms. It also meant a sharp increase in taxes specific to the oil industry. The total government take was increased to around 80 per cent.

A key aim of the new policy was to gain technological capabilities in oil relevant industries, including exploration, extraction, downstream processing as well as production of equipment for the offshore industry. As the Norwegian shipbuilding industry was hit by a major crisis in 1975, government increased its pressure on the oil companies to use domestic subcontractors. The nascent Norwegian oil-supply industry expanded strongly in the following years, to a large extent helped by protectionist measures (Hanisch and Nerheim 1992, pp. 188–264; 1996, pp. 74–122).

State ownership of oil production was increased throughout the 1970s. In late 1970, the state increased its shareholding in Norsk Hydro from 43 per cent to 51 per cent in order to pre-empt any foreign takeover of the new oil company. Eighteen months later, in June 1972, the parliament decided unanimously to establish a fully state-owned oil company, Statoil. A somewhat similar development took place in Great Britain, where a state-owned oil company BNOC was established in 1975. In addition, the British state owned half the stocks in BP (Andersen 1993, pp. 88–94). Interestingly, Danish oil policies came to follow a quite different trajectory. After the state had assigned the whole continental shelf to a single consortium in 1963, it refrained from any intervention in the oil sector up until the early 1980s. A "buy Danish" clause was only introduced in 1981 and oil taxes (on the top of mainland taxes) in 1982 (Andersen 1993, pp. 46–49, 81–87 and 119–130). However, it must be remembered that Denmark had much less oil than Norway. Danish politicians may have chosen differently if more had been at stake.

In Norway, Statoil developed into a vertically integrated oil company and gained a dominating position within the country's petroleum industry. It had particularly strong support from the Labour Party governments (1973–81). Statoil was however organized as a limited company and had an independent management. This made Statoil stand apart from many state oil companies in OPEC countries, where there were less clear distinctions between the government administration and the state oil companies (Johnsen 1989; Ryggvik 2009, pp. 40–41).

In addition to Statoil, the new oil policy gave other Norwegian oil companies preferential access to promising oil concessions. This included the partly state-owned Norsk Hydro and to a lesser extent, the privately owned Norwegian oil company Saga Petroleum. The international oil companies were of course allowed to keep the ownership rights, which they had been allotted in the 1960s and early 1970s, but their ownership shares in new oil fields declined steadily after 1973. While the state allotted enormous values to different companies in the oil concessions, no instances of major political corruption have been uncovered. As with the earlier concession law, oil and gas concessions were handled by the parliament, and the process remained fairly transparent – especially as there were very few governments with a ruling majority after oil was discovered. The preferences for Norwegian companies – and especially Statoil – did create strong domestic vested interest in the continuation of the status quo. However, over the years Norwegian politicians showed a remarkable willingness to implement practical reforms to the regulatory regime. After the sharp increase in resource nationalism in the early 1970s, the following decades saw a series of adjustments and reforms to the Norwegian oil policy to prevent inefficiency and unwanted concentration of power.

One of the earliest major reforms was to the extent of Statoil's privileges, which had become one of the most controversial parts of Norwegian oil policy in the late 1970s and early 1980s. The state company's foremost critic was Kåre Willoch, conservative prime minister from 1981 to 1986. He feared that Statoil – with its huge future petroleum revenues – would come to dominate Norwegian society. Under his watch, and with vehement opposition from Statoil and its political allies, the privileges were scaled back. Around half of the company's share in licences in the North Sea was transferred to direct state ownership, to the so-called State's Direct Financial Interest (SDFI). While its dominance was reduced, Statoil still remained the by far largest company (measured in licences) in the Norwegian oil industry (Willoch 1990, pp. 282–305; Lie 2012, pp. 149–151).

The creation of SDFI was the Norwegian solution to a perennial problem in many petro states; namely how to keep political control over the revenue streams. SDFI was initially administered by the Ministry for Petroleum and Energy, later it was spun off as an independent holding company (Petoro). SDFI did not develop any operating capacities, but came to be regarded as a successful and efficient instrument for collecting resource rent (Ryggvik 2010, pp. 98–99).

In the late 1980s developments outside Norway instigated a new round of policy changes. The oil price collapsed in 1986, and it remained low until the late 1990s, only with a temporary spike when Saddam Hussein attacked Kuwait in 1990. With low oil prices it became evident that the Norwegian oil companies and subcontractors were less cost efficient than their best foreign competitors, thus wasting the resource rent. Protectionism was softened and competition increased. In the 1990s foreign oil companies gained an increasing share of new licences, especially in the northernmost parts of the Norwegian continental shelf (Lie 2005, 2012, pp. 153–154).

The ongoing European integration also had a major impact on Norwegian oil policy. Norwegian EU membership was rejected in a 1994 plebiscite, but it did join the free trade European Economic Area (EEA). This meant that all remaining protectionist measures in the oil industry had to be scrapped.[11] It is difficult to say exactly how important the protectionism had been for the development of the domestic oil supply industry. What is clear is that the Norwegian oil supply industry continued to prosper after the markets were opened for foreign competition, expanding abroad as well as at home.

The state also changed its relationship with Statoil in order to improve the company's efficiency. In the 1980s the British government privatized the state-owned BNOC and sold its shares in BP (Andersen 1993, pp. 130–144). And while neo-liberal ideology was much weaker in Norway, public confidence in the economic efficiency of Statoil was nevertheless eroded, not the least due to some massive cost overruns on some of its large investment projects. In 2001, the company was partly privatized, that is, the government sold 33 per cent of the shares to private investors. The aim was not to raise capital for state coffers (which were quite full), but to make Statoil more competitive by introducing "stock market discipline". When shares were first traded, the government stated that it would not interfere in the company's activities. Statoil was to be run as an ordinary profit oriented oil company. In comparison, the partially privatized Brazilian company, Petrobras, continued to play a political role.[12] In Norway state majority ownership was thus adjusted to – or rather combined with – a more open, market oriented approach. While the means had been adjusted since the 1970s, the fundamental aim of making sure that the lion's share of the oil rent came to Norwegian hands remained unchanged.

In 2007 Norsk Hydro's oil division was merged with Statoil. The merger created a national giant, controlling more than 70 per cent of the Norwegian oil production. Some years later, in 2012, Statoil had become the world's 11th largest oil company by revenue.[13] Interestingly, and in contrast to the 1970s and early 1980s, the government was not swayed by concerns about this new concentration of market power. The main motivation behind the merger was to gain more strength to expand internationally. Neither Statoil nor Norsk Hydro had so far been very successful outside the protected realm of Norwegian territorial waters (Ryggvik 2010, pp. 109–110). Time will show if the privatization and the merger will help the company gain international success.

Managing the oil economy

When oil prices spiked in 1973 Norway was in its early stages as an oil producer. While Norway was still a net importer of oil, it rapidly became clear that future oil revenues could become so formidable that they would transform the country's economy, both for better and for worse. In early 1974 the government submitted a report to parliament on how the country should manage its oil industry and its future oil wealth. The report called for a slow expansion of the oil activity. This would help Norway avoid crowding out effects on other industries and what later became known as Dutch Disease. A "rapid and uncontrolled" growth of private consumption should be avoided. The resource rents should instead be spent in ways that would develop Norway into a "society of better quality" (Norw.: *et kvalitativt bedre samfunn*), that is, on social reforms.[14]

Government awareness of the dangers of the Dutch Disease did however not shield the country from its symptoms. Despite the best intentions, reality became somewhat different, especially with regard to economic policy. In 1975 the government embarked on counter-cyclical policies in order to mitigate the effects of the international recession, and it started paying generous subsidies to uncompetitive industries. This happened at the same time as wages spiked upwards and as costly social reforms were introduced (Lie and Venneslan 2010, pp. 192–304). As a result, Norway faced huge structural problems in the late 1970s.

The promise of future oil revenues was not the sole explanation for this loss of fiscal restraint. Historian Einar Lie (Lie 2012, pp. 123–132) argues that other factors played an important role, such as the disintegration of the Norwegian post-war political consensus from the late 1960s onwards and especially the radicalization of Norwegian politics because of the EEC referendum in 1972. It is however clear that, in a contra-factual reality without oil, the spending taps would have been turned off much sooner. Oil income thus contributed to aggravating the situation.

In retrospect, Hermod Skånland, manager of the Bank of Norway (1985–94), stated that Norwegian politicians had staked out a sensible course back in 1974, but quickly chose to follow a different path (Skånland 1988, p. 4).[15] Skånland was not alone in criticizing the economic policy decisions of the mid-1970s. Fiscal restraint was reintroduced in the years around 1980. However, it proved difficult over time to balance the budgets. Einar Lie (Lie and Venneslan 2010, pp. 255–238) remarks in the history of the Ministry of Finance that fiscal policy had to be adjusted to what "voters would accept in the oil age".[16] By the mid-1980s both fiscal and monetary policies were again very expansive. The electorate expected increasing state services and were not prepared to shoulder the bills.

In the 1970s and early 1980s the oil and gas industry contributed to substantial economic growth. For the first time in history, Norway became one of Europe's most affluent countries. By 1985 the petroleum sector generated 18 per cent of GNP and almost half the country's exports.[17] Norwegian wage costs increased more rapidly than those of her trading partners. While Swedish and Danish industrial exports expanded rapidly in the mid-1980s Norwegian exports stagnated. Norwegian competitiveness had been eroded.[18]

In the spring of 1986 oil prices suffered a deep decline. This had dramatic effects on the Norwegian economy. In June 1986 the currency was devalued by 10.5 per cent. Fiscal policy was tightened and interest rates were raised. In the following years the banking sector suffered enormous losses equalling 8.1 per cent of GDP and had to be rescued by the state in the early 1990s (Sandal 2004, pp. 103–104; Lie 2012, pp. 163–168).

It should be noted that Norway's neighbouring countries Sweden and Finland also encountered economic turbulence in the early 1990s. They experienced in fact higher losses in the banking sector than Norway. In all three countries the crises might be interpreted as unintended consequences of the transition from a managed social democratic economy to a more market based economy. While oil can explain some of the overheating of the Norwegian economy before 1986, the fall in the oil price meant that Norway started adjusting its policies at an earlier date than her neighbouring countries.

In spite of the turbulence, the Norwegian economy continued to grow, albeit at a lower rate than the European average for some years (Maddison 2010). Due to modest wage increases in the late 1980s and early 1990s, the non-oil parts of Norwegian industry regained some of their lost competitiveness.[19] However, the Norwegian government did not actively try to diminish the size of the oil sector. Instead, the government temporarily reduced tax rates on new oil fields and opened large new areas in the Norwegian waters for exploration.[20] As a result, investments in the North Sea remained high, notwithstanding the low oil prices. In contrast to many other resource dependent countries, Norway thus managed to reduce economic volatility if not its dependency on oil. However, this also meant that Norway depleted her petroleum reserves more rapidly than most other oil producing countries (Ryggvik 2010, pp. 88–91).

Norwegian authorities had long worried that the country was vulnerable to more or less random occurrences such as oil price fluctuations and discoveries in the North Sea. The fiscal excesses of the 1970s and the mid-1980s had not been forgotten. In 1990 parliament therefore decided, with overwhelming majority, to establish a petroleum fund. This was a major institutional innovation. The basic idea was to deposit the petroleum revenue in a designated fund and to invest the holdings of this fund in foreign countries. By investing the money abroad the government hoped to kill three birds with one stone; reducing the effects of Dutch Disease on the Norwegian economy, hindering currency revaluation and minimizing future political meddling with investment decisions. However, due to the low oil prices of the early 1990s payments into the fund only commenced in 1996 (Lie and Venneslan 2010, pp. 345–347; Lie 2012, p. 151, 153).

All Norwegian governments were happy to spend oil revenue on popular welfare programmes, especially in election years. This type of spending also followed the main trajectory in Norwegian (and for that matter Scandinavian) politics, namely building a generous redistributive welfare state aimed to benefit the whole population. However, the Scandinavian countries also have a tradition of prudent fiscal management. In the late 1990s the Norwegian government became concerned that it could become difficult to rein in state expenditure if the oil price surged upwards. In 2001 the parliament introduced new guidelines for the petroleum fund. A maximum 4 per cent of the oil fund, that is the anticipated return on the investments, could each year be transferred to state budgets.[21] The government has by and large managed to keep expenditure of petroleum revenue within this 4 per cent limit (Lie 2012, p. 181). Despite calls across the political spectrum for increased spending on favourite causes, the electorate has for the most part accepted that the 4 per cent spending limit is a sensible policy.[22] This arguably is a reflection of the high level of trust in the political institutions among the Norwegian populace, as the majority believes that the oil fund will not be siphoned off, but will actually be used to pay for welfare in the future.

While the guidelines have limited state expenditure of petroleum revenue, and thus the crowding out effects, there is no doubt that Norway became increasingly dependent on oil in the 2000s. Despite the 4 per cent spending limit, expenditure has nonetheless increased rapidly, as the total value of the petroleum fund has risen spectacularly thanks to high oil prices; from US$44 billion in 2000, to more than US$500 billion in 2010, and then to almost US$900 billion in 2014 (Figure 15.4). In 2004 state authorities calculated that wage costs for Norwegian blue collar workers were 30 per cent higher than among her main trading partners.[23] In the following years wages continued surging upwards. As a result the traditional mainland industries found it increasingly difficult to compete in international markets. By 2010 the petroleum sector accounted for 22 per cent of Norway's GNP, 27 per cent of state income, 26 per cent of total investments and 47 per cent of exports.[24]

Norwegian oil production peaked in 2001 and fell by 30 per cent over the following decade (Figure 15.5). The decline will probably continue, in spite of some recent discoveries in the North Sea.[25] Gas production has expanded, but cannot offset the decline of oil as the resource rent of gas is much lower. However, as oil prices surged upwards in the early 2000s, almost no one in Norway noticed the falling output of oil.

What effect the rising oil wealth will have had for the long-term prospects of the Norwegian economy is still hard to say. In February 2012 *The Economist* had a special report on Nordic countries. With regard to Norway's oil wealth the magazine commented with an element of surprise that "the most striking thing about Norway is how quintessentially Nordic it is. Oil may have filled its coffers and reconfigured its political economy, but it has not changed its culture."[26]

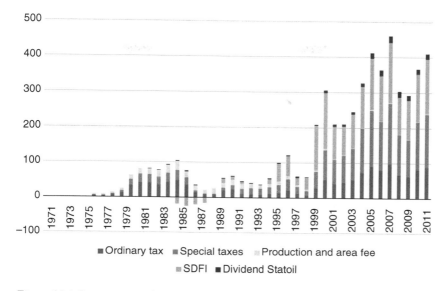

Figure 15.4 State revenue from the petroleum sector (billions of 2014 NOK) (source: Facts 2014: The Norwegian Petroleum Sector 2014: Table 1.1. Adjusted for inflation).

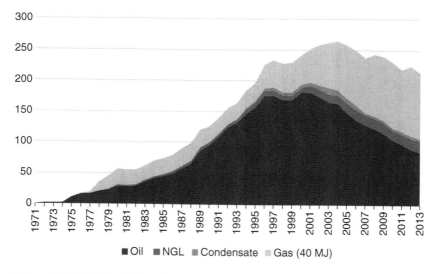

Figure 15.5 Mill. Sm³ oil equivalents per year (source: Facts 2014: The Norwegian Petroleum Sector 2014, Table 1.2).

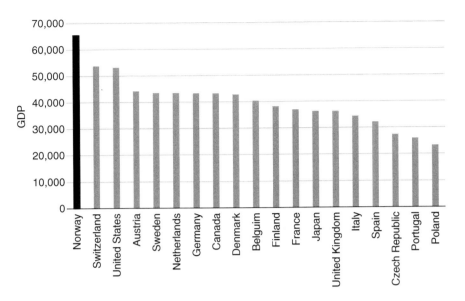

Figure 15.6 GDP per capita (PPP) in select countries, 2013 (source: World Bank 2014).

The latter point might be debatable; work ethics may have deteriorated and absenteeism has surged (Lie 2012, p. 186).

However, what may be remarkable is to what extent Norwegian politics have been focused on other economic issues than oil. Far-reaching market reforms were introduced in Norway's other resource based industries. The government believed that electricity had been sold too cheaply to metallurgical industries, which in essence had squandered much of the resource rent. In 1990 Norway therefore deregulated its electricity markets, it was in fact one of the first countries to do so (Nilsen and Thue 2006, pp. 282–284). Yet the power plants themselves remained in public hands. Publicly owned mines were also closed when they failed to produce a profit. In the fisheries and in fish farming production quotas became tradable. These two examples were a part of a general trend. Norwegian authorities strove to raise efficiency in all parts of the economy. They were also keen to stimulate innovation. According to *The Economist* Norwegians display the same enthusiasm for entrepreneurship as their Nordic cousins.[27] To what extent this eagerness can help Norway when oil revenues start falling is hard to foresee. However, the main point here is that while being awash with oil income, Norway has not developed into a typical rentier state.

Conclusion

Norway is arguably one of the most successful resource rich countries in the world. Several scholars have explained this success by the fact that the country already had a stable democracy and high quality institutions when oil was discovered in 1969. While there is obviously much truth in this explanation, it does in our view obfuscate what we believe are the key elements in the Norwegian development, namely the country's resource policies. These policies have had a major influence on the Norwegian resource industries, on ownership structures, distribution of resource rent, income volatility, etc.

From the early twentieth century onwards, Norway developed an interventionist regulatory regime for her natural resources. Norway has thus a very long history of resource regulation; it has been a recurring topic in Norwegian politics for more than a hundred years. The long tradition of resource regulation was in itself important, as it made Norwegian politicians and state servants well prepared when oil exploration started in the North Sea in the 1960s.

During the resource boom of the early twentieth century, the Norwegian Parliament established the principle that the state should regulate the country's natural resources. Throughout the century, the state has pursued a rather wide set of aims, including securing resource rents, employment, spill-over effects, national ownership and especially from the 1970s onwards environmental standards. While the emphasis of state policy has varied, over time as well as between the different resource based industries, the common denominator has been to maximize benefits for Norwegian society at large, not just for a political or an economic elite.

When studying Norwegian regulations of natural resources, it is possible to identify three policy goals, which to varying degree affected the regulation of the different resources. The first objective was to *ensure that natural resources would benefit or be accessible to a large part of the population*. State regulation ensured that natural resources that required little capital to exploit – like forests and fish – were not monopolized by large private enterprises. For the resource intensive sectors, such as hydropower, mining and oil, the state regulated the industries in the public interest, and acquired rents on behalf of the public, through taxes and public ownership. Redistribution of these rents to the population at large was done indirectly through public spending. Second, the state authorities strove to *secure domestic ownership of the natural resources*. This was mainly achieved through public ownership. This was in part due to the weakness of the Norwegian private sector, and in part because of a general high level of public trust in the state.

The third objective has been to *exploit natural resources to foster economic growth*. Throughout the century, the state has for the most part favoured growth through natural resource based exports. There has been comparatively little import substitution protectionism, even in the regulated economy of the post-war era. Rather than actively diversifying away from the resource exports, the country adopted policies focused on ensuring a higher level of spill-over effects from the resource-heavy exports to the rest of the economy. In addition to promoting domestic ownership, both the concession laws and later oil policy gave preferential access to Norwegian-made materials and machinery.

The first and second objectives were at times at odds with the third. In the case of fisheries, social considerations were more important than achieving maximum efficiency. Politicians were also willing to sacrifice some growth in order to increase domestic ownership over natural resources. This was the case in early twentieth century hydropower policy as well as in the oil policy of the 1970s and 1980s. In the case of oil, politicians were keenly aware that it would be impossible to develop the resources without the technical expertise of foreign oil companies. Foreign ownership was therefore accepted. Terms and taxes were at times adjusted in order to attract investments, but without ever fundamentally sacrificing the first and second policy objective.

In Norway state regulation has coexisted with respect for private property rights. Natural resources owned by domestic or foreign companies were not forcefully nationalized or confiscated. The comprehensive Norwegian concession laws did not apply to mines or hydropower plants built before the laws were passed and these plants were allowed to continue to operate without restrictions. Likewise, the property of foreign oil companies has always been respected. The government has done its utmost to appear as a trustworthy and reliable partner when it negotiated with foreign-owned companies. In essence, the Norwegian state has combined strict demands with the lure of a stable business environment. Contracts with the government have been respected regardless of who was in power. The strict and consistent principle established in the early twentieth century that the country's natural resources and the rents they generate should benefit the country at large can be thought to have pre-empted later popular demands for nationalization and renegotiations, which have been a destabilizing factor in many other resource rich countries. In these regards the Norwegian approach has been quite different from policies in many resource rich countries in Latin America or post-Soviet Russia.

It is possible to argue that the Norwegian political institutions made a crucial difference to the apparent success of the country's resource policies. The high levels of trust in a stable, pluralistic political system with little corruption or violence spared the country many of the problems common to other resource rich countries. This high level of trust allowed the state to act as a steady "harvester" of resource rent, and also made it easier for the electorate to accept the restraint of the 4 per cent budgetary rule. However, it is altogether less clear whether the reasons for the good institutions can be found in the "mechanics" of the Norwegian institutions, or within its institutional culture. For instance, the restrain and pragmatism shown by the successive Norwegian governments was not necessarily found in the laws themselves, but rather in the way the public authorities chose to enact them.

The exploitation of Norway's traditional natural resources (timber, fish, minerals and hydropower) has never led to any serious problems with Dutch Disease or to crowding out effects. Petroleum was different. This was acknowledged by state authorities from an early date. The resource rents were so high that they might cause considerable problems in the non-oil parts of the economy. However, when oil income was at hand, it proved politically difficult to rein in spending on popular measures. In order to limit expenditure of oil income the parliament established the Norwegian oil fund in 1990. When income from the petroleum sector surged upwards the fund's guidelines helped to keep state spending in check. The fund must be considered a success. However, expenditure was still so high that wages and prices increased rapidly, a development that has led to crowding out effects in the non-oil parts of the economy. Crowding out is of course a natural consequence of increasing wealth.

The question remains whether Norway has become too dependent on its petroleum wealth and whether the present development is sustainable. The Norwegian economy is clearly vulnerable to a drop in the oil price. Outside the efforts to limit the amount of oil revenue the state spends each year, the country has not engaged in an active economic diversification strategy. With a drop in oil prices, the state will not only lose revenue from the petroleum sector, but mainland industries will also suffer as they have become increasingly dependent on sales of services and equipment to the offshore sector. While the oil fund provides an important buffer against temporary shortfalls of oil income it will be of limited help if a prolonged downturn occurs in the oil market. Only the future will decide whether Norway has truly avoided the resource curse.

Notes

1 An updated overview of the sovereign wealth fund can be found at www.nbim.no/.
2 See for instance Mehlum *et al.* 2006; Bhattacharyya and Hodler 2010; Gylfason 2011).
3 This was primarily calcium carbide, nitrates and aluminium. Cheap power was also important to electro-metallurgical industries such as ferro-alloy production and the electrolysis of nickel.
4 For a complete overview of the law, see Amundsen (1918).
5 *Hjemfallsrett* in Norwegian. Sometimes also translated as "escheat".
6 *Odelstings Proposition 11*, 1908, Appendix 2, pp. 25–72, 129–131.
7 *Meddelte vasdragskoncessioner*, appendix to St. Prp. 1, 1915, Hovedpost IX A, chapter 9, pp. 125–134.
8 This is based on a close study of Norwegian concession practice in Annaniassen 1983; Dugstad 2011).
9 This point is made in Cappelen and Mjøset (2013). However, the effect is downplayed by Christensen and Rinde 2009, pp. 85–87).
10 A complete overview of all hydropower concessions can be found in *Meddelte vasdragskoncessioner*, appendix to St. Prp. 1 1915, Hovedpost IX A, chapter 9 and *Meddelte vasdragskoncessioner*, appendix to St. Prp. 1 1916, Hovedpost IX, chapter 9.
11 Odelstingsprop. 82, 1991–92.
12 Stortingsproposisjon 36, 2000–2001. See also Ryggvik (2010, pp. 103–107).
13 *Statoil Annual Report 2012*, p. 13.
14 *Stortingsmelding 25 1973/74 Petroleumsvirksomhetens plass i det norske samfunn* [The role of petroleum activities in Norwegian society]. See the discussion of this report in Hanisch and Nerheim (1992, pp. 406–450) and Lie and Venneslan (2010, pp. 163–176).
15 The original quote is "Tidlig og med betydelig klarsyn staket vi … ut vår kurs. Deretter tok vi en annen vei."
16 Lie and Venneslan (2010, pp. 255–328).The quote is from p. 313. The original quote is: "På mange måter var strategien tilpasset hva velgerne kunne tåle av endringer i oljealderen,…"
17 Statistics Norway, Historisk Statistikk 1994, Table 16.4, 18.1 and 22.1.

18 Ministry of Labour and Administration 2004, NOU 14 *Etter inntektsoppgjørene*, Table 5.1 (Lie and Venneslan 2010).
19 Ministry of Labour and Administration 2004, NOU 14 *Etter inntektsoppgjørene*, Table 5.1.
20 Stortingsmeld. 41, 1986–87.
21 The Ministry of Finance, 2001. Stortingsmelding nr. 29 *Retningslinjer for den økonomiske politikken*, 2000–2001.
22 Among the parties with parliamentary representation, only the populist right *Fremskritspartiet* has proposed to scrap the 4 per cent rule.
23 Ministry of Labour and Administration 2004, NOU 14 *Etter inntektsoppgjørene*, Sector 5.
24 The Ministry of Petroleum and Energy 2010, *Fakta Norsk Petroleumsverksemd 2010*, 14.
25 The Ministry of Petroleum and Energy 2010, *Fakta Norsk Petroleumsverksemd 2010*, 36.
26 "Norway, the rich cousin", *The Economist*, 2 February 2013.
27 "Norway, the rich cousin", *The Economist*, 2 February 2013.

References

Amundsen, O., 1918. *Lov om erhvervelse av vandfald, bergverk og anden fast eiendom: koncessions-loven av 14 december 1917: med kommentar*. Kristiania: Aschehoug.

Andersen, K.G., 2005. *Flaggskip i fremmed eie: Hydro 1905–1945*. Oslo: Pax forlag.

Andersen, S.S., 1993. *The Struggle Over North Sea Oil and Gas: Government Strategies in Denmark, Britain, and Norway*. Oslo: Scandinavian University Press.

Annaniassen, E., 1983. *Rettsgrunnlag og konsesjonspraksis: en undersøkelse av rettsgrunnlaget for vassdragskonsesjoner og dets håndhevelse i tidsrommet 1906–1910*. Unpublished master's thesis. University of Oslo.

Anonymus, 1957. *Bergverkenes Landssammenslutning, BVL., gjennom 50 år, 1907–1957*. Oslo: Grøndahl.

Bhattacharyya, S. and Hodler, R., 2010. Natural resources, democracy and corruption. *European Economic Review*, 54 (4), 608–621.

Cappelen, Å. and Mjøset, L., 2013. Can Norway be a role model for natural resource abundant countries? *In*: A.K. Fosu, ed. *Development Success: Historical Accounts from More Advanced Countries*. Oxford: Oxford University Press.

Christensen, P. and Hallenstvedt, A., 2005. *I kamp om havets verdier: Norges fiskarlags historie*. Trondheim: Norges fiskarlag.

Christensen, S.A. and Rinde, H., 2009. *Nasjonale utlendinger: ABB i Norge 1880–2010*. Oslo: Gyldendal.

Dugstad, A.R.S., 2011. *Chasing waterfalls: foreign direct investments and Norwegian watercourse concession policy, 1916–1926*. Unpublished master's thesis. NTNU.

Etemad, B. and Luciani, J., 1991. *World Energy Production, 1800–1985*. Geneva: Librairie Droz.

Facts 2014, 2014. *The Norwegian Petroleum Sector*. Edited by Yngvild Tormodsgard, Ministry of Petroleum and Energy.

Gylfason, T., 2011. Natural resource endowment: a mixed blessing? *In*: R. Arezki, T. Gylfason and A. Sy, eds. *Beyond the Curse: Policies to Harness the Power of Natural Resources*. Washington, DC: International Monetary Fund.

Haaland, A., 1995. *Fra konsesjonslov til "midlertidig trustlov" – norsk konkurransepolitikk 1905–1926*. Bergen: Stiftelsen for samfunns- og næringslivsforskning.

Haber, L.F., 1971. *The Chemical Industry, 1900–1930: International Growth and Technological Change*. Oxford: Clarendon Press.
Hanisch, T.J. and Nerheim, G., 1992. *Norsk oljehistorie: Fra vantro til overmot?*. Oslo: Norsk petroleumsforening.
Hanisch, T.J. and Nerheim, G., 1996. *Norsk oljehistorie: En gassnasjon blir til*. Oslo: Norsk petroleumsforening.
Historisk statistikk, 1978. Oslo: Central Bureau of Statistics of Norway.
Hodne, F., 1981. *Norges økonomiske historie 1815–1970*. Oslo: Cappelen.
Hodne, F. and Grytten, O.H., 2002. *Norsk økonomi i det 20. århundre*. Bergen: Fagbokforlaget.
Johannessen, F.E., Rønning, A. and Sandvik, P.T., 2005. *Nasjonal kontroll og industriell fornyelse, Hydro 1945–1977*. Oslo: Pax Forlag.
Johnsen, A., 1989. *Utfordringen: Statoil-år*. Oslo: Gyldendal norsk forlag.
Jónsson, G., 2009. Comparing the Icelandic and the Norwegian fisheries' responses to the economic crises of the 1930s. *In*: S.O. Olsson, ed. *Managing Crises and De-Globalisation: Nordic Foreign Trade and Exchange 1919–1939*. London: Routledge, 240.
Keilhau, W., 1938. *Det Norske folks liv og historie: I vår egen tid*. Oslo: H. Aschehoug & Company.
Knutsen, S., 2007. *Staten og kapitalen i det 20. århundre: regulering, kriser og endring i det norske finanssystemet 1900–2005*. Oslo: Scandinavian University Press, Humanistiske Fakultet.
Lange, E., 1977. The concession laws of 1906–09 and Norwegian industrial development. *Scandinavian Journal of History*, 2 (1–4), 311–330.
Leigh, G.J., 2004. *The World's Greatest Fix: A History of Nitrogen and Agriculture*. New York: Oxford University Press.
Lie, E., 2005. *Oljerikdommer og internasjonal ekspansjon: Hydro 1977–2005*. Oslo: Pax Forlag.
Lie, E., 2012. *Norsk økonomisk politikk etter 1905*. Oslo: Universitetsforlaget.
Lie, E. and Venneslan, C., 2010. *Over evne: Finansdepartmentet 1965–1992*. Oslo: Pax Forlag.
Maddison, A., 2010. Historical statistics. PIB and population data. [online]. Available from: www.ggdc.net/maddison/Historical_Statistics/horizontal-file_02-2010.xls.
Maloney, W.F., 2007. Missed opportunities: innovation and resource-based growth in Latin America. *In*: D. Lederman and W.F. Maloney, eds. *Natural Resources: Neither Curse nor Destiny*. Stanford, CA: Stanford University Press.
Mehlum, H., Moene, K. and Torvik, R., 2006. Institutions and the resource curse. *The Economic Journal*, 116, 1–20.
Mjeldheim, L., 2006. *Den gylne mellomvegen: tema frå Venstres historie 1905–1940*. Bergen: Vigmostad & Bjørke.
Myrvang, C., 1997. Falkeblikk og styringsteknikk. *In*: R.P. Amdam, D. Gjestland and A. Hompland, eds. *Årdal, verket og bygda 1947–1997*. Oslo: Samlaget.
Nilsen, Y. and Thue, L., 2006. *Statens kraft 1965–2006: miljö och marked*. Oslo: Universitetsforlaget.
Rinde, H., 1997. Årdal, verket og bygda 1947–1997. *In*: R.P. Amdam, D. Gjestland and A. Hompland, eds. *Årdal, verket og bygda 1947–1997*. Oslo: Samlaget.
Ryggvik, H., 2000. *Norsk oljevirksomhet mellom det nasjonale og det internasjonale*. Oslo: Universitetet.
Ryggvik, H., 2009. *Til siste dråpe: om oljens politiske økonomi*. Oslo: Aschehoug.

Ryggvik, H., 2010. *The Norwegian Oil Experience: A Toolbox for Managing Resources?*. Oslo: Senter for teknologi, innovasjon og kultur (TIK).

Sandal, K., 2004. The Norwegian banking crises in the early 1990s – resolution methods and fiscal costs. *In*: T. Moe, J. Solheim and B. Vale, eds. *The Norwegian Banking Crisis*. Oslo: Norges bank.

Sandvik, P.T., 2007. En mer demokratisk kapitalisme? Økonomi og samfunnsutvikling i Trøndelag 1750–1920. *Historisk Tidskrift*, 86 (1), 35–56.

Sandvik, P.T., 2008. European, global or Norwegian? The Norwegian aluminium companies 1946–2005. *In*: H. Schröter, ed. *The European Enterprise: Historical Investigation into a Future Species*. Berlin: Springer Science & Business Media, 297.

Sandvik, P.T. and Andresen, A., 2000. *Kristiansand energiverk: i elektrisitetens århundre; 1900–2000*. Kristiansand: Verket.

Skånland, H., 1988. Norge og oljen – gamle eller nye utfordringer. *Sosialøkonomen*, 11.

Skjold, D.O., 2006. *Statens kraft 1947–1965: For velferd og industri*. Oslo: Universitetsforlaget.

Sogner, K., 2012. *Andresens: en familie i norsk økonomi og samfunnsliv gjennom to hundre år*. Oslo: Pax.

Sogner, K. and Christensen, S.A., 2001. *Plankeadel: Kiær- og Solberg-familien under den 2. industrielle revolusjon*. Oslo: Andresen & Butenschøn for Handelshøyskolen, BI.

Stonehill, A.I., 1965. *Foreign Ownership in Norwegian Enterprises*. Statistisk sentralbyrå [I kommisjon hos Aschehoug].

Storli, E., 2010. *Out of Norway Falls Aluminium: The Norwegian Aluminium Industry in the International Economy, 1908–1940*. Unpublished PhD dissertation. NTNU.

Thue, L., 2003. *For egen kraft: kraftkommunene og det norske kraftregimet 1887–2003*. Oslo: Abstrakt forlag.

Thue, L., 2006. *Statens kraft 1890–1947: kraftutbygging og samfunnsutvikling*. Second edn. Oslo: Universiteitsforlaget.

Willoch, K., 1990. *Statsminister*. Oslo: Schibsted.

World Bank, I. C. P. d. 2014, 2014. *GDP per Capita, PPP (Current International $)*. In http://data.worldbank.org.

16 Water scarcity and agricultural growth in Spain

From curse to blessing?

Ignacio Cazcarro, Rosa Duarte, Miguel Martín-Retortillo, Vicente Pinilla and Ana Serrano

Introduction

Natural resource scarcity can be a major drawback for economic growth. When we consider pre-industrial economies, where the agricultural sector is the basis of most productive activities, environmental conditions are essential to explain the level of production, its composition and the pace of growth. The climate, soil and ruggedness of landscape are the main constraints to agricultural activities. In traditional economies, human beings have adapted to these environmental conditions by developing crops – or other activities – as close as possible to their ecological optimum (Grigg 1982, pp. 51–53). Nevertheless, history also shows that there have also been conscious and deliberate attempts to change these conditions. The use of the natural resource of water has been the most important way to increase land productivity and to ensure crops in arid and semi-arid regions.

This process has been conditioned by the particularities of water, such as its transformation following water cycles (naturally circulating resource, constantly recharged) and its irregular distribution over time and across geographies, which create shortages locally (Oki and Kanae 2006). Among the features that influence the economic characterization and management of water, we find the essentiality of water as an element for life, its mobility and its heterogeneity in terms of location and quality, variability, etc. Despite the fact that water is widely regarded as the most essential of natural resources, freshwater systems are – paradoxically – directly threatened by human activities (United-Nations-Water 2009; Vörösmarty *et al.* 2010), transformed through land cover changes, industrialization, urbanization, dams and other engineering works, irrigation and inter-basin transfers, all of which aim to increase human access to water (Meybeck 2003; Vörösmarty *et al.* 2004). The benefits of water provision to productivity improvements (UNDP 2006; United-Nations-Water 2009) often go along with harm to the environment and to biodiversity, with potentially serious costs (Abell *et al.* 2008; IUCN 2009), and all of these effects further shape water's relative scarcity and the environmental, economic, political and social responses to that scarcity.

In this context, the objective of this work is to analyse the process of frontier expansion, meaning the exploitation of new relatively abundant resources (water) for production purposes (Barbier 2011). Water for irrigated agriculture was obtained from ground sources identified as "vertically downward" sources (i.e. wells), and from "horizontally extensive" surface sources (such as dams and canals). The characterization of water as "new" is due to the fact that, although the use of this resource is very old, traditional technologies offered limited possibilities for its extraction and development. However, crucial technological changes in engineering, the use of new materials and the utilization of fossil fuel to power engines created significant expansion of ready access to water from the early decades of the twentieth century, making it possible to construct large reservoirs with a capacity to store, and therefore to regulate, large volumes of water. Furthermore, the introduction of steam (and, later, fossil fuels) to power machines to pump water, allowed the extraction of water from underground.

The case study chosen is Spain, a predominantly semi-arid country, with a long tradition of water "management", dating back to the Roman period. From the nineteenth century on, there was an intensification of effort to expand irrigation on a much larger scale. However, the effects of these efforts did not begin to be felt until the first decades of the twentieth century, coming to fruition after 1950.

Water use grew notably when economic growth accelerated after the Industrial Revolution. Population growth, of course, increased the demand for water, but the primary underlying factor was the great increase in per capita income. Growing per capita income not only increased the demand for food, but also modified consumption patterns. Consumption of water-intensive goods increased sharply, resulting in a significant increase in water use. However, the most serious strain on freshwater resources comes now from the mounting weight of meat in the consumption package (Duarte *et al.* 2013, 2014a).

To cope with the increase in demand, agriculture has substantially increased its production throughout the past century. The expansion of irrigation has contributed significantly to this increase in production; the global irrigated area jumped from approximately 48 million hectares in 1900 to 235 million in 1989 (Gleick 1993). The development of modern irrigation systems has also been identified as a necessary condition for the efficient use of the agricultural technologies that emerged in the second half of the twentieth century (Hayami and Ruttan 1985). In the case of the Green Revolution, the new high-yield crop varieties worked best where irrigation infrastructure was already available, and chemical fertilizers were widely used (Federico 2005). A great investment in dams and irrigations canals became necessary and, accordingly, food supply more than doubled and water withdrawal grew by 2.81 per cent annually during this period. It was the intensification of agriculture that made water withdrawal figures soar, as agricultural water use is the most important (Duarte *et al.* 2014a).

In this chapter we first explain why water scarcity is so important in Spain to understand its relative agricultural backwardness in the European context until late in the nineteenth century. It was not until the twentieth century that irrigation spread significantly. We then analyse the result of the increase of water use on agricultural crop production for the period 1935–2005. Subsequently, we focus on the compositional changes in agricultural production stemming from the greater availability of water. In addition, we examine the impact of the expansion of irrigation on the regional distribution of agricultural crop production. The last section deals with the negative effects generated by greater water availability: the development of irrigation could have caused significant environmental damage, and there were important conflicts over the control of, and access to, water resources, particularly from 1977 onwards.

Water as a constraint for agricultural growth

In pre-industrial Europe, the most significant agricultural innovations consisted of a sequence of changes introduced in England, and then in the Netherlands: changes in crop rotation and the introduction of forage pulses that fixed nitrogen to the soil were crucial, allowing for the elimination of fallow and a greater integration of livestock and crop farming, largely thanks to the greater availability of feed for cattle. At the same time, these changes led to greater access to organic fertilizers, and agricultural yields and production increased (Clark 1987; Allen 1994).

Spain is a semi-arid country characterized by variable and unequal rainfall, together with higher levels of evapotranspiration compared to the European average (González de Molina 2001). Spain stands out, not only for its semi-arid character, but also for its irregular distribution of water resources, both over time and in space. Figure 16.1 shows the average long-term precipitation for the period 1982–2002 (in mm) in the various Spanish regions, and clearly displays significant disparities in terms of water endowment. The North-West of Spain is the most humid area in the country, followed by the Cantabrican coast. Other regions in the north of Spain, particularly those in the Pyrenees and the Cantabrican mountains, also show important amounts of rainfall. However, as can be seen, most regions in Spain are arid or semi-arid, with low average annual precipitation. These differences have, historically, had a clear effect on regional grain yields (Santiago-Caballero 2013).

Aridity was one of the primary limiting factors of the adoption in Spain of the English mix of farming techniques, and hampered the introduction of fodder crops into the crop rotation system and the addition of nutrients to the soil (Garrabou 1994; Tortella 1994; Clar and Pinilla 2009). Throughout the nineteenth century, many European countries followed the English agricultural innovations, and thus increased productivity (Chorley 1981; Van Zanden 1991; Bairoch 1999; Lains and Pinilla 2008; Clar and Pinilla 2009). Production per hectare was significantly lower in Spain than in the rest of Europe, where these innovations were introduced (Pinilla 2004).

By the end of the nineteenth century, a political movement, Regenerationism, led by the thinker Joaquín Costa, viewed irrigation as a panacea for the serious problems affecting rural areas, especially the problem of poverty. The expansion

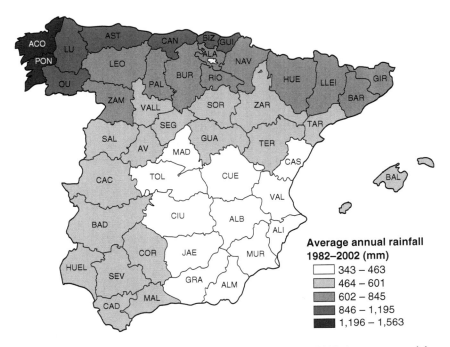

Figure 16.1 Long-term average annual rainfall (mm), 1982–2002 (source: own elaboration with data from Goerlich 2012).

Note
The list and codes of provinces are shown in the Appendix.

of irrigation during the nineteenth century was limited, for two reasons. First, the economic liberalism propounded by Adam Smith gave the state a very limited economic role; thus, large waterworks must be privately funded, and the cost of the initial investment, and its long amortization period, limited the increase in irrigated area – although with some regional differences (Pinilla 2008a; Ramón i Muñoz 2013). Second, from a technological viewpoint, the materials used and the development of engineering did not allow for the construction of large reservoirs. Thus, even the irrigation canals that were built did not have the ability to maintain a supply of water when, and where, it was most needed.

Both drawbacks were overcome in the early years of the twentieth century. Costa's ideas broke with the tradition of economic liberalism and instead granted the state a role in encouraging the economic development of the country. Consequently, from 1895 on, the state funded some hydraulic plans already under construction and notably boosted the expansion of irrigation.

Second, the new technologies that had recently appeared, as engineering techniques and new materials like reinforced concrete were introduced, allowed Spain to overcome these technological disadvantages. Furthermore, since the middle of the nineteenth century, the use of steam power to pump water from wells had spread, although the high costs involved considerably limited the process. This became less of a problem with the introduction of pumps driven by petrol, gas or electricity (Martínez Carrión and Calatayud 2005).

As a result of such technological improvement, and a substantial increase in public investment, the construction of hydraulic infrastructure accelerated, especially from the second half of the twentieth century, and Spain's irrigated area increased substantially (Herranz-Loncán 2004). The new reservoirs entailed an improvement in the quality of irrigation; it was now possible to go from irregular irrigation, when water could be harnessed only in the months of higher rainfall and snowmelt, to a permanent irrigation, when it was possible to supply water when, and where, it was needed for crop growth. The productivity of the land increased and new irrigated crops were introduced that would not have been feasible under rainfed conditions. In those places where it was possible to alleviate water scarcity by constructing waterworks, water went from being a limiting factor for agriculture to being essential, especially in combination with the Mediterranean climate characterized by high levels of sunshine hours.

The irrigated area increased rapidly between 1935 and 2006. As we can see in Figure 16.2, this growth was particularly intense from 1955. It seems quite clear that the development of the Spanish agricultural sector entailed large pressures on water resources, necessitating the construction of irrigation infrastructure and the expansion of irrigated land (Duarte *et al.* 2014c). The former phenomenon,

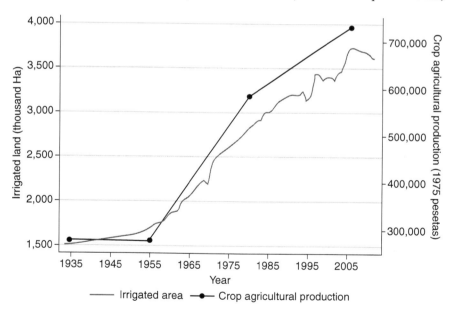

Figure 16.2 Trajectory of irrigated area in thousand ha (left axis) and agricultural production (in pesetas at 1975 prices) (right axis), 1935–2006 (source: data from 1935 to 1953 were not available. We linearly interpolated information between 1935 and 1954 (Irrigated area). Own calculation from Gallego Martínez 1993; MAGRAMA 2010 (Agricultural production)).

together with abundant sunshine, compared to other Western European countries, gave Spain a significant advantage in the production of certain agricultural goods.

During Franco's dictatorship, the construction of water infrastructure became an outstanding agricultural policy. Spain moved towards becoming a high-income country, and the development of the domestic market, together with integration in international markets as an exporter of high-value agricultural and food products, put increased pressure on domestic water resources and made it necessary to intensify the change from rainfed to irrigated agriculture.

The increase in agricultural production

Spanish agricultural production, following the depression at the end of the nineteenth century, grew at a significant pace during the next three decades (Clar and Pinilla 2009). This growth was based on Spain's growing presence in international agricultural markets, and on the development of the domestic market for both traditional and new products. In the first case, the success of Spain as an exporter of horticultural products was remarkable, with a notable increase in trade (Pinilla and Ayuda 2009, 2010), but this success was dependent on the expansion of irrigation, since the most important products, such as oranges and fruit and vegetables, required more water than could be supplied by the rain. It has been estimated that 32.4 per cent of the increase in irrigation water consumed in Spain between 1900 and 1935 was devoted to export products (Duarte et al. 2014b, p. 103).

Growth in Spanish agricultural production was halted from the beginning of the civil war in 1936 until the mid-1950s, but more important than the effects of the war itself, was the post-war situation; the autarkic policies of the Franco regime (a crude intervention in the markets that discouraged the production of key commodities such as wheat) and the difficulty in obtaining inputs such as fertilizers and machinery, led to a decline in production and a hiatus in agricultural modernization (Barciela 1986; Christiansen 2012).

The turnaround in agrarian policies from 1951 and the end of the international isolation of the Spanish economy allowed the resumption of agricultural transformations and a very rapid growth in production, both in the European context, and in absolute terms (Martín-Retortillo and Pinilla 2015). If we only consider crop production, it increased at 3 per cent annually, on average, from 1955 to 1975, and irrigated land grew at a 2.25 per cent annual rate. Finally, during the democratic period (1975–2006) agricultural production and land under irrigation continued to increase, but at a slower pace, 0.8 per cent and 1.1 per cent respectively. Accordingly, during these years, Spanish agriculture went from being a traditional sector in which production was allocated mostly depending on climatic characteristics to a modern sector, highly conditioned by the strong development of irrigation.

Irrigation played a key role in the growth of agricultural production. As we can see in Figure 16.3, rainfed agricultural production had a decreasing share

Water and agricultural growth in Spain 345

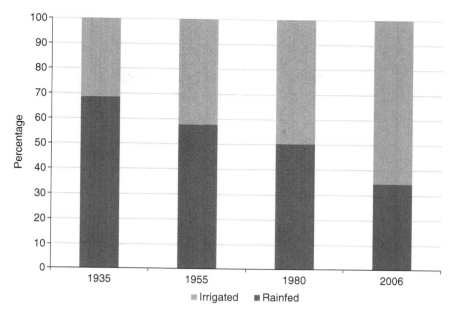

Figure 16.3 Percentage of crop production, ratios of rainfed to irrigated production (source: Own elaboration based on MAGRAMA 1935, 1955, 1975, 1980 and 2007).

from 1935 to the beginning of the twenty-first century. In fact, during these years it went from being around 70 per cent of total crop production in 1935 to slightly more than one third of the total output in 2006. Although the problem of Spanish aridity was partially overcome, the development of the agricultural sector led to greatly increased pressure on water resources (Duarte *et al.* 2014c).

An important aspect of this analysis is the quantification of the factors driving the growth in agricultural production during the period 1935–2006. Following a decomposition approach (Dietzenbacher and Los 1998), we assess to what extent changes in irrigation and rainfed crop yields, as well as variations in irrigated and rainfed area, contributed to the increase in agricultural production. Thus, we conduct the decomposition shown below:

$$\Delta P = \Delta Y_R (A_{R0} + A_{R1}) + \Delta A_R (Y_{R0} + Y_{R1}) + \Delta Y_I (A_{I0} + A_{I1}) + \Delta A_I (Y_{I0} + Y_{I1})$$

Changes in agricultural production (ΔP) between the periods $t=0$ and $t=1$ are explained on the basis of changes in the rainfed crop yield ($\Delta Y_R(A_{R0}+A_{R1})$), where Y is yield and R is rainfed; changes in the rainfed area ($\Delta A_R(Y_{R0}+Y_{R1})$), where A indicates area; changes in the irrigated crop yield ($\Delta Y_I(A_{I0}+A_{I1})$), where I indicates irrigation, and changes in the irrigated area ($\Delta A_I(Y_{I0}+Y_{I1})$).

As we can see in Table 16.1, three factors underlie the increase in agricultural production between 1935 and 2006. The increase in irrigated area accounted for 45 per cent, and from 1980 to 2006, it accounted for 71 per cent of the increase in agricultural production. The growth in the irrigated crop yield was 41 per cent of the total change in agricultural production. Great technological improvements occurred throughout this period, together with an important compositional change towards water-intensive crops. Technological development during this period also contributed to the increase in the rainfed crop yield, accounting for 33 per cent of the growth in agricultural production.

Changes in the crop mix

During the first third of the twentieth century, the Mediterranean regions tended to substitute traditional rainfed crops by irrigated production, with much of this being destined for export (Pinilla and Ayuda 2009; Duarte et al. 2014b). This was possible thanks to the use of new technologies (petrol engines, electric pumps, etc.), and private funding of irrigation was supplemented by state financing of the construction of waterworks (Pinilla 2006).

In fact, as we can see in Table 16.2, the distribution of agricultural production changed significantly from 1935 to 2006. First, there was a marked increase in the share of horticultural crops and fruit trees, while tubers – and to a lesser extent cereals and pulses – lost importance in the production structure. That is, there was a substitution from traditional crops to high-value-added Mediterranean horticultural products. This compositional change could be related to economic development, the associated dietary changes and the orientation of these products to foreign markets. Without the greater water availability that came from the expansion of irrigation, these changes would not have been possible. Furthermore, changes in the crop mixture on irrigated land (especially in fruit trees) led to an increase in irrigation productivity.

The most striking changes took place between 1980 and 2006. The entrance of Spain to the European Economic Community, and thus the Common Agricultural Policy (CAP), was a significant factor. The growing integration of European markets encouraged specialization in certain products (fruit trees, olives)

Table 16.1 Decomposition of agricultural production

	1935–1955	1955–1980	1980–2006	1935–2006
Change in rainfed yield (%)	−409	48	17	33
Change in rainfed area (%)	−281	−4	−46	−19
Change in irrigated yield (%)	501	24	58	41
Change in irrigated area (%)	289	32	71	45
Change in production (million pesetas at 1975 prices)	3,968	307,561	145,643	457,172

Source: Own elaboration. *As the change in production was insignificant between 1935 and 1955, the percentages of the effects of the explaining factors rise rapidly due to simple calculations.

Table 16.2 Crop production (million pesetas at 1975 prices) and percentage of group products in agricultural crop production

	1935	1955	1980	2006	1935	1955	1980	2006
Cereals	77,364	70,674	162,756	168,107	28.25	25.44	27.80	23.00
Legumes	7,514	13,542	9,414	5,515	2.74	4.87	1.61	0.75
Industrial crops	12,980	19,115	40,657	35,820	4.74	6.88	6.95	4.90
Tubers	32,921	31,835	43,130	18,971	12.02	11.46	7.37	2.60
Horticultural products	39,723	44,443	103,026	179,082	14.50	16.00	17.60	24.50
Fruit trees	38,127	34,980	82,731	147,253	13.92	12.59	14.13	20.14
Vineyard	20,450	20,112	50,867	44,810	7.47	7.24	8.69	6.13
Olive	32,474	19,519	35,443	87,981	11.86	7.02	6.05	12.03
Fodder crops	12,331	23,631	57,388	43,515	4.50	8.51	9.80	5.95
Total crop production	273,882	277,851	585,412	731,055	100	100	100	100

Source: Own elaboration based on MAGRAMA (1935, 1955, 1975, 1980 and 2007).

while the production of others (tubers, cereals, fodder crops) was discouraged (Pinilla and Serrano 2009; Clar et al. 2014).

In this regard, changes in the distribution of agricultural production had profound impacts on natural resources, especially in the case of water. In fact, the growing importance of horticultural and fruit products involved increasing pressure on water resources, which were particularly intense during the Franco dictatorship, but also in the subsequent democratic period. This marked compositional change towards water-intensive products, in a semi-arid country like Spain, came with a cost: the development of irrigation and therefore of an increase in the irrigated area.

As Table 16.3 shows, the percentage of rainfed agriculture dropped in all groups of products. Nonetheless, there are interesting differences among them. Fruit trees, tubers and vineyard products are the groups with a larger decrease in their share of rainfed production. The case of fruit products is notable since, in 2006, only 10 per cent were cultivated under rainfed conditions, having declined from almost 55 per cent in 1935. On the other hand, cereals, fodder crops and horticultural products had a lesser decline. However, an abrupt change in cereals grown under irrigation occurred; maize replaced wheat as the main cereal crop on Spanish irrigated land. As for horticultural products, despite that they show a smooth decrease, their weight during the whole period was the lowest, and rainfed production only accounted for 1.32 per cent by 2006.

Changes in the spatial distribution of agricultural production

In Figure 16.4, it is possible to distinguish that, in 1930, the value of agricultural production varied sharply from region to region The dispersion of agricultural production was significant, and it is important to highlight areas such as Valencia (centre east), Barcelona (the darkest in the north-east), A Coruña (the northernmost on the west) and Sevilla (the darkest in the south-west); these regions

Table 16.3 Percentage of rainfed production by group of products on total agricultural crop production

	1935	1955	1980	2006
Cereals	84.26	79.60	74.72	62.40
Legumes	99.00	78.94	74.51	71.94
Industrial crops	53.02	31.21	31.13	28.68
Tubers	66.50	52.00	43.30	13.39
Horticultural products	22.74	17.19	11.18	1.32
Fruit trees	54.65	41.89	22.83	10.12
Vineyard	93.86	93.91	89.54	66.73
Olive	92.91	92.54	88.62	69.84
Fodder crops	58.04	49.58	46.50	50.63
Total	68.57	57.74	50.22	34.52

Source: Own elaboration based on MAGRAMA (1935, 1955, 1975, 1980 and 2007).

Water and agricultural growth in Spain 349

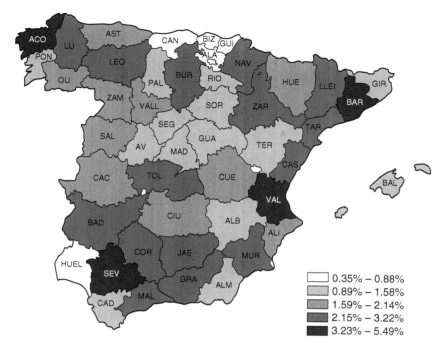

Figure 16.4 Regional distribution of agricultural crop production as percentage of the total, 1930 (source: own elaboration from Gallego Martínez 1993).

Note
The list and codes of provinces are shown in the Appendix.

accounted for 5.8 per cent, 4.14 per cent, 4.13 per cent and 3.7 per cent, respectively, of the value of total agricultural production in 1930.

The picture is very different when we consider the regional distribution of agricultural production in 2005 (Figure 16.5). From 1930 to 2005, a clear trend can be found. A reallocation of agricultural production took place, from humid to arid and semi-arid areas. Whereas in 1930 those areas with an average value of annual precipitation lower than 846 mm represented around 64 per cent of the value of agricultural crop production, these regions accounted for over 80 per cent of crop agricultural production in 2005. Humid areas in the North of Spain lost importance, mostly in favour of the arid regions in the South. The provinces in the South, and in the Ebro Valley in the North-East increased their proportion of total crop production. In other words, agricultural production became concentrated in certain provinces, especially those with the most arid climates.

The arid and semi-arid provinces of Badajoz, Sevilla, Almería, Jaén, Murcia, Córdoba and Ciudad Real doubled their share of national production between 1930 and 2005; they comprised 18.69 per cent of total Spanish production in 1930, rising to more than 40 per cent in 2005. Average annual rainfall in these seven provinces was 442 mm in 1982 and 2002, while the national average was

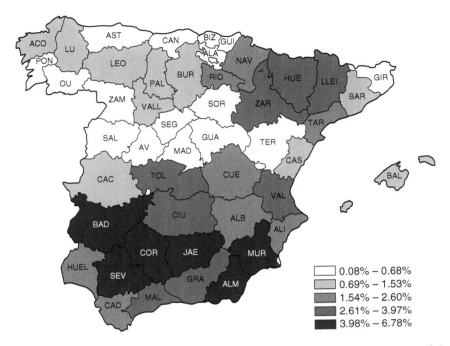

Figure 16.5 Regional distribution of agricultural crop production as percentage of the total, 2005 (source: own elaboration from MAGRAMA 2005).

Note
The list and codes of provinces are shown in the Appendix.

650mm (as indicated above). On the whole, these regions specialized in Mediterranean agricultural products, and these products experienced significant declines in rainfed production, especially in the period 1980–2006.[1] Hence, the role of irrigation in the development of the agricultural sector in arid regions in the South of Spain was essential. During these years, important investments in water infrastructure were carried out, which allowed an evolution from a traditional agriculture based on rainfed crops to a modern and productive irrigated sector.

Only certain regions in the North of Spain, such as those in the Ebro Valley, where irrigation infrastructure was intensively developed during the twentieth century, display shares of agricultural production greater than 1.5 per cent (Pinilla 2008b).

But what is the relationship between aridity and the distribution of agricultural production? As can be seen in Figure 16.6, throughout the years 1930–2005 there was a de-coupling between precipitation levels and the share of the value of agricultural production. The weight of the most humid areas in Spain in crop agricultural production decreased from 1930 to 2005, with this decline being particularly intense in the case of the provinces in Galicia (ACO, PON, LU and OU). Nevertheless, the most remarkable aspect is the large increase in the share

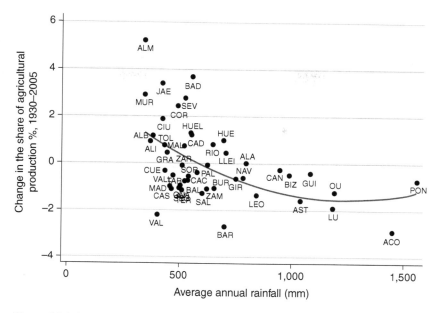

Figure 16.6 Average annual rainfall in Spain vs changes in the share of agricultural crop production (%) (source: own elaboration from Gallego Martínez 1993; MAGRAMA 2005, 2010; Goerlich 2012).

Note
The list and codes of provinces are shown in the Appendix.

of agricultural production of those arid areas located in the south of Spain. This is the case, for example, of the south-eastern provinces of Almeria and Murcia, two Mediterranean areas with the lowest levels of rainfall in Spain that have experienced a large rise in their weight of agricultural production, with shares of 5.2 per cent and 2.9 per cent, respectively. That is, whereas the dry provinces in the southern half of Spain and those in the (north-eastern) Ebro Valley gained share in agricultural production, in humid Spain, agriculture was losing importance.

This de-coupling would not have been possible without the key role of irrigation. The largest increase in the percentage of irrigated production took place between 1980 and 2006, jointly with the increase in the share of horticultural, fruit trees and olive products. In this sub-period, the existing trends were reinforced. It seems paradoxical that, in one of the driest countries in Europe, water resources have such intensive use.

In Figure 16.7, we can see the change in the provincial distribution of irrigated land during the twentieth century. With some exceptions (such as certain provinces in the North Meseta, centre-north of the peninsula and in Catalonia, north-eastern provinces), the general pattern was that irrigation grew more in the drier provinces. Where water was scarcer, more investments in irrigated land

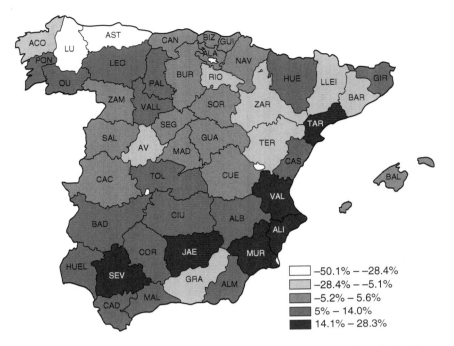

Figure 16.7 Change in the percentage of irrigated land on total agricultural area, 1916–2009 (source: own elaboration based on Junta Consultiva Agronómica 1918; INE 2009).

took place and more pressure on water resources was exerted. These resources included both surface and ground water. In some provinces, the exploitation of aquifers was significant, escalating the problems of pressure on water resources (Reig Martínez and Picazo Tadeo 2002).

Environmental impacts and water conflicts

As mentioned above, agricultural development in the twentieth century cannot be understood without a grasp of the policies of expansion of irrigated area and the concomitant increase in water capacity, especially from the 1950s on. This was a process of construction of reservoirs, dams, canals and irrigation infrastructure that allowed for the regulation of the water supply of the main Spanish rivers, and reducing the risks associated with the geographical and seasonal variations of water availability in Spain. However, the construction and extension of this infrastructure, while it has led to the consolidation of irrigated agriculture, greater associated income and the spread of a new energy source (hydropower), has not been at all conducive to the ecological preservation of the environment. Furthermore, the drilling of wells, many of them illegal, also entailed environmental problems.

As is well known, any river basin contains many natural ecosystems (aquatic habitats, headwaters, riparian areas, groundwater associated with the channel, estuary, wetlands,...) with different ecological and eco-social functions (flood control and storm protection, yield products such as wildlife, fisheries and forest resources, among others) that are seriously affected by large-scale irrigation infrastructure and dams. These effects mainly come from the required stabilization of runoff and the diversion of surface water for irrigation, implicit in irrigation infrastructures, which alter the natural hydrological cycle.

There is significant evidence of the global impacts of hydraulic engineering on the quantity and seasonal patterns of continental water flows. According to the World Commission on Dams (2000), these are clearly negative, complex, varied and profound, and include physical, chemical and geomorphological effects that alter the natural distribution and timing of flows, affect water quality, water quantity, the flow regime and sediment load (first-order impacts). A second group of impacts are changes in the biological productivity of ecosystems of the main channel, and of riparian land and wetlands (second-order impacts). Consequential to these impacts, significant effects on fish, vertebrates and other wildlife have been reported.

More specifically, problems of degradation of irrigated land (salinization, alkalization, waterlogging, over-exploitation of groundwater flows) have been observed in large-scale irrigation schemes (Dougherty and Hall 1995). Changes in the structure of soils, often with damage and degradation associated with intensive cultivation and improper irrigation management, directly reduce the fertility and productivity of irrigated areas, leading to additional stresses on land and water resources.

In this regard, according to FAO/IPGRI (1994), European Commission (2002) and Amezketa (2008), 3 per cent of the more than 3.5 million hectares of irrigated land in Spain are severely affected by salinity problems, and 15 per cent are seriously threatened. In the case of the Ebro basin, the acreage affected by salinity exceeds 300,000 hectares, representing around 30 per cent of the total irrigated area (Pinilla 2006).

Similarly, the over-exploitation of water has been drastic along the south-east coast (Doñana, Upper-Guadiana, Upper-Duero), with irreversible damage in some cases associated with wetland water tables. Moreover, over 125,000 hectares should be abandoned to achieve balance among the aquifers affected by over-exploitation (Oñate 2009).

The development of irrigated agriculture was also responsible for the problems of diffuse pollution, due to intensive use of fertilizers and pesticides, with the greatest impact on the underground areas being due to nitrates. It is estimated that more than 600,000 hectares in Spain are located in areas vulnerable to pollution. Severe impacts of pollution on the surface systems (rivers, wetlands, coastal lagoons) and ecosystems have also been reported for certain areas of the Spanish Mediterranean coast (MAPA 2002; Oñate 2009).

In this regard, the alteration of natural river flows, both spatially and temporally, and the associated impacts on water quality, salinity and temperature, have led to critical consequences for fish populations and wetland species. Thus, when the natural variability of the river is affected, biological communities in the area are seriously damaged. Moreover, the cut-off of migratory routes along the river associated with the diversion of water flows also contributes to isolate animal populations, impoverishing some ecological relationships. As an example, Ibáñez et al. (1999) estimate a reduction in fish catches in the lagoons of the Ebro delta from 300 tonne/year in the 1970s, to 50 tonne/year in the 1990s. Díaz et al. (1993) showed, in a study of Castilla-León, how the habitat transformation involved in the passage from extensive rainfed to intensive rainfed and, subsequently, irrigation, resulted in the replacement of steppe birds, as well as other species common in urbanized environments.

Habitat fragmentation, together with downstream effects, such as loss of floodplains, the reduction of surface water and the deterioration of river deltas and sea estuaries, have been seen as major ecological impacts of hydrological alterations (Rosenberg et al. 2000). As an example, the construction of the large dams of Ribarroja and Mequinenza, near the delta of the Ebro river, consolidated a slow and gradual process of reduction in sediment inputs to the delta, now discounted by 99 per cent compared to the original flows, from 22 million t/year in the 1940s, before the expansion of irrigation, to the current flow around 0.1 million t/year (Ibarra et al. 2008).

Other effects, such as the occupation of coastal lands, reducing the natural section avenues, and the modification of the natural landscape, also arise as a result of water regulation infrastructures. Finally, according to Vörosmarty and Sahagian (2000), from a global perspective, engineering-based control of drainage basins represents a significant alteration of the quantity and seasonal patterns of continental runoff.

From a socio-economic point of view, water regulation has allowed modernization of agriculture, with an associated increase in agriculture-based income. However, the construction of water infrastructures, and specifically water reservoirs, also left a trail of important socio-economic negative impacts in Spain. Forced population displacements as a consequence of the flooding of villages, and the disappearance of economic activities dependent on the river ecosystem, both upstream and downstream from a dam, can be seen as the most serious social effect of water resource development. The impact on the personal, social and cultural identity of displaced populations is difficult to measure, even though it may often be irreversible. In Spain, more than 400 villages disappeared due to the building of dams, with compensation and resettlement attempts often being insufficient for the affected populations.[2]

The Spanish economic growth model has encouraged, in certain regions, the development of high value-added and high water-intensive activities (recreation, intensive irrigation, urban centres, residential buildings, etc.) in recent decades. In this context, water appears as a newly valued element in the political arena, and territorial wars for water control within the river basin, or among regions throughout the Spanish rivers system, are exacerbated during periods of severe drought. Two types of conflict have arisen. First, inter-basin conflicts, as a result of the huge needs for water in the export-oriented Mediterranean region that demanded water transfers. Second, in some watersheds, there were disputes between supporters of continuing the implementation of water projects, mainly farmers, and protesters, mostly people living in the affected mountain areas.

Perhaps the most controversial – and most discussed – regional water conflicts have been those that involve inter-basin water transfers. The Tajo-Segura transfer[3] and the major water transfers drafted in the National Hydrological Plan are the best examples (Gil Olcina 1995; Arrojo 2001; Villarroya 2006). In the first case, the droughts in the donor basin in Castile-La Mancha (and other conflicts linked to the harnessing of the Júcar) have contributed to struggles between regions for the resource, and to major water transfers. The National Hydrological Plan, especially the planned extraction of 1,000 hm^3 per year from the Ebro river to the Mediterranean regions, generated many technical questions, and gave rise to serious concerns about sustainability. In this context, we can cite the claim of Aragon for the right to make use of the Ebro flows, the demands of Catalonia regarding security of supply and environmental flows at the delta, the demands of the Valencia Community to ensure the development of its economic and tourism activity, and those of the Murcia region to develop its horticulture.

Conclusions

The objective of this chapter has been to illustrate how the scarcity of an essential natural resource can encourage technological change in a process of frontier expansion, allowing the exploitation of new productive sources. On the basis of this debate, the question arises: is the availability of natural resources a blessing, or a curse, for economic and social development.

We consider water resources in a semi-arid Mediterranean country, Spain, as our case study. We discuss how the process of economic growth, and a public policy focused on the expansion of irrigation as a key element in boosting income growth and achieving national food security, encouraged throughout the twentieth century the development of technologies and infrastructures to dramatically increase the productivity of agriculture. Substantial public and private investments, sustained over several decades, led to a new geographical distribution of crop production, in which traditional relatively dry regions (though with relative abundance of other natural resources) took advantage of the new resource, regulated water. This reallocation of crop agricultural production was determined both by the availability of untapped water resources, rivers or aquifers, in drier regions, and its high agricultural potential if existing high insolation was combined with enough water resources. The results can be considered mixed.

On the one hand, the development and expansion of irrigation schemes allowed the Spanish agriculture, mainly during the second part of the twentieth century, to experience unprecedented economic growth. Undoubtedly, this allowed the Spanish economy to establish the basis of a more productive sector, better integrated in the production chain (while also facilitating the development of the agri-food industry) and crucially more competitive in international markets. Technological and structural changes in agriculture led to a significant increase in productivity, which supported the rise in agricultural incomes.

On the other hand, the development of this water-intensive agriculture has led to a significant mismatch between those areas with better natural endowments of water, and the areas that currently show higher agricultural productivity. The long-term process of nationwide expansion and intensification of irrigation, and the associated development of irrigation infrastructures (reservoirs, dams, canals, wells) to bring regulated water from its original sources to its users, has left behind important ecological and social impacts that in some cases are already irreversible. The development of irrigation in Spain has been associated with four main ecological problems, namely, salinity and erosion, over-exploitation of water sources, water pollution and damage to river eco-habitats. The severity of the salinity problem in the Spanish fields (affecting almost 20 per cent of irrigation), the over-exploitation of aquifers of major rivers (the cases of Almería, Upper-Duero and Upper-Guadiana are significant), the reduction of contributions to deltas (almost 100 per cent in the case of the Ebro delta) and the effects on wildlife and vegetation in specific areas (the disappearance of steppe bird species) are clear examples of the other side of the coin of agricultural development in Spain.

Additionally, the process of construction of reservoirs and dams, encouraged as a sort of national economic policy, is problematic. Although it was seen as a source of employment in the short term (mainly unskilled and sometimes underpaid work), it forced the displacement of rural populations, due to either the direct flooding of villages, or the effect on agricultural areas and pastures on which those populations depended. The negative consequences for those communities are immeasurable.

Finally, the availability of regulated water has been understood in recent decades as a powerful element of regional planning, which allows for the rapid economic growth of recipient regions (through the development of highly profitable and highly intensive water-economic activities), but which condemns other areas that cannot fully take advantage of its use as it passes through their territory. Thus, political promises and territorial expectations have situated water resources in the centre of the political debate, further intensifying the dissonance between natural availability and resource use. The project National Hydrological Plan of 2001, with the inclusion of a system of water transfers in the Ebro to supply Eastern Spain (Catalonia, Valencia and Murcia) and the transfers in the Tajo-Guadiana river system, generated major political and social confrontations among territories, on a scale never before seen regarding a natural resource.

Appendix

List and code of provinces:

ALB: Albacete, ALI: Alicante, ALM: Almería, AV: Ávila, BAD: Badajoz, BAL: Baleares, BAR: Barcelona, BUR: Burgos, CAC: Cáceres, CAD:

Cádiz, CAN: Cantabria, CAS: Castellón, CIU: Ciudad Real, COR: Córdoba, ACO: A Coruña, CUE: Cuenca, GIR: Girona, GRA: Granada, GUA: Guadalajara, GUI: Guipúzcoa, HUEL: Huelva, HUE: Huesca, JAE: Jaén, ALA: Álava, LEO: León, LLEI: Lleida, LU: Lugo, MAD: Madrid, MAL: Málaga, MUR: Murcia, NAV: Navarra, OU: Ourense, PAL: Palencia, PON: Pontevedra, AST: Asturias, RIO: La Rioja, SAL: Salamanca, SEG: Segovia, SEV: Sevilla, SOR: Soria, TAR: Tarragona, TER: Teruel, TOL: Toledo, VAL: Valencia, VALL: Valladolid, BIZ: Vizcaya, ZAM: Zamora, ZAR: Zaragoza

Acknowledgements

This work has been partially supported by the Ministry of Science and Innovation of the Spanish Government, projects ECO 2012–3328 and ECO 2010–14929 and the Department of Science, Technology and Universities of the Government of Aragon, the Research Group for "Agrifood Economic History" and the Research Group "Growth, Demand and Natural Resources". Ignacio Cazcarro acknowledges the support of the US National Science Foundation CNH grant #1115025, "Impacts of Global Change Scenarios on Ecosystem Services from the World's Rivers". Miguel Martín-Retortillo and Ana Serrano acknowledge the support of the Ministry of Science and Innovation of the Spanish Government grants. The usual disclaimers apply.

Notes

1 The provinces of Almería, Murcia and Badajoz had a clear horticultural specialization; in 2005 they produced 43 per cent of total horticultural production. Jaén, Sevilla and Córdoba were specialized in olive products, representing 61 per cent of the production of these crops in 2005. The importance of vineyard products in Ciudad Real is notable, since this province produced 20 per cent of total Spanish vineyard production in 2005.
2 See for the Aragonese Pyrenees, Herranz-Loncán (1995).
3 The Tajo-Segura was devised in the I National Plan of Hydraulic Works as the transfer of surplus from the Tajo (Tagus) to correct a hydrographic imbalance, taking almost half a century to complete (in 1979) and creating a 286-km canal.

References

Abell, R., Thieme, M.L., Revenga, C., Bryer, M., Kottelat, M., Bogutskaya, N., Coad, B., Mandrak, N., Balderas, S.C., Bussing, W., Stiassny, M.L.J., Skelton, P., Allen, G.R., Unmack, P., Naseka, A., Ng, R., Sindorf, N., Robertson, J., Armijo, E., Higgins, J. V., Heibel, T.J., Wikramanayake, E., Olson, D., López, H.L., Reis, R.E., Lundberg, J.G., Sabaj Pérez, M.H. and Petry, P., 2008. Freshwater ecoregions of the world: a new map of biogeographic units for freshwater biodiversity conservation. *BioScience*, 58 (5), 403–414.
Allen, R.C., 1994. Agriculture during the Industrial Revolution. *In*: R. Floud and D. McCloskey, eds. *The Economic History of Britain Since 1700: 1700–1860.* Cambridge, MA: Cambridge University Press, 96–122.

Amezketa, E., 2008. *Problemática relacionada con la Salinidad del Suelo en Navarra.* Sección de Evaluación de Recursos Agrarios (SERA). Navarra: Departamento de agricultura, Ganadería y Alimentación (DAGA).

Arrojo, P., 2001. *El Plan Hidrológico Nacional a debate.* Bilbao: Bakeaz y Fundación Nueva Cultura del Agua.

Bairoch, P., 1999. *L'agriculture des pays développés: 1800 à nos jours.* París: Editions Economica.

Barbier, E.B., 2011. *Scarcity and Frontiers: How Economies Have Developed through Natural Resource Exploitation.* New York: Cambridge University Press.

Barciela, C., 1986. Introducción. In: R. Garrabou, C. Barciela and I. Jiménez Blanco, eds. *Historia Agraria de la España contemporánea. 3. El fin de la agricultura tradicional (1900–1960).* Barcelona: Crítica, 383–454.

Chorley, G.P.H., 1981. The agricultural revolution in Northern Europe, 1750–1880: nitrogen, legumes, and crop productivity. *The Economic History Review*, 34 (1), 71–93.

Christiansen, T., 2012. *The Reason Why: The Post Civil-war Agrarian Crisis in Spain.* Zaragoza: Universidad de Zaragoza.

Clar, E. and Pinilla, V., 2009. Agriculture and economic development in Spain, 1870–1973. In: P. Lains and V. Pinilla, eds. *Agriculture and Economic Development in Europe since 1870.* London: Routledge, 311–332.

Clar, E., Pinilla, V. and Serrano, R., 2014. El comercio agroalimentario español en la segunda globalización, 1951–2011. *Historia Agraria*, 65, 113–145.

Clark, G., 1987. Productivity growth without technical change in European agriculture before 1850. *The Journal of Economic History*, 47 (2), 419–432.

Díaz, M., Naveso, M.A. and Rebollo, E., 1993. Respuesta de las comunidades nidificantes de aves a la intensificación agrícola en cultivos cerealistas de la Meseta Norte (Valladolid-Palencia, España). *Aegypius*, 11, 1–6.

Dietzenbacher, E. and Los, B., 1998. Structural decomposition techniques: sense and sensitivity. *Economic Systems Research*, 10 (4), 307–324.

Dougherty, C.T. and Hall, A.W., 1995. *Environmental Impact Assessment of Irrigation and Drainage Projects.* FAO Irrigation and Drainage paper. No. 53.

Duarte, R., Pinilla, V. and Serrano, A., 2013. Is there an environmental Kuznets curve for water use? A panel smooth transition regression approach. *Economic Modelling*, 31, 518–527.

Duarte, R., Pinilla, V. and Serrano, A., 2014a. Looking backward to look forward: water use and economic growth from a long-term perspective. *Applied Economics*, 46 (2), 212–224.

Duarte, R., Pinilla, V. and Serrano, A., 2014b. The effect of globalisation on water consumption: a case study of the Spanish virtual water trade, 1849–1935. *Ecological Economics*, 100, 96–105.

Duarte, R., Pinilla, V. and Serrano, A., 2014c. The water footprint of the Spanish agricultural sector: 1860–2010. *Ecological Economics*, 108, 200–207.

European Commission, 2002. *Towards a Strategy for Soil Protection.* COM. Brussels, European Commission.

FAO/IPGRI, 1994. *Genebank Standards.* Rome: Food and Agriculture Organization of the United Nations/International Plant Genetic Resources Institute.

Federico, G., 2005. *Feeding the World: An Economic History of Agriculture, 1800–2000.* Princeton, NJ: Princeton University Press.

Gallego Martínez, D., 1993. Pautas regionales de cambio técnico en el sector agrario español (1900–1930). *Cuadernos aragoneses de economía*, 3 (2), 241–276.

Garrabou, R., 1994. Revolución o revoluciones agrarias en el siglo XIX: su difusión en el mundo mediterráneo. *In*: A. Sanchez Picón, ed. *Agriculturas mediterráneas y mundo campesino. Cambios históricos y retos actuales*. Almería: Instituto de Estudios Almerienses, 93–110.

Gil Olcina, A., 1995. Conflictos autonómicos sobre trasvases de agua en España. *Investigaciones geográficas*, 13, 17–28.

Gleick, P.H., 1993. *Water in Crisis: A Guide to the World's Fresh Water Resources*. Oxford: Oxford University Press.

Goerlich, F.J., 2012. Datos climáticos históricos para las regiones españolas. CRU TS 2.1. *Investigaciones de Historia Económica – Economic History Research*, 8 (1), 29–40.

González de Molina, M., 2001. Condicionamientos ambientales del crecimiento agrario español (siglos XIX y XX). *In*: J. Pujol-Andreu, M. González de Molina and L.F. Prieto, eds. *El pozo de todos los males: Sobre el atraso de la agricultura española contemporánea*. Barcelona: Crítica, 43–94.

Grigg, D.B., 1982. *The Dynamics of Agricultural Change: The Historical Experience*. London: Hutchinson.

Hayami, Y. and Ruttan, V.W., 1985. *Agricultural Development: An International Perspective*. Baltimore, MA: Johns Hopkins University Press.

Herranz-Loncán, A., 1995. La construcción de pantanos y su impacto sobre la economía y población del Pirineo aragonés. *In*: L.J. Acín and V. Pinilla, eds. *Pueblos abandonados: ¿un mundo perdido?*. Zaragoza: Rolde de Estudios Aragoneses, 79–102.

Herranz-Loncán, A., 2004. *La dotación de infraestructuras en España, 1844–1935*. Madrid: Banco de España, Servicio de Estudios.

Ibáñez, C., Prat, N., Canicio, A. and Curcó, A., 1999. *El delta del Ebro: un sistema amenazado*. Bilbao: Bakeaz.

Ibarra, P., de la Riva, J., Iriarte, I., Rodrigo, V. and Rabanaque, I., 2008. Gestión del Agua y Medio Natural. *In*: V. Pinilla, ed. *Gestión y usos del agua en la Cuenca del Ebro en el siglo XX*. Zaragoza: Prensas Universitarias de Zaragoza, 609–657.

INE, 2009. Censo Agrario, Madrid: Instituto Nacional de Estadística.

IUCN, 2009. *The IUCN Red List of Threatened Species 2009*. International Union for Conservation of Nature and Natural Resources.

Junta Consultiva Agronómica, 1918. Medios que se utilizan para suministrar el riego a las tierras y distribución de los cultivos en la zona regable. Resumen hecho por … de las memorias de 1916, remitidas por los ingenieros del servicio agronómico provincial., Madrid: Imprenta de los hijos de M. G. Hernández.

Lains, P. and Pinilla, V., eds., 2008. *Agriculture and Economic Development in Europe Since 1870*. London and New York: Routledge.

MAGRAMA, 1935–2010. Anuario Estadístico de la Produccion Agraria. Available at: www.magrama.gob.es/es/estadistica/temas/publicaciones/anuario-de-estadistica/default.aspx.

MAPA, 2002. *Programa de vigilancia ambiental del PNR- Horizonte 2008*. Madrid: Ministerio de Agricultura, Pesca y Alimentación.

Martínez Carrión, J.M. and Calatayud, S., 2005. El cambio tecnológico en el uso de las aguas subterráneas en la España del siglo XX. Un enfoque regional. *Revista de Historia Industrial*, 28, 81–115.

Martín-Retortillo, M. and Pinilla, V., 2015. Patterns and causes of growth of European agricultural production, 1950–2005. *Agricultural History Review*, 63.

Meybeck, M., 2003. Global analysis of river systems: from Earth system controls to Anthropocene syndromes. *Philosophical Transactions of the Royal Society of London. Series B, Biological Sciences*, 358 (1440), 1935–1955.

Oki, T. and Kanae, S., 2006. Global hydrological cycles and world water resources. *Science (New York)*, 313 (5790), 1068–1072.

Oñate, J.J., 2009. Regadío y ecología: exigencias medio ambientales. *In*: J.A. Gómez-Limon, ed. *La economía del agua de riego en España*. Almería: Cajamar.

Pinilla, V., 2004. Sobre la agricultura y el crecimiento económico en España, 1800–1935. *Historia Agraria*, 34, 137–162.

Pinilla, V., 2006. The development of irrigated agriculture in twentieth-century Spain: a case study of the Ebro basin (English). *The Agricultural History Review*, 54 (1), 122–141.

Pinilla, V., ed., 2008a. *Gestión y usos del agua en la cuenca del Ebro en el siglo XX*. Zaragoza: Universidad de Zaragoza.

Pinilla, V., 2008b. Gestión y usos del agua en el siglo XX. Un estudio de caso: la Cuenca del Ebro. *In*: *Gestión y usos del agua en la Cuenca del Ebro en el siglo XX*. Zaragoza: Prensas Universitarias de Zaragoza, 9–35.

Pinilla, V. and Ayuda, M.I., 2009. Foreign markets, globalisation and agricultural change in Spain. *In*: V. Pinilla, ed. *Markets and Agricultural Change in Europe from the 13th to the 20th Century*. Turnhout: Brepols Publishers, 173–208.

Pinilla, V. and Ayuda, M.I., 2010. Taking advantage of globalization? Spain and the building of the international market in Mediterranean horticultural products, 1850–1935. *European Review of Economic History*, 14 (2), 239–274.

Pinilla, V. and Serrano, R., 2009. Agricultural and food trade in the European Community since 1963. *In*: K.K. Patel, ed. *Fertile Ground for Europe? The History of European Integration and the Common Agricultural Policy since 1945*. Baden-Baden: Nomos, 273–300.

Ramón i Muñoz, J.M., 2013. Cambio agrario, uso del suelo y regadío: el impacto del Canal de Urgell, 1860–1935. *Historia agraria: Revista de agricultura e historia rural*, 59, 43–94.

Reig Martínez, E. and Picazo Tadeo, A.J., 2002. *La agricultura española: crecimiento y productividad*. Alicante: Caja de Ahorros del Mediterráneo.

Rosenberg, D.M., McCully, P. and Pringle, C.M., 2000. Global-scale environmental effects of hydrological alterations: introduction. *BioScience*, 50 (9), 746.

Santiago-Caballero, C., 2013. Trapped by nature: provincial grain yields in Spain in the mid 18th century. *Revista de Historia Económica – Journal of Iberian and Latin American Economic History*, 31 (3), 359–386.

Tortella, G., 1994. Patterns of economic retardation and recovery in South-Western Europe in the nineteenth and twentieth centuries. *The Economic History Review*, 47, 1–21.

UNDP, 2006. *Human Development Report – Beyond Scarcity: Power, Poverty and the Global Water Crisis*. United Nations Development Programme.

United-Nations-Water, 2009. *World Water Development Report 3 "Water in a Changing World."* UN-Water (UNESCO) WWAP.

Van Zanden, J.L., 1991. The first green revolution: the growth of production and productivity in European agriculture. *The Economic History Review*, 44 (2), 215–239.

Villarroya, F., 2006. Los conflictos sobre el trasvase del Ebro y del Tajo. M+A. *Revista Electrónic@ de Medioambiente*, 2, 56–72.

Vörösmarty, C.J. and Sahagian, D., 2000. Anthropogenic disturbance of the terrestrial water cycle. *BioScience*, 50 (9), 753.

Vörösmarty, C.J., Lettenmaier, D., Leveque, C., Meybeck, M., Pahl-Wostl, C., Alcamo, J., Cosgrove, W., Grassl, H., Hoff, H., Kabat, P., Lansigan, F., Lawford, R. and Naiman, R., 2004. Humans transforming the global water system. *Eos, Transactions American Geophysical Union*, 85 (48), 509–514.

Vörösmarty, C.J., McIntyre, P.B., Gessner, M.O., Dudgeon, D., Prusevich, A., Green, P., Glidden, S., Bunn, S.E., Sullivan, C.A., Liermann, C.R. and Davies, P.M., 2010. Global threats to human water security and river biodiversity. *Nature*, 467 (7315), 555–561.

World Commission on Dams, 2000. *Dams and Development: A New Framework for Decision-making*. London: Earthscan Publications Ltd.

Index

Page numbers in *italics* denote tables, those in **bold** denote figures.

Aboyade, O. *104*, 105–6, 110
Acemoglu, D. 11, 13, 29, 40, 77, 79, 83, 86, 90, 95, 264
Africa 16, 37, 59, 86, 142, 248; booms 101; British colonial ambition 80; GDP wasted 290n13; natural resource wealth 61; newly independent economies 30; peasant economies 13; southern **62**, 79; underdeveloped countries 63; West 62, 73n7–8, 102, 105
African Economic Outlook 86, 89
agricultural 59, 69, 345, 356; colonial 54, 64; conversion of land **58**; development 154, 352; frontier **60–2**; European Common Agricultural Policy (CAP) 346; land 65–6, 104; production 155, 257, 261, 266, 341, **343**; productivity 43, 154; sector 45, 49, 80, 86, 93–4, 111, 141, 154, 253, 255, 261, 285, 339, 343, 350; Spanish production 344, *346*, 348–9, **350–1**, 355
agriculture 4, 12, 28, 45, 57, **84**, 123, 249, 252–3, 261, 275, 341, 356; American 129, 136n3; Australian **287**; Chilean **206**, 221n29; colonial administrative expenditure *81*; exporting sector 284–5; GDP *35*, 36–7, 78; Indonesia 243; irrigated 340, 344, 352–3; Latin America 161, 211; limiting factor 343; low productivity 35; modernization 354; Norwegian 302, 307; production 340; product levels 266; rents-wages ratio 255; slavery-based 65; Spanish 344, 348, **350–1**, 355; subsistence 87; technological revolutions 277; wages 263; water-intensive 356; workforce 50n2

Allen, L. 169–70
Allen, R.C. 133, 136n2, 341
Altman, M. 4–5
Álvarez, J. 262–3
Alvarez, R. 220n7
Amdam, R.P. 304–5
America Atlantic 59; Committee on the Machinery of the USA 119; international economic success 294; migration to 302; nineteenth century 134; North and South 4, 59, **60**, 62
American 55, 126; agriculture 129, 136n3; development 55–6, 119; economic development 294; exports 121; firms 130, 134; fracking 132; history 120, 294; industrialization 69; labour 290; Manufacturing Belt 133; property 165; South 65
American minerals 120, 128, 133; abundance 121; coal 122; copper 126; development 123; domestic-market orientation 134; expansion 124; mineral-based economy 68; oil 69, 128–30, 236; resources 125
American mining 134; engineers 302; executives 126; Institute of Mining Engineers 125, 133; regulation 135; sector 5
American Petroleum 69, 128; Institute *121*, **130**, 131
Andersen, S.S. 326–7
Annaniassen, E. 316–17, 319, 335n8
Arcilla Farias, E. 170–1
Argentina 6, 54, 63–4, 72, 86, 198n3, 248–9, 260, 262, 276; agricultural based economy 154; dollarization 279; education *195*; exports 277; gas exports

Index 363

to 190; GDP **175–6**; land distribution 263; land-resource/population ratios 272; rents of natural resources **153**; stratified universalism 156; structural productivity *151*; wheat exports 220n9
Atkinson, G. 11, 160
Austin, G. 101, 116n1
Australia 6, 13, 17, 123, 132–3, 145, 220n9, 248, 261–2, 265–6, 272, 282, 286, 290n11, 296, 299–301, 306; boom 54, 56, 289n6, 302; Broken Hill (New South Wales) 301; colonial 279; copper production 220n10; development 290n19; developmental state 276; economic situation 274; environmental movement 136; export dependence 273, 280; exports **285**; grain production 205; land distribution 263; Lucky Country 272, 281, 284, 289n4; regions of recent settlement 63–4; Reserve Bank of Australia (RBA) **287**; resource-rich 219n2, 219n4, 324; structural productivity *151*; technological knowledge 297; temperate 61; trepang trade 297; wealth 289n4; wealth structure *144*; wheat export industries 277; wool export 298
Australian 272, 295; colonial dominions 282; conditions 301–2; dollar 290n18; economy 286, 296; exports 298; industry and exports **287**; mining 301; overseas trade 299; per capita incomes 296; prospectors 301; public organisations 300; settler process 274; society 297
Australian economy 286, 296; natural resources-based 294; NRBKE 295, 309
Australian natural resources 298; knowledge economy (NRBKE) 295, 309; management 204
Auty, R.M. 2, 10–12, 16–17, 26, *27*, 30–2, 41, 46–7, 50, 73n2, 88, 92, 101, 108–9, 219n3, 250, 274
Azar, P. *192*, 267n1

Badia-Miró, M. 5–6, 10, 16, 198n1, 207, 209, 212, *213*, **213**, 214–15, **216**, 217, 219, 219n1, 220n18, 221n24
Bahl, R. 237–8
Bain and Company 77, 94
Bairoch, P. 142, 341
Bakken, G.M. 131, 135
Baland, J.M. 11
Baldwin, R.E. 32, 47

Baptista, A. 172–3
Barbier, E.B. 1, 4–5, 13–14, 16, 56–7, 59, 64–5, 67, 69–72, 73n3–4, 73n11, 204–5, 252, 289n8, 340
Beaulier, S.A. 77, 83
Berg, B.I. 306
Berry, S.S. 105
Bértola, L. 5, **143**, 145, 150, *151–2*, *157*, 159n1, 266n1
Beteta, M.R. 168
Bevan, D. 32, 47, 100, 106–7
BHP (Broken Hill Proprietaries) 302
Bjerke, E. 303
Black Death 65, 70
Blainey, G. 300–1
Bloom, D.E. 14, 37, 43
Bolivia 201n31; education 193, 194–5, *196*, 197, 201n34; education and health spending 191, *192*; exclusive system 156; external debt crisis 190; imports from Chile 207; natural resources-rich 198n3; revenues **187**; Stabilization Plan 189, 196; territorial dispute 208, 220n13
Bolivian 196–7; central government 187, 195, 198n8, 200n19; economic underdevelopment 189; economy 185; education 193, 201n35; elites 189; fiscal reliance 186–7, 190; GDP 200n22; government 185, 187–90, 193, 198n8, 199n11; Gulf Oil Co. 190; mining 188; mining taxes 200n28; natural resources revenues 191; non-oil industry 188; public finances 191, 197; public universities 201n36; tax legislation 199n11; tin quota 199n16; VAT 200n29
Bolt, J. 80, 82, 90
boom 28, 91, 101–2, 104, 106–8, 109, 127, 205, 214–15, 219, 315; commodity 26, 232, 243; days 321; domestic natural gas 132; economic 4, 56, 105; energy intensive industries 320; export 73n11, 220n8, 281, 284; gold 301–2; investment 107, 289n6; Latin American economy 152; mining 285; natural resources 54, 92, 204, 272; nitrate 207–9, 211, 217; Norway 319; potential 212; price 9, 66, 71, 73n11; resource 6, 111, 115, 275, 296, 313–14, 318, 333; silver 59; speculative 234; world transport and trade 73n11
booming cities 106, 272–3, 300; commodity revenue 28; export sector 9, 283, 289n5; mining cycles 219; sectors 278

Index

booms and busts 10, 47, 273, 279; risk 32
booms collapsed 278; Dutch Disease 205, 272; export 279, 283; mineral 300
Boone, P. 32
Booth, A. 226, 233
Bornhorst, F. 184, 186, 198n2, 199n9
Børresen, A.K. 307–8
Boschini, A.D. 12, 250–2
Botswana 5, 89, 274; cattle economy 88; Development Corporation (BDC) 93; diamond mining 84–5; diamond wealth 92, 94, 96; economic growth rate 86; economy 7, 29, 70, 79, 84, 87, 91; education 194, *195*; GDP growth **85**; Gini coefficient *83*; government 77, 84, 86, 90, 93; growth miracle 90, 96; industrialization 92–3; International Merchandise Trade Statistics (BIMTS) 78, 89; land-locked 85, 95; Meat Commission 83; natural resource trap 78
Boyce, J. 5, 267n8
Braütigam, D. 185
Brazil 37, 66, 70, 123, 132; agricultural based economy 154; diamond deposits 89; dual system 156; education *195*; GDP **175–6**; natural resources-rich 198n3, 272; partially privatized company 327; plantation economy 59; rents of natural resources **153**; structural productivity *151*; sugar economy **60**
Breistein, D. 304
Bretton Woods system 278; post-Bretton Woods era 279
Britain 129, 282, 298, 314, 322; Australian independence 299; coal mining 300; commodity dependence 273; expansion of agricultural land 65; immigration 61; manufacturing 296; mining nation 119; Nigerian Independence 100; nineteenth century 40; smelting ore 125; state-owned oil company 325
British 298; access to raw materials 103; American coal imports 119; companies 319, 324; distributive pattern 249, 262, 265; Empire 80, 123, 132, 279, 281; former possessions 248; government 104, 132, 327; immigration 281, 309; Industrial Revolution 120; mining traditions 300; movement 220n13; North Sea 325; state 326; trading firms 104; tradition 264
British colonial 281; convict colony 296–7; establishment 109; ambition 80; former colonies 249; imperial influence 274; power in North America 66; regime 263; settlement of southern Africa 62
Bruland, K. 306
Brunnschweiler, C.N. 3, 15, 31, 88–9, 198n4
Bulmer-Thomas, V. 207, 212
Bulte, E.H. 11–12, 250

Cain, L.P. 121
Canada 13–14, 17, 54, 59, 63–4, 66–7, 123, 132, 136, 136n6, *144*, 145, *151*, 248–9, 261, 266, 272–3, 277, 284; electricity production **316**; HDI and GDP **176**, 290n11, **332**
Canadian Anglo Canadian Cement Co **113**; economic development 63
Cariola, C. 207, 209, 211, 217, 220n6, 220n14
Carlsson, E. 80, 82, 95
Carreras-Marín, A. 198n1, 212, 221n27
Carrillo Batalla, T.E. 171–2
cartel 199n16; cartelization (cartelisation) 238, 273; international tin 242; *see also* tin cartel
Cashin, P. 47
cattle economy 79–80, 85, 88; colonial 78, 82
Cazcarro, I. 16–17
Central American republics 156
CEPAL 189
Chandler, A.D. 121, 127
Chile 50, 204, 220n13, 249, 267n4, 274, 276; competitive advantage lost 220n9; copper *121*, 126, **206**, *208*; Dutch Disease 220n20; economic development 205; economy 248; education *192*, 193, *194–5*; environmental movement 136, 136n6; GDP **175–6**; industrialization 16; industry *213*; land-resource/population ratios 272; natural resource rents **153**; nitrates 209, 211, 220n14; resource-based development 133; resource-rich 49, 198n3; revenues 207; stratified universalism 156; structural productivity *151*
Chilean 185, 187, 193, 220n13; economic history 208; economy 204–5, 209, 211–12, 217, 219; exports **206**, 207; foreign trade 214; government 220n13; industrial activity 217; industrial exports 221n27; industry 213, 216
China 37, 41, 123, 132, 142; dual track reform 50; economic development 243,

288n3; frontier-based development 69, 70; HDI/GDP **176**; migrant labour 240; pegged RMB 279; unstable 276; wealth structure *144*
Chinese: booming industrial exports 272–3; demand 284–5; immigrants 232
Christensen, P. 318, 324
Christensen, S.A. 315, 319, 335n9
CIA 78
Cimoli, M. 7, 9
civil war 106–7, 109, *112*; Chilean 209; Nigerian 113, 115; post 123; pre-civil war era 122; Spanish 344
Clar, E. 341, 344, 348
Clark, G. 73n6, 341
Colcough, C. **81**, 89, 95
Collett, J.P. 305, 307
Collier, P. 11, 32, 100, 184, 220n9
colonial 80, 82, 104, 110, 301; agricultural development 54, 64; Australia 279, 282; British Office 281; British regime 263; cattle economy 78; context 83; elites 95; era 91, 94, 114, 126, 226, 240, 290n10; expansion in Asia 61; heritage 264–5; Indonesia 236; influence 90; investment *81*, 86; legacy 14, 109; marketing boards 115; period 101; power 66; rule 230; settlement 296; settlers 13; territories 102
colonial government 103–4, 105–6, 109, 114, 265; administrations 80–1, 94; Dutch 230; expenditures *81*; institutions 102, 110
colonial institutions 29, 114–15; institutional framework 102; pre-colonial 79, 90
COMIBOL 189–90, 200n20
concessions 231, 318–19, 321; expiry 236; exploitation 235; government conditions 240; hydropower 335n10; laws 316, 320, 323, 325, 333–4; mining *231*, 232, **239**; Norwegian policy 324, 335n8; oil and gas 169, 326; right of reversion 317; tax 237
Connolly, E. **287**, 289n6
contract of work (CoW) *231*, 232–4, *235*, 236–40, 244
Corden, W.M. 9–10, 13, 91, 100, 205
Coronil, F. 172–4, 178–9, 180n1
Crafts, N. 73n4, 133, **176**
Crivelli, E. 184, 191, 198n2
Czelusta, J. 5, 16, 67–9, 284

Darmono, D. 233, 237–8, 244n2

David, P.A. 5, 55, 67–8, 120, 123, 132, 219n3, 294, 309
Davis, G.A. 160, 205
Dean, E. 111, *112*
Denoon, D. 248, 265, 267n4
Departemen Pertambangan 233
DESDM *235*
Deutsch.J.G. 104
developing countries 10, 17, 29–30, 32, 37–9, 47, 49, 70, 88, 92, 107, 134–5, 146, 191, 273, 288n1
DFAT **280**, **285**
di Tella, G. 5, 56, 63, 65, 71–2
diamonds 78, 92; Debswana Diamond Company Ltd. 84; deep mining 85; deposits 77, 84, 89, 95–6; economy 78, 84–6, 89, 94; export revenues 87; incomes 86, 90; industry 86; led growth 87, 91, 94; resources 77, 85, 95; sector 78, 85–6; wealth 92
diamonds 230, 232–3; extraction 93, 96; production 92
Díaz, J. 214, **215–16**, 220n19, 221n25
dictator 169; dictatorial periods 201n36
dictatorships 161, 276; Franco 344, 348; Gómez 169
Dike, K.O. 102, 104
Ding, N. 15–16
disequilibrium abnormal rents hypothesis 65, 71
Domar, E.D. 64–5, 71
Dosi, G. 9
Duarte, R. 340, 343–6
Ducoing, C. 5–6, 10, 16, 212, *213*, **213**, 214–15, **216**, 219, 220n18, 220n21, 221n24
Dugstad, A.R.S. 316–18, 321, 335n8
Dutch Disease 10, *42*, 91–2, 94, 164, 220n5, 220n20, 313, 321, 328; effects 16, 28, 32, 34, 40, 44–6, 49, 211, 319, 329; framework 209; problem 205, 334

East Asia 36, 50n4, 274; commodity-dependent countries 288n1; Newly Industrializing Economies 88; transformation 288n3
Easterly, W. 14, 290n10
Echevarria, C. 36, 167
economic crisis 89, 91; 1930s 8; Euro-American 275; macroeconomic 197
economic diversification 46, 71, 274; active strategy 335; competitive 17
economy 78, 84–5; agricultural based **154**; Australian 286, 296; Bolivian 185;

366 *Index*

economy *continued*
  boom 152; Botswana 7, 29, 70, 79, 84, 87, 91; cattle economy 78–80, 85, 88; Chilean 204–5, 209, 211–12, 217, 219, 248; diamond 78, 84–6, 89, 94; green 174; Indonesian 229; Latin American 140, 152, 161; Mexican 165; mineral 26–7, 32, 47, 68; natural resources 294; Newly Industrializing 88; Norwegian 289n6, 303, 319, 322, 329–30, 335; NRBKE 294–5, 309; oil 101, 294, 328; peasant 13; plantation 59, **60**, 65–6; sugar **60**; US 55, 68, *121*, 123, 295; Venezuelan 172; *see also* natural resource based economies, political economy
Ecuador 107, *151*, 156, 198n3, 201n31
Ehret, C. 73n8
electoral processes 17; democracy 282; governance 29; reform 40
El Serafy, S. 166, 174
Emerson, C. 237
employment 7, 28, 35, 37, 41, 86, 275, 277, 333; agricultural 45; creation 227; full 146, 283–4; generation 285, **286**; growth 36; intensive 93; mining sector *228*, 240; opportunities 92, 243; petroleum geologists 128; source 356; subsidies *42*; system 282
Engerman, S.L. 14, 66–7, 71, 264
Esping-Andersen, G. 146–7, 156
Europe 57, 59, 351; coal **122**; common currency 283; Eastern 314; emigration from 58; GDP 302, **315**; gold ore 125; inflation 173; market 73n5; mining 136n6, 307; mining schools 134; mining technology 301; modern 56; Northern 306, 309; north-western 299; pre-industrial 341; structural productivity *151*; transportation links 101–2; Western 4, 65, 70, 73n11, 170, **175**, 177, 274, 296; wool market 298
European 13, 58, 61, 306, 327, 340–1; average income 174; chemical industries 315; Commission 353; Common Agricultural Policy (CAP) 346; countries 271, 303, 314, 322; diseases 73n7; Economic Community 346; economic growth 324, 329; economies 57, 214; goods exported 116n2; industrializing 4; investments in US mining 134; mining engineers 127; monopolization of Asian trade routes 73n5; rulers 262; technologies 120, 301;

trading firms 102, 115; Union 32; Western 344
European colonies 14, 66; colonial era 290n10; colonists 61–2, 263; colonization 13, 280; settlement 29, **62**, 119, 262–3, 297
Ewell, J. 173
exploration licences 231, 235, 325
export tax 114, 185, 200n19–20, 242; nitrate 209, 211; silver 188–9, 199n11; tin 199n12–13

FAO/IPGRI 353
farmers 36, 47, 105, 355; adapted to conditions 136n3; clubs 299; export earnings 103, 106; faction 319; family 277, 281; forests owned 315, 318; inventions and improvements 304–5; lawsuit 135; native 55–6; peasant 34, 40; prices received 104; sedentary society 264; settlements 61; small 50, 265, 282; smallholder 108; trickle down impact 102; yeoman 29
Federal Office of Statistics 105, **113**
Federico, G. 141, 340
Fell, J.E. 124, 136n4
Filgueira, F. 156
Findlay, R. 5, 55, 57, 63–4, 68, 73n4, 73n11, 253
First World War (WWI) 4, 105, 248–9, 364, 319–20, 324
fisheries 58, 296, 302, 307, 315, 324, 332–3, 353; fish farming 332; licences 32; operations 237; trawlers 318, 324
foreign aid 27, 31–2, *33*, 48, 50, 111
foreign direct investment (FDI) 10, 134, 190, 235, 237, 317; inflows 233–4, 238
forestry 12, 237, 273, 302–3, 307, 309; companies 277, 315; Law 245n4; Norwegian industry 318; owners 305; products 277, 315; regulations 324
Forrest, T. 107–8
Frank, A.G. 8, 142, 220n6
Frankema, E. 80, 194, 201n31
Franklin, B. 119
Freeman, C. 9
Fundación Jubileo 196, 200n27

Gallego Martínez, D. **343**, **349**, **351**
Gallo, C. 185, 200n17, 211, 220n6
Gaolathe, B. 84, 92
García-Jimeno, C. 251, 256
gas 130, 227, 232, 330, 343; boom 289n5; concessions 326; development prospects

Index 367

132; exporters 274; exports 190, 241, 243, 290n16; firms 239; industry 329; Law 236–7; offshore 324; prices 229, **230**; production 200n21, 233; sector 313; state revenue **331**; technologies 131; value adding 240, **242**; *see also* liquefied natural gas, gasoline
gasoline: aviation 241; domestic price 190; taxes on consumption 200n21
Gelb, A.H. 11, 28, 45, 101, 107–8
Gillis, M. 13, 234
Goerlich, F.J. **342**, **351**
Gómez, J.V. 161, 169
Gómez, W. 200n18–20
Good, K. 87, 90
Goodman, L.W. 161, 178
Gorelick, S.M. 131
Greasley, D. 219n3, 248
Great Depression 16, 30, 187, 189, 199n16, 204, 211–12, 214, 219, 282
green economists 166; economy 174; standards 168
greenfield investments 321; exploration of deposits 238
Green Revolution 340
Gregorio, J. 12, 220n17
Gregory, R.G. 204, 219n2
gross value added (GVA) **227**, *228*, **229–30**, 238, **239**, **242**
Gylfason, T. 2, 10–13, 67, 70, 89, 250, 235n2

Habakkuk, H. 88, 219n4
Haber, S. 167, 186–7, 198n4
Hall, P. 147–8
Hallenstvedt, A. 318, 324
Hanisch, T.J. 325, 335n14
Hansen, B. 5, 63
Harris, J.R. 208, 220n12
Hartwick, J.M. 174, 177
Harvey, C. 81, 119
Heald, S. 90
Helleiner, G.K. 101–2, **103**, 106, 116n1
Herranz-Loncán, A. 198n1, 343, 357n2
high-rent 27–8, 39, 46, 321; economies 27, 31, 34–5, 37, 40–1, 44–6, 49–50; staple trap 28, 41, *42*, 44–5, 48
Hill, C.B. 91–2
Hill, H. 243
Hill, N.P. 124–5
Hillbom, E. 5, 7, 11, 16, 77–8, 80, 82, 86–7, 90, 93, 95–6
Hillman, J. 238, 242
Hirschman, A.O. 7, 92, 220n16, 271, 273,

288n1; Innis/Hirschman theory 277, 290n14; Innis/Hirschman/Krugman theme 279
Historisk statistikk **322**, 324
Hodne, F. 315, 320–1
Hong Kong 41, 279
Horne, D. 289n4
Hounshell, D.A. 120
Hubbert, M.K. 131
Huberman, M. 145, 156
Hujo, K. 6, 185, 198n7
Human Development Index (HDI) 161, 175, 177, 179, 273, 289n9, 290n11; GDP ranking **176**; inequality adjusted *157*
hydrocarbon 165, 190, 200n22, 200n26; exports 162; exploitation 199n9; GDP 188; industries 185, 199n10; international prices 200n23; Law of 1943 164, 170; production 196, 198n2; revenues *186*, 187; royalties 201n37; sector 198n5; taxes 200n21, 200n27
hydropower 309, 322–4, 333, 352; concessions 318, 335n10; investment in 320–1; plants 317, 319–20, 323, 334; policy 325, 334

Iceland 273, 324
IDE *228*, **230**
Iimi, A. 91–2
IMF 50n1, 90
income distribution 258, *260*, 261, 265–6; in agriculture 249; more equal 43, 172; worsening 252–3, 255, 267n5
income *per capita 35*, 249; average 174, 273, 282, 289n9
indicators 174–5, 177, 229, 259; economic 173, 180; fiscal and trade 164; income distribution 255–6; indirect 193; macroeconomic 178–9; misleading 161, 171; natural resource abundance 15; welfare 3, 12
Indonesia 6, 16, 29, 107, 226–7, 232, 242–3; aluminium 241; Constitution 244; exports 229; foreign trade statistics **230**; governments 235, 238; legislation 237; mineral deposits 240; National Labour Force Survey *228*; oil 245n3; oil companies 231, 233–4, 236; tin production 228, 234
Indonesian 244; companies 236; economy 229; exports 243; ventures 241
Indonesian mining 226, *228–9*, *231*, 233, 235, 237–8, 240, 244; commodities prices 243; legislation 230; miners 232

INE **352**
Inikori, J. 105, 116n2
Innis, H.A. 4, 63; Innis/Hirschman theory 277, 290n14; Innis/Hirschman/Krugman theme 279
irrigated 344–6, 348, 351–3; areas 340, 342, *346*; land **343**, **352**; paddy 69; production **345**; sector 350
irrigation 17, 73n6, 339–42, 344–6, 350, 356; development of 348; expansion 354–5; infrastructure 343, 352–3; role 351; systems 304
Isham, J. 11, 32, 40, 250
IUCN 339

Japan 242, 272, 274, 288n3; GDP **176**, **332**; industrialization 61, 73n6; Japanese groups 148; occupation of Indonesia 232; productivity *151*
Jerven, M. 77, 85
Jones, E.L. 58, 73n6
Joseph, R.A. 110–11
Junta Central Agronómica **352**
Jurajada, S. 54, 73n3

Karl, T. 11, 28, 173
Kaufmann, D. 11, 87
Kilby, P. 102, 105, 110, 113
Kirsch, H.W. 212, 221n22
Krueger, A.O. 11, 30–1, 34
Krugman, P. 7–8, 10, 133; Innis/Hirschman/Krugman theme of linkages 279
Kuznets, S. 295

labor (labour) market 255, 282; highly segmented 146; institutionalization 277; integration of women 158; opportunities 147; turning point *42*, 43
Latin America 14, 149, 178–9, 187, 220n17; commodity price shocks 31; copper extraction and exports 208; development 158; economy 161; education 142, **143**, 159n1, *194–5*; financial expansion 152; frontier-based development 59; GDP 193; import substitution 30; industrialization 171, 211; labor productivity *152*; natural resources 16; peasant economy 13; production sector 150; resource rich 324, 334; Social States 156–7; stagnation 88; underdeveloped countries 63; wealth structure *144*; welfare state 148

Latin American 65, 150; colonies 66; countries 30, 67, 73n2, 157, 172, 174, 193, 201n31; demands 149; development 142; economies 140, 152; education *192*, 194–5; exports 145; GDP **175**; nations 173; natural resource-rich countries 184; oil producers 187; production structure 148; Structuralist school 8; welfare state 156
least developed countries (LDCs) 274, 290n10
Leite, C. 11, 88
Leith, J.C. 77, 83–6, 91, 93
Lewin, M. 77, 93
Lewis, P. 81, 110, 114
Lewis, W.A. 7, 30, 43
Lie, E. 327–30, 332, 335n14, 335n16
Lieuwen, E. 169–71
Lindblad, J.T. 226, 241
Lindert, P.H. 193–4, 201n32–3
liquefied natural gas (LNG) 229, 233, 244, 289n6; production *228*, 237
Lizzeri, A. 40
Llona, A. 211, 220n20
Lloyd, B. 234
Lloyd, C. 16, 145, 156, 248, 265, 267n1, 276, 279, 283, 286, 288, 288n1, 290n12
low-rent competitive industrialisation 28, 41, *42*, 45, 48–9
low-rent economies 34, 37, 39–44, 48
Lucier, P. 122, 127
Lüders, R. 209, 220n6, 220n14, 220n19
Lundahl, M. 5, 55, 57, 63, 64, 68, 73n4, 253
Lustig, N. 168, 201n38

Mabogunje, A.L. 104–5
McCombie, J.S.L. 8
McKinsey 35–6
McLean, I.W. 5, 299
Maddison, A. 165, 174, **175**, 302, 314, **315–16**, 329
Magee, G.B. 298, 301–2
MAGRAMA **343**, **345**, *347–8*, **350–1**
Makgala, C.J. *81*, 87, 90
Malaysia 29, 49–50, 70, **176**, 242, 274
Maloney, W.F. 29, 313, 324
MAPA 353
markets 10, 34, 39–40, *42*, 54, 120, 127, 133–4, 277, 327, 346; absence of 11; broader 265; commodity 55; competitive 27, 32, 41, 46, 49; domestic 241, 244; electricity 332; export 306; financial 168; global 226; imperfect 250; international 330, 344, 356; labor

146; override 30, 48; overseas 165; productive factor 263; repressed 28; traditional 158; world 6, 8, 314
Martín-Retortillo, M. 344, 357
Marwah, H. 4, 11, 16, 100, 108
Masire, Q.K.J. 79, 82–3, 90
Mauritius 41, 46, 50, 93, 274
Mehlum, H. 267n3, 271, 335n2
Meinig, D.W. 59, 73n7
Mellor, J.W. 36, 50n2
MEMR 234
Méndez Beltrán, L.M. 208
Menghetti, D. 301–2
Meredith, D. 105, 297
Metzer, J. **176**, 248
Mexican 160, 166, 168, 179; energy development 162; economy 165; government 164, 167, 169; metals 161
Mexican oil 161, 165; exports and taxes **163**, 166, 168–9; nationalisation **162**, 170; PEMEX (*Petróleos Mexicanos*) 167; production 165; sector 179
Mexicans 160, 166, 168, 179
Mexico 6, 16, 126, 177; dual system 156; economic history 174; GDP **164, 175–6**; positive genuine savings **178**; rents of natural resources **153**; silver production *121*, 161; structural productivity *151*
Meyer, D.R. 133, 277
Mikesell, R.F. 87, 91–2, 160, 205
Miller, R. 207
Mining Law 233–4, 244; clarifications 235; Indonesia 236; Mineral and Coal 238; national 134
Ministerio de Hacienda 170
Mitchell, B.R. 54, 73n3, *121*, **122**
Moenir, A.S. 233, 244n2
Mokyr, J. 295, 297, 310n2
Moore, B. 273, 288n1
Moore, M. 184
Muñoz Gomá, Ó. 212, **213**, 215, **216**, 221n24
Myint, H. 4, 28, 63, 101, 116n1
Myrdal, G. 7–8
Myrvang, C. 307, 323

Naím, M. 173
natural gas 130; domestic 132; exploitation 198n5; exports 91; Indonesia 226, **227**, **228**, 231, 237; US production 131
natural resource based economies 294, 309; exports 320, 333; industries (NRBI) 17, 294–6, 303, 309; knowledge economy (NRBKE) 294–5, 309

natural resources 1–4, 6–7, 9–12, 13, 15, 54–5, 57, 78, 87–92, 94, 184, 197, 205, 248, 250, 266; abundance 5, 16–17, 66, 69, 145, 160, 249, 251–2, 261, 272, 302; curse 204, 219n2; curse literature 185, 191, 198n7; dependence 79, 82–3, 93, 95, 211, 324; endowment 70, 265, 274; exploitation 71; exports 209, 220n8; ownership 314; rents 30–2, *33*, 47–8; state ownership 188; trap 96; wealth 58, 61–2
Neary, J.P. 10, 91, 205
negative savings 161; genuine 177–9
Nelson, R.R. 9, 136n5
Neumayer, E. 160, 177
New Zealand 13, 56, **61**, *144*, *151*, **176**, 204, 219n3, 248, 262–3, 265–6, 273, 276, 281
Nigeria 16, 89, 104–6, 108–10, 115, 116n1, 272, 274; booms 101–2, 113; development 114; exports **103**; government loans 111; northern 102, 107, **113**; resource curse 100–1; wealth structure 144
nitrate 207, 209, 219, 220n5, 335n3, 353; boom 211; cycle 204–5, **206**, 208, 214, 216; Era 220n20, 221n28; mechanization 220n15; production *210*, 217, 320; taxation 220n14
non-boom tradables 28, 44, 49
Nordic 330, 332; countries 324, 330; neighbours 313; regions 274, 276, 288n1; societies 273–4, 286
North, D.C. 26, 29, 38, 148
North America 56, 59, **60**, 66, 264, 301; frontier expansion 64; northeastern 133; oil and gas development prospects 132; resource abundance 119; southern 65; *see also* America, Canada
North and South America 4, 56, 59, **60**, 62; North-South trade model 8
Norway 86, 299, 302, 306–7; Academy of Science 305; boom 319; commodity-dependence 289n6; Dutch Disease 328; egalitarian 314; electricity **316**, 332; environmental movement 136; exports 273, 313; foreign investment 316, 323; GDP **175–6**, 315, **332**; geological surveys 308; German occupation 322; GNP 330; HDI 290n11; HDI/GDP **176**; hydropower 324; interventionist regulatory regime 333; investment in knowledge foundations 133; local knowledge capabilities 296–7; national

370 *Index*

Norway *continued*
  independence movement 298; rejection of EEC membership 325, 327; state regulation 334; structural productivity *151*; wealth structure *144*
Norwegian 160, 295, 317, 324–6, 329–30; authorities 332; concession laws 318, 334; concession practice 335n8; economy 294, 322, 335; GDP 314; governments 306, 320–1; machinery 319, 333; pyrites 315; scientists 307–8; society 335n14; state 303
Norwegian continental shelf 313, 327; territorial waters 328–9
Norwegian electricity supplies 316; hydroelectricity production 323
Norwegian exports 315, 322, 324, 329; aluminium **322**; industry 313
Norwegian industry 304, 329; electrometallurgical 322–3, 335n3; energy intensive 318, 320, 322; export 313; growth 316, 320, 323; industrial company 325; metallurgical 322–3, 332; oil 325–9; resource 317, 319–22, 333; shipping 315, 324–5
Norwegian mining 315, 319, 323–4; industry 315, 319; managers 306
Norwegian oil 326; companies 326–7; dependence 335; economy 294; industry 325–9; policy 325; price collapse 327; production 327, 330; reserves 313; resources 89, 313; petroleum sector 329–30, **331**, 335
Norwegian politics 328, 330, 332–3; Labour Party 322; political institutions 334; political system 322; politicians 314, 319– 20, 326, 328, 333; post-war political consensus 328
Norwegian resources 320, 334; industries 319, 321, 333; management 204; NRBE 303, 309; NRBKE 295, 309; policies 313–14, 321, 324; regulatory regime 314
Nurkse, R. 7, 88

O'Callaghan, T. 237–8
O'Connell, J. 109, 111
O'Rourke, K.H. 4, 73n4, 73n11
Ocampo, J.A. 8, **143**, 145, 272
OECD 35, 290n11; countries 16, 39, 286
oil 164, 168, 171, 173, 179, 236, 240–1, 326, 328, 330; crude 106, 161, 229, 231, 233, **242**; curse 100–1, 115; cycle 16; domestic consumption 227, 238; economy 101, 294; extracted 128, 170; importers 31, 130; imports 131; palm 102, 241; rents 107, 327; resources 89, 166; revenues 108–9, 111, 114, 243, 332, 335; sector **164**, 226, 244, 329; tax **163**, 172; wealth 165, 169; windfalls 28
oil boom 109–12, 114, 168, 172, 220n7, 229, 313; **1917** 165; **1970s** 100, 106–8, 113, 229, 238, 243–4; Dutch disease effects 243; first 108, 164–5; post-oil boom crisis 161; second 167
oil exports 162, **163**, 168, 171–2, 241; exporters 8, 26, *27*, 28, 31–2, 89, 161, 169, 289n6; exporting 28–9, 47, 274
oil prices 106, 327, 329; decreased 31, 242, 335; fluctuations 115; high 173, 235, 330; international 237; low 330; quadrupled 325; revenues 114; rise 168, 172; spiked 328; unpredictable 107; volatility 100
oil production 237–8; crude 161, 236, 241; global 131; growth of 226; Indonesia 232–5; Mexican **162**, 165; Norwegian 325, 327, 330; US **130**, 131; Venezuelan **162**, 169
Olmstead, A.L. 136n3, 267n1
Olson, M. 38–40, 42, 44
Oñate, J.J. 353
Ooi, J.-B. 226, 245n3
Organization of Petroleum Exporting Countries (OPEC) 130, 162, 172, 234, 326
Ortega, L. 208–9, 212, 220n9, 220n15
Ossowski, R. 184–6, 191, 199n9
Owusu, F. 93

Palma, J.G. 6, 209, 211–12, 214–15, **216**, 220n6, 220n14, 221n27
Papyrakis, E. 12, 89
Parsons, Q.N. 77, 90, 95
patronage 29; channels 39, 46, 49; government 40; networks 27, 48, 114; primary tools 115
Paul, R. 124, 136n4
Paz Arauco, V. 201n38
Pedler, F. 102
PEMEX (*Petróleos Mexicanos*) 166–8
Peres Cajias, J.A. 16, 185, 189, 191, *192*, 196, 198n6, 198n8, 199n9, 199n16, 200n18, 200n22, 200n24, 200n30
Peters, P. 80, 82
Philip, G. 167
Philippines GDP per capita **176**
Philips Petroleum 313
Pinilla, V. 8, 341–2, 344, 346, 348, 350, 353

Pinto, J. 208, 212, 220n15, 221n28
Polanyi, K. 273, 277, 279, 288n1, 289n7
political 11, 17, 32, 45, 67, 90, 95, 189, 263, 273, 284, 330; competition 44; consensus 191, 325, 328; consent 197; economy 5, *33*, 148, 152, 155–6, 174, 190, 217, 226, 275, 281, 288n1, 290n14, 318, 322; instability 39, 196; institutional structure 87; institutions 79, 83, 92, 251, 334; power 40, 145, 158, 201n36, 262, 265; restrictions 198, 200n28; stability 77, 89, 96, 161; support 34, 48
population growth 37, 43, 46, 69, 302, 340
post-colonial context 273; legacy 109
post-war 36, 324; banking crises 321; decades 30, 49; depression 319–20; development 37; industrialisation of Latin America 171; industrialisation model 41; Norway 322–4, 328, 333; reconstruction of Western Europe 170; Spanish situation 344; world 55; years 47, 162
pre-colonial 80, 90, 95; era 94; institutions 79; society 82
property rights 41, 256; badly defined 10; breach 317; enforcement 17; guarantees 29; lobbying for 40, 43; protection 39; respect for 334; secure 89; systems 79
Przeworski, A. 37, 41
Przeworski, J.F. 126
pyrite claims 320, 324; Norwegian 315, 319

Rajan, R.G. 32, 34
Read, T.T. 127–8
Redfern, W.A. 236, 241
Reeves, W.P. 276, 282
rent 5, 11, 13, 26–8, 30–2, 34, 39–41, 43, 45–50, 63–5, 71, 152, 155, 238, 252, 261–2, 267n5, 334; appropriating 256, 266; capture 317–18, 320; concentrated 32; curse 249; extraction 156, 160; frontier 66, 73n11, 281; invest 86; labour *33*; land **154**, 255, *260*; land use 105; low 37; mineral 84; natural resources 3, 12, 16–17, **153**, 250, 314; oil 107, 327; resource 315, 324–5, 328, 333; share 226, 235; siphoning 38, *42*; transferring 101
rental differentials 249; land rental rates 255, 267n5; rentals/wages ratio 253
rent cycling 27; theory 27–8, 34, 41, 46–50
rent-driven models 36; development 37, 41, *42*

Index   371

rentier state 174, 275, 332; hypothesis 184–6, 191, 197–8
rent-rich exports 26
rent-seeking 11–12, 29, 39, 45, 50, 54, 88, 155, 273, 275, 284, 318, 321, 323; activity 10, 40; attitudes 204; behaviors 16, 191; blatant 237; elimination of 278; elites 101, 108, 276; increased 100; mismanaged 48; opportunities 17, 45–6, 250
Republic of Botswana 93; *see also* Botswana
resource curse 10, 12, 15, 29–31, 34, 73n2, 100, 132, 160–1, 177, 178, 272–3, 275, 284, 289n4, 294, 303, 313, 319; avoidance 168, 276, 335; effects 26, 49, 127; hypothesis 2, 6, 54, 248; literature 27–8, 174, 179–80, 185, 191, 198n7, 205, 271, 288n1–2; natural 88–92, 94, 184, 204, 219n2; symptoms 32, 48;
resource-dependent economies 13, 271, 283
resource rent 2, 11, 27, 226, 314, 319, 324, 327–8, 330, 334; conflicts 315; distribution 238–9, 333; natural 10, 30–2, *33*, 47–8, 250; potential 325; share 230, 235–6, 242, 244; squandered 332
restrictions 7, 16, 71, 106, 148; development 140; foreign exchange 242; land shares 253; operating without 334; political 189, 198, 200n28; quantitative 200n18, 201n36; structural 188; trawlers 324
restrictive policy 168, 324
reversion 170; right of reversion 317, 321
Richards, A. 108, 111
Richards, J.F. 56, 73n5–6
Rickard, T.A. 119, 125
Rinde, H. 319, 323, 335n9
Robinson, J.A. 29, 40, 77, 83, 90, 95, 219n3, 251, 256, 267n3, 271, 274
Rodríguez, F. 160, 170, 173, 220n17
Rodriguez, G. 195–6, 201n35
Román, C. 256, 267n1
Rosenberg, D.M. 354
Rosenberg, N. 119
Ross, M. 11, 40, 184, 197
Rostow, W.W. 7, 88
royalties 160, 186, 234–7; hydrocarbon 200n26–7, 201n37; raised 170
Rubio-Varas, M. del M. 5–6, 16, 165, 169, 177–8
Ryggvik, H. 325–9

Sachs, J.D. 2, 10–14, 28, 31, 36, 86, 88, 91–2, 160, 173, 178, 204, 219n2, 219n4, 220n8, 248, 250, 289n5, 294
Sala-i-Martin, X. 11, 100–1
Samatar, A.I. 77, 83, 86, 93
Sanders, A.R.D. 16, 160
Sandvik, P.T. 16, 160, 315, 321–2
Sater, W.F. 209, 220n9, 220n13
Schapera, I. 77, 79–80, 82
Schedvin, C.B. 5, 62, 248, 299
Schmitz, C.J. 123, 125
Schumpeter, J.A. 57; neo-Schumpeterian 9, 15; Schumpeterian 8, 150, 152, 154–5
Schwach, V. 307–8
Second World War (WWII) 30, 82, 102–4, 283, 322
serfdom 64–5, 71
Serrano, R. 8, 348
Sicotte, R. 211, 220n11, 220n14
Silitshena, R.M.K. 79, 82
silver 119; Australia 300; exploitation 198n5, 199n11; exports 199n11; gross value added (GVA) 227; Indonesia *228*, **229**, 230–3, 240–1; international prices 188, 197; Latin America 161; mining 124–5, **239**; Norway 306; Spanish mines 59, **60**; US production 121–5
Singapore 41, 242, 288n3
Singer, H.W. 8, 30; Prebisch-Singer Hypothesis 8, 272
Siwawa-Ndai, P. 84, 92–3
Skånland, H. 328
Skjold, D.O. 323
slaves **62**, 64, 71; exploited 62; plantation economy 59, **60**, 65–6; post-slave trade export boom 102; trans-Atlantic trade 66, 73n8
Smith, A. 4, 119, 271, 342
Smith, D. 134–5
Smith, G.O. 120, **121**
Smith, K. 306
Sociedad Nacional Minera 208, 220n10
Sogner, K. 315, 321
Sokoloff K.L. 14, 66–7, 71, 264, 298
Solow, R.M. 7, 177
South Africa 4, 56, 80, 84–6, 93–5, *121*, *144*, 267n4
South America **60**, 66; Second Industrial Revolution 248; southern border 145; Southern Cone 249, 266; temperate 56, 59; tropical and sub-tropical regions 59, 65
South American countries 211–12, 214, 249

South Korea 41, 43, *144*, 194, 272, 276, 288n3
Spain 15, 314, 316, 340, 342; crop production 345, 349–51; European Economic Community 346; farming techniques 341; forced population displacements 354; GDP **315**, **332**; HDI *157*; HDI/GDP **176**; international agricultural markets 344; irrigated area 343, 348, 353; irrigation development 356; silver boom 59; structural productivity *151*; water availability 352, 355; wealth structure *144*
Spanish 341; agriculture 343, 355; agricultural production 344, 349; aridity 345; conquest of Latin America 208; economic growth model 354; irrigated land 348; legal regime 263; pollution 353; salinity problem 356; silver mines 59, **60**; territorial wars for water control 354; vineyard production 357n1; water supply regulation 352
Spitz, P. 129
squatting 280; frontier 281; resource 273
state-owned enterprises (SOEs) 234, 236–7, 242; Indonesian 243–4; mining 232–3, 239
Stiglitz, J.E. 39, 273
Stonehill, A.I. 315, 321
Storli, E. 320–1
sub-Saharan Africa (SSA) 31, 34, 62, 77, 88
subsidies 28, 39, 41, 328; agricultural 278; public 196; urban 45, 49
Sunkel, O. 207, 209, 211, 217, 220n6, 220n14
surplus rural labour 48; absorption 43, 49
Syrquin, M. *35*, 36, 43, 50n1

Taiwan 41, 43, 276, 288n3
tax *42*, 43, 46–7, 82, 135, 160, 188–9, 234, 281, 286, 333–4; ad hoc 238; agricultural exports 106; agricultural income **103**; Bolivian legislation 199n11; burden 146; collection 196, 201n37; concession 237, 317, 319, 321; direct 41, 199n13; domestic 30, 184–6, 199n9; domestic effort 198–9; evasion 166; exemptions 200n20; export 114, 199n12, 200n19–20, 242; hydrocarbon 200n21, 200n27; income 38, 170, 236, 290n20, 323; inheritance 209, 211; land 262; low 12, 200n17; lower rates 325; mining 190, 199n16, 200n28, **239**;

natural resource 220n6; nitrate 220n14; oil **163**, 164, 171, 326; over-taxation 44; payers 40, 49; pressure 197, 200n23; receipts 6, 172; reduced 329; reform 200n24; revenues 36, 69, 80; shadow 187, 200n18; special 165, **331**; support 193; surplus 205; value-added 191, 200n29
Taylor, A. 285, **286**
territorial 356; empires 61–2; expansion 72; legislature 127; losses 189; Norwegian waters 328; wars 208, 354
The Economist 171, 330, 332
Thomas, A. 184, 186–7, 198n2, 198n7, 199n9
Thomas, B. 136n2
Thorp, R. 165
Thue, L. 303, 320, 332
tin 119, 188, 231, 234, 238, 240, 242, 244; exploitation 187, 198n5; export tax 199n12–13; gross value added **239**; International Tin Council 199n16; mining 232, 243; ore *228*, 230, 241; refined 226
tin cartel 199n16, 238, 242
Torvik, R. 10–11
Transparency International 77, 90
Turner, F.J. 55–6, 71, 251, 255

UDAPE 198n8, 201n37
UNDP 86, 339
unemployment 45, 146
United Kingdom 207; average income 174; coal production **122**; copper *126*; Dutch disease phenomenon 289n5; education 159n1; GDP **175**, **332**; HDI/GDP **176**; oil company 232; postwar labour government 111; structural productivity *151*; *see also* Britain, British
United Nations 175; Water 339
United Nations Economic Commission for Latin America (ECLAC) 171, *192*, 199n9
United States 4–5, 13–15, 54, 59, 63–4, 66–8, 72, 123–4, 161, 169, 205, 207–8, 219n3–4, 220n9–10, 284, 290n19, 296; chemical industry 129; coal production **122**; Columbia College 126–7; copper 125, *126*, 136n6, 233; economy 55; education 159n1, *195*; electricity production **316**; GDP **176**, **332**; Geological Survey (USGS) 120, 128, 133, 244n2; industrialization 119–20;

Index 373

inflation 173; Mid-West 277; minerals 68, *121*, 132; mining 134–5, 294–5, 302; natural resources 204, 272; oil production **130**, 131–2; petrochemical industry 69; petroleum industry 127; southern **60**; structural productivity *151*; wealth structure *144*; *see also* America, American, North America
Uruguay 145, 156, 193, 198n3, 248–9, 262–3; agro-based economy **154**; education *192*, *194–5*; health spending 193; land distribution 263; real price of land **155**; rents of natural resources **153**; stratified universalism 156; structural productivity *151*
Uslar Pietri, A. 169–70, 173

Van Bemmelen, R.W. 240, 244n1
van der Eng, P. 5–6, 16, **227**, **229–30**, **242**, 243
van der Ploeg, F. 10, 15, 47, 73n3, 88–9, 91, 204, 220n7, 250
van Zanden, J.L. 226, 341
Venezuela 6, 16, 107, *151*, 161, 166, 173; decline 179; GDP **175**, 177; impoverishment 172; negative savings **178**; resource curse 174; resources-rich 198n3; wealth indicators 171
Venezuelan 187; exceptionalism 174; governments 160, 164, 169–71, 179; history 161; investment 172–3; nationalisation **162**
Venezuelan institutions 179; *Cámara de Diputados* 170; *Ministerio de Trabajo* 171; Ministry of Mines and Hydrocarbons 170
Venezuelan oil 170–1; Banco Central 172; dependence 171; industry **162–4**, 169–70; wealth 173;
Venezuelans 160, 169, 171, 173
Ville, S. 17, 133, 205, 219n3, 294, 296, 298, 302–3, 309
Vörösmarty, C.J. 339, 354

wages 255, 265, 282, 330; bargaining on 147; driven up 91; high 207; higher 10, 205, 209, 217, 220n5, 283; increased 335; low 88, 165; of the poor 43, 45, 49; public sector 82; rents-wages ratio 253, *260*; rising 64; spiked upwards 328; total 267n5
Walker, G. 102
war 205, 232, 263, 320–1; Academy of 307; before the war 216; Chaco 189;

war *continued*
  efforts 199n16; Great 321; of independence 232, 267n10; interwar period 162, 276, 278, 319–21; Korean 232; Napoleonic 303; of the Pacific 207–9, 220n11, 220n13; pre-war 232–4; pre-war legislation 236; Spanish 344; territorial 354; World 30, 213; Yom Kippur 106; *see also* civil war, First World War, post-war, Second World War
Watkins, M.H. 4, 6
Watts, M. 106–7
Weaver, J.C. 73n11
Webb, W.P. 56–7, 63–4
welfare 1, 13, 27, 38, 109, 140, 146–7, 156–7, 198n6, 282, 288; conditions 15; enhancing 48; improved 304–5, 309; indicators 3, 12; levels 5; national 178, 307; redistributive state 330; requirements 317; social 158, 276, 302–4; Social Democratic Capitalism (SDWC) 274, 282; states 145, 148, 314
White, C.M. 297
White, G.T. 128–9
Wicken, O. 17, 133, 205, 219n3, 294, 296, 303, 309

Willebald, H. 5, 12, 16, 198n1, 248–50, 253, 256, 261–6, 267n5, 267n7
Williams, E.J. 167
Williams, G. 102, 104
Williams, M. 120, 264
Williamson, H.F. 128
Williamson, J.G. 4, 7–8, 10–11, 37, 43, 73n4, 73n11, 211, 248–9, 266, 267n5
Willoch, K. 326–7
windfall 54, 73n11; earnings 2, 9; gains 65, 69, 71; oil 28, 108, 235; rents 13, 26, 31, 46; resource 289n4, 319; revenue 27, 30, 34, 48
Wood, A. 12, 36
Woolcock, M. 12, 39, 250
World Bank 15, *27*, 29, 34, 37, 50n3, 77–8, **83–5**, 86–7, 89–94, 111, 142, *144*, **132**
World Commission on Dams 353
Wright, G. 5, 15–16, 55, 67–9, 120–3, 132, 219n3, 294, 309
Wrigley, E.A. 136n2
WTO 252

Yergin, D. 129, 131–2